4th
**edition**

# David W. Johnson
*The University of Minnesota*

# Frank P. Johnson

# JOINING TOGETHER

## Group Theory and Group Skills

Prentice Hall, Englewood Cliffs, New Jersey 07632

*Library of Congress Cataloging-in-Publication Data*

Johnson, David W., [date]

    Joining together : group theory and group skills / David W.
Johnson, Frank P. Johnson. — 4th ed.
      p.  cm.
    Includes bibliographical references and index.
    ISBN 0-13-511858-1
    1. Social groups.  2. Leadership.  3. Group relations training.
I. Johnson, Frank P. (Frank Pierce), [date].  II. Title.
HM131.J613    1991
302.3—dc20      90-48522

Editorial/production supervision
  and interior design:  *Edie Riker*
Cover design:  *Maureen Eide*
Cover photo: *"Scene De Fete," Sonia Delauney, Photo from Three Lions*
Prepress buyer:  *Debra Kesar*
Manufacturing buyer:  *Mary Ann Gloriande*

## This book is dedicated to our parents, who created the basic group to which we first belonged.

© 1991, 1987, 1982, 1975 by Prentice-Hall, Inc.
A Division of Simon & Schuster
Englewood Cliffs, New Jersey 07632

Printed in the United States of America

10  9  8  7  6  5  4  3  2  1

ISBN    0-13-511858-1

Prentice-Hall International (UK) Limited, *London*
Prentice-Hall of Australia Pty. Limited, *Sydney*
Prentice-Hall Canada Inc., *Toronto*
Prentice-Hall Hispanoamericana, S.A., *Mexico*
Prentice-Hall of India Private Limited, *New Delhi*
Prentice-Hall of Japan, Inc., *Tokyo*
Simon & Schuster Asia Pte. Ltd., *Singapore*
Editora Prentice-Hall do Brasil, Ltda., *Rio de Janeiro*

# Contents

# 2    Experiential Learning    37

# 3    Group Goals and Social Interdependence    57

# 4    Communication Within Groups    105

## 8   Conflicts of Interest   301

## 9   The Use of Power   361

## 10     Leading Learning and Discussion Groups      393

## 11     Leading Growth and Counseling Groups      411

## 12     Team Development      431

# List of Exercises

# Preface

We, the authors, know a great deal about groups. We grew up in one. There are seven children in our family. Frank is the oldest. David is in the middle. We are five years apart in age. Although Frank was very bossy as a child, and refused to ever believe that David was really not supposed to clean up his room, our relationship survived. As part of a group of seven children, we raised each other, and learned about group dynamics in the trenches of trying to decide as a group who gets the extra piece of pie, who sits by the windows in the car, who decides which game we are going to play, who sweeps and who mops, and whether we go to sleep with the light on or off.

Families are not the only group setting. Within all organizations and social systems, and throughout all walks of life, groups are the key setting in which things get done. The need for knowledge of group dynamics and skills in being part of small groups is more important than ever. Our original reasons for writing *Joining Together* included introducing readers to both the (1) theory and research findings needed to understand how to make groups effective and (2) skills required to apply that knowledge in practical situations. Expertise in working in groups is based on an integration of such knowledge and skills. *Joining Together* is more than a book reviewing current knowledge in the area of small groups, and it is more than a book of skill-building exercises. The theory and exercises are integrated into an inquiry or experiential approach to learning about the dynamics of small groups. Just as "the truth will make you free," *throughout one's life, choices, opportunities, and successes are created by*

*(1) knowledge of group dynamics and (2) mastery of the skills required to apply that knowledge in practical situations.*

Knowledge of how groups function is continually expanding. New theoretical explanations for group behaviors are being crafted. Researchers are subjecting these hypotheses to empirical test. Fresh insights and unexpected findings continue to be achieved. While many of the basic premises presented in the first edition of this book, published 16 years ago, remain unchallenged, others have been refined, augmented, or even disconfirmed in the intervening years. This book continues to keep pace with the new developments in theory and research by taking an updated look at what is known about group dynamics. While the readers of this book are diverse, *Joining Together* remains focused on the characteristic dynamics found in virtually all groups. Examples are used from all walks of life. Because this book is intended to serve as an introduction to the dynamics of groups, furthermore, we have maintained a balanced, integrative stance when presenting theories and research findings.

The authors wish to thank many people for their help in writing this book and in preparing the manuscript. We owe much to the social psychologists who have influenced our theorizing and to the colleagues with whom we have conducted various types of laboratory-training experiences. We have tried to acknowledge sources of the exercises included in this book whenever possible. Some of the exercises presented are so commonly used that the originators are not traceable. If we have inadvertently missed giving recognition to anyone, we apologize. Special thanks are extended to our wives, Linda Mulholland Johnson and Jane Miley Johnson, who contributed their support to the development and writing of this book. A special thanks to Judy Bartlett for clerical, proofreading, and administrative assistance, which has been invaluable. All photographs were taken by the authors. We wish to thank Nancy Valin Waller and Thomas Grummett who drew the cartoon figures appearing in the book.

*David W. Johnson*
*Frank P. Johnson*

# JOINING TOGETHER

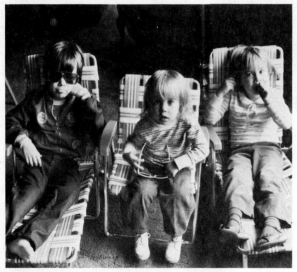

# 1

# Group Dynamics

## BASIC CONCEPTS TO BE COVERED IN THIS CHAPTER

In this chapter a number of concepts are defined and discussed. The major ones are listed below. The procedure for learning these concepts is as follows:

1. Divide into heterogeneous pairs.
2. The task for each pair is to
   a. Define each concept, noting the page on which it is defined and discussed.
   b. Ensure that both members of the pair understand the meaning of each concept.
3. Combine into groups of four. Compare the answers of the two pairs. If there is disagreement, the members look up the concept in the chapter and clarify it until they all agree on the definition and understand it.

### CONCEPTS

1. Group
2. Group dynamics
3. Group effectiveness
4. Interdependence
5. Sequential-stage theory of group development
6. Recurring-phase theory of group development
7. Individualistic orientation toward group dynamics
8. Group orientation toward group dynamics
9. Kurt Lewin
10. Role
11. Norm
12. Primary group
13. Reference group

# asic Elements Of Cooperative Learning

### Positive Interdependence

Students perceive that they need each other in order to complete the group's task ("sink or swim together"). Teachers may structure positive interdependence by establishing **mutual goals** (learn and make sure all other group members learn), **joint rewards** (if all group members achieve above the criteria, each will receive bonus points), **shared resources** (one paper for each group or each member receives part of the required information), and **assigned roles** (summarizer, encourager of participation, elaborator).

### Face-to-Face Promotive Interaction

Students promote each other's learning by helping, sharing, and encouraging efforts to learn. Students explain, discuss, and teach what they know to classmates. Teachers structure the groups so that students sit knee-to-knee and talk through each aspect of the assignment.

### Individual Accountability

Each student's performance is frequently assessed and the results are given to the group and the individual. Teachers may structure individual accountability by giving an individual test to each student or randomly selecting one group member to give the answer.

### Interpersonal And Small Group Skills

Groups cannot function effectively if students do not have and use the needed social skills. Teachers teach these skills as purposefully and precisely as academic skills. Collaborative skills include leadership, decision-making, trust-building, communication, and conflict-management skills.

### Group Processing

Groups need specific time to discuss how well they are achieving their goals and maintaining effective working relationships among members. Teachers structure group processing by assigning such tasks as (a) list at least three member actions that helped the group be successful and (b) list one action that could be added to make the group even more successful tomorrow. Teachers also monitor the groups and give feedback on how well the groups are working together to the groups and the class as a whole.

From D. W. Johnson, R. T. Johnson and E. Holubec, *Cooperation in the Classroom* (Edina, MN: Interaction Book Company, 1991). Used with permission of authors.

## THE IMPORTANCE OF GROUPS

In 12,896 B.C., a small group of hunters surround a band of reindeer as they ford an icy river. The hunters are armed with harpoons tipped with spearheads carved from reindeer antler. As the reindeer wallow in the water, the hunters run in and slaughter them. It is the coordinated action of the group of Cro-Magnon hunters that makes them more successful than their Neanderthal cousins, who hunt as individuals.

Our origins are somehow linked with the fate of the Neanderthals. We have never been proud of our extinct predecessors, partly because of their looks. Nevertheless, the Neanderthals represent a high point in the human story. Their lineage goes back to the earliest members of the genus *Homo*. They were the original pioneers. Over thousands of years Neanderthals moved out of Africa by way of the Near East into India and China and Malaysia, and into southern Europe. In recent times, 150,000 or so years ago, they pioneered glacial landscapes. The Neanderthals were the first to cope with climates hospitable only to woolly mammoths and reindeer.

There is no anatomical evidence that the Neanderthals were inferior to us (the Cro-Magnons) cerebrally, and no doubt whatever that they were our physical superiors. Their strongest individuals could probably lift weights of half a ton or so. Physically, we are quite puny in comparison. But we gradually replaced the Neanderthals during an overlapping period of a few thousand years. It may have mainly been a matter of attrition and population pressure. As the glaciers from Scandinavia advanced, northern populations of Neanderthals moved south while our ancestors were moving north out of Africa. We met in Europe. They vanished about 30,000 years ago.

There are numerous explanations for the disappearance of the Neanderthals. Perhaps they evolved into us. Perhaps we merged. Perhaps there was an intergroup

competition for food, with the Neanderthals unable to meet our challenge and dying off in marginal areas. Perhaps the Neanderthals were too set in their ways and were unable to evolve and refine better ways to cooperate while we were continually organizing better cooperative efforts to cope with changing climatic conditions. There seems to be little doubt that we were more able to form and maintain cooperative efforts within small groups.

During the time we (the Cro-Magnons) overlapped with the Neanderthals, our ancestors developed highly sophisticated cooperative effects characterized by social organization, group-hunting procedures, creative experimentation with a variety of materials, sharing of knowledge, divisions of labor, trade, and transportation systems. We sent out scouts to monitor the movements of herds of animals we preyed on. The Neanderthals probably did not. We cached supplies and first aid materials to aid hunting parties far away from our home bases. The Neanderthals did not. Neanderthals apparently engaged their prey chiefly in direct combat. We learned more efficient ways of hunting, such as driving animals over cliffs, that changed fundamentally our relationship with the rest of the animal kingdom (i.e., instead of behaving like lions and other carnivores, going after young and old and sick animals to weed out the less fit, large-scale game drives wiped out entire herds and perhaps entire species). We developed more sophisticated tools and weapons to kill from a distance such as the spear thrower and the bow and arrow. The Neanderthals probably did not. The Neanderthals used local materials to develop tools. We were more selective, often obtaining special fine-grained and colorful flints from quarries as far as 250 miles away. This took a level of intergroup cooperation and social organization that Neanderthals did not develop. We improved the tool-making process through experimentation and sharing knowledge. The Neanderthals did not. The Neanderthals used stone almost exclusively for tools. We used bone and ivory to make needles and other tools. We "tailored" our clothes and made ropes and nets. Our ability to obtain more food than we needed resulted in trading and the formation of far-ranging social networks. Status hierarchies, the accumulation of wealth, artistic efforts, laws, and story telling to preserve traditions followed, as more complex forms of cooperation were developed. Whether we replaced or evolved from the Neanderthals, our ingenuity was especially evident in organizing cooperative efforts to increase our standard of living and the quality of our lives. We excelled at organizing effective small-group efforts.

Humans are small-group beings. We always have been and we always will be. As John Donne said, "No man is an island, entire of itself." Throughout the history of our species we have lived in small groups. For 200,000 years humans lived in small hunting and gathering groups. For 10,000 years humans lived in small farming communities. It is only recently, the past 100 years or so, that large cities have become the rule rather than the exception.

The ubiquitousness of groups and the inevitability of being in them make groups one of the most important factors in our lives. All day long we interact first in one group and then in another. We live in a dwelling as part of a group, we learn in groups contained in the same classroom, we work in groups, we interact with friends in groups, and we spend much of our leisure time in groups. Our family life, our leisure time, our friendships, and our careers are all filled with groups. In fact, if a person from outer space conducted a study of the people of Earth, group membership would probably be the dominant characteristic noted. We are born into a group called the family, and we would not survive the first few minutes, the first few weeks, or even the first few years of our lives without membership in this group. It is within our family and peer groups that we are socialized into ways of behaving and thinking, educated, and taught to have certain perspectives on ourselves and our world. Our personal identity is derived from the way in which we are perceived and treated by other members of our groups. We learn, work, worship, and plan in groups. As humans we have an inherent social nature: our life is filled with groups from the moment of our birth to the moment of our death.

As the effectiveness of our groups go, so goes the our quality of life. In business, education, government, social work, churches, the military, and in all other aspects of our society there is great interest in improving the productivity of groups. There is great concern in our society with strengthening the family. Educators are striving to understand better how the classroom functions as a group and how to use cooperative learning groups. Drug abuse, delinquency and crime, and mental illness are all being treated through group procedures, and there is continued concern with making those procedures more effective. There are many settings in which groups are being seen as important elements of improving productivity and effectiveness.

## Groups in Business and Industry

> In an industrial organization it's group effort that counts. There's really no room for stars in an industrial organization. You need talented people, but they can't do it alone. They have to have help.
>
> *John F. Donnelly, president, Donnelly Mirrors*

The productivity of U.S. business and industry has been falling. The implementation of more effective work teams are one means to reverse this trend. During the first half of this century, the United States was without question the world leader in manufacturing. The United States had developed new technologies and translated them into products that were available nowhere else in the world. Today, the United States ranks fourth behind Europe, Japan, and Russia in manufacturing research, third in the consumption of machine tools, and fifth in the production of machine tools (National Center for Manufacturing Sciences, 1989). The U.S. share of the world automative market has dropped from 76 percent to 24 percent, machine tools from 100 percent to 35 percent, and color TVs from 90 percent to 10 percent. At one time 27 U.S. companies produced TVs—now only 1 does.

To halt the decline of the U.S. manufacturing industries, companies are turning to the high productivity generated by small groups. Teams are central to increasing productivity. Ford Industries, for example, formed **problem-solving groups** to deal with shop floor problems, **interface groups** to work on problems that cut across work groups, **opportunity teams** to oversee implementation of new technology and facilities improvements, **special project teams** to manage specific events such as auto shows, **linking teams** to deal with issues that require input from several shifts and departments, **launch teams** to coordinate across process and design needed to launch a successful new project, **vendor quality teams** to develop ongoing communication with suppliers both inside and outside the company, and **research committees** to provide consulting and training on request (Banas, 1988). A knowledge of group dynamics is thus central to running Ford Industries and any other company.

In the "excellent" companies, work is conducted in a variety of teams. This trend will continue and expand. What will make companies viable in the future is not their level of technology but rather their ability to establish a **culture of learning, continuous improvement,** and **adaptation** among their personnel. In the future excellent company, employees will continuously come up with ideas to improve quality and productiveness. Factory workers, for example, need the skills to build, debug, and improve their own machines so that a continuous redesign process occurs. Continuous learning from customers to fine-tune and adapt products to their needs will be required to keep a company in business. Quick adaptations to changing market conditions will be necessary. *The basic building block to create such a culture of learning, continuous improvement, and adaptation is the team.*

## Groups in Education

American education could be better. Education is tied with social work as the most labor-intensive business in the economy in the United States. Labor costs are equal to 93 percent of the output value. The U.S. Office of Technology Assessment figures indicate that formal instruction in the United States is a $400-billion-a-year industry, employing 10 percent of the work force. In the last 10 years, the cost of education has doubled. Productivity, however, has not doubled.

In some metropolitan areas, the dropout rate is over 50 percent. Nationwide it translates into 3,000 dropouts per day. One report placed 9th graders fifteenth in the world in scientific knowledge. Nearly 40 percent of our high school graduates cannot read at the 9th grade level. It is estimated that 750,000 are unable to read their diplomas. One-third of U.S. science classes are taught by teachers who hold majors in other disciplines. Fewer than half of the high school students take any math or science beyond the 10th grade. Only 9 percent of high school graduates are both interested in and prepared for entering science, engineering, and engineering technology careers. Remedial education and training is costing American firms over $30 million a year. A Hudson Institute report states that, viewed as an economic sector, education has the worst productivity record of any major U.S. industry.

*To improve the productivity of our educational system schools and colleges are turning to high productivity of cooperative learning* (Johnson, Johnson, & Holubec, 1990). Students work in small groups to maximize both their own learning and the learning of their classmates (see Chapter 10). Cooperative learning typically produces higher achievement, more positive relationships, and psychologically healthier members than do competitive or individualistic learning (Johnson & Johnson, 1989a).

## The Family as a Group

For thousands of years, family life has been one of the sustaining values of civilization. Anthropologist Margaret Mead observed that the family is the toughest institution humans have. Yet the structure of the family has been changing. To build and maintain a caring and loving family in which children and parents function as an effective group, knowledge of group dynamics and small-group skills are essential. Since the beginning of the human species most fathers and mothers worked side by side, in or near their homes, hunting and gathering, farming, or plying trades. Each contributed to family economic well-being, and—often with carefully delineated roles—they shared the responsibility of child rearing. Only with the advent of the Industrial Revolution did men go off to work in a distant place like a factory or an office (Footlick, 1989).

First, there was the demise of the extended family. Second, there was the demise of the nuclear family. In the United States, the automobile is as much to blame as anything. Each year one American family out of five moves. Children grow up and move away from home. They move a hundred miles. They move a thousand miles. Family ties are then loosened or even broken. Grandparents become part of the distant past—no longer able to give the love, wisdom, and advice that only time and experience brings. Parents often retain only occasional contact.

The traditional, "Leave It to Beaver," American family (the father working, the mother at home, and two children in school) characterized 58 percent of American families in the late 1950s. It now applies only to less than 14 percent of American families. In many families, two parents have become part of the distant past. Early in the 1900s divorce was rare. After World War I, upward of one-fourth of marriages ended in divorce. After World War II, Americans were shocked to discover nearly one-third of marriages were ending in divorce. By 1980, one-half of marriages were ending in divorce and six out of ten second marriages collapsed. One-third of all children born in the past decade will probably live in a stepfamily before they are eighteen. In addition, contact between parents and children has been decreasing. One out of four children today is being raised by a single parent. Two-thirds of all mothers are in the labor force, and more than half of all mothers of infants are in the work force.

With the changes in family structure have come a series of problems. Fractured relationships. Broken homes. Children of divorce. Out-of-wedlock births (one out of four children is born out of wedlock). Child abuse. Child neglect. Babies having babies. Kids refusing to grow up and leave home. Parents prizing their BMWs more than their children. Both rich and poor kids blotting their minds with drugs. Financial disasters. Unhappy lives. One out of five children lives in poverty. Divorce has left a devastated generation in its wake, and for many youngsters, the pain is compounded by poverty and neglect.

This is a period of historic change in American family life. Instead of the traditional American family, there are many American families, of diverse styles and shapes (Footlick, 1989). There are fathers working while mothers keep house, mothers working while fathers keep house, fathers and mothers both working away from home, single parents, second marriages bringing children together from unrelated backgrounds, childless couples, and unmarried couples with and without children. *In order to build and maintain a constructive family life within the diverse demands of modern life, individuals have to have a thorough knowledge of group dynamics and the small-group skills to forge caring and nurturing relationships within the new family structures.*

## Groups and Psychological Health

We are in an epidemic of depression, anxiety, and mental illness (Seligman, 1988). Two major surveys of mental illness in the United States, for example, showed that, contrary to expectations, younger people were much more likely to have had a depressive episode in their lives than were older people (Robins et al., 1984, reported in Seligman, 1988). The rate of depression over the last two generations has increased roughly tenfold as people are experiencing much more depression now than they did two generations ago, feeling hopeless, giving up, being passive, having low self-esteem, and committing suicide. The reason may be found in the breakdown of cooperative relationships within the family, neighborhood, community, work, church, and country. In modern society, each person is encouraged to live exclusively for him- or herself and, when adversity hits, lean exclusively on him- or herself.

To reduce this epidemic, more effective groups are needed. The psychological health, coping skills, and ego strength needed to develop, build, and maintain psychological health comes from being involved in caring and committed relationships within groups. Being involved in supportive groups prevents the occurrence of psychological problems and the use of supportive and caring groups is the ideal mode of treatment of psychological problems. *The more individuals understand about group dynamics and the more skillful they are in enhancing productivity and building supportive and caring relationships within groups, the more healthy they tend to be psychologically.*

## Complexity of Group Dynamics

Groups are the basic building blocks of human existence. Groups are ubiquitous. They are the key to more productivity in industry and education, higher quality of life within family and leisure groups, and greater individual psychological health. Despite the incalculable importance of groups, however, there are many puzzling contradictions in the findings of those who have studied groups. Does performing a task in the presence of others create anxiety and apprehension, or does it inspire and energize? Do people avoid close physical contact with others, or do they seek intimacy? Do people like to be part of groups, or do they enjoy being different and distinct from others? Do people enjoy and seek out crowded situations, or do they dislike and avoid them? The answers are, all are true under certain conditions. There is nothing particularly simple about the way in which human groups function.

It should come as no surprise, therefore, that disagreement exists among social scientists as to the importance and value of groups. Some social scientists think groups are the salvation of our species. They see groups as the basis for everything that is good in our lives. Other social scientists think groups are our bane. They see groups as destructive influences on our lives. Both views are oversimplified. Groups can have constructive or destructive effects depending on how they are used. The more you understand the dynamics of groups, the more you will be able to maximize the constructive aspects of groups and minimize the destructive ones. *When it comes to group functioning, knowledge does give power.* But knowledge of group dynamics in and of itself is not sufficient to promote effective functioning—social skills are also required. To promote effective group functioning, you must both know what an effective group is and have the social skills necessary to actualize group effectiveness.

*Knowing group dynamics theory and having small group skills can change your life.* They can make you more employable and lead to greater career success. They can lead to more caring and loving family relationships and greater competence as parents. They can lead to greater learning in school. They can promote greater psychological health and increased ability to cope with stress and adversity. There is no aspect of your life that is untouched by your knowledge of group dynamics and skills in effectively participating in group activities.

The effectiveness of our groups depends both on our knowledge of group dynamics and on our ability to behave effectively within groups. It takes both knowledge and skills to build and maintain effective group efforts. *This book, therefore, has two purposes:*

1. To provide you with a systematic analysis of the theory and research on group dynamics.
2. To provide you with simulations and exercises that will enable you to develop competent group skills.

## EXERCISE 1.1:
## YOUR SOLITARY ACTIVITIES

1. List everything you do in a typical day from the moment you wake up to the moment you fall asleep.
2. Delete from your list all the activities you perform with groups of people and see what is left.
3. Form a group of three and discuss the results.

## EXERCISE 1.2:
## WHO AM I?

We are all members of groups. If we are asked to describe who we are, most of us include information about the groups to which we belong. "I'm a student at the University of Minnesota," "I'm a member of the hockey team," "I'm a Johnson," "I'm a male," "I'm an American," and so forth. Membership in groups may be formal ("I'm an employee of IBM"), aspiring ("I want to be rich"), marginal ("Sometimes I'm invited to Ralph's parties, sometimes I'm not"), voluntary ("I'm a Baptist"), and nonvoluntary ("I'm a female"). To a large extent, our memberships define who we are as individuals.

1. We can all describe ourselves in many ways. Write ten different answers to the question, "Who am I?" on a sheet of paper. Answer in terms of groups you belong to, beliefs you hold, and your roles and responsibilities.
2. Rank your answers from most important to your sense of self to least important to your sense of self.
3. Form a group of three, and share your self-descriptions. Count how many memberships are represented in the triad. Discuss the role of groups in your view of who you are as a person.
4. Count how many group memberships are represented in the class.

## EXERCISE 1.3:
## WHAT IS A GROUP?

There has been considerable controversy as to what a group is. The purpose of this exercise is to structure a critical examination of the different definitions. The procedure is as follows:

1. The class forms groups of seven members.
2. Each member receives a sheet containing one of the seven definitions that appear on the following pages. Without interacting with the other group members, each member is to
   a. Study his or her definition until it is thoroughly understood.
   b. Plan how to teach the definition to the other members of the group.
   c. Name three examples of groups that meet the criterion contained in the definition.
   d. Name three examples of two or more people in close proximity who do not meet the criterion contained in the definition.
   e. Explain in what way(s) his or her group (doing this exercise) meets the criterion contained in the definition.
   About 10 minutes are allowed for this phase of the exercise.
3. Each group meets to derive a single definition of the concept group. Up to 20 minutes are allowed for this phase.
4. Each group reads its definition to the entire class.
5. If there is substantial disagreement, the class forms new groups (composed of one member from each of the previous groups). The task of the new group is to arrive at one definition of the concept group, each member representing the definition of his or her former group.
6. Each group reads its definition to the entire class.

### Interpersonal Interaction

A group may be defined as a number of individuals who are interacting with one another. According to this definition, a group does not exist unless the individuals are interacting with one another. Four psychologists who have defined group in this way are Hare, Bonner, Stogdill, and Homans.

For a collection of individuals to be considered a group there must be some interaction. (Hare, 1976, p. 4)

A group is a number of people in interaction with one another, and it is this interaction process that distinguishes the group from an aggregate. (Bonner, 1959, p. 4)

A group may be regarded as an open interaction system in which actions determine the structure of the system and successive interactions exert coequal effects upon the identity of the system. (Stodgill, 1959, p. 18)

> We mean by a group a number of persons who communicate with one another often over a span of time, and who are few enough so that each person is able to communicate with all the others, not at secondhand, through other people, but face-to-face. (Homans, 1950, p. 1)

All four of these definitions stress that the primary defining characteristic of a group is interpersonal interaction. It is questionable that a group can exist without its members interacting with one another.

### Perceptions of Membership

A group may be defined as a social unit consisting of two or more persons who perceive themselves as belonging to a group. According to this definition, the persons are not a group unless they perceive themselves to be part of a group. Two psychologists who have defined group in this way are Bales and Smith:

> A small group is defined as any number of persons engaged in interaction with one another in a single face-to-face meeting or series of such meetings, in which each member receives some impression or perception of each other member distinct enough so that he can, either at the time or in later questioning, give some reaction to each of the others as an individual person, even though it be only to recall that the other was present. (Bales, 1950, p. 33)

> We may define a social group as a unit consisting of a plural number of separate organisms (agents) who have a collective perception of their unity and who have the ability to act and/or are acting in a unitary manner toward their environment. (Smith, 1945, p. 227)

Both definitions stress that the primary defining characteristic of a group is that the members perceive themselves to be part of a group. It is questionable that a group could exist without its members being aware that they are members of a group.

### Interdependency

A group may be defined as a collection of individuals who are interdependent. According to this definition, the individuals are not a group unless an event that affects one of them affects them all. Four psychologists who have defined group in this way are Cartwright and Zander, Fiedler, and Lewin:

> A group is a collection of individuals who have relations to one another that make them interdependent to some significant degree. As so defined, the term group refers to a class of social entities having in common the property of interdependence among their constituent members. (Cartwright & Zander, 1968, p. 46)

> By this term [group] we generally mean a set of individuals who share a common fate, that is, who are interdependent in the sense that an event which affects one member is likely to affect all. (Fiedler, 1967, p. 6)

> Conceiving of a group as a dynamic whole should include a definition of group which is based on interdependence of the members (or better, the subparts of the group). (Lewin, 1951, p. 146)

All three definitions stress that the primary defining characteristic of a group is that the members are interdependent in some way. It is questionable that a group could exist without its members being interdependent.

### Goals

Groups exist for a reason. People join groups in order to achieve goals they are unable to achieve by themselves. A group may be defined as a number of individuals who join together to achieve a goal. Three psychologists who have defined group this way are Mills, Deutsch, and Freeman:

> To put it simply, they [small groups] are units composed of two or more persons who come into contact for a purpose and who consider the contact meaningful. (Mills, 1967, p. 2)

> A psychological group exists (has unity) to the extent that the individuals composing it perceive themselves as pursuing promotively interdependent goals. (Deutsch, 1949a, p. 136)

> Freeman, as early as 1936, pointed out that people join groups in order to achieve common goals.

These definitions stress that the primary defining characteristic of a group is the striving of its members to achieve a mutual goal. It is questionable whether a group could exist unless there was a mutual goal that its members were trying to achieve.

### Motivation

A group may be defined as a collection of individuals who are trying to satisfy some personal need through their joint association. According to this definition, the individuals are not a group unless they are motivated by some personal reason to be part of a group. Two psychologists who have defined group in this way are Bass and Cattell:

> We define "group" as a collection of individuals whose existence as a collection is rewarding to the individuals. (Bass, 1960, p. 39)

> The definition which seems most essential is that a group is a collection of organisms in which the existence of all (in their given relationships) is necessary to the satisfaction of certain individual needs in each. (Cattell, 1951, p. 167)

> Both definitions stress that the primary defining characteristic of a group is that its members belong to the group in order to obtain needed rewards or to satisfy other personal needs. It is questionable that a group could exist without its members' needs being satisfied by their membership.

### Structured Relationships

A group may be defined as a collection of individuals whose interactions are structured by a set of roles and norms. According to this definition, the individuals are not a group unless their interactions are structured by a set of role definitions and norms. Two sets of psychologists who have defined group in this way are McDavid and Harari and Sherif and Sherif:

> A social-psychological group is an organized system of two or more individuals who are interrelated so that the system performs some function, has a standard set of role relationships among its members, and has a set of norms that regulate the function of the group and each of its members. (McDavid & Harari, 1968, p. 237)

> A group is a social unit which consists of a number of individuals who stand in (more or less) definite status and role relationships to one another and which possesses a set of values or norms of its own regulating the behavior of individual members, at least in matters of consequence to the group. (Sherif & Sherif, 1956, p. 144)

Both these definitions stress that the primary defining characteristic of a group is that the interaction of its members is structured by role definitions and norms. It is questionable whether a group could exist unless role definitions and norms structured the interaction of its members.

### Mutual Influence

A group may be defined as a collection of individuals who influence each other. According to this definition, the individuals are not a group unless they are affecting and being affected by each other. Shaw (1976, p. 11) defined group in this way:

> A group is defined as two or more persons who are interacting with one another in such a manner that each person influences and is influenced by each other person.

This definition stresses that the primary defining characteristic of a group is interpersonal influence. It is questionable that a group could exist without its members influencing each other.

## WHAT IS A GROUP?

It takes two flints to make a fire.

*Louisa May Alcott*

In a bus trapped in a traffic jam, six passengers begin to talk to each other, comparing reactions and sharing previous similar experiences. They start to develop a plan of action to get the bus out of the heavy traffic. Is this a group? In Yellowstone National Park it is deep winter. Several cross-country skiers glide through an isolated, snow covered valley. They are participating in a Minnesota Science Museum tour to study winter ecology and photography. Periodically, they stop and cluster around a professional photographer as he explains the ways the winter scenes may be photographed. The vacationers admire and discuss the beautiful winter scenery as they photograph it. Is this a group? Do groups exist at all?

There are psychologists who like to work on the level of the individual, stressing each person's perceptions, beliefs, and actions. Some social psychologists have even suggested that groups are not real. The late Floyd Allport believed that groups existed only in the minds of people. He used to say, "You can't stumble over a group." To Allport, groups are no more than shared sets of values, ideas, thoughts, and habits that exist simultaneously in the minds of several persons. Other social psychologists stress the unique aspects of the group process in and of itself.

How do you tell when you are a member of a group? Not every collection of people can be considered a group. The term **aggregate** refers to collections of individuals who do not interact with one another. Individuals standing on a street corner, the members of an audience at a play, and students listening to a lecture are aggregates, not groups. Yet groups do exist. As you have learned from the preceding exercise, there are many different definitions of the concept group. The social scientists who have tried to define what a group is seem much like the blind men trying to describe an elephant. Each social scientist has taken some aspect of a group and assumed that aspect revealed the essence of a group.

One solution to the profusion of definitions is to combine them all into one definition. A group may be defined as two or more individuals who (1) interact with each other, (2) are interdependent, (3) define themselves and are defined by others as belonging to the group, (4) share norms concerning matters of common interest and participate in a system of interlocking roles, (5) influence each other, (6) find the group rewarding, and (7) pursue common goals. Not all of these characteristics are equally important, and while it is impossible to gain consensus among social scientists as to which characteristics are most important, the authors prefer the following definition: A group is two or more individuals in face-to-face interaction, each aware of his or her membership in the group, each aware of the others who belong to the group, and each aware of their positive interdependence as they strive to achieve mutual goals. Though there may be some groups that do not fully fit this definition, the most commonly recognized examples of groups do.

Based on the above definition, how do you tell the difference between an aggregate and a group? Is an audience at a concert a group? Are the people traveling in the same airplane a group? Are the children waiting in the same line to talk to Santa Claus a group? Are all 21-year-old males in our society a group?

## THE FIELD OF GROUP DYNAMICS

> Close cooperation between theorists and practitioners can be accomplished . . . if the theorist does not look toward applied problems with highbrow aversion or with a fear of social problems, and if the applied psychologist realizes that there is nothing so practical as a good theory.
>
> *Kurt Lewin (1951, p. 169)*

To understand group dynamics, it must be defined as a field of study, the theories that delineate the dimensions of effective groups must be identified, research to validate or disconfirm the theories must be reviewed, and the practical value of group dynamics theory and research must be established. The theory, research, and practical applications of group dynamics all interact and enhance each other (see Figure 1.1). Theory both guides and summarizes research. Research validates or disconfirms theory, thereby leading to its refinement and modification. Practice is guided by validated theory, and applications of the theory reveal inadequacies that lead to refining of the theory, conducting new research studies, and modifying the application. In this book theory, research, and practice are all emphasized.

**Group dynamics** is the scientific study of behavior in groups to advance our knowledge about the nature of groups, group development, and the interrelations between groups and individuals, other groups, and larger entities. Social scientists interested in group dynamics subject the many aspects of groups to scientific analysis through the construction of theories and the rigorous testing of the adequacy of these theories through empirical research. They then apply the validated theory to "real-world" situations. Group dynamics is an interdisciplinary field belonging to many

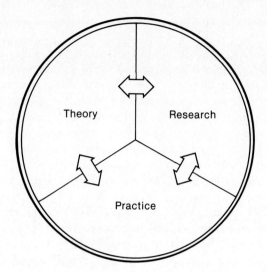

**FIGURE 1.1**   Relationship Among Theory, Research, Practice   From D. W. Johnson and R. T. Johnson, *Cooperation and Competition: Theory and Research* (Edina, MN: Interaction Book Company, 1989). Used with permission of the authors.

different branches of the social sciences. It is the common property of all social sciences.

There are two contrasting approaches to group dynamics. The **individualistic orientation** focuses on the individual in the group. To explain the functioning of the group, psychologists focus on the attitudes, cognitions, and personalities of the members. Floyd Allport used to say that groups had no nervous systems, only individuals have nervous systems. Allport believed that the actions of a group are nothing more than the sum of the actions of each member taken separately. The **group orientation** focuses on the group as a whole. In explaining the behavior of the members, social scientists focus on the influences of the group and the larger social systems of which it is part. In the late 1800s Emile Durkheim (1866) posited that small **primary groups** (small groups characterized by face-to-face interaction, interdependency, and strong group identification such as families and very close friends) were the building blocks of society, and he worked upward from this level to an analysis of social systems in general. He was convinced that a groupmind- or collective consciousness–dominated individual will in many situations. Lewin, as a Gestalt psychologist, noted that a group cannot be understood by considering only the qualities and characteristics of each member. When individuals merge into a group, something new is created that must be seen as an entity in and of itself. Changes in one aspect of a group will necessarily lead to changes in the other group features. Social scientists of both the individualistic and group persuasions have been productive in generating theories of group functioning and conducting research to validate or disconfirm the theories. They are both represented in this book.

To understand group dynamics you must know that all groups have a basic structure, you must know that groups change and develop over time, and you must comprehend the difference between effective and ineffective groups.

# GROUP STRUCTURE

Imagine you are living 300 years ago and you are an explorer who has viewed six of the seven corners of the world. You have encountered many strange and unique habitats in your travels, from thick rain forests to severe deserts, and as you approach the world's seventh corner, you look for features you have grown to expect: topography, weather patterns, plants, animals, and their interconnections. You have observed, for example, that plants and animals have certain territories that comprise an elaborate division of labor and broad symbioses and that plants and animals adapt over time so that they are uniquely suited to survive and flourish within their habitat. Thus, as a seasoned explorer, you expect to find a basic ecological structure within any corner of the world.

Now imagine you are an explorer of small groups. Needless to say, in your travels you have encountered many strange and unique groups. As you approach new groups you look for the features you have grown to expect: a group purpose that defines the territory of the group, different members of the group performing different functions that fit into an overall division of labor, a set of expectations concerning acceptable and unacceptable behavior by group members, and the adaptation of the group to the organization, society, and culture within which it is based. Once the basic structure has been identified, the nature of interpersonal relations in the group can be understood as clearly as the functioning of an ecosystem.

Just like ecosystems, groups have a structure. Observers of groups look beyond the unique features of the group to its basic structure. The **group structure** is a stable pattern of interaction among members. Groups function as members interact. Groups are networks of human relationships, and a group is effective only if members are effective in cooperating with each other. Whenever two or more individuals join together to achieve a goal, a group structure develops. Within any group, no matter which organization, society, or culture it is within, there are differentiated roles and integrating norms. The interaction among group members is structured by the group's roles and norms. Roles differentiate the responsibilities of group members while norms integrate members' efforts into a unified whole. Each is discussed briefly below.

## Roles: Differentiation Within Groups

Think of one of the groups to which you have belonged. Once you have a specific group in mind, answer this question: Did everyone in the group act in the same way or perform the same functions? In all likelihood, your answer is "no." Usually, a considerable degree of **differentiation** exists within groups so that different members work on different tasks and are expected to accomplish different things for the group. In other words, different group members play different roles. Roles define the formal structure of the group and differentiate one position from another. Formally, a **role** may be defined as a set of expectations defining the appropriate behavior of an occupant of a position toward other related positions. Often such roles are assigned in a relatively formal manner, such as appointing a president, secretary, treasurer, and so on. Other times individuals drift into various roles on the basis of their interests and skills. Once a role is assumed, however, the member is expected (by other group members) to behave in certain ways and members who conform to their role requirements are rewarded, while those who deviate are punished. Roles ensure that the task behaviors of group members are appropriately interrelated so that the group's goals are achieved. The roles are complementary in that one cannot be performed without the other (e.g., the roles of "teacher" and "student"). The expectations that define a role include both rights and obligations. The obligations of one role are the rights of other roles. One of the obligations of being a "teacher," for example, includes structuring a learning situation; one of the rights of being a "student" is to have learning situations structured by the teacher. Within a group, expectations of the obligations of a role can conflict (i.e., **role conflict**). What a principal and what students expect from a teacher, for example, can be contradictory.

## Norms: Integration of Members' Actions

While roles differentiate members' rights and obligations from each other, norms integrate the actions of all group members. Norms are rules, implicit or explicit, established by groups to regulate the behavior of their members. Norms tell group members how to behave, or how *not* to behave, in various situations. The **norms** of a group are the group's common beliefs regarding appropriate behavior for members. They are the prescribed modes of conduct and belief that not only guide the behavior of group members, but also help group interaction by specifying the kinds of responses that are expected and acceptable in particular situations. All groups have norms, set either formally or informally. A group of students that often parties together, for example, will have common ideas about what is acceptable and unacceptable behavior at a party, about what is expected of everyone. More formally organized groups, such as classrooms, will have norms about absence, tardiness, accomplishment of assigned work, and appropriate times to speak. In any group some norms specify the behavior expected of all group members and others apply only to persons in specific roles. In the classroom, for instance, some norms govern both the teacher's and the students' behavior, but others may apply only to the teacher or only to the students. Because norms refer to the expected behavior sanctioned (rewarded or punished) by a group, they have a specific "ought to" or "must" quality: group members must not disrupt the group's work, group members ought to participate in discussions, and so on. The norms of any group vary in importance. Those that are less important for the objectives and values of the group usually allow for a greater range of behavior and bring less severe pressures for members to conform than do norms that are highly relevant to group functioning. Since most groups insist on adherence to their norms as a basic requirement for membership, it is hardly surprising that individuals wishing to join or remain in specific groups generally follow these "rules of the game." If they do not, they may soon find themselves on the outside looking in.

For a group norm to influence a person's behavior, the person must recognize that it exists, be aware that other group members accept and follow the regulation, and accept and follow it himself. At first a person may conform to a group norm because the group typically rewards conforming behavior and punishes nonconforming behavior. Later the person may internalize the norm and conform to it automatically, even when no other group members are present. A regulation that all members should be on time for group meetings, for example, becomes a norm only to the extent that the individual group member accepts it, sees other group members accepting it, and sees them enforce the regulation among themselves.

Group norms help a group maintain behavioral consistency among its members. They provide a basis for predicting the behavior of other members and serve as guide for a member's own behavior. Norms thus help each group member anticipate how the others are going to behave in repetitive situations, and they reduce ambiguity concerning appropriate behavior within the group. Norms are formed only with respect to matters that have some significance for the group. Norms may apply to all members or only to certain members. Norms vary in the degree to which they are accepted by the group members. Some norms allow for more deviation by members than others. Some norms require strict adherence to a rule; others permit a wide range of behavior that is regarded as acceptable.

Norms cannot be imposed on a group, but rather develop out of the interaction among members. Norms are social products. This was demonstrated ingeniously by Muzafer Sherif (1936a). When a fixed point of light is viewed in total darkness, it appears to move spontaneously: a perceptual phenomenon known as the autokinetic effect. Sherif utilized this phenomenon in studying how group norms develop and how group members come to form coherent, shared beliefs about novel events. Sherif asked participants, first individually and then in groups, to note how much the light moved. When tested in groups the participants coalesced in their judgments on the amount of movement. Once a group decision was made about how much the light was moving, the norm persisted even when the group was not present. Individual participants used the group judgment as a frame of reference within which to evaluate the perceived movement of the light. Many of the judgments and values of individual group members that seem to be their own are shaped in part by the judgments of their fellow group members.

Another classic study on the impact of group norms on the beliefs and values of group members was conducted by Theodore Newcomb (1943). Born in 1903, Newcomb had studied with Goodwin Watson and Gardner Murphy at Columbia University. He was a pioneer of social psychology and a cofounder of the social psychology program at the University of Michigan. He conducted a number of studies on the impact of the college experience on students, the most famous of which was his classic study of group norms at Bennington College. The students, all females from mostly well-to-do and politically conservative families, lived in a community where most of the faculty and older students were somewhat amaterialistic and politically liberal. A majority of the Bennington students became progressively more liberal over their careers, but some did not. Newcomb was able to relate the student's ultimate political orientation to the group she identified with—liberal, if she thought of herself as foremost a member of the campus community, and conservative, if her primary identification was with her family. This study served as the basis on which the study of referenced groups began. A **reference group** is a group people identify with, compare their attitudes to, and use as a means to evaluate those attitudes.

## THE DEVELOPMENT OF GROUPS OVER TIME

Groups change over time. The kinds of developmental changes seen in most groups have been described by well over 100 theories. Most of these theories have taken one of two approaches (Hill & Gruner, 1973; Shambaugh, 1978). **Sequential-stage theories** specify the "typical" order of the phases of group development. Probably the most famous sequential stage theory was formulated by Bruce W. Tuckman (1965; Tuckman & Jensen, 1977). He stated that groups develop through five stages which he labeled forming, storming, norming, performing, and adjourning. The theory is described in some detail in Chapter 10. In the forming stage, members become oriented toward each other. In the storming stage, members often find themselves in conflict and its management becomes the focus of attention. In the norming stage, a role structure and a set of group norms are formulated. In the performing stage, the group works as a unit to achieve the group's goals. In the adjourning stage, the group disbands.

Recurring-phase theories specify the issues that dominate group interaction which reoccur again and again. Robert Freed Bales (1965), for example, stated that an equilibrium had to exist between task-oriented work and emotional expressions to build better relationships among group members. The group tends to oscillate between these two concerns, sometimes striving for more solidarity and sometimes striving for a more work-oriented focus. Bion (1961) stated that groups focus on the three basic themes of dependency on the leader, pairing among members for emotional support, and fight-flight reactions to a threat to the group.

Both the sequential-stage and the recurring-phase perspectives are useful for understanding group development. They are not contradictory. A group may move through various stages while dealing with basic themes that surface as they become relevant to the group's work. Because the issues underlying the themes are never completely resolved, they can recur later.

Roles and norms define the group's structure. The structure of a group changes over time. A group's structure is evaluated on the basis of how well it facilitates the achievement of the group's goals. In other words, the structure exists to ensure that the group is effective.

## EFFECTIVE GROUPS AND EFFECTIVE GROUP SKILLS

I will pay more for the ability to deal with people than for any other ability under the sun.

*John D. Rockefeller*

A small manufacturing firm in Milwaukee is in the midst of a literacy program to bring the reading level of their employees up to a 9th grade level and the math knowledge of employees up to a 10th grade level. Currently, their employees read at the 7th grade level and can do 6th grade math. Four employees are studying together to improve each other's math skills. As they work through the math text, they explain to each other how to solve the problems. Will the company program be successful?

Simply placing individuals in groups and telling them to work together does not in and of itself promote productivity. There are many ways in which group efforts may go wrong. Less able members sometimes "leave it to George" to complete the group's tasks thus creating a **free rider effect** (Kerr & Bruun, 1983) whereby group members expend decreasing amounts of effort and just go through the teamwork

**Table 1.1**   Comparison of effective and ineffective groups.

| Effective Groups | Ineffective Groups |
|---|---|
| Goals are clarified and changed so that the best possible match between individual goals and the group's goals may be achieved; goals are cooperatively structured. | Members accept imposed goals; goals are competitively structured. |
| Communication is two-way, and the open and accurate expression of both ideas and feelings is emphasized. | Communication is one-way and only ideas are expressed; feelings are suppressed or ignored. |
| Participation and leadership are distributed among all group members; goal accomplishment, internal maintenance, and developmental change are underscored. | Leadership is delegated and based upon authority; membership participation is unequal, with high-authority members dominating; only goal accomplishment is emphasized. |
| Ability and information determine influence and power; contracts are built to make sure individuals' goals and needs are fulfilled; power is equalized and shared. | Position determines influence and power; power is concentrated in the authority positions; obedience to authority is the rule. |
| Decision-making procedures are matched with the situation; different methods are used at different times; consensus is sought for important decisions; involvement and group discussions are encouraged. | Decisions are always made by the highest authority; there is little group discussion; members' involvement is minimal. |
| Controversy and conflict are seen as a positive key to members' involvement, the quality and originality of decisions, and the continuance of the group in good working condition. | Controversy and conflict are ignored, denied, avoided, or suppressed. |
| Interpersonal, group, and intergroup behaviors are stressed; cohesion is advanced through high levels of inclusion, affection, acceptance, support, and trust. Individuality is endorsed. | The functions performed by members are emphasized; cohesion is ignored and members are controlled by force. Rigid conformity is promoted. |
| Problem-solving adequacy is high. | Problem-solving adequacy is low. |
| Members evaluate the effectiveness of the group and decide how to improve its functioning; goal accomplishment, internal maintenance, and development are all considered important. | The highest authority evaluates the group's effectiveness and decides how goal accomplishment may be improved; internal maintenance and development are ignored as much as possible; stability is affirmed. |
| Interpersonal effectiveness, self-actualization, and innovation are encouraged. | "Organizational persons" who desire order, stability, and structure are encouraged. |

motions. At the same time, the more able group member may expend less effort to avoid the **sucker effect** of doing all the work (Kerr, 1983). High-ability group members may be deferred to and may take over the important leadership roles in ways that benefit them at the expense of the other group members (the **rich-get-richer effect**). In a learning group, for example, the more able group member may give all the explanations of what is being learned. Since the amount of time spent explaining correlates highly with the amount learned, the more able member learns a great deal while the less able members flounder as a captive audience. The time spent listening in group brainstorming can reduce the amount of time any individual can state their ideas (Hill, 1982; Lamm & Trommsdorff, 1973). Group efforts can be characterized by self-induced helplessness (Langer & Beneven to, 1978), diffusion of responsibility and social loafing (Latane, Williams, & Harkins, 1979), ganging up against a task, or reactance (Salomon, 1981), dysfunctional divisions of labor ("I'm the thinkist and you're the typist") (Sheingold, Hawkins, & Char, 1984), inappropriate dependence on authority (Webb, Ender, & Lewis, 1986), destructive conflict (Collins, 1970; Johnson & Johnson, 1979), and other patterns of behavior that debilitate group performance.

There are many ways, therefore, that groups can function in unproductive ways. Group effectiveness does not magically appear when a group is formed. Members must consciously work to build and maintain the effectiveness of their group. To work to make a group more effective, members must have a clear model of what an effective group is. Any **effective group** has three core activities: (1) accomplishing its goals, (2) maintaining good working relationships among members, and (3) developing and adapting to changing conditions in ways that improve its effectiveness. Group members must have the skills to eliminate barriers to the accomplishment of the group's goals, to solve problems in maintaining high-quality interaction among members, and to overcome obstacles to the development of a more effective group.

The dimensions of group effectiveness make up a model that can be used to diagnosis how well a group is functioning (see Table 1.1). The model provides a direction in building a productive group. An awareness of the difference between the ideal model and the actual group functioning motivates group members to improve their effectiveness. The dimensions of an effective group, discussed in detail in later chapters, are as follows (see Figure 1.2):

1. *Group goals must be clearly understood, be relevant to the needs of group members, highlight the positive interdependence of members, and evoke from every member a high level of commitment to their accomplishment.* Groups form for a cooperative purpose. When the personal goals of individual group members are interdependent a group goal results. Cooperation among group members is so fundamental that it is part of the definition of what is a group. It is our ability to engage in cooperative enterprises to achieve group goals that distinguishes us as a species. Cooperation, compared with competitive or individualistic efforts, tends to promote higher achievement and productivity, more caring and committed relationships among group members, and greater member psychological health and social competence. Group goals and social interdependence are discussed in Chapter 3.

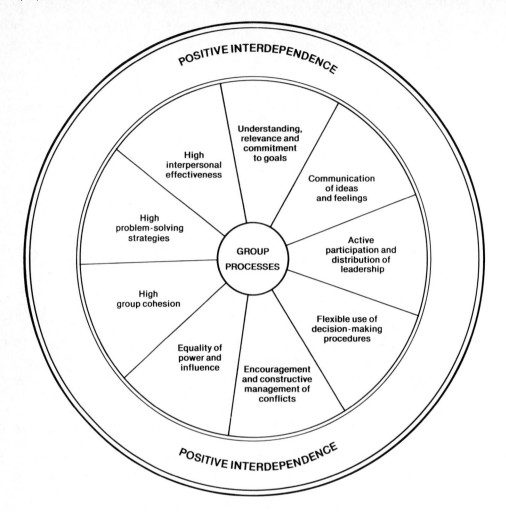

**FIGURE 1.2.** Components of an Effective Group   From D. W. Johnson and R. T. Johnson, *Cooperation and Competition: Theory and Research* (Edina, MN: Interaction Book Company, 1989). Used with permission of the authors.

2. *Group members must communicate their ideas and feelings accurately and clearly.* Effective, two-way communication is the basis of all group functioning and interaction among group members. Communication among group members is discussed in Chapter 4.

3. *Participation and leadership must be distributed among members.* All members should participate, and all should be listened to. As leadership needs arise, all members should feel responsible for meeting them. The equalization of participation and leadership makes certain that all members are involved in the group's work, committed to implementing the group's decisions, and satisfied with their member-

ship. It also (a) assures that the resources of every member are fully utilized and (b) increases the cohesiveness of the group. Leadership is discussed in Chapter 5.

4. *Appropriate decision-making procedures must be used flexibly to match them with the needs of the situation.* There must be a balance between the availability of time and resources (such as members' skills) and the method of decision making used. Another balance must be struck among the size and seriousness of the decision, the commitment needed to put it into practice, and the method used for making the decision. The most effective way of making a decision is usually by consensus (unanimous agreement). Consensus promotes distributed participation, the equalization of power, productive controversy, cohesion, involvement, and commitment. Decision making is discussed in Chapter 6.

5. *Conflicts should be encouraged and managed constructively.* Constructive management of conflicts are an important aspect of promoting the productivity of the group. Conflicts are inevitable within groups. And the occurrence of a conflict is a "moment of truth" within a group that determines whether the productivity of the group will increase or decrease. **Controversies** (conflicts among opposing ideas and conclusions) promote involvement in the group's work, quality and creativity in decision making, and commitment to implementing the group's decisions. Minority opinions should be accepted and used. All decisions are by their very nature controversies. Yet intellectual conflict is rarely created, managed, and resolved within decision-making situations. Conflicts promoted by incompatible needs or goals, by the scarcity of a resource (money or power), and by competitiveness (i.e., **conflicts of interest**), must be negotiated in a manner that is mutually satisfying and does not weaken the cooperative interdependence of group members. Controversy is discussed in Chapter 7 and conflicts of interest are discussed in Chapter 8.

6. *Power and influence need to be approximately equal throughout the group.* Power should be based on expertise, ability, and access to information, not on authority. Coalitions that help fulfill personal goals should be formed among group members on the basis of mutual influence and interdependence. Power is discussed in Chapter 9.

7. *Group cohesion needs to be high.* Consider two groups: in the first, members like one another and are strongly committed to the goals the group is seeking and, therefore, they believe that they could not possibly find another group that better fills their needs; in the second, members dislike each other and do not share common goals and, therefore, they are seeking alternative groups that may offer them a better deal. Which group would be more productive and exert stronger effects on its members? The answer is obvious. Generally, the higher the cohesiveness of a group, the more productive it tends to be. **Cohesion** is based on members liking each other, desiring to continue as part of the group, and being satisfied with their group membership. It is all the forces, both positive and negative, that cause individuals to remain in a group. On the positive side are such factors as attraction among members, a good match between individual needs and the group's goals, and high costs associated with leaving. On the negative side are low attraction among members, a poor match between individual needs and group goals, and low costs of withdrawing and seeking membership in other groups. The more cohesive the group,

the more influence it will have on the behavior, judgments, and attitudes of its members. Members of cohesive groups rely on each other for defining their social reality. That is, when they cannot test a belief or perception against physical reality they will validate it on the basis of the consensual agreement of other group members—social reality. Festinger (1954) developed a theory of social comparison based on this phenomenon. The norms of a group may be so strong that new leaders coming into the group need to accommodate themselves to the well-established customs and traditions. Cohesiveness is discussed in Chapter 12.

8. *Problem-solving adequacy should be high.* Problems must be solved with minimal energy and in a way that eliminates them permanently. Procedures should exist for sensing the existence of problems, inventing and implementing solutions, and evaluating the effectiveness of the solutions. When problems are dealt with adequately, the problem-solving ability of the group is increased, innovation is encouraged, and group effectiveness is improved. Problem solving is discussed in Chapter 12.

9. *The interpersonal effectiveness of members needs to be high.* Interpersonal effectiveness is a measure of how well the consequences of your behavior match your intentions. Johnson (1990) has focused on this subject and, therefore, it will not be discussed at length in this book.

## EXERCISE 1.4:
## DEVELOPING AN EFFECTIVE GROUP

The purpose of this exercise is to give participants some practice in planning how to develop an effective group. The procedure for the exercise is as follows:

1. The class forms groups of four.
2. Groups read and discuss the paragraph below, and then answer the following questions about the situation:
   a. What should the goals of the group be?
   b. How should leadership be managed?
   c. Who should have the most power in making decisions?
   d. What decision-making procedure should be used?
   e. How should conflicts be managed?
3. Each group decides whether its answers to the above questions are indicative of an effective or an ineffective group.
4. Each group shares its answers with the rest of the class.

### Sinking Boat Situation

On a dark summer night seven persons cling to a swamped and slowly sinking boat on a black tropical sea. They are not alone. A large shark glides below them, and soon, perhaps, there will be more. With fear thick in their salt-swollen throats, the seven are faced with a difficult choice. If they kick in unison, they may be able to fight the fierce current and tides driving them away from the shore and all make it to safety; if they stick together they have an equal chance to survive or drown. If they split up, each going it alone, one or two of the stronger swimmers might make it to safety, but the majority will certainly drown or be devoured by sharks.

Which alternative would you choose if you were there? What kind of people would you want as companions in such a situation?

# KURT LEWIN AND THE FIELD OF GROUP DYNAMICS

Group dynamics is a relatively young field, one that is rooted in a wide range of traditionally separate fields. Although the earliest existing philosophical literature contains a great deal of wisdom about the nature of groups, and although the basic assumptions that guide the field of group dynamics were discussed from the sixteenth through the nineteenth centuries, the field of group dynamics is strictly a twentieth-century development.

The first focus of researchers was on the question, "What change in an individual's normal solitary performance occurs when other people are present?" In the late nineteenth century, Norman Triplett, an Indiana University psychologist, became interested in the effects of other people on individual performance. In studying the records of the Racing Board of the League of American Wheelmen, Triplett observed that cyclists' times were faster when they were racing against each other than when the cyclists simply raced against the clock. He hypothesized that the presence of other people (i.e., competitors) acts as a stimulant to the performer. If the hypothesis were valid, Triplett reasoned, it would hold for activities other than bicycle racing. Creating an analogy to bicycle racing, Triplett (1898) asked children to wind fishing reels and compared their performance when alone with their performance when another child was present. This experiment was the first attempt to investigate the impact of social interdependence (i.e., competitive versus individualistic efforts) on achievement on a motor performance task.

If you were running a mile, would an audience make you run faster or slower? If you were asked to assemble a complex new machine you had never seen before, would an audience increase or decrease the speed with which you assembled the machine? Early in the 1900s a number of psychologists continued the investigation of whether the presence of other people facilitated or inhibited performance on a variety of tasks (Allport, 1924; Moede, 1920). They found that on simple tasks an audience increased speed of performance, while on complex tasks an audience decreased the speed of performance. A related line of research compared the performance of individuals and groups to determine which were more productive (Gordon, 1924; Shaw, 1932; Watson, 1928). Overall, the results indicated that groups were more productive than were individuals.

At the end of the 1930s a rapid advance in the field took place, due largely to the efforts of three sociologists. Sherif (1936a) studied the impact of group norms on perception of an ambiguous stimulus. In an ingenious experiment he demonstrated that the judgments made by individuals were influenced by the judgments of their fellow group members. During the years 1935 to 1939, Newcomb (1943) conducted a field study investigating the impact of social norms concerning political issues on the students at Bennington College. Most of the students came from politically conservative homes, but the prevailing political attitudes among them were liberal. Newcomb documented how the interaction of the students changed their attitudes so that they become more congruent with the prevailing norms of the peer group. In 1937 W. F. Whyte moved into one of the slums of Boston and began a three-and-a-half-year study of social clubs, political organizations, and racketeering. Whyte (1943) reported in vivid detail the structure, culture, and functioning of the Norton Street gang and the Italian Community Club. His study dramatized the great significance of groups in the lives of individuals and in the functioning of larger social systems.

By far the most influential study of group dynamics in the late 1930s, however, was that of three psychologists, Lewin, Lippitt, and White (1939). They studied the influences on groups and group members of different leadership patterns. Groups of 10- and 11-year-old children met regularly for several weeks under the leadership of an adult, who behaved in one of three ways: in a democratic, autocratic, or a laissez-faire manner. The effects of these leadership styles on the behavior of group members were large and dramatic. Severe forms of scapegoating, for example, occurred in the autocratic groups, and at the end of the experiment the children in some of those groups destroyed the things they had constructed. This study made it clear that important social issues could be produced in the laboratory and studied experimentally.

Almost immediately Lewin and his students and associates began a number of research studies aimed at developing a theory of group dynamics. French (1941) conducted a laboratory experiment comparing the effects of fear and frustration on organized versus unorganized groups. Bavelas (1942) conducted an experiment to determine whether the behavior of leaders of youth groups could be significantly modified through training. With the entry of the United States into World War II, Lewin, French, and Marrow (Marrow, 1957) explored group decision procedures as a means of improving industrial production, and Lewin, Radke, and others (Lewin, 1943a; Radke & Klisurich, 1947) conducted a number of experiments on group decision as a means of changing eating habits related to wartime food shortages.

In the 1940s, after a worldwide depression, the rise of dictatorship in Europe, and World War II, most Americans were worried about the fate of their country and the future of democracy. There was general agreement that a better understanding was needed of how democratic organizations could be made to function more effectively. Scientists had helped win the war, many people said, and now research should improve democracy. The field of group dynamics was thought to have significant potential for improving democracy. The health of a democratic society was seen as depending on the effectiveness of its component groups. Strengthening the family, the community, and the multitude of groups within our society was viewed as the primary means of ensuring the vitality of our democracy. At the same time, the notion that the scientific method could be employed in the task of improving group life gained popularity. People began to see that the scientific method could be applied to important social issues involving the functioning of groups, for example, leadership, decision making, and productivity. The belief that the solution of social problems could be facilitated by systematic research gained acceptance.

The drive to strengthen democracy by using the scientific method to strengthen groups resulted in two movements within psychology. The first was the scientific study of group dynamics. Social psychologists (a newly arrived group of specialists) began to conduct studies of group discussion, group productivity, attitude change, and leadership. They developed experimental methods of studying group dynamics, hoping thereby to find ways of strengthening democracy. Concurrently, the second movement began deriving methods for training leaders and group members in the social skills they would need to promote the effective functioning of democratic groups.

At the head of both movements was one of the most important psychologists of the twentieth century, Kurt Lewin. Lewin was born on September 9, 1890, in the tiny village of Mogilno in the Prussian province of Posen (now part of Poland), where his father owned and operated a general store. In 1910 Lewin began studying for a doctorate in philosophy and psychology at the University of Berlin. After finishing his doctoral work in 1914 he entered the Kaiser's army as a private and fought for four years in World War I in the infantry. He left the army as a lieutenant with an Iron Cross and returned to the University of Berlin to teach. There he became part of the Psychological Institute, where Max Wertheimer, Kurt Koffka, and Wolfgang Kohler were formulating their Gestalt theory. Lewin became one of the Gestaltists, but he was never an orthodox follower of their early leaders. His interests were in the area of motivation, and his work was directed more to practical application than to understanding for its own sake. In 1933, as Hitler was rising to power, Lewin migrated to the United States. He subsequently worked at Cornell University, the University of Iowa (where he taught at the Child Welfare Research Station), and the Massachusetts Institute of Technology, where he set up and headed the famous Research Center for Group Dynamics (which later moved to the Institute for Social Research at the

Kurt Lewin

University of Michigan). On February 11, 1947, Lewin died unexpectedly of a heart attack.

It was Lewin more than anyone else who stressed the importance of applying existing knowledge to the training of leaders and members to promote effective functioning of democratic groups. In 1942, for example, World War II had just begun for America, and travel was restricted. The Society for the Psychological Study of Social Issues had canceled its annual convention and was holding a single dinner session for members who lived in the Washington, D.C., area. On that warm September evening, Kurt Lewin spoke to an audience deeply concerned about the fate of their country and the future of democracy. His listeners welcomed his brave prediction:

> Although the scientific investigations of group work are but a few years old, I don't hesitate to predict that group work—that is, the handling of human beings not as isolated individuals, but in the social setting of groups—will soon be one of the most important theoretical and practical fields. . . . There is no hope for creating a better world without a deeper scientific insight into the function of leadership and culture, and of other essentials of group life.
>
> *(Lewin, 1943b)*

Lewin's prediction came true. From 1890 to 1940 there had been a gradual growth in the number of published studies on group behavior from 1 per year to approximately 30 per year. By the late 1940s, 55 studies were being published annually, and by the end of the 1950s the rate had skyrocketed to about 150. During the 1960s and 1970s the rate of research studies on group dynamics persisted at about 125 per year.

The interest in applied psychology and social reform evident in Lewin's early work continued throughout his life. He believed that social psychology could provide the information and understanding required for the solution of society's fundamental problems. In his advocacy of the study of group dynamics Lewin was noted for three things: his early championing of the use of experimental methodology, his development of theory, and his insistence that theory and research be relevant to social practice.

Lewin had a genius for thinking of ways to study his ideas experimentally, and he inspired in his students something of this ability. It was Lewin's study of different leadership strategies that proved that complex social phenomena could be studied with experimental methods. Lewin was convinced that the use of experimental methods in researching the dynamics of groups would revolutionize the field, and he was right.

Lewin, however, was above all a theorist. Throughout his career he was concerned primarily with the problem of constructing an empirically based theory of human behavior. He did not see his commitment to theory as irrelevant to, or in any way incompatible with, his concern for the solution of social problems. He was convinced that the interests of the theorist and the practitioner were inextricably interrelated. Lewin assumed that every field of science must be concerned primarily with theory, because it is theory that illuminates the causal structure of the empirical world. He believed that social science theory should do more than advance knowledge—it should also provide the sort of understanding required for action. To advance knowledge and solve social problems, however, the theorist and the practitioner must work together. As Lewin (1951, p. 169) stated, close cooperation between theorists and practitioners "can be accomplished . . . if the theorist does not look toward applied problems with highbrow aversion or with a fear of social problems, and if the applied psychologist realizes that there is nothing so practical as a good theory." Lewin coined the term **action research** for the use of the scientific method in solving research questions that have significant social value. He urged social scientists to develop theories that can be applied to important social problems.

Lewin saw clearly that theorists and practitioners share a common interest in understanding reality and acting competently. He viewed them as having interdependent tasks: practitioners identify significant problems to be solved, theorists develop a valid view of reality that contains the keys for solving the problems, and practitioners apply the theory. Practitioners keep theorists in contact with social reality, and theorists provide practitioners with a deeper understanding of the social problems that confront them. Lewin believed that theorists have a special obligation: to provide the kind of theory that can be used in solving social problems. Lewin was a doer, and he wanted to conduct and inspire research that made a difference in the real world of human affairs. He was constantly suggesting ways to bridge the gap between theoretical science and public policies and practices. And the particular applications he suggested were infused with democratic values. He had a profound faith in democracy, which to him was much more than just a political system. It was also a way of life, based on mutual participation and continual interaction in decision making for purposeful change.

Lewin was in his element with an informal seminar group. He was not at his best in a formal lecture, as he was not highly organized. But he had an enthusiasm for psychological analysis that was contagious. His contacts with his students were so strong that sometimes an afternoon discussion would last beyond midnight. Informal group discussions reflected not only Lewin's style of interacting with other people but also his beliefs in democracy. Given his style of working with groups, his interests in social action, and his concern for democratic decision making, it was not surprising that Lewin turned increasingly to the study of group dynamics in his years in America. Although Lewin did not create the field of group dynamics (it was the result of many developments that occurred over a period of several years and in several different disciplines and professions), he was the major link between much of the theorizing and much of the practical application in the field. The contents of this book as well as the entire field of group dynamics are heavily influenced by Lewin and his work.

The use of experiential procedures to learn about behavior in groups was greatly influenced by Lewin. When Lee Bradford and Ken Benne were looking for help in training community leaders in leadership and group decision-making skills, they approached Kurt Lewin. What resulted was, of course, the experiential learning method. Lewin's colleagues and students have been the chief promoters of experiential learning in the area of group theory and group skills. One of Lewin's characteristics was to discover valuable concepts and principles by observing his own and other people's experiences. The most trivial event, the most casual comment, might spark a thought in Lewin's mind that would result in a new theoretical breakthrough in the social psychology of groups. Those associating with Lewin never knew when he might make an important discovery, and this produced an excitement rare in a relationship with a colleague or teacher. Students and colleagues learned from Lewin how important it is to examine one's own experiences for potential principles about the way in which groups develop and work. Thus, Lewin's personal style focused on experiential learning.

Much of Lewin's research highlighted the importance of active participation in groups in order to learn new skills, develop new attitudes, and obtain new knowledge about groups. His research demonstrated that learning is achieved most productively in groups whose members can interact and then reflect on their mutual experiences. In this way members are able to spark one another's creativity in deriving conclusions about group dynamics. From Lewin, therefore, came an emphasis on studying one's own experiences in order to learn about group dynamics, on discussing mutual experiences with associates in order to increase mutual creativity and learning, and on behaving democratically in structuring learning situations.

The development of groups over time is briefly discussed next. The chapter concludes with a procedure for reflecting on your behavior in groups, and a learning contract for you to sign. Because an experiential approach to learning about group theory and developing group skills is taken in this book, it is necessary to explain what is meant by action theories and experiential learning, how they relate to skill learning, and what motivates students to learn experientially. All this is covered in Chapter 2.

## NATURE OF THIS BOOK AND HOW TO USE IT

This is not a book that you can read with detachment. It is written to involve you with its contents. By reading this book you will not only be able to learn the theoretical and empirical knowledge now available on group dynamics, but you will also learn to apply this knowledge in practical ways within the groups to which you belong. Often in the past, group dynamics practitioners did not pay attention to the research literature, and group dynamics researchers neglected to specify how their findings could be applied. Thus, the knowledge about effective groups and the learning of group skills was often divided. In this book we directly apply existing theory and research to the learning and application of effective group skills. As you participate in the exercises, use diagnostic procedures for assessing your current skill levels, and discuss the relevant theory and research provided, you will bridge the gap between theory and practice.

In selecting exercises to include in this book, we tried to include exercises that were original, short, relevant to the theory and research being discussed, clear and simple, and easy to prepare. We intended each exercise to be like a supporting actor; it should do its work effectively, unobtrusively, and without upstaging the theory and research being presented. Each exercise is also aimed at promoting the development of group skills. The book defines the skills needed for effective group functioning and provides opportunities for readers to practice the skills for themselves and to receive feedback on their performance.

The purpose of this book is to bring together the theory and research of group dynamics and structured exercises aimed at building practical group skills and illuminating the meaning of the theory and research presented. The central aim of each chapter is to review the most important theory and research, analyze basic issues in group dynamics, and provide structured skill-building exercises and other instructional aids. The format of each chapter is based on sound pedagogy and the principles of experiential learning. Most chapters begin with a discussion task involving the concepts presented in the chapter. At the beginning of most chapters is a short diagnostic instrument that will help you become more aware of your current behavior in the area discussed in the chapter. Also in most chapters is a controversy in which you and your classmates argue different sides of one of the central issues of the chapter. Exercises aimed at developing skills and understanding in the topic of the chapter are then provided. The relevant theory and research is presented. At the end of many of the chapters there is a procedure for examining the changes in your knowledge and skills.

In using this book you should diagnose your present knowledge and skills in the areas that are covered, actively participate in the exercises, reflect on your experiences, read the chapters carefully, and integrate the information and experiences into action theories related to group dynamics. You should then plan how to continue your skill- and knowledge-building activities after you have finished the book.

## EXERCISE 1.5:
## ARE GROUPS BENEFICIAL OR HARMFUL?

This exercise consists of a structured controversy over the possible constructiveness or destructiveness of group membership. The objective of the exercise is to promote a thoughtful examination of the benefits and costs of being a member of a group, whether it is a learning, career, family, friendship, or leisure group. The procedure for the exercise is as follows:

1. The class forms groups of four.
2. Each group is ultimately to write a report summarizing its position on whether groups are constructive or destructive. The report is to contain the group's overall conclusion and the facts and rationale supporting its position. The supporting facts and rationale may be obtained from the accompanying briefing sheets, the entire book, and outside reading.
3. First, each group divides into two pairs. One pair is assigned the position that groups are beneficial and the other pair the position that groups are harmful. The coordinator gives each pair the appropriate briefing sheet, explains the procedure, and reviews the rules for constructive controversy listed below.
4. The pairs meet separately to prepare as forceful a presentation of their position as possible. They are to make sure that both members have contributed to building a persuasive case for their position and that it includes as many facts and research findings as possible. Both members need to understand all the rationale supporting

their position. About ten minutes should be allowed for this phase of the exercise.

5. The group of four meets. Each pair presents its position, being as forceful and persuasive as possible, while the other pair takes notes and asks for clarification of anything that is not fully understood. Each pair has about three minutes to present its position.

6. The group of four has an open discussion on whether groups are harmful or beneficial. Each side should present as many facts and research findings as it can to support its point of view. Members should listen critically to the opposing position, asking for facts that support any conclusions advanced by the opposing pair. All the facts supporting each side should be brought out and discussed. The rules of constructive controversy appearing at the end of the exercise should be followed. About ten minutes should be allowed for this phase.

7. The perspectives in each group are now reversed, each pair arguing the opposing pair's position. Members should be as forceful and persuasive as they can in arguing for the opposing pair's position. They should elaborate on the opposing position, seeing if they can think of any new arguments or facts that the opposing pair did not present. Each pair has about three minutes for its presentation.

8. Each group of four should come to a group position that all members can agree on. The members should summarize the best arguments for each point of view, detailing what they know about the benefits and costs of group membership. When they have consensus in their group they should organize their arguments for presentation to the rest of the class. Because other groups will have other conclusions, each group may need to explain the validity of its position to the class. About ten minutes should be allowed for this phase.

9. The coordinator samples the decisions made by the groups of four by having several of them report briefly (not more than two minutes) to the class. The class then discusses similarities and differences.

10. The coordinator summarizes what participants have learned about the benefits and costs of group membership.

## Rules for Constructive Controversy

1. I am critical of ideas, not individuals. I challenge and refute the ideas of the opposing pair, but I do *not* indicate that I personally reject the members of the pair.
2. I focus on coming to the best decision possible, not on "winning." I remember that we are all in this together.
3. I encourage everyone to participate and to master all the relevant information.
4. I listen to everyone's ideas, even if I don't agree.
5. I paraphrase or restate what someone has said if it is not clear to me.
6. I first bring out *all* the ideas and facts supporting both sides, and then I try to put them together in a way that makes sense.
7. I try to understand both sides of the issue.
8. I change my mind when the evidence indicates that I should do so.

## Briefing Sheet: Groups Are Good for Humans

Groups are good for humans. The following overview of important research in social psychology clearly supports this point of view.

1. Under most conditions, the productivity of groups is higher than the productivity of individuals working alone.
2. Groups make more effective decisions and solve problems more effectively than individuals working alone.

3. It is through group memberships that the values of altruism, kindness, consideration for others, responsibility, and so forth, are socialized in us.
4. The quality of emotional life in terms of friendship, love, camaraderie, excitement, joy, fulfillment, and achievement is greater for members of groups than for individuals functioning alone.
5. The quality of everyday life is greater in groups because of the advantages of specialization and division of labor. Our material standard of living, for example—our housing, food, clothing, transportation, entertainment, and so forth—would not be possible for a person living outside of a society.
6. Conflicts are managed more productively in groups. Social influence is better managed in groups. Without group standards, social values, and laws, civilization would be impossible.
7. A person's identity, self-esteem, and social competencies are shaped by the groups of significance to him or her.
8. Without cooperation, social organization, and groups of various kinds, humans would not survive. Humans have a basic social nature, and our survival and evolution are the results of the effectiveness of our groups.

### Briefing Sheet: Groups Are *Not* Good for Humans

Groups are *not* good for humans. The following overview of important social-psychological research clearly supports this point of view.

1. People in groups are more likely to take greater risks than they would alone. Groups tend to take more extreme positions and indulge in more extreme behavior than their members would alone.
2. In groups there is sometimes a diffusion of responsibility such that members take less responsibility for providing assistance to someone in need or for rewarding good service.
3. In large groups individuals can become anonymous and therefore feel freer to engage in rowdy, shocking, and illegal behavior. When one member engages in impulsive and antisocial behavior, others may do likewise. Riots are often initiated and worsened by such modeling effects.
4. Being identified as part of a group may increase the tendency of nonmembers to treat one in impersonal and inhumane ways. It is easier, for example, to drop a bomb on the "enemy" than on a person.
5. Group contagion often gives rise to collective panic.
6. Millions of people have been swept into mass political movements only to become unhappy victims of their distorted visions of the leaders.
7. Groups often influence their members to conform. One type of conformity, obedience to authority, can cause a person to act in cruel and inhumane ways to others. The identity of the individual can be threatened when conformity is too extreme.

## KEEPING A PERSONAL JOURNAL

As you read this book you will be asked to keep a journal in which you record what you are learning about group dynamics and about how you behave in group situations. You may also wish to include specific information you have learned about the social psychology of groups, effective behavior in groups, and the extent to which you have developed the group skills you want. A **journal** is a personal collection of writing and thoughts that have value for the writer. It has to be kept up on a regular basis. Entries are evaluated by whether they are valuable to the author, have some possibilities for sharing with others, and reflect significant thinking. Such a journal will be of great interest to you after you have finished this book. You may also wish to include specific information you have learned about group dynamics. *The purposes of the journal are*

1. To keep track of the activities related to group dynamics.
2. To answer in writing some of the questions that are important for a clear understanding of the book's content (these will often be suggested, but others can be selected by you).
3. To collect thoughts that are related to the book's content (the best thinking often occurs when you are driving to or from school, about to go to sleep at night, and so forth).
4. To collect newspaper and magazine articles and references that are relevant to the topics covered in each chapter.
5. To keep summaries of conversations and anecdotal material that are unique, interesting or illustrate things related to group dynamics.

(If you publish your journal as did John Holt, Hugh Prather, and others, all we ask is a modest 10 percent of the royalties.)

The journal is an important part of this book. It is not an easy part. The entries should be important to you in your effort to make this course useful to you, and since this is a cooperative course, useful to your fellow participants. You may be surprised how writing sharpens and organizes your thoughts.

## LEARNING CONTRACT

Before beginning the next chapter, we would like to propose a learning contract. The contract is as follows:

> I understand that I will be taking an experiential approach to learning about group dynamics and to developing the skills needed to function effectively in groups. I willingly commit myself to the statements hereunder.

1. I will use the structured experiences in this book to learn from. This means I am willing to engage in specified behaviors, seek out feedback about the impact of my behavior on others, and analyze my interpersonal interactions with other class members in order to make the most of my learning.
2. I will make the most of my own learning by (a) engaging in specified behaviors and in being open about my feelings and reactions to what is taking place in order that others may have information to react to in giving me feedback and in building conclusions about the area of study, (b) setting personal learning goals that I will work actively to accomplish—which means that I will take responsibility for my own learning and not wait around for someone else to "make me grow," (c) being willing to experiment with new behavior and to practice new skills, (d) seeking out and being receptive to feedback, and (e) building conclusions about the experiences highlighted in the exercises.
3. I will help others make the most of their learning by (a) providing feedback in constructive ways, (b) helping to build the conditions (such as openness, trust, acceptance, and support) under which others can experiment and take risks with their

behavior, and (c) contributing to the formulation of conclusions about the experiences highlighted in the exercises.

4. I will use professional judgment in keeping what happens among group members in the exercises appropriately confidential.

Signed: _____

## YOUR SKILL LEVEL

Before going on, it will be useful for you to assess your current group skill level. Answer the following questions, describing yourself as accurately as you can:

1. How do you see yourself as a group member? What is your style of functioning within groups?
2. What are your strengths in functioning in groups? How do they fit into how you see yourself as a group member?
3. What situations within groups do you have trouble with and why? How do you feel when faced with them? How do you handle them? How would you like to handle them?
4. In what group skills do you wish to grow and develop? What changes would you like to make in your present group behavior? What new strengths in group behavior would you care to develop? What new group skills would you like to acquire?

You now have a basic understanding of what makes a group effective and what group dynamics is. In the next chapter you will learn what experiential learning is to prepare you for the experiential kind of learning expected of you. In Chapter 3 you will learn how to define and develop group goals and the social interdependence essential to effective group functioning.

# 2

# Experiential Learning

In this chapter a number of concepts are defined and discussed. The major ones are listed below. The procedure for learning these concepts is as follows:

1. Divide into heterogeneous pairs.
2. The task for each pair is to
   a. Define each concept, noting the page on which it is defined and discussed.
   b. Ensure that both members of the pair understand the meaning of each concept.
3. Combine into groups of four. Compare the answers of the two pairs. If there is disagreement, the members look up the concept in the chapter and clarify it until they all agree on the definition and understand it.

### CONCEPTS

1. Action theory
2. Experiential learning
3. Role playing
4. Process observation
5. Feedback
6. Content
7. Process
8. Participant-observer
9. Observation procedures
10. Procedural learning

## PROCEDURAL LEARNING

> Knowing is not enough; we must apply. Willing is not enough; we must do.
>
> *Goethe*

> One learns by doing the thing; for though you think you know it, you have no certainty until you try.
>
> *Sophocles*

> The hand is the cutting edge of the mind.
>
> *Jacob Bronowski*, Ascent of Man

Increasing your expertise in group dynamics requires procedural learning. Learning how to implement group dynamics theory and research is very similar to learning how to play tennis or golf, how to perform brain surgery, or how to fly an airplane. It involves more than simply reading material for a recognition level or even a total recall level of mastery. **Procedural learning** exists when you study group dynamics to

1. Learn conceptually group dynamics theory and research.
2. Translate your conceptual understanding into a set of group skills.
3. Actually use your group skills.
4. Eliminate errors in using your group skills to move through the initial awkward and mechanical stages of mastery to attain a routine-use, automated level of mastery.

In other words, you must acquire an understanding of group dynamics theory and research, develop a conceptualization of group skills, engage in guided practice to enact the skills and eliminate implementation errors, and persevere in using the group skills so that you can use them appropriately in a more and more automated fashion.

Procedural learning differs from simply learning facts and acquiring knowledge due to a heavier reliance on feedback about performance and the modification of implementation efforts until the errors of performance are eliminated. Procedural learning involves a progressive refinement of knowledge and skill as the procedures are practiced, practiced, and practiced.

It is the procedural nature of mastering group dynamics that makes this book different from most other textbooks. This may seem strange at first. Traditionally, in the United States, we have made a separation between "head" learning and "hand" learning. "Real" classes are supposed to be head learning while "vocational" classes are supposed to be hand learning. Thus, there is a focus on the head and a denial that the hand is present and important. In learning group dynamics, however, you should remember Jacob Bronowski's (1973) observation that it is the "hand" that drives the subsequent evolution of conceptual understanding. The "hand" becomes an instrument of vision, revealing the conceptual nature of the procedure being used. To "understand," you have to "do." True understanding only results from doing. *It is from using group skills that you will gain an understanding of what group dynamics is and how useful it can be.*

Procedural learning is based on experiential learning. The Russian cognitive theorist L. S. Vygotsky stated that learning from experience is the process whereby human development occurs. Your development and continual improvement of group skills depends on your participation in the skill-building exercises included in this book. Those exercises, and the links they provide with the theory and research discussed, are based on experiential learning. In experiential learning the responsibility for your learning lies with you, not with the teacher or instructor. Experiential exercises are structured so that you can experiment with your behavior, try things out, see what works, build skills, and develop action theories out of your own experiences. Appropriate theory is then presented so that you can summarize your learning and build conceptual frameworks within which you can organize what you know. Although experiential learning is a stimulating and involving activity, it is important to remember always that experience alone is not beneficial. You learn from the combination of experience and the conceptualization of your experiences.

In this chapter the nature of action theories and experiential learning is discussed. The procedures through which group skills are learned are presented. In addition, directions for how to conduct a skill-training experience and the ethics of doing so are discussed. First, to understand experiential learning you must first know what an action theory is.

## ACTION THEORIES

Change and growth take place when a person has risked himself and dares to become involved with experimenting with his own life.

*Herbert Otto*

All humans need to become competent in taking action and simultaneously reflecting on their action to learn from it. Integrating thought with action requires that we plan our behavior, engage in it, and then reflect on how effective we were. When we learn a pattern of behavior that deals effectively with a recurrent situation, we tend to repeat it over and over until it functions automatically. Such habitual behavioral patterns are based on theories of action. An **action theory** is a theory as to what actions are needed to achieve a desired consequence in a given situation. All theories have an "if . . . then . . . " form. An action theory states that in a given situation if we do $x$, then $y$ will result. Our theories of action are normative. They state what we ought to do if we wish to achieve certain results. Examples of action theories can be found in almost everything we do. If we smile and say hello, then others will return our smile and greeting. If we apologize, then the other person will excuse us. If we steal, then we will be punished. If a person shoves us, then we should shove back. All our behavior is based on theories that connect our actions with certain consequences. In essence we build an action theory. As our behavior becomes habitual and automatic our action theories become tacit (we are not able to put them into words). When our behavior becomes ineffective, we become aware of our action theories and modify them.

As children we are taught action theories by parents and other socializing agents. As we grow older we learn how to modify our action theories and develop new ones. We learn to try to anticipate what actions will lead to what consequences, to try out and experiment with new behaviors, to experience the consequences, and then to reflect on our experiences to determine whether our action theory is valid or needs modification. Experiential learning is a procedure based on the systematic development and modification of action theories.

We all have many action theories, one for every type of situation we regularly find ourselves in. This does not mean that we are aware of our action theories. An action is usually based on tacit knowledge—knowledge that we are not always able to put into words. Because most of our action theories function automatically, we are rarely conscious of our assumed connections between actions and their consequences. One of the purposes of this book is to help you become more conscious of the action theories that guide how you behave in small-group situations, test these theories against reality, and modify them to make them more effective.

## GAINING EXPERTISE THROUGH
## EXPERIENTIAL LEARNING

> We shall not cease from exploration
> And the end of all our exploring
> Will be to arrive where we started
> And know the place for the first time.
> *T. S. Eliot, "Four Quartets"*

Aesop tells the story of the lion, the bear, and the fox. The bear was about to seize a stray goat when the lion leaped from another direction on the same prey. The bear and the lion then fought furiously for the goat until they had received so many wounds that both sank down unable to continue the battle. Just then the fox dashed up, seized the goat, and made off with it as fast as he could go, while the lion and the bear looked on in helpless rage. "How much better it would have been," they said, "to have shared in a friendly spirit." The bear and the lion had learned from their direct experience an important lesson in the advantages of cooperation over competition.

We all learn from our experiences. From touching a hot stove we learn to avoid heated objects. By dating we learn about male-female relationships. Every day we have experiences we learn from. Many aspects of group dynamics can be learned only by experience. Hearing a lecture on resisting group pressure is not the same as actually experiencing group pressure. Seeing a movie on how to manage conflict is not the same as facing an angry neighbor who is yelling in your face. Reading a description of leadership is not the same as leading the charge up San Juan Hill. It takes more than listening to explanations to learn group skills.

**Experiential learning** may be defined as generating an action theory from your own experiences and then continually modifying it to improve your effectiveness. The purpose of experiential learning is to affect the learner in three ways: (1) the learner's cognitive structures are altered, (2) the learner's attitudes are modified, and (3) the learner's repertoire of behavioral skills is expanded. These three elements are interconnected and change as a whole, not as separate parts. Working on any one part in the absence of the other two will be ineffective:

1.  Information and knowledge can generate interest in changing, but will not bring about change. Knowing a rationale for change is not sufficient for motivating a person to change.
2.  Firsthand experience alone will not generate valid knowledge. For hundreds of years, for example, scientists believed that there were four elements in the world—earth, air, fire, and water. Experience with different types of gases and different types of matter did not generate a correct theory of physics. Besides experience there must be a theoretical system that the expertise tests out and reflection on the meaning of the experience.
3.  It takes more than engaging in a new behavior to result in permanent change. New skills may be practiced and mastered but will fade away unless action theories and attitudes also change.

To learn leadership skills, for example, the learner must develop a concept of what leadership is (knowledge), an action theory concerning what leadership behaviors will lead to effective group functioning, positive attitudes toward new leadership procedures, and perceptions that the new leadership actions are appropriate and that she is capable of performing them. Finally, the learner must develop the skills needed to perform the new leadership actions.

The process of experiential learning is shown in Figure 2.1. When you generate an action theory from your own experiences and then continually modify it to improve its effectiveness, you are learning experientially. Experiential learning can be conceived of in a simplified way as a four-stage cycle: (1) take action on the basis of one's current action theory, (2) assess consequences and obtain feedback, (3) reflect on how effective actions were and reformulate/refine the action theory, and (4) imple-

**FIGURE 2.1**  Experiential Learning Cycle

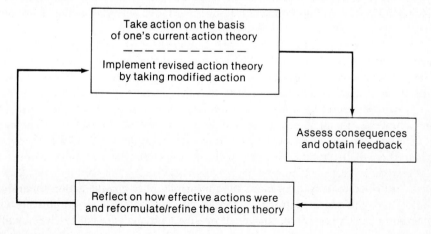

ment the revised action theory by taking modified action. As learners engage in these four steps, they must perceive themselves as being capable of implementing the procedures and strategies contained in the theory, perceive these procedures and strategies as being appropriate to their social world, and develop positive attitudes toward the theory and its implementation. This process of continuous improvement is repeated over and over again until expertise in the use of group skills is developed.

The experiential learning process of formulating an action theory, testing it out behaviorally, assessing consequences and obtaining feedback, reflecting, and modifying and refining the theory is based on a number of principles that need to be understood and followed. These principles are based on the theorizing of Kurt Lewin (Lewin, 1935; Lewin and Grabbe, 1945).

**Principle 1: Effective experiential learning will affect the learner's cognitive structures (action theories), attitudes and values, perceptions, and behavioral patterns.**    To learn to be a more effective decision maker, for example, the learner must develop a concept of what decision making is (knowledge), an action theory concerning what decision-making behaviors will lead to effective group decision making, positive attitudes toward new decision-making procedures, perceptions that the new decision-making actions are situationally appropriate and that one is capable of performing them, and the behavioral skills needed to perform the new decision-making actions.

**Principle 2: People will believe more in knowledge they have discovered themselves than in knowledge presented by others.**    Lewin was a great believer in experimental procedures whereby a person behaviorally validates or disproves a theory. He believed that such procedures needed to be introduced into the educational process so that students could test alternative behavioral patterns within controlled conditions. An approach to learning based on inquiry and discovery has been found to increase students' motivation to learn and their commitment to implement their conclusions in the future.

**Principle 3: Learning is more effective when it is an active rather than a passive process.**    When a learner can take a theory, concept, or practice and "try it on for size," he or she will understand it more completely, integrate it more effectively with past learning, and retain it longer. Many concepts (such as mathematical procedures) are never really learned until one uses them.

**Principle 4: Acceptance of new action theories, attitudes, and behavioral patterns cannot be brought about by a piecemeal approach—one's whole cognitive-affective-behavioral system has to change.**    The three elements are interconnected, and they change as a whole rather than as separate parts. Like any system, a cognitive-affective-behavioral system demands coherence, consistency, orderliness, and simplicity. Trying to change part of the system will not be effective. The need for consistency creates resistance to the item-by-item approach to new learning. Only when the whole system changes will the new learning be fully accepted and integrated.

**Principle 5: It takes more than information to change action theories, attitudes, and behavioral patterns.**    Telling people about the desirability of change does not mean that they will change. Providing a rationale for change is not sufficient to motivate people to change. Reading a book or listening to a lecture does not result in mastery and retention of the material, does not promote attitude change, and does not increase social skills. Information does generate interest in learning more about the desired changes.

**Principle 6: It takes more than firsthand experience to generate valid knowledge.** Lewin used to state that thousands of years of human experience with falling bodies did not bring humans to a correct theory of gravity. Besides experience, there needs to be a theoretical system that the experience tests out and reflection on the meaning of the experience.

**Principle 7: Behavior changes will be temporary unless the action theories and attitudes underlying them are changed.** New behavioral skills may be practiced and mastered, but without changes in the person's action theories and attitudes, the new behavior patterns will fade away.

**Principle 8: Changes in perceptions of oneself and one's social environment are necessary before changes in action theories, attitudes, and behavior will take place.** Learners must perceive themselves as capable of doing the needed behaviors and must see the behaviors as being appropriate to the situation before they will engage in them. Lewin believed that behavior, action theories, and attitudes are all steered by perception. Your perceptions of yourself and your immediate situation affect how you behave, what you believe, and how you feel.

**Principle 9: The more supportive, accepting, and caring the social environment, the freer a person is to experiment with new behaviors, attitudes, and action theories.** As the need to justify oneself and protect oneself against rejection decreases, it becomes easier to experiment with new ways of behaving, thinking, and valuing.

**Principle 10: For changes in behavior patterns, attitudes, and action theories to be permanent, both the person and the social environment have to change.** The person's role definitions, the expectations of the person held by colleagues and friends, and the general values of career and social settings all must change if the person is to maintain these changed behaviors, attitudes, and action theories. Team training is more effective than individual training because it changes both individuals and their social environment at the same time.

**Principle 11: It is easier to change a person's action theories, attitudes, and behavioral patterns in a group context than in an individual context.** The discussion and consensual validation that takes place within a group provides a personal commitment and encouragement for change that is not present when only one person is being changed.

**Principle 12: A person accepts a new system of action theories, attitudes, and behavioral patterns when he or she accepts membership in a new group.** New groups with new role definitions and expectations for appropriate behavior are helpful in educational efforts. A person becomes socialized by internalizing the normative culture of the groups to which one belongs. As the person gains membership in a new group, a new normative culture is accepted and internalized.

Experiential learning procedures are especially useful when you want to learn new skills. In the next section we shall review how skills are learned.

## LEARNING GROUP SKILLS

> For things we have to learn before we can do them, we learn by doing them.
>
> *Aristotle*

You are not born with group skills, nor do they magically appear when you need them. You have to learn them. Group skills are learned just as any other skill is learned. Learning how to lead a group is no different from learning how to play the piano or throw a football. All skills are learned the same way, according to the following steps:

1. *Understand why the skill is important and how it will be of value to you.* To want to learn a skill, you must see a need for it. You need to know that you will be better off with the skill than without the skill.

2. *Understand what the skill is, what are the component behaviors you have to engage in to perform the skill, and when it should be used.* To learn a skill, you must have a clear idea of what the skill is and you must know how to perform it. Often it is helpful to observe someone who has already mastered the skill perform it several times while describing it step by step. Apprentices, for example, watch masters of their craft perform the skill over and over again.

3. *Find situations in which you can practice the skill over and over again while a "coach" watches and tells you how well you are performing the skill.* There are four levels of **guided practice.** The *first* level of guided practice consists of practicing successive approximations of the group skill while others provide scaffolding on how to do so. **Scaffolding** is support, in the form of reminders, prompts, and help that you require to approximate the expert use of the group skills. As you practice the skills again and again, the scaffolding is gradually faded until you use the skill by yourself, which is called **soloing.** The *second* level of guided practice consists of using the group skills while **articulating** and **explaining** out loud how to do so to your "coach." This ensures that the scaffolding is internalized and **self-monitoring** and

**self-correcting** on how to engage in the skill takes place. The *third* level is independent practice. You engage in the skill while self-monitoring and self-correcting your efforts. In effect, you give yourself feedback. This solidifies your sense of self-efficacy and commitment to use the skills. *Finally,* you **decontextualize** your use of the skills by using them in a variety of groups and in a variety of different situations. Try practicing the skill for a short time each day for several days until you are sure you have mastered it completely.

4. *Assess how well the group skills are being implemented.* The key to assessing how well you engage in the skill is to realize that you can never fail. Rather, your behavior approximates what you ideally wish, and, through practice and the process of experiential learning (i.e., progressive refinement), the approximations get successively closer and closer to the ideal. *You have to sweat in practice before you can perform in concert!* Short-term failure is part of the process of gaining expertise and long-term success is inevitable when short-term failure is followed by persistent practice, obtaining feedback, and reflecting on how to implement the group skills more competently. Receiving feedback, furthermore, is necessary for correcting mistakes in learning a skill and for identifying problems you are having in mastering the skill. Through feedback you find out how much progress you are making in mastering the skill. Feedback lets you compare how well you are doing with how well you want to do.

5. *Keep practicing until the skill feels real and it becomes an automatic habit pattern.* Most skill development goes through the following steps:

1. Self-conscious, awkward engagement in the skill. Practicing any new skill feels awkward and group skills are no exception. The first few times someone throws a football, plays a violin, or paraphrases, it feels strange.
2. Feelings of phoniness while engaging in the new skill. After a while the awkwardness passes and enacting the skill becomes more smooth. Many individuals, however, feel that the skill is unauthentic or phony. Encouragement is needed to move the members through this stage.
3. Skilled but mechanical use of the skill.
4. Automatic, routine use where the skill is fully integrated into your behavioral repertoire and seems like a natural action to engage in.

You have to practice the skills long enough to go through the stages of skill development. The more you use a skill, the more natural it feels. It is then, when you apply the skills to real situations, that the skills will gain the fire and life that may sometimes be lacking when you practice.

6. *Load your practice toward success.* Set up practice units that you can easily master. It always helps to feel like a success as you practice a skill.

7. *Get friends to encourage you to use the skill.* Your friends can help you learn by giving you encouragement to do so. The more encouragement you receive, the easier it will be for you to practice the skill.

8. *Help others learn the group skills.* Harvey S. Firestone said, "It is only when we develop others that we permanently succeed." Nothing is completely learned until it is taught to someone else. By helping others learn group skills, you will enhance your own expertise.

In the learning of most skills there is a period of slow learning, then a period of rapid improvement, then a period where performance remains about the same (a plateau), then another period of rapid improvement, then another plateau, and so forth. Plateaus are quite common in skill learning. You have to persevere in practicing the skill until the next period of rapid improvement begins.

For you to move from awkwardness to the automatic use of the skills, sustained practice of the skills over a long period of time has to be encouraged. The goal for all skill learning is to reach the state where you automatically and naturally engage in the small-group skills while working with others to achieve mutual goals.

This book is designed to provide you with information about the nature of and the need for the group skills discussed. The behaviors needed to engage in the skills are specified. Questions that test your comprehension and understanding of the material presented are included in most chapters. You are given instructions for participating in exercises that provide you with a chance to practice the skills and receive feedback on how well you are mastering them. It is up to you, after engaging in the exercises, to practice the skills until you feel comfortable performing them. At the end of most chapters you will be asked to evaluate the extent to which you have mastered the skills presented in the chapter.

In short, this book provides you with guidance for increasing your group skills. It is up to you to take advantage of the material and exercises presented and use them in ways that will increase your group skills. The extent of your learning and skill development rests entirely on your commitment to use this book in fruitful ways.

## EXPERIENTIAL LEARNING AND MOTIVATION

All men by nature desire to learn.

*Aristotle*

What motivates you to learn concepts and skills? If someone offered you the opportunity either to earn a great deal of money or to experience a basic sense of accomplishment and satisfaction from learning a skill, which would you choose? Some educators seem to believe that students must be forced or persuaded into learning; others seem to believe that learning is fun and enjoyable in its own right. What do you believe? Experiential learning stresses the intrinsic sense of success of accomplishment in learning. Motivation is based upon what you see as desirable learning goals and the method you choose to accomplish them. The goal-directed aspect of motivation places an emphasis upon your feelings of success or failure in the learning situation. What leads to a psychological feeling of success in a learning situation? Kurt Lewin and his associates (1944) came up with four factors. They found evidence that you will experience psychological success (as opposed to psychological failure) if

1. You are able to define your own goals.
2. The goals are related to your central needs and values.
3. You are able to define the paths that lead to the accomplishment of the goals.
4. The goals represent a realistic level of aspiration for you—neither too high nor too low, but high enough to test your capabilities.

Feelings of success will be promoted when you are encouraged to take as much responsibility for your own behavior as you can handle. You must believe that you are in control of (or at least have some influence over) your learning in order to feel psychological success. Experiential learning offers the opportunity for experiencing success by allowing you freedom to decide what aspects of your experience you wish to focus upon, what skills you wish to develop, and how you conceptualize the conclusions drawn from your experiences. This is quite different from the traditional lecture approach to learning, in which you are a passive listener and the control of the material being presented is in the hands of the instructor. When an instructor decides what material will be presented and how it will be presented without letting learners have any influence over the decision, learners will experience psychological failure, no matter how entertaining the presentation is.

Although the primary motivation for learning in experiential situations is psychological success, there are extrinsic factors that will encourage further learning. The approval and support of other learners is an example of extrinsic motivators that facilitate learning without interfering with intrinsic motivators, such as a sense of accomplishment. As you participate in the exercises in this book, your learning will accelerate if other participants give you approval and recognition for successful learning. You should consciously try to give approval to other readers who are seriously trying to increase their group skills. Few influences on our behavior are more powerful than the support and approval of a group of friends or acquaintances. Using such group influences to help individuals learn is one of the most constructive ways of assuring the development of group skills and knowledge.

## ROLE PLAYING

In this and the following sections two important procedures for experiential learning are briefly discussed: role playing and observation of the dynamics of a group. Role playing is a tool for bringing a specific skill and its consequences into focus and thus is vital for experiential learning. It is a way in which you can experience concretely the type of interaction under examination. An imaginary life situation is set up in which you act and react in terms of the assumptions you are asked to adopt, the beliefs you are asked to hold, and the character you are asked to play. Role playing is intended to give you experience in practicing skills and in discussing and identifying effective and ineffective behavior. The outcome of a role-playing situation is not determined in advance, and the situation is not rehearsed. Initial instructions are given, and the role players determine what happens. When participating in a role-playing exercise, remain yourself and act as you would in the situation described. You do not have to be a good actor or actress to play a role; you need only accept the initial assumptions, beliefs, background, or assigned behaviors and then let your feelings, attitudes, and behavior change as circumstances seem to require. The role-playing instructions describe the point of departure and the beginning frame of reference; you and the situation then take over.

What happens in group role playing may lead you to change behaviors and attitudes, and you may have emotional experiences that you did not expect when the role playing began. The more real the role playing and the more effective the exercise, the more emotional involvement you will feel and the more you will learn. That role playing can simulate real-life situations makes it possible for you to try new ways of handling situations without suffering any serious consequences if the methods fail.

In role playing, questions may be raised in discussions that are not covered by the instructions given in this book. When this happens, role players are free to make up facts or experiences that accord with the circumstances; they should avoid making up experiences or facts that do not fit the role. In participating in a role-playing exercise, you should not consult or look at your role instructions after you have used them to start the action; you should be yourself. You should not act the way you feel a person described in the instructions should behave; you should act as naturally as possible merely by following the instructions.

The coordinator of the exercise should help involve the role players in the situation by introducing it in such a way that the players are emotionally stimulated. Using name tags and asking the players questions to help them get a feeling for the part are helpful. Introduce the scene to the role players and the observers. Always "derole" after the role playing has ended.

## PROCESS OBSERVATION

Within a group a distinction can be made between the content the group is discussing and the process by which the discussion is being conducted. Group process involves such things as leadership, decision making, communication, and controversy. **Content** is what is being discussed; **process** is how the group is functioning. To observe the group process is to observe how the group is functioning. A person highly skilled in process observation can both participate in group work and observe group process at the same time, thus becoming a **participant-observer.**

**Observation procedures** are aimed at describing and recording behavior as it occurs. From the behavior of group members an observer can make inferences about the group process—the way in which the group is functioning. The problem with observation of groups is the potential for lack of objectivity by the observers. An example of biased observing may be seen in a study conducted by Hastorf and Cantril (1954). They asked Dartmouth and Princeton college students to watch a film of the football game between the two schools. The game was an unusually rough one in which many penalties had been called. The Princeton quarterback, an all-American, left the game in the second quarter with a broken nose and a mild concussion. The Dartmouth quarterback left the game in the third quarter with a broken leg. The Dartmouth and Princeton college students were asked to watch the film and record the number and severity of the infractions committed by the two teams. Dartmouth won the game and its students saw the two teams committing an equal number of violations. The Princeton students saw the Dartmouth players as committing more than twice as many fouls as the Princeton team. A solution to the problem of bias is the use of **structured coding systems,** which require observers to categorize each group behavior into an objectively definable category.

Five steps are usually involved in observation, the first being to decide which aspects of a group process you wish to observe. The model of effective groups presented in Table 1.1 covers the basic aspects of group process that you will be interested in observing. By the time you finish this book, you will have a clear understanding of the aspects of group process that are important to observe.

The second step in observation is to find or construct an observation sheet that specifies observable and countable behaviors reflecting the aspect of group process to be studied. Numerous observation sheets are included in this book. The third step is to observe the group and count the number of members engaged in one of the specified behaviors. When there is more than one observer, you may be able to focus only on some of the group members. The fourth step is to look at the frequency with which group members are engaged in the specified behaviors and then infer how well the group is functioning in that aspect of the group process under observation. The final step is to summarize the observations in a manner that is clear and useful and then present the summary to the group as feedback. The group can then discuss the observations and revise the group process to make it more effective.

The **purpose** of process observation is to clarify and improve the ways in which the group is presently functioning through an objective assessment of the interaction among members. Information about group process is collected and then openly discussed so that modifications in group procedures and members' behavior can be made to improve the group's effectiveness.

By the time you finish this book, you will have developed skills in observing group process. At first the observation tasks specified in the exercises will seem difficult, but gradually you will find them easier and more helpful as your skills develop. As effective future behavior depends upon awareness of the nature and consequences of current behavior, there is no substitute for direct observation in skill development and in the facilitation of group effectiveness. Any effective group member must be aware of group process while participating in the group, and it is through observation practice that such skills are developed.

## CONDUCTING SKILL-TRAINING EXERCISES

### A Typical Skill-Training Session

Before discussing how to conduct a skill-training session, it may be helpful to review the overall structure of a group exercise. A typical session would involve the following procedures:

1. Participants are presented with an introduction by a coordinator, who then conducts a warm-up discussion. The introduction should include the objectives of the session, an outline of what will happen, and a description of the specific skills with which the participants will be concerned during the exercise: The warm-up discussion sets the stage for the exercise, engenders participant involvement, and promotes some sort of

emotional connection among participants. The warm-up could take the form of a brief exchange of current feelings among participants or an interesting anecdote about group skills told by the coordinator. The expectations of the participants should be set at this point.

2. The exercise is then conducted.
3. After the exercise is completed, the participants are asked to conceptualize, analyze, and summarize their experience. This step may be structured through discussion questions or data feedback about how each person and the group behaved. The personal learnings of each participant, their application to his or her life, and the theoretical principles into which the participants gained insight as a result of their experience can be focused upon.
4. In a general session participants should talk over the experience and summarize their ideas about their experience. The coordinator should integrate appropriate theory and cognitive frameworks into the participants' statements. The emphasis at this point is upon integrating the important learnings, theory, and research with their experiences.
5. The coordinator should then discuss the issues of applying the learnings and skills to the participants' specific life situation.
6. An evaluation of the success of the session in accomplishing its objectives should be made.
7. At the end of the session a sense of closure needs to be provided by the coordinator. This may be achieved by a short, fun, involving experience. Or the coordinator may simply say that the training exercise is over.

## Designing a Skill-Training Session

A skill-training program could involve any number and combination of the exercises presented in this book. It could consist of a single exercise or of several exercises drawn from different chapters. It could last a few minutes or several days. Whatever the length of the session and the number of exercises used, the basic design of the training process is the same. The following elements need to be considered when the coordinator designs a skill-training session:

1. The coordinator-participant relationship must be examined. Useful questions to be cleared up include the following: What is the purpose of the session? Why is the coordinator conducting it? What is the contract between the coordinator and the participants? What is the relationship between the coordinator and the participants? Your motivation as coordinator, hidden agendas (if any), explicit and implicit assumptions about the session and the participants, and your limitations and competencies should be reviewed. It is also helpful to know the following information about the participants:
   a. Expectations: What do the participants hope, believe, or fear will happen or not happen?
   b. Experience: What kinds of previous training have the participants had?
   c. Relevance: How might the learnings be used after the session?
   d. Relationships: What are the participants' past and future relationships with each other?
   e. Needs: What specific learnings, and what general kinds of learnings, do the participants want or need?
   f. Vital data: sex, age, marital status, general attitudes, physical or emotional problems and pressures, back-home support possibilities, and so on.
   g. Motivation: What is the level of the participants' motivation?

    h. Recruitment: How were the participants recruited? Did they all voluntarily agree to attend the session?

2. The desired outcomes of the session should be specified; they are usually discussed as objectives or goals. They should specify who is to be trained and what is to be the direction and magnitude of the desired learning. Clearly specified goals are useful when you are deciding upon the components of the session and its evaluation. All the criteria for clear goals given in Chapter 3 are of importance when you are stating the session's objectives. Participants should be able to spell out the learnings they will try to achieve.

3. Detail the constraints on the session. These include the time periods available, the location, the facilities, and your range of competencies.

4. Generate a list of alternative exercises and activities that can be used in the skill-training session. These alternatives may include a variety of exercises and theory sessions. This list can be put together from two sources: the desired outcomes of the session and the resources and preferences of the coordinator(s). All the exercises in this book and in the author's *Reaching Out* (Prentice Hall, 1990) are possibilities.

5. Make a tentative design for the session. Evaluate it in terms of these questions:
    a. Is it appropriate for accomplishing the desired outcomes?
    b. Are the activities within your range of competencies?
    c. Is there an opportunity for participants to express their needs or expectations or both?
    d. Does it enable the participants to make the transition from the "outside" world to the session and back to the "outside" world?
    e. Does it encourage the transfer of learnings?
    f. Does it have high personal relevance for the participants, and will it enable them to function better in their day-to-day life?
    g. If there is more than one coordinator, does it allow time for you to check signals with each other?
    h. Are high- and low-tension activities appropriately placed within the design?
    i. Are the assumptions about the skill and background of the participants appropriate?
    j. Does the overall design provide a sense of continuity, appropriate transitions among activities, a good "flow"?
    k. Are participants able to see the relationship between the exercises and the desired outcomes of the session?
    l. Does it allow for a logical flow of experiences?
    m. Does it offer flexibility in case of unexpected and emerging needs?
    n. Is it consistent with the principles of experiential learning?
    o. Is there opportunity for ongoing participant feedback and evaluation?
    p. Are you prepared to recognize and deal with unanticipated learning outcomes?
    q. Are all the necessary materials and facilities available?

6. Make sure you are highly committed to the final design. If there is more than one coordinator, assign responsibilities. Arrange for the materials and facilities.

7. If there is more than one coordinator, assess how you function as a staff. See if any team development needs to take place among the staff before the skill-training sessions begin.

## Evaluation

Evaluation is the process of determining how successful—or unsuccessful—a group was in achieving its goal or objective. In the case of a skill-training session, it is the process by which evidence is gathered about whether the desired outcomes of the session were accomplished, what unanticipated learnings were accomplished, how the activities involved in the session contributed to its success or failure, and what the coordinator(s) could do to improve their competencies. In an evaluation there must be a clear, operational statement of the desired outcomes, ways to measure how nearly the desired outcomes were achieved and what activities and coordinator behaviors contributed to the session's success or failure, time for the participants to give feedback on the effectiveness of the session, and time following the session for the data to be analyzed and conclusions drawn.

In evaluation it is helpful to know such things as the emotional reactions of the participants (how they feel now), the specific or significant learnings the participants have obviously achieved, the amount of increased participant competence in performing the skills, what sort of future experiences the participants now see the need for, the degree to which the desired outcomes were accomplished, the participants' reactions to various parts of the session, and what the coordinator(s) did that was helpful or unhelpful to the participants.

A variety of data collection procedures can be used by the coordinator(s) to evaluate a session: interviews, general statements made by the participants, questionnaire responses, observation of how skills were applied, and so on. All sessions do not have to be evaluated at a high level of proficiency, but more than the general impressions of the coordinator(s) should be used. At the very least, the coordinator(s) should be able to direct the same session in the future in a more effective and efficient way.

## Helpful Guidelines

In conducting the exercises in this book the coordinator will have a set of general responsibilities. These include

1. Organizing the materials, procedures, and facilities he or she will need to manage the exercise.
2. Introducing, ending, and tying together the experiences involved in the exercise.
3. Keeping time in a task-oriented way to prevent the participants from getting sidetracked.
4. Restating and calling attention to the main learnings of the exercise, which include relating the experiences to the theory.
5. Setting a climate of experimentation, acceptance, openness, and warmth so that participants will be encouraged to try out new skills and improve their competencies.
6. Serving as an anchor point by being reliable, knowledgeable, trustworthy, and responsible.
7. Modeling the skills he or she wishes to teach.
8. Following the general outlines of experiential learning.
9. Being enthusiastic about the value of the exercise.
10. Knowing and understanding the material well.
11. Making sure everyone understands his or her instructions and responsibilities.
12. Being sensitive to the differences in participation, needs, and styles of the participants.
13. Remaining flexible so that the preplanned procedures do not interfere with the participants' learning.

14. Enjoying himself or herself and making sure that he or she also learns and benefits from the exercises.

# ETHICS OF EXPERIENTIAL LEARNING

All learning activities require a code of ethics, either implicit or explicit. A great deal of attention has been paid to the ethics of growth-group leaders, but little consideration has been given to the ethics of conducting experiential-learning activities. Some of the ethical issues relevant to the type of skill-training exercises included in this book are as follows.

The most serious ethical issue involved in teaching group skills is determining the value and necessity of such cognitive and behavioral changes for the participants. Attempting to teach another person carries with it a responsibility not to work against that person's best interests and needs. It should also be noted that the only way to promote ethical standards in teaching-learning relationships is for the teachers to enforce their code of ethics on themselves and to use good judgment in what they do. As long as a teacher's behavior is based on care, respect, and regard for participants, ethical violations will be minimized. Persons leading experiential-learning activities must therefore develop a personal code of ethics to which they hold themselves accountable. The following points should provoke some thought as to what that personal code of ethics might include.

## The Contract: Informed Consent and Mutual Agreement

1. The coordinator's intentions and objectives should be clearly communicated to the participants. The participants should understand that they are going to participate in an experiential exercise in which they will be expected to examine their own behavior and the behavior of others and analyze the behaviors for purposes of learning.
2. The nature of the contract should be easily understood by the coordinator and the participants. The number of experiences, the length of each session, and the appropriateness and the objectives of each exercise should be agreed on.
3. The point at which the contract is terminated should be clear to both the coordinator and the participants.

## The Activities

1. The participants' freedom of choice should be respected. Participation should be voluntary. A participant's freedom to choose whether or not to become involved in an exercise or part of an exercise should be respected. This freedom includes advising the participants on how they can say "no" to the instructions of the coordinator.
2. The coordinator should have an explicit reason for conducting the exercise and be prepared to state it publicly.
3. Only exercises the coordinator is competent to direct should be conducted. If the coordinator lacks certification and competence in psychotherapy, for example, exercises aimed at exposing deep psychodynamics of participants should not be held (and there are no such exercises in this book).
4. The coordinator should present relevant theory and research when it is appropriate to the participants' learning and increased effectiveness.

5. The coordinator should be constantly aware of his or her behavior styles and personal needs and deal with them productively in the performance of his or her role. The coordinator should also be aware of the impact of his or her needs and style on the participants.

6. The coordinator should assess all experiences by discussing the participants' feelings and reactions to them and by asking the participants what can be learned from the experiences. Adequate time must be programmed into the design of the session for this purpose.

7. The coordinator should not initiate confrontations between participants, which may damage their future relationship. This does not mean that coordinators should discourage risk taking in giving feedback, the making of honest disclosures, or attempts to face conflicts and improve the relationship. It simply means that confrontation should originate with the participants, not the coordinator.

8. If any personal information is revealed, the coordinator should make sure that the possibility of it being used in any way to damage the participants is minimized.

9. Ideally, the coordinator should be able to recognize symptoms of serious psychological stress and be able to make responsible decisions when such problems arise. At the very least, the coordinator should know where emergency psychological services are available.

10. Sessions should be evaluated in such a way that the coordinator receives feedback that will improve his or her performance. The sessions should be open to scrutiny by competent professionals interested in the effectiveness of experiential learning.

11. Follow-up interviews with the participants should be made possible so that the impact of the sessions on them can be assessed and their feelings and reactions to the sessions discussed.

## The Coordinator's Knowledge, Skills, and Needs

1. What the coordinator does needs to be based on empirically validated knowledge. Folklore, superstition, common sense, fads, popular gimmicks, and personal experiences are not adequate bases for teaching others. The coordinator should thoroughly understand the principles of experiential learning, the steps of skill development, and the knowledge that the exercise is designed to teach.

2. In addition to knowledge, the coordinator should have some experience in conducting exercises and some skills in helping participants reflect on their behavior and that of others and learn from it. Knowing the steps of experiential learning is not enough: the coordinator should also have some skills and competencies in applying the principles of experiential learning.

3. At any time during the exercises the coordinator should be able to explain the theory she is operating by and the way in which current activities relate to the theory. This does not mean that the coordinator will not use her intuition and impulses when conducting an exercise, but she should be able to reconstruct the theory behind her intuitive actions.

4. The coordinator should be aware of his behavior style and personal needs and deal with them productively in the performance of the teaching style. He should also be aware of the impact of his personal needs and styles on the participants.

## Final Notes

The ability of most of you to conduct and coordinate experiential-learning exercises should improve if you apply the material in this book with intelligence and caution. If you are interested in other skill-building exercises, see Johnson (1987, 1990). You do not have to be a skilled teacher to conduct the exercises contained in this book, but constant concern for increasing your knowledge and skills in experiential learning is helpful.

The preceding statements are meant to be guidelines, not rigid rules. The only effective way to enforce ethical standards in educational activities is for the persons conducting the educational problems to enforce their code of ethics on themselves and use good judgment in what they do. Again, as long as a coordinator's behavior is based on care, respect, and regard for the participants, ethical violations will probably be avoided. It is hoped that the guidelines will be provocative in helping the users of this book build a personal code of ethical conduct.

## SUMMARY

To master the field of group dynamics you must conceptually learn the relevant theory and research and master the skills that put that knowledge into action. Such procedure learning results from skill building experiences as well as academic study. Procedural learning involves a progressive refinement of knowledge and skill as the procedures are practiced, practiced, and practiced. In other words, this book focuses on both "head" and "hand" learning.

Experiential learning begins with the formulation of an action theory. Action theories specify what actions are needed to achieve a desired consequence in a given situation. The next step is to take action and engage in the relevant group skills. The success or failure of the actions is assessed. Upon reflection, the action theory is refined and reformulated. Then the group skills are used again in a modified and improved way. This cycle is repeated over and over again as the skills are refined and continuously improved upon. This continuous improvement process eventually results in expertise in the use of group skills as changes in cognitive understanding, attitudes, and behavioral patterns result. While learning experientially, you experience psychological success. While mastering group skills, furthermore, you need to observe how they are being used by other group members while you fully participate in the group. Such participant observation enables you to know when to use various group skills and how to help others to do so in order to improve the ways in which the group is functioning. To learn the group skills discussed in this book, the skill-building exercises need to be conducted competently and ethically.

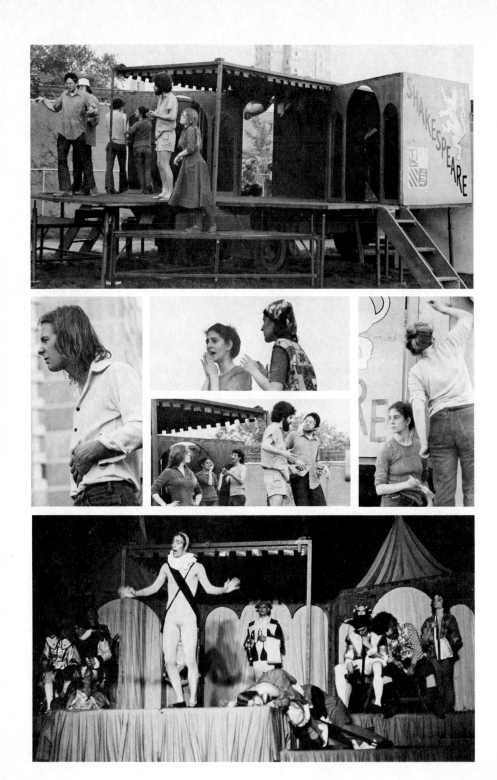

# 3

# Group Goals
# and
# Social Interdependence

## BASIC CONCEPTS TO BE COVERED IN THIS CHAPTER

In this chapter a number of concepts are defined and discussed. The major ones are listed below. The procedure for learning these concepts is as follows:

1. Divide into heterogeneous pairs.
2. The task for each pair is to
   a. Define each concept, noting the page on which it is defined and discussed.
   b. Ensure that both members of the pair understand the meaning of each concept.
3. Combine into groups of four. Compare the answers of the two pairs. If there is disagreement, the members look up the concept in the chapter and clarify it until they all agree on the definition and understand it.

### CONCEPTS

1. Goal
2. Group goal
3. Social interdependence
4. Operational goal
5. Hidden agenda
6. Cooperation
7. Goal structure
8. Competition
9. Individualistic efforts
10. Distributive justice
11. Merit system
12. Equality system
13. Need system
14. Level of aspiration

## INTRODUCTION

> The honor of one is the honor of all.
> The hurt of one is the hurt of all.
> *Creek Indian Creed*

Groups form for a cooperative purpose. Since our beginnings, humans have joined together to cooperate to achieve goals that each individual member could not achieve alone. While elephants have size and cheetahs have speed, it is our ability to engage in cooperative enterprises to achieve group goals that distinguishes us as a species. Social interdependence defines the ways in which the goals of individuals are related. Social interdependence is the heart of all human interaction, and cooperation is the heart of all small-group efforts. To be effective, groups must set group goals that all members commit themselves to cooperate in achieving. There are two steps to do so:

1. Operational goals and the paths to achieving the goals are clearly specified.
2. Cooperative interdependence is structured among group members.

### EXERCISE 3.1:
### ORIENTATIONS TOWARD SOCIAL INTERDEPENDENCE

This exercise has two purposes: (1) to make you more aware of your orientation toward goal interdependence with others and (2) to make your group more aware of members' orientations toward social interdependence. The procedure is as follows:

1. Working by yourself, complete the following questionnaire.
2. Using the scoring table that follows the questionnaire, determine your score and then determine the group average for each scale.
3. Have a group discussion concerning the orientations toward social interdependence of group members.

### Social Interdependence Questionnaire

For each item below, indicate your *general* perceptions about each statement. In the appropriate space, write down the number that most accurately describes your actions. 1 = Never, 2 = Seldom, 3 = Sometimes, 4 = Mostly, 5 = Always.

1. I like to compare myself with others to see who is best.
2. In my situation, people spend a lot of time working by themselves.
3. In my situation, people share their ideas and resources with each other.
4. In my situation, people are motivated to see who can do the best job.
5. In my situation, individuals like to work by themselves.
6. In my situation, individuals learn lots of important things from each other.
7. In my situation, individuals want to do better than the others.
8. In my situation, it bothers individuals when they have to work with each other.
9. In my situation, individuals help each other do a good job.
10. In my situation, individuals are encouraged to outperform each other.
11. In my situation, individuals would rather work alone than work together.
12. In my situation, individuals believe that they are more productive when they work with each other.

| Competitive | Individualistic | Cooperative |
|---|---|---|
| 1. _____ | 2. _____ | 3. _____ |
| 4. _____ | 5. _____ | 6. _____ |
| 7. _____ | 8. _____ | 9. _____ |
| 10. _____ | 11. _____ | 12. _____ |
| Total _____ | Total _____ | Total _____ |

## EXERCISE 3.2:
## ARE GROUP GOALS NECESSARY?

There has been some controversy over whether group goals are necessary. The purpose of this exercise is to structure a critical discussion of the issue. The procedure is as follows:

1. The class forms groups of four.
2. Each group is ultimately to write a report summarizing its position on whether group goals are necessary for a group to be effective. The report is to contain the group's overall conclusions and the facts and rationale supporting its position. The supporting facts and rationale may be obtained from the accompanying briefing sheets, the entire book, and outside reading.
3. First, each group divides into pairs. One pair is assigned the position that group goals are of no use and the other pair the position that groups cannot function without goals. Each pair reviews the appropriate briefing sheet, the procedure for the exercise, and the guidelines for constructive controversy (p. 282).
4. The pairs meet separately to prepare as forceful a 3-minute presentation of their position as possible. They are to make sure that both members have contributed to building a persuasive case for their position and that it includes as many facts and research findings as possible. Both members need to master all the rationale supporting their position. Ten minutes are allowed for this phase.
5. The group of four meets. Each pair presents its position, being as forceful and persuasive as possible, while the other pair takes notes and asks for clarification of anything that is not fully understood. Each pair is allowed about 3 minutes to present its position.
6. The group of four has an open discussion on whether group goals are necessary for a group to be effective. Each side presents as many facts and research findings as it can to support its point of view. Members listen critically to the opposing position and ask for facts to support any conclusions made by the opposing pair. Participants should ensure that all the facts supporting both sides are brought out and discussed, and should follow the guidelines for constructive controversy on page 282. About 10 minutes are allowed for this phase.
7. The perspectives in each group are now reversed, each pair arguing the opposing pair's position. Members should be as forceful and persuasive as they can in arguing for the opposing pair's position. They should elaborate on the opposing position, seeing if they can think of any new arguments or facts that the opposing pair did not present. Each pair has about 3 minutes for its presentation.
8. Each group of four should derive a position that all members can agree to. The members should summarize the best arguments from each position, detailing as many facts as they can on whether group goals are necessary for a group to be effective. When they have consensus in their group, they should organize their arguments for presentation to the rest of the class. Because other groups will have other conclusions, each group may need to explain the validity of its position to the class. About 10 minutes are allowed for this phase.
9. The coordinator samples the decisions made by the groups of four by having several of them present their position to the class. The class then discusses similarities and

differences, and the coordinator summarizes what the participants have learned about group goals.

**Briefing Sheet: Groups Cannot Function Without Goals**

Your position is that a group cannot function without having at least one goal understood and accepted by several of its members. To support your position, use the rationale given below, any material from this chapter that is applicable, and what you know from your outside reading.

The rationale for your position is as follows: Group goals guide the actions of members and allow them to plan and coordinate their efforts. Group goals direct, channel, motivate, coordinate, energize, and guide the behavior of group members. Groups cannot exist unless the activities of their members are directed toward achieving something (a goal). It is the power of goals to influence members to engage in needed behaviors that makes goals essential to an effective group.

**Briefing Sheet: Group Goals Are of No Use**

Your position is that a goal is never useful to a group and may even be a concept that has no basis in reality. To support your position, use the rationale given below, any material from this chapter that is applicable, and what you know from your outside reading.

The rationale for your position is as follows: Group goals are often stated in such vague terms that they could not possibly be effective guides for the actions of members. Many members of groups, furthermore, cannot accurately describe the goals of their group when asked, and thus the goals can have no impact on these persons. In certain cases goals are not determiners of members' efforts because they do not come close to describing what is being done in the group. Appraisals of group progress, moreover, usually reveal that groups have fallen short of their goals, which suggests that the goals are not being closely followed. It may even be that groups do not try to accomplish anything; they just exist and use up resources. All in all, it is not useful to try to describe the goals of a group.

# WHAT IS A GOAL?

> No wind favors him who has no destined port.
> *Montaigne*

Although the sky was clear, the pilot of a chartered flight from Uruguay to Chile miscalculated his position (Read, 1974). Rather than descending for his final landing approach, the pilot was actually flying into an extinct volcano, Tinguiririca. Both wings and the tail section were sheared off on impact, and the airplane's fuselage plummeted down the side of the mountain at a speed exceeding 200 miles per hour. It came to rest on the side of a 12,000-foot mountain, surrounded on three sides by other mountain peaks. None of the plane's crew survived long after the crash, but 32 of the 40 passengers lived. The passengers were the members of an amateur rugby team and their families and friends. They were trapped in the subzero temperatures of winter in the Andes with only some wine and candy to live on. The remnants of the plane's fuselage was their only shelter.

The passengers' overall goal was survival. There were, however, a series of short-term goals around their immediate problems. Their first problems were water, shelter, caring for the injured, and food. The captain of the rugby team assumed leadership and divided the survivors into teams with specific responsibilities such as caring for the injured and melting snow for drinking water. They constructed a rude shelter inside the battered fuselage. The only source of food available was the meat from the dead bodies of their fellow passengers and the airline crew. Group unity and support was essential to overcome the guilt and revulsion felt. A second problem was an avalanche on the seventeenth day of their ordeal that filled the fuselage with snow and smothered many of the survivors, including the rugby captain. The leadership was assumed by three cousins. The third problem was sending two of their fittest members to make the trip down the mountain to search for help. After 10 days of walking and sleeping in the open at night, the two managed to reach a small farm on the edge of the mountain range. The other survivors were rescued after 70 days of the ordeal. The survivors later pointed out "that it was their combined efforts that saved their lives" (Read, 1974, p. 310).

Groups exist for a reason. People join groups to achieve goals they are unable to achieve by themselves. The goal may be to build a better mousetrap, to climb a mountain, to get the most pay for the least amount of work, or to apply the material being presented in this book. The goal may even be to survive a disaster, such as a plane crash in the Andes. The essence of a **goal** is that it is an ideal. It is a desired

place toward which people are working, a state of affairs that people value. *The goals of individuals are related through social interdependence.* There may be a positive correlation among individuals' goal attainments (i.e., cooperation), a negative correlation among individuals' goal attainments (i.e., competition), or no correlation among individuals' goal attainments (i.e., individualistic efforts). Such **goal structures** specify the type of social interdependence among individuals as they strive to accomplish their goals. They specify the ways in which individuals will interact with each other. The goals of survival of the individuals involved in the plane wreck were positively correlated, and, therefore, a cooperative group effort existed. Social interdependence is discussed in depth in a later section of this chapter. When a positive correlation exists among individuals' goal attainments, a group goal results. A **group goal** is a future state of affairs desired by enough members of a group to motivate the group to work toward its achievement. Ever since there were two humans on earth, we have joined together to achieve mutual goals and to maximize our joint welfare. In the plane wreck example, the group goal was to ensure the survival of as many of the passengers as possible.

## A Joint Vision

Goals are not intellectual, cold, or analytical. Goals enlist the emotions of group members and point them toward coordinated efforts. The more the goal elicits emotions the more it is a vision. Group members share a vision as to what they can accomplish when they work together. A **vision** is an ideal and unique image of the future. The vision clarifies the mission and goals of the group. Stephen Wasniack and Stephen Jobs shared a vision as they invented the Apple computer in a garage. They took their dream from a garage to a multinational computer company. To end world hunger, to prevent the pain and anguish of children dying of cancer, to allow the deaf to hear with an artificial ear, to allow people to live with an artificial heart, to find a drug to prevent the body's rejection of transplanted organs, are all visions that bring tears, laughter, bitter disappointment, determination, hope, depression, enthusiasm, and joy. The vision tells group members what is uniquely possible if all work together for a common purpose. It shows members how their values and interests will be served by the accomplishments they are striving for. The goal of the group creates a compelling vision that focuses the passion of members and ignites the flame of inspired work. The vision binds members through a shared, **emotional** commitment. Group goals breathe life into the hopes and dreams of group members and enable them to see the exciting possibilities of their joint efforts.

## Do Group Goals Exist?

Each individual survivor of the plane crash in the Andes wanted to live. They formed a group to do so. There may be some disagreement as to whether there was an overall group goal or only the combination of the goals of individuals. Do groups have goals? Or are there only the various individual goals of the group's members? As dry as these questions may seem, social psychologists have hotly debated this issue for decades. Emmy Pepitone (1980), for example, insists that group goals can be identified, that they function as an important source of member interdependence in groups, and that they denote a common, central focus that is present most of the time and is readily identifiable as an objective reality. She states that group goals provide an aspect of unity, of a common fate, that one cannot readily convey simply by noting the individual goals of group members. Lewin (1944) noted that there are situations in which group members do seem to act to maximize joint outcomes or accomplish group goals rather than to maximize their individual outcomes or achieve their individual goals. Both Horwitz (1954) and Pepitone (1952) conducted studies that indicated that group members become motivated to have their group achieve its goal and are personally satisfied when the group does so. The success of the group, rather than their personal gain, seems to be the major source of their satisfaction. Numerous other studies have demonstrated that individuals do focus on joint outcomes rather than individual outcomes when they are placed in situations requiring cooperation with others.

Many social scientists, however, believe that a group goal is a combination of the individual goals of all group members. People, therefore, become group members because they have certain goals and motives that they wish to express or fulfill through group membership. Each person brings to the group a wish to satisfy personal goals. These goals are not always clearly known to the member—he or she may be completely aware, partially aware, or totally unaware of his or her goals and motives during a group meeting.

There is no definitive answer to whether group goals exist in and of themselves or are simply a reflection of the overlap among the personal goals of the group's members. It is safe to conclude, however, that both group and individual goals exist and the group goals must be relevant to the individual needs of the members. Group members try usually to achieve both individual and group goals, and the degree to which they can accomplish this through the same activities determines how effective the group will be in attaining its goals. The situation is further complicated by the fact that most groups and individuals have several goals and different members value different goals at different times and even the same member places different values on the same goal at different times.

Whether group goals are entities in and of themselves or simply a combination of the individual goals of members, they are important for numerous reasons.

## EXERCISE 3.3:
## YOUR GOAL-RELATED BEHAVIOR 1

The purpose of this exercise is to allow you to examine your group-goal-related behavior in problem-solving groups. Working by yourself, answer the following three questions. Be honest. Check as many responses to each question as are characteristic of your usual and regular behavior. Then form a group with two of your classmates and discuss your answers to the questions and why you answered them as you did. Try to develop as much awareness of your behavior in goal-related situations as possible.

1. When I am a member of a group that does not seem to have a clear awareness of what its goals are or how they are to be achieved, I usually

_____   ask the group to stop and discuss its goals until all group members clearly understand what they are and what actions the group needs to take to accomplish them.

_____   feel disgusted and refuse to attend meetings.

_____   state as specifically as possible what I consider the goals of the group to be, and comment on how the present actions of the group relate to goal accomplishment.

_____   ask the designated leader to stop messing around and tell the group what it is supposed to be doing.

2. When I am a member of a group that has a clear understanding of its goals but seems to have little commitment to accomplishing them, I usually

_____   try to shame other group members into being more motivated.

_____   blame the designated leader for being incompetent.

_____   ask the group members to look at how meaningful, relevant, and acceptable the goals are to them.

_____   try to change the group's goals in order to make them more relevant to the members' needs and motives.

_____   point out the sacrifices some members have made in the past toward goal accomplishment and hope that all members become more committed.

3. When I am a member of a group that has conflicting opinions on what its goals should be, or that has members with conflicting needs and motives, I usually

_____   figure out how much cooperative and competitive behavior exists in the group and give the group feedback based on my observations in an attempt to increase cooperativeness among its members.

_____   start a group discussion on the personal goals, needs, and motives of each group member in order to determine the extent to which there are competing goals among them.

_____   declare one member of the group to be the winner and ask all other group members to work toward accomplishing the person's goals.

_____   ask the group to determine how the members' actions can become more coordinated.

_____   form a secret coalition with several other group members so that our goals will become dominant in the group.

## Importance of Group Goals

There are a number of reasons why group goals are important. First, goals are guides for action, and it is through group goals that the efforts of group members are planned and coordinated. Roles and responsibilities are assigned to members on the basis of what needs to be done in order for the group's goals to be accomplished.

Second, the efficiency and usefulness of group procedures are evaluated on the basis of how they facilitate goal accomplishment. In other words, not only must the goals be clear, the path to reaching the goal must be clear. Perhaps the General Motors executives were not clear as to how to proceed to achieve the corporation's goals. Clear goals are not enough. The paths to these goals must be clear also.

The third reason why group goals are important is that conflicts among group members are resolved on the basis of what helps the group achieve its goals (see Chapter 7).

Fourth, and most important, group goals direct and motivate members' behavior. Many analyses of motivation overlook group goals as motivators and emphasize only individual psychological factors such as the need for achievement or drive to self-actualization. Frequently, people are as interested in working to achieve group goals as they are in striving to meet their own personal needs. When Zander (1971, 1974, 1977), for example, asked assembly-line workers to rate the importance of personal success and their group's success, the workers strongly emphasized their group's goals. A similar study in a Swedish brewery found that workers viewed the success of their team as very important, even when they were not concerned with the company as a whole. Executives serving on the boards of 46 United Funds agencies stated that "team spirit" may be as important in determining productivity as the striving for individual achievement. As members commit themselves to achieving a goal, an inner tension is aroused that continues until the goal has been accomplished or until some sort of psychological closure is achieved concerning the goal. It is this internal tension that motivates group members to work toward goal accomplishment. Thus, when group members commit themselves to a group goal, internal tension arises that makes them restless and dissatisfied until the group completes its plans. Members' commitment to accomplishing a group goal depends on several factors, such as

1. How desirable the goal seems.
2. How likely it seems that the group can accomplish the goal.
3. How challenging the goal is (a moderate risk of failure is more challenging than a high or low risk of failure).
4. Being able to tell when the goal has been achieved.
5. The satisfaction or reward the member expects to feel or receive when the goal is achieved.
6. The ways in which the member will relate to other members in working toward the accomplishment of the goal (some ways of relating to other members are more fun and involving than others).
7. The extent to which members participated in setting the goals. This increase in motivation comes in part from the fact that participation produces (a) a better matching of the group goals to the motives of members, which brings about greater acceptance of the goals, (b) a better understanding of the group actions needed to achieve the goals, and (c) a better appreciation of how individual behavior contributes to the necessary group action.
8. The level of cohesiveness that exists within the group (see Chapter 12).

If they are accepted, understood, and desired by group members, group goals direct, channel, motivate, coordinate, energize, and guide the behavior of group members. The goals of a group, therefore, are the beginning point in evaluating a group's effectiveness. Goals, however, must be clear rather than ambiguous and operational rather than nonoperational.

## EXERCISE 3.4:
## CLEAR AND UNCLEAR GOALS

This exercise shows the contrasting behavioral consequences of having clear and unclear goals. Approximately 1 hour is needed to complete it. Here is the procedure for the coordinator:

1. Seat the participants in groups of six to eight, formed into circles.
2. Introduce the exercise as focusing upon clear and unclear group goals.
3. Have each group select an observer, who reports to a designated place for instructions. While the observers are being briefed, urge the group members to get acquainted with one another.
4. Give each observer a copy of the observation guide and tell them that the groups will work on two tasks. The first task will be unclear, the second clear. Their job is to make careful observations of group behavior on the two tasks. The observers then return to their groups, but sit outside the circle.
5. Brief all groups as follows: "We are going to study group behavior by working on two brief tasks. Your observer will not participate, but will report to you at the end of the second task. Your first task will take about eight minutes. I will give you a warning a minute before the time is up. The task is: list the most appropriate goals to govern the best developmental group experiences in order to maximize social development in a democratic society."
6. While the groups work on the task, the observers should take notes. After 7 minutes give the warning and after 8 minutes end the discussion.
7. Give Task 2: "List as many of the formally organized clubs or organizations that exist in a typical community as you can." State that the groups will have 6 minutes to work on the task. At the end of 5 minutes give a 1-minute warning and after 6 minutes end the discussion.
8. Give a copy of the observation form to all participants. Then have each group discuss its experience, using the information obtained by the observers as its major resource. This discussion should last 10 to 15 minutes.
9. Form clusters by asking one group to pull its chairs in a circle around another group. The inner group becomes group A and the outer group becomes group B. Instruct group A to produce a list of characteristics of clear and unclear goals with one person recording them on newsprint in two columns. Allow 6 minutes for this task. Group B is to listen to group A, take notes, and be ready to add to the list. After 6 minutes instruct group B to comment on the list and have both groups jointly select the four or five most important characteristics of clear and unclear goals from the list. Give them 9 minutes to do so.
10. Groups A and B then change places, with group B now in the center. Group B is told to list behavioral symptoms of each of the characteristics of clear and unclear goals listed on the newsprint, beginning with the most important characteristics. After 9 minutes group A joins the discussion, which should take another 6 minutes.
11. Each cluster presents its work to the other group. Hold a general discussion on the nature of group goals and their consequences in feeling and behavior, using the material in the following section.

### Clear and Unclear Goals Exercise: Observation Guide

During this exercise the groups will work on two tasks. The first task will be unclear, and the second will be clear. Your job as an observer is to make careful notations of group behavior on the two tasks. When you understand the form below, return to your group but sit outside the circle.

## Clarity of Goals

To be useful, goals have to be clear. If you have done the preceding exercise, you will have a list of both the characteristics of clear and unclear goals and the behavioral symptoms of groups with clear and unclear goals. Remember that some of the symptoms of unclear goals are a high level of group tension, joking or horseplay, distraction into side issues, and the failure to use, support, and build on good ideas. The importance of clear goals may be seen when groups lose their direction. John De-Lorean (Wright, 1979) describes how highly qualified executives in General Motors held numerous pointless meetings where trivial issues were discussed at length. These highly paid executives forgot their true goal of planning for the corporation's future. Latham and Baldes (1975), on the other hand, report the beneficial effects of clear goals. When truck drivers who hauled logs from the woods to the mill were told to "do their best" when loading the logs they carried about 60 percent of what they could legally haul. When they were later encouraged to reach a goal of 94 percent of the legal limit, they met this specific goal. In financial terms, this clarification of goals earned the company more than a quarter of a million dollars. Goals become clarified as they are made more specific, operational, workable, measurable, and observable.

For individual members to perform effectively within a group, they must know what the group's goals are, understand what actions need to be taken to accom-

|  | First Task | Second Task |
|---|---|---|
| 1. Number of times a member clarified the goal or asked that it be clarified. |  |  |
| 2. Assessment of "working" climate of the group: Was it cooperative, hostile, pleasant, critical, accepting, and so forth?     At the beginning?    At the middle?    At the end? |  |  |
| 3. Frequency of verbal behavior not directly related to getting the job done (side conversation, jokes, comments). |  |  |
| 4. Frequency of nonverbal behavior not related to getting the task done (looking around the room, horseplay, bored withdrawal, hostility). |  |  |
| 5. How much progress did the group make in getting the task done? (Make an estimate.) |  |  |

plish them, know the criteria by which the group can tell when they have been reached, and be aware of how their own behavior can contribute to group actions. Goal and task accomplishment depend upon members' coordinating and synchronizing their actions. The clarity of the group goal and the clarity of the actions required to achieve it are important if individual members are to accept the group goal, to experience a feeling of group belongingness, to be interested in goal-related behaviors, and to be willing to accept influence from the group. One of the most common practical problems of groups is trying to keep up with precisely where the group is in relation to its goals and what steps need to be taken by group members to reach them. The group and the group's tasks become more attractive as the goal becomes clearer and as the nature of the tasks and the responsibilities of each member within the group are made more tangible.

## Operational Goals

**Operational goals** are goals for which specific steps to achievement are clear and identifiable. **Nonoperational goals** are abstract in that the specific steps required to achieve them are not discernible. Broad, long-range goals are often nonoperational and can be related to specific actions only through the formation of subgoals. Subgoals are often substituted for the more general goals of a group so that the group can gain operational advantages. An example of an operational goal is "Name three qualities of a good group member." An example of a nonoperational goal is "Make conclusions about the theoretical and empirical findings of qualities of effective actions by a group member."

If a goal is stated in an operational way, then it is easy to tell when it has been accomplished. There is no sense in going somewhere if you do not know when you have arrived. An operational goal has indicators that will make it evident when it has been achieved. The goal "Name three qualities of a good group member" is operational in that when you have listed three items, and if they refer to group membership, you will know the goal has been reached. The goal "Make conclusions about the theoretical and empirical findings of qualities of effective actions by a group member" is nonoperational in that it may be difficult to tell when such a goal has been achieved. Whatever indicators are used to tell when a group has accomplished its goals, several of them are better than one, and indicators that are observable, countable, and specific are better than those that are nonobservable, noncountable, and ambiguous. Usually the goal of a problem-solving group will have indicators that reflect both the accomplishment of the goal (profit, new members gained, problems solved) and group processes and group maintenance (group cohesion, communication effectiveness, decision-making ability, level of trust among members).

There are several advantages for a group in having operational goals. The first advantage is in helping communication among its members and between the group and other groups. A goal must be stated in such a way that it succeeds in telling what the group intends to accomplish, and this communication is successful when any knowledgeable person can look at the group's behavior or products and decide whether or not the goal has been reached. When the goal has been made sufficiently workable—in the sense that a series of behaviors for achieving it have been identified—that others can reliably agree on whether a group's performance or product fulfills the goal, then the goal is sufficiently specific.

The second advantage in having operational goals is that they help to guide the group in planning and carrying out its tasks. If a group is not certain what outcomes it is trying to effect, it will have difficulty planning how it will do its work. Operational goals help a group to select and to organize the appropriate resources and methods it will need in working on its tasks. They make it easier for a member to diagnose what leadership behaviors are needed and to accept responsibility for achievement. The more group members know what they are trying to accomplish with any specific task, the better they can direct their attention and efforts. Finally, the problems of revision, modification, and change in the group are helped when the overall effort is broken down into smaller operational parts.

The third advantage of operational goals is that they help the group to evaluate both the group process and the group outcome or product. By specifying its goals and the criteria by which it will know when it has reached them, the group can evaluate how well it has accomplished them. Similarly, operational goals facilitate feedback among group members about the accomplishments resulting from their behavior and the effectiveness of current procedures.

A fourth advantage is that when goals are operational, conflicts and differences about the course of group action are more likely to be decided by rational, analytic processes. When goals are not operational or when the operational subgoals are not relevant to most group members, differences are less likely to be adjusted through negotiation. If goals are operational, members can more readily see the logic of different courses of action. If goals are nonoperational, there is no logical and testable answer to such differences of judgment, and it is likely not only that a compromise result will be based upon concessions and trading but that a greater emphasis will be placed upon maintaining harmony within the group than upon accomplishing its goals.

How are clear, operational goals developed? It must be recognized that for most groups clear goals cannot always be determined in advance, especially if they are to be acceptable to all or most of the members. The first job of any group, therefore, is to modify any stated goal until all the group members understand it and a consensus exists concerning how it is to be operationalized or put into practice. Through such discussions, commitment to goals is built and the goals become acceptable to the group members. The more time a group spends establishing agreement on clear goals, the less time it needs in achieving them—and the more likely it will be that the members will work effectively for the common outcome.

How do you tell whether a group's goals are sufficiently understood and operationalized? If you have done the preceding exercise, you will have a list of both the characteristics of clear and unclear goals and the behavioral symptoms of groups with clear and unclear goals. Remember that some of the symptoms of unclear goals are a high level of group tension, joking or horseplay, distraction of the group by side issues, and the group's failure to use, support, or build on good ideas.

## Group Goals and Level of Aspiration

Kurt Lewin and his associates developed a theory of level of aspiration to explain how people set goals for themselves and their groups (Lewin, Dembo, Festinger, & Sears, 1944). **Level of aspiration (LOA)** may be defined as the compromise between ideal goals and more realistic expectations. The theory generally predicts that individuals enter situations with an ideal outcome in mind (for example, earning a "B" in this course) but revise their goals upward after success and downward after failure (if they get "A's" on the first two tests, they change their LOA to aspire for an "A," but if they get "C's" on the first two tests, they change their LOA to aspire for a "C"). As they gain experience, individuals revise their ideal expectations to match the reality of the situation.

Groups, like individuals, develop levels of aspirations. Alvin Zander conducted a series of studies with populations as diverse as high school boys batting a ball down a runway as a team (Zander & Medow, 1963) and United Fund chapters setting their fund-raising goals (Zander, 1971). He demonstrated that groups set goals that are slightly optimistic and revised their goals as feedback about performance levels became available. Groups tended to lower their level of aspiration somewhat less after failure than they raised it after success. In the United Fund study, for example, of the chapters that failed to reach their goal, only 40 percent lowered their goal for the next year. Of the chapters that succeeded in reaching their goal, 80 percent raised their goal. While this optimistic bias is constructive in most circumstances, there are times when it leads to a cycle of failure. When unsuccessful United Fund chapters set overoptimistic goals year after year, the continued failure decreased morale, work enjoyment, and group efficiency. While optimistic goal setting challenges members to work hard to improve performance, the refusal to revise overly idealistic goals in unsuccessful groups can set the stage for future failure and its consequences.

## Dealing with Hidden Agendas

The personal goals of the group members can be homogeneous (alike) or heterogeneous (different). Homogeneity of individual members' goals (or consensus about what the group's goals should be) usually helps group functioning, whereas heterogeneity of individual members' goals (or disagreement about what the group's goals should be) usually interferes with group functioning. Individual group members with homogeneous goals are usually happier with the group and its tasks than are members of groups with heterogeneous individual goals. Heterogeneous goals may easily become **hidden agendas**—personal goals that are unknown to all the other group members and are at cross-purposes with the dominant group goals. Hidden agendas can greatly hinder, indeed destroy, group effectiveness. Yet they are present in almost every group. A group, therefore, must both increase consensus among group members on what the group's goals should be and decrease disagreement among different members' goals. Some procedures for doing this are as follows:

1. When you first form a group, thoroughly discuss its goals, even when they are prescribed by superiors or by the constitution of the group. Such a discussion will clarify the members' understanding of the goals and help to clear away any misunderstandings concerning the tasks necessary to reach them. During the discussion the group should reword, reorganize, and review the goals until the majority of members feel a sense of "ownership" toward them.

2. As the group progresses in its activities, remember that it is continuously working on two levels at once: toward the achievement of the group's goals and toward the achievement and satisfaction of the individual members' goals and motives. Look for hidden agendas. The recognition of a group problem is the first step in diagnosing and solving it.

3. Bear in mind that there are conditions under which hidden agendas should be brought to the surface and rectified and conditions under which they should be left undisturbed. A judgment must be made about the consequences of bringing hidden agendas to the attention of the entire group. One way in which to tell how willing other group members are to deal with hidden agendas is to initiate a discussion on the subject, taking care not to force anyone into admitting their own hidden agendas. A statement like this one may be helpful: "I wonder if we've said all that we feel like saying about the issue. Maybe we should take time to go around the table so that any further thoughts can be brought up."

4. Do not scold or pressure the other group members when hidden agendas are recognized. They are present and legitimate and must be worked on in much the same manner that group tasks are. Hidden agendas should be given different amounts of attention at different times, depending upon their influence on the group's effectiveness and upon the nature of the group and its members.

5. Spend some time evaluating the ability of the group to deal productively with hidden agendas. Each experience the group has should reveal better ways in which to handle agendas more openly. As groups mature, hidden agendas are reduced.

## Effective Group Goals

Research has shown that the effectiveness of group goals depends on several variables:

1. The extent to which the goals are operationally defined, countable, and observable.
2. The extent to which group members see the goals as being meaningful, relevant, realistic, acceptable, and attainable.
3. How cooperative the goal structure is and how cooperatively oriented the group members are.
4. The degree to which both group goals and individual members' goals can be achieved by the same tasks and activities.
5. The degree to which conflict exists among the group members about the group's goals and the tasks the group must complete to achieve the goals.
6. The extent to which the goals are challenging and offer a moderate risk of failure.
7. The degree of coordination achieved among group members.
8. The availability of the resources needed for accomplishing the group's tasks and goals.
9. How specific the goals are, because specific goals indicate what needs to be done next.
10. How easily the goals can be modified and clarified.
11. How long a group has to attain its goals.

## Helping Groups Set Effective Goals

The first job of any group is to clarify and modify stated goals until they are clear and acceptable. The two methods of helping groups set effective goals are the survey-feedback method and program evaluation and review.

The **survey-feedback method** begins with the consultant or leader interviewing the individual members of the group about group goals and the priorities of the group as they see them. These interviews are conducted before a periodic meeting of the group (such as annually or semiannually). On the basis of the information collected, and working within the organizational goals, the consultant conducts a group session in which the group sets its goals and priorities for the next six months or year. During this meeting the group plans its short-term goals, defines specific responsibilities for working on the tasks, ranks the tasks and goals in terms of priority to the group, and sets group-development goals for more effective group work. Special attention is paid to specifying the leadership and membership-role relationships necessary not only for working on the tasks, but also for developing ways in which to identify and solve group relationship problems that might hinder goal achievement.

In program evaluation and review—or the **critical path method,** as it is sometimes called—groups are helped by a consultant to set effective goals by first specifying the end state they want to achieve. Working backward from this final goal, the group then details what must happen immediately before it is achieved, and the tasks and subgoals needed to accomplish it are all spelled out. The group decides which of the activities and subgoals are most critical for final goal accomplishment and allocates resources accordingly. A timetable for accomplishing each subgoal is set. The whole process is then reviewed and responsibilities assigned.

**EXERCISE 3.5:**
**PLANE WRECK**

The purpose of this exercise is to provide participants with an opportunity to experience cooperation based on a division of labor as well as a joint goal. The procedure is as follows:

1. The class forms groups of three. One member plays the role of observer, another member the role of A, and the third member B.
2. Each group of three needs the following materials:
   a. a blindfold
   b. five or six odd-sized pieces of cardboard
   c. a roll of cellophane tape or masking tape
   d. a piece of rope at least 3 feet long
3. *The situation:* A and B were flying a plane, which suddenly developed engine trouble and crashed on a desert island with no water. They will be rescued in a few days, but they must have water if they are to survive. They have some materials for making a container to hold rainwater. The only problem is that B received a heavy blow on her head and is now both blind and mute. A burned both his hands badly and is not able to use them at all. But they must build the container if they are to live. A rain cloud is quickly approaching, and they must have the container finished before it reaches the island. A few drops are already beginning to fall.
4. The observer ties A's hands behind his back and blindfolds B. B is not to say a word during the entire building process.
5. The observer takes notes on how well the two persons work together. How good are the directions? How well are they carried out? How cooperative are the two persons? What communication problems exist? What could they have done differently?
6. If the container is not finished in 20 minutes, the two persons stop. The group then combines with another group of three and the two groups discuss the following questions:
   a. How did the person playing A feel?
   b. How did the person playing B feel?
   c. What does the container look like? If it were made of wood and nails instead of cardboard and tape, would it hold water? (If there is a hole in the bottom, the answer is no).
   d. What would have improved the cooperation between A and B?
   e. What did you learn about the division of labor in a cooperative task?
7. Each group of six shares its major conclusions and experiences with the rest of the class.

## EXERCISE 3.6: BROKEN SQUARES

The purpose of this exercise is to explore the results of cooperation and competition among group members in solving a group problem. The exercise is done in groups of five participants and two observers. Tables that seat five should be used. At least four groups are recommended, but two may do in a pinch. Place the tables far enough apart so that members of one group cannot observe the activities of the other groups. One set of squares is needed for each group of five. (Instructions for making a set of squares may be found in the appendix on page 490). Approximately one hour is needed for the exercise. The procedures for the coordinator are as follows:

1. Introduce the exercise as one that focuses upon the way in which goals are defined by members of a group. State that it will consist of completing a group task involving a puzzle.
2. Hand out the observation instructions to the observers. Within each group give each participant an instruction sheet and an envelope containing pieces of the puzzle (see the directions for making a set of squares). Half of the groups should receive instructions that they are to act cooperatively, and half instructions that they are to act competitively. State that the envelopes are not to be opened until the signal is given.

Review the instructions with each group in such a way that cooperative groups do not hear the instructions to the competitive groups, and vice versa. Ask if the observers understand their role.

3. Give the signal to begin. The groups are to work until all of them have solved the puzzle. Each group should be carefully timed by its observers. If a group becomes deadlocked for more than 25 minutes, this phase of the exercise should be ended.

4. Collect the observation sheets and record the information in the table below. While you are doing this the groups should pair off, a cooperative group with a competitive group, and share and discuss their instructions and experiences with each other. Group observers are to participate fully in this discussion. By the end of the discussion the groups should have recorded their conclusions about the differences between working in a cooperatively oriented and a competitively oriented problem-solving group.

5. Share the results of the discussions among all the groups. Then present the information gathered by the observers. Using the material in the following section on goal structures, define cooperation and competition and discuss the impact of goal structures on group functioning and effectiveness.

You may conduct this exercise with only one group by leaving out the instructions about cooperative and competitive orientations and the comparison between cooperative and competitive groups. The issue of goal structure can still be discussed profitably.

## Broken Squares Exercise: Instructions to Each Member of the Cooperative Group

Each member of your group has an envelope containing pieces of cardboard for forming squares. When the signal is given to begin, the task of the group is to form one square in front of each member. Only parts of the pieces for forming the five squares are in each envelope. The exercise has two goals: your individual goal of forming a square in front of yourself as fast as possible and the group's goal of having squares formed in front of every member as fast as possible. The individual goal is accomplished when you have a completed square in front of you. The group goal is accomplished when all group members have completed squares in front of them.

You are to role-play a member of a group whose members are all highly cooperative. To you the group goal is far more important than the individual goal. Your job is to cooperate with the other group members as much as possible in order to accomplish the group goal in the shortest period of time possible. To you the other group members are your partners, and you are concerned with helping them put together a completed square. All members of your group have received the same instructions.

Data from Observation Sheets

|  | Cooperative | Competitive |
|---|---|---|
| Number of groups completing the task |  |  |
| Time for task completion |  |  |
| Number of times a member gave away a puzzle piece |  |  |
| Number of times a member took a puzzle piece |  |  |
| Number of members who cut themselves off from others |  |  |
| Cooperative behaviors |  |  |
| Competitive behaviors |  |  |

The specific rules for the exercise are as follows:

1. No talking, pointing, or any other kind of communication is allowed among the five members of your group.
2. No person may ask another member for a piece of the puzzle or in any way signal that another person is to give her a puzzle piece.
3. Members may give puzzle pieces to other members.
4. Members may not throw their pieces into the center for others to take; they have to give the pieces directly to one person.
5. Anyone may give away all the pieces of his puzzle, even if he or she has already formed a square.
6. Part of the role of the observers is to enforce these rules.

## Broken Squares Exercise: Instructions to Each Member of the Competitive Group

Every person in this group has an envelope that contains pieces of cardboard for forming squares. When the signal is given to begin, your task is to form a square in front of you. Only parts of the pieces for forming the five squares are in each envelope. The exercise has two goals: your individual goal of forming a square in front of you as fast as possible and the group's goal of forming squares in front of every member as fast as possible. The individual goal is accomplished when you have a completed square in front of you. The group goal is accomplished when all group members have completed squares in front of them.

You are to role-play a member of a group whose members are all highly competitive. To you the individual goal is far more important than the group goal. Your job is to compete with the other group members to see who can get a complete square in front of himself first. At the end of the exercise group members will be ranked on the basis of their speed in completing their square. The member finishing first will be labeled the "best" person in the group, the person finishing second will be labeled "second best" person in the group, and so on, with the last person finishing being labeled the "worst" person in the group. The other group members are your competitors, and you are concerned with completing your square before they do. If you complete your square and then decide to give a piece of it away, you lose your previous rank in terms of the order of members completing their squares and must start over. All members of your group have received the same instructions.

The specific rules for the exercise are as follows:

1. No talking, pointing, or any other kind of communicating is allowed among the five members of your group.
2. No person may ask another member for a piece of the puzzle or in any way signal that another person is to give him or her a puzzle piece.
3. Members may give puzzle pieces to other members.
4. Members may not throw their pieces into the center for others to take; they have to give the pieces directly to one person.
5. Part of the role of the observers is to enforce these rules.

## Broken Squares Exercise: Instructions for Observers

Your job is part observer, part recorder, and part rule enforcer. Do your best to strictly enforce the rules on the instruction sheet for participants. Then observe and record as accurately as possible the items listed below. The information you record will be used in a discussion of the results of the exercise.

1. Did the group complete the task? _____ Yes _____ No

2. How long did it take the group to complete the task? _____ minutes, _____ seconds

| 3. | Number of times a group member took a puzzle piece from another member: | Number of times a group member gave a puzzle piece to another member: |
|----|----|----|
| | | |

4. Number of members who finished their square and then divorced themselves from the struggles of the rest of the group? _____

5. Were there any critical turning points at which cooperation or competition increased? _____

_____

_____

6. What behaviors in the group showed cooperativeness or competitiveness? _____

_____

_____

_____

## EXERCISE 3.7:
## COOPERATIVE, COMPETITIVE, AND
## INDIVIDUALISTIC GOAL STRUCTURES

The purposes of this exercise are (1) to provide an experiential definition of the three goal structures and (2) to direct participants' attention to the contrasting patterns of interaction created by these three structures. (The correct answers are in the appendix on page 491.) The procedure for the coordinator is as follows:

1. Assign participants to heterogeneous groups of three.
2. Conduct a competitive task experience as follows:
   a. State that the members of each triad are to compete to see who is best in identifying how many squares are in a certain geometric figure. The criterion for winning is simply to identify more correct squares than the other two triad members. Ask the participants to turn their "square figure" right side up, and tell them to begin.
   b. At the end of 4 or 5 minutes instruct the participants to stop. Ask them to determine who is the winner of each triad, ask the winners to stand, and then have everyone applaud.
   c. Tell the participants to turn away from their triad and, working by themselves, write down (1) how they felt during the competition and (2) what they noticed during the competition. Give them another 3 or 4 minutes to do this.
3. Conduct an individualistic task experience as follows:
   a. State that participants are to work individualistically to find as many two-sided figures in a geometric figure as they can. All participants who find 95 percent of the biangles will receive an evaluation of "excellent," all those who find 90

percent will receive an evaluation of "good," and so forth. Tell the participants to turn their "biangles figure" right side up and begin.

   b. At the end of 4 or 5 minutes ask the participants to stop. Then announce the number of biangles in the figure. Ask the participants to leave their triad and, working by themselves, describe (1) how they felt and (2) what they noticed during this task. Give them another 3 or 4 minutes to do this.

4. Conduct a cooperative task experience as follows:

   a. State that the participants are to reform their triads and work as a group to identify as many triangles in a geometric figure as they can, making sure that all members of the triad can correctly identify all the triangles. When they are finished, the members of each triad should sign the group's paper to indicate their agreement with the group's answer. All members of the groups finding 95 percent of the triangles will receive an evaluation of "excellent," all members of the groups finding 90 percent of the triangles will receive an evaluation of "good," and so forth. Tell the participants to turn their "triangles figure" right side up and begin.

   b. At the end of 9 or 10 minutes tell the participants to stop. Inform them of the number of triangles in the figure. Then ask them to turn away from their triad and, working by themselves, write down (1) how they felt and (2) what they noticed during the cooperative task. Give the participants 4 minutes to do this.

5. Instruct the participants to share their reactions to the three types of task situations with the other members of their triad. Give them 10 or 12 minutes to do so. Then sample the reactions of the triads in a class discussion. Ask the participants to make conclusions about the reactions of the triads to the three task experiences.

6. Instruct the triads to fill out the table below on the basis of their experiences in the three goal structures and the comments made by the other triads. In the spaces provided, they should summarize their observations of the interaction that occurred in three task situations.

## Goal Structure and Interaction Among Group Members

| | Goal Structures | | |
| --- | --- | --- | --- |
| | *Cooperative* | *Competitive* | *Individualistic* |
| Interaction | | | |
| Communication | | | |
| Facilitation of others' efforts | | | |
| Peer influence | | | |
| Utilization of others' resources | | | |
| Divergent thinking | | | |
| Emotional involvement in task | | | |
| Acceptance and support among members | | | |
| Trust among members | | | |
| Conflict management | | | |
| Division of labor | | | |
| Fear of failure | | | |

In the spaces provided, summarize your observations of the three types of task situations.

7. Review with the entire class the conceptual definitions of the three goal structures and discuss their views of the impact of each of these structures on group functioning and productivity.

**Goal Structures Exercise: Squares**

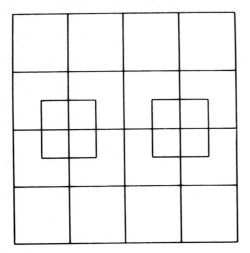

How did I feel?
What did I notice?

**Goal Structures Exercise: Biangles**

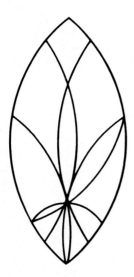

How did I feel?
What did I notice?

**Goal Structures Exercise: Triangles**

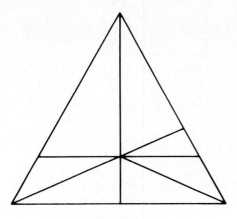

How did I feel?
What did I notice?

## EXERCISE 3.8:
## SUBSISTENCE

The purpose of this exercise is to observe the effect of unequal resources on the development of cooperation or competition within a group. The exercise simulates the effects of poverty and affluence in a life and death situation. The procedure is as follows:

1.  Form groups of seven. One member should volunteer to be the recorder and another member should volunteer to be the observer. Each group should have five participants, one recorder, and one observer.
2.  To play the game contained in this exercise the group needs a pack of blank 3- × 5-inch index cards to serve as food cards. The group also needs a pack of hunting and gathering cards. Each card should have one of the statements listed on page 81 written on it.
3.  The basic procedure of the game is as follows:
    a.  Each participant receives three food cards.
    b.  The recorder shuffles the hunting and gathering cards and places them in the center of the group.
    c.  Each participant draws a card in turn (going counterclockwise), reads it to the group, and receives from or gives to the recorder the required number of food cards.
    d.  The day's hunting and gathering is over when every participant has drawn one card. Participants may give any number of food cards to each other. At the end of the day they must give one food card to the recorder. Failure to do so results in death by starvation and dropping out of the game.
    e.  After seven rounds the week's hunting and gathering is over. Points are awarded to group members.
    f.  The game is played for a minimum of two weeks.
4.  The role of the observer is to record the frequency of the behaviors listed on the observation sheet. The frequencies are reported to the group during the concluding group discussion.

5. The role of the recorder is to
   a. Read the Subsistence Instruction Sheet to the group.
   b. Review the rules with participants.
   c. Give each participant three food cards.
   d. Shuffle the hunting and gathering cards and place them in the center of the group.
   e. Distribute and collect food cards on the basis of the cards drawn.
   f. At the end of each round collect one food card from each participant.
   g. Ensure that each participant announces how many food cards they have at the end of each round.
   h. Announce how many participants starved to death and who has the most food cards at the end of each week (seven rounds).
6. When the game is over, discuss the following questions:
   a. Who survived and who died?
   b. How was a cooperative or a competitive strategy decided on?
   c. How did participants feel about the impending death by starvation?
   d. How did the dead feel when they knew others could have saved them?
   e. How did the survivors feel when others died when they had extra food cards?
   f. Who organized the group to create a "just" distribution of food?
   g. What real-life situations parallel this exercise?

## Subsistence Instruction Sheet

A severe drought has devastated your world. Because food is so scarce you have banded together into a hunting and gathering group. It is more efficient for several people to coordinate their hunting and gathering so that more territory may be covered in any one day. There are five members of your hunting and gathering group. The food cards in your hands represent all you have left of your dwindling food supply. Because you are already weakened by hunger, you must eat at the end of each day (round) or die. At that time, you must give up one food card. When you are out of cards, you will die of starvation. A member who does not have one food card at the end of a day (round) is considered to be dead and can no longer participate in the group. Members with only one food card may not talk. Only members with two or more food cards may discuss their situation and converse with each other. You may give food cards to each other whenever you wish to do so.

## Rules for Subsistence Exercise

1. The game begins when the recorder gives all participants three food cards, shuffles the hunting and gathering cards, and places them in the center of the group.
2. The purpose of the game is to gain points. You receive eight points if at the end of the week of hunting and gathering (seven rounds) you have more food cards than does any other participant in your group. If no one in your group has starved at the end of the week of hunting and gathering, all participants receive five points.
3. The game is played for a minimum of two weeks. At the beginning of each week all participants begin with three food cards and with all five participants alive.
4. You draw one card during each round. You read it aloud to the group and receive from or give to the recorder the number of food cards indicated.
5. During a round you may give food cards to other participants if you wish to.
6. All participants read the hunting and gathering cards aloud. Only those with two or more food cards, however, may discuss the game with each other. Participants with one or no food cards must be silent.
7. At the end of each round participants hold up their food cards and announce to the group how many food cards they have.
8. At the end of each round participants give one food card each to the recorder. This symbolizes the food eaten during the day to stay alive.

9. If a participant cannot give a food card to the recorder at the end of a round, the participant dies of starvation and is excluded from further rounds during that week.
10. At the end of each week of hunting and gathering (seven rounds) the recorder announces who has the most food cards and how many participants starved to death. Points are then awarded.

Subsistence Record Sheet

| Name | Round 1 | Round 2 | Round 3 | Round 4 | Round 5 | Round 6 | Round 7 |
|------|---------|---------|---------|---------|---------|---------|---------|
|      |         |         |         |         |         |         |         |
|      |         |         |         |         |         |         |         |
|      |         |         |         |         |         |         |         |
|      |         |         |         |         |         |         |         |
|      |         |         |         |         |         |         |         |

Subsistence Observation Sheet

|  | Round 1 | Round 2 | Round 3 | Round 4 | Round 5 | Round 6 | Round 7 |
|--|---------|---------|---------|---------|---------|---------|---------|
| Number of cards given away |  |  |  |  |  |  |  |
| Number of cards taken away |  |  |  |  |  |  |  |
| Number of people starved |  |  |  |  |  |  |  |
| Cooperative strategy suggested |  |  |  |  |  |  |  |
| Competitive comment |  |  |  |  |  |  |  |
| Other |  |  |  |  |  |  |  |
| Other |  |  |  |  |  |  |  |

### Subsistence Exercise: Hunting and Gathering Cards

You found no food today.

You made a beautiful shot at what looked like a deer, but it turned out to be a strangely shaped rock. You got no food today.

You shot a bird. You get one food card from the recorder.

Wild dogs chased you and to get away you threw them one day's food. Give the recorder one food card. If you do not have a food card, and if no one will give you one, you die of starvation.

You fell asleep and slept all day. You got no food today.

Excellent shot. You killed a deer worth two days' food. You get two food cards from the recorder.

You met a member of another group and fell in love. To impress your new love you gave him or her one day's food. Give the recorder one food card. If you do not have a food card, and no one will give you one, you die of starvation.

You shot a snake. You get a food card from the recorder.

Army ants chased you and to get away you threw them one day's food. Give the recorder one food card. If you do not have a food card, and if no one will give you one, you die of starvation.

You shot a lizard. You get one food card from the recorder.

While running away from a lion, you took refuge in a peach tree. You receive one food card from the recorder.

You shot a deer but missed. You got no food today.

Lucky fluke! You shot at a deer and hit a rabbit. You get one food card from the recorder.

While you were hunting, a skunk broke into your hut and ate two days' worth of food. Give two food cards to the recorder. If you do not have two food cards, and if no one will give you one, you die of starvation.

While you were hunting, a lion ate you and all your food. Give all your food cards to the recorder and drop out of the game. Since you did not starve, your group's points are not affected. You are reborn the next week.

You found a nest of field mice and bopped them on their heads. You get one food card from the recorder.

You found no food today.

You shot a bird. You get one food card from the recorder.

You found a berry bush. Berries are in season. You get one food card from the recorder.

Lucky fluke! You shot at a wild pig and hit a rabbit. You get one food card from the recorder.

Excellent shot. You aimed at a bird you thought was standing on a rock. Your arrow hit the rock, which turned out to be a wild pig. You get two food cards from the recorder.

You found a deer, but a bear scared it away before you could shoot at it. You got no food today.

Excellent shot. Just as you shot at a deer, a wild pig ran in the way and got killed. You receive two food cards from the recorder.

You shot a rabbit. You get one food card from the recorder.

You found no food today. Probably too hot for anything to be out and around.

You found some wild carrots. You get one food card from the recorder.

You found an apple tree. Birds had eaten almost all of them. You get one food card from the recorder.

Excellent shot. You killed a wild pig. You get two food cards from the recorder.

While hunting, you accidentally stepped on a snake and killed it. You receive one food card from the recorder.

On your way home you fell into a swamp. You lost two days' worth of food to a hungry crocodile. Give two food cards to the recorder. If you do not have them, and if no one will give them to you, you die of starvation.

Excellent shot. You killed a deer. You get two food cards from the recorder.

You found some wild lettuce. You get one food card from the recorder.

You shot a rabbit. You get one food card from the recorder.

You shot a bird. You get one food card from the recorder.

You shot an aardvark. You get one food card from the recorder.

While hunting, you found a berry bush. Berries are in season. You get one food card from the recorder.

Best of luck! You found a deer with a broken leg. You killed it with your stone club. You get two food cards from the recorder.

You looked and looked and looked but found no food today.

You shot at a rabbit but it zigged instead of zagged. You got no food today.
You walked for miles and found nothing to gather or shoot at. You got no food today.

# GROUP GOALS AND SOCIAL INTERDEPENDENCE AMONG MEMBERS

> Two are better than one, because they have a good reward for their toil. For if they
> fall, one will lift up his fellow; but woe to him who is alone when he falls and has not
> another to lift him up. . . . And though a man might prevail against one who is alone,
> two will withstand him. A threefold cord is not quickly broken.
>
> *Ecclesiastes 4:9–12*

Examples of social interdependence abound. The scenes are familiar:

1. Six executives sit around a table. "How are we going to dispose of the mine tailings in a way that meets the environmental protection requirements and still makes a profit?" they ask. They begin to discuss three alternative disposal plans, sketching out the responsibilities of each person present in ensuring that the plans are implemented properly. After prolonged consideration, one plan is tentatively adopted and each executive leaves to mobilize their subordinates to put the plan into action.
2. The official shouts, "Ready, set, go!" and the runners explode out of the blocks, race down the track, and lean forward into the tape in an attempt to win over their opponents.
3. A young adult sits alone at the piano. For the eighteenth time he begins a concerto by Chopin. His attention is focused on the music, yet part of his brain is monitoring the quality of his playing. After 2 or 3 minutes he stops. "I am going to do this over and over again until I get it right!" he says to himself.

When individuals take action there are three ways that what they do may be related to the actions of others. One's actions may promote the success of others, obstruct the success of others, or not have any effect at all on the success or failure of others. Whenever people strive to achieve a goal, they may engage in cooperative, competitive, or individualistic efforts. Such social interdependence exists continually.

Social interdependence to humans is like water to fish. Because we are immersed in it, social interdependence can escape our notice. Whether it is quite personal or so impersonal that we are barely aware of it, we regularly underestimate the role that social interdependence plays in human life. Since we cannot imagine its absence, we often do not consider its presence. **Social interdependence** exists when the outcomes of individuals are affected by each other's actions. There are two types of social interdependence: (1) positive or cooperative and (2) negative or competitive (see Figure 3.1). In addition, there is the absence of interdependence or individualistic efforts. In most groups positive interdependence is obvious. In sports, for example, the outcomes of the team are closely tied to the outcomes of each individual player. No matter how well a quarterback throws the football, unless there is a receiver who can catch it and offensive linemen who can block to give the quarterback enough time to throw, a pass will never be completed. As Harold Kelley (1968,

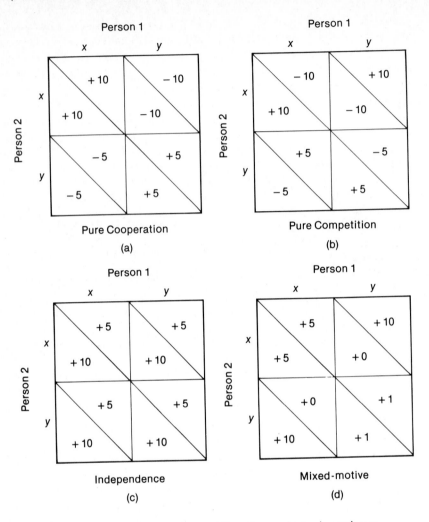

**FIGURE 3.1**  Matrix Representations of Four Types of Interdependence
Assuming that two persons (1 and 2) have only two choices (x and y) in a
group situation, four types of interdependence can be charted in simple
matrices. The numbers in each cell of the matrix represent possible outcomes
that vary in magnitude. In matrix A, for example, if person 1 chooses x while
person 2 chooses y, then both 1 and 2 will experience a −10 outcome. If,
however, both 1 and 2 choose y, then both will experience a +10 outcome.
Each matrix represents a different type of interdependence. Matrix A
represents pure cooperation because 1's actions directed toward achieving a
positive outcome also improve 2's chances of achieving a similarly positive
outcome—both individuals succeed or fail together. Matrix B represents pure
competition, since the success of one individual necessarily requires the
failure of the other. Matrix C represents independence, since the group
members' outcomes are not influenced by the other's choice. Matrix D is a
mixed-motive situation since some aspects of the outcomes encourage
competition and other aspects encourage cooperation.

p. 399) explains, individuals are positively interdependent when the "satisfaction of each person's needs is dependent in some manner upon the actions of other persons."

Social interdependence theory has evolved from Kurt Lewin's (1935) field theory. Lewin (1948) stated that the essence of a group is the interdependence among members which results in the group being a "dynamic whole" so that a change in the state of any member or subgroup changes the state of any other member or subgroup. For interdependence to exist, there must be more than one person or entity involved, and the persons or entities must have impact on each other in that a change in the state of one causes a change in the state of the others. In addition, Lewin stated that individuals are made interdependent through their common goals.

According to Lewin's (1935) theory of intrinsic motivation, a state of tension within an individual motivates movement toward the accomplishment of desired goals. Ouisiankian (1928) demonstrated that interrupted tasks were almost always resumed when the subjects were left free to do as they wished. Lissner (1933), Mahler (1933), and many others investigated the conditions under which one activity can substitute for and, hence, release the tension connected with another, interrupted activity. The substitute value was measured by the amount of decrease in resumption or recall of the interrupted original activity after a substitute activity had been completed. Helen Block Lewis (Lewis, 1944; Lewis & Franklin, 1944) demonstrated that cooperative work that is interrupted and not completed can lead to a persisting force to recall that is not much different from the pressure to recall induced by interrupted individual work. In other words, if a collaborator completes the original activity, his or her actions substitute for one's own, and the tension induced by being interrupted before the task was completed is released. From Lewin's field theory, and the research of these and other students and colleagues of Lewin, it may be concluded that it is the drive for goal accomplishment that motivates cooperative, competitive, and individualistic behavior.

Deutsch (1949a, 1962), in his theory of how the tension systems of different people may be interrelated, conceptualized two types of social interdependence—cooperative and competitive—and individualistic efforts as the absence of interdependence. Deutsch was born in 1920, graduated from City College of New York in 1939, and obtained a masters degree from the University of Pennsylvania in 1940. After serving in the U.S. Air Force from 1942 to 1945 he entered the doctoral program in social psychology at M.I.T. to study with Kurt Lewin. Deutsch has received a variety of professional rewards during his career, including the prestigious Kurt Lewin Memorial Award for contributions to the solution of social problems through theory and research and the Gordon Allport Memorial Award for contributions to constructive intergroup relations through theory and research. Following in Lewin's footsteps, Deutsch has become noted as an outstanding social psychologist because of his commitment to the development of theory about complex social issues, his ability to find ways to study these issues in a laboratory setting, and his dedication to the solution of social problems.

Deutsch's theory was based on two basic continua: one relating to the type of interdependence among the goals of the people involved in a given situation and one relating to the type of actions taken by the people involved. He identified as the ends

**Morton Deutsch**

of one continuum two basic types of goal interdependence: **promotive** (where the goals are positively linked in such a way that the probability of one person obtaining his or her goal is positively correlated with the probability of others obtaining their goals) and **contrient** (where goals are negatively linked in such a way that the probability of one person obtaining his or her goal is negatively correlated with the probability of others obtaining their goals). He identified as the ends of the second continuum two basic types of actions by an individual: **effective** (which improves the person's chances of obtaining his or her goal) and **bungling** (which decreases the person's chances of obtaining his or her goal). He then combined the two continua to posit how they jointly affect three basic social psychological processes: **substitutability, cathexis** (i.e., the investment of psychological energy in objects and events outside of oneself), and **inducibility** (i.e., openness to influence). Within a cooperative situation, ineffective actions by a collaborator do not substitute for one's own actions; rather one will expend extra effort to make up for the ineffective actions of others. In a relay race, for example, if one member of a team runs slowly, the others will try all the harder. Within a competitive situation, ineffective actions by a competitor do substitute for effective actions on your part (having an opponent run slowly substitutes for a person running fast). Within cooperative situations, effective actions are cathected positively, and bungling actions are cathected negatively, while within competitive situations the opposite is posited to be true. Finally, within a cooperative situation, collaborators are easily induced to help a participant but will work to prevent or obstruct a bungling action. In a competitive situation, competitors resist attempts to induce their assistance and work to prevent or obstruct a participant's effective actions, but will be willing to assist a participant's bungling actions. Deutsch (1949a, 1949b) formulated a series of hypotheses from substitutability, cathexis, and inducibility and tested them in his dissertation. Deutsch's (1949a) original theory has served as a major conceptual structure for this area of inquiry for the past 40 years. His theory and his research pioneered future work on social interdependence. Since his initial theorizing, Deutsch has extended his theory of social interdependence to include trust, conflict resolution, and systems of distributive justice. The progression of his theorizing over the past 40 years is one of the seminal works in the history of psychology.

Interaction among individuals may be structured cooperatively, competitively, or individualistically (Deutsch, 1949a, 1962; Johnson & Johnson, 1989a). In other words, there may be positive, negative, or no interdependence among the goals of individuals. **Cooperation** is working together to accomplish shared goals. It is the use of small groups so that individuals work together to maximize their own and each other's productivity and achievement. Thus, an individual seeks an outcome that is beneficial to him- or herself *and* beneficial to all other group members. In cooperative situations, individuals perceive that they can reach their goals if and only if the other group members also do so (Deutsch, 1962). Their goal attainments are positively correlated, and, consequently, individuals discuss their work, help and assist each other, and encourage each other to work hard. When a team of mountain climbers, for example, reaches the summit of a mountain, the success is experienced by all members of the team.

A **competitive goal structure** exits when there is a negative correlation among group members' goal attainments—that is, when group members perceive that they can obtain their goals if and only if the other members with whom they are competitively linked fail to obtain their goal. Individuals work against each other to determine who is best. Individuals are evaluated on how their performance compares with the performance of others and are expected to work faster and more accurately than their peers to achieve outcomes that are personally beneficial but detrimental to others. When one runner wins a race, for example, all the other runners in the race fail to win. An **individualistic goal structure** exists when there is no correlation among group members' goal attainments—that is, when group members perceive that obtaining their goal is unrelated to the goal achievement of other members. Individuals work by themselves to accomplish goals unrelated to the goals of others. Because their goal achievements are unrelated, individuals seek outcomes that are personally beneficial and they ignore as irrelevant the goal achievements of their peers. A person's success in swimming 50 yards, for example, is unrelated to whether others swim 50 yards or not.

## OUTCOMES OF SOCIAL INTERDEPENDENCE

Pull together. In the mountains you must depend on each other for survival.

*Willi Unsoeld*

Within Yosemite National Park lies the famous Half Dome Mountain. The Half Dome is famous for its 2,000 feet of soaring, sheer cliff wall. Unusually beautiful to the observer, and considered unclimbable for years, the Half Dome's northwest face was first scaled in 1957 by Royal Robbins and two companions. This incredibly dangerous climb took five days, with Robbins and his companions spending four nights on the cliff, sleeping in ropes with nothing below their bodies but air. Even today, the northwest face is a death trap to all but the finest and most skilled rock climbers. And far above the ground, moving slowly up the rock face, are two climbers.

The two climbers are motivated by a shared vision of successfully climbing the northwest face. As they move up the cliff they are attached to each other by a rope (the life line). As one member climbs (the lead climber), the other (the belayer) ensures that the two have a safe anchor and that he or she can catch the climber if the climber falls. The lead climber does not begin climbing until the belayer says "go." Then the lead climber advances, puts in a piton, slips in the rope, and continues to advance. The pitons help the belayer catch the climber if the climber falls, and they mark the path up the cliff. The life line (i.e., rope) goes from the belayer through the pitons up to the climber. When the lead climber has completed the first leg of the climb, he or she becomes the belayer and the other member of the team begins to climb. The pitons placed by the lead climber serve to guide and support the second member of the team up the rock face. The second member advances up the route marked out by the first member until the first leg is completed and then leapfrogs and becomes the lead climber for the second leg of the climb. The roles of lead climber and belayer are alternated until the summit is reached.

All human life is like mountain climbing. The human species seems to have a **cooperation imperative:** We desire and seek out opportunities to operate jointly with others to achieve mutual goals. We are attached to others through a variety of "life-lines," and we alternate supporting and leading others to ensure a better life for ourselves, our colleagues and neighbors, our children, and all generations to follow. Cooperation is an inescapable fact of life. From cradle to grave we cooperate with others. Each day, from our first waking moment until sleep overtakes us again, we cooperate within family, work, leisure, and community by working jointly to achieve mutual goals. Throughout history, people have come together to (1) accomplish feats that any one of them could not achieve alone and (2) share their joys and sorrows. From conceiving a child to sending a rocket to the moon, our successes require cooperation among individuals. The cooperation may be less clear than it is in climbing up a cliff, but it exists nonetheless.

Considerable research based on Deutsch's classic work on cooperation and competition has been conducted during the past 30 years. Working together to get the job done can have profound effects. In trying to understand how cooperation works, and in continually refining our understanding of how to implement cooperation most effectively, we have (1) reviewed over 520 experimental and over 100 correlational research studies conducted during the last 90 years comparing cooperative, competitive, and individualistic efforts and (2) conducted a 25-year program of research that has resulted in over 80 published studies. The numerous variables that are affected by cooperation may be subsumed within three broad and interrelated outcomes (see Figure 3.2) (Johnson & Johnson, 1989a):

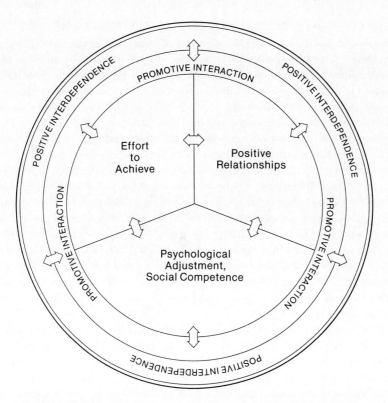

**FIGURE 3.2.** Outcomes of Cooperation   From D. W. Johnson and R. T. Johnson, *Cooperation and Competition: Theory and Research* (Edina, MN: Interaction Book Company, 1989). Used with permission of authors.

1. Effort exerted to achieve
2. Quality of relationships among participants
3. Participants' psychological adjustment and social competence

## Effort to Achieve and Produce

Two heads are better than one.

*John Heywood*

When asked how a small country like Japan with almost no natural resources could become such an economic power, a Japanese businessman replied, "Our people's hard work is our most important resource." Achievement comes from hard, intense, persistent, long-term efforts. Productivity depends on the physical and psychological energy individuals are willing to commit toward achievement. In U.S. schools, for example, many students spend very little time studying, avoid hard subjects such as math and science, and do far less than they are capable of doing. Some students do no schoolwork at all. No matter how intellectually capable or skilled individuals are, if they do not exert considerable effort and seek to achieve challenging goals, their productivity will be low.

*Working together to achieve a common goal produces increased effort, high-er achievement, and greater productivity than does working alone* (Johnson & Johnson, 1989a). Over the past 90 years over 375 studies on the relative impact of cooperative, competitive, and individualistic efforts have been conducted. The over-all effect size is 0.67 when cooperative and competitive efforts are compared, 0.64 when cooperative and individualistic efforts are compared, and 0.30 when competitive and individualistic efforts are compared (see Table 3.1). These effect sizes are weighted for the number of findings within each study and for effect-size variances. When only the methodologically high-quality studies are included, the effect sizes for the cooperative/competitive and the cooperative/individualistic comparisons change to 0.88 and 0.61, respectively. There are numerous dynamics within cooperative groups that result in higher achievement and greater productivity. Positive interde-pendence among group members' goals results in their encouraging and facilitating each others' efforts to produce. Group members seek more information from each other, utilize each other's information, engage in oral rehearsal of the information being exchanged, and influence each other's attitudes and conclusions. Group mem-bers become intrinsically motivated to succeed, have high expectations for success, strive for mutual benefit, have continuing motivation to complete the task, persist, and are committed to success.

While cooperation tends to promote higher achievement and productivity, its superiority over competitive and individualistic learning is most clearly seen in conceptually complex and problem-solving tasks. Cooperation, cognition, and meta-cognition are all intimately related. Cooperative efforts provide the context within which cognition and metacognition best take place. The interpersonal exchange with-

**Table 3.1**  Mean Effect Sizes for Comparison of Cooperative, Competitive, and Individualistic Learning

|  | Coop vs. Comp | Coop vs. Ind | Comp vs. Ind |
|---|---|---|---|
| Achievement |  |  |  |
| Overall | 0.67 | 0.64 | 0.30 |
| High quality | 0.88 | 0.61 | 0.07 |
| Pure | 0.71 | 0.65 | — |
| Mixed | 0.40 | 0.42 | — |
| Interpersonal attraction |  |  |  |
| Overall | 0.66 | 0.60 | 0.08 |
| High quality | 0.82 | 0.62 | 0.27 |
| Pure | 0.79 | 0.66 | — |
| Mixed | 0.46 | 0.36 | — |
| Self-esteem |  |  |  |
| Overall | 0.58 | 0.44 | −0.23 |
| High quality | 0.67 | 0.45 | −0.25 |
| Pure | 0.74 | 0.51 | — |
| Mixed | 0.33 | 0.22 | — |

Note: Coop vs. Comp = cooperative versus competitive; Coop vs. Ind = cooperative versus individualistic; Comp vs. Ind = competitive versus individualistic.

Source: D. W. Johnson and R. T. Johnson, *Cooperation and Competition: Theory and Research* (Edina, MN: Interaction Book Company, 1989).

in cooperative learning groups, and especially the intellectual challenge resulting from conflict among ideas and conclusions (i.e., controversy), promotes critical thinking, higher-level reasoning, and metacognitive thought. The divergent thinking and inspiration that spark creativity result from the oral explanations and elaboration acquired within cooperative groups. Explaining what one knows to his or her groupmates facilitates the understanding of how to apply one's knowledge and skills in one's work and community settings.

A number of the studies conducted operationally defined cooperation in a way that included elements of competition and individualistic work. The original jigsaw studies, for example, operationalized cooperative learning as a combination of positive resource interdependence and an individualistic reward structure (Aronson et al., 1978). Teams-Games-Tournaments (TGT) (DeVries & Edwards, 1974) and Student-Team-Achievement-Divisions (STAD) (Slavin, 1986) operationalized cooperative learning as a combination of ingroup cooperation and intergroup competition, while Team-Assisted-Individualization (TAI) (Slavin, 1986) is a mixture of cooperative and individualistic efforts. When such "mixed" operationalizations were compared with "pure" operationalizations, the effect-sizes for the cooperative versus competitive comparison were 0.45 and 0.74, respectively, $t(37) = 1.60$, $p < 0.06$ (Johnson & Johnson, 1989a). The effect-sizes for the cooperative versus individualistic comparisons were 0.13 and 0.61, respectively, $t(10) = 1.64$, $p < 0.07$.

Since the most credible studies (due to their high-quality methodologically) and the "pure" operationalizations of cooperative learning produced stronger effects, considerable confidence can be placed in the conclusion that cooperative efforts promote more positive cross-ethnic relationships than do competitive or individualistic efforts.

Not all research supporting the use of a cooperative goal structure has been experimental. Balderston (1930) conducted a study of group-incentive plans by collecting written descriptions of such plans from a number of companies. In each instance, the pay of all members depended on the productivity of the group as a whole. Balderston found that this method of work doubled the efficiency of the workers, increased their pay about 25 percent, and reduced their costs substantially compared to the flat rate previously paid to each individual. The users of group-incentive methods stated that their plans were valuable because they increased cooperation and team spirit among members, reduced monotony on the job, and caused workers to focus on a common goal.

## Quality of Relationships: Shelter Against the Cold

> A faithful friend is a strong defense, and he that hath found him, hath found a treasure.
>
> *Ecclesiastics 6:14*

We are created, not for isolation, but for relationships. At heart, we are not a thousand points of separated light but, rather, part of a larger brightness. *Within schools caring and committed relationships are not a luxury. They are a necessity.*

Children who are poorly accepted by their peers, for example, were found to be more likely to drop out of school than children who are better accepted. Recent national surveys indicate that it is feeling valued, loved, wanted, and respected by others that gives life meaning and purpose, and it is intimate relationships that create happiness. This is as true within schools as it is in general.

*Individuals care more about each other and are more committed to each other's success and well-being when they work together to get the job done than when they compete to see who is best or work independently from each other* (Johnson & Johnson, 1989a). Cooperative experiences, compared with competitive and individualistic ones, result in more positive relationships among members, relationships characterized by mutual liking, positive attitudes toward each other, mutual concern, friendliness, attentiveness, feelings of obligation to each other, and a desire to win each other's respect. These results hold even when group members are of different sexes and from different ethnic groups, social classes, and ability levels, especially when individuals are heterogeneous (differing in terms of intellectual ability, handicapping conditions, ethnic membership, social class, and sex), cooperating on a task results in more realistic and positive views of each other than do competing or working individualistically. Over 190 studies have been conducted on the relative impact of cooperative, competitive, and individualistic efforts on relationships among individuals. The weighted effect sizes for cooperation versus competition and cooperation versus individualistic efforts are 0.65 and 0.64, respectively. When only the methodologically high-quality studies are examined, the effect sizes go up to 0.77 and 0.67. "Pure" cooperation results in greater effects than do mixtures of cooperative, competitive, and individualistic efforts (cooperative versus competitive, pure = 0.75 and mixed = 0.48; cooperative versus individualistic, pure = 0.67 and mixed = 0.36).

The more frequently cooperation occurs, the more positive relationships become. Cooperation, compared with competitive and individualistic efforts, promotes greater liking, social support, caring, mutual commitment, and cohesion among group members. *Within cooperative efforts, every person can form friendships.* As relationships become more positive, furthermore, there are corresponding increases in productivity, feelings of personal commitment and responsibility to do the assigned work, willingness to take on and persist in completing difficult tasks, higher morale, and greater commitment to peers' success and growth.

Cooperative experiences, compared with competitive and individualistic ones, also promote more positive attitudes toward supervisors and organization superiors (Johnson & Johnson, 1989a). Superiors are viewed as being more supportive and accepting in cooperative situations. Such positive perceptions by group members of their relationship with superiors are important for many reasons, not the least of which is that the more positive the relationship is between a group member and an organizational superior, the less the superior has to rely on direct power and coercion to motivate group members to comply with organizational norms and role definitions. Members of cooperative groups not only like the group better but also their tasks and the organization that houses the group.

## Psychological Adjustment and Social Competence

> All for one, one for all.
>
> *Alexandre Dumas*

**Psychological health** is the ability to build, maintain, and appropriately modify interdependent relationships with others to succeed in achieving goals. Social competence is an essential aspect of psychological health, and self-esteem is often used as an index of how psychologically adjusted a person is. *Working cooperatively with peers, and valuing cooperation, results in greater psychological health, higher self-esteem, and greater social competence than do competing or working independently* (Johnson & Johnson, 1989a). When children, adolescents, and young adults are graduated from school, they need enough psychological stability to build and maintain career, family, and community relationships; to establish a basic and meaningful interdependence with other people; and to participate effectively within their society and world. States of depression, anxiety, and anger, furthermore, interfere with classroom functioning. The more positively individuals see themselves, the greater their productivity, acceptance and support of others, and autonomy and independence.

Self-esteem is often used as an index of psychological health and adjustment. Over 77 studies have been conducted on the relative impact of cooperative, competitive, and individualistic efforts on self-esteem (Johnson & Johnson, 1989a). The weighted effect sizes for cooperation versus competition and cooperation versus individualistic efforts are 0.60 and 0.44, respectively. When only the methodologically high-quality studies are examined, the effect sizes go up to 0.63 and 0.46. "Pure" cooperation results in greater effects than do mixtures of cooperative, competitive, and individualistic efforts (cooperative versus competitive, pure = 0.78 and mixed = 0.33; cooperative versus individualistic, pure = 0.51 and mixed = 0.22).

An important aspect of psychological health is social competence. *Social skills and competencies tend to increase more within cooperative than in competitive or individualistic situations* (Johnson & Johnson, 1989a). Members of groups dominated by a cooperative rather than a competitive or individualistic goal structure typically view the issues from a number of different perspectives and resolve conflicts more constructively. Members of groups dominated by cooperation are more willing to be influenced by other group members and are better able to influence their fellow members. The influence tends to be based on persuasion and reason rather than coercion. Cooperative experiences also promote greater increases in social skills such as communication, leadership, and decision making. Working together to get the job done increases individuals' abilities to provide leadership, build and maintain trust, communicate effectively, and manage conflicts constructively. Employability and career success depend largely on such social skills. Most modern work occurs within teams. Intelligence and technical expertise are of no use if individuals are not skillful group members. The social skills learned within cooperative groups, furthermore, provide the basis for building and maintaining lifelong friendships, loving and caring families, and cohesive neighborhoods.

## RECIPROCAL RELATIONSHIPS
## AMONG THE THREE OUTCOMES

> The reason we were so good, and continued to be so good, was because he (Joe Paterno) forces you to develop an inner love among the players. It is much harder to give up on your buddy, than it is to give up on your coach. I really believe that over the years the teams I played on were almost unbeatable in tight situations. When we needed to get that six inches we got it because of our love for each other. Our camaraderie existed because of the kind of coach and kind of person Joe was.
>
> *David Joyner*

There are bidirectional relationships among efforts to achieve, quality of relationships, and psychological health (Johnson & Johnson, 1989a). Each influences the others. Since each outcome can induce the others, they are likely to be found together. They are a package with each outcome a door into all three. And together they induce positive interdependence and promotive interaction.

### Joint Efforts to Achieve Promote Positive Relationships

> From the standpoint of everyday life . . . there is one thing we do know; that man is here for the sake of other men—above all, for those upon whose smile and well-being our own happiness depends, and also for the countless unknown souls with whose fate we are connected by a bond of sympathy. Many times a day I realize how much my own outer and inner life is built upon the labors of my fellow men, both living and dead, and how earnestly I must exert myself in order to give in return as much as I have received.
>
> *Albert Einstein*

*Joint efforts to achieve mutual goals tend to create caring and committed relationships.* From working together to get the job done individuals develop camaraderie and friendships. Caring does not come from memos or announcements. It comes from a sense of mutual accomplishment, mutual pride in joint work, and the bonding that results from joint efforts. More specifically, the actions of other individuals that facilitate the achievement of one's goals are liked and accepted. These feelings are then generalized to the individuals engaging in the actions. In addition, the more frequent interaction, the helping and support received, the more accurate understanding of others' perspectives, and the more differentiated and multidimensional view of others resulting from cooperative efforts creates liking among collaborators.

### Positive Relationships Promote Joint Efforts to Achieve

*Long-term, persistent, committed efforts to achieve are powered by caring and committed personal relationships* (not tangible rewards or intellectual rationales). Long-term and persistent efforts to achieve do not come from the head. They come from the heart. Individuals seek out opportunities to work with those they care about. Caring and committed friendships come from a sense of mutual accomplishment, mutual pride in joint work, and the bonding that results from joint efforts. The more individuals care about each other, on the other hand, the harder they will work to achieve mutual learning goals. Long-term and persistent efforts to achieve do not come from the head, they come from the heart (Johnson & Johnson, 1989b). Individuals seek out opportunities to work with those they care about. As caring increases, so do feelings of personal responsibility to do one's share of the work, willingness to take on difficult tasks, motivation and persistence in working toward goal achievement, and willingness to endure pain and frustration on behalf of the group. As relationships among members become stronger, members feel more united in a common effort and the energy they commit increases. Highly cohesive groups, where members like each other, are characterized by more uniform levels of achievement (Seashore, 1954) and greater susceptibility to influence by groupmates (Schachter, Ellertson, McBride, & Gregory, 1951). The most frequently used term to describe a sense of caring for and commitment to other group members is **cohesiveness.** Groups become cohesive by formulating and working together on issues that are specific, immediate, and realizable. As cohesiveness increases, absenteeism and turnover of membership decrease, member commitment to group goals increases, feelings of personal responsibility to the group increase, willingness to take on difficult tasks increases, motivation and persistence in working toward goal achievement increase, satisfaction and morale increase, willingness to endure pain and frustration on behalf of the group increases, willingness to defend the group against external criticism or attack increases, willingness to listen to and be influenced by colleagues increases, commitment to each other's professional growth and success increases, and productivity increases (Johnson & F. Johnson, 1987; Watson & Johnson, 1972). Cohesiveness within a group, team, department, business, classroom, or school is determined by how well members like each other as people and colleagues.

*Within cooperative efforts genuine acts of caring draw people together and forward.* When asked about their success, for example, the chief executives of the companies that have the best track records in North America state that they have been successful because they are able to create teams in which members care about each other on a personal as well as a professional level (Kouzes & Posner, 1987). The successful chief executives create a "family" within which members care deeply about each other and the mutual goals they are striving to achieve.

## Joint Efforts to Achieve Promote Psychological Health

*Working together cooperatively, and the accompanying mutual success, tends to increase participants' psychological health* through enhancing social competencies, achievement and productivity, intrinsic and achievement motivation, constructively coping with failure and anxiety, helping others succeed, feeling in control of one's life, constructive conflict management, and enhanced social skills.

Joint efforts to achieve mutual goals promote psychological health and social competence. The more successful the group, the higher participants' self-esteem, self-efficacy, personal control, and confidence in their competencies. Contributing to others' success, furthermore, can cure the blues.

## Psychological Health Promotes Joint Efforts to Achieve

If you want one year of prosperity, grow grain.
If you want ten years of prosperity, grow trees.
If you want one hundred years of prosperity, grow people.

*Chinese proverb*

*Psychological health tends to increase the productiveness of cooperative efforts and psychological illness tends to inhibit the productiveness of cooperative efforts.* The healthier psychologically individuals are, the better able they are to work with others to achieve mutual goals. People seek out cooperative relationships because they have goals they wish to pursue that require the participation of other people as well as themselves. Joint efforts require coordination, effective communication, leadership, and conflict management. The higher the level of an individual's psychopathology, the less able he or she is to coordinate efforts with others to achieve mutual goals. States of depression, anxiety, guilt, shame, and fear decrease the energy available to contribute to a cooperative effort. Being emotionally immature, socially maladjusted, alienated from oneself, self-rejecting, and prone to distort reality and hallucinating all interfere with working together to get the job done. So does distrusting others, avoiding interaction, expressing anger and frustration inappropriately, violating social rules and customs in resolving interpersonal problems, and being unable to provide leadership or communicate effectively. Thus, the psychological health of participants influences the productivity of a cooperative group.

## Positive Relationships Promote Psychological Health

A real friend is one who walks in when the rest of the world walks out.
*Walter Winchell*

*Caring and committed relationships tend to increase participants' psychological health.* Friendships are developmental advantages that promote self-esteem, self-efficacy, and general psychological adjustment. Psychological health and the ability to cope with adversity and stress are built through the internalization of positive relationships, direct social support, shared intimacy, expressions of caring, viewing situations from a variety of perspectives, intimate conversations in which personal feelings and thoughts are shared, seeking help to find meaning in stressful life events, and giving help to others who need to understand and cope with the stressful events in their life. The absence of caring and committed relationships, or destructive relationships, tend to increase psychological pathology.

## Psychological Health Promotes Positive Relationships

*Psychological health tends to promote the development of caring and committed relationships and psychological pathology tends to inhibit the development of positive interpersonal relationships.* The more psychologically healthy a person is, the better able he or she is to initiate, build, and maintain caring and committed relationships. People seek out caring and committed relationships because they have human needs that can only be satisfied within such relationships. The higher the level of a person's psychological health, the more willing the person is to take the risks required to initiate, build, and maintain caring and committed relationships.

The higher the level of an individual's psychopathology, the less able he or she is to develop and maintain caring and committed relationships. The higher the level of a person's pathology (e.g., depression, anger, anxiety), the less able he or she is to develop and maintain caring and committed relationships. The association between antisocial behavior and rejection by the normal peer group, for example, is well documented (Cantrel & Prinz, 1985; Dodge, Coie, & Bakke, 1982; Roff & Wirt, 1984). Inappropriately aggressive behavior leads to rejection by peers (Coie & Kupersmidt, 1983; Dodge, 1983). Rejected children are also deficient in a number of social-cognitive skills, including peer group entry, perception of peer group norms, response to provocation, and interpretation of prosocial interactions (Asarnow & Calan, 1985; Dodge, 1983; Putallaz, 1983). Among children referred to child guidance clinics, 30 to 75 percent (depending on age) are reported by their parents to experience peer difficulties (Achenbach & Edelbrock, 1981). These difficulties are roughly twice as common among clinic children as among nonreferred youngsters. Moreover, referred children have fewer friends and less contact with them than do nonreferred children, their friendships are significantly less stable over time, and their understanding of the reciprocities and intimacies involved in friendships is less mature (Selman, 1981).

States of depression, anxiety, guilt, repressed anger, shame, hopelessness, meaninglessness, and fear decrease the energy available to contribute to a relationship. Being emotionally immature, socially maladjusted, alienated from oneself, self-rejecting, prone to distort reality, and hallucinating all interfere with relating appropriately to others. So does distrusting others, avoiding interaction, expressing anger and frustration inappropriately, violating social rules and customs in resolving interpersonal problems, and being unable to communicate effectively. Troubled children, furthermore, have difficulties in forming and maintaining friendships. Thus, the psychological health of participants influences the development and maintenance of positive relationships.

## OTHER WAYS TO ACHIEVE COOPERATIVE INTERDEPENDENCE

The fundamental facts that brought about cooperation, society, and civilization and transformed the animal man into a human being are the facts that work performed under the division of labor is more productive than isolated work and that man's reason is capable of recognizing this truth. But for these facts men would have forever remained deadly foes of one another, irreconcilable rivals in their endeavors to secure a portion of the scarce supply of means of sustenance provided by Nature. Each man would have been forced to view all other men as his enemies; his craving for the satisfaction of his own appetites would have brought him into an implacable conflict with all his neighbors. No sympathy could possibly develop under such a state of affairs. . . . We may call consciousness of kind, sense of community, or sense of belonging together the acknowledgment of fact that all other human beings are potential collaborators in the struggle for survival because they are capable of recognizing the mutual benefits of cooperation.

*Ludwig Von Mises (1949)*

Cooperation may be structured among group members in a number of ways other than through the group's goal structure. Through a division of labor, group members can be cooperatively interdependent. The resources or information the group needs to complete the task can be divided among group members, thereby creating cooperative interdependence. The role assignments of group members can be such that a positive interdependence results. Finally, rewards can be distributed in ways that promote positive or negative interdependence among group members. Through task, resource, role, and reward interdependence as well as through goal interdependence, cooperation may be structured within a group. The way in which the distribution of rewards affects the productiveness and morale of groups, however, has been of special interest to social psychologists concerned with cooperation and will be discussed in the next section.

Within group efforts cooperation has to evolve (Axelrod, 1984). The pursuit of self-interest by each group member leads to a poor outcome for all. The problem is that while an individual can benefit from mutual cooperation, each one can also do even better by exploiting the cooperative efforts of others. But when the interactions are repeated, both participants attempt to exploit the other, leading to mutual poor outcomes. Exploiting the cooperative efforts of others may pay off when there is a *known and limited number* of interactions between yourself and the other group members and when you can remain lost in a sea of anonymous others, and, therefore, other individuals cannot retaliate effectively. Cooperation, however, pays off when

1. The number of interactions are not fixed in advance. Cooperation requires that individuals have a sufficiently large chance to meet again so that they have a stake in their future interaction. Cooperation is very difficult to establish in one-time encounters. An important way to promote cooperation is to arrange that the same two people meet each other again, be able to recognize each other from the past, and recall how the other has behaved until now. This continuing interaction is what makes it possible for cooperation based on reciprocity to be stable. In other words, make the future more important relative to the present. *Enlarge the shadow of the future.* There are two ways of doing this. The first is by making the interactions more durable: pro-

longed interaction allows patterns of cooperation that are based on reciprocity to be worth trying and allows them to become established. The second is by making the interactions more frequent: the more frequent the interactions, the more important future cooperation is. One way to increase the frequency of interactions is to keep others away. By breaking cooperation into small pieces, the potential gain from competition in any one interaction is small compared to the future gains from continued cooperation.

2. You and the other group members are easily identifiable to each other. That is, because of continuing contact and other factors such as a fixed meeting place, each group member must realize that retaliation is possible. When interaction among group members is durable and frequent, cooperation is the only behavior that makes sense. Improve recognition abilities. The ability to recognize the other people from past interactions, and to remember the relevant features of those interactions, is necessary to sustain cooperation. Exploitative behavior must be recognized when it occurs. The scope of sustainable cooperation can be expanded by any improvements in the individuals' ability to recognize each other from the past and to be confident about the prior actions that have actually been taken.

3. Group members emotionally identify with the other and with the group so that they value each other's well-being and want to promote each other's long-term welfare and the long-term success of the group. Group members need to care about each other and about the group. An excellent way to promote cooperation is to teach people to care about the welfare of others. The greater the altruistic motives of the individuals involved, the more stable the cooperation.

4. Group members understand the value of reciprocity and are able and willing to reciprocate both cooperation and competition. One of the basic principles of cooperation is reciprocation. Practice reciprocity. Follow a tit-for-tat strategy so that both cooperation and competition are reciprocated.

5. The temptation to exploit the cooperative efforts of group members is reduced by
   a. Changing the payoffs so that competition is too costly to be considered. The short-term incentive for cooperation should ideally be greater than the short-term incentive for competition.
   b. Not being envious. You should be more concerned as to how you are doing relative to individualistic and competitive alternatives than whether another group member is benefiting more than you from the collaboration.
   c. Not being the first to exploit another member's cooperative efforts. It pays to cooperate as long as the other group members are doing so. You will avoid much unnecessary conflict by keeping a clear cooperative orientation.

# GOAL STRUCTURES AND THE ALLOCATION OF REWARDS AMONG GROUP MEMBERS

Aesop tells a story of a man who had four sons. The father loved them very much, but they troubled him greatly, for they were always fighting with each other. Nothing the father said stopped their quarreling. "What can I do to show my sons how wrong it is to act this way?" the father thought. One day he called his sons to him and showed them a bundle of sticks. "Which of you, my sons, can break this bundle of sticks?" he asked them. All the boys tried in turn, but not one of them could do it. Then the father untied the bundle and gave each son a single stick. "See if you can break that," he said. Of course, they could easily do it. "My sons," the father said, "each of you alone is weak. He is as easy to injure as one of these sticks. But if you will be friends and stick together, you will be as strong as the bundle of sticks."

Individuals join groups because in the long run they are better off being part of the group than not. The better the group functions, the better off the individual members are; the better off the individual members are, the more they can contribute to the group's efforts, and therefore the better the group functions. Part of the process whereby effective cooperation among members is promoted in order to ensure their individual well-being is the distribution of rewards. The way in which rewards are distributed among group members can have a marked effect on how members behave toward one another in the future and how effective the group is (Deutsch, 1975, 1979). Depending on the circumstances, rewards may be distributed according to merit, equality, or need.

The **equity or merit view of distributing rewards** has been presented by Homans (1961) as a basic rule of distributive justice and equity theory—in a just distribution, rewards will be distributed among individuals in proportion to their contributions. In other words, those members who contribute the most to the group's success should receive the greatest benefits. It is commonly assumed that when rewards (for example, bonuses, salaries, advancement, grades) are contingent on performance, productivity will increase. Individual incentive plans, however, sometimes run into problems as individuals restrict output out of fear of being rejected by colleagues, intrinsic motivation is replaced with extrinsic motivation, and the negative consequences of competition may surface within the group. There are a number of other problems with the merit approach to distributing rewards within a group. One is that the economic values upon which equity theory is based can have unfortunate effects on group members' views of themselves and each other as well as on the relationships among members. From a utilitarian, economic point of view, group members are of value only to the extent that they contribute to the group's success. Such a view results in a depersonalization of both self and others and the attitude that different members have different value. Depersonalization and differential value undermine respect for self and other group members. Members may view their self-worth as being related to the rewards they receive, which in turn are related to the contributions they make to group goal accomplishment. Other members are viewed in the same way. Thus, if a member contributes little to group success and receives disproportionately small rewards, he or she is viewed as having little personal worth. Diesing (1962) describes such a situation as being alienated from oneself and others.

From the equity point of view, rewards have value only because they are a scarce commodity that one competes with others to obtain. Any intrinsic value is ignored. The utilitarian value of a reward increases with the number of persons who want the reward; the reward becomes a scarce commodity when its supply is far less than the demand for it. The symbolic meaning of the reward may become far more important than the intrinsic value of the reward. Children fight over being first in line, not because of the intrinsic value of the position, but rather because it symbolizes that they are winners, superior to those who are positioned behind them. Diesing (1962) describes such a situation as being alienated from one's possessions and creations. Thus, the competition among group members that is fostered by rewards being proportionate to members' contributions may seriously reduce the cohesiveness of the group, cause morale problems, and undermine group effectiveness as trust and communication among members deteriorate.

Group members who are successful under a merit system of distributive justice often misattribute their success to their efforts rather than to their talents. Certain group members will have more resource attractors than others. A **resource attractor** is an attribute that tends to attract other resources because it gives the possessor an advantage in a competition for these other resources. Examples of resource attractors are ability, training, previous experience, drive, and character. Group members with a high number of resource attractors often get higher rewards than do members with few resource attractors and may attribute their success to their worthiness and effort (implying that those who have fewer resource attractors are less worthy and more lazy).

Finally, a merit system often results in a situation in which the group members who are rewarded the most are given the power to distribute future rewards on the basis of their assessment of how much each member is contributing to the group effort. Deutsch (1975, 1979) notes that this allows those who are in power to bias the system of allocation to perpetuate their disproportionate rewards and power even when they are no longer making relatively large contributions to the group's well-being.

An **equality system of distributive justice** rewards all group members equally. If a football team wins the Super Bowl, all members receive a Super Bowl ring. If a learning group completes an assignment at an A level, all members of the group receive an A. To prevent the problems of the merit system, group incentive systems may be used. In most stores, for example, salesclerks are on individual commission systems. What happens when they are switched to a group commission system? Babchuk and Goode (1951) decided to find out. Sales were good with the individual incentive program, but the clerks avoided maintenance duties, competed with one another for customers, and suffered low morale. Under the group plan a sense of teamwork developed and the sales clerks reported greater feelings of satisfaction. Blau (1954) compared two groups of interviewers in an employment agency. In one, there was fierce competition to fill job openings. In the other, the interviewers worked cooperatively. Members of the competitive group, who were personally ambitious and extremely concerned about productivity, hoarded job notifications rather than posting them so everyone could see them, as they were supposed to do. This practice eventually was used defensively and so became self-perpetuating. Members of the cooperative group, by contrast, told each other about vacancies and encouraged each other to fill them. The cooperators ended up filling significantly more jobs. Deutsch (1975, 1979) notes that consequences of an equality system of distributive justice are mutual esteem, equal status, and mutual respect among members. He states that the principle of equality is more congenial to the fostering of enjoyable, personal relationships, group loyalty, and cooperativeness.

The **distribution of rewards according to need** results in a situation in which the group members who are most in need of the rewards receive a disproportionate amount of them. The member who has the largest family may receive the highest monetary bonus, the member who is grieving for the death of her parents may be asked to do the least work, or the member who has the least ability will be given the most support and assistance for completing his or her assigned tasks. A student who has never received an A might be given the highest grade in the group. Rawls (1971) pointed out that one of the natural duties of members of a group is to help another member who is in need or in jeopardy, providing one can do so without excessive loss or risk to oneself. The gain to the member who needs help is seen as far outweighing the loss or risk to oneself. The gain to the member who needs help is seen as far outweighing the loss of that required to assist that person. Such a system of distributive justice emphasizes the confidence and trust members may have in their colleagues' good intentions. Deutsch (1975, 1979) notes that a caring-oriented group will stress responsibility for each other, permissiveness toward members expressing their needs, heightened sensitivity to each other's needs, and support and nurturance of each other's legitimate needs.

Whatever system of distributing rewards a group uses, it has to be perceived as "just" by group members. When rewards are distributed unjustly, the group may be characterized by low morale and high conflict among its members, which in turn may decrease productivity. The evidence indicates that before a task is performed, there is a general perception that an equity or competitive reward system is fairest, but after a task is completed, an equality of cooperative reward system in which all group members receive the same reward is viewed as the fairest (Deutsch, 1979, 1985; Johnson & Johnson, 1983; Johnson, Johnson, Buckman, & Richards, 1986; Wheeler & Ryan, 1973).

## SOCIAL INTERDEPENDENCE AND THE REAL WORLD

In real life all three types of interdependence exist simultaneously and continuously. All individuals within a modern industrial/information–based society need to be able to work cooperatively with peers, superiors, and subordinates; compete for fun and enjoyment; and work autonomously on his or her own. In most situations, group members will usually have a mixture of cooperative, competitive, and individualistic motives. They may be committed to group goals and work to maximize joint outcomes while at the same time seeking to outperform a peer and to meet personal needs unrelated to the concerns of other members. Frank Pierce, for example, as a division chief for Skidmore Corporation, has cooperative interests in ensuring a high level of productivity for his division, competitive interests in being seen as the most productive division head within the company, and individualistic interests in keeping blocks of time free to write a book on successful management. Within a basketball team a player may be focused on the cooperative goal of ensuring the team wins, a competitive goal of being the best player on the team, and an individualistic goal of perfecting a jump shot. Mixtures of the three types of social interdependence are continually present in any situation. Which one dominates the situation, however, has important implications for individual, group, and organization productivity, morale, and well-being.

The effectiveness of a group can be easily damaged when an individual dominated by competitiveness joins the group. Kelley and Stahelski (1970) found that several things happen in such a situation. First, the cooperative members begin behaving in competitive ways, violating trust, hiding information, and cutting off communication. Second, the competitive person sees the formerly cooperative members as having always been competitive. Third, the cooperative members are aware that their behavior is being determined by the other's competitive behavior, but the competitive person is not aware of his or her impact on cooperative members. Cooperativeness needs to dominate group life. Effective patterns of interaction among members are usually far easier to destroy than to build.

## SUMMARY

Groups exist for a reason. People join groups to achieve goals they are unable to achieve by themselves. The personal goals of individual group members are linked together by positive interdependence. Group goals result. Group goals direct, channel, motivate, coordinate, energize, and guide the behavior of group members. To be useful, however, group goals have to be clear and operational. The group level of aspiration is continually being revised on the basis of success and failure.

The basis for the group goals is the positive interdependence among group members. Social interdependence theory originated from Kurt Lewin's field theory and was formalized by Morton Deutsch. In the past 90 years over 600 studies have been conducted. The numerous variables that are affected by cooperation may be subsumed within three broad and interrelated outcomes: effort to achieve, quality of relationships among participants, and psychological health and social competence. Within cooperative groups, as opposed to competitive and individualistic efforts, achievement is higher, committed and caring relationships form, and the self-esteem and social competence required to cope with stress and adversity are increased. Each of these outcomes affects the others. The more group members work together to get the job done, the more members care about each other. The more members care about each other, the harder they work to get the job done. The more group members work together to get the job done, the greater their social competencies and psychological health become. The healthier they are psychologically, the harder they will work to get the job done. The more caring and supportive the relationships, the greater the psychological health and the greater the psychological health the more caring and support individuals can give to each other. When individuals join into a cooperative effort, the whole Gestalt results. Finally, while group members will have cooperative, competitive, and individualistic goals, the cooperative goals must dominate. The cooperative effort to achieve group goals requires frequent, clear, and accurate communication. Group members must be able to communicate and listen clearly and effectively. You will learn how to do this in the next chapter.

# 4

# Communication Within Groups

## BASIC CONCEPTS TO BE COVERED IN THIS CHAPTER

In this chapter a number of concepts are defined and discussed. The major ones are listed below. The procedure for learning these concepts is as follows:

1. The class forms heterogeneous groups of four.
2. Each group divides into two pairs.
3. The task for each pair is to
   a. Define each concept, noting the page on which it is defined and discussed.
   b. Make sure that both members of the pair understand the meaning of each concept.
4. In each group, members compare the answers of the two pairs. If there is disagreement, the members look up the concept in the chapter and clarify it until they all agree on the definition and understand it.

### CONCEPTS

1. Interpersonal communication
2. Effective communication
3. Sender
4. Receiver
5. Message
6. Channel
7. Defensive behavior
8. One-way communication
9. Two-way communication
10. Communication network
11. Information gatekeepers
12. Leveling
13. Sharpening
14. Assimilation

## INTRODUCTION AND DEFINITIONS

Communication is the basis for all human interaction and for all group functioning. Every group must take in and use information. The very existence of a group depends on communication, on exchanging information and transmitting meaning. All cooperative action is contingent upon effective communication, and our daily lives are filled with one communication experience after another. Through communication members of groups reach some understanding of one another, build trust, coordinate their actions, plan strategies for a goal accomplishment, agree upon a division of labor, conduct all group activity—even exchange insults. It is through communication that the members interact, and effective communication is a prerequisite for every aspect of group functioning.

One primary difficulty in discussing communication within groups is that there are so many definitions of communication and so little agreement about which definition is the most useful. Dance (1970), for example, did a content analysis of 95 definitions of communication that he found published in several different academic fields. Among these definitions were several distinct concepts of communication. He noted that this variety of definitions has taken different theorists and researchers in different and sometimes contradictory directions. Dance concluded that the concept of communication is overburdened and that a family of concepts needs to be developed to replace it. Despite the difficulties in defining communication, however, there are ways in which to view the process of transmitting information that are helpful in discussing interpersonal and group communication skills.

Two persons seeing each other have a continuous effect on each other's perceptions and expectations of what the other is going to do. Interpersonal communication, then, can be defined broadly as any verbal or nonverbal behavior that is perceived by another person (Johnson, 1973, 1990). Communication, in other words, is much more than just the exchange of words: All behavior conveys some message and is, therefore, a form of communication. **Interpersonal communication,** however, is more commonly defined as a message sent by a person to a receiver (or receivers) with the conscious intent of affecting the receiver's behavior. A person sends the message "How are you?" to evoke the response "Fine." A teacher shakes his head to get two students to stop throwing erasers at him. Under this more limited definition, any signal aimed at influencing the receiver's behavior in any way is communication.

This definition of communication does not mean that there is always a sequence of events in which a person thinks up a message, sends it, and someone else receives it. Communication among persons is a process in which everyone receives, sends, interprets, and infers all at the same time: There is no beginning and no end; all communication involves persons sending one another symbols to which certain meanings are attached. These symbols can be either verbal (all words are symbols) or nonverbal (all expressions and gestures are symbols). The exchange of ideas and experiences between two persons is possible only when both have adopted the same ways of relating a particular nonverbal, spoken, written, or pictorial symbol to a particular experience.

How do you tell when communication is working effectively and when it is not? What is effective communication? What is ineffective communication? **Effective communication** exists between two persons when the receiver interprets the sender's message in the same way the sender intended it. If John tries to communicate to Jane that it is a wonderful day and he is feeling great by saying "Hi" with a warm smile, and if Jane interprets John's "Hi" as meaning John thinks it is a beautiful day and he is feeling well, then effective communication has taken place. If Jane interprets John's "Hi" as meaning he wants to stop and talk with her, then ineffective communication has taken place.

The model of communication presented by Johnson (1986) is typical of the applied approaches to interpersonal communication. In this model (Figure 4.1) the communicator is referred to as the **sender** and the person at whom the message is aimed is the **receiver.** The **message** is any verbal or nonverbal symbol that one person transmits to another; it is subject matter being referred to in a symbolic way (all words are symbols). A **channel** can be defined as the means of sending a message to another person: the sound waves of the voice, the light waves that make possible the seeing of words on a printed page. Because communication is a process, sending and receiving messages often take place simultaneously: A person can be speaking and at the same time paying close attention to the receiver's nonverbal responses.

Figure 4.1 represents a model of the process of communication between two persons. The model has seven basic elements:

1. The intentions, ideas, and feelings of the sender and the way he or she decides to behave lead him to send a message.
2. The sender encodes a message by translating his or her ideas, feelings, and intentions into a message appropriate for sending.
3. The sender sends the message to the receiver.
4. The message is sent through a channel.
5. The receiver decodes the message by interpreting its meaning. The receiver's interpretation depends on how well he or she understands the content of the message and the intentions of the sender.
6. The receiver responds internally to this interpretation of the message.
7. Noise is any element that interferes with the communication process. In the sender, noise refers to such things as his or her attitudes and frame of reference and the appropriateness of his or her language or other expression of the message. In the receiver, noise refers to such things as attitudes, background, and experiences that affect the decoding process. In the channel, noise refers to (a) environmental sounds, such as static or traffic, (b) speech problems, such as stammering, and (c) annoying or distracting mannerisms, such as a tendency to mumble. To a large extent, the success of communication is determined by the degree to which noise is overcome or controlled.

## EXERCISE 4.1:
## YOUR COMMUNICATION BEHAVIOR (I)

What is your communication behavior like in a group? How would you describe your communication actions? Begin a discussion of communication within groups by answering the following questions as honestly as possible:

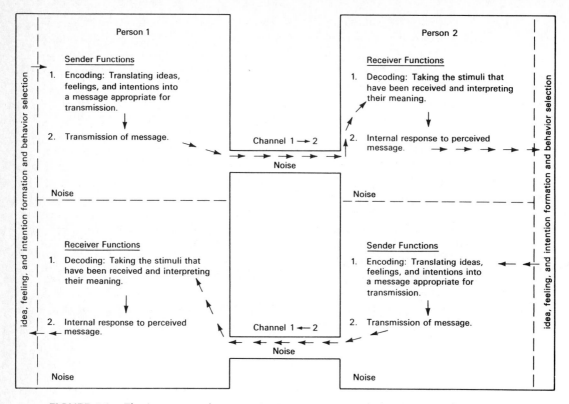

**FIGURE 4.1.**   The interpersonal communication process   From David W. Johnson, *Reaching Out,* 4th ed. (Englewood Cliffs, NJ: Prentice Hall, 1990), p. 107.

1. If I as group chairperson were giving a set of instructions and the other group members sat quietly with blank faces, I would

   _____   state the instructions clearly and precisely and then move on.

   _____   encourage members to ask questions until I was sure that everyone understood what they were supposed to do.

2. If the group chairperson gave a set of instructions to the group that I did not understand, I would

_____    keep silent and later ask another group member what he or she meant.

_____    immediately ask the chairperson to repeat the instructions and answer my questions until I was sure I understood what he or she wanted me to do.

3. How often do you let other group members know when you like or approve of something they say or do?
   Never  1 : 2 : 3 : 4 : 5 : 6 : 7 : 8 : 9   Always

4. How often do you let other group members know when you are irritated or impatient with, embarrassed by, or opposed to something they say or do?
   Never  1 : 2 : 3 : 4 : 5 : 6 : 7 : 8 : 9   Always

5. How often do you check out what other group members are feeling and how they are reacting rather than assuming that you know?
   Never  1 : 2 : 3 : 4 : 5 : 6 : 7 : 8 : 9   Always

6. How often do you encourage other group members to let you know how they are reacting to your behavior and actions in the group?
   Never  1 : 2 : 3 : 4 : 5 : 6 : 7 : 8 : 9   Always

7. How often do you check to make sure you understand what other group members mean before agreeing or disagreeing?
   Never  1 : 2 : 3 : 4 : 5 : 6 : 7 : 8 : 9   Always

8. How often do you paraphrase or restate what other members have said before responding?
   Never  1 : 2 : 3 : 4 : 5 : 6 : 7 : 8 : 9   Always

9. How often do you keep your thoughts, ideas, feelings, and reactions to yourself in group sessions?
   Never  1 : 2 : 3 : 4 : 5 : 6 : 7 : 8 : 9   Always

10. How often do you make sure that all information you have about the current topic of discussion is known to the rest of the group?
    Never  1 : 2 : 3 : 4 : 5 : 6 : 7 : 8 : 9   Always

These questions deal with several aspects of communication in groups that will be discussed in this chapter. The first two questions refer to whether communication is one-way (from the chairperson to the rest of the group members) or two-way. The third and fourth questions focus on your willingness to give feedback to other group members on how you are receiving and reacting to their messages. Questions 5 and 6 refer to your willingness to ask for feedback about how other group members are receiving and reacting to your messages. Questions 7 and 8 focus on receiving skills, and the final two questions relate to your willingness to contribute (send) relevant messages about the group's work. Review your answers to these questions and summarize your present communication behavior in a group.

## EFFECTIVE INTERPERSONAL COMMUNICATION

All communication within groups is between individuals and is, therefore, interpersonal communication. There are many discussions of the skills needed for effective interpersonal communication. One of the authors, for example, has published a training program for interpersonal skill development that includes communication skills (Johnson, 1986). The focus in this chapter is on the unique aspects of communication among members of a problem-solving group, including the communication of task-relevant information among group members and the passage of messages through several authority levels. An example of the latter would be the passage of a chairperson's message to a vice-chairperson, who sends it to a committee chairperson, who sends it to the rest of the group.

## Sending Messages Effectively

The first aspect of effective communication is the sending of a message. The three basic requirements for sending a message so that it will be understood are to phrase the message so it may be comprehended, have credibility as a sender, and ask for feedback on how the message is affecting the receiver. Research supports the following conclusions about the sending of messages (Johnson, 1974):

1. *Clearly "own" your messages by using first-person singular pronouns ("I," "my").* Personal ownership includes clearly taking responsibility for the ideas and feelings that one expresses. People disown their messages when they use phrases such as "most people," "some of our friends," and "our group." Such language makes it difficult for listeners to tell whether the individuals really think and feel what they are saying or whether they are repeating the thoughts and feelings of others.
2. *Make your messages complete and specific.* Include clear statements of all necessary information the receiver needs to comprehend the message. Being complete and specific seems too obvious, but often people do not communicate the frame of reference they are using, the assumptions they are making, the intentions they have in communicating, or the leaps in thinking they are making.
3. *Make your verbal and nonverbal messages congruent.* Every face-to-face communication involves both verbal and nonverbal messages. Usually these messages are congruent: The person who is saying that he appreciates your help is smiling and expressing warmth in other nonverbal ways. Communication problems arise when a person's verbal and nonverbal messages are contradictory. If a person says, "Here is some information that may be of help to you" with a sneer on his face and a mocking tone of voice, the meaning you receive is confused by the two different messages being sent.
4. *Be redundant.* Sending the same message more than once and using more than one channel of communication (such as pictures and written messages as well as verbal and nonverbal cues) will help the receiver understand your messages.
5. *Ask for feedback concerning the way your messages are being received.* To communicate effectively you must be aware of how the receiver is interpreting and processing your messages. The only way to be sure is to continually seek feedback as to what meanings the receiver is attaching to your messages.
6. *Make the message appropriate to the receiver's frame of reference.* Explain the same information differently to an expert in the field and a novice, to a child and an adult, to your boss and coworker.
7. *Describe your feelings by name, action, or figure of speech.* When communicating your feelings it is especially important to be descriptive. You may describe your feelings by name ("I feel sad"), by actions ("I feel like crying"), or by figures of speech ("I feel down in the dumps"). Description will help communicate your feelings clearly and unambiguously.
8. *Describe others' behavior without evaluating or interpreting.* When reacting to the behavior of others be sure to describe their behavior ("You keep interrupting me") rather than evaluating it ("You're a rotten, self-centered egotist who won't listen to anyone else's ideas").

One of the most important elements in interpersonal communication is the credibility of the sender. **Sender credibility** refers to the attitude the receiver has toward the perceived trustworthiness of the sender's statements. Sender credibility has several dimensions:

1. The reliability of the sender as an information source—the sender's dependability, predictability, and consistency.
2. The sender's motives. The sender should be open as to the effect she wants her message to have upon the receiver.
3. The expression of warmth and friendliness.
4. The majority opinion of others concerning the trustworthiness of the sender. If most of our friends tell us the sender is trustworthy, we tend to believe it.
5. The sender's expertise on the topic under discussion.
6. The dynamism of the sender. A dynamic sender is seen as aggressive, emphatic, and forceful and tends to be viewed as more credible than a passive sender.

There is little evidence from the studies on sender credibility to suggest which of these dimensions is the most important. It seems that a highly credible sender is one who is perceived in a favorable light in *all* of these dimensions. A sender low in credibility, on the other hand, is one who is perceived in a negative light in *any one* of the dimensions. Unless we appear credible to a receiver, he or she will discount our message and we will not be able to communicate effectively with that person. Sender credibility, in short, might be defined as the perceived trustworthiness of the sender.

Effective message-sending skills are prerequisite to the skills covered in this chapter. Sending skills are examined in detail in Johnson (1986), which discusses the basic theory behind sending effective verbal and nonverbal messages and includes specific exercises for developing these skills. You should learn and review these skills before (or in combination with) the skills presented in this chapter.

## Receiving Messages Effectively

Developing sending skills meets only half the requirements for communicating effectively; you must also have receiving skills. The skills involved in receiving messages are based on giving feedback about the reception and the message in ways that clarify and aid continued discussion. Receiving skills have two basic parts: (1) communicating the *intention* of wanting to understand the ideas and feelings of the sender and (2) understanding and interpreting the sender's ideas and feelings. Of the two, many theorists consider the first—communicating the intention to understand correctly, but not evaluate, a message—to be the more important. The principal barrier to building effective communication is the tendency of most persons to judge or evaluate the message they are receiving: the sender makes a statement and the receiver responds inwardly or openly with "I think you're wrong," "I don't like what you said," "I think you're right," or "That is the greatest (or worst) idea I have ever heard!" Such evaluative receiving will make the sender defensive and cautious, and thereby decrease the openness of the communication. Though the tendency to give evaluative responses is common in almost all conversations, it is accentuated in situations where emotions are deeply involved. The stronger the feelings, the more likely two group members will evaluate each other's statements from their own point of view only. Thus it is highly important for the receiver to indicate that he or she wants to understand the sender fully before making an evaluation.

The specific receiving skills are paraphrasing, checking one's perception of the sender's feelings, and negotiating for meaning. Let's look at each of these skills in turn.

1. *Paraphrase accurately and nonevaluatively the content of the message and the feelings of the sender.* The most basic and important skill in receiving messages is paraphrasing—restating the words of the sender. Paraphrasing should be done in a way that indicates an understanding of the sender's frame of reference. The basic rule to follow in paraphrasing is this: *Speak for yourself only after you have first restated the ideas and feelings of the sender accurately and to the sender's satisfaction.* When paraphrasing, it is helpful to restate the sender's expressed ideas and feelings in your own words rather than repeating her words exactly, avoid any indication of approval or disapproval, neither add nor subtract from her message, and try to place yourself in her shoes to understand what she is feeling and what her message means.

2. *Describe what you perceive to be the sender's feelings.* Sometimes it is difficult to paraphrase the feelings of the sender if they are not described in words in the message. Thus a second receiving skill is to check your perception of the sender's feelings simply by describing that perception. This description should tentatively identify those feelings without expressing approval or disapproval and without attempting to interpret them or explain their causes. It is simply saying, "Here is what I understand your feelings to be; am I accurate?"

3. *State your interpretation of the sender's message and negotiate with the sender until there is agreement as to the message's meaning.* Often the words contained in a message do not carry the actual meaning. A person may ask, "Do you always shout like this?" and mean "Please quiet down." Sometimes, therefore, paraphrasing the content of a message will do little to communicate your understanding of it. In such a case, you must negotiate the meaning of the message. You may wish to preface your negotiation for meaning with "What I think you mean is. . . ." If you are accurate, you then make your reply; if you are inaccurate, the sender restates the message until you can state what its essential meaning is. Keep in mind that it is the process that is important in negotiating meaning, not the actual phrasing you use. After the process becomes natural a variety of introductory phrases will be used. Be tolerant of others who are using the same phrases over and over as they are developing their skill.

A complete treatment of these basic receiving skills, so important to effective communication, can be found in Johnson (1990), which also contains exercises for developing verbal and nonverbal competence in them. These skills should also be learned and reviewed as a prerequisite for the skills discussed in this chapter.

One of the major influences upon the reception of a message is the usefulness of its content in accomplishing the receiver's goals and tasks. All messages may be evaluated in terms of whether they help or hinder the receiver's task performance within the group, and messages that are seen as helping goal and task accomplishment are comprehended most accurately and easily. Of course, it is quite common for group members to misunderstand the usefulness of certain messages. Opposition and disagreement, for example, are often seen as short-term obstructions instead of the long-term aids they might be by generating new and better ways of accomplishing tasks and goals.

## EXERCISE 4.2:
## BEWISE COLLEGE

The purpose of this exercise is to examine the communication patterns within a task-oriented group. Our objectives are to see how task-relevant information is shared within a work group and to explore the effects of collaboration and competition in group problem solving. The materials to be used in the exercise are a briefing sheet, a series of data sheets, a candidate summary sheet, and an observer frequency chart. The exercise takes about two hours. Participants are organized into groups of five role players and two observers. An unlimited number of groups may be directed at the same time. The procedure for the coordinator is as follows:

1. Introduce the exercise as focusing upon communication within a problem-solving situation. Set the stage for the role playing by reviewing the briefing sheet in a realistic manner.
2. Divide the class into groups of seven—five participants plus two observers. Instruct the groups to choose the correct president based upon the data they will receive. Suggest that there is one correct solution to their problem and caution them that they must reach their solution independent of the other groups. Then distribute a briefing sheet, a candidate summary sheet, and one data sheet to each participant. Ensure that the five differently coded data sheets are distributed to different members in each group. Each sheet is coded by the number of dots, ranging from one to five, following the second sentence in the first paragraph. Part of each sheet contains data unique to that sheet. Tell the participants not to let other group members read their sheets.
3. While the five role players are studying their sheets, meet with the observers. Dis-

tribute copies of the frequency chart and brief observers on how they are used. A copy of the chart appears below. All observers will need several copies of the chart, so time should be given for them to make their extra copies.

4. Give the signal to begin the group meeting. You may introduce an element of competition by posting groups' solutions in order of completion and by posting the number of minutes used by each group in solving the problem.

5. After all the groups have submitted their solution to the problem, review the answers and compare them with the correct answer, which appears on page 491 in the appendix. Then ask the group to discuss their experience, using the observations of the observers. Here are some relevant questions for discussion:

   a. What were the patterns of communication within the group? Who spoke to whom? Who talked, how often did they talk, and for how long? Who triggered whom in what ways? How did members feel about the amount of their participation? What could have been done to gain wider participation?

   b. Was the needed information easily obtained by all the group members? Did group members share their information appropriately, request each other's information, and create the conditions under which the information could be shared?

   c. Were the resources of all group members used? Was everyone listened to?

   d. How cooperative or competitive were the group members?

   e. How did the group make decisions?

   f. What problems did the group have in working together?

   g. What conclusions about communication can be made from the group's experience?

6. Have all the groups share their conclusions with one another. Review the observation sheets and discuss the nature of communication within goal-oriented groups.

**Observer Frequency Chart: Patterns of Communication**

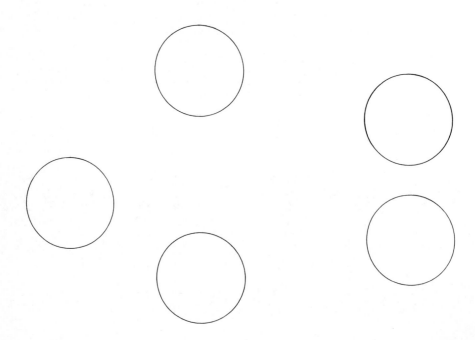

Interval _____ (Use one sheet for each 5-minute interval.) Label the circles with the names of the group members. Indicate a message from a sender to a receiver with an arrow; when someone sends a message to the entire group, indicate this with an arrow to the center. Indicate frequency of message sending with tally marks ( ‖‖ ‖ ). Place an "x" in the member's circle every time he or she interrupts or overrides another group member; place a check "√" in the member's circle every time he or she encourages another member to partici- pate. Here is an example:

### Bewise College Briefing Sheet

1. This is the first meeting of your group.
2. Basically, the data you bring with you are in your head.
3. Assume there is one solution.
4. Assume that all information in your data sheet is correct.
5. There must be substantial agreement within the group when the problem has been solved.
6. You must work on the problem as a group.

### Bewise College Data Sheet

Your group is a committee consisting of college board members, administrators, faculty, and students of Bewise College. Your group has been authorized by the Board of Regents to select a new president of the college from the list of candidates.

Each of the represented groups (Board of Regents, administrators, faculty, students) has its own list of requirements for the new president. Insofar as possible, your group is pledged to select a candidate who meets these requirements.

Bewise College was established in 1969. It is located in the heart of an industrial city with a population of about 100,000. In addition to a standard liberal arts curriculum, Bewise College offers a curriculum in which students can receive college credit for work and learning experiences outside the college. There is only one other college in the same city; it is the smallest college in the state, and until 1954 all students attending it were black Americans.

The new president faces a series of challenges. The Board of Regents wants a presi- dent who can raise money for the college, as the college is now in a desperate financial position. The college administration is very much afraid of a president who will not be a competent administrator. Students are dissatisfied with faculty teaching, and faculty members are dissatisfied with student unresponsiveness to their teaching. Both students and faculty see the necessity of having a president who comes from a background that would provide insights into the type of student attending Bewise.

### Bewise College Data Sheet

Your group is a committee consisting of college board members, administrators, faculty, and students of Bewise College. Your group has been authorized by the Board of Regents to select a new president of the college from the list of candidates.

Each of the represented groups (Board of Regents, administrators, faculty, students) has its own list of requirements for the new president. Insofar as possible, your group is pledged to select a candidate who meets these requirements.

Bewise College was established in 1969. It is located in the heart of an industrial city with a population of about 100,000. In addition to a standard liberal arts curriculum, Bewise College offers a curriculum in which students can receive college credit for work and learning experiences outside the college. Within the state, only Brown College, Samuels College, and Holubec College are larger, which makes Bewise one of the largest colleges in the state; Andrews is the smallest.

The new president faces a series of challenges. The Board of Regents wants a president who can raise money for the college. The college administration will not accept a new president who does not have administrative experience. The faculty is upset about the difficulty in teaching the students and, therefore, wants a president with experience in teaching the type of student who attends Bewise. Teaching experience is also considered crucial because it would make the president sympathetic to the problems of the faculty.

### Bewise College Data Sheet

Your group is a committee consisting of college board members, administrators, faculty, and students of Bewise College. Your group has been authorized by the Board of Regents to select a new president of the college from the list of candidates. . .

Each of the represented groups (Board of Regents, administrators, faculty, students) has its own list of requirements for the new president. Insofar as possible, your group is pledged to select a candidate who meets these requirements.

Bewise College was established in 1969. It is located in the heart of an industrial city with a population of about 100,000. In addition to a standard liberal arts curriculum, Bewise College offers a curriculum in which students can receive college credit for work and learning experiences outside the college. Since universities are always larger than colleges, Bewise is smaller than the State University, but it is growing rapidly.

The new president faces a series of challenges. The students are dissatisfied with the faculty's teaching and have stated that the only qualification they will recognize as valid for judging faculty teaching ability is for the president to have an education degree. The faculty, on the other hand, demands that the new president have experience in working with the type of student attending Bewise. The Board of Regents sees the need for a president who can raise money to support the college.

### Bewise College Data Sheet

Your group is a committee consisting of college board members, administrators, faculty, and students of Bewise College. Your group has been authorized by the Board of Regents to select a new president of the college from among the list of candidates. . . .

Each of the represented groups (Board of Regents, administrators, faculty, students) has its own list of requirements for the new president. Insofar as possible, your group is pledged to select a candidate who meets these requirements.

Bewise College was established in 1969. It is located in the heart of an industrial city with a population of about 100,000. In addition to a standard liberal arts curriculum, Bewise College offers a curriculum in which students can receive college credit for work and learning experiences outside the college. The faculty at Bewise College is made up primarily of young and dedicated but not highly experienced teachers.

The new president faces a series of challenges. The Board of Regents is most concerned about the ability of the president to be a public relations person for the college and raise money. The college has been in the "red" for the past two years and may have to close if it cannot balance its budget. The new president will be expected to make many public speeches to raise money from the community. The students are angry about the quality of teaching and want a president who can judge the teaching ability of faculty. Members of the college administration have nightmares about getting a president who is an incompetent administrator.

## Bewise College Data Sheet

Your group is a committee consisting of college board members, administrators, faculty, and students of Bewise College. Your group has been authorized by the Board of Regents to select a new president of the college from among the list of candidates. . . . .

Each of the represented groups (Board of Regents, administrators, faculty, students) has its own list of requirements for the new president. Insofar as possible, your group is pledged to select a candidate who meets these requirements.

Bewise College was established in 1969. It is located in the heart of an industrial city with a population of about 100,000. In addition to a standard liberal arts curriculum, Bewise College offers a curriculum in which students can receive college credit for work and learning experiences outside of the college. Bewise College was established to provide higher education for persons such as minority group members, working-class and lower-income students, the elderly, and dropouts from other colleges and universities.

The new president faces a series of challenges. The Board of Regents is most concerned about the ability of the president to be a public relations person for the college and raise money. The college has been losing money for the past two years. The college administration is very much afraid of a president who will not be a competent administrator. Students are dissatisfied with the quality of teaching. Faculty members are having a very difficult time in the classroom and want to make sure the new president has a background that includes experience in working with the type of students attending Bewise College.

## Bewise College Candidate Summary Sheet

| | |
|---|---|
| Name: | David Wolcott |
| Education: | Graduated from Andrews College in liberal arts in 1962; Master of Education from Winfield University in English in 1964; doctorate in political science from Winfield University in 1973. |
| Employment: | Instructor in English at Winfield University, 1964–1968; taught political science at James University, 1968–1977; representative in state legislature, 1970–1972; chairman of the department of political science at James University, 1975–1982; dean of students at James University, 1982 to the present. |
| Other: | Is well-known for his scholarship and intelligence. |
| | |
| Name: | Roger Thornton |
| Education: | Graduated from Samuels College in industrial arts in 1955; Master of Education in chemistry from Smith University in 1962; doctorate in administration from Smith University in 1976. |
| Employment: | High school chemistry teacher, 1962–1969; high school principal, 1969–1976, school superintendent, 1976 to the present. |
| Other: | Very innovative and efficient administrator; very successful political speaker (the superintendent of schools is elected in his district); his father is vice-president of a large bank. |
| | |
| Name: | Edythe Holubec |

| | |
|---|---|
| Education: | Graduated from Brown College in liberal arts in 1965; Master's in accounting from Smith University in 1970; doctorate in administration in 1978 from Smith University. |
| Employment: | Insurance agent, 1965–1970; certified public accountant, 1970–1978; vice-president of finance, Williams College 1978 to the present. |
| Other: | Taught accounting in night school for eight years; volunteer director of a community center in a lower-class neighborhood for four years; has a competing job offer from a public relations firm for which she has worked part time for two years. |

| | |
|---|---|
| Name: | Frank Pierce |
| Education: | Graduated from Smith University in liberal arts in 1968; Master of Education in mathematics in 1971 from Smith University; doctorate in administration from Johnson Institute in 1977. |
| Employment: | Neighborhood worker, 1968–1971; coordinator of parent-volunteer program for school system, 1971–1975; assistant superintendent for community relations, 1975 to the present. |
| Other: | Has written a training program for industrial education. |

| | |
|---|---|
| Name: | Helen Johnson |
| Education: | Graduated from Brown College in social studies education in 1966; Master of Education in social studies in 1970 from Brown College. |
| Employment: | Teacher of basic skills in a neighborhood center run by school system, 1966–1970; chairwoman of student teaching program, Smith University, 1970–1974; dean of students, Smith University, 1976–1980; vice-president for community relations and scholarship fund development, Smith University, 1980 to the present. |
| Other: | Grew up in one of the worst slums in the state; has written one book and several scholarly articles. Given award for fund-raising effectiveness. |

| | |
|---|---|
| Name: | Keith Clement |
| Education: | Graduated in biology education from Mulholland College in 1967; Master's in administration from Mulholland College in 1969. |
| Employment: | Biology teacher in a high school, 1966–1972; consultant in fund raising, public relations firm, 1972 to the present. |
| Other: | Is recognized as one of the best fund raisers in the state; has written a book on teaching working-class students; extensive volunteer work in adult education. |

# EXERCISE 4.3:
# SOLSTICE-SHENANIGANS MYSTERY

The purpose of this exercise is to study the way in which information is communicated in problem-solving groups. A mystery situation is used. Each of the accompanying clues should be written on a separate card. (The answers appear on page 491 in the appendix.) The procedure is as follows:

1. The class forms heterogeneous groups of six. One member should volunteer to be an observer. The observer's task is to record the communication patterns of the group, using the observation chart from the previous exercise.
2. The task of each group is to work cooperatively to solve a mystery. Each group is to decide
   a. What was stolen.
   b. How it was stolen.
   c. Who the thief was.
   d. What the thief's motive was.
   e. What time the crime took place.
3. Each group receives a deck of cards. On each card is written a clue to the mystery. Keeping the cards face down so that the clues cannot be read, one member deals them all out so that each member has several clues.
4. Each group member is to read aloud the clues on his or her cards, but not show them to anyone else. Members may take notes, but may not show them to other members. All communication in the group is to be verbal.
5. When a group has answered the five questions above, it may wish to answer the following two questions if the other groups are not yet done:
   a. What happened to the other items?
   b. Who was present at the party?
6. Each group is to discuss the communication patterns they used in solving the mystery. Members may use the following questions to structure the discussion.
   a. What were the patterns of communication within the group? Who spoke to whom? Who talked, how often did they talk, and for how long? Who triggered whom in what ways? How did members feel about the amount of their participation? What could have been done to gain wider participation?
   b. Was the needed information easily obtained by all the group members? Did group members share their information appropriately, request each other's information, and create the conditions under which the information could be shared?
   c. Were the resources of all group members used? Was everyone listened to?
   d. How did the group make decisions?
   e. What problems did the group have in working together?
   f. What conclusions about communication can be made from the group's experience?
7. Each group shares its conclusions with the rest of the class.

## Solstice-Shenanigans Mystery Clues

Mr. Purloin showed great interest in Mrs. Klutz's expensive diamond ring.
Mr. Purloin danced all evening with Ms. Beautiful.
Mrs. Klutz was always losing things.
Mrs. Klutz could not find her diamond ring after leaving the party.
The Hosts had a big party to celebrate the summer solstice.
The Hosts had a painting by Artisimisso.
Artisimisso was a sixteenth-century Italian artist.
Paintings by sixteenth-century Italian artists are quite valuable.
Mr. Avarice was heard to say that he would do anything for a valuable painting.
Mr. Klutz is a dealer in fine art.
Mr. Klutz needed money badly to keep his business from failing.
Mr. Klutz always carried his briefcase with him.
Mr. Avarice is known to be very rich.
All of Artisimisso's paintings are small.
Mrs. Klutz spent most of the evening in a dark corner of the patio with Mr. Handsome.

Ms. Perceptive saw something glitter in a corner of the patio as she was getting ready to leave the party.

Ms. Perceptive admired a painting by Artisimisso when she arrived at the party.

Ms. Perceptive noticed that the picture she admired was not there when she left the party.

Ms. Perceptive left the party at 10:00.

Ms. Wealthy brought her dog to the party.

Ms. Wealthy could not find what she had brought to the party.

The Neighbors owned three dogs.

The Neighbors found four dogs in their back yard after the party.

Mrs. Klutz admired the painting by Artisimisso when she left the party.

Mrs. Klutz left about 9:30.

Mr. Handsome was a kleptomaniac.

Mr. Handsome left the part 20 minutes after Mrs. Klutz.

Mr. and Mrs. Klutz left the party together.

Mr. Purloin was a jewel thief.

Ms. Beautiful noticed the painting when she left the party at 9:45.

Ms. Beautiful left the party with Mr. Purloin.

Ms. Wealthy and Mr. Avarice left the party together.

Ms. Wealthy left the party about the time Mr. Klutz did.

## EXERCISE 4.4:
## LIEPZ AND BOUNZ

The following exercise is based on the same principle as the mystery exercise. It may be conducted in 45 minutes. Use the same procedures, observation tasks, and discussion tasks as used in the mystery exercise. Use six group members (including one observer). The solution is on page 491 in the appendix.

The instructions for the exercises are as follows:

Pretend that liepz and bounz are new ways of measuring distance and that hobz, skibz, and jumpz represent a new way of measuring time. David jogs from Farmland through Parker and Selma to Muncie. The task of your group is to determine how many jumpz the entire trip took. You will be given cards containing information related to the task of the group. You may share this information orally, but do not show your cards to anyone. You have twenty minutes for the task. The information for individual group members is as follows:

Each of the following pieces of information is to be placed on a card. The cards are randomly distributed among the five group members.

It is 5 liepz from Farmland to Parker.
It is 8 liepz from Parker to Selma.
It is 9 liepz from Selma to Muncie.
A liepz is 10 bounz.
A liepz is a way of measuring distance.
There are 4 bounz in a mile.
A hobz is 10 skibz.
A skibz is 10 jumpz.
A jumpz is a way of measuring time.
There are 4 jumpz in an hour.
A hobz is a way of measuring time.
A skibz is a way of measuring time.
David jogs from Farmland to Parker at the rate of 25 liepz per jumpz.
David jogs from Parker to Selma at the rate of 20 liepz per jumpz.
David jogs from Selma to Muncie at the rate of 15 liepz per jumpz.

## COMMUNICATING INFORMATION
## IN A PROBLEM-SOLVING GROUP

For any problem-solving group to be effective, the members have to obtain the information they need to solve the problem and they have to put it together in such a way that an accurate or creative solution results. The previous exercises focused on the communication of information within a group. The situation in each exercise can be seen in Figure 4.2.

In most problem-solving groups, some information is shared by everyone, some information is known only to a few members, and each member has information that no one else in the group knows. Each member is responsible for communicating what he or she knows to the other members of the group. Each member is also responsible for seeking out the information known by the other members but not by that person. Thus, effective sending and receiving skills are both essential for all group members. What makes the exchange of information problematic is the "noise" that is usually present in problem-solving groups. Noise is defined as anything that gets in the way of effective communication. Determinants of noise include how a group member is perceived, how much information a group member thinks each of the others has, how trustworthy a member has been in the past, how the messages are formulated and sent, what receiving skills are used, how cooperative the group is, and whether the member believes his or her information will contribute to the group's efforts.

The coordination of information, ideas, experiences, and opinions is an essential part of problem solving in a group. How successful a group is with such coordination depends on the skills of the group members in sending and receiving messages and on the group norms about and procedures for communicating.

## PATTERNS OF COMMUNICATION
## AMONG GROUP MEMBERS

The patterns of communication among group members are an important aspect of group process to observe and discuss. There are several patterns of communication within a group that are often helpful to observe. (The frequency chart in the Bewise

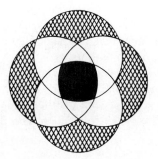

**FIGURE 4.2.** Communication of information: the shaded area represents information known to all group members; the crosshatched area represents information known to only one group member; the unmarked but enclosed area represents information known to two or more members of the group.

College exercise is one means of distinguishing them.) One of these patterns is the relative frequency and length of communication acts—who talked, how often he or she talked, and how much of the total available time that person used. A second pattern to figure out is who communicates to whom. Some persons speak to those they are trying to impress, others to those from whom they want support, and still others to those from whom they expect opposition. Information on this pattern of communication among group members is often helpful in pinpointing conflicts that must be resolved and increasing the group members' understanding of how they are relating to one another.

A third pattern of communication to observe is who "triggers" whom and in what ways. There are clear patterns of triggering. For example, whenever one member speaks another may always speak next, even if the remarks are not initially directed to her. This kind of triggering may reflect either support ("Attaboy") or a desire to undo the point ("Yeahbut") that has just been made. Schein (1969) quotes a businessman as saying that in group discussions in his company it takes at least three attaboys to undo the damage of one yeahbut. Another type of triggering is when one member of a group interrupts other members. Knowing who interrupts whom gives the observer clues as to how members see their own status or power in the group relative to that of other members. Generally, high-authority members feel freer to interrupt low-authority members and vice versa. Interrupting others is one of the more common and more destructive kinds of communication behavior, and observing the patterns of interruption often reveals a great deal about relationships among members.

## EFFECTS OF COMPETITION ON COMMUNICATION

A considerable body of research shows that when a situation within a group is cooperatively structured, relevant information is communicated openly, accurately, and honestly; in a competitively structured situation, communication is either lacking or misleading. With a cooperative structure each group member is interested in informing as well as being informed by others. Competition, on the other hand, gives rise to (1) espionage or other techniques for getting information another group member is unwilling to communicate and (2) tactics for misleading other group members about oneself. The more intense the competition, the more likely communication will be blocked or, if group members have to communicate with one another, the more likely they will communicate only lies and threats. The very nature of competition, in which one works to gain an edge toward winning and fears the possibility of losing, promotes a great deal of defensiveness among group members.

**Defensive behavior** in a group is behavior that occurs when a person feels threatened or anticipates a threat. Competition is inevitably accompanied by defensive behavior, and defensive individuals, even if they work on the group's tasks, devote a lot of energy just to defending themselves. They think about how they look to others, how they may win over or dominate their peers, how they may impress their superiors, how they may keep from losing, and how they may protect themselves from anticipated attacks. As a person becomes more and more defensive, furthermore, he or she becomes less and less able to see correctly the motives, values, emotions, and content involved in messages of other group members. Gibb (1961) demonstrated that defensive behavior is correlated positively with losses in efficiency and effectiveness of communication. Thus as people become less defensive their communication behavior becomes more efficient and effective. Competitiveness in one group member breeds competition in all group members, and defensiveness will continue to spiral as long as competition thrives among members.

The arousal of defensiveness makes it difficult, if not impossible, to communicate ideas clearly and move purposefully toward accomplishing the group's goals. In an eight-year study of communication behavior in groups, Gibb (1961) found several behaviors that prompt defensiveness among group members as well as other behaviors that lessen defensiveness. For example, if one group member sends messages that she is evaluating or judging other group members, they will become defensive. Descriptive messages, on the contrary, tend to arouse little uneasiness. Messages that try to control other group members increase their defensiveness, especially if the control attempts are subtle and denied. Yet if the sender is oriented toward the group problem, communicates a desire to help in defining and solving it, and implies that she has no predetermined solution, attitude, or method to impose upon the other group members, the same problem orientation tends to be created in the receivers. When the sender is seen as being engaged in a strategy involving many ambiguous motives, the receivers again tend to become defensive: No one likes to be the victim of some hidden motivation, and most groups dislike deceit. Behavior that seems to be spontaneous and free of deception reduces defensiveness in the receivers.

Gibb also found that when neutrality in communication appears to the receiver to evidence lack of concern for one's welfare, that person becomes defensive. Communications that are particularly persuasive in reducing defensiveness are those that show empathy with the feelings of the receiver and respect for the receiver's worth. When a person communicates that he or she feels superior in some way to the receiver, defensiveness is aroused. When the sender communicates a willingness to enter into participative planning with others in mutual trust and respect, on the other hand, defensiveness is lessened. Finally, those who seem to know the answers, who need no additional information, and who see themselves as teachers rather than coworkers tend to arouse defensiveness in others. A person minimizes that defensiveness of receivers by communicating that he or she is willing to experiment with his or her own behavior, attitudes, and ideas. These behaviors, which are characteristic of either a competitive or a cooperative orientation in a group, are summarized below.

| *COMPETITIVE ORIENTATION* | *COOPERATIVE ORIENTATION* |
| --- | --- |
| evaluation | description |
| control | problem orientation |
| strategy | spontaneity |
| neutrality | empathy |
| superiority | equality |
| certainty | provisionalism |

Groups that display a high cooperative orientation, groups whose members are good listeners, more accepting of the ideas of others, and less possessive of their own, generally demonstrate greater sending and receiving skills. Achievement will be higher in a cooperative group than in a competitive one, more attentiveness will be paid to members' ideas, and a friendlier climate will prevail. A cooperative orientation leads to increased cohesiveness and greater group productivity. One sound means of improving the communication among group members is to increase their cooperativeness and decrease their competitiveness.

## PHYSICAL BARRIERS TO COMMUNICATION

Physical factors can also block effective communication within a group. Group members should pay attention to the acoustics of the room in which they are meeting; how members are seated; the duration of the meeting; the ventilation, temperature, and lighting in the room; and what time of day it is. All these are potential physical barriers to effective communication among members. Once noted, of course, they can usually be changed or compensated for.

### EXERCISE 4.5:
### TRANSMISSION OF INFORMATION

The objective of this exercise is to show the effects of using one-way and two-way communication to pass information through a series of group members. At least ten persons and two observers are required. The time needed to complete the exercise is approximately one hour, and the procedure for the coordinator is as follows:

1. Introduce the exercise as an example of information being passed from member to member within a group.
2. Ask ten persons to leave the room. They are to constitute two groups of five members each. The first group is to demonstrate *one-way communication*. Entering the room one by one, each is to listen to a brief story and repeat it to the next person in his or her own way without help from other participants or the group's observer. The receiver cannot ask questions or comment: He or she must simply listen to the story and then repeat it to the next person. The second group is to demonstrate *two-way communication*. Entering the room one by one, each is to listen to the story and ask questions about it to clarify its meaning and to make sure that he or she knows what the story is about. The person then repeats the story to the next person in the group in his or her own way without help from other participants or the group's observer; the receiver can ask as many questions as he or she wants. You may wish to record the whole experience so that it can be played back for the participants' benefit.
3. After the ten participants have left the room, pass out copies of the accompanying observation sheets and a copy of "The Story" to the observers. Discuss the use of the observation sheet and read the story aloud. Explain the basic concepts of leveling, sharpening, and assimilation (these are discussed in the section on the effects of one-way communication on a message).
4. Begin the demonstration of one-way communication. Ask the first person to enter the room, read the story once, ask the second person to enter, have the first person repeat the story to the second person, and so on until the fifth person repeats the story to the observers.

5. Begin the demonstration of two-way communication. Ask the first person to enter the room, read the story once, answer all questions he or she has about the story, ask the second person to enter, have the first person repeat the story to the second person and answer all of the second person's questions, and so on until the fifth person repeats the story to the observers.

6. Reread the original story out loud. Using the results recorded by the observers and the following summary tables and summary graph, chart the percentages of original details retained correctly in the successive reproductions and compare the one-way and two-way communications. Discuss the results, incorporating the material in the sections on the characteristics of communication within an authority hierarchy and the effects of one-way communication on a message. Ask the group for further evidence that leveling, sharpening, and assimilation occurred. Then ask what conclusions about one-way and two-way communication can be made on the basis of the results of the demonstration. Finally ask the group what conclusions can be made about communication in authority hierarchies.

Other stories can be used in this exercise. Often, the more the cultural background of the story differs from the listener's culture the more the story is taken in. A story from the Eskimo culture that might be used in this exercise appears below "The Story."

Summary Table: One-Way Communication

| Person | Details Correct | | Details Incorrect | | Details Left Out | | Total Details |
|---|---|---|---|---|---|---|---|
| | *Number* | *Percentage* | *Number* | *Percentage* | *Number* | *Percentage* | |
| 1 | | | | | | | 20 |
| 2 | | | | | | | 20 |
| 3 | | | | | | | 20 |
| 4 | | | | | | | 20 |
| 5 | | | | | | | 20 |

Summary Table: Two-Way Communication

| Person | Details Correct | | Details Incorrect | | Details Left Out | | Total Details |
|---|---|---|---|---|---|---|---|
| | *Number* | *Percentage* | *Number* | *Percentage* | *Number* | *Percentage* | |
| 1 | | | | | | | 20 |
| 2 | | | | | | | 20 |
| 3 | | | | | | | 20 |
| 4 | | | | | | | 20 |
| 5 | | | | | | | 20 |

**Summary Graph**

On this graph plot the percentages of original details retained correctly in one-way and two-way communication. Connect the one-way results with a solid line and the two-way results with a broken line.

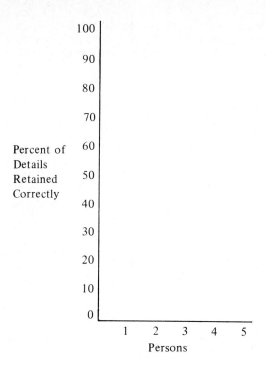

## The Story*

A *farmer* in *western Kansas* put a *tin roof on his barn*. Then a *small tornado blew* the roof off, and when the farmer found it *two counties away,* it was *twisted and mangled* beyond repair.

A *friend and a lawyer* advised him that the *Ford Motor Company* would pay him a *good price* for the scrap tin, and the farmer decided he would *ship the roof* up to the company to see *how much he could get for it.* He crated it up in a *very big wooden box* and sent it off to *Dearborn, Michigan,* marking it plainly with his *return address* so that the Ford Company would know where to *send the check.*

*Twelve weeks passed,* and the farmer didn't hear from the Ford Company. Finally, he was just on the *verge of writing them* to find out what was the matter, when he *received an envelope* from them. It said, "We don't know *what hit your car,* mister, but we'll have it fixed for you by the *fifteenth of next month.*"

## The War of the Ghosts

One night two young men from Egulac went down to the river to hunt seals, and while they were there it became foggy and calm. Then they heard war cries, and they thought: "Maybe this is a war party." They escaped to the shore, and hid behind a log. Now canoes came up,

---

*This story by Samuel J. Sackett, whose actual title is "Tin Lizzie," is included in Botkin (1957). This title should not be mentioned until the end of the exercise.

and they heard the noise of paddles, and they saw one canoe coming up to them. There were five men in the canoe and they said:

"What do you think. We wish to take you along. We are going up the river to make war on the people."

One of the young men said: "I have no arrows."

"Arrows are in the canoe," they said.

"I will not go along. I might be killed. My relatives do not know where I have gone. But you," he said, turning to the other, "may go with them."

So one of the young men went, but the other returned home.

And the warriors went on up the river to a town on the other side of Kalama. The people came down to the water and they began to fight, and many were killed. And presently the young man heard one of the warriors say: "Quick, let us go home. That Indian has been hit." Now he thought, "Oh, they are ghosts." He did not feel sick, but they said he had been shot.

So the canoes went back to Egulac, and the young man went ashore to his house and made a fire. And he told everybody: "Behold, I accompanied ghosts, and we went to fight. Many of our fellows were killed, and many of those who attacked us were killed. They said I was hit, but I did not feel sick."

He told it all, and then he became quiet. When the sun rose he fell down. Something black came out of his mouth. His face became contorted. The people jumped up and cried.

He was dead.

### Observation Sheet: One-Way Communication

List in the first column the 20 specific details of the story (these appear in italics in the story). Verify the list when the coordinator reads the story to the first person. As person 1 repeats the story to person 2, note the mistakes in person 1's version by writing the wrong words or phrases in the proper row and column. To help in scoring, use a checkmark for details correctly reported and a zero for details left out. Repeat this procedure for the rest of the participants.

### Observation Sheet: Two-Way Communication

List in the first column the 20 specific details of the story (these appear in italics in the story). Verify the list when the coordinator reads the story to the first person. As person 1 repeats the story to person 2, note the mistakes in person 1's version by writing the wrong words or phrases in the proper row and column. To help in scoring, use a check mark for details correctly reported and a zero for details left out. Repeat this procedure for the rest of the participants.

### EXERCISE 4.6:
### ONE- AND TWO-WAY COMMUNICATION

This is another exercise that contrasts the impact of one-way and two-way communication on communication effectiveness. For this exercise each participant needs two sheets of paper and a pencil. The coordinator needs copies of the accompanying square arrangements, which are given on pages 492–93 in the appendix. The coordinator may wish to copy the three summary tables below onto a blackboard or a large sheet of paper. The procedure for the coordinator is as follows:

1. Select a sender and two observers (if the group has less than seven members, select only one observer). The sender should be a person who communicates well and who speaks clearly and loudly enough to be heard.

| Detail | Original Story | Version 1 | Version 2 | Version 3 | Version 4 | Version 5 |
|--------|----------------|-----------|-----------|-----------|-----------|-----------|
| 1 | | | | | | |
| 2 | | | | | | |
| 3 | | | | | | |
| 4 | | | | | | |
| 5 | | | | | | |
| 6 | | | | | | |
| 7 | | | | | | |
| 8 | | | | | | |
| 9 | | | | | | |
| 10 | | | | | | |
| 11 | | | | | | |
| 12 | | | | | | |
| 13 | | | | | | |
| 14 | | | | | | |
| 15 | | | | | | |
| 16 | | | | | | |
| 17 | | | | | | |
| 18 | | | | | | |
| 19 | | | | | | |
| 20 | | | | | | |

2. Have the sender sit either with her back to the group of receivers or behind a screen. Give her the first square arrangement, being careful that the group members do not see it. Tell her to study the arrangement of squares carefully for two minutes in order to be prepared to instruct the group members on how to draw a similar set of squares on their paper.

3. Ask the first observer to note the behavior and reactions of the sender during the exercise and to make notes for later comments. Ask the second observer to make notes on the behavior and reactions of the group members. Facial reactions, gestures, posture, and other nonverbal behaviors may be observed.

4. Give the group these instructions: "The sender is going to describe a drawing to you. You are to listen carefully to her instructions and draw what she describes as accurately as you can. You will be timed, but there is no time limit. *You may ask no questions of the sender and give no audible response.* You are asked to work independently."

5. Display the three summary tables in the front of the room. Then tell the sender to proceed to give the instructions for drawing the first arrangement of squares as quickly and accurately as she can. Make sure that there are no questions or audible reactions from the group members.

6. When the sender has completed giving the instructions for the first square arrangement, record the time it look her to do so in the proper space in the first table. Ask all

| Detail | Original Story | Version 1 | Version 2 | Version 3 | Version 4 | Version 5 |
|---|---|---|---|---|---|---|
| 1 | | | | | | |
| 2 | | | | | | |
| 3 | | | | | | |
| 4 | | | | | | |
| 5 | | | | | | |
| 6 | | | | | | |
| 7 | | | | | | |
| 8 | | | | | | |
| 9 | | | | | | |
| 10 | | | | | | |
| 11 | | | | | | |
| 12 | | | | | | |
| 13 | | | | | | |
| 14 | | | | | | |
| 15 | | | | | | |
| 16 | | | | | | |
| 17 | | | | | | |
| 18 | | | | | | |
| 19 | | | | | | |
| 20 | | | | | | |

**Table A:** Medians for Trials I and II

| Medians | I | II |
|---|---|---|
| Time elapsed: | | |
| Guess accuracy: | | |
| Actual accuracy: | | |

**Table B:** First Trial

| Number Correct | Guess | Actual |
|---|---|---|
| 5 | | |
| 4 | | |
| 3 | | |
| 2 | | |
| 1 | | |
| 0 | | |

**Table C:** Second Trial

| Number Correct | Guess | Actual |
|---|---|---|
| 5 | | |
| 4 | | |
| 3 | | |
| 2 | | |
| 1 | | |
| 0 | | |

members of the group to write down the number of squares they think they have drawn correctly in relation to the preceding square.

7. Instruct the sender to face the group members. Give her the second square arrangement and tell her to study the relationship of the squares in this new diagram for two minutes in preparation for instructing the group members on how to draw it.

8. Give the group these instructions: "The sender is going to describe another drawing to you. This time she will be in full view of you and you may ask as many questions as you wish. She is free to reply to your questions or amplify her statements as she sees fit. She is not, however, allowed to make any hand signals while describing the drawing. You will be timed, but there is no time limit. Work as accurately and rapidly as you can."

9. Tell the sender to proceed.

10. When the sender has completed giving instructions for the second figure, record the time in the appropriate space in Table A. Ask the group members to guess the number of squares they have drawn correctly and to record the number on their papers.

11. Obtain a median for guessed accuracy on the first drawing by recording the number of group members who guessed zero, the number who guessed one, and so on in Table B. Find the median guessed number by counting from zero the number of group members guessing each number until you reach half the members of the group. Then record the median in Table A.

12. Repeat this method to get the median of accurate guesses for the second drawing.

13. Show the group members the master drawing for the first set of squares, and point out the relationship of each square to the preceding one. Each square must be in the exact relationship to the preceding one as it appears on the master drawing in order to be counted as correct. When this step has been completed ask the members to count and record the actual number right. Have them make a similar count for the second square arrangement.

14. Obtain the median for accuracy for the first and second arrangements and place them in Table A.

15. Discuss the following questions with the class:
    a. What may be concluded from the results in terms of time, accuracy, and level of confidence?
    b. What did the observers record during the exercise? How did the behavior of the sender and the group members vary from one situation to the other? What were the group members and the sender feeling during the two situations?
    c. How does this exercise compare with situations you find yourself in at work, school, or at home? How might you change your behavior in relating to your friends and acquaintances as a result of what you have experienced during this exercise?

## COMMUNICATION WITHIN AN AUTHORITY HIERARCHY

Within every organization and in many groups there is an authority hierarchy. An authority hierarchy exists when role requirements are established in such a way that different members perform different roles and members performing particular roles supervise the other members to make sure they fulfill their role requirements. If a group, for example, is divided into several committees, each responsible for a different aspect of the group's work, its role structure would look like Figure 4.3. The members are supervised by the committee chairpersons and the committee chairper-

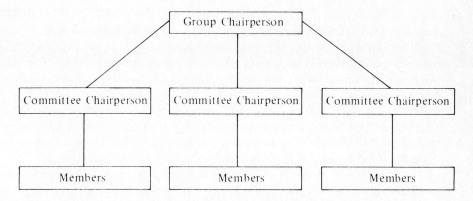

**FIGURE 4.3.** A group and its internal authority hierarchy

sons are supervised by the group chairperson. Within an authority hierarchy a system of rewards and punishments is usually established so that a supervisor will have some power over the persons he or she is supervising. Although authority hierarchies are established to facilitate the effectiveness of the group, they can often interfere with its effectiveness by undermining necessary processes such as distributed participation and leadership, equalization of power, controversy procedures, and communication. In this chapter we will focus on the effect of authority hierarchies upon communication within a group and thus elaborate on the conclusions resulting from the previous exercises.

To organize itself to accomplish its goals, maintain itself in good working order, and adapt to a changing world, a group must structure its communication. Meetings will be scheduled; reports from group members will be requested; conferences among members will be set up; summaries of group progress may be written and sent to all members. All these activities are structured communication opportunities. The **communication network** thus created determines the amount and type of information a group member will receive from the other members. The very nature of a group implies that communication is selective, that a communication network exists, that incentives to use it properly are present, and that members must use certain procedures for communicating with each other. Thus, a college seminar will schedule meetings and teacher-student conferences as the communication network, be selective in the material upon which communication will be based, use learning and grades as incentives for participating in the network, and encourage certain procedures (for example, when the teacher talks, students listen). The formal network, incentives, and procedures are established to coordinate members' efforts to accomplish goals. In addition to the formal communication network, in many groups there is an informal network, which includes patterns of friendship and social contact among group members.

The procedures used within a formal communication network of a group can be examined in several different ways; the approach most relevant to a discussion of authority hierarchies focuses on three types: one-way, one-way-with-feedback, and two-way. In an authority hierarchy a one-way communication procedure is characterized by a group chairperson giving instructions or making announcements to the other group members, who are not allowed to communicate with her. The listeners, then, are entirely passive, and communication effectiveness is determined by how the messages are created and presented. Usually there is someone higher in the authority hierarchy who communicates messages to the chairperson, who then communicates them to the group members. One-way communication takes little time compared with the other two procedures, but it is less effective. And though it is less frustrating for the sender, it is far more unsatisfactory for the receivers.

One-way-with-feedback communication is often called **directive** or **coercive communication** (McGregor, 1967). In this communication procedure within an authority hierarchy, the chairperson presents the message and the group members give feedback on how well they understand it. The exchange is completed when the group members indicate to the chairperson that they have received the message correctly. This procedure is called coercive because no provision exists for mutual influence or exchange: Communication begins with the belief that the chairperson's position is correct and that the only information he or she needs from the group members is that they correctly understand and accept the message. The chairperson influences while the group members merely understand. This second procedure is, in the short run, faster than two-way communication and less frustrating for the chairperson, but also less accurate and more frustrating for the group members.

When one-way and one-way-with-feedback communication procedures are used in groups, communication can be so poor that informal communication among group members is necessary in order for them to complete the group's tasks adequately. This reduces the long-term effectiveness of these procedures. The original messages can become distorted as they pass through the informal network and this can hinder the coordination of member behavior. Such distortion and misunderstanding are most frequent when the most influential members of the informal network disagree with the decisions and points of view of the chairperson and his or her superiors (if he or she has them), or when distrust and competition exist among group members or between the chairperson and the group members. Unless group members have the opportunity to communicate freely with the chairperson, the informal network may become more influential, powerful, important, and effective than the group's formal network.

Two-way communication is a reciprocal process in which each member starts messages and tries to understand the other members' messages. In a two-way communication procedure the chairperson and the other group members freely exchange ideas and information in a productive discussion. Both sending and receiving skills are needed. All members are able to participate at will, and minority opinions are encouraged and more apt to be expressed. Feelings of resistance or doubt can be discussed and resolved at the time they are experienced so that they are not potential barriers to commitment. Two-way communication encourages open and candid member interaction, distributed participation and leadership, consensual decision making, and other elements of group effectiveness. Although two-way communication is much more time-consuming than the one-way procedures and more frustrating for the chairperson, it is less frustrating for the group members and much more effective in the long run. Any goal-directed, problem-solving group that hopes to be effective must use two-way communication procedures.

Even when a two-way communication procedure is encouraged, the authority hierarchy will influence communication among group members. High-authority group members usually do most of the talking, and most of the messages are directed at them. Low-authority members often do not communicate very much with each other during a group meeting, preferring to address their remarks to high-authority members. Because they generally fear evaluation by those with power, members without power can be expected to take few risks, speak inconsequentially, and avoid frankness in their remarks. High-authority members often hesitate to reveal any of their own limitations or vulnerability, a tendency that also decreases open and effective communication among group members. Thus, several influences push the group's use of communication procedures toward practices that thwart the kind of discussion and problem solving needed for it to function effectively.

How can these tendencies be avoided so that communication within a group is effective? There are two answers to this question. The first is to establish a cooperative group climate that encourages the equal participation of all members. The second is to promote group norms that foster the feeling that a member's ideas and views, no matter what his or her authority level, are of real interest to other group members. If a group is to function effectively, it must adopt a two-way communication procedure and develop a cooperative group climate and group norms that facilitate interaction among members. Because communication is an interpersonal phenomenon, furthermore, anything that interferes with the relationships among group members interferes with their communication. Much attention, therefore, must be paid to the interpersonal relationships of group members.

# INFORMAL COMMUNICATION NETWORKS
# AND OPINION LEADERS

When one-way communication procedures are used in a group, comprehension of messages is often so poor that group members turn to the informal communication network to clarify what has been communicated. Often certain group members will be better able to interpret messages from higher-ups. In such cases other members will seek them out and ask them what the higher-ups meant by the latest communication. Such members are called **opinion leaders** or **gatekeepers** because they have more influence over members' comprehension of messages than do the persons in higher-authority positions who originated the messages. There are two common types of opinion leaders: **information gatekeepers,** who receive messages from superiors and outside sources or who read, listen, and reflect upon written reports and verbal messages to a greater extent than other group members, and **technological gatekeepers,** who read more of the theory and research literature in their field and consult more with outside sources than do the other group members.

Opinion leaders frequently serve as **translators** by taking messages from superiors and rephrasing them into more understandable form and into the specific meanings they have for different group members. When one-way communication procedures are being used, the original source is often not available for questioning and clarification of messages; group members, therefore, must rely on the opinion leaders to clarify the messages and what meanings they have for the specific group members. Group members, furthermore, may remember an opinion leader's interpretation of a message they themselves heard, better than the original message! Research on testimony in court cases indicates that people remember initial reports of events they witnessed better than the events themselves (Jones & Gerard, 1967). If the opinion leader misconstrues the message, errors in understanding are amplified as interpretations are passed from member to member. Even within a two-way communication procedure, group members will at times be unable to clarify a message and will use opinion leaders to help them do so.

# EFFECTS ON THE MESSAGE OF A ONE-WAY
# COMMUNICATION PROCEDURE

Some basic research has been conducted on what happens to information when it is passed through several persons with little or no clarification. The more the message is passed from person to person, the more distorted and changed it will become. Three psychological processes characterize the communication between persons who are unable to communicate directly with the original source of a message (Allport & Postman, 1945; Bartlett, 1932). These three processes are attempts to reduce the message to a simple one that has significance for the receiver in terms of his or her own interests, experience, frame of reference, and tasks. The three processes are as follows:

**Leveling.** The receiver tends to reduce the amount of information he or she receives by remembering much less of the message than was presented by the sender. The message tends to grow shorter, more concise, and more easily grasped and told. In successive versions, fewer words are used and fewer details are mentioned.

**Sharpening.** The receiver sharpens certain parts of the information so that a few high points are readily remembered while most of the message is forgotten. Sharpening, then, is the selective retaining, perceiving, and reporting of a limited number of details from a larger context. It is the reciprocal of leveling: One cannot exist without the other. Certain points become dominant, and all the others are grouped about them.

**Assimilation.** The receiver takes much of the message into her own frame of reference and personality. Thus, her interpretations, and memories of what she heard are affected by her own thoughts and feelings. This process involves not only changing the unfamiliar to some known context, but also leaving out material that seems irrelevant and substituting material that gives meaning in the person's own frame of reference.

Because these three processes are at work whenever one-way procedures are being used, inefficient and ineffective communication usually results. This is true even when opinion leaders supplement the procedure.

## EXERCISE 4.7:
## GROUP OBSERVATION

Review the material in the last three sections by taking the frequency chart used in the Bewise College exercise and observing at least two groups of which you are a member—one group in which there is a chairperson (such as a teacher) who dominates the meeting and another group in which free and open discussions are held among members. Observe the communication patterns in both groups and compare them. Write a description of the communication patterns in each group and discuss them with other members of your class.

## EXERCISE 4.8:
## NORMS AND COMMUNICATION

This exercise should develop participants' awareness of how group norms affect communication among group members. The participating groups must be groups that have worked together for several hours. Observation sheets similar to the frequency chart used in the Bewise College exercise are needed; participants can construct their own. The exercise will take approximately one hour to complete. The procedure for the coordinator is as follows:

1. Introduce the exercise as a structured experience in learning how group norms affect communication among group members.
2. Have each group select two observers. The observers need to construct six observation sheets, making the number of circles on the sheets equal to the number of members in the group they are observing. Explain the use of these sheets.
3. Give each group a copy of the accompanying discussion sheet and state that the groups have 30 minutes to discuss the topic. Give the signal to begin.

4. At the end of 30 minutes ask the observers to report to their groups. Groups are to discuss the communication pattern among their members and how it relates to the group norms they have been listing. Each group should also discuss how its members feel about the amount of their participation and how it could change group norms so as to gain more widespread participation and more effective communication among members. Each group should then revise its list of group norms in light of the discussion. Allow twenty minutes for this discussion.
5. Have the groups share their conclusions in a general discussion.


### Discussion Sheet: What is Norm?

Norms develop in groups so that members will know how they are expected to behave and what is appropriate member behavior. They are common rules or customs followed by group members. In some groups, for example, members address each other by their last names; in other groups first names are used. All groups have norms, and usually these norms are eventually followed without conscious thought. Norms can develop so that every member does the same thing (dressing formally for a group meeting) or something different (dressing differently for a group meeting).

Norms are not built from scratch, but develop from the values, expectations, and learned habits that the members bring with them when the group is first formed. "Don't interrupt the chairperson," an expression of respect for authority, is a norm that most persons bring with them into new groups. Norms can also be implied by the setting in which the group meets. Most persons do not sit on the floor in a room that appears to be arranged formally. Most persons do not remain standing when their group is meeting at a beach.

Norms have a powerful influence upon communication within a group. Such influences are seldom examined. It is even rarer that a group attempts to change its norms so as to facilitate goal accomplishment. Usually group members simply follow norms without question. This does not mean that norms do not change. Norms do change as expectations of appropriate member behavior change, but this is commonly an unobtrusive process.

What norms have developed in your group? Do you all sense where you are supposed to sit? Do you all sense who should be listened to and who should be ignored? Do you interrupt each other, or is politeness a group norm? Are jokes allowed, or is the tone of the group serious? How do discussions usually start? How are boredom and frustration generally expressed, if at all? Are certain topics permissible to talk about and others avoided? Is the emotional involvement of members supposed to be high or low? In answering these questions you will become more conscious of the norms that are present in your group.

Spend the next 30 minutes discussing your group norms and making a list of what they are.


### EXERCISE 4.9:
### SITTING IN A CIRCLE

How a group sits has a great deal of influence on how its members communicate. This exercise focuses upon the effects of sitting in a circle. The procedure for each group is to engage in three 5-minute discussions. After each one, each member writes down several adjectives to describe his or her reactions to the discussion. A different position is to be used for each discussion: (1) circle in which everyone's back is to the center, (2) circle with members face to face and a large rectangular table between them, and (3) circle with members face to face and nothing between them.

After the 15 minutes of discussion members compare their reactions to the three positions. What were the differences in feelings? Was there any difference in how productive the discussion was? What effects did the different positions have upon the discussion? How was communication affected? The advantage of sitting close together in a circle with nothing between members is that their unobstructed view of one another increases their opportunities to receive and send nonverbal messages. This type of circular seating arrangement also encourages more equal participation because there is no podium or seat at the head of a table to suggest that a particular member should assume leadership.

## EXERCISE 4.10
## COMMUNICATION NETWORKS

The purpose of this exercise is to compare the impact of four different communication patterns on productivity and morale. The procedure is as follows:

1. The class forms heterogeneous groups of six. One member needs to volunteer to be an observer. The task of the observer is to time how long it takes the group to complete its task and to make notes about the behavior and apparent feelings of the participants.
2. The five participants in each group place themselves in a straight line with everyone facing the same way. Each member receives five cards from a regular deck of playing cards. No verbal communication is allowed, but members may write notes to the person in front of or behind them. Members may pass cards to the person in front of or behind them. The *group task* is to select one card from each member's hand in order to make the highest-ranking poker hand possible. After the group has decided on a poker hand each member should write an answer to the following questions:
   a. How satisfied are you with the group and its work?
   b. How did you feel?
   c. What did you observe?
3. The same task with the same rules is repeated, but this time the group members arrange themselves in a circle. Members may pass notes and cards only to the person on their left or right. No verbal communication is allowed. After the group has completed the task each member writes answers to the same three questions.
4. The same task with the same rules is repeated, but this time the group members arrange themselves in a wheel, as in Figure 4.4. Members on the outside may pass notes and cards only to the person in the middle; the member in the middle may pass notes and cards to anyone. No verbal communication is allowed. After the group has decided on a poker hand each member answers the same three questions.
5. The same task is repeated, this time with the members sitting in a circle. Any member may communicate with anyone else in the group. Members may pass cards and notes, and may speak to whomever they wish in the group. After the group has decided on a poker hand each member answers the same three questions.
6. Using the reactions of the group members and the observer's impressions, the group

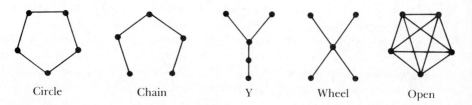

Circle        Chain        Y        Wheel        Open

**FIGURE 4.4.**  Communication networks

should discuss the advantages and disadvantages of each communication pattern. Here are some questions the group may wish to talk about:

  a. What were the feelings of the members in the middle of a communication pattern? What were the feelings of those on the fringe?

  b. In what communication pattern was the shortest amount of time needed to arrive at a group poker hand?

  c. If you were in charge of a company, which communication pattern would you try to use?

  d. How many messages were sent in each type of communication pattern?

  e. Did each pattern have a leader? For those patterns that did, what position did the leader occupy?

7. Each group shares its conclusions with the rest of the class.

## COMMUNICATION STRUCTURES AND NETWORKS

If a group is to function effectively, its members must be able to communicate easily and efficiently. Communication within the group needs to be arranged so that ideas, knowledge, and other information may flow freely among group members. To this end a number of studies has been conducted on the physical arrangement of communication networks—that is, who can communicate with whom and whether the communication is direct or via another group member. Typically, these studies imposed various communication networks on groups in order to determine their effects on group process. Some of the networks that have been investigated are diagrammed in Figure 4.4. The circles represent individual group members and the lines represent links in the communication network. The most common procedure for imposing communication networks was first formulated by Alex Bavelas (1948). He suggested placing group members in cubicles connected by slots in their walls, through which written messages could be passed. When all slots are open every group member can communicate directly with every other member. Other patterns are formed merely by selection of the appropriate slots.

Communication networks have been found to influence the emergence of leadership, the development of organization, the morale of group members, and the efficiency of problem solving (Leavitt, 1951; Shaw, 1964). The group member who occupies a central physical position in a communication network usually emerges as the leader of the group. Because the central member has more information, he or she can coordinate group activities.

A group becomes organized when it follows a consistent pattern of information exchange during the course of a problem solution. Research has found two basic patterns of organization in communication networks: **centralized** and **each-to-all.** In the centralized pattern all information is funneled to one person, who solves the problem and distributes the answer to the other group members. In the each-to-all pattern all available information is communicated to all group members, each of whom solves the problem independently. When a centralized communication network is imposed on a group, the group adopts a centralized organization. When a decentralized communication network is imposed on a group, each-to-all organization tends to develop.

Members who occupy a central position in a communication network are usually more satisfied with the group's work than members who occupy fringe positions. Typically, the morale of a group is higher in decentralized (circle, open) communication networks than in centralized ones (chain, Y, wheel).

Finally, when a task is simple and requires only the collection of information, a centralized network is more efficient in terms of speed and lack of errors. But when the task is complex and requires the analysis of information, the decentralized networks are more efficient, as we can see in Table 4.1. The problem with centralized communication networks is that the members in the centralized positions may easily receive more messages than they can handle. Any extra demands, furthermore, that must be addressed by a member in a centralized position are likely to interfere with the efficiency of the network.

## SEATING ARRANGEMENTS

The way in which group members seat themselves in relation to each other exerts significant influences on their perceptions of status, patterns of participation, leadership activities, and affective reactions (Gardin, Kaplan, Firestone, & Cowan, 1973; Howells & Becker, 1962; Myers, 1962); Steinzor, 1950; Strodtbeck & Hook, 1961). Members who perceive themselves to have relatively high status in the group select positions (such as the head of the table) that are in accord with this perception. Members sitting at the end positions of a rectangular arrangement participate more

**Table 4.1**  Differences between Centralized (wheel, chain, Y) and Decentralized (circle, open) Communication Networks as a Function of Task Complexity

|  | Simple Problems* | Complex Problems† | Total |
|---|---|---|---|
| Time |  |  |  |
| Centralized faster | 14 | 0 | 14 |
| Decentralized faster | 4 | 18 | 22 |
| Messages |  |  |  |
| Centralized sent more | 0 | 1 | 1 |
| Decentralized sent more | 18 | 17 | 35 |
| Errors |  |  |  |
| Centralized made more | 0 | 6 | 6 |
| Decentralized made more | 9 | 1 | 10 |
| No difference | 1 | 3 | 4 |
| Satisfaction |  |  |  |
| Centralized higher | 1 | 1 | 2 |
| Decentralized higher | 7 | 10 | 17 |

*Simple problems: symbol, letter, number, and color identification tasks.

†Complex problems: arithmetic, word arrangement, sentence construction, and discussion problems.

Source: M. E. Shaw, 2 "Communication Networks." in L. Berkowitz (Ed.), *Advances in Experimental Social Psychology*, Vol. 1 (New York: Academic Press, 1964). Reprinted with permission.

in the group and are seen as having more influence on the group decision than members seated at the sides. There is a strong tendency for members to communicate with members facing them rather than with members adjacent to them. Easy eye contact among members enhances frequency of interaction, friendliness, cooperativeness, and liking for the group and its work. The more formal a seating arrangement, the more anxious members may feel. The group's formal leader usually sits at the head of the table, and the member sitting at the head of the table is usually perceived to be the leader.

## TAKING A SURVEY

Group effectiveness is always improved when members have clear expectations of the kinds of behaviors expected of them as group members. One way to clarify such expectations is the survey method. In this method any member may ask for the opinion of all the others at any time. Each member then states in two or three sentences his or her current position on the topic under discussion. A survey is not a vote, and it does not bind the group members to a fixed position; it is a device to help communication and problem solving within a group.

## IMPROVING COMMUNICATION AMONG GROUP MEMBERS

To improve communication among group members, one must observe their communication behavior in order to diagnose possible sources of difficulty. Once a diagnosis has been made and enough data have been gathered to confirm existing problems, both communication skills and the group's awareness of its present behavior need to be examined. If certain members—or all of them—lack some basic skills, this situation can be easily corrected by a training program. If members have the skills but are not fully aware that they are not using them, an analysis of the communication behavior in the group can be a great help. After examining member self-awareness and skills one may analyze the effect of group norms and traditional practices to find out if they are suppressing effective communication behaviors and promoting ineffective ones. Group norms can then be adjusted so that communication effectiveness among members will increase.

Because communication is interpersonal, whatever interferes with the relationships among group members interferes with their communication. Changes in the relationships in a group can result in basic improvements in communication. And as we have noted before, perhaps the most powerful influence on the relationships among members and on communication in a group is the members' orientation toward participation in the group and toward its goal structure. Cooperativeness helps a group's effectiveness. Competitiveness, either in goal structure or member orientation, is highly destructive of communication and relationships.

**EXERCISE 4.11:**
**YOUR COMMUNICATION BEHAVIOR (II)**

How would you now describe your communication behavior in a problem-solving group? What are your strengths in communicating, and in what areas do you still wish to build skills? After completing the exercises in this chapter take 20 minutes or so to write a description of how you see your communication behavior in problem-solving groups. Include a description of the way you formulate and send messages, the receiving skills you use, the way in which you contribute your information and ideas to the group, the way in which you receive information about group meetings and group business, and so on.

After you have written your description, meet with two persons who know you well and discuss it with them. Is it accurate? Can they add anything? Do they have other ideas that might help clarify your communication behavior?

# SUMMARY

Now you are aware of the problems of communicating within a group and have had an opportunity to diagnose and practice effective and ineffective communication patterns. The next chapter will discuss the nature of leadership within groups.

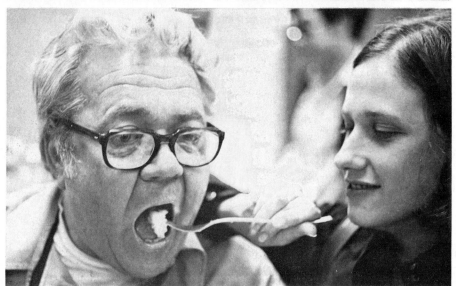

# 5

# Leadership

## BASIC CONCEPTS TO BE COVERED IN THIS CHAPTER

In this chapter a number of concepts are defined and discussed. The major ones are listed below. The procedure for learning these concepts is as follows:

1. Divide into heterogeneous pairs.
2. The task for each pair is to
   a. Define each concept, noting the page on which it is defined and discussed.
   b. Ensure that both members of the pair understand the meaning of each concept.
3. Combine into groups of four. Compare the answers of the two pairs. If there is disagreement, the members look up the concept in the chapter and clarify it until they all agree on the definition and understand it.

### CONCEPTS

1. Trait approach to leadership
2. Charismatic leadership
3. Machiavellian leadership
4. Leadership styles
5. Initiating structure
6. Influence leadership
7. Role position approach to leadership
8. Distributed-actions approach to leadership
9. Task actions
10. Relationship actions
11. Member maturity
12. Telling
13. Selling
14. Participating
15. Delegating

# LEADERSHIP ISSUES

1. How to *challenge the status quo* of the traditional competitive/individualistic organization. The old competitive/individualistic mass production organizational model that emphasizes "lone rangers" just does not work well any more.

2. How to *inspire a clear mutual vision* of what the organization should and could be, a clear mission that all members are committed to achieving, and a set of goals that guides members' efforts. It is the long-term promise of achieving something worthwhile and meaningful that powers an individual's drive toward greater expertise.

3. How to *empower members through cooperative teamwork*. Doing so enables each individual member to take action to increase his or her expertise and effectiveness, both technically and interpersonally. To be effective, a cooperative team must be carefully structured to include positive interdependence, face-to-face promotive interaction, individual accountability, social skills, and group processing.

4. How to *lead by example* by (a) using cooperative team procedures and (b) taking risks to increase expertise. You begin leadership by becoming a role model who exemplifies the organizational and leadership values you believe are important.

5. How to *encourage the heart* of members to persist and keep striving to improve their technical and interpersonal expertise. Within cooperative enterprises, genuine acts of caring draw people together and forward. Love of their work and each other is what inspires many members to commit more and more of their energy to their jobs.

# WHAT IS LEADERSHIP?

> Leadership begins where management ends, where the systems of rewards and punishments, control and scrutiny, give way to innovation, individual character, and the courage of convictions. Your challenge is to lead your staff to get extraordinary things done. This requires inspiring and motivating your staff toward a common purpose and building a cohesive and spirited team.
>
> *David and Roger Johnson (1989b)*

What is a leader? What is leadership? Are leaders born, or are they made? Does effective leadership originate in a person or in a set of actions and behaviors? The concepts leader and leadership have been defined in more different ways than almost any other concept associated with group dynamics. Curiosity about leaders is not confined to social scientists. A preoccupation with leadership occurs throughout countries with an Anglo-Saxon heritage. The *Oxford English Dictionary* notes the appearance of the word leader in the English language as early as 1300. The word leadership, however, did not appear until about 1800. When one reads the historical as well as the current literature on leaders and leadership, it seems as if there are as many different definitions as there are persons who have attempted to define the concepts. Perhaps an example will help clarify who is a leader and what leadership is.

Before Benjamin Franklin reached 30 years of age he had been chosen public printer for the colony of Pennsylvania, had founded the famous and influential Junto Club, and created and published *Poor Richard's Almanac* (the most widely read publication in America), had founded the first circulating library, and had been elected grand master of the Freemasons Lodge of Pennsylvania. The next year he inaugurated the first fire-fighting company in Pennsylvania and was chosen clerk of the Pennsylvania Assembly. He was one of the most successful businessmen in the colonies, but had enough interest in scholarship and research to be the founder (at age 37) of the American Philosophical Society. He continued to serve in a variety of leadership posts in politics, the army, science, diplomacy, and education (founding the academy that became the University of Pennsylvania). At 80 he led the group enterprise of writing the Constitution of the United States. A biographer noted, "Nobody could approach him without being charmed by his conversation, humor, wisdom, and kindness" (Fay, 1929).

How would you explain Benjamin Franklin's success as a leader? Was it due to his (pick only one)

1. Inborn, genetic traits?
2. Style of leadership?
3. Ability to influence others?
4. Occupation of positions of authority?
5. Ability to provide helpful behaviors in diverse situations?

In selecting one of these alternatives, you have decided on a theory of leadership. In this chapter we shall review each of these theories.

## EXERCISE 5.1:
## THE NATURE OF LEADERSHIP

There has been considerable controversy as to the nature of leadership. The purpose of this exercise is to structure a critical discussion of the different views of leadership. The procedure is as follows:

1. The class forms groups of four.
2. Each group is ultimately to write a report summarizing its position on the nature of leadership. The report is to contain the group's overall conclusions and the facts and rationale supporting its position. The supporting facts and rationale may be obtained from the accompanying briefing sheets, the entire book, and outside reading.
3. The sequence of the exercise contains two controversies:
   a. Are leaders pawns of history or are they origins (creators and controllers) of history?
   b. Are leaders born or made?
   For each controversy two briefing sheets are given, one representing one side of the argument and one the other.
4. Each group divides into pairs. One pair is assigned the position that leaders are pawns of history and the other pair the position that leaders are the origins of history. The coordinator gives each pair the appropriate briefing sheet, explains the procedure, and reviews the guidelines for constructive controversy (p. 282).
5. The pairs meet separately to prepare as forceful a 3-minute presentation of their position as possible. They are to make sure that both members have contributed to building a persuasive case for their position and that it includes as many facts and research findings as possible. Both members need to master all the rationale supporting their position. About 10 minutes should be allowed for this phase of the exercise.
6. The group of four meets. Each pair presents its position, being as forceful and persuasive as possible, while the other pair takes notes and asks for clarification of anything that is not fully understood. Each pair has about 3 minutes to present its position.
7. The group of four has an open discussion on whether leaders are pawns or origins. Each side should present as many facts and research findings as it can to support its point of view. Members should listen critically to the opposing position, asking for facts to support any conclusions made by the opposing pair. Participants should ensure that all the facts supporting both sides are brought out and discussed. The rules for constructive controversy should be followed. About 10 minutes should be allowed for this phase.
8. The perspectives in each group are now reversed, each pair arguing the opposing pair's position. Members should be as forceful and persuasive as they can in arguing for the opposing pair's position. They should elaborate on the opposing position, seeing if they can think of any new arguments or facts that the opposing pair did not present. Each pair has about 3 minutes for its presentation.
9. Each group of four should come to a group position that all members can agree on. The members should summarize the best arguments from each position, detailing as many facts as they can on whether leaders are pawns or origins. When they have consensus in their group they should organize their arguments for presentation to the rest of the class. Since other groups will have other conclusions, each group may need to explain the validity of its position to the class. About 10 minutes should be allowed for this phase.
10. The coordinator samples the decisions made by the groups of four by having several of them present their position to the class. The class then discusses similarities and differences, and the coordinator summarizes what participants have learned about leadership.

11. Steps 1–10 are repeated for the issue of whether leaders are born or made.
12. The coordinator summarizes what the participants have learned from the two controversies.

### Briefing Sheet: Leaders Control Fortune

Your position is that leaders basically control fortune and that it really matters who is elected president of the United States or president of General Motors, as they determine the future. To support your position, use the following quotations from *The Prince* by Machiavelli and any material from this chapter that is applicable.

> One who adapts his policy to the times prospers, and likewise . . . one whose policy clashes with the demands of the times does not.

> It can be observed that with two circumspect men, one will achieve his end, the other not; and likewise two men succeed equally well with different methods, one of them being circumspect and the other impetuous. This results from nothing else except the extent to which their methods are or are not suited to the nature of the times.

> If a man behaves with patience and circumspection and the time and circumstances are such that this method is called for, he will prosper, but if the time and circumstances change he will be ruined because he does not change his policy. Thus a man who is circumspect, when circumstances demand impetuous behavior, is unequal to the task, and so he comes to grief. If he changed his character according to the time and circumstances, then his fortune (that is, prosperity) would change.

### Briefing Sheet: Leaders Are Pawns of Fortune

Your position is that leaders are basically pawns of fortune and that it does not really matter who is president of the United States or president of General Motors, because the future turns out the same regardless of who is in charge. To support your position, use the following quotations from *War and Peace* by Leo Tolstoy and any material from the chapter that seems applicable.

> Man lives consciously for himself, but is an unconscious instrument in the attainment of the historic, universal, aims of humanity. . . . The higher a man stands on the social ladder, the more people he is connected with and the more power he has over others, the more evident is the predestination and inevitability of his every action.

> A king is history's slave.

> History . . . uses every moment of the life of kings as a tool for its own purposes.

### Briefing Sheet: Leaders Are Born, Not Made

Your position is that leaders are basically born, not made. To support your position, use the information given below, any material from this chapter or the rest of the book that seems applicable, and any information from your outside reading that is appropriate.

> Throughout history there has been a continuing popular belief that leaders possess unique, inborn traits. Aristotle, for example, once remarked, "From the moment of their birth, some are marked for subjugation and others for command." There are individuals who seem to rise to leadership in a range of settings. Woods (1913) studied 14 nations over periods of five to ten centuries. The conditions of each reign

were found to reflect the ruler's capabilities. The brothers of the more successful kings, furthermore, were found to be men of power and influence in their time. Woods concluded that the person makes the nation and shapes it in accordance with his or her abilities. Wiggam (1931) concluded that the survival of the fittest and marriage among them produce an aristocratic class that differs biologically from the lower classes. Thus an adequate supply of superior leaders depends on a proportionately high birth rate among the abler classes. The best predictor of leadership ability, therefore, may be family background.

### Briefing Sheet: Leaders Are Made, Not Born

Your position is that leaders are basically made, not born. To support your position, use the information given below, any material from this chapter or the rest of the book that seems applicable, and any information from your outside reading that is relevant.

Leadership competencies and skills are learned, and anyone with certain minimal requirements can acquire them. A number of studies have demonstrated that schoolchildren are more successful and effective leaders after receiving training in leadership skills (Cassel & Shafer, 1961; Eicher & Merrill, 1933; Zeleny, 1940). It is not uncommon for individuals to practice and master the skills of leadership needed by the groups to which they belong. Schneider (1937) found that the number of great military leaders in England was proportional to the number of conflicts in which the nation engaged. Since leadership skills can be taught and individuals can become more successful leaders through training, and since individuals may deliberately develop the leadership competencies needed by the groups to which they belong, it may be concluded that leaders are made, not born.

### EXERCISE 5.2:
### OUR IDEAL LEADERS

The purpose of this exercise is to identify the traits possessed by ideal leaders in our society. The procedure for the exercise is as follows.

1. The class forms heterogeneous groups of four.
2. Each group is to
   a. Read the assignment sheet that appears below.
   b. Pick at least five great leaders who have lived in the last 50 years.
   c. List the qualities of each that made him or her great.
   d. Decide by consensus the ten most important traits of a great leader.
3. Each group reads its list to the class. Note differences and similarities.
4. Compare the qualities identified by the groups with the material in this chapter.

### Ideal Leaders Assignment Sheet

Every society identifies traits characteristic of its ideal leaders. The ancient Egyptians, for example, attributed three qualities of divinity to their king (Frankfort, Frankfort, Wilson, & Jacobsen, 1949): "Authoritative utterance is in thy mouth, perception is in thy heart, and thy tongue is the shrine of justice." An analysis of leaders in Homer's Iliad resulted in four sets of ideal leadership qualities admired by ancient Greeks (Sarachek, 1968): (1) justice and judgment (Agamemnon), (2) wisdom and counsel (Nestor), (3) shrewdness and cunning (Odysseus), and (4) valor and action (Achilles). What are the qualities we most admire in our outstanding leaders?

# TRAIT THEORIES OF LEADERSHIP

Perhaps Benjamin Franklin was one of the greatest leaders of the eighteenth century because he was genetically superior to his contemporaries. Throughout history many people have believed that leaders are born, not made, and that great leaders are discovered, not developed. Especially in times of great social upheaval and trouble many people have looked for a great leader who has unique, inborn traits. This is the "great-man" or "great-woman" theory of leadership. Royalty, members of elite social classes, older siblings, and early maturers are likely to believe in this approach to leadership. One of the strongest advocates of this theory of leadership was Aristotle, who once stated, "From the moment of their birth, some are marked for subjugation and others for command." There do seem to be individuals who dominate others through the force of their personality, their charisma, what they stand for, or their ability to manipulate others. And there have been historical periods when the prevailing ideology was that leaders are superior to other human beings.

In the early twentieth century there were many strong advocates of the trait theories of leadership. Wiggam (1931), for example, concluded that the survival of the fittest and marriage among them produce an aristocratic class that differs biologically from the lower classes. Advocating the social Darwinism that was popular at that time, Wiggam took the position that an adequate supply of superior leaders depended on a proportionately high birth rate among the abler classes. Henry Ford remarked, "The question 'Who should be boss?' is like asking 'Who ought to be the tenor in the quartet?' Obviously, the man who can sing tenor." He was suggesting the boss is a person who has the natural ability to lead. The historian Thomas Carlyle believed that genius would exert its influence wherever it was found.

Hundreds of research studies have been conducted to identify the personal attributes of leaders. In one of the more interesting ones, Frederick Adams Woods (1913), an early-twentieth-century American historian, examined 386 rulers in 14 countries in Western Europe who lived between A.D. 1000 and the French Revolution. All these rulers had absolute power over their kingdoms. Each was classified as strong, weak, or mediocre on the basis of knowledge about his or her intellectual and personal characteristics (which were presumably independent of the strength or weakness of the nation at that time). The condition of each country was also classified as prosperous, declining, or lacking a clear indication of either. (This classification was based on the country's economic and political status, not on its artistic, educational, and scientific development.) Woods found a relationship between the monarchs' personalities and the state of the countries. He summarized his results as follows: "Strong, mediocre, and weak monarchs are associated with strong, mediocre, and weak periods respectively" (p. 246). Although the correlation coefficient was reasonably strong (between $+0.60$ and $+0.70$), as with any correlation we cannot infer a direct relationship between cause and effect. However, Woods favored the interpretations that strong leaders cause their countries to flourish.

The typical research studies on trait theories have compared the characteristics of a leader (defined as an individual holding a position of authority, such as the president of the United States) with the characteristics of a follower (defined as an individual not holding a position of authority, such as a low-level government employee). The findings of these studies are somewhat contradictory and inconclusive. Bird (1940) analyzed the results of 20 studies that had considered 79 leadership traits. He found little consistency in the results from one study to another. Of the 79 traits, 51 made a difference in only one study each. High degrees of 4 traits—intelligence, initiative, sense of humor, and extroversion—were identified often enough in leaders for Bird to consider them "general traits of leadership." Mann (1959) reviewed 125 studies of leadership and personality characteristics representing over 700 findings (see Table 5.1). He concluded that intelligence and personal adjustment seem to be correlated with leadership.

There may be leaders who are more intelligent than nonleaders, yet it is evident that many of the most intelligent people never obtain positions of leadership. Intelligence may have been a prerequisite for Benjamin Franklin's type of leadership, but it is doubtful whether Franklin or John Adams or George Washington possessed the highest IQ of their period (Cox, 1926). A follow-up study of 1,000 highly intelligent children from California showed that in 25 years relatively few of them had reached the roster of famous leaders (Terman & Odor, 1947). None had attained high political office or the presidency of a corporation or college. Only 5 percent were in *Who's Who* and only 13 percent were in *American Men of Science*. And despite the findings that leaders are better adjusted psychologically than nonleaders, many leaders (such as Adolf Hitler) showed signs of being emotionally disturbed.

Stimulated by the personnel testing and selection programs begun during World War I, social scientists attempted to identify the distinguishing traits of leaders. On these tests leaders were found to score higher than followers on a wide variety of characteristics, including intelligence and aptitude, personality, task motivation and performance, and social competence (Stogdill, 1974). Despite the great

**Table 5.1**  Percentage of Significant Relationships Reported in a Positive or Negative Direction for 125 Studies, Representing 751 Findings on the Relationship of Various Personality Characteristics and Leadership.

| Personality Factors and Number of Studies of Each | Number of Findings | Percent Yielding Sig. Positive Relationship | Percent Yielding Sig. Negative Relationship | Percent Yielding Neither |
|---|---|---|---|---|
| Intelligence, 28 | (196) | 46% (91) | 1%[1] (1) | 53% (104) |
| Adjustment, 22 | (164) | 30% (50) | 2%[1] (2) | 68% (112) |
| Extroversion, 22 | (119) | 31% (37) | 5% (6) | 64% (76) |
| Dominance, 12 | (39) | 38% (15) | 15% (6) | 46% (18) |
| Masculinity, 9 | (70) | 16% (11) | 1%[1] (1) | 83% (58) |
| Conservatism, 17 | (62) | 5% (3) | 27% (17) | 68% (42) |
| Sensitivity, 15 | (101) | 15% (15) | 1%[1] (1) | 84% (85) |

[1]Rounded upward.

Source: R. Mann, "A Review of the Relationship Between Personality and Performance in Small Groups." *Psychological Bulletin*, 1959, 56, 241–270. Reprinted by permission.

ingenuity displayed in the development of tests to measure these characteristics, however, such instruments have not proved reliably useful in the selection of leaders.

Although the correlations between individual traits and leadership measures are not large, some conclusions may be made. Stogdill (1974) divided the research on this subject into two periods: studies conducted between 1904 and 1947 and studies conducted between 1948 and 1970. The former body of research, he noted, revealed that leaders who participated actively in organizing cooperative tasks and carrying them through to completion were characterized by intelligence, alertness to the needs and motives of others, insight into situations, and such habits as responsibility, initiative, persistence, and self-confidence. The trait studies conducted between 1948 and 1970 indicated that leaders who have the capacity for organizing and expediting cooperative efforts are characterized by a strong drive for responsibility and task completion, vigor and persistence in pursuit of goals, venturesomeness and originality in problem solving, a drive to exercise initiative in social situations, self-confidence and a sense of personal identity, willingness to accept the consequences of decisions and actions, readiness to absorb interpersonal stress, readiness to tolerate frustration and delay, ability to influence the behavior of others, and the capacity to structure social systems according to the purpose at hand.

These characteristics seem to differentiate (1) leaders from nonleaders, (2) effective from ineffective leaders, and (3) higher-echelon from lower-echelon leaders. Stogdill (1974) added, however, that when these characteristics are considered singly they hold little diagnostic or predictive significance. In combination they appear to be advantageous to the person seeking the responsibilities of leadership. Stogdill also noted that whether any one person with these characteristics rises to a leadership position depends considerably on chance: one must not only have the traits but also be in the right place at the right time. Perhaps the safest conclusion to draw from the trait and personality studies of leadership is that individuals who have the energy, drive, self-confidence, and determination to succeed will become leaders, because they work hard to get leadership positions.

Simon Bolivar once said, "Man is the weak toy of fortune." The trait theory of leadership gains some support when it is combined with social determinism. The **social determinism** or Zeitgeist theory of history states that historic events are determined by social forces, social movements, and changing social values. *Zeitgeist* means "spirit of the times" or "temper of the times." Leaders simply play out roles designed for them by broad social forces. As Victor Hugo wrote, "there is nothing in this world so powerful as an idea whose time has come." Dean Simonton (1979), for example, analyzed why certain scientists rise notably above their peers and suggested that sheer chance and the influence of the Zeitgeist and previous technological discoveries are more important determinants of scientific eminence than personal traits. The trait and social determinism views are combined in the view that the great person plays a unique and decisive role only when the historical situation permits major alternative paths of development (Hook, 1955). Only when choices exist does the great person influence history.

What makes one person a successful leader while another person fails in the same position? Some leaders (Napoleon, Hitler, Mao Tse-tung) have been able to control the destinies of millions of people. There are, however, at least four problems with trying to identify the traits of leaders: (1) an unlimited number of leadership traits may be identified, (2) different traits may be needed under different conditions, (3) "great" leaders are identified after the fact, but who will become a great leader cannot be predicted ahead of time, and (4) a match between the Zeitgeist and the great person may be required for great leadership to occur. In addition, there has been a biased focus on "great men" as leaders and a relative inattention to "great women." Perhaps the best predictor of leadership success is prior success in leadership roles (Stogdill, 1974).

Besides the extensive research trying to differentiate leaders from non-leaders on the basis of personal attributes, there has been considerable discussion and research on two major traits of some leaders: charisma and Machiavellianism.

## Charismatic Leaders

One of the dictionary definitions of **charisma** is "an extraordinary power, as of working miracles." Sometimes charismatic leaders seem to inspire their followers to love and be passionately devoted to them. Other times charismatic leaders offer their followers the promise and hope of deliverance from distress. Charismatic leaders are saviors who say in essence, "I will make you safe," "I will give you identity," or "I will give your life significance and meaning."

Charisma does not seem to be correlated with any one personality type. The personalities of Alexander, Julius Caesar, George Washington, Robespierre, Bolivar, Sun Yat-sen, and Gandhi were widely different, yet these individuals were all able to inspire confidence in their followers and to demand from them the sacrifice even of life itself. Garibaldi won the loyalty of his Roman soldiers with an unusual appeal: "What I have to offer you is fatigue, danger, struggle, and death; the chill of the cold night in the fall air, and heat under the burning sun; no lodgings, no provisions, but forced marches, dangerous watchposts, and the continual struggle with the bayonet against batteries—those who love freedom and their country may follow me!"

Winston Churchill offered "blood, sweat, and tears," but sustained the faith and courage of millions.

Attempts to define charisma specifically and to measure the degree of charisma possessed by various leaders have failed. In general, however, a **charismatic leader** has (1) an extraordinary power or vision and is able to communicate it to others or (2) unusual powers of practical leadership that will enable her to achieve the goals that will alleviate followers' distress. The charismatic leader has a sense of mission, a belief in the social-change movement he or she leads, and confidence in himself or herself as the chosen instrument to lead the movement to its destination. The leader appears extremely self-confident in order to inspire others with the faith that the movement he or she leads will prevail and ultimately reduce their distress.

## Machiavellianism

Current theories of leadership ignore not only the irrational aspects of leadership and followership reflected in charisma but also the realities of how power is often handled. If charismatic leaders found social movements and bring them to power, it is the Machiavellian leaders who consolidate and wield the power the charismatic leaders obtain. The essence of **Machiavellian leadership** is believing (1) that people are basically weak, fallible, and gullible, and not particularly trustworthy; (2) that others are impersonal objects; and (3) that one should manipulate others whenever it is necessary in order to achieve one's ends.

Niccolo Machiavelli (1469–1527) was a Florentine statesman whose treatise *The Prince* advocated the use of craft, duplicity, and cunning by rulers as political principles for increasing their power and success. He did not originate such an approach. Throughout history there have been theorists who conceived of leadership essentially in terms of the possession and exercise of power for self-enhancement. After analyzing the historical literature on how political leaders should govern, Richard Christie (Christie & Geis, 1970) concluded that Machiavellian leaders who manipulate their followers for political and personal reasons have four characteristics. First, they have little emotional involvement in their interpersonal relationships, as it is easier to manipulate others if they are viewed as objects rather than as fellow humans. Second, since they take a utilitarian rather than a moral view of their interactions with others, they are not concerned with conventional morality. Third, because successful manipulation of followers depends on an accurate perception of their needs and of "reality" in general, they will not be grossly psychopathological. Finally, since the essence of successful manipulation is a focus on getting things done rather than achieving long-term ideological goals, Machiavellian leaders will have a low degree of ideological commitment.

## EXERCISE 5.3:
## INTERPERSONAL PATTERNS

This exercise focuses on your interaction with other members of your group. It may help you think about how you conduct yourself in a group. The procedure for the exercise is as follows:

1. The class divides into groups of three. Each person fills out the adjective checklist below.
2. Analyze the meaning of the adjectives you checked by following the instructions below the checklist.
3. Share with the other two members of your triad the results of the exercise, and ask for their comments on whether they perceive you in the same way or differently.

The 20 verbs listed below describe some of the ways people feel and act from time to time. Think of your behavior in groups. How do you feel and act in groups? Check the five verbs that best describe your behavior in groups as you see it.

| | | | |
|---|---|---|---|
| _____ | acquiesce | _____ | disapprove |
| _____ | advise | _____ | evade |
| _____ | agree | _____ | initiate |
| _____ | analyze | _____ | judge |
| _____ | assist | _____ | lead |
| _____ | concede | _____ | oblige |
| _____ | concur | _____ | relinquish |
| _____ | coordinate | _____ | resist |
| _____ | criticize | _____ | retreat |
| _____ | direct | _____ | withdraw |

There are two underlying patterns of interpersonal behavior represented in the list of objectives: *dominance* (authority or control) and *sociability* (intimacy or friendliness). Most individuals tend either to like to control things (high dominance) or to let others control things (low dominance). Similarly, most persons tend either to be warm and personal (high sociability) or to be somewhat cold and impersonal (low sociability). In the diagram below,

| | HIGH DOMINANCE | LOW DOMINANCE |
|---|---|---|
| **HIGH SOCIABILITY** | advises<br>coordinates<br>directs<br>initiates<br>leads | acquiesces<br>agrees<br>assists<br>complies<br>obliges |
| **LOW SOCIABILITY** | analyzes<br>criticizes<br>disapproves<br>judges<br>resists | concedes<br>evades<br>relinquishes<br>retreats<br>withdraws |

circle the five verbs you used to describe yourself in group activities. The set of ten verbs—horizontal for the dominance dimension and vertical for the sociability dimension—in which three or more are circled represents your tendency in that pattern of interpersonal behavior.

## LEADERSHIP STYLES

Perhaps Benjamin Franklin became a leader through his style of relating to others. Franklin was noted for his charm, conversational skills, humor, wisdom, and kindness. But was Franklin's leadership style the same as George Washington's or Thomas Jefferson's? Even casual observation of leaders in action reveals marked differences in their styles of leadership. Some leaders seem autocratic: they dictate orders and determine all policy without involving group members in decision making. Some leaders seem democratic: They set policies through group discussion and decision, encouraging and helping group members to interact, requesting the cooperation of others, and being considerate of members' feelings and needs. Finally, some leaders take a laissez-faire approach: They do not participate in their group's decision making at all. It seems obvious that such differences in leadership style should affect group productivity and the attitudes of group members.

The pioneering study of whether leadership styles do in fact make a difference in group functioning was conducted by Lewin, Lippitt, and White (1939). Although the study has many shortcomings, it demonstrated strikingly that the same group of individuals will behave in markedly different ways under leaders who behave differently. As we have seen in Chapter 1, groups of 10- and 11-year-olds were run by three adult leaders who adopted each of three leadership styles for a specified period: autocratic, democratic, or laissez-faire. When the groups were under an autocratic leader, they were more dependent on the leader and more egocentric in their peer relationships. When rotated to a democratic style of leadership, the same children evidenced more initiative, friendliness, and responsibility and continued to work even when the leader was out of the room. Their interest in their work and in the quality of their product was higher. Aggressive acts were more frequent under autocratic and laissez-faire leaders than they were under a democratic leader. Hostility was 30 times as great in the autocratic groups than in either of the other two: Frequently one group member was made the target of hostility and aggression until he or she left the group, and then another member would be chosen to perform the same function. Nineteen of 20 members liked the democratic leader better than the autocrat, and 7 of 10 liked the laissez-faire leader better than the autocrat.

Since this classic study a number of researchers have investigated the relative impact of democratic and autocratic leaders on group functioning. In reviewing these studies Stogdill (1974) noted that neither democratic nor autocratic leadership can be advocated as a method for increasing productivity, but that member satisfaction is associated with a democratic style of leadership. Satisfaction with democratic leadership tends to be highest in small, interaction-oriented groups. Other studies have compared permissive, follower-oriented, participative, and considerate leadership styles with restrictive, task-oriented, directive, socially distant, and structured leadership styles. After reviewing the studies in each of these areas, Stogdill (1974) reached the following conclusions:

1. Person-oriented styles of leadership are not consistently related to productivity.
2. Among the work-oriented leadership styles, socially distant, directive, and structured leader behaviors that tend to maintain role differentiation and let members know what to expect are consistently related to group productivity.
3. Among the person-oriented leadership styles, only those providing for member participation in decision making and showing concern for members' welfare and comfort are consistently related to group cohesiveness.
4. Among the work-oriented leadership styles, only the structuring of member expectations is uniformly related to group cohesiveness.
5. All of the person-oriented leadership styles tend to be related to member satisfaction.
6. Only the structuring of member expectations is related positively to member satisfaction among the work-oriented leadership styles.

Initiating structure by clearly defining one's role as a leader and what one expects from the other members of the group is the single style of leadership that contributes positively to group productivity, cohesiveness, and satisfaction. The most effective leaders may be those who show concern for the well-being and contributions of group members and at the same time structure members' role responsibilities.

The Lewin, Lippitt, and White (1939) study, along with other research conducted by Lewin and his colleagues, helped to inspire and initiate the training programs in applied group dynamics and conducted for the past 30 years at Bethel, Maine, by the National Training Laboratories Institute of Applied Behavioral Science. Immediately after World War II, a group of adult educators and Kurt Lewin and his associates began conducting workshops aimed at developing the leadership competencies of participants. These workshops formed the basis for the explosion of small-group methods for personal and organizational change that took place during the 1960s and the growth in the number of consultants concerned with improving the development and planned change of organizations.

The major shortcomings of the style approach to leadership are that (1) different styles are effective under different conditions and (2) an unlimited number of styles may be identified. Certain conditions exist, for example, under which autocratic leadership seems more effective (such as when an urgent decision has to be made). In other conditions a democratic style may be most effective (such as when considerable member commitment to the implementation of the decision needs to be built). There are even conditions in which the laissez-faire style seems best (such as when the group is committed to a decision, has the resources to implement it, and needs a minimum of interference to work effectively). Because different leadership styles seem to be required in different situations, even with the same group, the attention of many social scientists has moved to situational approaches to leadership. But before considering such approaches, two other theories of leadership are briefly discussed.

# THE INFLUENCE THEORY OF LEADERSHIP

> A leader is a man who has the ability to get other people to do what they don't want to do, and like it.
>
> *Harry S Truman*

> Leadership is the ability to decide what is to be done, and then to get others to want to do it.
>
> *Dwight D. Eisenhower*

> Leadership appears to be the art of getting others to want to do something that you are convinced should be done.
>
> *Vance Packard, The Pyramid Climbers*

Benjamin Franklin may have been an outstanding leader because he knew how to influence people. An **influence leader** may be defined as a group member who exerts more influence on other members than they exert on him or her. A number of studies have examined the factors affecting the amount of influence a leader has on the attitudes and behaviors of groupmates. Michener and Burt (1975), for example, found that the compliance of members is greater when a leader justifies his demands as being good for the group, has the power to punish members who do not do as he has asked, and has a legitimate right to make demands of subordinates. The success or failure of the group does not seem to affect a leader's ability to influence, nor does approval of him by subordinates.

An **influence approach to leadership** implies that there is a reciprocal role relationship between leaders and followers in which an exchange, or transaction, takes place. Without followers there can be no leader, and without a leader there can be no followers. The leader and the followers both give something to and receive something from each other. As Homans stated, "Influence over others is purchased at the price of allowing oneself to be influenced by others" (1961, p. 286). While leadership may be defined as the successful influencing of other group members, the followers also influence the leader. The leader receives status, recognition, esteem, and other reinforcement for contributing his or her resources to the accomplishment of the group's goals. The followers obtain the leaders' resources and ability to structure the group's activities toward the attainment of a goal. The leader provides structure, direction, and resources. The followers provide deference and reinforcement. Because both the leader and the followers control resources that the other desires, they can each influence the other's behavior.

The interdependence of leader and followers has been demonstrated by a number of studies. Research indicates, for example, that leaders tend both to talk more than other group members and to receive more communications than do other group members (Zander, 1979). When a person is reinforced and encouraged by other group members to engage in active leadership behaviors, the person's proportion of talking time increases as one's perceived leadership status increases (Bavelas, Hostorf, Gross, & Kite, 1965; Zdep & Oakes, 1967). Pepinsky and his associates (1958) demonstrated that individuals who have previously exhibited few leadership

behaviors were influenced to behave far more actively in such behaviors by the group's evident support for their assertions; individuals who had previously exhibited many leadership behaviors in earlier situations were affected in precisely the opposite way by the group's evident disagreement with their statements. From these and other studies, it may be concluded that (1) the amount of participation and influence by a leader affects members' perceptions of his or her leadership, and (2) the amount of encouragement and support by followers affects the amount of a person's participation and perceived leadership status.

Viewing leadership as a reciprocal influence between a leader and a set of followers does not necessarily mean that leadership is based on domination. Hitler, for example, defined leadership as the ability to move the masses (either through persuasion or violence). Ho Chi Minh once stated that a good leader must learn to mold, shape, and change the people just as a woodworker must learn to use wood. Both views are erroneous. Leaders do not influence through domination and coercion. The influence of leaders is directed toward persuading group members to cooperate in setting and achieving goals. Leadership is thus the art of ensuring that group members work together with the least friction and the most cooperation. This often means that leaders need to persuade and inspire members to follow their views of what needs to be done in order to achieve a group's goals.

## ROLE POSITION/GROUP STRUCTURE APPROACH TO LEADERSHIP

Perhaps Benjamin Franklin was known as a leader simply because he was appointed to various leadership positions. Whenever two or more individuals join together to achieve a goal, a group structure develops. The **group structure** consists of role definitions and group norms that structure the interaction among group members. A **role** is a set of expected behaviors associated with a position within a group. A **norm** is essentially a rule that specifies acceptable behavior in the group. Once a formal structure is established, it is largely independent of the particular individuals who compose the group. The formal role system (for example, president, vice-president, manager, supervisor, worker) defines the hierarchy of authority. **Authority** is legitimate power, power vested in a particular position to ensure that individuals in subordinate positions meet the requirements of their organizational role. A supervisor, for example, is given the authority to ensure that workers are doing their job. Because organizational law demands that subordinates obey their supervisors in matters of role performance, a person with authority will influence his or her subordinates. A person who is directly above you in the authority hierarchy, therefore, is your leader.

There are at least three problems with the role position approach to leadership. First, it is unclear how individuals are appointed to high-authority positions. It does not have to be for leadership ability. Second, it does not explain how the leader can engage in nonleadership behaviors and the subordinates can engage in leadership actions. Not all of the appointed leader's actions are leadership behaviors. In addition, subordinates can provide leadership. Third, the role behavior of subordinates is influenced by outsiders who have no direct authority over them.

**EXERCISE 5.4:**
**YOUR LEADERSHIP ACTIONS I**

Any action that helps a group complete its task is a leadership action. Any action that helps a group maintain effective working relationships among its members is a leadership action. When you are a member of a group, what leadership actions do you engage in? How do you influence other group members to complete the task and maintain collaborative relationships? This exercise has two purposes: (1) to make you more aware of your typical leadership actions and (2) to make your group more aware of its patterns of leadership. The procedure for the exercise is as follows:

1. Working by yourself, complete the following questionnaire.
2. Determine your score and place it on the task-maintenance grid in Figure 5.1
3. In your group, place all members' scores on the task-maintenance grid. With the other members of your group, write a description of the leadership pattern of your group. Then write a description of how this pattern may be improved.

## Understanding Your Leadership Actions Questionnaire

Each of the following items describes a leadership action. In the space next to each item write 5 if you *always* behave that way, 4 if you *frequently* behave that way, 3 if you *occasionally* behave that way, 2 if you *seldom* behave that way, and 1 if you *never* behave that way. When I am a member of a group:

_____  1. I offer facts and give my opinions, ideas, feelings, and information in order to help the group discussion.

_____  2. I warmly encourage all members of the group to participate. I am open to their ideas. I let them know I value their contributions to the group.

_____  3. I ask for facts, information, opinions, ideas, and feelings from the other group members in order to help the group discussion.

_____  4. I help communicate among group members by using good communication skills. I make sure that each group member understands what the others say.

_____  5. I give direction to the group by planning how to go on with the group work and by calling attention to the tasks that need to be done. I assign responsibilities to different group members.

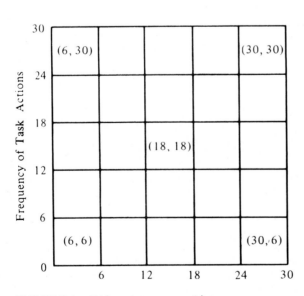

**FIGURE 5.1.**   Task-maintenance grid.

_____ 6. I tell jokes and suggest interesting ways of doing the work in order to reduce tension in the group and increase the fun we have working together.

_____ 7. I pull together related ideas or suggestions made by group members and restate and summarize the major points discussed by the group.

_____ 8. I observe the way the group is working and use my observations to help discuss how the group can work together better.

_____ 9. I give the group energy. I encourage group members to work hard to achieve our goals.

_____ 10. I promote the open discussion of conflicts among group members in order to resolve disagreements and increase group cohesiveness. I mediate conflicts among members when they seem unable to resolve them directly.

_____ 11. I ask others to summarize what the group has been discussing in order to ensure that they understand group decisions and comprehend the material being discussed by the group.

_____ 12. I express support, acceptance, and liking for other members of the group and give appropriate praise when another member has taken a constructive action in the group.

To obtain a total score for task actions and maintenance actions, write the score for each item in the appropriate column and then add the columns.

*TASK ACTIONS*

_____ 1. information and opinion giver
_____ 3. information and opinion seeker
_____ 5. direction and role definer
_____ 7. summarizer
_____ 9. energizer
_____ 11. comprehension checker

_____ Total for Task Actions

*MAINTENANCE ACTIONS*

_____ 2. encourager of participation
_____ 4. communication facilitator
_____ 6. tension reliever
_____ 8. process observer
_____ 10. interpersonal problem solver
_____ 12. supporter and praiser

_____ Total for Maintenance Actions

### Description of Task-Maintenance Patterns

(6,6) Only a minimum effort is given to getting the required work done. There is general noninvolvement with other group members. The person with this score may well be saying, "To hell with it all." Or he or she may be so inactive in the group as to have no influence whatsoever on other group members.

(6,30) High value is placed on keeping good relationships within the group. Thoughtful attention is given to the needs of other members. The person with this score helps create a comfortable, friendly atmosphere and work tempo. However, he or she may never help the group get any work accomplished.

(30,6) Getting the job done is emphasized in a way that shows very little concern with group maintenance. Work is seen as important, and relationships among group members are ignored. The person with this score may take an army-drillmaster approach to leadership.

(18,18) The task and maintenance needs of the group are balanced. The person with this score continually makes compromises between task needs and maintenance needs. Though a great compromiser, this person does not look for or find ways to creatively integrate task and maintenance activities for optimal productivity.

(30,30) When everyone plans and makes decisions together, all the members become committed to getting the task done as they build relationships of trust and respect. A high value is placed on sound, creative decisions that result in understanding and agreement. Ideas and opinions are sought and listened to, even when they differ from one's own. The group as a whole defines the task and works to get it done. The creative combining of both task and maintenance needs is encouraged.

## Matching Exercise 1

To help you learn the task and maintenance actions, match the following terms with their definitions (answers on page 193).

### TASK ACTIONS

_____ 1. Information and opinion giver
_____ 2. Information and opinion seeker
_____ 3. Direction and role definer
_____ 4. Summarizer
_____ 5. Energizer
_____ 6. Comprehension checker

### MAINTENANCE ACTIONS

_____ 7. Encourager of participation
_____ 8. Communication facilitator
_____ 9. Tension releaser
_____ 10. Process observer
_____ 11. Interpersonal problem solver
_____ 12. Supporter and praiser

a. Makes sure all group members understand what each other says.
b. Pulls together related ideas or suggestions and restates them.
c. Offers facts, opinions, ideas, feelings, and information.
d. Expresses acceptance and liking for group members.
e. Uses observations of how the group is working to help discuss how the group can improve.
f. Lets members know their contributions are valued.
g. Asks for facts, opinions, ideas, feelings, and information.
h. Asks others to summarize discussion to make sure they understand.
i. Encourages group members to work hard to achieve goals.
j. Calls attention to tasks that need to be done and assigns responsibilities.
k. Helps resolve and mediate conflicts.
l. Tells jokes and increases the group fun.

## Matching Exercise 2

Match the following statements with the task or maintenance action they best seem to fill (answers on page 193).

### TASK ACTIONS

_____ 1. Information and opinion giver
_____ 2. Information and opinion seeker
_____ 3. Direction and role definer
_____ 4. Summarizer
_____ 5. Energizer
_____ 6. Comprehension checker

### MAINTENANCE ACTIONS

_____ 7. Encourager of participation
_____ 8. Communication facilitator
_____ 9. Tension releaser
_____ 10. Process observer
_____ 11. Interpersonal problem solver
_____ 12. Supporter and praiser

a. "Does everyone in the group understand Helen's idea?"
b. "How about giving our report on yoga while standing on our heads?"
c. "Edye's idea seems like Buddy's; I think they could be combined."
d. "I think we should openly discuss the conflict between Dave and Linda to help resolve it."
e. "Before we go on, let me tell you how other groups have solved this task."
f. "We need a time-keeper. Keith, why don't you do that?"
g. "I really enjoy this group. I especially enjoy Roger's sense of humor."
h. "I think we'd find a good solution if we put a little more work into it."
i. "Frank, tell us what we've said so far to see if you understand it correctly."
j. "We seem to be suggesting solutions before we're ready. Let's define the problem first."
k. "I don't understand. What do you mean?"
l. "Helen, I'd like to hear what you think about this; you have such good ideas."

## SITUATIONAL THEORIES OF LEADERSHIP

Perhaps Benjamin Franklin became a renowned leader because he was able to vary his behavior systematically from situation to situation so as to provide the appropriate leadership actions at the appropriate time. There is currently a consensus among social scientists that leadership skills and competencies are not inherited from one's ancestors, that they do not magically appear when a person is assigned to a leadership position, and that the same set of competencies will not provide adequate leadership in every situation. Different situations require different approaches to leadership. We shall discuss five situational theories in this chapter: the distributed-actions theory, Bale's interaction-process analysis, Fiedler's situational theory, and Hersey and Blanchard's situational theory, and Vroom's normative model of leadership.

## The Distributed-Actions Theory of Leadership

> Not the cry, but the flight of the wild duck, leads the flock to fly and follow.
> *Chinese proverb*

Groups have at least two basic objectives: to complete a task and to maintain effective collaborative relationships among the members. The **distributed-actions theory of leadership** emphasizes that certain functions need to be filled if a group is to meet these two objectives. It defines leadership as the performance of acts that help the group to complete its task and to maintain effective working relationships among its members. For a group to complete its task successfully, group members must obtain, organize, and use information to make a decision. This requires members to engage in the **task-leadership actions** of contributing, asking for, summarizing, and coordinating the information. Members have to structure and give direction to the group's efforts and provide the energy to motivate efforts to make the decision. For any group to be successful, such task-leadership actions have to be provided.

But it does no good to complete a task if the manner of doing so alienates several group members. If a number of group members refuse to come to the next meeting, the group has not been successful. Thus, members must pay attention to maintaining good working relationships while working on the task. The task must be completed in a way that increases the ability of group members to work together effectively in the future. For this to happen, certain **maintenance-leadership actions** are needed. Members have to encourage one another to participate. They have to relieve tension when it gets too high, facilitate communication among themselves, and evaluate the emotional climate of the group. They have to discuss how the group's work can be improved, and they have to listen carefully and respectfully to one another. These leadership actions are necessary for the maintenance of friendly relationships among members and, indeed, for the success of the group.

Leadership actions tend to be performed by the individuals most concerned with achieving the group's goals. Among the survivors of the plane crash in the Andes (Read, 1974), Marcelo took responsibility for organizing the group into work squads and controlled the rationing of their meager food supplies. Marcelo turned out to be

an admirable leader in terms of getting many necessary tasks accomplished such as finding drinking water and caring for the injured. But he did not satisfy the emotional needs of the group. By the ninth day, the survivors were becoming more and more depressed and discouraged, and Marcelo began crying silently to himself at night. Several members, as if to offset Marcelo's inability to cheer up the survivors, become more positive and friendly, actively trying to reduce conflict. The only surviving female (Liliana Methol), for example, became a "unique source of solace" for the men and seemed to take the place of their mothers and sweethearts. One of the younger boys "called her his god-mother, and she responded to him and the others with comforting words and gentle optimism" (Read, 1974, p. 74). In this extreme setting, where the lives of the group's members were at stake, both task and maintenance leadership actions were required.

The distributed-actions theory of leadership includes two basic ideas: (1) any member of a group may become a leader by taking actions that help the group complete its task and maintain effective collaborative relationships; (2) any leadership function may be fulfilled by different members performing a variety of relevant behaviors. Leadership, therefore, is specific to a particular group in a particular situation. Under specific circumstances, any given behavior may or may not be helpful; under another set, it may impair the effectiveness of the group. For example, when a group is trying to define a problem, suggesting a possible solution may not be helpful; however, when the group is making various solutions to a defined problem, suggesting a possible solution may indeed be helpful.

From the perspective of this theory, leadership is a learned set of skills that anyone with certain minimal requirements can acquire. Responsible group membership and leadership both depend on flexible behavior, the ability to diagnose what behaviors are needed at a particular time in order for the group to function most efficiently, and the ability to fulfill these behaviors or to get other members to fulfill them. A skilled member or leader, therefore, has to have diagnostic skills in order to be aware that a given function is needed in the group, and he or she must be sufficiently adaptive to provide the diverse types of behaviors needed for different conditions. In addition, an effective group member or leader must be able to utilize the abilities of other group members in providing the actions needed by the group.

For at least three reasons, it is usually considered necessary for the behaviors that fulfill group functions to be distributed among group members. First, if members do not participate, then their ideas, skills, and information are not being contributed. This hurts the group's effectiveness. The second reason is that members are committed to what they help build. Members who participate become more committed to the group and what the group has done. Members who remain silent tend not to care about the group and its effectiveness. The more members feel they have influenced the group and contributed to its work, the more committed they will be to the group. The third reason is that active members often become worried or annoyed about the silent members and view them as unconcerned about task completion. Unequal patterns of participation can create maintenance problems within the group.

Sometimes actions within a group not only help it to operate but serve oneself as well. Such individually oriented behavior sometimes involves issues of personal identity (Who am I in this group? Where do I fit in?), personal goals and needs (What do I want from this group? Are the group's goals consistent with my personal goals?), power and control (Who will control what we do? How much power and influence do I have?), and intimacy (How close will we get to each other? How much can I trust the other group members?).

The distributed-actions theory of leadership is one of the most concrete and direct approaches available for improving a person's leadership skills and for improving the effectiveness of a group. People can be taught the diagnostic skills and behaviors that help a group accomplish its task and maintain effective collaborative relationships among its members. There is, however, some criticism of the approach. There are so many different actions members can take to help in task achievement and group maintenance that specific ones are hard to pin down. What constitutes leadership then depends on the view of the person who is listing the leadership behaviors.

## Interaction-Process Analysis

If you put five strangers together and assign them a task that requires them to cooperate, something quite remarkable but very predictable happens: The social interaction among them becomes patterned and a leadership structure emerges. One variable that is consistently related to the emergence of leadership is the amount of talking a group member does. The person who talks the most in the group is the most likely to emerge as leader (Burke, 1974; Stein & Heller, 1979). The average correlation between participation and leadership is 0.65. Group members attribute leadership qualities to certain behaviors they observe in the group. Quantity of participation is attributed to be a sign of motivation, involvement, willingness to share resources with the group, and seriously trying to contribute to the group's goals (Sorrentino & Boutillier, 1975).

Whether it is a work group, discussion group, learning group, recreation group, one of the common forms this leadership structure takes is for one person to assume a **task-leadership role** that includes behaviors oriented primarily to task achievement (such as directing, summarizing, and providing ideas) and another person to assume a **social-emotional-leadership role** that includes behaviors oriented primarily to the expressive, interpersonal affairs of the group (such as alleviating frustrations, resolving tensions, and mediating conflicts).

Robert Bales (1950, 1952, 1955), in a series of studies in the late 1940s and early 1950s, was among the first to focus on task and social-emotional leadership. His work has been corroborated and extended by Burke (1972). The basic interaction-process theory consists of the following points:

1. When a group has a task to complete, its members engage in task-related behaviors on an unequal basis.
2. The members who are high on task behaviors tend to create some tension and hostility on the part of members who are less committed to the task.
3. There is a need for actions that help maintain effective working relationships among members.

4. Social-emotional actions are engaged in by members other than those high on task actions.
5. These differentiated roles (task and social-emotional) are stabilized and synchronized as the task and social-emotional leaders reinforce and support each other.

When the group has no task to achieve, or no commitment to achieve its assigned task, a task leader is not needed and will not appear. Correspondingly, with no commitment to a goal, there is no need to maintain relationships among members and a social-emotional leader will not evolve.

In his research Bales developed an observational instrument for identifying task and social-emotional behaviors within a small group (Figures 5.2 and 5.3). The instrument consists of several categories that are designed to allow a systematic classification of all the acts of participation in a group. As you can see in Figure 5.2, the categories are polarized: Category 1 is the opposite of category 12, 2 is the opposite of 11, and so on. The first three categories are positive emotions, the last three negative emotions. Categories 7, 8, and 9 request aid, whereas categories 4, 5, and 6 offer it.

Bales's research indicates that positive emotions (categories 1, 2, and 3) are usually expressed more than twice as often as negative emotions (10, 11, and 12). Opinions and information are much more often volunteered (46 percent of all partici-

---

*Social-Emotional Area: Positive*
  **1.** Shows solidarity, raises others' status, gives help, rewards

  **2.** Shows tension release, jokes, laughs, shows satisfaction

  **3.** Agrees, shows passive acceptance, understands, concurs, complies

*Task Area: Neutral*
  **4.** Gives suggestions, direction, implying autonomy for others

  **5.** Gives opinions, evaluation, analysis: expresses feeling, wishes

  **6.** Gives orientation, information, repeats, clarifies, confirms

*Task Area: Neutral*
  **7.** Asks for orientation, information, repetition, confirmation

  **8.** Asks for opinions, evaluation, analysis, expressions of feeling

  **9.** Asks for suggestions, direction, possible ways of action

*Social-Emotional Area: Negative*
  **10.** Disagrees; shows passive rejection, formality, withholds help

  **11.** Shows tension, asks for help, withdraws, leaves the field

  **12.** Shows antagonism, deflates others' status, defends or asserts self

---

**FIGURE 5.2.** Bales's system of categories used in observation.   Source: R. Bales, *Interaction Process Analysis* (Reading, MA: Addison-Wesley, 1950).

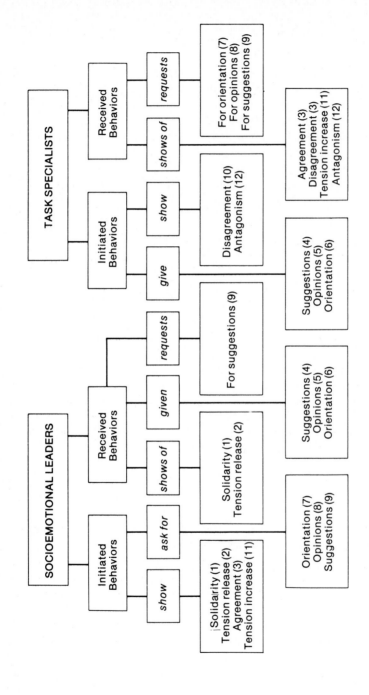

**FIGURE 5.3.** How Behaviors Differ for Socioemotional Leaders and Task Specialists. (Numbers in parentheses indicate category number from Bales's interaction process analysis.)

pant behaviors observed) than asked for (7 percent). Problem-solving groups tend to progress through three stages: orientation (What is the problem?), evaluation (How do we feel about it?), and control (What should we do about it?). As the discussion moves from the intellectual examination of the problem (the orientation phase) to evaluation and decision (the control phase), emotions are expressed more often.

Bales's observation form may be found in Figure 5.4. Why not try using it to observe a number of group meetings?

## Fiedler's Situational Theory of Leadership

Social psychologist Fred Fiedler did a series of studies on leadership (1964, 1967, 1969) in many different situations and groups. Defining a leader's effectiveness in terms of the group's performance in achieving its goals, Fiedler divided leaders into those who were task oriented and those who were maintenance oriented. He found no consistent relationship between group effectiveness and leadership behaviors, the reason being that maintenance-oriented leaders were more effective in certain situations and task-oriented leaders more effective in other situations.

A **task-oriented leader** is effective under two sets of conditions. Under the first, he or she is on very good terms with the group members, the task is clearly structured, and the leader has a position of high authority and power. Under such conditions the group is ready to be directed and is willing to be told what to do. Under the second set of conditions, the leader is on poor terms with group members, the task is ambiguous, and he or she has a position of low authority and power. Under these conditions the leader can also be effective in taking responsibility for making decisions and directing group members. When moderately good or poor relations exist between leader and the group members, when the leader has a position of moderate authority and power, and when the task is moderately clear, the **maintenance-oriented leader** who emphasizes member participation in decision making seems to be the most effective type of leader.

Fiedler's results imply that the distributed-functions theory of leadership needs to be modified to take into account the situational conditions influencing the impact of leadership style upon a group. There are some difficulties with this theory, however. For example, how can a person tell if the situational conditions of leadership—member relations, task clarity, and leader power are high, moderate, or low? Almost all group situations fall into the moderate range; in only the most extreme cases are the sets of conditions in the high or low categories. A second difficulty is that although the theory is more complex than the outdated leadership-style theory, which held that a leader should always be democratic, it may not be complex enough. A good leader is always paying attention to the situational conditions that influence the group, modifying his or her behavior to make it effective. Moreover, leader-member relations, task clarity, and leader power may be only three of many different situational factors that group leaders should be aware of.

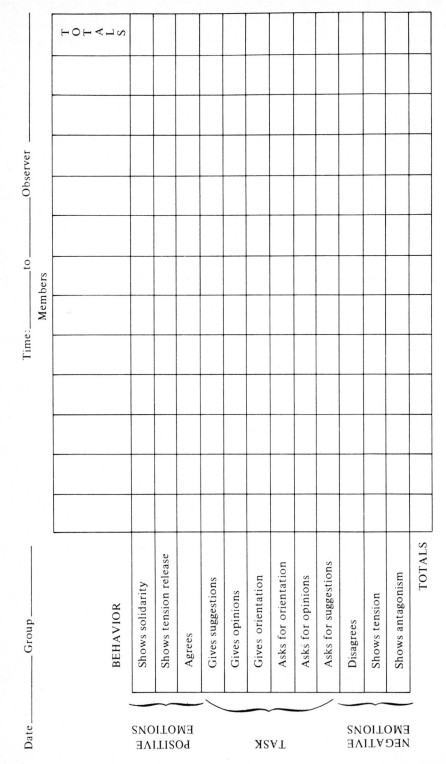

Date _____ Group _____ Time: _____ to _____ Observer _____

Members

| BEHAVIOR | | | | | | | | | | | TOTALS |
|---|---|---|---|---|---|---|---|---|---|---|---|
| Shows solidarity | | | | | | | | | | | |
| Shows tension release | | | | | | | | | | | |
| Agrees | | | | | | | | | | | |
| Gives suggestions | | | | | | | | | | | |
| Gives opinions | | | | | | | | | | | |
| Gives orientation | | | | | | | | | | | |
| Asks for orientation | | | | | | | | | | | |
| Asks for opinions | | | | | | | | | | | |
| Asks for suggestions | | | | | | | | | | | |
| Disagrees | | | | | | | | | | | |
| Shows tension | | | | | | | | | | | |
| Shows antagonism | | | | | | | | | | | |
| TOTALS | | | | | | | | | | | |

POSITIVE EMOTIONS — Shows solidarity, Shows tension release, Agrees

TASK — Gives suggestions, Gives opinions, Gives orientation, Asks for orientation, Asks for opinions, Asks for suggestions

NEGATIVE EMOTIONS — Disagrees, Shows tension, Shows antagonism

**FIGURE 5.4.** Cumulative interaction form.

# EXERCISE 5.5:
## THE LEAST PREFERRED COWORKER SCALE

Fiedler (1978) developed an indirect measure of leadership style known as the **Least Preferred Coworker Scale (LPC).** See Figure 5.5. Think of a person with whom you can work least well. The person may be someone you work with now or someone you knew in the past. This person need not be the person you liked least well, but should be the person with whom you have had the most difficulty working to get the job done.

Your score will fall somewhere in between 16 and 128. To calculate your score, add up the numbers you have circled for each of the adjective pairs. If your score is 56 or less, then you are a low-LPC leader. The lower your score, the more "task oriented" you are. If your score is 63 or above, then you are a high-LPC leader. The higher your LPC score, the more "relationship oriented" you are. If your score falls between 56 and 63, then you do not fit easily into either category and may call yourself "socioindependent."

According to Fiedler (1978) people who describe their least preferred coworker in very negative, rejecting terms are so oriented toward completing the task that it completely determines their perception of coworkers who they have trouble working with. In effect, they say, "If I cannot work with you, if you frustrate my need to get the job done, then you cannot be any good in other respects. You are unfriendly, unpleasant, cold, and nasty." People who describe their least preferred coworkers in positive terms are relationship oriented. In effect,

**FIGURE 5.5.** The LPC Scale. Think of a person with whom you can work least well. She or he may be someone you work with now or someone you knew in the past. He or she does not have to be the person you like least well, but should be the person with whom you have had the most difficulty in getting a job done. Describe this person by circling one of the numbers between each pair of adjectives.

To calculate your score, add up the numbers you have circled for each of the adjective pairs. According to Fiedler, if your score is 56 or less, then you are a low-LPC leader. If, however, your score is 63 or above, then you are a high-LPC leader. If, unfortunately, your score falls between 56 and 63, then you don't fit easily into either category (a motivational style tentatively labeled *socioindependent*). (Source: F. Fiedler, "Recent Developments in Research on the Contingency Model," in L. Berkowitz (Ed.), *Group Processes* (New York: Academic Press, 1978).]

| | | | | | | | | | | |
|--|--|--|--|--|--|--|--|--|--|--|
| Pleasant | : | 8 7 6 5 4 3 2 1 | : | Unpleasant |
| Friendly | : | 8 7 6 5 4 3 2 1 | : | Unfriendly |
| Rejecting | : | 1 2 3 4 5 6 7 8 | : | Accepting |
| Tense | : | 1 2 3 4 5 6 7 8 | : | Relaxed |
| Distant | : | 1 2 3 4 5 6 7 8 | : | Close |
| Cold | : | 1 2 3 4 5 6 7 8 | : | Warm |
| Supportive | : | 8 7 6 5 4 3 2 1 | : | Hostile |
| Boring | : | 1 2 3 4 5 6 7 8 | : | Interesting |
| Quarrelsome | : | 1 2 3 4 5 6 7 8 | : | Harmonious |
| Gloomy | : | 1 2 3 4 5 6 7 8 | : | Cheerful |
| Open | : | 8 7 6 5 4 3 2 1 | : | Guarded |
| Backbiting | : | 1 2 3 4 5 6 7 8 | : | Loyal |
| Untrustworthy | : | 1 2 3 4 5 6 7 8 | : | Trustworthy |
| Considerate | : | 8 7 6 5 4 3 2 1 | : | Inconsiderate |
| Nasty | : | 1 2 3 4 5 6 7 8 | : | Nice |
| Agreeable | : | 8 7 6 5 4 3 2 1 | : | Disagreeable |
| Insincere | : | 1 2 3 4 5 6 7 8 | : | Sincere |
| Kind | : | 8 7 6 5 4 3 2 1 | : | Unkind |

they say, "Even though I cannot work with you, getting the job done is not everything, and I can still see you as friendly, relaxed, and interesting."

### Hersey and Blanchard's Theory of Situational Leadership

On the basis of studies of leadership conducted at Ohio State University, Paul Hersey and Kenneth Blanchard (1977) concluded that they can classify most of the activities of leaders into two distinct behavioral dimensions: initiation of structure (task actions) and consideration of group members (relationship of maintenance actions). They define **task behavior** as the extent to which a leader engages in one-way communication by explaining what each follower is to do as well as when, where, and how tasks are to be accomplished. They define **relationship behavior** as the extent to which a leader engages in two-way communication by providing emotional support and facilitating behaviors. According to Hersey and Blanchard, the Ohio State University studies found that some leaders focus mainly on directing task-accomplishment–related activities for their followers, whereas other leaders concentrate on providing emotional support through relationships with their followers. Still other leaders engage in both task and relationship behaviors, or in neither. Hersey and Blanchard determined that task and relationship behaviors are two separate dimensions, which can be portrayed as in Figure 5.6.

Hersey and Blanchard's situational-leadership theory assumes that any of the four combinations of leadership behaviors shown in Figure 5.6 may be ineffective or

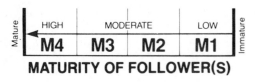

**FIGURE 5.6.** Situational leadership. Source: P. Hersey and K. Blanchard, *Management of Organizational Behavior: Utilizing Human Resources,* 3rd ed. (Englewood Cliffs, NJ: Prentice-Hall, 1977). Reprinted by permission.

effective, depending on the situation. Which combination of behaviors is appropriate depends on the level of maturity of the group. They define **maturity** as the capacity to set high but attainable goals (achievement motivation), willingness and ability to take responsibility, and the education and/or experience of group members. Maturity is determined only in relation to a specific task to be performed. On one task a member may have high maturity, on another task low maturity.

The essence of Hersey and Blanchard's theory is that when group members have low maturity in terms of accomplishing a specific task, the leader should engage in high-task and low-relationship behaviors. When members are moderately mature, the leader moves to high-task and high-relationship behaviors and then to high-relationship and low-task behaviors. When group members are highly mature in terms of accomplishing a specific task, then low-task and low-relationship behaviors are needed. Hersey and Blanchard refer to high-task/low-relationship leadership behavior as telling, because it is characterized by one-way communication in which the leader defines the roles of group members and tells them how, when, and where to do various tasks. As the members' experience and understanding of the task goes up, so does their task maturity. High-task/high-relationship leadership behavior is referred to as selling, because while providing clear direction as to role responsibilities the leader also attempts through two-way communication and socioemotional support to get the group members to psychologically buy into decisions that have to be made. As group members' commitment to the task increases, so does their maturity. Low-task/high-relationship leadership behavior is referred to as participating, because the leader and group members share in decision making through two-way communication and considerable facilitating behavior from the leader, since the group members have the ability and knowledge to complete the task. Finally, low-task/low-relationship leadership behavior is referred to as delegating, because the leader allows group members considerable autonomy in completing the task, since they are both willing and able to take responsibility for directing their own task behavior.

## VROOM AND YETTON'S NORMATIVE MODEL OF LEADERSHIP

Vroom and Yetton (1973) developed a normative model of leadership that has three key features: a taxonomy of leadership methods, the problem attributes, and the decision tree.

Five key types of leadership methods are identified (Vroom & Yetton, 1973):

*Autocratic I:* Making the decision using information currently available to the leader.

*Autocratic II:* Making the decision using information available to all group members without informing them of the purpose of their information.

*Consultative I:* Sharing the problem with relevant individuals, getting their ideas and suggestions without getting them together as a group, and then making the decision.

*Consultative II:* Sharing the problem with the group, obtaining their ideas and suggestions during a group discussion, and then making the decision.

*Group II:* Sharing the problem with the group, chairing a group discussion, and accepting and implementing any decision by the entire group.

None of these leadership methods is best in all situations. The leader must match the leadership method with the situation. Seven attributes of the situation must be taken into account in deciding which leadership method to use (Vroom & Yetton, 1973):

1. Is there a quality requirement such that one solution is likely to be more rational than another?
2. Do I have sufficient information and expertise to make a high-quality decision?
3. Is the problem structured?
4. Is acceptance of the decision by subordinates critical to its effective implementation?
5. If I were to make the decision by myself, is it reasonably certain that it would be accepted by my subordinates?
6. Do subordinates share the organizational goals to be attained in solving this problem?
7. Is conflict among subordinates likely in preferred solutions?

The answers to these questions specify which method of leadership is appropriate for the situation. Answering each question "yes" or "no" leads to a decision tree that tells the leader how to proceed.

## ORGANIZATIONAL LEADERSHIP

Whenever anyone asks me (how to be a leader) I tell them I have the secret to success in life. The secret to success is to stay in love. Staying in love gives you the fire to really ignite other people, to see inside other people, to have a greater desire to get things done than other people. A person who is not in love doesn't really feel the kind of excitement that helps them to get ahead and lead others and to achieve. I don't know any other fire, any other thing in life that is more exhilarating and is more positive a feeling than love is.

*Army Major General John H. Stanford (Kouzes & Posner, 1987)*

On July 15, 1982, Don Bennett, a Seattle businessman, was the first amputee ever to climb Mount Rainier (reported by Kouzes & Posner, 1987). He climbed 14,410 feet on one leg and two crutches. It took him five days. When asked to state the most important lesson he learned from doing so, without hesitation he said, "You can't do it alone."

What did he mean? There were many ways in which others helped him achieve his goal, including his daughter. During one very difficult trek across an ice field in Don Bennett's hop to the top of Mount Rainer, his daughter stayed by his side for four hours and with each new hop told him, "You can do it, Dad. You're the best dad in the world. You can do it, Dad." There was no way Bennett would quit hopping to the top with his daughter yelling words of love and encouragement in his ear. The encouragement by his daughter kept him going, strengthening his commitment to make it to the top. The team and the organization are similar. With members of their cooperative group cheering them on, members amaze themselves and their superiors with what they can achieve.

*There is growth and decline. Staying the same is not an option.* Growth takes leadership, not management. There is a difference. Some individuals manage, some individuals lead. The difference may be found in the root meanings of "lead" and "manage" (Kouzes & Posner, 1987). The root origin of *lead* is a word meaning "to go," denoting travel from one place to another. Leaders are those who "go first," pioneering unexplored territory and showing others the direction they should take. By comparison, the root origin of *manage* is a word meaning "hand." Managing seems to connote "handling" things by controlling and maintaining the status quo. Managers tend to handle things, leaders tend to get us going somewhere. *The unique role of the leader is to take us on journeys to places we have never been before.*

The metaphor of the journey may be the most appropriate metaphor for discussing the tasks of leaders. Individuals can manage what now exists, the status quo, or take staff members on a journey to increase their expertise and create a new and better organization.

Perhaps more than anything else, leadership is about the creation of a new way of life within organizations. Leadership is inextricably connected with the process of innovation, of bringing new ideas, methods, or solutions into use. Leaders are agents of change. Change requires leadership, a "prime mover" to push for implementation of strategic decisions. The leader highlights the challenges the organization faces and makes them shared challenges for the staff. *Leaders create a "family" within which staff members care deeply about each other and the mutual vision they are trying to actualize.* Managers get other people to do, but leaders get other people to *want* to do.

There are a series of leadership issues that must be faced in order to maximize the productivity of the organization (Kouzes & Posner, 1987; Johnson & Johnson, 1989b):

1. How to *challenge the status quo* of the traditional competitive and individualistic models of management.
2. How to *inspire a clear mutual vision* of what the organization should and could be, a clear mission that all members are committed to achieving, and a set of goals that guides members' efforts.
3. How to *empower members through cooperative teamwork.* Doing so enables each individual member to take action to increase his or her expertise and effectiveness, both technically and interpersonally.
4. How to *lead by example* by (a) using cooperative team procedures and (b) taking risks to increase expertise.
5. How to *encourage the heart* of members to persist and keep striving to improve their technical and interpersonal expertise.

## Challenging the Status Quo

Organizations (and groups) are sites for an inevitable and external conflict. On one side are the forces of maintenance and continuity (i.e., the status quo), which strive to create and sustain the use of orderly and predictable procedures. Opposing them are the forces of innovation and discontinuity, which seek to alter established practices.

Both seek the same goal of team and organizational productivity. Both are needed. The creative tension between the two is what powers considered and thoughtful development and change.

These same two forces operate within the individual member. Group members will experience the conflict between the security of the past and the satisfactions of growth in expertise and accomplishment. The status quo side wants to continue what he or she has done in the past. The enhanced expertise side strives for growth, change, and increased competence. Leaving the status quo and risking one's current success against the potential of being even better in the future requires courage.

Leaders challenge the status quo and inspire team and organization members to recognize that *if they are not working to increase their expertise, they are losing their expertise.* Expertise is a process, not an end product. Any person or organization is constantly changing. If expertise is not growing, then it is declining. The minute a person believes he or she is an expert and stops trying to learn more, then he or she is losing their expertise. *Leaders must lead members toward enhanced expertise, not manage for bureaucratic control. And the clearest and most direct challenge to traditional competitive and individualistic actions is the adoption of cooperative teams within the organization.* The organization needs to be transformed into an interlocking network of cooperative teams in order to increase productivity, promote more supportive and committed relationships, and increase members' psychological adjustment and self-esteem.

## Creating a Shared Vision

The second leadership responsibility is to create a joint vision of what the team or organization should and could be, a clear mission that all members are committed to achieving, and a set of goals that guides members' efforts. *To do so a leader must*

1. Have a vision/dream of what the organization could be.
2. Communicate that vision with commitment and enthusiasm.
3. Make it a *shared* vision that staff members adopt as their own.
4. Make it a rational vision based on theory and research and sound implementation procedures.

Leaders enthusiastically and frequently communicate the dream of the team and organization being places where individuals share, help, encourage, and support each other's efforts to achieve and succeed, places where *we* dominates *me*, where working together to get the job done creates caring and committed relationships that propel people forward in their mutual search for excellence.

Leaders inspire a *shared* vision. It is the common vision that creates a basic sense of "sink or swim together" (i.e., positive interdependence) among members. Leaders breathe life into the hopes and dreams of others and enable them to see the exciting possibilities the future holds by striving for a common purpose. *The vision and its advocacy, furthermore, has to be rational.* The new practices have to be backed up with a knowledge of the relevant research and theory. A person with no followers is *not* a leader, and people will not become followers until they accept a vision as their own. It is the long-term promise of achieving something worthwhile and meaningful that powers an individual's drive toward greater expertise. *You cannot command commitment, you can only inspire it!*

## Empowering Members Through Cooperative Teams

*The most important of all the five leadership practices is empowering individuals by organizing them into cooperative teams.* To be effective, a cooperative team must be carefully structured to include positive interdependence, face-to-face promotive interaction, individual accountability, social skills, and group processing (Johnson, Johnson, & Holubec, 1988, 1990).

The one-word test to detect whether someone is on the road to becoming a leader is *we*. Leaders do not achieve success by themselves. It is not *my* personal best leaders inspire, it is *our* personal best. The most important thing a leader can do is to organize members so that they work cooperatively with each other, for at least two reasons.

*The first is to promote committed and caring relationships among organization members.* This is achieved through a "team" approach. Having members work as part of cooperative teams fosters committed and caring relationships. Cooperative efforts result in trust, open communication, and interpersonal support, all of which are crucial ingredients for productivity. When trust is broken by competition, harsh feelings, criticism, negative comments, and disrespect, productivity suffers.

*The second is to empower staff members through teamwork.* The "real world" involves working with and through many different people to get the job done. By organizing members into cooperative teams, leaders increase members' confidence that if they exert effort, they will be successful. Teams empower their members to act by making them feel strong, capable, and committed. Being part of a team enables members to innovate, experiment, take risks, and grow professionally.

## Leading by Example

> One does not improve through argument but through examples. . . . Be what you wish to make others become. Make yourself, not your words, a sermon.
>
> *Henri Frederic Amiel*

To provide leadership, you will need to model (1) using cooperative procedures and (2) taking risks to increase your technical and interpersonal expertise. You model the way by practicing what you are preaching. *You lead by example.* To do so, you must be clear about your belief in cooperative efforts, you must be able to speak coherently about your vision and values, and your actions must be congruent with your words. *You begin leadership by becoming a role model that exemplifies the organizational and leadership values you believe are important.* You show your priorities through living your values.

One thing you can count on for certain. *Every exceptional leader is a learner.* The self-confidence required to lead comes from trying, failing, learning from mistakes, and trying again. We are all involved in a continuous process of increasing our technical and interpersonal expertise. From making your own journey to actualize your vision, you model the way for others. Remember, it is not the cry, but the flight of the wild duck that leads the flock to fly and follow (a Chinese proverb).

## Encouraging the Heart of Staff Members

> Love 'em and lead 'em.
>
> *Major General John H. Stanford, Commander, U.S. Army*

Leaders are vigilant about the little things that make a big difference. Each spring at Verstec, annual bonuses are given to about 2,000 nonmanagerial personnel (Kouzes & Posner, 1987). In a recent year, the president arrived at the celebration dressed in a satin costume, riding atop an elephant, and accompanied by the Stanford Marching Band. The president frequently says, "If you are going to give someone a check, don't just mail it. Have a celebration."

This example may seem extreme. It usually does not take a marching band and an elephant to make organizational members feel appreciated. *What makes a difference to each individual staff member is to know that his or her successes are perceived, recognized, and celebrated.* Leaders search out "good news" opportunities and orchestrate celebrations. Striving for increased technical and interpersonal expertise is an arduous and long-term enterprise. Members become exhausted, frustrated, and disenchanted. They often are tempted to give up. *Leaders must inspire members to continue the journey by encouraging the heart* (Kouzes & Posner, 1987). Leaders inspire staff members by giving them the courage and hope to continue the quest. This does not require elephants and marching bands (although they are not a bad idea). What it does require is

1. The recognition of individual contributions to the common vision.
2. Frequent group celebrations of individual and joint accomplishments.

Members do not start the day with a desire to fail. It is the leader's job to show them that they can succeed. *The primary tools for doing so are individual recognition and group celebration.* A leader becomes a master of celebration. Leaders should give out stickers, T-shirts, buttons, and every other conceivable award when members achieve a milestone. One leader sends out cards that have "I heard something good about you" printed at the top. *Leaders find ways to celebrate accomplishments.* If you do not show your appreciation to your members, they are going to stop caring, and then, in essence, you are going to find yourself out of business.

To give individual recognition and have a group celebration requires a cooperative organizational structure. In competitions, to declare one person a winner is to declare all others losers. Group celebrations do not take place in competitive/individualistic organizations. In such environments, praise may be perceived to be phony or satirical, and recognition may be the source of embarrassment and anxiety about future retaliation by colleagues. *Within cooperative enterprises, however, genuine acts of caring draw people together and forward. Love of their work and each other is what inspires many members to commit more and more of their energy to their jobs.* Establishing a cooperative structure and encouraging the development of caring and committed relationships among members may just be the best-kept secret of exemplary leadership.

### Leaping the Abyss of Failure

> When you look into the abyss, the abyss is looking into you.
>
> *Nietzsche*

*Leaders give organizational members the courage they need to take the risks neces-*
*sary to increase technical and interpersonal expertise.* Members can choose to play it
safe in the short-run by traveling on the path of the status quo, thereby facing
guaranteed long-term failure through obsolescence, atrophy, and burnout. Adherents
to the status quo slowly and gradually descend into the abyss of failure. They are
descending even though they may not always realize it. Managers organize the easy
walk downward into the abyss of failure along the path of the status quo. Leaders
encourage and inspire members to take the difficult leaps toward increased technical
and interpersonal competence. They take a leap over the abyss of failure to reach
enhanced expertise. Sometimes their leap falls short and they fail. Sometimes they
soar high above the abyss to land safely on the other side. Leaders encourage the
risks of short-term failure in order to enhance long-term productivity.

## WHAT IF YOU DO NOT WANT TO BE A LEADER?

If you follow the following rules carefully, you can be guaranteed to never be a leader:

1. Be absent from group meetings as frequently as possible.
2. When you do attend, contribute nothing.
3. If you do participate, come on strong early in the discussion. Demonstrate your
   knowledge of everything, including your extensive vocabulary of big words and technical jargon.
4. Indicate that you will do only what you have to and nothing more.
5. Read the paper or knit during meetings.

### EXERCISE 5.6:
### HOW DO YOU EXPLAIN THIS LEADER?

Form a group of three. Read the following case study. Review the theories of leadership
presented in this chapter and develop an explanation of the leadership demonstrated within
the following situation. Then join with another group and compare your explanations.

Jim Jones was ordained as a minister in the Disciples of Christ Christian Church. In
the early 1960s, he built his California-based church into a massive organization of
dedicated followers. Preaching a mixture of Christianity and Marxism, he emphasized interracial harmony. He was a dynamic, entrancing speaker who could hold an
audience in rapt attention. In 1963 he formed his own church, the People's Temple
Full Gospel Church, and soon had 8,000 members. While the People's Temple was
considered to be civic-minded and altruistic for some time, rumors began to surface
concerning Jones's demands for absolute dedication from his followers and the punishment he would inflict on members. Ex-members reported that he demanded to be

called father, frequently made sexual demands on both male and female members, and required large financial contributions of even the poorest members.

Jones was reported to be obsessed with suicide. Occasionally, he would announce that the sacramental wine the congregation had drunk had been poison and all would be dead in a half hour. Jones even had confederates in the congregation simulate collapse, complete with stage blood flowing from their mouths. After convincing everyone that they were dying, he would announce that he was merely testing their faith in him. Through repetition of this ceremony the thought of mass suicide became commonplace to his church members.

Feeling persecuted, Jones moved his church and congregation to the South American country of Guyana and established Jonestown in the jungle. His press releases described the settlement as a utopian community. Rumors, however, kept surfacing that the community was a prison in which members were brutalized. Armed guards to prevent desertion were reported and the suicide rituals were practiced repeatedly. In response to the rumors congressional representative Leo Ryan visited Jonestown and was murdered. Realizing that a full investigation would be made of his church, he ordered a suicide ritual. Over the loudspeaker system Jones explained the need for the "revolutionary suicide of the faithful" and ordered his followers to take their own lives and the lives of their children.

The next day, when authorities reached the settlement, they viewed a scene of unbelievable ghastliness. More than 900 people from infants to adults, as well as Jones himself, had committed suicide. Whole families had taken the poison on Jones's orders and died side by side. (See Krause, 1978, for a detailed description of the development and demise of Jones's cult.)

# EXERCISE 5.7:
# THE FURNITURE FACTORY

The purpose of this exercise is to give participants an opportunity to observe task-leadership and maintenance-leadership actions within a decision-making group. The procedure is as follows:

1. The class divides into groups of seven. Two members should volunteer to be observers. The task of the observers is to record the frequency of task and maintenance actions within the group. The observation sheets to be used are on pages 182–83.
2. The task of each group is to read and discuss the problem description that follows and rank the five possible solutions on the basis of how effective they would be in ensuring the least resistance to the proposed changes in work procedures. Each member of the group must be willing to sign the group answer sheet, indicating that he agrees with the group's ranking and can explain the rationale for ranking the possible solutions in the order that the group did so.
3. After deciding how the possible solutions are to be ranked, members discuss the nature of leadership within the group. The following questions may be used as a starter:
   a. What leadership actions were present and absent in the group?
   b. What leadership actions did each member engage in?
   c. How do the members feel about their participation in the group?
   d. How might the task effectiveness of the group be improved?
   e. How might the relationships among group members be improved?
4. Each group shares its conclusions with the class.
5. The ranking of possible solutions by experts on organizational change appears on page 488.

**Problem Description: Furniture Factory Exercise**

Lazy-Days Manufacturing Company is located in a small northern town. This small, family-owned business manufactures school furniture. Because of the opportunities for work available in a larger town located about 50 miles away, Lazy-Days must attract whomever it can and train them to do the job. Most of the 400 workers are women and young people just out of high school. Lazy-Days also hires some physically handicapped and mentally retarded adults as part of a special community program.

Observation Sheet for Task Actions

| Actions | *Group Members* | | | | |
|---|---|---|---|---|---|
| Information and opinion giver | | | | | |
| Information and opinion seeker | | | | | |
| Direction and role definer | | | | | |
| Summarizer | | | | | |
| Energizer | | | | | |
| Comprehension checker | | | | | |

Observation Sheet for Maintenance Actions

| Actions | *Group Members* | | | | |
|---|---|---|---|---|---|
| Encourager of participation | | | | | |
| Communication facilitator | | | | | |
| Tension releaser | | | | | |
| Process observer | | | | | |
| Interpersonal problem solver | | | | | |
| Supporter and praiser | | | | | |

Observation Sheet for Task and Maintenance Actions

| Actions | Group Members | | | | |
|---|---|---|---|---|---|
| Information and opinion giver | | | | | |
| Information and opinion seeker | | | | | |
| Direction and role definer | | | | | |
| Summarizer | | | | | |
| Energizer | | | | | |
| Comprehension checker | | | | | |
| Encourager of participation | | | | | |
| Communication facilitator | | | | | |
| Tension releaser | | | | | |
| Process observer | | | | | |
| Interpersonal problem solver | | | | | |
| Supporter and praiser | | | | | |

Until now, Lazy-Days has manufactured school furniture but, because of a tightening of the economy, management has realized a dire need to diversify its manufacturing capabilities. After a study of the market, the decision was made to add showroom display cases as a new product. If well made, this line will bring increased income and security to Lazy-Days Manufacturing.

Because of the difficulties in getting new workers, particularly trained ones, Lazy-Days would like to divert current personnel to the new jobs. However, the current workers are very set in their ways and are highly resistant to and suspicious of changes at work. The last time changes were needed, workers demanded higher wages, threatened to unionize, and a few key people quit. If the new line is successful, Lazy-Days could raise wages, but this is not possible under current conditions that require using available income to help purchase the new equipment and finance necessary remodeling to accommodate the new equipment.

Michael Days, president of Lazy-Days, has listed several ways of approaching the workers about the needed changes. He has asked you to decide which alternative to use. As a group, rank these alternatives from 1 to 5 in terms of their effectiveness in bringing about the desired changes with the least resistance from the workers. Number 1 would be the most effective, 2 the next most effective, and so on through 5, the least effective. Remember, your decision can make the difference between the success or failure of Lazy-Days Manufacturing Company.

_____ a. Mr. Days would send a written memo to all employees that would tell them about the needed changes. He would then make the changes and lay off any employees who did not comply with the changes in their jobs.

_____ b. Mr. Days would meet with small groups of employees. He would explain the need for the changes and the reasoning behind the changes. He would then ask everyone to help in designing and implementing the new jobs.

_____ c. Mr. Days would meet with large groups of his employees. He would enthusiastically describe the needed changes and present multicolored charts and filmclips to make his points dramatically and forcefully. He would then implement the changes.

_____ d. Mr. Days would send a written memo to all employees that would explain the need for the changes and ask the employees to go along with the changes for the good of the company.

_____ e. Mr. Days would meet with large groups of his employees. He would explain the need for the changes and the reasoning behind the changes. He would then have the employees select representatives to work with him in designing and implementing the new jobs.

## EXERCISE 5.8:
## TOWER BUILDING

This exercise is aimed at providing participants with an opportunity to observe leadership behavior in a situation of intergroup competition in which verbal communication is not allowed. Several groups are need for this exercise, all of which should have at least seven members. The task of each group is to build a tower from supplied materials. A large room is needed so that the groups can work separately (but within sight of one another). The time needed to complete the exercise is approximately 1 hour. The procedure is as follows:

1. Two judges are selected to determine which one tower is (a) the highest, (b) the strongest, (c) the most beautiful, and (d) the cleverest.
2. The class forms groups of at least seven members.
3. Each group selects two of its members to observe leadership in the group. The observers (using the observation sheets on pages 182–83) are to note:
   a. How the group organizes for work.
   b. How decisions are made by the group.
   c. Whether participation and influence is distributed throughout the group, or whether a few members dominate.
   d. What task and maintenance actions are needed to improve the functioning of the group.
   e. How the group reacts to winning or losing.
4. Each group receives a box of supplies containing construction paper, newsprint, tape, magazines, crayons, pipe cleaners, scissors, and glue.
5. The groups have 20 minutes to build their towers. This is a *nonverbal* exercise: *No talking among group members or between groups is allowed.*

6. During the 20 minutes the judges meet to decide how they will evaluate the towers on the basis of the four criteria given. At the end of the 20 minutes the judges decide which tower wins and award a box of candy (provided by the person conducting the exercise) to the winning group.
7. The groups meet with their observers and discuss the exercise. All impressions concerning how the group functioned and what leadership patterns were present and absent should be presented and reviewed.

## EXERCISE 5.9:
## SELECTING A CITY

The purposes of this exercise are for participants to develop through role playing an under-standing of the distributed-actions theory of leadership and to observe task and maintenance actions in a decision-making group. Instructions for the coordinator are as follows:

1. Introduce the exercise by stating the objectives. Then explain the following leader-ship actions (see page 162 for definitions):
   a. Information and opinion giver
   b. Information and opinion seeker
   c. Direction and role definer
   d. Summarizer
   e. Encourager of participation
   f. Communication facilitator
   g. Process observer
   h. Tension reliever
2. Form heterogeneous groups of eight. Two members from each group should volun-teer to be observers.
3. Explain the task-behavior and maintenance-behavior observation form to the ob-servers and instruct them to look for
   a. What leadership actions are present and absent in the group.
   b. How well participation is distributed among group members.
   c. What specific leadership actions each group member provides.
4. Place a large envelope containing role-playing instruction envelopes in the center of each group; give no further instructions or information.
5. After the exercise has been completed, instruct each group to discuss its experience, using the following questions as a starter:
   a. What leadership actions was each member supposed to role-play, and how were they carried out?
   b. What leadership actions were present and absent in the group decision making, and what were the consequences of the presence or absence of these actions?
   c. What were the feelings and reactions of the group members?
   d. What conclusions about leadership and group functioning can be drawn from this exercise?
6. Have each group share its conclusions with the class.

### Envelope Instructions

*Instructions written on the large envelope, which contains all other envelopes:*

Enclosed you will find three envelopes containing directions for the phases of this group session. You are to open the first one (labeled Envelope I) at once. Later instructions will tell you when to open the second (Envelope II) and third (Envelope III).

Selecting a City Exercise Observation Sheet

| Actions | *Group Members* | | | | |
|---|---|---|---|---|---|
| Information and opinion giver | | | | | |
| Information and opinion seeker | | | | | |
| Direction and role definer | | | | | |
| Summarizer | | | | | |
| Encourager of participation | | | | | |
| Communication facilitator | | | | | |
| Process observer | | | | | |
| Tension reliever | | | | | |

*Envelope I contains the following directions:*

**DIRECTIONS FOR ENVELOPE I:**

Time allowed: 15 minutes
Special instructions: Each member is to take one of the enclosed envelopes and
    follow the individual role-playing instructions contained in it.
Task: The group is to select a city.
DO NOT LET ANYONE ELSE SEE *YOUR* INSTRUCTIONS!
(After 15 minutes, go on to the next envelope.)

*Envelope II contains the following directions:*

**DIRECTIONS FOR ENVELOPE II:**

Time allowed: 5 minutes
Task: You are to choose a group chairperson.
(After 5 minutes go on to the next envelope.)

*Envelope III contains the following directions:*

**DIRECTIONS FOR ENVELOPE III:**

Time allowed: 10 minutes
Task: You are to evaluate the first phase of this group session.
Special instructions for the second phase: The newly selected chairperson will lead a

discussion on the roles and actions of group members in the process of decision making and their feelings and reactions to that process. The discussion should begin with the report of the observers.

(After 10 minutes return the directions to their respective envelopes and prepare for a general discussion of the exercise.)

**Role-Playing Instruction Envelopes for Phase I**

Here are the contents of the six individual instruction envelopes to be used in the first phase of the exercise. Each envelope contains an assigned leadership action and a position concerning which city to select. Two of the envelopes also contain special knowledge concerning the selection process.

1. *Leadership Action:* Direction and Role Definer
   *Position:* Introduce and support Albuquerque. Oppose San Diego.
2. *Leadership Action:* Encourager of Participation
   *Position:* Introduce and support San Diego. Oppose Albuquerque.
   *Special Knowledge:* The group is going to select a chairperson later in the exercise. You are to conduct yourself in such a manner that they will select you.
3. *Leadership Action:* Information and Opinion Seeker
   *Position:* Introduce and support New York City.
4. *Leadership Actions:* Summarizer and Process Observer
   *Position:* Oppose New York City.
5. *Leadership Action:* Communication Facilitator
   *Position:* When there seems to be a clear polarity in the discussion, suggest a compromise city, such as Minneapolis or Frameswitch, Texas.
6. *Leadership Action:* Tension Reliever
   *Position:* Support San Diego.
   *Special Knowledge:* The group is going to select a chairperson later in the exercise. You are to conduct yourself in such a manner that they will select you.
7. (if needed) *Leadership Action:* Any
   *Position:* Any

# EXERCISE 5.10:
# ARE GROUPS RUN BY GREAT PERSONS?

The purpose of this exercise is to compare two opposing theories of leadership: the great-person theory and the interaction-process-analysis theory. According to the great-person theory, the leader is the best-liked member of the group and is perceived as being the most important member for achieving the group's goals. The interaction-process-analysis theory suggests that task actions and maintenance actions are ordinarily executed by different persons, so that a group will usually have two complementary leaders. The procedure for the exercise is as follows:

1. Each participant locates a group that has worked together for some time and has a stable group structure. The group should be small enough so that every member knows every other member well enough to evaluate them on likability and task ability.
2. Give every member of the group a questionnaire consisting of two items:
   a. Rank-order the members of the group from best to worst at helping the group complete its tasks.
   b. Rank-order the members of the group from most to least likeable.
3. Construct two sociometric matrices from the group. The task-ability matrix is constructed by:

a. Listing the names of the group members down the left-hand side of the matrix and also across the top of the matrix.
b. Listing the ranks given by each group member to all other members on task ability in the rows. Each column then represents the rankings received for one member by all the other members of the group.
c. Compute the mean rank of each member.
4. Repeat this process for the likability rankings.
5. By graphing the mean ranking of the members on the two dimensions the answer to which theory holds in that group can be determined. If the two sets of rankings correspond, the graph should resemble a straight line, and the great-person theory of leadership is confirmed. If any pattern other than a straight line results, the theory of two complementary leaders or another theory of leadership is supported.
6. The class divides into groups of five. Share with each other your graphs. Discuss the following questions:
a. How do the graphs of the different groups compare with one another?

### Example of Sociometric Task-Ability Matrix

Members Being Ranked

| Members Doing Ranking | John | Sue | Fred | Ralph | Betsy | Helen |
|---|---|---|---|---|---|---|
| John | | | | | | |
| Sue | | | | | | |
| Fred | | | | | | |
| Ralph | | | | | | |
| Betsy | | | | | | |
| Helen | | | | | | |
| Mean Ranking | | | | | | |

### Example of Sociometric Graph

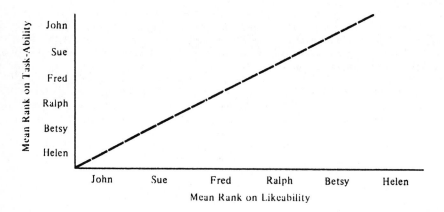

    b. What overall conclusions concerning group leadership can be made from the five graphs?

    c. What have you learned about leadership by analyzing and comparing the leadership patterns of the five groups?

## EXERCISE 5.11: HOLLOW SQUARE

The Hollow Square Exercise is a problem-solving situation in which you can observe leadership functions. You can see the processes of group planning, the problems of communication between a planning group and an implementing group, and the problems with which an implementing group must cope when carrying out a plan it did not make itself, all of which requires effective leadership behavior. The specific objectives for the exercise are to provide a problem-solving task in which you can observe leadership behavior, to increase your awareness of the problems involved in using a formal hierarchy in group problem solving, and to give you practice in observing groups and in giving the group feedback on your observations.

    The exercise is carried out in clusters of 10 to 12 persons. Each cluster is divided into three subgroups: 4 persons are planners, 4 are implementers, and the rest observers. The planners decide how they will instruct the implementers to do a task, the implementers carry through the task as best they can, and the observers watch the process of both groups in the two phases. Here is the specific procedure for the coordinator of the exercise:

1. Tell the participants the objectives of the exercise and divide them into four-person planning teams, four-person implementing teams, and observers. Each team goes to a separate room or different parts of a large room (out of earshot) to await instructions.

2. Hand out the appropriate instruction sheets to each team. Give them adequate time to read them, then review them with each team. The observers should be fully briefed first, the planners next, and the implementers last.

3. The planners are given the general diagram sheet and the pieces of the puzzle and are instructed to begin phase I. Each planner is given four pieces of the puzzle. The exact distribution of the pieces is not crucial, but they should not have any labels marked on them. Phase I lasts 45 minutes. All information the planners need to know is on their briefing-sheet. The answer as to how the puzzle fits together is on page 494.

4. At the end of phase I the planning team gives the implementing team its instructions. The planners are then prohibited from giving any further help; they must remain silent and uninvolved as the implementing team works.

5. Implementers are to finish the task, phase II, according to their instructions, taking as much time as necessary.

6. When the task is completed a discussion is held involving all the members of each cluster. This discussion is to include reports from the observers, planners, and implementers, and a comparison of similarities between the exercise and other organizational and group experiences of the members. Questions for the discussion should include:

    a. What leadership functions were present and absent in the planning and implementing teams? What were the consequences of the functions being present or absent?

    b. What leadership functions were needed for each type of activity?

    c. How could the functioning of each team have been improved?

    d. Were the leadership functions distributed among all the team members? Was participation and influence evenly distributed throughout the team?

    e. How was communication between the planning and implementing teams handled? How could it have been improved?

    f. What did it feel like to wait for the planners' instructions, and what did it feel like to watch the implementers carry them out?

7. The major points of the discussion should be summarized with an emphasis placed upon the conclusions about the leadership functions being present, absent, and distributed within the teams. Other types of learning that typically take place during the exercise are

    a. Planners often place limitations on team behavior that do not appear in the instructions, thereby making their task harder. They could, for example, ask the implementing team to observe their planning meeting.

    b. There is considerable frustration in planning something that others will carry out without yourself being involved. The commitment to implement a plan is usually built through the planning process, and when the planners cannot put the plan into effect they often experience frustration.

    c. Planning is so interesting and absorbing that planners can forget what their implementing team is experiencing. Implementers can become anxious because they do not know what the task will be, though this concern does not usually enter the minds of the planners.

    d. Planners often fail to use all the resources at their disposal to solve the problem, such as getting the silent members of the planning team to participate.

    e. Planners can spend so much time planning the task that they do not allow enough time to communicate their plans adequately to the implementers, which results in wasting much of their effort.

    f. In communicating their plan to the implementing team the planning team often does not take into account the implementers' anxieties, their needs for being physically comfortable, and so on. Their preoccupation with giving information under pressure blinds them to the needs of the members of the implementing team, which reduces the effectiveness of the communication.

    g. Implementers usually develop some feelings of antagonism or hostility toward their planners while they are waiting for their instructions. This antagonism increases if they are given complex instructions in a short amount of time and left confused as they take responsibility for finishing the task.

## Instruction Sheet for Observers

You will be observing a situation in which a planning team decides how to solve a problem and gives instructions to an implementing team. The problem consists of assembling 16 flat pieces into a square containing an empty square in its middle. The planning team is supplied with a general diagram of the assembled pieces. The planners are *not* allowed to put the puzzle together themselves; they are to instruct the implementing team on how to assemble the pieces in minimum time. You will be silent observers throughout the process. Half of you should observe the planners throughout the entire exercise and half of you should observe the implementers. Observation sheets focusing upon task and maintenance leadership behaviors are provided to help you observe. Make sure you understand the behavioral roles before you begin. Some suggestions for observers are

1. Each observer should watch the general patterns of leadership behavior.
2. During phase I, consider the following questions:
    a. What kinds of behavior block or help the process?
    b. Are the team members participating equally?

    c. How does the planning team divide its time between planning and instructing?

    d. What group functions are not provided by the group members?

3. During the instructing process, note these behavioral questions:

    a. At the beginning of the instruction, how do the planners orient the implementers to their task?

    b. What assumptions made by the planning team are not communicated to the implementing team?

    c. How effective are the instructions?

    d. Does the implementing team appear to feel free to ask questions of the planners?

    e. What leadership functions are present and absent?

4. During the assembling period, seek answers to the following questions:

    a. How does the implementing team show that instructions were clearly understood or misunderstood?

    b. What nonverbal reactions do planning team members show as they watch their plans being implemented or distorted?

    c. What leadership functions are present and absent?

5. You should each have two copies of the observation sheets, one for phase I and one for phase II.

## Instruction Sheet for Planners

Each of you will be given a packet containing four pieces of a puzzle. When all the pieces from all four packets are properly assembled, they will form a large square containing an empty place in the middle. A sheet bearing a diagram of the completed puzzle is provided for your team. Your task is to

1. Plan how the 16 pieces distributed among you can be assembled to solve the puzzle.
2. Decide on a plan for instructing your implementing team on how to carry out your plan for putting the puzzle together.
3. Call the implementing team and begin instructing them at any time during the next forty minutes.
4. Give them at least 5 minutes of instructions; the implementing team must begin assembling the puzzle 45 minutes from now.

Before you begin, read these rules:

1. During planning,

    a. Keep the pieces from your packet in front of you at all times.

    b. Do not touch the pieces nor trade any with other persons, either now or during the instruction period.

    c. Do not assemble the square; that is the implementers' job.

    d. Do not mark any of the pieces.

2. During instruction,

    a. Give all instructions in words. Do not show the diagram to the implementers; hide it. Do not draw any diagrams yourselves, either on paper or in the air with gestures. You may give your instructions orally or on paper.

    b. The implementing team must not move the pieces until the signal is given to start phase II.

    c. Do not show any diagram to the implementers.

    d. After the signal is given for the assembly to begin, you may *not* give any further instructions; stand back and observe. You may not touch the pieces or in any way join in the implementers' work.

**Hollow Square Pattern**

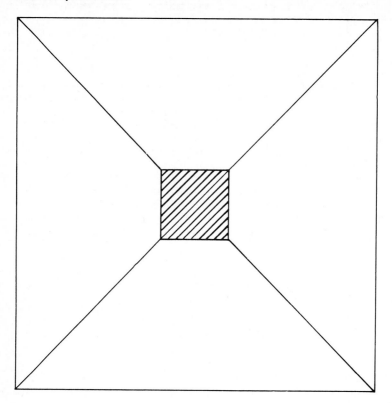

**Instruction Sheet for Implementers**

1. Your team will have the responsibility of carrying out a task in accordance with instructions given you by your planning team.
2. Your task will begin 40 minutes from now.
3. Your planning team may call you in for instruction at any time during the next 40 minutes.
4. If they do not call you during the next 40 minutes, you must report to them on your own at the end of that time.
5. You may send notes to the planners and they may send notes in reply.
6. Once you have begun the task of assembling the puzzle, your planning team will not be allowed to give you any further instructions. Finish the assigned task as quickly as possible.
7. While you wait for a call from your planning team, do the following:
   a. Individually, write on a piece of paper the concerns you feel while waiting for instructions.
   b. As a group, think of anything you can that might help you follow instructions or keep you from doing so. Write actions that will help you on one sheet of paper and those that will hinder you on another.
   c. Make notes on how the four of you can organize as a team to receive and follow the instructions.

d. Keep handy the sheets on which you have written these notes. You may find them useful during the discussion that takes place after you have completed the task.

## OTHER LEADERSHIP EXERCISES 5.12

1. An exercise for an ongoing group is to place the task and maintenance functions singly on 3- × 5-inch cards, shuffle the cards, and deal each member one or two of them face down. During a meeting of the group, each member then practices the task or maintenance function on the card he or she received. There must be at least two observers. After the meeting the group discusses which functions different members fulfilled and which ones they were trying to fulfill.
2. The class forms groups of six. Each group chooses a leader and then analyzes why it selected that person.
3. Members lie on the floor with their heads toward the center of the group and begin a group fantasy about what the perfect leader for this group would have to be like. When the fantasy is over the group reviews the experience.
4. Working as a group, members paint or draw a picture of the perfect leader for their group. Members then discuss both the process of making the picture and the picture itself.

## EXERCISE 5.13:
## YOUR LEADERSHIP BEHAVIOR (II)

Now that you have completed some or all of the exercises in this chapter and have read some or all of the information presented, it may be helpful for you to again take stock of your leadership behavior. Here is a procedure for doing so.

1. Describe the task and maintenance actions in which you usually engage.
2. Describe the task and maintenance actions you would like to practice and become better at.
3. Ask other members of your group to describe your usual task and maintenance actions and help you decide which ones would be helpful for you to practice.
4. Plan how you can practice being a process observer in order to determine which task and maintenance actions would be most helpful for the group to focus on.
5. Plan how you can encourage other group members to engage in needed task and maintenance actions.

## SUMMARY

Now you have learned about the different theories of leadership and assessed your own style of leadership. You are probably aware of some group actions in which you would like to improve your skill. Continue to practice these areas as you learn about decision making, the subject of the next chapter.

## ANSWERS

*Page* 162: 1. c; 2. g; 3. j; 4. b; 5. i; 6. h; 7. f; 8. a; 9. l; 10. e; 11. k; 12. d.
*Page* 163: 1. e; 2. k; 3. j; 4. c; 5. h; 6. a; 7. l; 8. i; 9. b; 10. f; 11. d; 12. g.

# 6

# Decision Making

## BASIC CONCEPTS TO BE COVERED IN THIS CHAPTER

In this chapter a number of concepts are defined and discussed. The major ones are listed below. The procedure for learning these concepts is as follows:

1. Divide into heterogeneous pairs.
2. The task for each pair is to
   a. Define each concept, noting the page on which it is defined and discussed.
   b. Ensure that both members of the pair understand the meaning of each concept.
3. Combine into groups of four. Compare the answers of the two pairs. If there is disagreement, the members look up the concept in the chapter and clarify it until they all agree on the definition and understand it.

### CONCEPTS

1. Decision
2. Effective decision
3. Consensus
4. Majority vote
5. Minority control
6. Averaging opinions

7. Defensive avoidance
8. Groupthink
9. Dissonance reduction
10. Concurrence seeking
11. Critical evaluation
12. Vigilance

## MAKING EFFECTIVE DECISIONS

Imagine yourself driving down the street. A police officer stops you for a minor traffic violation and then notices that your appearance matches the description of a person who has just robbed a nearby bank. He arrests you and, to your horror, no fewer than six eyewitnesses identify you as the bank robber. You cannot provide a good alibi for the time of the robbery (you were driving around by yourself), and no one pays any attention to your protestations of innocence. The ordeal drags on until the day you go on trial and face your accusers. As the trial begins, you realize that the only barrier between you and a prison sentence is a small group of your peers. The jury members are strangers to one another, chosen randomly from your community, unschooled in legal principles, and unpracticed in group decision making. They hold your fate, your future, your well-being in their hands.

Trial by a jury of peers to determine guilt and innocence has formed the foundation of judicial systems for hundreds of years. As far back as the eleventh century, juries were used to both provide information about the actions of the accused and to weigh the evidence. Gradually, juries evolved into finders of fact that weight the testimony of each person before deciding if a law had in fact been broken.

A jury is only one of the small groups in our society that have to make vital decisions. Governments, large corporations, military units, and virtually all other social entities entrust their key decisions to groups. As a result, most of the laws, policies, and practices that affect our daily lives (as well as the future course of society) are determined by teams, committees, boards of directors, and similar groups, *not* by single individuals. Many groups exist to decide in our society. Thousands of small groups are making vital decisions every day. Most of the important decisions made in our society are made by small groups. How good the decisions are depends on how effective the group is. Groups are continually making decisions, some as important as whether a peer accused of a crime will live or die, others as ordinary as when and where the group will meet, what course of action it will take toward accomplishing goals, and what procedures it will use in discussions.

The purpose of group decision making is to decide upon well-considered, well-understood, realist action toward goals every member wishes to achieve. A **group decision** implies that some agreement prevails among group members as to which of several courses of action is most desirable for achieving the group's goals. Making a decision is just one step in the more general problem-solving process of goal-directed groups—but it is a crucial one. After defining a problem or issue, thinking over alternative courses of action, and weighing the advantages and disadvantages of each, a group will decide which course is the most desirable for them to implement.

Typically, groups try to make their decisions as effectively as possible. There are five major characteristics of an **effective decision:**

1. The resources of group members are fully utilized.
2. Time is well used.
3. The decision is correct, or of high quality.

4. The decision is implemented fully by all the required group members.
5. The problem-solving ability of the group is enhanced, or at least not lessened.

A decision is effective to the extent that these five criteria are met; if all five are not met, the decision has not been made effectively.

Some groups have a difficult time making decisions; members do not agree on what the decision should be. There are several reasons for indecisiveness—fear of the consequences of the decisions, members' loyalties to other groups that undermine their commitment to making good decisions, conflicts among members that destroy their ability to reach decisions cooperatively and implement them, and rigid methods of decision making that do not fit the immediate situation. To help assure that their group will arrive at effective decisions, members must not only pay attention to the factors that may block effective decision making but also take advantage of the factors that facilitate effective decision making.

In this chapter we shall discuss the comparative effectiveness of individual and group decision making. Then we shall consider the factors that facilitate and hinder an effective group discussion. We next explain the different methods a group can use to arrive at a decision, under what circumstances each method is useful and productive, and what the likely outcomes are for these methods. The next topic is the effects on group members of their involvement in the group's decision making. Finally, we detail a process groups may use to ensure effective decision making.

## EXERCISE 6.1:
## INDIVIDUAL VERSUS GROUP DECISION MAKING

There has been some controversy over whether individual or group decision making is more effective. The purpose of this exercise is to structure a critical discussion of the issue. The procedure is as follows:

1. The class forms groups of four.
2. Each group is ultimately to write a report summarizing its position on whether individual or group decision making is more effective. The report is to contain the group's overall conclusions and the facts and rationale supporting its position. The supporting facts and rationale may be obtained from the accompanying briefing sheets, the entire book, and outside reading.
3. First each group divides into pairs. One pair is assigned the position that individuals are superior to groups in making decisions, and the other pair the position that groups are superior to individuals in making decisions. Each pair takes the appropriate briefing sheet and reviews the procedure and the guidelines for constructive controversy (p. 282).
4. The pairs meet separately to prepare as forceful a 3-minute presentation of their position as possible. They are to make sure that both members have contributed to building a persuasive case for their position and that it includes as many facts and research findings as possible. Both members need to master all the rationale supporting their position. Ten minutes is allowed for this phase.
5. The group of four meets. Each pair presents its position, being as forceful and persuasive as possible, while the other pair takes notes and asks for clarification of anything that is not fully understood. Each pair is allowed about 3 minutes to present its position.

6. The group of four has an open discussion of whether individuals or groups make the best decisions. Each side should present as many facts and research findings as it can to support its point of view. Members should listen critically to the opposing position, asking for facts to support any conclusions made by the opposing pair. Participants should ensure that all the facts supporting both sides are brought out and discussed, and should follow the rules for constructive controversy. About 10 minutes are allowed for this phase.

7. The perspectives in each group are now reversed, each pair arguing the opposing pair's position. Members should be as forceful and persuasive as they can in arguing for the opposing pair's position. They should elaborate on the opposing position, seeing if they can think of any new arguments or facts that the opposing pair did not present. Each pair has about 3 minutes for its presentation.

8. Each group of four should derive a position that all members can agree on. The members should summarize the best arguments from both positions, detailing as many facts as they can on whether individuals or groups make the best decisions. When they have consensus in their group they should organize their arguments for presentation to the rest of the class. Because other groups will have other conclusions, each group may need to explain the validity of its position to the class. About 10 minutes are allowed for this phase.

9. The coordinator samples the decisions made by the groups of four by having several of them present their position to the class. The class then discusses similarities and differences.

10. The coordinator summarizes what participants have learned about decision making.

## Briefing Sheet: Individuals Make Superior Decisions

Your position is that individuals make higher-quality decisions than groups. To support your position, use the two quotations below, any material from this chapter that is applicable, and what you know from your outside reading.

> If anything, group membership blunts ethical perception and fetters moral imagination, because we then uncritically and passively let others think for us.
>
> Weston LaBarre (1972, p. 14)

> When a hundred clever heads join a group, one big nincompoop is the result, because every individual is trammelled by the otherness of the others.
>
> C. G. Jung (Illing, 1957, p. 80)

## Briefing Sheet: Groups Make Superior Decisions

Your position is that groups make higher-quality decisions than individuals. To support your position, use the quotation below, any material from this chapter that is applicable, and what you know from your outside reading.

> Group operations have two kinds of potential advantage over action by a single individual. One is the caliber of thinking, the range of resources, and the critical scrutiny which enter the problem solving. The other is the willingness with which people carry out decisions they have helped to make. . . . Groups may sometimes be more sane, moderate, well-balanced and wise than their average member. . . . A thoughtful group may make its members more rational, more self-critical, and more ready to revise personal prejudices in the light of objective evidence, than these members would be if they were studying alone.
>
> Watson and Johnson (1972, pp. 130–131)

## INDIVIDUAL VERSUS GROUP DECISION MAKING

> Achievement is a we thing, not a me thing, always the product of many heads and hands.
>
> *Atkinson and Raynor (1974)*

There is little doubt that groups typically perform higher than do individuals on almost all types of tasks (with the possible exception of brainstorming) (Johnson & Johnson 1989a; Watson & Johnson, 1972). As early as the 1930s, Thorndike (1938) considered the superiority of group to individual problem solving and decision making to have been proved. As is discussed in Chapter 3, there is substantial evidence that working in groups promotes higher individual achievement, greater group productivity, more frequent discovery and use of higher-quality reasoning strategies, greater metacognitive thought, process gain, and more frequent transfer of learning, all of which contribute to higher quality group decisions.

Within a group, chance errors among members can be corrected (Ziller, 1957). Blind spots may be corrected, as it is usually easier to see others' mistakes than one's own. Members can remedy each other's mistakes. Bekhterev (1924) briefly showed a picture to groups. Members then wrote down all the details they could remember from the picture. A discussion period followed in which the group tried to reach a consensus about each item. The group decision corrected many of the mistaken recollections of the members. Villasenor (1977) notes that the jurors in the Juan Corona trial remembered far more recollectively about the evidence and the testimony than they did individually. Shaw (1932), furthermore, concluded from a study on group decision making that a group is better able to recognize and reject incorrect solutions and suggestions than are individuals working alone. A number of studies have found that groups discussing problems derive more crucial insights into how best to solve the problems than do individuals working alone (Johnson, Skon, & Johnson, 1980; Skon, Johnson, & Johnson, 1981). Falk and Johnson (1977) found that group discussions led to decisions that none of the participants had thought of before the discussion.

One of the earliest studies to compare individual and group decision making was conducted by Goodwin Watson (1931). Watson received his Bachelor of Arts degree from the University of Wisconsin and his masters and doctorate from Columbia University. He taught at Columbia University from 1925 to 1962. In 1970 he founded and became director of the Union Graduate School of the Union for Experimenting Colleges and Universities. A vigorous, dedicated psychologist, Watson fought against all types of discrimination and challenged the value of standardized intelligence tests. In his study he used three equivalent forms of an intelligence test, each consisting of nine tasks suited to bright adults. Sixty-eight graduate students participated in the study. Each student took the first test alone, students then joined with one another in groups of four or five to solve the second test cooperatively. The third form of the test was taken by each individual alone. The two individual performances were averaged. Groups had no previous practice in working together and were allowed only 10 minutes per task. Eleven of the 15 groups excelled their average member in score; 6 of the 15 excelled their best individual performer. The typical group attained a level of effective intellectual performance of about the seventieth percentile of its members. The subsequent research generally confirms Watson's findings. Barnlund (1959), for example, found that after a group discussion, decisions surpassed both the average of the decisions of individual members and the best individual answers.

# FACTORS ENHANCING EFFECTIVE GROUP DECISION MAKING

> Two heads are better than one.
>
> *Heywood*

It is only under certain conditions that group decisions are better than individual ones.

## Positive Interdependence

The first step in ensuring that group decisions are of high quality is to structure positive interdependence within the group. **Positive interdependence** exists when group members perceive that each is linked with the others in a way that one cannot succeed unless they all do and/or that each must coordinate his or her efforts with the efforts of the others to complete a task (see Chapter 3). Positive goal interdependence may be supplemented by joint rewards, dependence on each other's resources, assigning complementary roles, and divisions of labor. Positive interdependence has numerous effects on members' motivation and productivity, not the least of which is to highlight the fact that the efforts of all group members are needed for group success. In a series of studies on the impact of positive interdependence (see Johnson & Johnson, 1989a), it was demonstrated that neither group membership nor interaction among members was sufficient to produce higher-quality decisions—a perception of positive interdependence was needed to do so.

## Individual Accountability

Group members share responsibility for the group's success. Each group member, therefore, has to take personal responsibility for (1) contributing his or her efforts to accomplish the group's goals and (2) helping other group members do likewise. The shared responsibility structured by positive interdependence adds the concept of **ought** to members' motivation—one *ought* to do one's part, pull one's weight, and contribute one's share. **Individual accountability** exists when the quality and quantity of each member's contributions are assessed and the results given to all group members. The reasons for doing so are to

1. Inform the group which members need more assistance or encouragement in completing their work.
2. Increase members' perceptions that their contributions to the group effort are identi-

fiable and they must fulfill their responsibilities in order for the group (and themselves) to be successful.
3. Reduce duplication of each other's efforts.
4. Highlight and clarify the responsibilities of each member.
5. Minimize the likelihood of social loafing and free riders.

The smaller the size of the group the easier it is to ensure that members are individually accountable.

## Promotive (Face-to-Face) Interaction

**Promotive interaction** may be defined as members encouraging and facilitating each other's efforts to achieve, complete tasks, and produce in order to reach the group's goals. Promotive interaction is characterized by individuals

1. Providing each other with efficient and effective help and assistance.
2. Exchanging needed resources such as information and materials and processing information more efficiently and effectively. The rehearsal of information relevant to the decision and the elaboration of the information's meaning both increase members' comprehension, deeper-level understanding, and retention of the information being discussed (Johnson & Johnson, 1989a).
3. Providing each other with feedback in order to improve their subsequent performance of their assigned tasks and responsibilities.
4. Challenging each other's conclusions and reasoning in order to promote higher-quality decision making and greater insight into the problems being considered.
5. Advocating the exertion of effort to achieve mutual goals.

In most decision-making groups, members with incomplete information interact with others who have different facts and perspectives relevant to the decision. The quality of decision making in such a situation depends on the processes of information exchange. If a high-quality decision is to be made, the resources of each member have to be judged correctly, the participation of all members has to be encouraged, all contributors must be listened to carefully, and the complementary knowledge must be coordinated properly. Thus, the pooling of resources results in a better decision (Laughlin, Branch, and Johnson, 1969; Goldman, 1965). Group discussion often stimulates ideas that might not occur to the individual working alone. In a musical jam session, for example, each member responds continuously to the stimulation of others in building a creative product.

In groups there is usually more support and encouragement for contributing to high-quality decision making than when individuals are working alone (Johnson & Johnson, 1989a). This social encouragement may be the reason that members of groups, compared with individuals working alone, are more optimistic that a successful decision will be made, are more intrinsically motivated to make a high-quality decision, and are more emotionally involved in the decision-making process (Johnson & Johnson, 1989a). Interaction among group members also allows members to imitate the actions of more highly motivated members (Bandura, 1965) and to compare contributions with those of other members (Festinger, 1954), both of which inspire greater efforts.

Certain decision-making situations that are labeled group decision making in fact do not allow members to interact with one another. Making decisions by decree of the designated leader (without group discussion), by edict of an expert, or by averaging members' opinions does not require any group interaction. The **Delphi method of group decision making,** in which members generate ideas independently, read a summary of the ideas of other members, and then vote, is another example. The evidence supporting the superiority of group decision making to individual decision making is based primarily on situations in which group members do interact with one another.

### Socially Skilled Group Members

If group members lack the necessary social skills to interact effectively, groups will not be productive. Individuals must be taught the interpersonal and small-group skills needed for high-quality cooperation and be motivated to use them. Numerous studies (e.g., Lew, Mesch, Johnson & Johnson, 1986a, 1986b; Mesch, Lew, Johnson & Johnson, 1986; Mesch, Johnson, & Johnson, 1988; Putnam, Johnson, Rynders, & Johnson, 1988) have demonstrated that when group members are taught small-group skills, their groups are more productive. Obviously, when members cannot communicate or manage conflicts constructively, or when they deliberately sabotage the efforts of the group, the group's decisions may not be superior to those made by individuals.

### Group Processing

The quality of group decision making is enhanced when group members regularly discuss how effectively members are working together and what skills need to be employed to improve the functioning of the group in the future. Effective work is influenced by whether or not groups reflect on (i.e., process) how well they are functioning. A **process** is an identifiable sequence of events taking place over time, and **process goals** refer to the sequence of events instrumental in achieving goals. Members engage in group processing when they discuss (1) how well their group is functioning and (2) how they may improve the group's effectiveness. More specifically, **group processing** may be defined as reflecting on a group session to (1) describe what member actions were helpful and unhelpful and (2) make decisions about what actions to continue or change. The purpose of group processing is to clarify and improve the effectiveness of the members in contributing to the collaborative efforts to achieve the group's goals. It is a truism in group dynamics that to be productive groups have to "process" how well they are working and take action to resolve any difficulties members have in collaborating together productively.

No direct evidence existed as to whether group processing did in fact improve productivity until a study was conducted by Stuart Yager (Yager, Johnson, & Johnson, 1985). He examined the impact on achievement of (1) cooperative learning in which members discussed how well their group was functioning and how they could improve its effectiveness, (2) cooperative learning without any group processing, and (3) individualistic learning. Eighty-four 3rd grade students were randomly assigned to the conditions stratifying for sex and ability level. Subjects studied a transportation unit for 35 minutes a day for 25 instructional days. The results indicated that the high-, medium-, and low-achieving individuals in the cooperation-with-group-processing condition achieved higher on daily achievement, postinstructional achievement, and retention measures than did the individuals in the other two conditions. Subjects in the cooperation-without-group-processing condition, furthermore, achieved higher on all three measures than did the subjects in the individualistic condition (see Figure 6.1).

**FIGURE 6.1**   The Impact of Cooperative Learning and Group Processing on Academic Achievement   From D. W. Johnson & R. T. Johnson, *Cooperation and Competition: Theory and Research* (Edina, MN: Interaction Book Company, 1989). Used with permission of the authors.

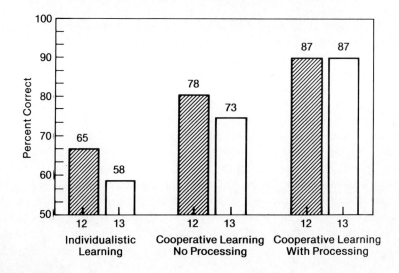

Johnson, Johnson, Stanne, and Garibaldi (in press) conducted a follow-up study comparing cooperative learning with no processing, cooperative learning with teacher processing (teacher specified cooperative skills to use, observed, and gave whole-class feedback as to how well individuals were using the skills), cooperative learning with teacher and student processing (teacher specified cooperative skills to use, observed, and gave whole-class feedback as to how well individuals were using the skills, and learning groups discussed how well they interacted as a group), and individualistic learning. Forty-nine high-ability high school black American seniors and entering college freshmen at Xavier University participated in the study. A complex computer-assisted problem-solving assignment was given to all individuals. All three cooperative conditions performed higher than did the individualistic condition. The combination of teacher and student processing resulted in greater individual and group problem-solving success than did the other cooperative conditions.

While these five conditions (positive interdependence, individual accountability, promotive interaction, small-group skills, and group processing) are the primary determiners of group effectiveness, there are other variables that should be mentioned.

### Controversy

When groups first begin to discuss an issue, members rarely voice unanimous agreement. Rather they support a wide range of views and favor competing courses of action. This disagreement provides the basis for controversy—conflict among ideas, opinions, and conclusions—which motivate group members to rethink their decision and to obtain more information about the problem. Controversy has such powerful and important effects on group decision making that it is discussed in depth in the next chapter.

### Motivation to Make a High-Quality Decision: Social Facilitation

Individuals working in groups often tend to be more motivated to make a high-quality decision than do individuals working alone. In the social facilitation research, the individual or "alone" condition typically involves the performance of an individual in front of an observant experimenter, whereas the group condition involves people working in the presence of coactors and an experimenter on similar yet independent tasks. The participants in the groups can see and be seen by one another, which produces an implicitly competitive situation (Geen, 1980).

Social facilitation researchers have shown that working in the presence of others improves performance in a variety of tasks such as fishing-reel winding (Triplett, 1898), dressing in familiar clothes (Markus, 1978), recognition of salient stimuli (Cottrell, Wack, Sekerak, & Rittle, 1968), negotiating simple mazes (Hunt & Hillery, 1973), and copying simple material (Sanders & Baron, 1975). On the other hand, they have found that working in the presence of others hampers performance on other tasks, such as solving difficult anagrams (Green, 1977), dressing in unfamiliar clothes

(Markus, 1978), recognition of novel stimuli (Cottrell et al., 1968), negotiating difficult mazes (Hunt & Hillery, 1973), and copying difficult material (Sanders & Baron, 1975). The underlying reason that has been offered to explain this effect is that feelings of competition increase anxiety, evaluation apprehension, and drive, which increase the likelihood that the dominant or most probable response will occur. If the dominant response includes behaviors that lead to successful performance (as in the case of simple tasks), then people do better when in a drive state. If the dominant response primarily includes behaviors that lead to poor performance (as in the case in difficult tasks), then people do worse when in a drive state (Zajonc, 1965).

## Group Polarization

Groups seem to be more secure than individuals in adopting positions that are more liberal or conservative than those originally held by the members (Myers & Lamm, 1976). A group discussion can polarize decisions by causing the group to adopt a position more extreme that those of the individual members beforehand. When divergent and creative thinking is required and new perspectives are needed, such risk-taking enhances the quality of group decisions.

More than 300 research studies have originated in a surprising finding by James Stoner (1961), then an M.I.T. graduate student in industrial management. For his master's thesis, Stoner decided to compare risk taking by individuals and groups. He wanted to test the commonly held belief that groups were more conservative in their decisions than individuals were. Stoner's procedure, which was followed in dozens of later experiments, posed some decision dilemmas to people by themselves (see Figure 6.2). Each problem described a decision faced by a fictitious person. The subject's task was to advise the person how much risk to take. For example, what advice would you give the person in this item:

> Henry is a writer who is said to have considerable creative talent but who so far has been earning a comfortable living by writing cheap Westerns. Recently he has come up with an idea for a potentially significant novel. If it could be written and accepted, it might have considerable literary impact and be a big boost to his career. On the other hand, if he is not able to work out his idea or if the novel is a flop, he will have expended considerable time and energy without remuneration.

Imagine that you are advising Henry. Please check the **lowest** probability that you would consider acceptable for Henry to attempt to write the novel.

> Henry should attempt to write the novel if the chances that the novel will be a success are at least:

> \_\_\_\_\_ 1 in 10    \_\_\_\_\_ 4 in 10    \_\_\_\_\_ 7 in 10
> \_\_\_\_\_ 2 in 10    \_\_\_\_\_ 5 in 10    \_\_\_\_\_ 8 in 10
> \_\_\_\_\_ 3 in 10    \_\_\_\_\_ 6 in 10    \_\_\_\_\_ 9 in 10
> \_\_\_\_\_ 10 in 10 (Place a check here if you think Henry should attempt the
> novel only if it is certain that the novel will be a success.)

**FIGURE 6.2**   A Choice-Dilemma Questionnaire Item

Mr. A., an electrical engineer who is married and has one child, has been working for a large electronics corporation since graduating from college five years ago. He is assured of a lifetime job with a modest, though adequate, salary and liberal pension benefits upon retirement. On the other hand, it is very unlikely that his salary will increase much before he retires. While attending a convention, Mr. A. is offered a job with a small, newly founded company which has a highly uncertain future. The new job would pay more to start and would offer the possibility of a share in the ownership if the company survived the competition of the larger firms.

Imagine that you are advising Mr. A. Listed below are several probabilities or odds of the new company proving financially sound.

*Please check the lowest probability that you would consider acceptable to make it worthwhile for Mr. A. to take the new job.*

_____   The chances are 1 in 10 that the company will prove financially sound.
_____   The chances are 3 in 10 that the company will prove financially sound.
_____   The chances are 5 in 10 that the company will prove financially sound.
_____   The chances are 7 in 10 that the company will prove financially sound.
_____   The chances are 9 in 10 that the company will prove financially sound.
_____   Place a check here if you think Mr. A. should not take the new job no matter what the probabilities.

Source: M. Wallach, N. Kogan, and D. Bem) "Group Influence on Individual Risk Taking," *Journal of Abnormal and Social Psychology,* 65 (1962), 75–86.

After marking their advice on a dozen items similar to this one, subjects would be placed in groups of five or so members and discuss each item and reach an unanimous decision on how much risk the person should take. Much to everyone's surprise, the decisions chosen by the group were by and large riskier than those selected before discussion. The finding was immediately dubbed the "risky-shift" phenomenon. Most studies that used this method found that group decisions were indeed riskier, and other research indicates that group decision intensifies all sorts of attitudes, beliefs, values, judgments, and perceptions (Myers, 1982).

More recently, researchers have realized that although group discussion often produces a shift in individual opinions, such a shift is not necessarily in the direction of greater risk. It could be in the direction of greater cautiousness (a **caution shift**). If the initial opinions of the group tend toward conservatism, then the shift resulting from group discussion will be toward a more extreme conservative opinion (Fraser, 1971; Myers & Bishop, 1970). The term **group polarization,** therefore, has replaced the term "risky shift." When people discuss issues in groups, there is a tendency to decide on a more extreme course of action than would be suggested by the average of their individual judgments, but the direction of this shift depends on what was initially the dominant point of view (see Figure 6.3). Groups seem to be more secure than individuals in adopting positions that are more liberal or conserva-

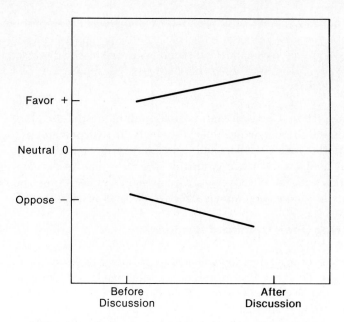

Favor +

Neutral 0

Oppose −

Before Discussion

After Discussion

**FIGURE 6.3** The group-polarization hypothesis predicts that an attitude shared by group members will usually be strengthened by discussion. For example, if people initially tend to favor risk on a life dilemma question (such as that concerning Henry), they tend to favor it even more after discussion. If initially they tend to oppose risk (as in the case of Roger's decision about selling his life insurance), they tend to oppose it even more after discussion.

tive than those originally held by the members (Myers & Lamm, 1976). A group discussion can polarize decisions by causing the group to adopt a position more extreme than those of the individual members beforehand.

At least three explanations have been given for the group polarization effect: interpersonal comparison, informational influence, and social identification. Groups may polarize because members want to create a favorable impression on others and, therefore, compare their opinions to those of other group members and modify their opinions to be a strong advocate of the group's position. Or groups may polarize because in the discussion group members learn new information that causes them to modify their opinions. Finally, groups may polarize because individuals want to identify with the group and be considered members.

## FACTORS HAMPERING EFFECTIVE GROUP DECISION MAKING

Although groups tend to make higher-quality decisions than do individuals working alone, there is nothing magical about groups. There are conditions under which groups function inefficiently and ineffectively. As we saw in the previous section, 6 of the 15 groups in the Watson (1931) study excelled the decision of their best member. There are a number of possible reasons why more of the groups did not do so. The potential barriers of group-decision making effectiveness are briefly discussed below.

## Lack of Group Maturity

In the study conducted by Goodwin Watson (1931) and in most of the other studies conducted on group decision making, college students are assigned groups in which they know none of the other members and in which they stay together for only one hour or so. Such temporary, ad hoc groups do not have time to develop enough maturity to function with full effectiveness. Group members need time and experience working together to develop into an effective decision-making team.

## Uncritically Giving One's Dominant Response

A central barrier to successful decision making includes uncritically giving the dominant response to the situation. Poor decisions are often made because group members quickly decide on a solution based on their dominant response and, therefore, do not think of the proper alternatives or do a poor job of evaluating and choosing among alternatives being considered (Maier & Thurber, 1969). Both Berlyne (1965) and Maier (1970) have theorized that responses are hierarchically arranged, and when confronted with a problem, individuals may place low probabilities on the correct solution. Dominant responses may be based on (1) physical states such as hunger that affect which stimuli a person attends to (Levine, Chein, & Murphy, 1942; McClelland & Atkinson, 1948), (2) psychological states such as attitudes and beliefs that affect what one perceives (Allport & Postman, 1945; Iverson & Schwab, 1967), (3) general cultural perspectives that lead to distortions in information perceived (Bartlett, 1932), (4) mental sets that cause the same words to have different meanings for different persons (Foley & MacMillan, 1943), (5) expectations that bias how ambiguous events are interpreted (Bruner & Minturn, 1955) and create a sensitivity to perceiving some stimuli and not others (Neisser, 1954), (6) fixation on the first reasonable solution thought of (Simon, 1976), (7) laziness that results in available information not being cognitively processed and alternative ways of understanding such information not being fully considered (Langer, Blank, & Chanowitz, 1978; Taylor, 1980), and (8) adoption of solutions that have been previously useful (Luchins, 1942).

## Social Loafing

A barrier to high-quality decision making in groups is the possibility of some members loafing. **Social loafing** is a reduction of individual effort when working with others on an additive group task. **Addition tasks** require the summing together of individual group members' inputs to maximize the group product. Each group member performs a simple individual task, such as pulling on a rope, cheering at a football game, clapping after a concert, or raking leaves in a yard. When the efforts of each member are added together, more is accomplished than any one person can achieve alone. In other words, "many hands make light the work." This does not mean, however, that groups will work with complete efficiency because of (1) group process problems such as difficulty in coordinating the efforts of group members (on pulling a rope, for example, everyone has to position himself or herself to get a good hold on the rope and then they have to pull and pause at the same time) and/or (2) some group members loafing. The productivity of the group, under these circumstances is (Steiner, 1972, 1976)

Actual productivity = potential productivity − losses due to faulty group processes

One of the first studies of group-process problems reducing group productivity was conducted by a German psychologist named Ringelmann, who studied additive tasks by having individuals and groups pull on a rope attached to a pressure gauge (reported in Moede, 1927). Two people, of course, pull harder than one person. And three people pull harder than two people. Individuals, on the average, exerted 63 kilograms (kg) of pressure, dyads about 118 kg, triads about 160 kg, and groups of eight about 248 kg of pressure. The intriguing aspect of these findings was that each person added did not increase the performance by 63 kg. Triads, for example, only performed at 2.5 times as much as the performance of one individual. The inverse relationship between the number of people in a group and the quality and/or magnitude of individual performance on additive tasks was dubbed the **Ringelmann effect.** The research on social loafing extended this research.

**Social loafing** has been demonstrated on a variety of additive tasks such as rope pulling, shouting, clapping, evaluation of poems and editorials, cheering, cycling, pumping air or water, producing ideas, typing, and detecting signals. In some four dozen studies we see that, when individuals who are working on additive tasks believe that they are lost in a crowd and, therefore, are not accountable and cannot evaluate their own efforts, responsibility is diffused across all group members (see Figure 6.4). Several situational and social factors appear to have an important impact on the magnitude of the effect. For instance, social loafing has been shown to occur

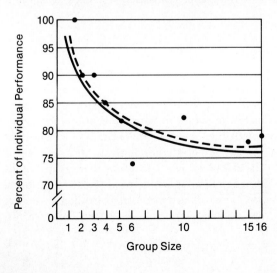

**FIGURE 6.4** This chart represents a summary of 49 studies involving more than four thousand participants and disclosed that effort decreases (loafing increases) as the size of the group increases. Each X represents the aggregate data from one of these studies From J. Jackson and K. Williams, "A Review and Theoretical Analysis of Social Loafing."

especially when group members lack identifiable contributions (Williams, Harkins, & Latane, 1981); when there is an increased likelihood of redundant efforts (Harkins & Petty, 1982); when there is a lack of cohesiveness among group members (Williams, 1981); when there is lessened responsibility for the final outcome (Petty et al., 1977); when the task is boring (as opposed to challenging, appealing, or involving) (Brickner, Harkings, & Ostrom, 1986); when there is no spirit of commitment to the team (Hackman & Walton, 1986); and when group members believe that others are loafing (Zaccaro, 1984).

In essence, social loafing is related to social facilitation through evaluation apprehension. When people believe that their individual performance is being closely monitored by others, their concern about being evaluated goes up and their performance on simple additive tasks may increase. But when they believe that their efforts are lost in a crowd, their evaluation concerns decrease and social loafing may occur.

## Conflicting Goals of Group Members

Members bring to a group a variety of motives. Some may wish, consciously or unconsciously, to sabotage the group effort. Others have self-oriented needs that may interfere with attention to making an effective decision. Members may be competing with one another in ways that reduce their effectiveness in working together. Even when members are genuinely work oriented and anxious to achieve results, they may have different ideas about how to proceed.

## Failure to Communicate and Utilize Information

Not all members participate equally in a group, and not all contributions are listened to carefully by group members. In many decision-making groups, members fail to communicate through shyness or reluctance to participate. Lack of communication skills may add further problems.

## Egocentrism of Group Members

A critical aspect of effective decision making is the ability to view the issues being discussed from a variety of points of view. When members egocentrically present their opinions and coldly evaluate the extent to which the information and conclusions of other members agree with their own, a competition over whose ideas are going to dominate develops. A number of studies indicate that an egocentric approach to decision making results in lower-quality decisions than an approach emphasizing understanding of other members' perspectives (Falk & Johnson, 1977; Johnson, 1972, 1977). The more members are embedded in their own perspective and the more they refuse to consider the perspectives of others, the lower the quality of the group's decisions will be.

## Concurrence Seeking Within the Group

**Concurrence seeking** occurs when members of a group inhibit discussion in order to avoid any disagreement or arguments, emphasize agreement, and avoid realistic appraisal of alternative ideas and courses of action. Quick compromises and censorship of disagreement are characteristic of groups dominated by concurrence seeking. Concurrence seeking typically results in poor decision making, a fact that will be discussed thoroughly in Chapter 7.

## Lack of Sufficient Heterogeneity

Whether a group will be optimally productive depends on how fully the necessary information, skills, and viewpoints are represented. The more homogeneous the participants, the less each member adds to the resources present in the others. In general, homogeneous groups make less effective decisions than heterogeneous groups (Johnson, 1980a).

## Interference

Because only one person can talk (and be heard by all the others) at any one time, participants in a discussion often have to wait to make their point. Sometimes the delay is so long that the whole course of the discussion has changed before the would-be speaker gets a chance to be heard. He or she may then drop the idea entirely, which deprives the group, or may bring the idea belatedly, which causes the others to backtrack from the issues they have moved on to. There are times when the participation of one member may interfere with the participation of other members and lower the decision-making effectiveness of the group.

## Inappropriate Group Size

Some decisions require that a large number of persons participate; other decisions need only one or two individuals. An inappropriate group size may interfere with effective group decision making. The smaller the size of the group, furthermore, the greater the individual accountability (Messick & Brewer, 1983). Seta, Paulus, and Schkade (1976) found that for a complex task, larger groups performed worse than smaller groups when given competitive instructions and better when given cooperative instructions. They also found that cooperative groups performed better when they were in close proximity and competitors performed better when they were not in close proximity. In groups of more than eight or nine members, a few participants are likely to dominate and others are likely to remain passive (Watson & Johnson, 1972). It is important that decision-making groups be large enough so that needed resources and diversity are present, but small enough so that everyone's resources are fully utilized, participation is high, acceptance and support by all members are possible, and coordination is easy (Johnson, 1980a).

## No Need for Deliberations

When the correct decision is already known by one or more members, the process of decision making becomes less an aspect of problem solving and more a persuasive situation. Laughlin (1980) has noted that when one person in a group knows the answer to a problem, members who do not know the answer often do not agree to the correct solution.

## Power Differences and Distrust

The quality of group decision making often suffers because of differences in power among members and lack of trust in what the high-power person will do if other members actively disagree with him or her. Those in high-power positions can talk freely and be listened to, but often this is a one-way affair. Many groups have explicit or implicit power structures that impede free communication. Torrance (1954), for example, studied the decision making of B-26 combat crews, in which the pilot was the commanding officer, the navigator was a commissioned officer, and the gunner was an enlisted man inferior in status to the two officers. He found that when one of the men had the right answer and the other two were mistaken, the pilots were almost always successful in persuading the other two to accept their view (94 percent), the navigators not quite as successful (80 percent), and the gunners much less persuasive (63 percent). It is not uncommon in decision-making groups for a low-power person to have a critical insight or piece of information and be ignored.

## Premature Closure and Dissonance Reduction

Making a decision prematurely and then reducing any dissonance felt by group members can contribute to ineffective decision making. According to the dissonance theory developed by Leon Festinger (1957), any time one is forced to choose between two attractive options, postdecision dissonance is present. **Cognitive dissonance** exists when a person possesses two cognitions that contradict each other. Dissonance exists, for example, if a group member knows the group selected one alternative as the most desirable option when other attractive alternatives also exist. A state of dissonance is assumed to motivate group members to reduce or eliminate it. One way to reduce the dissonance is to increase the perceived desirability of the decision made and decrease the perceived desirability of the alternatives that were not adopted. The more difficult or important the decision, the more likely group members are to find reasons that support the choice that was made and to minimize the attractive qualities of the forgone choice. This spreads apart the alternatives so that the one chosen is viewed as more attractive (in comparison with the other alternatives) after the decision than before it. If the group needs to reconsider the decision or reopen the decision making, dissonance reduction may interfere with their doing so.

## Lack of Sufficient Time

The superiority of group to individual decision making depends in part on having enough time. A short work period favors the individual response; it takes time for group members to become adjusted to one another, to express ideas, to assimilate one another's contributions, to interact, to criticize, and to integrate proposals. The larger the group, the longer the time required. Groups need enough time to thoroughly discuss the issues, especially when their task does not have a clear answer (Fox & Lorge, 1962; South, 1972).

## Summary

Although groups tend to make higher-quality decisions than do individuals working alone, there is nothing magical about groups. For high-quality decision making to take place within a group, the group needs to work together long enough to mature and to develop effective patterns of interaction among members. Any tendency toward uncritically giving the dominant response to the situation or social loafing needs to be avoided. Conflicting goals of individual members need to be resolved. All members need to participate and have the necessary social skills to present their information and ensure that it is incorporated into the group's deliberations. Egocentric refusal to consider any ideas but one's own needs to be avoided by group members. Avoidance and suppression of conflict and disagreement must also be avoided. A group needs sufficient heterogeneity among its members to ensure that different viewpoints and resources will be contributed to the discussion. Participation of members needs to be managed so that all members contribute without interfering with one another's thinking processes. Group size needs to be appropriate to the problem, the problem has to be important to group members, and there needs to be sufficient time to deal with the problem. Power within the group needs to be managed constructively, and members' motivation needs to be sustained. Quick decisions and premature closures need to be avoided.

## EXERCISE 6.2:
## THE BEAN JAR (I)

The purpose of this exercise is to compare the reactions of group members to the seven methods of decision making discussed in the next section of this chapter. A large jar full of a known quantity of beans is required for the exercise. The procedure for the coordinator is as follows:

1. Set a large jar of beans in front of the participants. You need to know exactly how many beans are in the jar. Inform the participants that they will be asked to estimate how many beans the jar contains.
2. Divide the participants into heterogeneous groups of six. Seven groups are ideal for this exercise. Appoint one member of the group to be the recorder. After the group has made its decision and all group members have completed the postdecision questionnaire (at the end of this exercise), the recorder collects the results and

computes a group average for each question by totaling the individual scores for each question and dividing the sum by the number of members in the group.

3. State that each group has to estimate the number of beans the jar contains. Assign one method of decision making to each group. The instructions of each method are as follows:

   a. The member with the most authority makes the decision. One member is appointed leader by the coordinator. This person should exercise control by such means as telling the group how to sit while waiting for the decision to be made and how to use their time while she is deciding. The leader then estimates how many beans are in the jar and announces her decision to the group. All members of the group then complete the postdecision questionnaire.

   b. The member with the most expertise makes the decision. The coordinator appoints the member with the most training in mathematics to be the leader. The expert then considers how many beans are in the jar, makes a decision, and announces it to the group. All group members then complete the postdecision questionnaire.

   c. The opinions of the individual members are averaged. Each member of the group backs away from the group so that he cannot see the answers of other group members and they cannot see his answer. Each member independently estimates the number of beans in the jar without interacting with the other group members. The recorder then asks each member for his estimate, adds the estimates, and divides the sum by the number of members. The resulting number is announced as the group's decision. All group members then complete the postdecision questionnaire.

   d. The member with the most authority makes the decision following a group discussion. One member is appointed leader by the coordinator, and she calls the meeting to order. She asks the group to discuss how many beans are in the jar. When she thinks she knows how many beans are in the jar, she announces her decision to the group. This is not consensus or majority vote—the leader has full responsibility and makes the decision she thinks is best. All members of the group then complete the postdecision questionnaire.

   e. A minority of group members makes the decision. The coordinator appoints an executive committee of two members. The committee meets away from the group to decide how many beans are in the jar. They announce their decision to the group. All group members then complete the postdecision questionnaire.

   f. Majority vote. Each group member estimates the number of beans in the jar, and the group then votes on which estimate is to be its decision. When the majority of members agree on an estimate, the group decision is made. All group members then complete the postdecision questionnaire.

   g. Consensus. All members of the group participate in a discussion as to how many beans are in the jar. Discuss the issue until all members of the group can live with and support the group's estimate. Follow the basic guidelines for consensual decision making given on page 220. When an estimate is agreed on, all members of the group complete the postdecision questionnaire.

4. Collect the results from the postdecision questionnaires and enter them in the summary table below. Instruct each group to make four conclusions as to what is to be learned from these results. Have each group share its conclusions with the class. Then conduct a class discussion on how the conclusions agree or disagree with the material presented in this chapter. Point out the following relationships:

   a. The extent to which a member feels understood and influential in the group is related to how well his or her resources are utilized.

   b. The extent to which a member is committed to the decision and responsible for its implementation is related to his or her commitment to implement the decision.

   c. The extent to which a member is satisfied with his or her participation and the

positiveness of the atmosphere of the group is related to the future problem-solving ability of the group.
5. Note how accurate each group's estimate was. Usually, the more group members directly involved in the decision making the more effective the decision is.

**Postdecision Questionnaire**

On a sheet of paper record your answers to the following questions. Then hand the paper to the recorder in your group.

1. How understood and listened to did you feel in your group?
Not at all   1 : 2 : 3 : 4 : 5 : 6 : 7 : 8 : 9   Completely
2. How much influence do you feel you had in your group's decision making?
None   1 : 2 : 3 : 4 : 5 : 6 : 7 : 8 : 9   A great deal
3. How committed do you feel to the decision your group made?
Very uncommitted   1 : 2 : 3 : 4 : 5 : 6 : 7 : 8 : 9   Very committed
4. How much responsibility do you feel for making the decision work?
None   1 : 2 : 3 : 4 : 5 : 6 : 7 : 8 : 9   A great deal
5. How satisfied do you feel with the amount and quality of your participation in your group's decision making?
Very dissatisfied   1 : 2 : 3 : 4 : 5 : 6 : 7 : 8 : 9   Very satisfied
6. Write one adjective that describes the atmosphere in your group during the decision making

---

# METHODS OF DECISION MAKING

Think about the groups to which you belong. How do they make decisions? Do different groups use different methods? Does your family use the same procedure for making decisions that you and your friends do? Among the alternatives listed below, which decision-making method would you prefer for the groups to which you belong?

1. Rely on the person in charge of the group because she should have the power to make the decision she believes is best, no matter what the rest of the group members think. The designated leader has the responsibility; she should also have the power to make the decisions.
2. Postpone making a decision and wait it out. Time takes care of everything; with a little luck a decision will never have to be made if the group waits long enough.
3. Let the expert make the decision. Give the person with the most expertise in the group the authority to make whatever decision he or she thinks best.
4. Find out what each member thinks, and then choose the most popular alternative. With this method the group does not even have to meet; members are polled individually.
5. Flip a coin, roll the dice, or pick a number out of a hat.
6. Rely on the person in charge of the group to make the decision, but only after the group has thoroughly discussed the issue with that person.
7. Put the decision in the hands of a knowledgeable and qualified committee that will look at the issues, decide what the group should do, and tell the group members its decision.
8. Take a vote and let the majority rule. The issues should be presented to the group, discussed, and then a vote held with the majority deciding.

Results of Postdecision Questionnaire

| Method of Decision Making | Understanding | Influence | Commitment | Responsibility | Satisfaction | Atmosphere |
|---|---|---|---|---|---|---|
| Decision by authority without discussion | | | | | | |
| Expert member | | | | | | |
| Average member | | | | | | |
| Decision by authority after discussion | | | | | | |
| Minority rule | | | | | | |
| Majority vote | | | | | | |
| Consensus | | | | | | |

9. Ask the group next door what it is going to do and then do just the opposite.
10. Obtain a basic agreement among everyone in the group as to what the decision should be. The issues should be thoroughly discussed, each member participating, until all agree on what the group should do.

There are many ways in which a group can make a decision. We shall take up seven of the major ones. Do not judge which methods are desirable and undesirable. Each decision-making method has its uses and is appropriate under certain circumstances. Each also has its particular consequences for the group's future operation. An effective group understands each method of decision making well enough to choose the method that is best for

1. The type of decision to be made.
2. The amount of time and resources available.
3. The history of the group.
4. The nature of the task being worked on.
5. The kind of climate the group wishes to establish.
6. The type of setting in which the group is working.

## Method 1: Decision by Authority Without Group Discussion

In this method the designated leader makes all the decisions without consulting the group members in any way. This method is quite common in organizations. It is an efficient method in the sense that it can take a short time to execute, but it is not very effective. Even if the designated leader is a good listener who sorts out the correct information upon which to make his or her decision, it is still the group that has to act on the decision, and under this method the involvement of the other group members is very small. Furthermore, when the designated leader makes the decision, not all members of the group may understand what it is; they may not, therefore, be able to implement it. And if they disagree with it, they may not want to implement it. Under this method, how well the decision is implemented is particularly crucial.

## Method 2: Decision by Expert

Group decisions can be made by letting the most expert member in the group decide what the group should do. The procedure for this method is to select the expert, let him or her consider the issues, and then have that person tell the group what the decision is. The group does not discuss the issue, but rather lets the expert decide on his or her own.

There is one major problem with this method: how to tell which member has the most expertise. On most complex issues, individuals disagree as to what the best approach is, and this makes it difficult for them to identify the expert among them. Personal popularity and the amount of power a person has over the group members often interfere with the selection of the most expert member. The classic illustration of this point is the story of the general with a high school education and several captains with Ph.D.s in engineering discussing how a bridge should be built. Needless to say, it is the general who designs the bridge, simply because he has the most power. Individuals with a lot of power are notorious for overestimating their expertise while underestimating that of others. Unless there is a clear and effective way to determine who the expert is, this method does not work very well. Moreover, it too fails to win the involvement of other group members, which is necessary for implementing the decision.

## Method 3: Decision by Averaging Individuals' Opinions

This method consists of separately asking each group member her opinion and then averaging the results. When a chairwoman of a group, for example, calls each member on the telephone, asks what the member's opinion is, and then takes the most popular opinion as the group's decision, she is using the averaging method. This procedure is like majority voting, except that the group's decision may be determined by less than 50 percent of the members (the most common opinion is not necessarily the opinion of more than half of the members) and no direct discussion is held among members as to what decision the group should make.

Because individual errors and extreme opinions tend to cancel themselves out under this method, it is usually a better procedure to follow than the designated-leader method (without a group discussion). At least members are consulted in this method. The disadvantage of the method is that the opinions of the least knowledgeable members may annul the opinions of the most knowledgeable members. Letting the most expert member make the decision is always better than using a group average to decide. And although group members are consulted before the decision is made, they are still little involved in the decision making itself. Consequently, their commitment to the decision is not very strong. If implementation of a decision made by this method requires the efforts of all group members, the effectiveness of the decision will probably be slight.

## Method 4: Decision by Authority After Group Discussion

Many groups have an authority structure that clearly indicates that the designated leader will make the decisions. Groups that function within organizations such as businesses and government agencies usually employ this method of decision making. The group does not originate ideas and hold discussions, but it is the designated leader who makes the final decision. Under this method the designated leader calls a meeting of the group, presents the issues, listens to the discussion until he is sure of what he thinks the decision should be, and then announces his decision to the group.

Listening to a group discussion will usually improve the accuracy of a decision made by the group's leader. The greater the designated leader's skill as a listener, the greater will be the benefits of the group discussion. But although members can become involved in the discussion, they have no part in the decision making, which does not help the decision's effectiveness. As a result, the group members tend to either compete to impress the leader or tell the leader what they think he wants to hear.

## Method 5: Decision by Minority

A minority—two or more members who constitute less than 50 percent of the group—can make the group's decisions in several ways, some legitimate and some illegitimate. One legitimate method is for the minority to act as an executive committee composed of only a few members, making all but the most important decisions for the group. Another is for the minority to act as a temporary committee that considers special problems and decides what action the group should take. The illegitimate methods involve railroading. For instance, two or more members may come to a quick agreement on a course of action, challenge the rest of the group with a sudden "Does anyone object?" and, if no one replies fast enough, proceed with a "Let's go ahead, then." Or a minority may forcibly recommend a course of action—implying that anyone who disagrees is in for a fight—and then move ahead before other members can consider the issue carefully. We shall focus on the legitimate methods of minority decision making; group members should be able to tell when they are being railroaded.

The minority members who make the decision may be committed to it, but the majority may not only be uncommitted, they may even want to keep the decision from being implemented. When a few members railroad a decision, furthermore, they seem to assume that persons who are silent agree. But often a majority of group members need more time to organize their thoughts against a proposal, or sometimes members keep silent because they are afraid they are the only ones who disagree. When a group has a large number of decisions to be made and not enough time to deal with them all, decision-making committees can be efficient. This method may also be effective if a large number of decisions do not need member involvement in order to be implemented. In general, however, decision by minority is not a good method of decision making.

## Method 6: Decision by Majority Vote

Majority vote is the method of group decision making most commonly used in the United States. Its procedure is to discuss an issue only as long as it takes at least 51 percent of the members to decide on a course of action. This method is so common in our society—indeed, it is almost a ritual—that it is often taken for granted as the natural way for any group to make decisions. And it is certainly one of the methods that is used most often. On the surface, majority voting resembles our election system, but critical differences exist between elections and the use of majority vote in most groups. In our political system minority rights are carefully protected through the Bill of Rights and the Constitution, and political minorities always have the right to compete on equal terms in the next election in order to become a majority. In most groups, however, minority opinions are not always safeguarded. Thus, majority voting often splits a group into "winners" and "losers," encourages "either/or" thinking (when there may be other ways of looking at a problem), and fosters blind arguments rather than rational discussion. A minority that has often been outvoted is not contributing its resources toward influencing the decision. This circumstance not only reduces the quality of the decision but often creates coalitions of individuals who resent losing the vote and who try to regroup, pick up support, and overturn the decision. When a task needs the support of everyone in the group, when the lack of support, or sabotage, by one or more members could seriously damage the undertaking, a decision by vote can be dangerous. Where commitment by everyone is not essential, of course, a majority vote can serve very well. If majority voting is to be used, however, the group must be sure that it has created a climate in which members feel they have had their day in court and will feel obliged to support the majority decision.

## Method 7: Decision by Consensus

Consensus is the most effective method of group decision making, but it also takes the most time. Perfect consensus means that everyone agrees what the decision should be. Unanimity, however, is often impossible to achieve. There are degrees of consensus, all of which bring about a higher-quality decision than majority vote or other methods of decision making. Consensus is more commonly defined as a collective opinion arrived at by a group of individuals working together under conditions that permit communications to be sufficiently open—and the group climate to be sufficiently supportive—for everyone in the group to feel that he or she has had a fair chance to influence the decision. When a decision is made by consensus, all members understand the decision and are prepared to support it. In operation, consensus means that all members can rephrase the decision to show that they understand it, that all members have had a chance to tell the group how they feel about the decision, and that those members who continue to disagree or have doubts will nevertheless say publicly that they are willing to give the decision a try for a period of time.

To achieve consensus, members must have enough time to state their views and, in particular, their opposition to other members' views. By the time the decision is made they should be feeling that others really do understand them. Group members, therefore, must listen carefully and communicate effectively. Decisions made by consensus are sometimes referred to as synergistic decisions, because the group members working together arrive at a decision of higher quality than the decision they would obtain if each one worked separately. In reaching consensus, group members need to see differences of opinion as a way of (1) gathering additional information, (2) clarifying issues, and (3) forcing the group to seek better alternatives.

The basic guidelines for consensual decision making are as follows:

1. Avoid arguing blindly for your own opinions. Present your position as clearly and logically as possible, but listen to other members' reactions and consider them carefully before you press your point.
2. Avoid changing your mind *only* to reach agreement and avoid conflict. Support only solutions with which you are at least somewhat able to agree. Yield only to positions that have objective and logically sound foundations.
3. Avoid conflict-reducing procedures such as majority voting, tossing a coin, averaging, and bargaining.
4. Seek out differences of opinion. They are natural and expected. Try to involve everyone in the decision process. Disagreements can improve the group's decision because they present a wide range of information and opinions, thereby creating a better chance for the group to hit upon more adequate solutions.

5.  Do not assume that someone must win and someone must lose when discussion reaches a stalemate. Instead, look for the next most acceptable alternative for all members.
6.  Discuss underlying assumptions, listen carefully to one another, and encourage the participation of *all* members.

Consensus is the best method for producing an innovative, creative, and high-quality decision that (1) all members will be committed to implementing, (2) uses the resources of all group members, and (3) increases the future decision-making effectiveness of the group. Consensus is not easy to achieve (Kerr et al., 1976), but is worth the time and trouble as it is characterized by more conflict among members, more shifts of opinion, a longer time to reach a conclusion, and more confidence by members in the correctness of their decision (Nemeth, 1977). Consensus requires a fairly sophisticated understanding of the dynamics of controversy, distributed participation and leadership, communication, and all other group interpersonal skills. All group members must participate actively, and power must be distributed evenly among them.

Decisions by consensus take a great deal of time and member motivation, and often prove frustrating to designated leaders. But in terms of the future ability of the group to make high-quality decisions, consensus productively resolves controversies and conflicts—which majority vote, minority rule, and all other methods of decision making do not. Research shows that the more effective groups tend to have designated leaders who allow greater participation, and more differences of opinions and who express greater acceptance of different decisions (Torrance, 1957). Effective leaders have been shown to encourage minority opinions and conflict to a greater extent than less effective leaders (Maier & Solem, 1952). Groups members with little influence over a decision not only fail to contribute their resources to it, but usually are less likely to carry it out when action is required (Coch & French, 1948). If consensus is to be used effectively, all group members must contribute their views on the issue and their reactions to proposed alternatives for group action; no one should be allowed to remain silent. For a group to achieve consensus, furthermore, time must be allowed for all members to state their opposition fully enough to feel that the others understand them—a procedure that requires careful listening and effective communication by the group members.

The advantages and disadvantages of consensus and the other six methods of decision making discussed above are summarized in Table 6.1.

## THE RELATION BETWEEN TIME AND DECISION METHOD

Every method of decision making takes a different amount of time to carry out. Obviously, methods that involve group discussion take more time than methods that do not. Usually, the more persons involved in the decision making the longer it will take to reach a decision. Figure 6.5 summarizes the relationship among the number of persons involved, the type of method used, the quality of the decision, and the

**Table 6.1**  Advantages and Disadvantages of Decision-Making Methods

| Method of Decision Making | Disadvantages | Advantages |
|---|---|---|
| 1. Decision by authority without discussion | One person is not a good resource for every decision; advantages of group interaction are lost; no commitment to implementing the decision is developed among other group members; resentment and disagreement may result in sabotage and deterioration of group effectiveness; resources of other members are not used. | Applies more to administrative needs; useful for simple, routine decisions; should be used when very little time is available to make the decision, when group members expect the designated leader to make the decision, and when group members lack the skills and information to make the decision any other way. |
| 2. Expert member | It is difficult to determine who the expert is; no commitment to implement the decision is built; advantages of group interaction are lost; resentment and disagreement may result in sabotage and deterioration of group effectiveness; resources of other members are not used. | Useful when the expertise of one person is so far superior to that of all other group members that little is to be gained by discussion; should be used when the need for membership action in implementing the decision is slight. |
| 3. Average of members' opinions | There is not enough interaction among group members for them to gain from each other's resources and from the benefits of group discussion; no commitment to implement the decision is built; unresolved conflict and controversy may damage group effectiveness in the future. | Useful when it is difficult to get group members together to talk, when the decision is so urgent that there is no time for group discussion, when member commitment is not necessary for implementing the decision, and when group members lack the skills and information to make the decision any other way; applicable to simple, routine decisions. |
| 4. Decision by authority after discussion | Does not develop commitment to implement the decision; does not resolve the controversies and conflicts among group members; tends to create situations in | Uses the resources of the group members more than previous methods; gains some of the benefits of group discussion. |

*(continued)*

**Table 6.1** (*Continued*)

| Method of Decision Making | Disadvantages | Advantages |
|---|---|---|
| | which group members either compete to impress the designated leader or tell the leader what they think he or she wants to hear. | |
| 5. Majority control | Usually leaves an alienated minority, which damages future group effectiveness; relevant resources of many group members may be lost; full commitment to implement the decision is absent; full benefit of group interaction is not obtained. | Can be used when sufficient time is lacking for decision by consensus or when the decision is not so important that consensus needs to be used and when complete member commitment is not necessary for implementing the decision; closes discussion on issues that are not highly important for the group. |
| 6. Minority control | Does not utilize the resources of many group members; does not establish widespread commitment to implement the decision; unresolved conflict and controversy may damage future group effectiveness; not much benefit from group interaction. | Can be used when everyone cannot meet to make a decision, when the group is under such time pressure that it must delegate responsibility to a committee, when only a few members have any relevant resources, and when broad member commitment is not needed to implement the decision; useful for simple, routine decisions. |
| 7. Consensus | Takes a great deal of time and psychological energy and a high level of member skill; time pressure must be minimal, and there must be no emergency in progress. | Produces an innovative, creative, and high-quality decision; elicits commitment by all members to implement the decision; uses the resources of all members; the future decision-making ability of the group is enhanced; useful in making serious, important, and complex decisions to which all members are to be committed. |

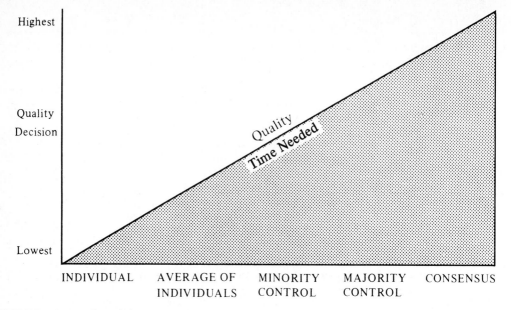

**FIGURE 6.5** Quality of decision and time needed, as a function of number of decision makers.

time needed to arrive at a decision. If the time needed for both making and implementing a decision is considered, however, the time factor becomes less clear. Often the extra time taken to make a consensual decision will greatly reduce the time needed to implement it. Thus, many group authorities insist that if the whole process of decision making and implementation is considered, consensus is the *least* time-consuming method.

## EXERCISE 6.3:
## WINTER SURVIVAL

The purpose of this exercise is to compare the effectiveness of five different methods of making decisions. Three of the methods do not utilize group discussion; the others do. The methods compared are (1) decision by a designated leader before a discussion, (2) decision by averaging members' opinions, (3) decision by expert member, (4) decision by a designated leader after a discussion, and (5) decision by consensus. At least four groups of eight to twelve members each should take part. Inasmuch as the results are very predictable, however, fewer groups with fewer members may be used if necessary. The exercise takes approximately two hours. The materials needed are as follows:

Instructions for observers
A description of the situation and a decision form
A group summary sheet
Instructions for groups that decide by consensus
Instructions for groups whose leader decides
A summary table

The coordinator for the exercise should use the following procedure:

1. State that the purpose of the exercise is to compare several different methods of decision making. Set the stage by pointing out that group decision making is one of the most significant aspects of group functioning, that most consequential decisions are made by groups rather than individuals, that though many decisions are routine others are extremely crucial, and that participants in this exercise are now in a situation where the decisions they make as a group may determine whether or not they survive.

2. Divide the participants into groups of approximately eight members—six participants and two observers. Give each group a number or name for purposes of identification, ask the observers to meet at a central place to be briefed, and then distribute the description and decision forms to the participants. Review the situation with the participants, again emphasizing that their survival depends upon the quality of their decision. In half the groups designate one person as the leader; in the other groups make no mention of leadership. Then instruct the participants to complete the decision form quietly and by themselves so that the results indicate their own decisions. They have 15 minutes to complete the decision form and make a duplicate copy of their ranking. The designated group leaders should write "leader" on their duplicate copy, and all participants must write their group designation on their duplicate copy. At the end of the 15 minutes, collect the duplicate copies.

3. While the participants are completing their decision forms, brief the observers. Give each a copy of the instructions for observers and copies of the description and decision form (to orient them to the group task). Review the instructions to make sure the observers understand their task.

4. Distribute one copy of the group summary sheet and the appropriate instruction sheet to each participant. (The groups with a leader receive one instruction sheet and the groups without a leader the other instruction sheet.) Observers should also receive a copy of the instructions for their group. The groups should be placed far enough apart so that they cannot hear each other's discussions or be aware that they have different instructions. The groups have 45 minutes to decide upon a group ranking of the items on the decision form. They are to make a copy of their group ranking with their group designation clearly written on the top.

5. While the groups are working on their rankings, score the individual decision forms in the following way:
   a. Score the net difference between the participant's answer and the correct answer. For example, if the participant's answer was 9 and the correct answer is 12, the net difference is 3. Disregard all plus or minus signs; find only the net difference for each item. (The correct ranking appears in the appendix.)
   b. Total these scores; the result is the participant's score. The lower the score the more accurate the ranking.
   c. To arrive at an average member score, total all members' scores for each group and divide by the number of members.
   d. Put the scores in order from best to worst for each group. This ranking will be used to compare how many members, if any, had more accurate scores than the group's score.
   e. In the summary table that follows the instruction sheets for the groups, enter the average member's score for each group and the score of the most accurate group member. Then, for the groups with a designated leader, enter the score of that person.

6. At the end of 40 minutes, give a 5-minute warning. After 45 minutes instruct the groups to complete their ranking in the next 30 seconds and, with the group number or name clearly marked on the paper, to turn in their group ranking. Quickly score

the groups' rankings and enter them in the appropriate place in the summary table. Recruit one or two observers to help if you need them.

7. In a session with all the participants, give the correct ranking and the rationale for each item. The correct ranking and the rationale appear on page 495 in the appendix. Then explain how the rankings are scored so that each person can determine his or her score.

8. Present the data in the summary table, preferably on a blackboard or a sheet of newsprint so that everyone can see it. Review the purpose of the exercise (to compare five different methods of making decisions), and then present the data in this order:

   a. State that one way to make a decision is to have the designated leader make it, and that this is a very common practice in most organizations. Write in the leader scores, and compare them to see which group had the most accurate leader.

   b. Move on to the next column, which is reserved for another way in which to make a decision: to poll the group and take the average opinion. Enter these data in the table and compare them with the leader scores. Usually the group average will be better than the designated leader's scores.

   c. Refer to the third column as a third decision-making method: to let the most expert member make the decision. Enter the scores of the most accurate group members in the summary table and compare with the other two methods. The expert score is usually far superior to the other two. The problem, however, is that it is often hard to identify who the most expert member of the group is; the person with the most power often believes he or she is the most expert.

   d. Point out that these first three methods represent decision procedures that do not require group interaction, that the next two procedures do involve interaction among group members and discussion as to what the decision should be, and that research on decision making overwhelmingly indicates that under most conditions discussion methods are better than nondiscussion methods.

   e. Review the instructions to the "leader" groups. Then state that a fourth way of making decisions is to have a designated leader make the decision after a group discussion. This method is also very common in most organizations. Enter the relevant data and compare them with the first three methods.

   f. Explain that the fifth column represents another way of making decisions: by group consensus. Review the instructions for the "consensus" groups. Enter the appropriate data and compare with the other four methods. When a group is functioning well, the consensus score should be better than the scores resulting from all the other methods.

9. Give the groups 20 minutes to discuss the data presented and the way in which they functioned, using as a basis of their discussions the notations of the observers. Ask each group to write out on newsprint a list of conclusions that they can share with the other groups. Here are some questions the group might discuss:

   a. How well did the group use its resources? Was there anyone who had valuable information who could not persuade others to his or her point of view? If so, why? How were silent members treated by the group: Were they encouraged to participate or left alone?

   b. What factors caused the group to use its resources well—or not well? Who behaved in what ways to influence group functioning?

   c. Was there anyone who forced his or her opinion on the group? If so, why was he or she able to do this?

   d. Did the group follow its instructions in making decisions? What influence did the instructions have on the way the group functioned?

   e. What were the personal reactions of one particular group member to the group decision making? How did this person feel? What was he or she thinking?

   f. How similar were the behaviors in this exercise to those in other group sessions? What implications does this exercise have for group meetings?

10. Share the conclusions of each group in a general session and discuss the material on decision making included in this chapter.

**Instruction to Observers**

This exercise looks at the process by which groups make decisions. Crucial issues are how well the group uses the resources of its members, how much commitment to implement the decision is mustered, how the future decision-making ability of the group is affected, and how members feel about and react to what is taking place. As an observer, you may wish to focus on the following issues:

1. Who does and does not participate in the discussion? Who participates the most?
2. Who influences the decision and who does not? How is influence determined (expertise, sex, loudness of voice)?
3. Who is involved and who is uninvolved?
4. What are the dominant feelings of the group members? How would you describe the group atmosphere during the meeting?
5. What leadership behaviors are present and absent in the group? You may wish to use the task-behavior and maintenance-behavior observation sheets on pages 182–83.
6. What are the basic causes for the members' resources being used or not being used?

**Winter Survival Exercise: The Situation**

You have just crash-landed in the woods of northern Minnesota and southern Manitoba. It is 11:32 A.M. in mid-January. The light plane in which you were traveling crashed on a lake. The pilot and copilot were killed. Shortly after the crash the plane sank completely into the lake with the pilot's and copilot's bodies inside. None of you are seriously injured and you are all dry.

The crash came suddenly, before the pilot had time to radio for help or inform anyone of your position. Since your pilot was trying to avoid a storm, you know the plane was considerably off course. The pilot announced shortly before the crash that you were 20 miles northwest of a small town that is the nearest known habitation.

You are in a wilderness area made up of thick woods broken by many lakes and streams. The snow depth varies from above the ankles in windswept areas to knee-deep where it has drifted. The last weather report indicated that the temperature would reach minus 25 degrees Fahrenheit in the daytime and minus 40 at night. There is plenty of dead wood and twigs in the immediate area. You are dressed in winter clothing appropriate for city wear— suits, pantsuits, street shoes, and overcoats.

While escaping from the plane, the several members of your group salvaged 12 items. Your task is to rank these items according to their importance to your survival, starting with 1 for the most important item and ending with 12 for the least important one.

You may assume that the number of passengers is the same as the number of persons in your group, and that the group has agreed to stick together.

**Winter Survival Decision Form**

Rank the following items according to their importance to your survival, starting with 1 for the most important one and proceeding to 12 for the least important one.

_____   ball of steel wool

_____   newspapers (one per person)

_____   compass

————————   hand ax

————————   cigarette lighter (without fluid)

————————   loaded .45-caliber pistol

————————   sectional air map made of plastic

————————   20-ft by 20-ft piece of heavy-duty canvas

————————   extra shirt and pants for each survivor

————————   can of shortening

————————   quart of 100-proof whiskey

————————   family-size chocolate bar (one per person)

## Instructions for Groups Without a Leader

This is an exercise in group decision making. Your group is to employ the method of group consensus in reaching its decision. This means that the ranking for each of the 12 survival items *must* be agreed upon by each group member before it becomes a part of the group decision. Consensus is difficult to reach. Therefore, not every ranking will meet with everyone's complete approval. Try, as a group, to make each ranking one with which all group members can at least partially agree. Here are some guidelines to use in reaching consensus:

1. Avoid arguing *blindly* for your own opinions. Present your position as clearly and logically as possible, but listen to other members' reactions and consider them carefully before you press your point.
2. Avoid changing your mind just to reach agreement and avoid conflict. Support only

Winter Survival: Group Summary Sheet

| Item | Members | | | | | | Summary |
|------|---------|---|---|---|---|---|---------|
| | 1 | 2 | 3 | 4 | 5 | 6 | |
| Ball of steel wool | | | | | | | |
| Newspapers | | | | | | | |
| Compass | | | | | | | |
| Hand ax | | | | | | | |
| Cigarette lighter | | | | | | | |
| .45-caliber pistol | | | | | | | |
| Sectional air map | | | | | | | |
| Canvas | | | | | | | |
| Shirt and pants | | | | | | | |
| Shortening | | | | | | | |
| Whiskey | | | | | | | |
| Chocolate bars | | | | | | | |

Summary Table: Accuracy of Decisions

| Group | Before Group Discussion | | After Group Discussion | | Gain or loss over designated leader's score | Gain or loss over average member's score | Gain or loss over most accurate member's score | Number of members superior to group score |
| | Designated leader's score | Most accurate member's score | Leader-group score | Consensus-group score | | | | |
| | | Average member's score | | | | | | |
| 1 | | | | | | | | |
| 2 | | | | | | | | |
| 3 | | | | | | | | |
| 4 | | | | | | | | |

solutions with which you are able to agree to at least some degree. Yield only to positions that have objective and logically sound foundations.

3. Avoid conflict-reducing procedures such as majority voting, tossing a coin, averaging, and bargaining.

4. Seek out differences of opinion. They are natural and expected. Try to involve everyone in the decision process. Disagreements can improve the group's decision because a wide range of information and opinions improves the chances of the group to hit upon more adequate solutions.

5. Do not assume that someone must win and someone must lose when discussion reaches a stalemate. Instead, look for the next most acceptable alternative for all members.

6. Discuss underlying assumptions, listen carefully to one another, and encourage the participation of *all* members—the especially important factors in reaching decisions by consensus.

### Instructions for Groups with a Leader

This is an exercise in how a leader makes decisions after participating in a group discussion. Your group is to discuss what the ranking of the survival items should be, but the final decision rests with the designated leader of your group. At the end of 45 minutes your group's leader will hand in what he or she considers to be the best ranking of the items. The role of the group members is to provide as much help as the leader wants in trying to determine how the items should be ranked.

### EXERCISE 6.4:
### THEY'LL NEVER TAKE US ALIVE
### (see page 495 for correct ranking)

This exercise uses the same procedure as the Winter Survival Exercise.

### They'll Never Take Us Alive Ranking Sheet

In a recent survey *Dun's Review* lists the most perilous products or activities in the United States, based on annual death statistics. Below are listed 15 of these death-causing hazards. Your task is to rank them in order of dangerousness according to the number of deaths caused each year. Place the number "1" by the most dangerous, the number "2" by the next most dangerous, and so forth:

| | |
|---|---|
| _____ | swimming |
| _____ | railroads |
| _____ | police work |
| _____ | home appliances |
| _____ | alcohol |
| _____ | nuclear power |
| _____ | smoking |
| _____ | motor vehicles |
| _____ | pesticides |

| | |
|---|---|
| _____ | handguns |
| _____ | bicycles |
| _____ | firefighting |
| _____ | mountain climbing |
| _____ | vaccinations |
| _____ | surgery |

## INVOLVEMENT IN DECISION MAKING

There are at least three important reasons for involving all group members in decision making: to improve the quality of the decision, to increase members' allegiance to the group, and to increase the commitment of group members to implement the decision. In general, the more group members participating in the making of a decision, the more effective the decision will be. High involvement in decision making increases the use of the members' resources, which in turn increases the quality of the decision. The members responsible for implementing the decision, furthermore, may be especially knowledgeable about what the decision should be. Many groups, while deliberating over what the decision should be, ignore those members who have to carry out the decision, thus losing their special expertise. Involvement in decision making also tends to increase members' allegiance to the group.

One of the most famous research studies of the 1940s dealt with involving workers in decisions about how their work should be conducted. An associate of Kurt Lewin and the personnel manager of a clothing factory teamed up to do a study on overcoming the resistance of workers to changes in their work activities (French & Coch, 1948). The workers in question resisted management's changes in work activities by quitting their jobs, lowering their level of production, and expressing verbal hostility toward the plant and coworkers. French and Coch decided to try out three methods of instituting changes in job duties. One group of workers was simply told about the planned changes in their jobs and what was expected of them; they did not participate in the decision making. The second group appointed representatives from among themselves to meet with management to consider problems involved in changing work methods. All members of the third group met with management, participated actively in discussions, shared many suggestions, and helped plan the most efficient methods for mastering the new jobs. The differences in outcome were dramatic. Average production in the nonparticipating group dropped 20 percent immediately and did not regain the prechange level. Nine percent of the group quit. Morale fell sharply, as evidenced by marked hostility toward the supervisor, by slowdowns, by complaints to the union, and by other instances of aggressive behavior. The group that participated through representatives required two weeks to recover its prechange output. Their attitude was cooperative, and none of the members quit their jobs. The consequences in the total participation group were even more positive. Members of this group regained the prechange output after only two days, and then climbed steadily until they reached a level of about 14 percent above the earlier average. No one quit, all members of the group worked well with their supervisors, and there were no signs of aggression. Zander and Armstrong (1972), furthermore, found that when work groups in a slipper factory were asked to set their own daily production goals, they tended to aim for goals even higher than the standard set by the manager.

Perhaps the only times decisions should be made by one or a few persons are (1) when the decisions are about matters that do not need committed action by most members of the group, (2) when the decisions are so simple that coordination among group members and understanding of what to do are easy, and (3) when the decisions have to be made quickly.

## CHANGING BEHAVIORAL PATTERNS AND ATTITUDES

Participating in a decision-making discussion within a group can have an impact on a person's subsequent behavior and attitudes. The classic experiments demonstrating this were conducted by Kurt Lewin and his associates. During World War II there was considerable concern in the U.S. government about the reactions of the public to food rationing and the need to promote the use of foods not ordinarily eaten by U.S. citizens. Lewin was persuaded to come to Washington and help. He and his associates conducted a series of experiments to determine (1) what procedures were most effective in changing behavioral patterns and attitudes and (2) what methods of persuading citizens to eat foods they consider undesirable to recommend to the government. In the first study Lewin (1943) attempted to encourage housewives to use less popular meat products, such as kidneys and sweetbreads. The subjects were six groups of Red Cross volunteers ranging from 13 to 17 members each. Half the groups were given an interesting lecture arguing for greater use of these meat products, and the other half were led through a group discussion that developed the same arguments as those presented in the lecture. At the end of the group discussion, the group leader asked for a show of hands by those willing to try one of the undesirable meat products. A follow-up survey revealed that only 3 percent of those in the lecture groups had served one of these meats, whereas 32 percent of those in the group-decision groups had served them.

A second study was conducted with six groups of housewives, ranging from six to nine members (Radke & Klishurich, 1947). The attempt in this study was to increase the consumption of milk. The groups were temporary and the same person served as both lecturer and group-decision leader. Again, an interesting lecture was given to half of the groups and the other half participated in a group discussion about the use of milk. A follow-up was made after two weeks and again after four weeks. In both cases the increase in the use of milk was greater among those in the group-decision situation.

A third study was conducted in which an attempt was made to increase the consumption of orange juice and cod-liver oil by babies (Radke & Klishurich, 1947). In this study farm mothers with their first baby either examined interesting materials on the use of orange juice and cod-liver oil or participated in group discussions covering the same material. Again, the group-decision procedure was more effective in getting the mother to actually use more orange juice and cod-liver oil.

A number of studies have confirmed the findings of Lewin and his associates (Kostick, 1957; Levine & Butler, 1952), although subsequent work indicates that later use of the foods may have been influenced by the commitment of the public to use them and the degree of perceived consensus in the group as well as by participation in the discussion (Bennett, 1955; Pelz, 1958; Pennington, Haravey, & Bass, 1958). In a related study, Preston and Heintz (1949) compared the impact of participatory- and supervisory-leadership roles on students' attitudes. The participatory leader was told to be sure that each member of his or her group was considered, to encourage all members to take part in the discussion, to discourage chance methods of decision making, and to complete the group's assigned work in the allotted time. The supervisory leader was instructed not to participate in the discussion and to limit his or her responsibility to seeing that the work was done in the allotted time. The results showed that participatory leadership was more effective than supervisory leadership in changing students' attitudes. Participatory-group members also were more satisfied with their group's decision than members of the supervisory groups, found the task more interesting and meaningful, and rated their group discussions as more friendly and enjoyable.

Overall, the results of these and other studies indicate that if you wish to change people's behaviors and attitudes, you should involve them in group discussions that lead to public commitment to (1) the new behaviors and attitudes and (2) the perception that all members of the group support the new behaviors and attitudes. A participatory-leadership pattern may facilitate this process.

## APPROACHES TO DECISION MAKING

> Neither life nor liberty nor sacred honor are safe while the legislature is in session.
> *Revere's Canon*

> This country has come to feel the same when Congress is in session as when a baby gets hold of a hammer.
> *Will Rogers*

Involving all group members in the decision making ensures that a considered and thoughtful decision is made that everyone is committed to implementing. Making a considered and thoughtful decision is much harder than it sounds. Many times decisions are made by trying to

1. *Stay with the status quo.* The decision makers complacently decide to continue whatever they have been doing, clinging to tradition, ignoring information about its ineffectiveness and the risks of losses. This is often a nonrational resistance to change, such as clinging to tradition, inertia and habit, overdependence on authority, illusions of powerlessness, or insecurity about the consequences of the change for oneself.

2. *Change as little as possible.* The decision makers adopt a new course of action that requires as little effort to implement as possible. Lindblom (1959) notes that decision makers engage in "disjointed incrementalism" where decisions differ incrementally from existing policies and, therefore, only small changes ever result.

3. *Delay and avoid making the decision.* The decision makers believe that they are "damned if they change and damned if they don't." Because they believe there are serious risks no matter what they do, they defensively avoid the decision. **Defensive avoidance** is characterized by (a) procrastination (turning attention away from the conflict to other less distressing matters), (b) shifting of responsibility or "buck passing" to someone else (enabling them to evade the dilemma and providing them with a handy scapegoat should the decision prove to have undesirable outcomes), or (c) psychological escape by means of inventing fanciful rationalizations in support of one of the choice alternatives (selectively attending to only the good aspects of that alternative and ignoring or distorting negative information about it so that decision makers feel invulnerable to threat and danger) (Mann & Janis, 1983). This latter procedure is often known as groupthink.

4. *Choose the first likely solution without considering all alternatives.* The decision makers feel pressure to make the decision immediately. Fear and anxiety about the consequences of the decision may result in vacillation, panic, and impulsively seizing a hastily contrived solution without understanding its full implications. The new course of action that requires minimal change, is most salient, or is most strongly advocated is uncritically adopted action without much thought. Hoffman (1961) notes that decisions are adopted when they reach a minimum level of support necessary for acceptance. There is a reduced time perspective, reduced memory span, simplistic and repetitive thinking, and cognitive rigidity, all of which leads to a higher value on immediate goals, premature closure, restricted search for alternatives, and less rigorous evaluation of alternatives and their consequences (Janis & Mann, 1983).

5. *Considered and thoughtful decision making in which all major alternatives are given a fair and thorough hearing.* Group members search for relevant information, assimilate it in a relatively unbiased way, and carefully evaluate the major alternatives before making a choice. Considered and thoughtful decision making can be best achieved from the small-group/large-group decision-making procedure using advocacy subgroups. This procedure is discussed in depth in Chapter 7.

The first four methods are so easy but so inadequate compared to considered and thoughtful decision making.

## GROUPTHINK AS DEFENSIVE AVOIDANCE

Decision makers are often reluctant to take action; are beset by conflict, doubts, and worry; and struggle with incongruous longings, antipathies, and loyalties (Janis & Mann, 1977). They seek relief by procrastinating, rationalizing, or denying responsibility for their own choices, that is, **defensive avoidance.** When group decision making is dominated by defensive avoidance, poor decisions are often made. Perhaps the most destructive form of defensive avoidance in group decision making is groupthink. Janis (1972, 1982) defines **groupthink** as a collective striving for unanimity that overrides group members' motivation to realistically appraise alternative courses of action and thereby leads to (1) a deterioration of mental efficiency, reality testing, and moral judgment and (2) the ignoring of external information inconsistent with the favored alternative course of action.

Social psychologist Irving Janis (1971, 1982) coined the word "groupthink" in his study of decision making. He analyzed the decision-making procedures that led to several major fiascos, such as

1. *Pearl Harbor.* In the weeks preceding the 1941 Pearl Harbor attack, military commanders in Hawaii were fed a steady stream of information about Japan's preparations for attack—somewhere. Then military intelligence lost radio contact with Japanese aircraft carriers, which had begun moving full steam straight for Hawaii. Air reconnaissance could have spotted the carriers, or at least provided a few minutes of warning of the impending attack. But the commanders decided against such precautions.
2. *Bay of Pigs Invasion.* "How could we have been so stupid?" asked President John Kennedy after the 1961 invasion of Cuba by 1,400 CIA-trained Cuban exiles. Nearly all the invaders were soon killed or captured, the United States was humiliated, and Cuba allied itself even closer to the USSR.
3. *Vietnam War.* From 1964 to 1967 President Lyndon Johnson and his "Tuesday lunch group" of policy advisors escalated the Vietnam war on the assumption that the escalations (U.S. aerial bombardment, defoliation, and search and destroy missions) were likely to bring North Vietnam to the negotiating table. The escalation decisions were made despite warning from government intelligence experts as well as from leaders of nearly all U.S. allies. The resulting disaster cost 56,500 American and more than 1 million Vietnamese lives, drove Lyndon Johnson from office, and created huge budget deficits that helped fuel inflation in the 1970s.

concurrence and avoid disagreement within the group. The concurrence seeking is reflected in eight symptoms of groupthink:

Janis believes that these blunders were bred by the groupthink syndrome. The **groupthink syndrome** is promoted when the group is highly cohesive, when it is insulated from outside criticism, when the leader is directive and dynamic, and when the group does not search for and critically evaluate alternatives (see Figure 6.6). Instead, group members rely on shared illusions and rationalizations to bolster whatever opinion is preferred by the leader. In other words, there is a tendency to seek

1. *Self-censorship.* Each member minimizes any doubts about the apparent group consensus.
2. *Illusion of unanimity.* Each member assumes that everyone (except oneself) is in agreement. There is a state of pluralistic ignorance where members falsely assume that the silence of other members implies consent and agreement.
3. *Direct pressure on dissenters.* Anyone expressing doubts is pressured to conform.
4. *Mindguards.* Certain group members try to prevent dissenters from raising objections.

---

### Antecedent Conditions

1. High cohesiveness
2. Insulation of the group
3. Lack of methodical procedures for search and appraisal
4. Directive leadership
5. High stress with a low degree of hope for finding a better solution than the one favored by the leader or other influential persons

↓

### Concurrence-Seeking Tendency

↓

### Symptoms of Groupthink

1. Illusion of invulnerability
2. Collective rationalization
3. Belief in inherent morality of the group
4. Stereotypes of outgroups
5. Direct pressure on dissenters
6. Self-censorship
7. Illusion of unanimity
8. Self-appointed mind guards

↓

### Symptoms of Defective Decision Making

1. Incomplete survey of alternatives
2. Incomplete survey of objectives
3. Failure to examine risks of preferred choice
4. Poor information search
5. Selective bias in processing information at hand
6. Failure to reappraise alternatives
7. Failure to work out contingency plans

---

**FIGURE 6.6** A Model of Groupthink

5. *Illusion of invulnerability.* Members develop an illusion of invulnerability, characterized by unwarranted optimism and excessive risk taking. They often believe that the group is above attack and reproach.
6. *Rationalization.* Group members invent justifications for whatever action is about to be undertaken, thus preventing misgivings and appropriate reconsideration.
7. *Illusion of morality.* Members ignore the ethical consequences of the favored alternative and assume that the group's actions are morally justified.
8. *Stereotyping.* Group members dismiss competitors, rivals, and potential critics as too weak to react effectively or as too evil to warrant genuine attempts at negotiation.

These aspects of groupthink lead to a number of defects in the decision-making process including an incomplete survey of alternatives and objectives, failure to examine risks of the preferred choice, poor information search, selective bias in processing information, failing to reappraise alternatives, and making no contingency plans.

## CONSIDERED AND THOUGHTFUL DECISION MAKING

Decision making occurs within the context of problem solving. To consider the steps to making considered and thoughtful decisions, the whole problem-solving procedure has to be discussed (Johnson & Johnson, 1989b).

### Establishing Positive Interdependence

Thoughtful and considered decision making begins with ensuring that the group is well structured. A classic error often made is assuming that individuals will work cooperatively if they are part of a decision-making group. What often results is competition at close quarters. The group goal of coming to a joint conclusion as to what course of action will best solve a problem must be accepted by all members. Group members must perceive that they sink or swim together. In addition, sufficient face-to-face interaction time must be scheduled for members to exchange views and challenge each other's thinking, members must be individually accountable for doing their share of the work, members must be responsible for using small-group skills, and a procedure for periodic group processing of how well the group is functioning must exist.

### Identifying and Defining the Problem or Issue

Once upon a time, a young rabbit decided to go out into the world and seek his fortune. His parents gave him $500, wished him well, and he began his search. Before he had traveled very far he met a pack rat. "Hey, little rabbit, where are you going?" asked the pack rat. "I'm seeking my fortune," replied the young rabbit. "You're in luck," said the pack rat. "I have here a suit of beautiful clothes that I will sell to you for only $100. Then you can go seeking your fortune looking prosperous and stylish!" "Say, that's fantastic!" replied the young rabbit, who immediately brought the clothes, put them on, and continued his search for his fortune.

    Soon he met a deer. "Hey, little rabbit, where are you going?" asked the deer. "I'm seeking my fortune," replied the young rabbit. "You're in great luck," said the deer. "For only $300, I will sell you this motorcycle so you can go seeking your fortune at great and exciting speeds!" "Say, that's fantastic!" replied the young rabbit, who immediately bought the motorcycle and went zooming across the countryside.

    Soon he met a coyote. "Hey, little rabbit, where are you going?" asked the coyote. "I'm seeking my fortune," replied the young rabbit. "You're in great luck!"

said the coyote. "For a measly $100, I will let you take a shortcut," said the coyote, pointing to his open mouth, "and you will save yourself years of time!" "Say, that's fantastic!" replied the young rabbit. And paying his last $100 he put his head into the coyote's mouth, and was immediately devoured.

The moral of this story is: If you don't know where you are going, you are likely to end up somewhere you do not want to be!

The first step of a decision-making group is to identify and define the problem. A **problem** is a discrepancy or difference between an actual state of affairs and a desired state of affairs. Problem solving requires both an idea about where the group should be and valid information about where it is now. The more clear and accurate the definition of the problem, the easier it is to do the other steps in the problem-solving processes. The group's vision, mission, and goals are relevant to defining the problem. There are three steps in defining the problem:

1. Reaching agreement on what the desired state of affairs is.
2. Obtaining valid, reliable, directly verifiable, descriptive (not inferential or evaluative), and correct information about the existing state of affairs.
3. Discussing thoroughly the difference between the desired and actual state of affairs, because it is from the awareness of this discrepancy that the commitment and motivation to solve the problem is built.

Because problem-solving groups often progress too quickly toward a solution to the problem without first getting a clear, consensual definition of the problem itself, members of the group should see to it that everyone understands what the problem is before trying to assess its magnitude.

*Defining a workable problem is often the hardest stage of the problem-solving process.* Suggestions for procedures are as follows:

1. List a series of statements about the problem. Describe it as concretely as possible by mentioning people, places, and resources. There should be as many different statements of the problem as the members are willing to give. Write them on a blackboard where everyone can see them. Avoid arguing about whether the problem is perfectly stated.
2. Restate each problem statement so that it includes a description of both the desired and actual state of affairs. Take out alternative definitions that are beyond the resources of the group to solve. Choose the definition that the group members agree is most correct. *The problem should be important, solvable, and urgent.*
3. Write out a detailed description of what group life will be like when the problem is solved. The more detailed and specific the scenario is, the better.

There are a number of potential barriers to identifying and defining problems. The first is **prematurely defining the problem.** The direction a group first takes in defining the problem may keep it from finding a successful solution (Maier, 1930); therefore, the group should be careful not to agree prematurely on the definition of its problem. The second is a **lack of clarity in stating the problem.** Much of the initial effort of groups in solving a problem is directed toward orienting members to what the problem is. This phase is extremely important, and it deserves sufficient time and effort to identify the problem, to define it, and, through this process, to get the members involved in and committed to solving it. Often, groups are doomed to failure when they inadequately define the nature of their problem. Third, **a critical, evaluative, competitive climate** prevents creative and workable solutions from being discovered. A supportive, trusting, cooperative atmosphere is necessary for solving problems successfully. If group members are afraid that other members are evaluating their ideas, effective problem solving is destroyed. Fourth, if group members have **inadequate motivation to solve the problem,** a compelling solution will not be found. Any problem-solving group must have the motivation to solve its problems. If the group members are not motivated, they must be persuaded to see the importance of the problem and the necessity for seeking a solution. Members who leave the work to others clearly lack motivation.

## Gathering Information About the Existence of the Problem

The second step in the problem-solving process is diagnosing the existence, magnitude, and nature of the problem. Valid information must be gathered. Then the information must be thoroughly discussed and analyzed to ensure that all task force members understand it. Actual frequency of occurrence of the problem, the magnitude of the forces helping the school to move toward the desired state of affairs, and the forces hindering this movement need to be documented. Determining what forces are acting upon the problem situation is called **force field analysis** (Lewin, 1944; Myrdal, 1944). In force field analysis the problem is seen as a balance between forces working in opposite directions—some helping the movement toward the desired state of affairs and others restraining such movement. The balance that results between the helping and restraining forces is the actual state of affairs—a **quasi-stationary equilibrium** that can be altered through changes in the forces (see Figure 6.7).

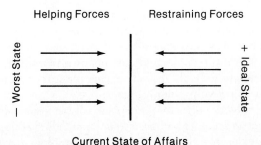

**Helping Forces**   **Restraining Forces**

Worst State   + Ideal State

**Current State of Affairs**            **FIGURE 6.7**   Force Field Analysis

The ideal state of affairs toward which the group is working is on the right side and is represented by a plus sign. The worst state of affairs, on the left side of the figure, is represented by a minus sign. The vertical line in the middle signifies the current state of affairs—a middle ground. On any problem numerous forces are at work, some restraining change and others helping change. There are two basic steps for a group to follow in doing a force field analysis.

1. Make up lists of forces by first brainstorming all the helping forces and then all the restraining forces. The list should include all possible forces, whether psychological, interpersonal, organizational, or societal. If a force seems to be a complex of variables, each variable should be listed separately. Critical judgment should be avoided; it is essential that every member's ideas are publicly requested and aired.
2. Rank the forces according to their importance in affecting the present situation. Agree on the most important helping and restraining forces, which may total from three to six each. Rate the important forces according to how easily they can be resolved, and avoid spending time discussing those that the group cannot influence with their current resources.

An example is as follows. The implementation of cooperative learning within a school may be seen as a balance between forces helping teachers implement cooperative learning and restraining teachers from using cooperative learning (see Figure 6.8). The use of cooperative learning is promoted by the teachers' awareness that it will increase student achievement, higher-level reasoning, social skills, self-esteem, and social support. The use of cooperative learning is restrained by teachers habitually using other instructional procedures, not being willing to commit the time to learn how to use cooperative learning, inherent fear of change, lack of willingness to revise their standard lessons, and incomplete understanding of what cooperative learning is.

There are two major *barriers* to gathering valid information about the nature and magnitude of the problem. The first is *not getting the needed information*. When information is minimal, the definition of the problem will be inadequate, fewer alternative strategies for the solution will be generated, and potential consequences of those alternatives will not be properly explored. The result is relatively low-grade solutions. Great emphasis must be placed on fact finding in order to solve a problem effectively. The second barrier is *poor communication within the group*. Poor communication among group members has the same effect as the lack of information, with the added problem that it makes the implementation of any action that requires coordination among group members difficult. Effective communication among all group members is necessary for effective problem solving.

Without defining the problem correctly and specifically, it cannot be adequately understood. And without an accurate and precise understanding of the forces involved, the alternative strategies for the solution of the problem cannot be formulated.

**FIGURE 6.8**   Implementing Cooperative Learning

|  | HELPING FORCES | | RESTRAINING FORCES | |
|---|---|---|---|---|

| No Use — | Achievement increases ▶ | Habit of status quo | + Skilled Use |
| | Higher level reasoning ▶ | ◀ Time needed to learn how | |
| | Improved social skills ▶ | ◀ Fear of change | |
| | Increased self-esteem ▶ | ◀ Time to revise lessons | |
| | More social support ▶ | ◀ Lack of understanding | |
| | Liking for school ▶ | ◀ Teacher isolation | |

Current Level of Use

## Formulating and Considering Alternative Solutions

The overall purpose of a decision-making group is to make a free and informed choice of a solution to the problem based on having and understanding the relevant information. To achieve that purpose a cooperative structure must be established, the problem must be accurately identified and defined, and valid information about the existence, magnitude, and nature of the problem must be gathered and organized so it is easily understood. Once the nature and magnitude of the problem are accurately understood, alternative ways to solve it may be identified.

The fourth step in problem solving is identifying and analyzing alternative ways to solve the problem. Groups often make poor decisions because they (1) do not think of the proper alternative solutions and /or (2) do a poor job of evaluating and choosing among alternatives considered. *Systematically evaluating each alternative and analyzing the advantages and disadvantages of each alternative before making a final decision are the most important factors in effective decision making.* The more explicit the systematic evaluation, the less likely that an alternative will be overlooked or rationalized away. If decision makers do know what the alternatives are and have correctly diagnosed each alternative's inherent advantages and disadvantages, they will not choose a certain course of action unless its advantages are expected to exceed its disadvantages.

Identifying and analyzing alternative ways to solve the problem requires creative, divergent, and inventive reasoning. Such "higher-level" thinking and analysis comes primarily from intellectual disagreement and challenge, that is, controversy. Controversy is discussed in Chapter 7. By definition, all decisions involve controversy as decision making is a choice among alternative courses of action. Controversy is structured within problem-solving groups through the use of advocacy subgroups. To participate competently in the controversy process group members must be able to prepare a position, advocate it, defend it from criticism, critically evaluate the alternative positions, view the problem from all perspectives, and synthesize and integrate the best parts of all solutions.

## Force Field Analysis

Force field analysis is a particularly useful way of specifying alternative strategies for solving a problem. It is based on the assumption that changes in the present situation will occur only as the helpful and restraining forces are changed so that the level where they are balancing is altered. *There are two basic methods for changing the equilibrium point between the two sets of forces:* increasing the strength or number of the helping forces and decreasing the strength or number of the restraining forces. Of the two, the preferable strategy is to reduce the strength or eliminate the restraining forces. Increasing the pressure for change in the present situation by strengthening the helping forces also increases natural resistances to change, reducing the strategy's effectiveness. Restraining forces may be reduced or eliminated without creating resistance. *Reducing the restraining forces, therefore, is usually the more effective of the two strategies.* The fewer the forces acting upon the present situation, furthermore, the lower the tension level of the people in the situation.

The two methods are not mutually exclusive. Often you will wish to reduce restraining forces and increase helping forces at the same time. When this can be done, it is very effective. One way of intervening simultaneously with both types of forces is to modify a restraining force so that it becomes a helping force. One of the most successful strategies for changing the direction of a restraining force is to involve the group members who are resisting the desired changes in diagnosing the problem situation and in planning the solutions (Watson & Johnson, 1972). *People enjoy and affirm the changes they make themselves, and they resist changes imposed upon them by others.* Involvement of resisters in the diagnosing and planning of change often means a more difficult planning process, but it virtually guarantees that they are committed to the proposed changes. It also helps clear up any misunderstandings and differences of opinion before the strategies are implemented, and it uses the resources of the "opposition."

*Force field analysis is useful for two reasons.* First, it avoids the error of a single-factor analysis of a problem; using it will keep attention on the problem situation until a number of relevant factors are identified. Second, by helping to identify a number of problem-related factors, it gives group members several points at which they may intervene in their attempt to produce a change. Because any change is the result of a number of factors, an effective change strategy involves plural actions that are directed toward several of those factors. When an approach is made through modifying several factors at the same time, the possibility is increased that the improvement will be permanent.

In specifying alternative strategies for change, group members should think of as many ways as possible in which the forces holding the group from moving toward the desired state might be reduced. They should obtain ideas from everyone in the group. If group members do not have many ideas, outside consultants can always be invited to lend assistance. Bringing in an expert who knows a lot about the substance of the problem is often extremely helpful at this point. Group members should try to take each restraining force in turn and think up ways to reduce its strength or to eliminate it altogether. Divergent thinking should be encouraged.

## Vigilant Analysis

Janis and Mann (1977) recommend a procedure they believe eliminates the possibility of defensive avoidance and ensures that vigilant consideration of each alternative solution takes place. The group systematically evaluates each alternative solution on the basis of four factors:

1. The tangible gains and losses for the school staff.
2. The tangible gains and losses for significant others such as parents and other members of the school district.
3. Staff self-approval or self-disapproval. (Will we feel proud or ashamed if we choose this alternative?)
4. The approval or disapproval of the school by significant others. (Will important people we are connected with think we made the right decision?)

To ensure that these four factors are used to analyze each alternative,

1. A balance sheet is completed for each course of action considered. A balance sheet consists of listing the tangible gains from adopting the alternative on one side and the tangible losses on the other.
2. Each gain or loss is rated in terms of its importance on a ten-point scale from 1 (no importance) to 10 (extremely important).
3. After a balance sheet is completed for each alternative course of action, the balance sheets are compared and the alternatives are ranked from "most desirable" to "least desirable."

Using a balance sheet to ensure systematic evaluation has been found to be related to level of satisfaction with a decision, commitment to a decision, and security about the correctness of a decision (Janis & Mann, 1977).

Other procedures for ensuring that high-quality decisions are made by preventing groupthink and by structuring systematic evaluation include the following (Janis & Mann, 1977; Mann & Janis, 1983):

1. *Impartial Leadership.* The leader abstains from communicating his or her position at the outset so that members cannot adopt it uncritically. By not stating preferences and expectations at the outset and by not advocating specific proposals, the leader allows members to develop an atmosphere of open inquiry and to explore impartially a wide range of policy alternatives.
2. *Critical Evaluator Role for Every Member.* Group members are encouraged to express doubts and objections freely. The leader assigns each member the role of critical evaluator, giving high priority to the airing of objections and doubts and accepting criticism of judgments in order to discourage group members from softpedaling their disagreements.
3. *Devil's Advocate.* One or more group members are assigned the role of challenging the testimony of all those who support the majority opinion. Members are chosen to represent unpopular positions in the group.
4. *Outside Experts.* Outside experts are invited to group meetings and asked to challenge the views of group members.

## Barriers

There are a number of barriers to formulating and considering alternative solutions to the problem. The first is a *failure to identify the proper alternative courses of action.* If a course of action is not identified, it cannot be considered and evaluated. The second is *premature elimination of course of action without proper analysis and evaluation, or uninformed and premature choice.* Groups often make poor decisions, not because they did not think of the proper alternatives, but because they did a poor job of evaluating and choosing among the alternatives they considered (Maier & Thurber, 1969). For most people, ideas are fragile creations, easily blighted by a chill, or even indifferent, reception. As groups proceed in their problem-solving activities, they must avoid all tendencies to squelch each idea as it comes along;

instead, they should create an atmosphere that supports the presentation and the pooling of a wide assortment of ideas. All alternative solutions should receive a fair hearing. Only then can the group avoid becoming fixated on the first reasonable solution suggested and critically evaluate the worth of all alternatives. The third is *pressures for conformity.* Pressures for conformity and compliance slow down the development of different and diverse ideas. Divergent thinking as well as convergent thinking are necessary for sound problem solving. The fourth is *a lack of inquiry and problem-solving skills.* Some groups may need special training in how to use inquiry and problem-solving methods to advantage. Training may be accomplished through an expert member of the group, or the group may wish to call in an outside consultant. The fifth is *a lack of procedures to aid analysis and synthesis.* The forces creating the problem must be understood and systematically analyzed in order for new alternatives to be created.

## Deciding on a Solution

Once all the possible solutions have been identified and formulated in specific terms, the group needs to select the solution it will implement. Making a decision involves considering possible alternatives and choosing one. The purpose of group decision making is to decide on well-considered, well-understood, realistic action toward goals every member wishes to achieve. Whenever possible, decisions by task forces should be made by consensus. Consensus is not easy to achieve as it is characterized by more conflict among members, more shifts of opinion, a longer time to reach a conclusion, and more confidence by members in the correctness of their decision. It is, however, worth the time and trouble.

## Second-Chance Meeting

Even when decisions are made by consensus, there are times when members fixate on an alternative without thinking through all its consequences. One procedure for ensuring that a decision is not made too hastily is **second-chance meetings.** Alfred Sloan, when he was chairman of General Motors, once called an executive meeting to consider a major decision. He concluded the meeting by saying, "Gentlemen, I take it we are all in complete agreement on the decision here. . . . Then I propose we postpone further discussion until our next meeting to give ourselves time to develop disagreement and perhaps gain some understanding of what the decision is all about." After a preliminary consensus on the best alternative, a second-chance meeting can be held in which all members are encouraged to express any remaining doubts and criticisms. Second chance meetings help prevent premature consensus and concurrence seeking.

There are a number of societies that have assumed that under the influence of alcohol there would be fewer inhibitions against expressing residual doubts about a preliminary decision made when everyone was sober. According to Herodotus, the ancient Persians would make important decisions twice—first sober and then drunk. According to Tacitus, the Germans in Roman times also followed this practice. In Japan, where an emphasis is placed on harmony and politeness, a decision is frequently reconsidered after work in a bar. "Sake talk" takes place after each person has had a couple of cups of sake and, therefore, is no longer required to be polite. How group members really feel about the decision is then revealed.

## Presenting the Recommendation to the Organization

It is not enough to make a decision. All persons who need to implement the decision need to be convinced that it is the best thing to do. Thus, the solution recommended has to be communicated clearly to the organization as a whole, and the relevant others must have an opportunity to modify the decision if they are to be committed to implementing it. If the people who must implement the decision are not involved in making it, they will have little or no commitment to help implement the decision. People tend to affirm, support, and implement decisions they have helped make while they tend to resist implementation of decisions imposed on them. The key to this step is to ensure that everyone participates, everyone is involved in making the decision, and, therefore, everyone is committed to implementing the decision once it is made. The barrier to effective decision making at this point is inadequate involvement of the individuals who have to implement the decision.

## Evaluating Extent and Success of Implementation

The responsibilities of the group members do not end when the group makes a decision. The decision has to be implemented. **Decision implementation** is a process of taking the necessary actions that result in the execution of the decision. *Decision implementation requires internal commitment by relevant group members to the decisions made.* No decision is worthwhile unless it is implemented. Once the group decides, the next step is going out and doing what members have decided to do.

To evaluate the success of the solution the group has decided to implement, members must determine (1) whether the solution was successfully implemented and (2) what the effects were. The first activity is sometimes called **process evaluation** because it deals with the process of implementing a strategy. The second is called **outcome evaluation** because it involves assessing or judging the consequences of implementing the strategy. Planners should establish criteria for or ways in which to judge the effectiveness of their actions in implementing the strategy and review their progress as each action step occurs. The major criterion for assessing the outcome of an implemented strategy is whether the actual state of affairs is closer to the desired state of affairs than it was before the strategy was carried out. The group documents the extent to which implementation takes place, notes barriers to implementation, and evaluates the success of the decision.

If the group finds that its solution has been successfully implemented, but has failed to change substantially the current situation into the ideal state of affairs, a new solution must be chosen and implemented until the group finds one that is effective. The solution of one set of problems, however, often brings other problems into the open, and in trying out various strategies the group may find that it has not been working for the solution of the most critical problem in the situation. The final result of the evaluation stage, therefore, should be to show the group what problems have been solved and to what extent, what problems still need to be solved, and what new problems have come up. Evaluation should result in a new definition of a problem, a rediagnosis of the situation, and beginning of a new problem-solving sequence.

# TWO PROBLEMS WITH THE THEORIZING ON DECISION MAKING

There are at least two major problems with the theorizing and research on decision making in small groups. The first is that much of the research has focused on whether the decisions made by groups are of high or low quality. In the real world many decisions cannot be objectively evaluated in terms of success or failure because their long-term effects cannot be fully measured. To evaluate long-term success or failure, one would need to take into account the negative consequences of the decision made, the positive consequences that would have resulted if each of the other alternatives had been adopted as the decision, the positive consequences of the decision, and the negative consequences that would have resulted if each of the other alternatives had been adopted. Obviously, it is difficult if not impossible to quantify these factors.

The second problem is that much of the theorizing and research on decision making has assumed that decision makers are completely informed (that they know all the possible courses of action and the potential outcomes of each), infinitely sensitive (they see each alternative in all its complexity), and always rational (they always maximize the outcomes of their action). Real-life decision makers, however, are not always completely informed (they do not or cannot know all courses of action and their potential outcomes), do not understand fully the intricacies of various alternatives, and are rarely completely rational. Real-life decision makers often seem beset by conflicts, doubts, and worries: they struggle with conflicting loyalties, antipathies, and longings and engage in procrastination, rationalization, and denial of responsibility for their decisions. Instead of determining the solution that maximizes their outcomes, many decision makers look only for the alternative that meets a minimal set of requirements (this is called satisficing) and make quick decisions (Hoffman, 1961; Simon, 1976). Ineffective groups seem to operate under a variety of decision-making rules, such as "tell a qualified expert about the problem and do whatever he or she says—that will be good enough" and "Do what we did last time if it worked, and the opposite if it didn't work." Real-life decision makers also realize how expensive it is in time, effort, and money to collect and dissect the huge amounts of information a group needs in order to use an ideal form of decision making.

Researchers can alleviate these two problems by studying the process of decision making rather than focusing on quality, and by specifying procedures that encourage real-life decision makers to become more systematic and rational in their decision making.

## EXERCISE 6.5:
## A PROBLEM DIAGNOSIS PROGRAM

This program is designed to help you in diagnosing a problem that involves people working together in a group. In this program eleven separate steps are presented, each of which contains a complete and separate idea, question, or instruction. Be sure that you understand and complete each step before going on to the next one.

1. Identify the problem you wish to work on. Describe the problem as you now see it.

   _____

   _____

   _____.

2. Most problem statements can be rephrased so that they describe two things:
   a. The situation as it is now.
   b. The situation as you would like it to be (the ideal).

   Restate your problem situation in these terms. _____

   _____

   _____

   _____

   _____.

3. Most problem situations can be understood in terms of the forces that push toward and against change—in other words, helping forces and restraining forces. It is useful to analyze a problem by making lists of the helping and restraining forces affecting a situation. Think about these now, and list them. Be sure to list as many as you can, not worrying at this point about how important each one is. Use additional paper if you need to.

| **Helping** | **Restraining** |
|---|---|
|  |  |
|  |  |
|  |  |
|  |  |
|  |  |

4. Review the two lists. Underline those forces that seem to be the most important right now, and that you think you might be able to influence constructively. Depending on the problem, there may be one specific force that stands out, or there may be two or three helping forces and two or three restraining forces that are particularly important.

5. Now, for each restraining force you have underlined, list some possible courses of action that you might be able to plan and carry out to reduce the effect of the force or to eliminate it completely. Brainstorm. List as many action steps as possible, without worrying about how effective or practical they would be. You will later have a chance to decide which are the most appropriate.
   Restraining force A. Possible action steps to reduce this force:

   _____

   _____.

Restraining force B. Possible action steps to reduce this force:

_____

_____.

Restraining force C. Possible action steps to reduce this force:

_____

_____.

6. Now do the same with each helping force you underlined. List all the action steps that come to mind that would increase the effect of each helping force.
Helping force A. Possible action steps to increase this force:

_____

_____.

Helping force B. Possible action steps to increase this force:

_____

_____.

Helping force C. Possible action steps to increase this force:

_____

_____.

7. You have now listed actions steps to change the key forces affecting your problem situation. Review these possible action steps and underline those that seem promising.
8. List the steps you have underlined. Then for each action step list the materials, people, and other resources available to you for carrying out the action.

| Action Steps | Resources Available |
| --- | --- |
|  |  |
|  |  |
|  |  |

9. Review the list of action steps and resources and think about how each might fit into a comprehensive action plan. Take out those items that do not seem to fit into the overall plan, add any new steps and resources that will round out the plan, and think about a possible sequence of action.

_____

_____

_____

_____

10. Plan a way of evaluating the effectiveness of your action program as it is implemented. Think about this now, and list the evaluation procedures you will use.

   _____

   _____

   _____

   _____

11. You now have a plan of action to deal with the problem situation. The next step is for you to implement it.


**EXERCISE 6.6**
**THE BEAN JAR (II)**

The purpose of this exercise is to show that the involvement of more persons in the decision-making process affects the accuracy of the decision. The exercise can be done in an hour, and it requires only a large jar full of a known quantity of beans. The procedure for the coordinator is as follows:

1. Explain that the exercise focuses on the accuracy of the decisions made by different combinations of individuals. Then set a large jar of beans in front of the participants. You need to know exactly how many beans are in the jar. Tell the participants they will be asked to estimate how many beans the jar contains.
2. Have each person estimate the number of beans, working alone. Record the estimates.
3. Have each participant pick a partner. Have the 2-person teams work out a system for estimating how many beans are in the jar, and record their estimates.
4. Have each pair pick another twosome and the 4-person teams estimate the number of beans. Record their estimates.
5. Have each quartet pick another foursome and the 8-member groups estimate the number of beans. Record their estimates.
6. Have each octet pick another group and the 16-member groups estimate the number of beans. Record their estimates.
7. Ask for the final estimates and then tell the participants the number of beans in the jar. Have the class form groups of 8 and discuss their experience, how they felt during the decision making, and the way in which they operated in the groups. Finally, ask the groups of eight to build a set of conclusions about the effect that an increasing number of members has on the accuracy of the decision and why the number of members influenced decision accuracy in the way it did. Have each group share its conclusions with the rest of the participants, and then have a class discussion of the conclusions.


**EXERCISE 6.7:**
**YOUR DECISION-MAKING BEHAVIOR**

Before this chapter ends it might be useful for you to consider your decision-making behavior.

How do you usually behave in a decision-making group? How would you like to behave? Here is a closing exercise for you to do in a group with two of your classmates:

1. Throw all your loose change into the center of the group. Decide (using consensus) how to use the money. Then look at the group decision in terms of the behaviors of each member. How did each of you behave? What task and maintenance functions did you yourself fulfill? How did you feel about your participation? How did your usual behavior reveal itself in the group decision making?
2. Review as a group the task and maintenance functions listed in the previous chapter. Discuss what other functions could be added. Examples are
   a. *Clarification or elaboration.* Interpret or reflect ideas or suggestions; clear up confusion; bring up alternatives and new issues before the group; give examples.
   b. *Summarization.* Pull together related ideas; restate suggestions after the group has discussed them.
   c. *Consensus testing.* Check with the group to see how much agreement has been reached; test to see if the group is nearing a decision.
   d. *Communication of feeling.* Express your feelings about the issues the group is discussing and the way in which it is functioning.
   e. *Verification of feeling.* Ask other members how they are feeling; check to see if your perception of their feelings is correct.
   Pick the task and maintenance functions you usually engage in; pick those you would like to perform better. Give one another feedback about each member's behavior.
3. Have you received any feedback on your behavior that has increased your awareness of how you behave? How would you now describe your behavior in decision-making situations?
4. Decide as a group when to end this exercise.

## HOW I BEHAVE QUESTIONNAIRE

The purpose of this questionnaire is to help you look at how you behave in a group that is making a decision. Different persons act in different ways when they are members of groups that are making decisions. Moreover, the same person may act differently at different times, depending on the group, the decision to be made, and the circumstances. But in general, how do you act when a group in which you are a member is making a decision? In each of the following three statements, choose the best description of the way in which you behave when a group to which you belong is making a decision. Be as objective and honest as you can; the results are for your use only.

1. When my group is making a decision, I

   _____ passively defer to others.

   _____ work for a decision that satisfies everyone without worrying about how good it is.

   _____ look entirely at the merits of the alternatives without thinking about how the members of the group feel or how satisfied they are.

   _____ look for alternatives that work, though I might not personally think they are the best.

_____   work for a strong, creative decision having a common basis of understanding among group members.

2. When my group is facing a decision, I

_____   show little interest in the decision or the other group members.

_____   think mostly about how the members of the group are getting along, without worrying about what the decision will be.

_____   push for a really good decision and view the other members only as contributors of resources that will help make a better decision.

_____   work for good relations among the members and a good solution, though I am willing to sacrifice a little of each to get the job done.

_____   avoid compromise and try to get everyone to agree to and be satisfied with a decision that is based upon looking at the situation in a realistic way.

3. When my group is making a decision, I

_____   wait for the group to tell me what to do and accept what they recommend for me.

_____   help others participate by giving them moral support and by testing to see if members can agree.

_____   give information, evaluate how well the group is working toward completing the task, set ground rules for behavior, and see that everyone stays at the task.

_____   summarize periodically what has been discussed, call for things to be made clearer, and encourage members to compromise.

_____   help the group think of alternatives, discuss how practical the alternatives are, and work out ways in which the group can come to an agreement.

You can plot this self-assessment on the task-maintenance grid in Figure 5.1. Each of the preceding statements can be completed in five possible ways. The first alternative for each statement is a (6,6) response; it shows that this person has little or no interest in either maintaining the group or helping it accomplish its task of making a decision. The second alternative is a (6,30) response, showing that this member emphasizes group maintenance while ignoring the task. The third alternative is a (30,6) response; here the person focuses on getting the task done but ignores group maintenance. The fourth alternative is an (18,18) response, indicating a member who compromises on both task and maintenance in order to reach a decision. The fifth alternative for each question is a (30,30) response; this person tries to achieve a creative, consensual decision, and emphasizes both the task and maintenance functions of the group.

Look at your three responses. Locate each on the task-maintenance grid. Then discuss the results in groups of three, comparing your responses here with those you gave on the leadership surveys in the previous chapter, and with the way you would like to act in groups.

## SUMMARY

This chapter dealt with effective decision making and gave you practice in skills needed for being an effective group decision maker. As groups become more developed they must learn to deal with controversy and maximize their opportunities for creativity. This will be discussed in the next chapter.

# Controversy and Creativity

## BASIC CONCEPTS TO BE COVERED IN THIS CHAPTER

In this chapter a number of concepts are defined and discussed. The major ones are listed below. The procedure for learning these concepts is as follows:

1. Divide into heterogeneous pairs.
2. The task for each pair is to
   a. Define each concept, noting the page on which it is defined and discussed.
   b. Ensure that both members of the pair understand the meaning of each concept.
3. Combine into groups of four. Compare the answers of the two pairs. If there is disagreement, the members look up the concept in the chapter and clarify it until they all agree on the definition and understand it.

### CONCEPTS

1. Controversy
2. Conceptual conflict
3. Epistemic curiosity
4. Perspective taking
5. Open-mindedness
6. Dogmatism
7. Cognitive perspective
8. Differentiation of positions
9. Integration of positions
10. Creativity
11. Brainstorming

## EXERCISE 7.1:
## CONTROVERSY

1. Form a group of five members. Your group is to make a decision as to what the answer of the following question is:

   ***ASSERTION* IS TO *DISPROVED* AS *ACTION* IS TO**

   a. hindered
   b. opposed
   c. illegal
   d. precipitate
   e. thwarted

2. Assign each alternative answer to a group member who is told to plan and present the best case for that alternative being the correct answer.
3. Each member then presents the "best case" for their alternative. After all alternatives have been advocated, members are to point out why each of the other alternatives is incorrect and defend their alternative from attacks by other group members.
4. Each member is assigned a different alternative and reverses perspectives by presenting the best case for the previously opposing answer.
5. Members drop all advocacy and decide by consensus on the correct answer.

The answer, by the way, is "thwarted."

## EXERCISE 7.2:
## YOUR BEHAVIOR IN CONTROVERSIES (I)

This exercise has two purposes: (1) to make you more aware of your typical actions when you are involved in a controversy and (2) to make your group more aware of the patterns of behavior of its members when they are involved in a controversy. The procedure is as follows:

1. Working by yourself, complete the following questionnaire.
2. Using the scoring table that follows the questionnaire, determine your score and then the group average for each of the controversy-managing strategies.
3. Discuss with the other members what strategies are used most frequently in your group and how controversies among members can be managed more constructively. Then write a description of the pattern your group exhibits in managing controversies among members. Finally, write a description of how this controversy pattern may be improved.

### Understanding My Controversy Behavior

Each of the following questions describes an action taken during a controversy. On a sheet of paper write down the numbers 1 through 30 in a column at the left-hand side of the page. For each question put a 5 if you *always* behave that way, 4 if you *frequently* behave that way, 3 if you *occasionally* behave that way, 2 if you *seldom* behave that way, and 1 if you *never* behave that way.

1. When I disagree with other group members, I insist that they change their opinions to match mine.
2. If someone disagrees with my ideas and opinions, I feel hurt and rejected.
3. I often infer that persons who disagree with me are incompetent and ignorant.
4. When others disagree with me, I try to view the issue from all points of view.
5. I try to avoid individuals who argue with me.

6. When others disagree with me, I view it as an interesting opportunity to learn and to improve the quality of my ideas and reasoning.
7. When I get involved in an argument with others, I become more and more certain that I am correct and argue more and more strongly for my own point of view.
8. When others disagree with my ideas, I get hostile and angry at them.
9. When I disagree with others, I am careful to communicate respect for them as persons while I criticize their ideas.
10. I am careful to always paraphrase thinking and feelings of others when they present ideas and opinions that are different from mine.
11. When others disagree with me, I generally keep my ideas and opinions to myself.
12. When others disagree with me, I encourage them to express their ideas and opinions fully, and seek to clarify the differences between their position and perspective and mine.
13. I view my disagreements with others as opportunities to see who "wins" and who "loses."
14. I often insult those who criticize my ideas and opinions.
15. When another person and I disagree, I carefully communicate, "I appreciate you, I am interested in your ideas, but I disagree with your current position."
16. When others disagree with me, I keep thinking of my ideas and opinions so that I do not forget them or get confused.
17. I am careful not to share my ideas and opinions when I think others may disagree with them.
18. When I disagree with others, I listen carefully to their ideas and opinions and change my mind when doing so is warranted by their information and reasoning.
19. When others and I disagree, I try to overpower them with my facts and reasoning.
20. I tend to dislike those who disagree with my ideas and opinions.
21. When I am disagreeing with and criticizing others' ideas and opinions, I let them know that I like them as persons.
22. I try to view the situation and issue from my opponent's shoes when involved in a disagreement about ideas and opinions.
23. I refuse to get into an argument with anyone.
24. When others disagree with me, I try to clarify the differences among our ideas and opinions, clarify the points of agreement, and seek a creative integration of all our ideas and information.
25. When others and I disagree, I have to convince them that I am right and they are wrong.
26. When others disagree with my ideas and opinions, it means that they are angry with me and dislike me.
27. While I am disagreeing with others I let them know that I appreciate their ability to present a challenging and thought-provoking position.
28. When I am involved in an argument, I restate and summarize the opposing positions.
29. When others disagree with me I stay very quiet and try to avoid them in the future.
30. When I am involved in an argument, I never forget that we are trying to make the best decision possible by combining the best of all our facts and reasoning.

## Scoring

Write your answer for each question in the space provided and total your answers for each controversy-managing strategy. The higher the total score for each controversy strategy, the more frequently you tend to use that strategy; the lower the total score for each controversy strategy, the less frequently you tend to use it. Add the scores of all group members for each strategy and divide by the number of members in the group. This will give you group average for each strategy.

| Win-Lose | Rejection | Confirmation |
|---|---|---|
| _____ 1. | _____ 2. | _____ 3.* |
| _____ 7. | _____ 8. | _____ 9. |
| _____ 13. | _____ 14. | _____ 15. |
| _____ 19. | _____ 20. | _____ 21. |
| _____ 25. | _____ 26. | _____ 27. |
| _____ TOTAL | _____ TOTAL | _____ TOTAL |
| _____ GROUP AVERAGE | _____ GROUP AVERAGE | _____ GROUP AVERAGE |

| Perspective Taking | Avoidance | Problem Solving |
|---|---|---|
| _____ 4. | _____ 5. | _____ 6. |
| _____ 10. | _____ 11. | _____ 12. |
| _____ 16.* | _____ 17. | _____ 18. |
| _____ 22. | _____ 23. | _____ 24. |
| _____ 28. | _____ 29. | _____ 30. |
| _____ TOTAL | _____ TOTAL | _____ TOTAL |
| _____ GROUP AVERAGE | _____ GROUP AVERAGE | _____ GROUP AVERAGE |

*Reverse the scoring on this question by substituting 1 for 5, 2 for 4, and so on.

### Controversy Questionnaire

Write your scores in the spaces provided below. If your score is above 15, it means that you are likely to engage in this strategy. If your score is less than 15, it means that you are not likely to engage in this strategy. Add the scores of all group members for each strategy and divide by the number of members in the group. This will give you your group average for each strategy.

| Constructive Strategy | Your Score | Group Average | Destructive Strategy | Your Score | Group Average |
|---|---|---|---|---|---|
| Problem solving | _____ | _____ | Win-lose | _____ | _____ |
| Confirmation | _____ | _____ | Rejection | _____ | _____ |
| Perspective taking | _____ | _____ | Avoidance | _____ | _____ |

### Procedure

1. Compare your scores for the constructive and destructive strategies.
2. Compare your scores with your actual behavior (as reported by observer) in the controversy exercise.
3. Discuss the strategies that are difficult for you to engage in.
4. On the basis of the group average scores and on the actual behavior of the group members in the controversy exercise, characterize the group's tendencies toward constructive and destructive controversy.

## CONTROVERSY AND DECISION MAKING

Since the general or prevailing opinion on any subject is rarely or never the whole truth, it is only by the collision of adverse opinion that the remainder of the truth has any chance of being supplied.

*John Stuart Mill*

A large pharmaceutical company faced the decision of whether to buy or build a chemical plant (*The Wall Street Journal,* October 22, 1975). To maximize the likelihood that the best decision was made, the president established two advocacy teams to ensure that both the "buy" and the "build" alternatives received a fair and complete hearing. An **advocacy team** is a subgroup that prepares and presents a particular policy alternative to the decision-making group. The "buy" team was instructed to prepare and present the best case for purchasing a chemical plant, and the "build" team was told to prepare and present the best case for constructing a new chemical plant near the company's national headquarters. The "buy" team identified over 100 existing plants that would meet the company's needs, narrowed the field down to 20, further narrowed the field down to 3, and then selected 1 plant as the ideal plant to buy. The "build" team contacted dozens of engineering firms and, after four months of consideration, selected a design for the ideal plant to build. Nine months after they were established, the two teams, armed with all the details about cost, (1) presented their best case and (2) challenged each other's information, reasoning, and conclusions. From the spirited discussion, it became apparent that the two options would cost about the same amount of money. The group chose therefore, the "build" option because it allowed the plant to be conveniently located near company headquarters. This procedure represents the structured use of controversy to ensure high-quality decision making.

In almost every meeting room within every organization, people are disagreeing with each other. Whether the organization is a business, an industry, a government agency, a hospital, a school, a law firm, or a family, disagreements occur as decisions are made and problems are solved. Involved participation in such situations means that different ideas, opinions, beliefs, and information will surface and clash. The result is **controversy**—the conflict that arises when one person's ideas, information, conclusions, theories, and opinions are incompatible with those of another person, and the two seek to reach an agreement.

Controversies are common within decision-making situations. In the mining

industry, for example, engineers are accustomed to address issues such as land use, air and water pollution, and health and safety. The complexity of the design of production processes, the balancing of environmental and manufacturing interests, and numerous other factors often create controversy. Most groups waste the benefits of such disputes, but every effective decision-making situation thrives on what controversy has to offer. Decisions are by their very nature controversial, as alternative solutions are suggested and considered before agreement is reached. When a decision is made, the controversy ends and participants commit themselves to a common course of action.

## THE STEPS OF STRUCTURED CONTROVERSY

> Conflict is the gadfly of thought. It stirs us to observation and memory. It instigates invention. It shocks us out of sheep-like passivity, and sets us at noting and contriving . . . conflict is a "sine qua non" of reflection and ingenuity.
>
> *John Dewey*

Involved participation in groups will inevitably produce conflicts among ideas, opinions, conclusions, theories, and information of members. Using controversies to promote creative syntheses results in high productivity. Suppressing controversies to create a superficial sense of unity results in low productivity. Yet groups cannot always count on controversies naturally occurring. And group members need a structure and a set of social skills in managing controversies when they do occur. For these and other reasons, controversies need to be carefully structured into group life.

An example of controversy is when a decision is to be made about how best to manage the disposal of hazardous wastes produced by the company's manufacturing processes. A manager may structure a controversy by holding a group discussion and identifying a number of options for disposing of the hazardous waste, such as building a plant to burn the waste, seeking a permit to bury it, or hiring a disposal company to ship it to a dump hundreds of miles away. The manager makes clear that the goal is to prepare a group report reflecting the best possible decision the group members are able to agree on. To do so requires that all alternatives get a fair and complete hearing. Members of the group are then assigned to advocacy subgroups and given the responsibility to prepare the "best case" for the alternative assigned. All available relevant information is then gathered and organized in order to advocate that alternative to the whole group. Phase 1 consists of giving the advocacy subgroups time to find all the supporting facts, information, and evidence available for their alternative. They organize what is known into a coherent and reasoned position. They plan how to present their case so that all members of the decision-making group understand thoroughly the team's position and are convinced of its soundness.

The second phase consists of (1) having the advocacy teams present their positions forcefully, sincerely, and persuasively while keeping an open mind, while (2) critically listening and attempting to refute the positions of the other advocacy teams and (3) experiencing conceptual conflict and uncertainty. Each team presents its position and reasoning to the opposition, thereby engaging in considerable cognitive rehearsal and elaboration of their position and its rationale. When the other team presents, members' reasoning and conclusions are challenged by the other members. Group members then engage in a general discussion in which they advocate their position, defend it against refutation, rebut the opposing position, and seek to reach the best decision possible about the need to regulate hazardous waste management. During this initial presentation and discussion members experience **conceptual conflict** and **uncertainty.** When members are challenged by conclusions and information that are incompatible with and do not fit with their reasoning and conclusions, conceptual conflict, uncertainty, and disequilibrium result.

The third phase consists of group members experiencing epistemic curiosity. As a result of their uncertainty, members actively (1) search for more information and experiences to support their position and (2) seek to understand the opposing position and its supporting rationale. The fourth phase is having group members **reverse perspectives.** Each advocacy team has to take one of the opposing positions and summarize and present it as forcefully, sincerely, and accurately as they can. This results in freeing them from their original position and helping them view the issue from more than one perspective. The fifth phase is reaching a consensus and preparing a group report on how the hazardous wastes should be disposed of. This requires reconceptualizing the issue by synthesizing and integrating the best information and reasoning from all sides. The group's decision then reflects their best reasoned judgment.

Within a controversy there is positive goal interdependence (coming to a consensus on how hazardous waste should be managed), resource interdependence (different members have different information), and conflict (group members advocating different perspectives and positions). When controversies are structured, group members are required to rehearse orally the information they are dealing with; advocate a position; teach their knowledge to peers; analyze, critically evaluate, and rebut information; reason both deductively and inductively; and synthesize and integrate information into factual and judgmental conclusions that are summarized into a joint position on which all sides can agree. These skills are important in almost any conflict within a group.

Controversy can be contrasted with debate, concurrence seeking, and individualistic decision making. **Debate** exists when group members argue for positions that are incompatible with one another and a winner is declared on the basis of who presented the best position; individuals within a decision-making group present opposing positions for a judge to decide which position is most correct. In a debate, group members compete to see who is best in presenting their position. An example of a debate is when two advocacy subgroups present their positions to the best of their ability and the chair of the group decides which alternative to adopt. **Concurrence seeking** occurs when members of a decision-making group inhibit discussion to avoid any disagreement or arguments and emphasize agreement; there is a suppression of different conclusions, an emphasis on quick compromise, and a lack of disagreement within a decision-making group. An example of concurrence seeking is when a decision-making group is assigned the task of formulating recommendations concerning hazardous waste regulation with the stipulation that they do not argue but rather compromise quickly whenever opposing positions are expressed. Most group decision-making situations are dominated by concurrence seeking (Walton, 1987). **Individualistic decision making** occurs when isolated individuals independently decide on a course of action without any interaction or consultation with each other; each decision maker comes to his or her decision without interacting with others or discussing the information upon which the decision is being made. The processes generated by each type of conflict are summarized in Table 7.1.

A key to the effectiveness of conflict procedures is the mixture of cooperative and competitive elements within the procedure. The greater the cooperative elements and the less the competitive elements, the more constructive the conflict tends to be (Deutsch, 1973). Cooperative elements alone, however, do not ensure maximal productivity out of a decision-making group. There has to be both cooperation and conflict (see Table 7.2).

**Table 7.1**    Processes of Controversy, Debate, Concurrence Seeking, and Individualistic Efforts

| Controversy | Debate | Concurrence Seeking | Individualistic |
|---|---|---|---|
| Categorizing and organizing information to derive conclusions | Categorizing and organizing information to derive conclusions | Categorizing and organizing information to derive conclusions | Categorizing and organizing information to derive conclusions |
| Presenting, advocating, elaborating position and rationale | Presenting, advocating, elaborating position and rationale | Active presentation of position | No oral statement of positions |
| Being challenged by opposing views | Being challenged by opposing views | Quick compromise to one view | Presence of only one view |
| Conceptual conflict and uncertainty about the correctness of own views | Conceptual conflict and uncertainty about the correctness of own views | High certainty about the correctness of own views | High certainty about the correctness of own views |
| Epistemic curiosity and perspective taking | Epistemic curiosity | No epistemic curiosity | No epistemic curiosity |
| Reconceptualization, synthesis, integration | Closed-minded adherence to own point of view | Closed-minded adherence to own point of view | Closed-minded adherence to own point of view |
| High achievement, positive relationships, psychological health/social competences | Moderate achievement, relationships, psychological health | Low achievement, relationships, psychological health | Low achievement, relationships, psychological health |

Source: D. W. Johnson and R. T. Johnson *Cooperation and Competition: Theory and Research* (Edina, MN: Interaction Book Company, 1989). Used with permission of the authors.

**Table 7.2**   Nature of Decision-Making Methods

| | Controversy | Debate | Concurrence Seeking | Individualistic |
|---|---|---|---|---|
| Positive goal interdependence | Yes | No | Yes | No |
| Resource interdependence | Yes | Yes | No | No |
| Negative goal interdependence | No | Yes | No | No |
| Conflict | Yes | Yes | No | No |

## THE AVOIDANCE OF CONTROVERSY

Within most organizations there is considerable conflict that is managed in costly and time-consuming ways. Thomas and Schmidt (1976) found that between 20 and 25 percent of managers' time is spent dealing directly with conflicts. Accountemps, a division of Robert Half International, Inc., found in a recent survey that managers of America's leading corporations spend over four working weeks a year dealing with the problems caused by employees who just don't get along with each other. Janz and Tjosvold (1985) determined in an interview study the cost of interpersonal conflicts in employee time, materials, and project days. Included in their broad definition of conflict was refusing to communicate directly, ignoring advice and suggestions, being disinterested in learning from others, viewing problems from only one's own point of view, involving only others that support one's point of view, embarrassing and blaming others, and seeing design flaws but not bringing them up because of wanting others to look bad. They estimated that the cost in employee time and materials for ineffectively managing interpersonal conflicts was about $15,000 (Canadian dollars) per employee per year and over $40,000 per employee per year if project days were taken into account. Conflicts, therefore, are pervasive within most organizations and frequently mismanaged. There is a need to train managers and other organizational personnel in the procedures and skills needed to manage conflicts constructively.

If a group is to make effective decisions and solve problems competently, controversies should not only be encouraged and sought out, but deliberately structured. Yet too few organizational members seek to stimulate or structure controversy. There are at least three reasons why. The first reason is that too few people understand controversy to be able to accept and utilize it effectively. There is insufficient knowledge and understanding of the procedures involved in controversy and the advantages and potentially constructive outcomes that can result from disagreements. A second reason is that many people seem to lack the interpersonal skills and competencies needed to stimulate controversy and ensure that it is managed constructively. Although most managerial training programs, for example, spend years providing technical training, the interpersonal skills needed to manage decision-making and problem-solving situations are not systematically and extensively taught.

Third, the discussion of conflicting ideas may not be a standard and common practice within decision-making and problem-solving situations because of the fear and anxiety most people seem to feel in conflict situations. A general feeling in our society is that conflicts are bad and should be avoided; consequently, many people believe that an effective group is one in which there are no conflicts among members. Many discussions of conflict see it only as causing divorce, separation, psychological distress, social disorder, violence, divisiveness, and even war. The disintegration of many groups and organizations have been blamed on conflict. Within most groups, members either try to shun conflict or crush it. Neither strategy works. Avoidance or force only raises the level of the conflict and becomes part of the problem rather than being the solution.

A healthy group does not suffer from a lack of conflict. Rather, the absence of conflict may signal apathy, disinterest, noninvolvement, and alienation—not maturity. In a healthy group, conflicts among members are inevitable. Thus, the issue is not whether conflicts can be prevented, but rather how they are managed, for conflicts can have both highly constructive and highly destructive effects on group and organizational functioning. Initiating conflicts and capitalizing on their constructive outcomes are essential group and managerial skills. Nowhere is that more true than in decision-making situations.

Not all executives are afraid of controversy. Alfred Sloan, a former chairman of General Motors, once stated at an executive meeting in which a major decision was being considered (cited in Drucker, 1974, p. 472):

> I take it we are all in complete agreement on the decision here. . . . Then I propose we postpone further discussion until our next meeting to give ourselves time to develop disagreement and perhaps gain some understanding of what the decision is all about.

## EXPERTS AND GROUP DECISION MAKING

When two men in business always agree, one of them is unnecessary.
*William Wrigley, Jr.*

Organizations are filled with individuals who have expertise in their limited areas and must interact and make joint decisions with each other. Important decisions are typically made by small groups of individuals with diverse expertise. To maximize the quality of the decision, expertise must be exchanged. Most important group decisions involve more than one expert, and, as Tversky and Kahneman (1981) note, most decision makers are normally unaware of alternative perspectives and frames of reference and of their potential effects on the relative attractiveness of options. Thus, two different experts, with different information and perspectives, can make directly opposing decisions without recognizing the limitations of their frames of reference. Each expert does not see the "whole world"; each sees only the part in which he or she specializes. Because they are capable of all sorts of rationalizations about their areas of expertise—mainly in the direction of enhancing its importance—any decision made by a single expert is suspect. Lord, Ross, and Lepper (1979) found that individuals who hold strong beliefs about an issue are apt to examine relevant evidence in a biased manner, by accepting confirming evidence at face value and subjecting disconfirming evidence to highly critical evaluation.

When experts with different information and perspectives come together to make a joint decision, conflict and disagreement result. Their points of departure need to be explicitly highlighted so that they will be able to sort out their differences and arrive at a mutually acceptable synthesis. Most decisions have to be made under the condition of uncertainty (the probability of desired outcomes resulting from the alternative course of action are unknown). Individuals with a wide variety of expertise and frames of reference are brought together to make such decisions. Conflict among their ideas, information, opinions, preferences, theories, conclusions, and perspectives is inevitable. Having the skills to manage the controversies constructively and knowing the procedures for exchanging information and perspectives among individuals with differing expertise are essential for organizational effectiveness and growth.

Expertise is not only developed but it must be maintained. If experts are not gaining new information and knowledge, not refining their theories and conceptual frameworks, and not challenging their conclusions, they may soon lose their expertise. With the rapid growth of knowledge in almost all fields, individuals can quickly lose their expertise if they do not stay current and push beyond their present levels of understanding. To do so they must generate an epistemic curiosity about their field of knowledge, promote their internal conceptual conflict by seeking out different perspectives and theories that contradict their own, adopt new and broader perspectives, and incorporate new information into their conceptual frameworks. Controversy is an essential factor in obtaining and maintaining expertise.

## EXERCISE 7.3:
## STRANDED IN THE DESERT

There is nothing as beautiful as a desert night. And there are few places more dangerous to be stranded than the desert during the night or day. In such a situation effective decision making is a matter of life or death, and since the emotional content of the arguments over what a stranded group should do will be high, skills in managing controversies constructively are essential. The purpose of this exercise is to examine the dynamics of controversy and its effects on the decision making of a group caught in a survival dilemma. The materials needed for the exercise are a description of the situation, a group decision form, a postdecision questionnaire, a summary table, a controversy-observation form, and a constructive-controversy checklist. Approximately 90 minutes are needed for the exercise. The procedure for the coordinator is as follows:

1. Introduce the exercise by stating its objective and reviewing the overall procedure and tasks.
2. Form groups of six. Ideally, the total number of groups should be divisible by five. One member from each group should volunteer to be an observer. The observer's role is to record the nature of each member's participation in the group, using the accompanying observation form. Each observer needs two copies of this form.
3. Introduce the situation, have the groups read the description of the situation, and assign each group one of these five basic positions:
   a. Your position is that the group members have to walk to the nearest ranch if they

are to survive. Plan carefully the best procedure for doing so. Select the five or six possessions of the group that are most important for implementing your plan and rank them from 1 (the most important) to 5 or 6 (the least important).

b. Your position is that the group members have to gather food and water if they are to survive. Plan carefully the best procedure for doing so. Select the five or six possessions of the group that are most important for implementing your plan and rank them from 1 (the most important) to 5 or 6 (the least important).

c. Your position is that the group members have to signal search planes and vehicles if they are to survive. Plan carefully the best procedure for doing so. Select the five or six possessions of the group that are most important for implementing your plan and rank them from 1 (the most important) to 5 or 6 (the least important).

d. Your position is that the group members have to protect themselves from the heat of the day and the cold of the night if they are to survive. Plan carefully the best procedure for doing so. Select the five or six possessions of the group that are most important for implementing your plan and rank them from 1 (the most important) to 5 or 6 (the least important).

e. Your position is that the group members must stay by the wreck and keep physical movement to a minimum if they are to survive. Plan carefully the best procedure for doing so. Select the five or six possessions of the group that are most important for implementing your plan and rank them from 1 (the most important) to 5 or 6 (the least important).

4. Instruct the groups to build as good a rationale for their position as possible. Give them 20 minutes to do so.

5. Form new groups of five by taking one participant from each of the previous groups and placing them together in a new group. All participants should now be in a new group, and each member in a group should be representing a different position. Assign a group to each observer. The observer's role is to record the nature of each member's participation on a copy of the controversy-observation form.

6. Instruct the new groups to read the situation description and then rank the 12 possessions of the group from 1 (the most important possession for the survival of the group members) to 12 (the least important possession). The group is to derive one ranking to which every members agrees. Moreover, every member should be able to explain why each item is ranked where it is. There is a correct ranking in the appendix according to which the group's ranking will be evaluated. Give the groups 30 minutes to decide on their ranking. After 25 minutes, announce that they have 5 minutes left.

7. Instruct participants to complete the postdecision questionnaire. Then have the observers determine the group mean for each question in the questionnaire while you inform the class of the correct ranking of the 12 items (see page 498 in the appendix).

8. In front of the whole class compile the results for each group using the summary table.

9. Instruct each group to discuss its experiences, using
   a. The decision and questionnaire results.
   b. The information collected by the observers.
   c. The impressions of the group members.
   c. The constructive-controversy checklist.
   The following questions may help the groups discuss how they managed the controversy:
   a. How did the group manage disagreements among its members? (Use the checklist for constructive controversy as a guide.)
   b. From its experience, what conclusions can the group make about the constructive handling of controversies?
   c. Did the opinions of group members change as a result of the group's discussion during the ranking task? Did members gain insight into other points of view? Did they learn new things about survival in the desert?

      d. What did members learn about themselves and other group members? How did each member react to the controversy?

10. Have each group share its conclusions about the constructive management of controversy with the rest of the class.

## Stranded in the Desert Situation

You are one of the members of a geology club that is on a field trip to study unusual formations in the New Mexico desert. It is the last week in July. You have been driving over old trails, far from any road, in order to see out-of-the-way formations. At about 10:30 A.M. the specially equipped minibus in which your club is riding overturns, rolls into a 20-foot ravine, and burns. The driver and professional advisor to the club are killed. The rest of you are relatively uninjured.

You know that the nearest ranch is approximately 45 miles east of where you are. There is no closer habitation. When your club does not report to its motel that evening you will be missed. Several persons know generally where you are, but because of the nature of your outing they will not be able to pinpoint your whereabouts.

The area around you is rather rugged and very dry. There is a shallow water hole nearby, but the water is contaminated by worms, animal feces and urine, and several dead mice. You heard from a weather report before you left that the temperature would reach 108 degrees, making the surface temperature 128 degrees. You are all dressed in light-weight summer clothing and you all have hats and sunglasses.

While escaping from the minibus each member of your group salvaged a couple of items; there are 12 in all. Your group's task is to rank these 12 items according to their importance to your survival, starting with 1 for the most important and proceeding to 12 for the least important.

You may assume that the number of club members is the same as the number of persons in your group and that the group has agreed to stick together.

## Stranded in the Desert Decision Form

Rank the following items according to their importance to your survival, starting with 1 for the most important and proceeding to 12 for the least important:

_____ magnetic compass

_____ 20-ft by 20-ft piece of heavy-duty, light-blue canvas

_____ book, *Plants of the Desert*

_____ rearview mirror

_____ large knife

_____ flashlight (four-battery size)

_____ one jacket per person

_____ one transparent, plastic ground cloth (6 ft by 4 ft) per person

_____ .38-caliber loaded pistol

_____ one 2-quart plastic canteen per person, full of water

_____ accurate map of the area

_____ large box of kitchen matches

### Stranded in the Desert Postdecision Questionnaire

1. To what extent did other members of the group listen to, and understand your ideas?
   Not at all                          1 : 2 : 3 : 4 : 5 : 6 : 7 : 8 : 9                     Completely
2. How much influence do you feel you had on the group's decision?
   None at all                         1 : 2 : 3 : 4 : 5 : 6 : 7 : 8 : 9                     Complete
3. To what extent do you feel committed to, and responsible for the group's decision?
   Not at all                          1 : 2 : 3 : 4 : 5 : 6 : 7 : 8 : 9                     Completely
4. To what extent are you satisfied with your group's performance?
   Very dissatisfied                   1 : 2 : 3 : 4 : 5 : 6 : 7 : 8 : 9                     Very satisfied
5. How much did you learn about the issue under discussion?
   Nothing at all                      1 : 2 : 3 : 4 : 5 : 6 : 7 : 8 : 9                     A great deal
6. Write two adjectives describing the way you now feel. _____

### Constructive-Controversy Checklist

_____     1. There was no winner or loser, only a successful, creative, and productive solution. The cooperativeness of group members should outweigh by far their competitiveness.

_____     2. Disagreements among members' positions were initiated.

_____     3. All members actively participated in the group discussions, sharing their information, conclusions, and perspectives.

_____     4. Every member's contributions were listened to, respected, and taken seriously.

_____     5. Effective communication skills were used, including paraphrasing and other listening skills and "I" messages and other sending skills.

_____     6. Issues and problems were viewed from all available perspectives.

_____     7. Group members criticized ideas and positions, not individuals. Members disagreed with each other while confirming each other's competence.

_____     8. Group members viewed disagreement as an interesting situation from which something could be learned, not as personal rejection or a sign that they were being perceived as incompetent or ignorant.

_____     9. There was appropriate pacing of differentiation and integration of member's positions. Differentiation took place first, followed by integration.

_____    10. Emotions were allowed and members were encouraged to express them.

_____    11. The rules of rational argument were followed. Members presented organized information to support their positions, reasoned logically, and changed their minds when others presented persuasive and convincing arguments and proof.

_____    12. The arguments of all members were given equal consideration, regardless of how much formal power a member had.

Summary Table: Response to Postdecision Questionnaire

| Group | Group Score | Understanding | Influence | Commitment | Satisfaction | Learning | Feelings |
|-------|-------------|---------------|-----------|------------|--------------|----------|----------|
| 1     |             |               |           |            |              |          |          |
| 2     |             |               |           |            |              |          |          |
| 3     |             |               |           |            |              |          |          |
| 4     |             |               |           |            |              |          |          |

Determine the group means from the questionnaire responses and record them in the appropriate column, except for the first and the last columns. In the "Feelings" column put representative adjectives from the questionnaires.

Controversy-Observation Form

| Behaviors | Participants | | | | | |
|---|---|---|---|---|---|---|
| Contributes ideas and opinions | | | | | | |
| Asks others for their ideas and opinions | | | | | | |
| Emphasizes mutual goals | | | | | | |
| Emphasizes win-lose competition | | | | | | |
| Asks others for proof, facts, and rationale | | | | | | |
| Paraphrases, summarizes | | | | | | |
| Criticizes and disagrees with others' ideas | | | | | | |
| Criticizes other members as persons | | | | | | |
| Differentiates positions | | | | | | |
| Integrates positions | | | | | | |
| Other | | | | | | |

Insert the name of each group member above the columns. Then record the frequency with which each member engages in each behavior.

## EXERCISE 7.4:
## WHO SHOULD GET THE PENICILLIN

The purpose of this exercise is to examine the dynamics of controversy within the context of a social studies lesson. The materials needed for the exercise are a description of the situation, a briefing sheet for the military point of view, a briefing sheet for the medical point of view, a postdecision questionnaire, a summary table, a controversy-observation form, and a constructive-controversy checklist. (The last four items are the same as in the previous exercise, and are also used in the following three exercises.) Approximately 90 minutes are needed for the exercise. The procedure for the coordinator is as follows:

1. Introduce the exercise by stating its objective and reviewing the overall procedure.
2. Form groups of five members. One member from each group should volunteer to be an observer. The observer's role is to record the nature of each member's participation in the group, using the controversy-observation form.
3. Divide the remaining four members of each group into two pairs. Give one pair a copy of the medical viewpoint and the other pair a copy of the military viewpoint.
4. Introduce the situation. Instruct the pairs to build as good a rationale for their assigned position as they can in 15 or 20 minutes, using the information on the briefing sheet as a guide.

5. Instruct the pairs to meet together as a group of four. The group is to come to a decision that all four members can agree to. The decision should reflect the best reasoning of the entire group. The group discussion should follow these steps:
   a. Each pair presents its position as forcefully and persuasively as it can while the opposing pair takes notes and clarifies anything the two members do not fully understand.
   b. Have an open discussion in which members of each pair (1) argue forcefully and persuasively for their position, presenting as many facts as they can to support it and (2) listen critically to members of the opposing pair, asking them for the facts that support their point of view. This is a complex issue and members need to know both sides in order to come to a thoughtful decision.
6. Instruct the pairs to reverse their perspectives by switching sides and arguing for the opposite point of view as forcefully and persuasively as possible. Members should see if they can think of any new facts that the opposing pair did not present in support of its position, and should elaborate on that position.
7. Instruct the groups to come to a joint decision by
   a. Summarizing the best arguments for both points of view.
   b. Detailing the facts they know about World War II and the African campaign.
   c. Achieving consensus among the members.
   d. Organizing the rationale supporting the decision that they will present to the rest of the class. They should be ready to defend the validity of their decision to groups who may have come to the opposite decision.
8. Instruct participants to complete the postdecision questionnaire. Then have the observers determine the group mean for each question.
9. Summarize the decision of each group in front of the entire class. Then summarize the results of the postdecision questionnaire, using the summary table.
10. Instruct each group to discuss their experience, using
    a. The decision and questionnaire results.
    b. The information collected by the observers.
    c. The impressions of the group members.
    d. The constructive-controversy checklist.
    The following questions may help the groups discuss how they managed the controversy:
    a. How did the group manage disagreements among its members? (Use the checklist for constructive controversy as a guide.)
    b. From its experience, what conclusions can the group make about the constructive handling of controversies?
    c. Did the opinions of the group members change as a result of the group's discussion? Did members gain insight into the other point of view through the perspective-reversal procedure? Did members learn anything new about World War II?
    d. What did members learn about themselves and other group members? How did each member react to the controversy?
11. Have each group share its conclusions about the constructive management of controversy with the rest of the class.

### Who Should Get the Penicillin Exercise Situation

In 1943 penicillin, which is used for the prevention of infection, was in short supply among the U.S. armed forces in North Africa. Decisions had to be made whether to use this meager supply for the thousands of hospitalized victims of venereal disease or for the thousands of victims of battle wounds at the front. If you were a member of a team of medical and military personnel, whom would you use the penicillin for?

——————    victims of venereal disease

——————    victims of battle wounds

Share your position and rationale with your group. Stick to your guns unless logically persuaded otherwise. At the same time, help your group achieve consensus on this issue.

### Briefing Sheet: The Medical Viewpoint—Who Should Get the Penicillin Exercise

Your position is to give the penicillin to the battle-wounded. Whether or not you agree with this position, argue for it as strongly and as honestly as you can, using arguments that make sense and are rational. Be creative and invent new supporting arguments. Seek out information; ask members of other groups who may know the answers to your questions. Remember to learn the rationale for both your position and the military position. Challenge the military position; think of loopholes in its logic; demand facts and information that back up its arguments.

1. Our responsibility is to treat the wounded and save as many lives as possible. Without the penicillin many of the wounded will die needlessly. Minor wounds will get infected and become major, life-threatening wounds.
2. Our strategies must be based on the premise that human life is sacred. If one person dies needlessly, we have failed in our responsibility. The soldiers who have sacrificed so much to help us win the war must be treated with all the care, concern, and resources we can muster. Our soldiers must be able to fight harder than the German soldiers.
3. Troop morale is vital. Nothing raises troop morale as much as the men's knowledge that if they are wounded they will receive top-notch medical treatment.
4. Morale at home is vital. People must make sacrifices to produce the goods and materials we need to win the war. Nothing raises morale at home more than knowing that sons and brothers are receiving the most effective medical care that is humanly possible. It would be devastating for word to reach the United States that we were needlessly letting soldiers die for lack of medical care.
5. Even though we are at war, we must not lose our humanity. It will do no good to defeat Germany if we become Nazis in the process.
6. At this point the war is going badly in North Africa. Rommel and the German army are cutting through our lines like butter. We are on the verge of being pushed out of Africa, in which case we will lose the war. Rommel must be stopped.
7. Fresh troops and supplies are unavailable. The German submarines control the Atlantic, and we cannot get troop ships or supply ships into African ports. We have to make do with what we have.
8. Penicillin is a wonder drug that will save countless lives if it is used to treat the wounded.

### Briefing Sheet: The Military Viewpoint—Who Should Get the Penicillin Exercise

Your position is to give the penicillin to the VD patients. Whether or not you agree with this position, argue for it as strongly and as honestly as you can, using arguments that make sense and are rational. Be creative and invent new supporting arguments. Seek out information that supports your position. If you do not have needed information, ask members of other groups who may. Remember to learn the rationale for both your position and the medical position. Challenge the medical position; think of loopholes in its logic; demand facts and information that back up its arguments.

1. Our responsibility is to win the war for our country at all costs. If we lose Africa, we will lose Europe to Hitler, and eventually we will be fighting in the United States.
2. Our strategies to win must be based on the premise of "the greatest good for the greatest number." We may have to sacrifice soldiers in order to win the war, save our democracy, and free Europe.
3. Troop morale is vital. Our soldiers must be able to fight harder than the German soldiers. Nothing raises troop morale like seeing fresh troops arrive at the front.
4. Morale at home is vital. People must make sacrifices to produce the goods and materials we need to fight the war. Nothing raises morale at home like hearing of battles won and progress being made in winning the war. Victories give our people at home more dedication.
5. At this point, the war is going badly in North Africa. Rommel and the German army are cutting through our lines like butter. We are on the verge of being pushed out of Africa, in which case we will lose the war. Rommel must be stopped at all costs!
6. Penicillin is a wonder drug that will send VD into remission, and within 24 hours the VD patients will be free from pain and able to function effectively on the battlefield.

## EXERCISE 7.5:
## FALLOUT SHELTER

The purpose of this exercise is to provide a decision-making situation in which controversy will occur. The procedure for the exercise is as follows:

1. Form groups of six. One member should volunteer to be an observer. The observer should use the Controversy-Observation Form on page 270.
2. Each group member individually completes the Fallout Shelter Ranking Task.
3. The group decides by consensus on the best ranking possible on the Fallout Shelter items. There should be one ranking for the group, every member should agree with the ranking, and be able to explain the rationale behind the ranking of each item.
4. Members complete the Postdecision Questionnaire. Compute the group means for each question and place them in the summary table.
5. Score the accuracy of the group's ranking by comparing it with the experts' ranking on page 499 in the appendix. Find the absolute difference between the group's ranking and the experts' ranking for each item and add them together. The lower the score the more accurate the group's ranking.
6. Using the observer's information, the postdecision questionnaire results, the members' impressions, and the accuracy score for the ranking, discuss the way in which controversy was managed in the group. The constructive-controversy checklist and the discussion questions given on page 268 may be helpful. The group should write down its conclusions about the constructive management of controversy.
7. Groups should share their conclusions with the entire class.

**Fallout Shelter Exercise: Ranking Task**

The possibility of a nuclear war has been announced and the alert signal has been sounded. You and the members of your group have access to a small basement fallout shelter. When the attack warning signal is announced, you must immediately go to the shelter. In the meantime, you must decide what to take with you to help you survive during and after the attack. You are outside the immediate blast areas. The greatest danger facing you is from radioactive fallout. In order to help in your decision making, rank the following items in order of their importance to your survival in the shelter:

_____ one large and one small garbage can with lids

_____ broom

_____ containers of water

_____ blankets

_____ canned heat stove

_____ matches and candles

_____ canned and dried foods

_____ liquid chlorine bleach

_____ vaporizing liquid fire extinguisher

_____ flashlight and batteries

_____ battery-powered radio

_____ soap and towels

_____ first-aid kit with iodine and medicines

_____ cooking and eating utensils

_____ Geiger counter

## OUTCOMES OF CONTROVERSY

Have you learned lessons only of
those who admired you, and were tender
with you, and stood aside for you?

Have you not learned great lessons
from those who brace themselves
against you, and disputed the passage
with you?

*Walt Whitman (1860)*

When controversy is suppressed and concurrence seeking is emphasized, several defects in making decisions will appear. When NASA, for example, decided to launch the space shuttle *Challenger,* engineers at the Morton Thiokol Company (which makes the shuttle's rocket boosters) and at Rockwell International (which manufactures the orbiter) had opposed the launch because of dangers posed by the subfreezing temperatures. The Thiokol engineers feared that the cold would make the rubber seals at the joints between the rocket's four main segments too brittle to contain the rocket's superhot gases. Several months before the doomed mission, the company's top expert had warned in a memo that it was a "jump ball" as to whether the seal would hold and that if it failed "the result would be a catastrophe of the highest order" (Magnuson, 1986). In a group discussion the night before the launch, the engineers argued for a delay with their uncertain managers and the NASA officials who wanted to launch on schedule. Since the engineers could not *prove* there was danger, they were silenced (illusion of invulnerability). Conformity pressures were aimed at the engineers, such as when one of the NASA officials complained, "My God, Thiokol, when you do want me to launch, next April?" The NASA managers made a coalition with the Thiokol managers to shut the engineers out of the decision making (illusion of unanimity). Finally, to mindguard, the top NASA executive who made the final decision to launch was never told about the engineers' concerns, nor about the reservations of the Rockwell officials. Protected from the disagreeable information, he confidently gave the go-ahead to launch the *Challenger* on its tragic flight.

How could such faulty decision making take place? The answer is, because of the lack of controversy. NASA officials never gave the alternative of delaying the launch a fair and complete hearing. Disagreement was stifled rather than utilized. Often in group discussions, if a margin of support for one alternative develops, then better ideas have little chance of being accepted. In mob lynchings, for example, misgivings, if not immediately expressed, were drowned out. Drawing on biased information is evident in some group polarization experiments; often the arguments that surfaced in group discussion tended to be more one sided than did those volunteered by individuals privately. Group discussions can exacerbate tendencies toward overconfidence, thereby heightening an illusion of judgmental accuracy (Dunning & Ross, 1988). Minority opinions can be suppressed. When initially only one member of a six-member group knew the correct answer, in almost 75 percent of the time the single member failed to convince the others because they were not given a fair and complete hearing (Laughlin, 1980; Laughlin & Adamopoulos, 1980). Group decision making often goes wrong because alternatives are not considered carefully, minority opinions are silenced, and disagreement among members' conclusions is suppressed.

Without controversy, group decisions may always be less than optimal. Over the past 20 years there have been more than 23 experimental studies on controversy. The nature and results of those studies are summarized in Johnson and Johnson (1989a). These studies form a solid body of evidence that controversy promotes high productivity, positive interpersonal relationships, and psychological health and social competence.

The evidence concerning the overall impact of controversy on productivity and achievement may be found in Table 7.3. Controversy typically produced higher group productivity, individual achievement, and quality of decision making than did concurrence seeking, debate, or individualistic efforts (Johnson & Johnson, 1989a). Controversy not only resulted in greater mastery and retention of the material being discussed, but also greater ability to transfer learning to new situations, and more frequent use of higher-level reasoning strategies. Controversy generated more potential solutions and more creative insight into the problem by influencing group members to view the problem from different perspectives and reformulate the problem in ways that allowed the emergence of new orientations. The number, quality, variety, and novelty of ideas, the feelings of stimulation and enjoyment, and originality of

**Table 7.3**    Mean Effect Sizes of Controversy
on Productivity

| Condition | Mean | SD | *n* |
|---|---|---|---|
| Controversy/concurrence | 0.42 | 0.57 | 49 |
| Controversy/debate | 0.77 | 0.41 | 20 |
| Controversy/individualistic | 0.65 | 0.32 | 20 |
| Debate/individualistic | 0.36 | 1.03 | 3 |

Source: D. W. Johnson and R. T. Johnson (1989), *Cooperation and Competition: Theory and Research* (Edina, MN:
Interaction Book Company, 1989). Used with permission of
the authors.

expression in creative problem-solving were all increased by controversy. Finally,
group members exerted more physical and psychological energy in working on the
decision when controversy occurred.

It is often assumed that the presence of conflict within a group will lead to
difficulties in establishing good interpersonal relationships and will promote negative
attitudes toward groupmates. It is also assumed that arguing leads to rejection,
divisiveness, and hostility among peers. The research indicates otherwise (Johnson &
Johnson, 1989a). Controversy has been found to promote greater liking among group
members than debate, concurrence seeking, and individualistic efforts. Spirited disagreement and intellectual challenge cannot only be fun, it can bind people into
deeper and more meaningful relationships. Finally, being able to manage conflicts is
an essential coping skill that increases psychological health and adjustment as well as
self-esteem (Johnson & Johnson, 1989a).

## PROCESS OF CONTROVERSY

Difference of opinion leads to inquiry, and inquiry to truth.

*Thomas Jefferson*

The process by which controversy sparks high-quality decision making, increased productivity, better relationships, increased psychological health, and other
positive outcomes for the group is outlined in Figure 7.1. During a constructive
controversy, decision makers proceed to do the following (Johnson & Johnson, 1987;
Johnson & Johnson, 1989a):

1. Controversy begins when your group, faced with a decision that has to be
made, assigns the major alternatives to advocacy subgroups and has each subgroup
(a) develop its alternative in depth and (b) plan how to present the best case possible
for its alternative to the rest of the group. You develop your assigned position by

    a. Formulating a thesis statement or claim. A **thesis statement/claim** is a statement that
the person wants accepted, but which he or she expects to be challenged. It often
includes qualifiers and reservations. **Qualifiers** are those ways of communicating how

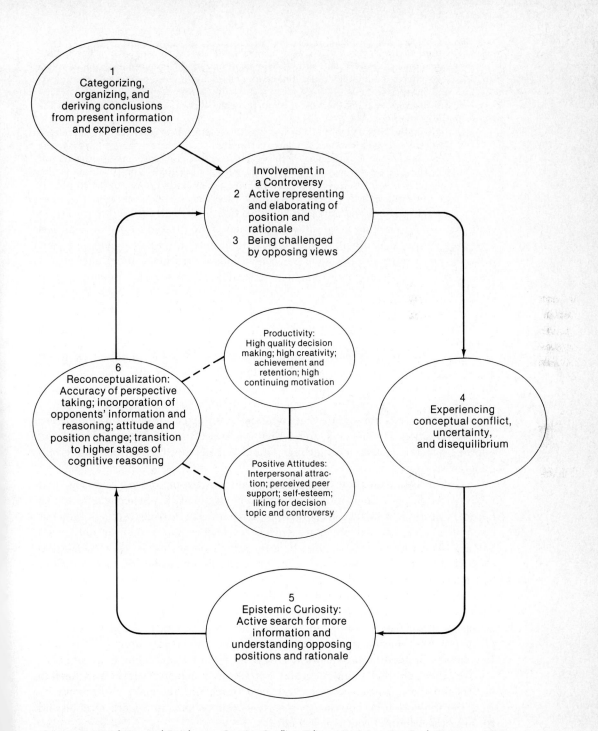

1
Categorizing, organizing, and deriving conclusions from present information and experiences

Involvement in a Controversy
2  Active representing and elaborating of position and rationale
3  Being challenged by opposing views

Productivity:
High quality decision making; high creativity; achievement and retention; high continuing motivation

6
Reconceptualization: Accuracy of perspective taking; incorporation of opponents' information and reasoning; attitude and position change; transition to higher stages of cognitive reasoning

4
Experiencing conceptual conflict, uncertainty, and disequilibrium

Positive Attitudes: Interpersonal attraction; perceived peer support; self-esteem; liking for decision topic and controversy

5
Epistemic Curiosity: Active search for more information and understanding opposing positions and rationale

Source: D. W. Johnson and R. Johnson, *Creative Conflict*, (Edina, MN: Interaction Book Company, 1987).

confident the speaker is in his or her claim and involve words such as "probably," "sometimes," "never," and "always." **Reservations** are the circumstances under which the speaker would decide not to defend a claim and involve words such as "unless" and "until."

b. Listing and detailing the facts, information, and theories gathered that validate the thesis statement.

c. Linking the facts together in a logical structure that leads to conclusions. The isolated facts are arranged, composed, and structured into conceptual systems that make the case for the thesis statement. Solid evidence and sound reasoning are strived for. Conclusions are derived based on the principles of scientific inquiry and deductive and inductive logic. In essence, you prepare a position to present to the rest of the group based on your current information, experiences, and perspective.

2.  You present and advocate your position to the rest of the group who, in turn, are advocating opposing positions. **Advocacy** is the presenting of a position and providing reasons why others should adopt it. You present, teach, and advocate your position and its rationale. Decisions and conclusions are reached through a process of argument and counterargument aimed at persuading others to adopt, modify, or drop positions. Advocating a position and defending it against refutation require engaging in considerable cognitive rehearsal and elaboration, which in turn results in increased understanding of the position and the more frequent use of higher-level reasoning processes.

3.  You are confronted by other group members with different positions based on their information, experiences, and perspectives. They advocate their positions just as you are advocating yours. Your position is challenged as group members critically analyze each other's positions in attempts to discern weaknesses and strengths. Members attempt to refute opposing positions while rebutting the attacks on their position. At the same time, they are aware that they need to learn the information being presented and understand the perspective of the other group members.

4.  Faced with these opposing positions, criticisms of your position, and information that is incompatible with and does not fit with your conclusions, you become uncertain as to the correctness of your views. A state of conceptual conflict or disequilibrium is aroused. You experience conceptual conflict and uncertainty when you are faced with (a) opposing positions with their rationales and (b) challenges to the validity of their own position and its rationale. Being challenged by conclusions and information that are incompatible with and do not fit with your reasoning and conclusions results in conceptual conflict, uncertainty, and disequilibrium.

5.  Your uncertainty, conceptual conflict, and disequilibrium motivates an active search for more information, new experiences, and a more adequate cognitive perspective and reasoning in hopes of resolving the uncertainty. Berlyne (1971) calls this active search **epistemic curiosity.** Divergent attention and thought are stimulated. You search for more information and experiences to support your position, seek to understand the opposing positions and their supporting rationale, and attempt to view the problem from opposing perspectives. This results in a reorganization and reconceptualization of your conclusions.

6.  You adapt your cognitive perspective and reasoning through understand-

**FIGURE 7.2**    Process of Controversy

ing and accommodating the perspective and reasoning of others to derive a new, reconceptualized, and reorganized conclusion and to detect novel solutions and decisions. The purpose of controversy is *not* to choose the best of the alternatives. The purpose of controversy is to create a synthesis of the best reasoning and conclusions from all the various alternatives. **Synthesizing** occurs when group members integrate a number of different positions containing diverse information and conclusions into a new, single, inclusive position that all group members can agree on and commit themselves to. This process is repeated until the differences in conclusions among group members have been resolved, a decision is reached, and the controversy has ended.

## CONDITIONS DETERMINING
## THE CONSTRUCTIVENESS OF CONTROVERSY

Although controversies can operate in a beneficial way, they will not do so under all conditions. As with all types of conflicts, the potential for either constructive or destructive outcomes is present in a controversy. Whether there are positive or negative consequences depends on the conditions under which controversy occurs and the way in which it is managed. These conditions and procedures include

1. The goal structure within which the controversy occurs.
2. The heterogeneity of group members. Differences among individuals in personality, sex, attitudes, background, social class, reasoning strategies, cognitive perspectives, information, ability levels, and skills lead to diverse organization and processing of information and experiences, which, in turn, begin the cycle of controversy. Heterogeneity among members also leads to more diverse interaction patterns and resources for decision making and problem solving.
3. The amount of relevant information distributed among members. The more information individuals have about an issue, the higher quality their decision making could be. Having relevant information available, however, does not mean that it will be listened to and utilized. All alternatives need to have a fair and complete hearing if all individuals are to contribute their relevant information and if all information is synthesized effectively.
4. The social skills of group members, especially their ability to disagree with each other without creating defensiveness.
5. The ability of members to engage in rational argument.

## Cooperative Goal Structure

Deutsch (1973) emphasizes that the context in which conflicts occur has important effects on whether the conflict turns out to be constructive or destructive. There are two possible contexts for controversy: cooperative and competitive. A cooperative context facilitates constructive controversy, whereas a competitive context promotes destructive controversy in several ways (Johnson & Johnson, 1987; Johnson & Johnson, 1989a):

1. For controversy to be constructive, information must be accurately communicated. Communication of information is far more complete, accurate, encouraged, and utilized in a cooperative context than in a competitive context.
2. Constructive controversy requires a supportive climate in which group members feel safe enough to challenge each other's ideas. Cooperation provides a far more supportive climate than competition.
3. For controversy to be constructive, it must be valued. Cooperative experiences promote stronger beliefs that controversy is valid and valuable.
4. Constructive controversy requires dealing both with feelings and with ideas and information. There is evidence that cooperativeness is positively related and competitiveness is negatively related to ability to understand what others are feeling and why they are feeling that way.
5. How controversies are defined has a great impact on how constructively they are managed. Within a cooperative context, controversies are defined as problems to be solved, while in a competitive situation controversies tend to be defined as "win-lose" situations.
6. Constructive controversy requires a recognition of both similarities and differences between positions. Group members participating in a controversy within a cooperative context identify more of the similarities between their positions than do members participating in a controversy within a competitive context.

In a series of studies, Dean Tjosvold and his associates studied the impact of cooperative and competitive contexts (Tjosvold, 1982; Tjosvold & Johnson, 1978; Van

Blerkom & Tjosvold, 1981). They found that controversy within a **competitive context** promoted closed-minded disinterest and rejection of the opponent's ideas and information. Competitors tend to refuse to incorporate any of the opponents' viewpoints into their own position. The increased understanding that resulted from controversy tended to be ignored for a defensive adherence to the competitors' own positions. When competitors were unsure of the correctness of their position, they selected to be exposed to disconfirming information when it could easily be refuted, presumably because such refutation could affirm their own beliefs. Avoidance of controversy resulted in little interest in or actual knowledge of opposing ideas and information and the making of a decision that reflected one's own views only. Within a cooperative context, controversy induced feelings of comfort, pleasure, and helpfulness in discussing opposing positions, an open-minded listening to the opposing positions, motivation to hear more about the opponent's arguments, more accurate understanding of the opponent's position, and the reaching of more integrated positions where both one's own and one's opponent's conclusions and reasoning are synthesized into a final position.

## Skilled Disagreement

Controversy requires a complex set of procedures and skills. For controversies to be managed constructively, people need collaborative and conflict-management skills (Johnson, 1990; Johnson & Johnson, 1987, 1989a). One of the most important skills is to be able to *disagree with each other's ideas while confirming each other's personal competence*. Disagreeing with others, and at the same time imputing that others are incompetent, tends to increase their commitment to their own ideas and their rejection of the other person's information and reasoning. Disagreeing with others while simultaneously confirming their personal competence, however, results in being better liked and in opponents being less critical of others' ideas, more interested in learning more about others' ideas, and more willing to incorporate others' information and reasoning into their own analysis of the problem.

Another important set of skills for exchanging information and opinions within a controversy is **perspective taking.** More information, both personal and impersonal, is disclosed when one is interacting with a person who is engaging in perspective-taking behaviors, such as paraphrasing, which communicate a desire to understand accurately. Perspective-taking ability increases one's capacity to phrase messages so that they are easily understood by others and to comprehend accurately the messages of others. Engaging in perspective taking in controversies results in increased understanding and retention of the opponent's information and perspective (Johnson, 1971a). Perspective taking facilitates the achievement of creative, high-quality problem solving (Falk & Johnson, 1977; Johnson, 1977). Finally, perspective taking promotes more positive perceptions of the information-exchange process, of fellow group members, and of the group's work. To obtain a creative synthesis of all positions in a controversy, group members must obtain a clear understanding of all sides of the issue and an accurate assessment of the validity and relative merits of each position. To do this fully, they must accurately perceive the frame of reference from which the other person is viewing and analyzing the situation and problem.

A third set of skills involves the *cycle of differentiation of positions and their integration*. Group members should ensure that there are several cycles of differentiation (bringing out differences in positions) and integration (combining several positions into one new, creative position). Differentiation must precede integration. Differentiation involves seeking out and clarifying differences among members' ideas, information, conclusions, theories, and opinions. It involves highlighting the differences among members' reasoning and seeking to understand fully what the different positions and perspectives are. All different points of view must be presented and explored thoroughly before new, creative solutions are sought. Integration involves combining the information, reasoning, theories, and conclusions of the various group members so that all members are satisfied. After it has differentiated positions, the group needs to seek a new, creative position that synthesizes the thinking of all the members. The group should never try to integrate members' positions before adequate differentiation has taken place. *The potential for integration is never greater than the adequacy of the differentiation already achieved.* Most controversies go through a series of differentiations and integrations before reaching a final decision.

### Rational Argument

During a controversy, group members have to follow the canons of rational argumentation. Within a controversy group members present their position and its rationale while asking other members for proof that their analyses and conclusions are valid. Rational argumentation includes generating ideas, collecting and organizing relevant information, using inductive and deductive logic, and making tentative conclusions based on current understanding. Rational argumentation requires that participants keep an open mind, changing their conclusions and positions when others are persuasive and convincing in their presentation of rationale, proof, and logical reasoning. The abilities to gather, organize, and present information, to challenge and disagree, and to engage in reason logically are essential for the constructive management of controversies.

## GUIDELINES FOR CONSTRUCTIVE CONTROVERSY

There are no cookbook rules for making controversies productive, but the following guidelines can help group members argue more constructively and transform disagreement among themselves into a positive experience:

1. *Emphasize your common ground of making the best possible decision.* Statements such as "We are all in this together" and "Let's make the best possible decision" should dominate the group, not "I am right and you are wrong." The

context within which the controversy takes place should be cooperative, not competitive. The issue is not to establish who has the best answer but to make the best group decision possible by exploring different perspectives and integrating different information.

2. *Look for opportunities to engage in controversy.* Highlight contrasting viewpoints, point out disagreements, and promote challenging tasks. Include diverse people in the group. People who differ in background, expertise, opinions, outlook, and organizational position are likely to disagree.

3. *Prepare the best case possible for your position.* Develop your thesis statement and research the best rationale possible to support it. It is up to you to ensure that your position is seen in its best light. Consult relevant articles, books, and experts to compile information and experiences to support your position. List relevant facts, information, and theories.

4. *Advocate your position forcefully but with an open mind.* Speak up. Make sure everyone listens. It is up to you to ensure that your position gets a fair and complete hearing.

5. *Encourage others to advocate their positions forcefully.* Express a warm, intense interest in all contributions. Every member should share his or her position and ideas in order to get comments and reactions from other members that will help improve the quality of group work. Value, respect, and take seriously everyone's contributions. Help all members, regardless of their status, to speak out confidently.

6. *Understand, then challenge opposing ideas and positions.* Ask questions. Ask for the supporting facts, information, and theories in order to understand the opposing positions more thoroughly. Understanding the statements of another group member is not enough; the frame of reference from which the member is speaking must also be clearly understood. View the issue under discussion from a variety of perspectives. Then, point out fallacies in information and logic. Try to refute their thesis statements and claims. Group members should be critical of ideas, not of persons. Arguments should concern ideas, not personality traits. Group members should be highly critical of each other's ideas at the same time affirming each other's competence and communicating respect and appreciation for the member as a person. Any inference of incompetence or weakness and any hint of rejecting another member should be avoided. *Criticize opposing ideas while confirming the competence of the other group members.* Combine personal regard with intellectual challenge. Say, "We are friends," "I am interested in what you have to say." Then say, "I do not agree with you on that point," "I have come to a different conclusion," "I appreciate you, I am interested in your ideas, but I disagree with your current position." Do not say, "You are stupid and ignorant and I do not like you!" Insults or imputations that challenge another member's integrity, intelligence, and motives are to be avoided.

7. *Do not take personally other members' disagreements and rejection of their ideas.* That other members disagree with your ideas and conclusions should be taken as an interesting situation from which something can be learned, not as a personal attack. Do not confuse rejection of your ideas and opinions with personal

rejection. Separate the validity of your thinking from your competence and worth as a person.

8. *Ensure that there are several cycles of differentiation and integration.* **Differentiation** involves bringing out differences in positions, and **integration** involves combining several positions into one new, creative position. Differentiation must come before integration is attempted.

9. *Put yourself in the other member's shoes.* Controversy is an opportunity to improve the quality of your own reasoning by seeing the issue from a variety of perspectives. Ensure that you understand the perspectives underlying positions as well as their content.

10. *Follow the canons of rational argument.* Generate ideas, collect and organize relevant information, use deductive and inductive logical procedures, and make tentative conclusions. Avoid premature evaluations.

11. *Synthesize the best ideas from all viewpoints and perspectives.* The end result is a synthesis that is better than any single position advocated. Think creatively until it is discovered.

## Summary

Decision making typically involves considering possible alternatives and choosing one. By definition, all decision-making situations involve some conflict as to which of several alternatives should be chosen. Within decision-making groups conflict takes the form of controversy. **Controversy** exists when one individual's ideas, information, conclusions, theories, and opinions are incompatible with those of another, and the two seek to reach an agreement. Such intellectual conflict among individuals may be avoided and suppressed or it may be structured and encouraged. Simply by emphasizing concurrence seeking, intellectual conflict among group members may be avoided. And if it does occur, it may be suppressed by stating that it is against the rules.

Most intellectual conflicts are avoided and suppressed. Yet there is evidence that controversy can be a powerful tool. Conflicts among ideas, conclusions, theories, information, perspectives, opinions, and preferences are inevitable. Such conflicts are (1) an inherent aspect of decision making, problem solving, reasoned judgment, and critical thinking and (2) inevitable. If individuals get intellectually and emotionally involved in cooperative efforts, controversies will occur no matter what participants do. They are critical events that may bring (1) increased learning, creative insight, high-quality problem solving and decision making; (2) closer and more positive relationships; and (3) greater social competence and psychological health. Or they may bring closed minds and poorly conceived decisions, lasting resentment and smoldering hostility, and psychological scars, rigidly ineffectual behavior, and a refusal to change or learn.

Controversy begins when your group, faced with a decision that has to be made, assigns the major alternatives to advocacy subgroups and has each subgroup (1) develop its alternative in depth and (2) plan how to present the best case possible for its alternative to the rest of the group. First, group members prepare a position to present to the rest of the group based on their current information, experiences, and perspective. Second, they then present and advocate their position to the rest of the group who, in turn, are advocating opposing positions. High-quality decisions and conclusions are reached through a process of argument and counterargument aimed at persuading others to adopt, modify, or drop positions. Third, group members are confronted by other group members with different positions based on their information, experiences, and perspectives. Members attempt to refute opposing positions while rebutting the attacks on their position.

Fourth, faced with these opposing positions, criticisms of your position, and information that is incompatible with and does not fit with their conclusions, they become uncertain as to the correctness of your views. A state of conceptual conflict or disequilibrium is aroused. Group members experience conceptual conflict and uncertainty when faced with (1) opposing positions with their rationales and (2) challenges to the validity of their own position and its rationale. Being challenged by conclusions and information that are incompatible with and do not fit with their reasoning and conclusions results in conceptual conflict, uncertainty, and disequilibrium. Fifth, members' uncertainty, conceptual conflict, and disequilibrium motivates an active search for more information, new experiences, and a more adequate cognitive perspective and reasoning in hopes of resolving the uncertainty. Epistemic curiosity, divergent attention and thought are stimulated. Members search for more information and experiences to support your position, seek to understand opposition positions and rationales, seek to understand the opposing positions and their supporting rationale, and attempt to view the problem from opposing perspectives. This results in a reorganization and reconceptualization of their conclusions.

Finally, members adapt their cognitive perspective and reasoning through understanding and accommodating the perspective and reasoning of others and derive a new, reconceptualized, and reorganized conclusion. Novel solutions and decisions that, on balance, are qualitatively better are detected. The purpose of controversy is not to choose the best of the alternatives. The purpose of controversy is to create a synthesis of the best reasoning and conclusions from all the various alternatives. To do so, members have to keep conclusions tentative, accurately understand opposing perspectives, incorporate new information into their conceptual frameworks, and change their attitudes and position. This process is repeated until the differences in conclusions among group members have been resolved, a decision is reached, and the controversy has ended.

Controversies tend to be constructive when the situational context is cooperative, there is some heterogeneity among group members, information and expertise is distributed within the group, members have the necessary conflict skills, and the canons of rational argumentation are followed. An essential aspect of controversy is the creativity that is derived from the collision of adverse opinion.

## EXERCISE 7.6:
## THE JOHNSON SCHOOL

Form groups of six. Give one set of cards to each group. Each member should take one of the cards. The cards should contain the following statements, one on each card:

1.  The strongest coach coached wrestling second.
    Track was a sport coached at the Johnson School.
    Dale offered to recruit cheerleaders for the school.
2.  Members of your group have all the information needed to find the answer to the following question. (Only one answer is correct.) *In what sequence did the Johnsons coach the sports taught at their school?* Some of the information your group has is not relevant and will not help your group solve the problem.
3.  Frank coached wrestling third.
    The strongest coach had been coaching longer than the other coaches.
    Edye's favorite sport was eating.
4.  The strongest coach coached first the sport that David liked the best.
    All coaches coached all the sports.
    Keith preferred telling others what to do rather than doing it himself.
5.  Helen had been coaching longer than any of the other coaches.
    David coached basketball third.
    Each coach coached the sport they liked best second.
6.  Roger preferred to coach golf more than the other sports.
    All coaches preferred or liked one sport above the others.
    All coaches coached at the same time.

Give the following instructions: You have all the information you need to define a problem and solve it. You have 20 to 40 minutes. One rule you must follow: Although you may tell your group what is on your card, you may not pass it around for others to read. All communication in the group is to be verbal. I repeat, you may not let others read what is on your card, you may only tell them what it says.

## EXERCISE 7.7:
## AVOIDING CONTROVERSIES

People often find ingenious methods to keep from having to deal directly with controversies. How do you behave when you want to avoid a dispute? How do the other members of your group behave?

The following exercise is designed to produce feedback about how other group members see your behavior when you want to avoid a controversy. Its objective is for participants to examine their own behavior in controversies and disagreements. Understanding avoidance behavior, or how people avoid responding, can be as helpful as increasing their awareness of constructive behaviors. The procedure for the coordinator is as follows:

1. Introduce the exercise as a chance for each group member to get feedback from other group members on his or her behavior.
2. Tell each group member to place a sheet of newsprint on the wall with his or her name clearly written at the top.
3. Have group members walk around the room writing down their impressions on the newsprint of how each of the others behaves when he or she wants to avoid a controversy. You may wish to use the checklist below to start ideas.
4. All members should classify themselves according to the checklist below and then read the remarks other group members have written on their sheet.
5. Divide the participants into groups of three and have them discuss the content of the remarks written on their sheets, their own perceptions of their behavior, and the feelings generated by the exercise. Note that although the defenses against directly facing controversy are not helpful to the group and will promote destructive outcomes, they are at times very helpful and of constructive value to the individual. Participants should ask themselves whether there are ways to protect themselves without being harmful to the group.

**Defenses Against Controversy**

1. *Ostrich:* deny the controversy exists; refuse to see the potential or actual disagreement.
2. *Turtle:* withdraw from the issue and the persons disagreeing with you.
3. *Lemming:* give in and accept the other person's point of view or ideas.
4. *Weasel:* rationalize by stating that the issue is not important, that you really don't hold an opposing opinion, that the issue is one on which you have no expertise, and so on.
5. *Gorilla:* overpower the other members by forcing them to accept your ideas and point of view.
6. *Owl:* intellectualize about the issue and ideas so that all feelings and emotions are hidden.
7. *Sheep:* formulate, support, and conform to group norms forbidding the expression of opposition and disagreement in the group.

## EXERCISE 7.8: BELIEFS ABOUT CREATIVITY

The purpose of this exercise is to provoke a discussion concerning the nature of creativity. The procedure is as follows:

1. Working by yourself, answer the following questions about creativity.
   a. Creativity and intelligence are (1) unrelated, (2) highly related to each other in the sense that creativity promotes cognitive development.
   b. Creativity is a (1) stable trait that some persons are born with and others lack, (2) process of problem solving characterized by an interaction between group members and the challenges of their environment.

    c. Creativity: (1) is at the same level across situations—a creative person is creative in every situation—(2) varies a great deal from situation to situation, depending on the problem-solving process being used.

    d. Creativity is something that (1) cannot be taught because it is an inborn trait, (2) can be taught because it is a problem-solving process.

    e. The role of the school is to (1) discover or identify creative students and place them in accelerated programs to that their creativity is utilized, (2) develop creative competencies in all students by providing the needed challenges and teaching them the problem-solving skills necessary for a creative response.

2. Form heterogeneous groups of six and arrive at a group consensus for each question.
3. Compare your group's answers with those of the other groups in the class.

## CREATIVITY

*Creativity* is a *process* of bringing something new into existence. Group creativity results from productive controversy during the problem-solving process. The creative process consists of a sequence of overlapping phases:

1. Recognizing and experiencing a problem challenging enough to motivate members of a group to solve it.
2. Gathering the necessary knowledge and resources within the group and planning an intense, long-term effort to solve the problem.
3. Experiencing an incubation period during which group members feel frustration, tension, and discomfort due to their failure to produce an adequate solution to the problem and temporarily withdraw from the issue.
4. Seeing the problem from different perspectives and reformulating it in a way that lets new orientations to a solution emerge. This phase usually results from controversy among diverse points of view. The controversy produces a moment of insight or inspiration by one or more group members. The insight is often accompanied by intense emotional experiences of illumination and excitement and leads to the formulation of a tentative solution.
5. Elaborating, detailing, and testing the solution against reality.
6. Giving the validated solution to relevant audiences.

    There are several key elements in such a process of creative problem solving: motivation to persist in trying to solve a challenging problem, the availability of diverse information and viewpoints, controversy among persons with diverging ideas and perspectives, and open-mindedness in viewing the problem from diverse perspectives.

    For the possibility of creativity to exist, group members need to be aroused to a level of motivation sufficient to sustain problem-solving efforts despite frustrations and dead ends (Deutsch, 1969). This level of motivation, however, cannot be so intense that it overwhelms members or keeps them too close to the problem. The motivation to persist is increased by both controversy and a group tradition supporting the view that with time and effort constructive solutions can be discovered or invented for seemingly insoluble problems. The more varied the members of a group, the more likely the group will arrive at a creative solution. Both male and female, lower-class and middle-class, white and minority, high-achieving and low-achieving persons should be placed in the same cooperative problem-solving groups so as to maximize the possibility of creative solutions being found.

Once diverse ideas and perspectives are available, they need to be presented so that they can be put together into new and varied patterns. As the differences among group member's perspectives and ideas are understood, the range of available solutions will broaden. The debate among group members in and of itself will tend to spark new ideas and approaches. As with all productive controversies, each group member needs the freedom, support, and self-confidence to express herself without being afraid of censure. The exchange of ideas has to be encouraged. And controversy has to be an exciting and accepted procedure for the group.

Disagreements, arguments, debates, and diverse information and ideas are all important aspects of gaining creative insight. There is evidence that such interpersonal interaction increases the number and quality of ideas, feelings of stimulation and enjoyment, and originality of expression in creative problem solving (Bahn, 1964; Bolen & Torrance, 1976; Dunnette, Campbell, & Jaastad, 1963; Triandis, Bass, Ewen, & Mieksele, 1963). And there is evidence that controversies result in more creative solutions and more member satisfaction, compared with group efforts that do not include controversies (Glidewell, 1953; Hoffman, Harburg, & Maier, 1962; Maier & Hoffman, 1964; Rogers, 1970). Controversies have been shown to encourage group members to dig into a problem, raise issues, and settle them in ways that show the

benefits of a wide range of ideas being used. Controversies also result in a high degree of emotional involvement in and commitment to solving the problems the group is working on.

For group members to derive creative answers to problems they are working on, they must be allowed time to reflect. Instant answers should not be demanded. Creative thinking "is commonly typified by periods of intense application and periods of inactivity" (Treffinger, Speedie, & Brunner, 1974, p. 21). After all sides of a controversy have been presented, group members should be allowed to think about solutions for a day or so before trying to put things together in new and varied patterns.

For controversy to result in creativity, group members must be open-minded about different beliefs, opinions, information, ideas, perspectives, and assumptions. Group discussion must be such that members do not feel threatened or under too much pressure (Deutsch, 1969; Rokeach, 1960; Stein, 1968). Feeling threatened prompts defensiveness and reduces both tolerance of ambiguity and receptiveness to the new and the unfamiliar. Too much tension leads to stereotyping of thought processes. Feeling threatened and under pressure prevents group members from becoming sufficiently detached from their original viewpoint to be able to see the problem from new perspectives.

Group members must seek out different perspectives and different ways of viewing the problem when analyzing it. The extent to which a member can receive, evaluate, and act on relevant information on its *own* merits (as opposed to viewing it only from his or her own perspective) defines the extent to which the student is *open-minded* (as opposed to being closed-minded) (Rokeach, 1960). Without seeing the problem from several perspectives, members will not be able to analyze it and synthesize various ideas so as to produce creative solutions. Controversy is an essential ingredient in discovering new perspectives on the problem being solved.

How do you tell if a group is open- or closed-minded? Closed-minded groups are characterized by (1) emphasis on the differences between what they believe and what they do not believe, (2) denial of information that is contrary to what they believe, (3) the existence of contradictory beliefs that go unquestioned, (4) the discarding as irrelevant of similarities between what they believe and what they reject, and (5) avoidance of exploring differences in beliefs and distortion of information that does not fit their beliefs. Open-minded groups are characterized by (1) the seeking out of opposing and differing beliefs, (2) the discovery of new beliefs, (3) the remembering of information that disagrees with currently held beliefs, and (4) the organization of new beliefs that lead to the solution of the problem. Open-mindedness is an important aspect of controversy, creativity, and problem solving.

## DEVELOPING AND FOSTERING CREATIVITY

From the process perspective, leaders are given the responsibility for developing creative skills and attitudes in group members and fostering creative problem solving. Here is a set of procedures that can be used to promote creativity:

1. Using a cooperative goal structure, give members problems to be solved through the use of inquiry procedures.
2. Structure the cooperative groups as heterogeneously as possible.
3. Promote controversy among ideas, opinions, information, theories, and perspectives.
4. Model curiosity and inquiry, the ability to shift perspectives, the recombining of already known facts into new combinations and relationships, and general open-mindedness.
5. Allow members time to reflect on their ideas after periods of intense work.
6. Encourage persistence in the face of failure to solve problems: do not take members off the hook by giving them answers; let them struggle and support such struggling; communicate to them that creative individuals such as Einstein and Picasso experienced great difficulties before achieving insight.
7. Be enthusiastic about originality in thinking and problem solving. Reinforce it whenever you see it.
8. Introduce members to provocative ideas, books, persons, things, and procedures.
9. Encourage manipulation of objects and ideas.
10. Encourage members to immerse themselves in a specific area of interest if they become excited about it.
11. Communicate that creative insights are valuable by such procedures as having members keep a personal notebook of their new and important ideas.

David and Houtman (1968) are the authors of a book intended to teach creativity. They suggest four methods of generating novel ideas that can be taught: part changing, using a checkerboard figure, using a checklist, and finding something similar. The *part-changing method* involves group members in identifying the parts or attributes of something that might be changed. The following is an example:

> Four qualities of a chair are color, shape, size, and hardness. Invent a new kind of chair by listing 15 different colors, 10 different shapes, 5 sizes, and 5 grades of hardness. Try to think of different ideas, and do not worry about whether or not they are any good. Think of different ways to change each part of the chair. Use your imagination.

The *checkerboard method* involves making a checkerboard figure with spaces for entering words or phrases on the vertical and horizontal axes. Different sets of properties or attributes are listed on the axes. Then group members examine the interaction or combination of each pair of things or attributes. For example,

> Your group is to invent a new sport. Place materials and equipment along the top, horizontal axis, and place the things the players do (such as running, batting, kicking, hanging from their knees) down the side or vertical axis. Then examine the combination of each item on each axis with all the other items on the other axis.

The *checklist method* involves developing and using checklists to make sure that something is not left out or forgotten. David and Houtman suggest a checklist that includes these procedures:

1. Change color.
2. Change size.
3. Change shape.

4. Use new or different material.
5. Add or subtract something.
6. Rearrange things.
7. Identify a new design.

A group can apply this checklist to any object or problem.

The *find-something-similar method* involves encouraging group members to come up with new ideas by thinking of other persons, animals, or social units in the world that perform the same acts the group wants to perform. Here is an example:

> Imagine your city has a parking problem. Find ideas for solving this problem by thinking of how bees, squirrels, ants, shoe stores, clothing stores, and so on store things.

Another technique designed to enhance the creativity of students is *synectics*, developed by William J. Gordon (1961). Gordon stresses the importance of psychological states in achieving creativity and the use of metaphor in achieving the proper psychological state. He suggests using three interrelated techniques for making the strange appear familiar and the familiar strange:

1. Personal analogy in which persons imagine how it feels to be part of the phenomenon they are studying. Asking them how they would feel if they were an incomplete sentence or if they were Paul Revere's horse are examples.
2. Direct analogy, in which group members are asked to think about a parallel situation in order to gain insight into what they are studying. Asking them to describe how a book is like a lightbulb or how a beaver chewing on a log resembles a typewriter are examples.
3. Compressed conflict, in which group members are forced to perceive an object or concept from two frames of reference. Asking them to give examples of "repulsive attraction" or "cooperative competition" are illustrations.

## EXERCISE 7.9:
## CREATIVITY

This problem requires creativity on the part of the group that is attempting to solve it. The class should divide into groups of three. Each group's assignment is to connect all nine dots with only four straight and connected lines. (Answer A on page 501 in the appendix).

**EXERCISE 7.10:**
**JOE DOODLEBUG**

This problem also requires group creativity to solve. It is taken from Rokeach (1960). The procedure for the coordinator is as follows:

1. Have the class divide into groups of three.
2. Hand out copies of the problem sheet and state that it contains all the necessary information. The problem is *why* Joe *has* to take *four* jumps to reach the food, which is only 3 feet away. The groups have 30 minutes to come up with an answer. Explain that you will give hints after 15, 20, and 25 minutes if the groups have not solved the problem.
3. After 15 minutes give the first hint, after 20 minutes the second, and after 25 minutes the third (see page 495 in the appendix).
4. At the end of 30 minutes stop the groups and give them the answer (it appears on page 495 in the appendix). After clarifying the answer, conduct a discussion of moving outside one's belief system to solve a problem. Then ask the group to discuss how they worked together, listened to each other, handled controversies, and so on.

**The Problem**

Joe Doodlebug has been jumping all over the place getting some exercise when his master places a pile of food 3 feet directly west of him. Joe notices that the pile of food is a little larger than he. As soon as Joe sees all this food he stops dead in his tracks facing north. After all his exercise Joe is hungry and he wants to get the food as quickly as possible. Joe examines the situation and then says, "I'll have to jump four times to get the food." Why does Joe have to take four jumps to get to the food?

Joe Doodlebug, a strange sort of imaginary bug, can and cannot do the following things: (1) he can jump only in four different directions: north, south, east, and west (he cannot jump diagonally, such as southwest); (2) once he starts in any direction he *must* jump four times in that direction before he can change direction; (3) he can only jump, not crawl, fly, or walk; (4) he cannot jump less than 1 inch per jump or more than 10 feet per jump; (5) Joe cannot turn around.

## OPEN VERSUS CLOSED BELIEF SYSTEMS

For controversy to be constructive, group members must be receptive to information, ideas, perspectives, assumptions, beliefs, conclusions, and opinions different from their own. They must be willing to modify their cognitive structures so that they will be able to incorporate this new information. The systematic personality differences that exist among people affect their openness to new information that may modify their attitudes and cognitive structures. These personality differences may also affect the extent to which constructive consequences result from controversy.

Rokeach (1954, 1960) has developed the concept of *dogmatism* to categorize persons in terms of the openness or closedness of their belief system. He defines dogmatism as "(a) a relatively closed cognitive organization of beliefs and disbeliefs about reality, (b) organized around a central set of beliefs about absolute authority which, in turn, (c) provides a framework for patterns of intolerance toward others." In discussing dogmatism, Rokeach (1960, p. 57) states that every person must be able to evaluate adequately both the relevant and irrelevant information he receives from every situation. This leads us to suggest a basic characteristic that defines the extent to which a person's system is open or closed, namely, the extent to which the person can receive, evaluate, and act on relevant information received from the outside on its own intrinsic merits, unencumbered by irrelevant factors in the situation, within the person, or from the outside.

When a group member is willing to attend to, comprehend, and gain insight into information, ideas, perspectives, assumptions, beliefs, conclusions, and opinions discrepant from her own, she is open-minded. When she resists such opportunities, she is closed-minded and dogmatic. Numerous studies on dogmatism have been reviewed by Ehrlich and Lee (1969) and by Vacchiano, Strauss, and Hochman (1968). This research indicates that closed-minded persons, compared with open-minded individuals,

1. Are less able to learn new beliefs and to change old beliefs.
2. Are less able to organize new beliefs and integrate them into their existing cognitive systems during problem solving, and thus take longer to solve problems involving new beliefs.
3. Are less accepting of belief-discrepant information.
4. Are more resistant to changing their beliefs.
5. More frequently reject information that is potentially threatening to their perceptual and attitudinal organization.
6. Have less recall of information that is inconsistent with their beliefs.
7. Evaluate information that is consistent with their beliefs more positively.
8. Have more difficulty in discriminating between the information received and its source, so that the status of an authority is confused with the validity of what the authority is stating; in other words, dogmatic persons tend to accept what authorities say as the truth and discount what low-status individuals say as invalid.
9. Resolve fewer issues in conflict situations, are more resistant to compromise, and are more likely to view compromise as defeat.

The solution of the Joe Doodlebug problem requires open-mindedness in that group members must give up a series of beliefs about the situation and replace them with a set of new beliefs. They must then synthesize the new beliefs in order to solve the problem.

In solving the problem group members must first overcome three beliefs, one by one, and replace them with three new beliefs. The first is the *facing belief*. In everyday life we have to face the food we are to eat. But Joe does not have to face the food in order to eat it—he can land on top of it. The second is the *direction belief*. In everyday life we can change direction at will. But Joe is not able to do this because he must forever face north. The only way Joe can change direction is by jumping sideways and backward. The third belief that must be replaced is the *movement belief*. When we wish to change direction in everyday life, there is nothing to stop us from doing so immediately. But Joe's freedom of movement is restricted by the fact that once he moves in a particular direction (north, south, east, or west) he has to continue four times in that direction before he can change it. Many group members assume that Joe is at the end rather than possibly in the middle of a jumping sequence.

The replacement of old beliefs with new beliefs is called the *analytic phase* of the problem-solving process. Once new beliefs have superseded the old ones, group members must organize them in a way that leads them to the solution. This organizational step is called the *synthesizing phase* of the problem-solving process. In creative problem solving, controversies and open-mindedness help a group obtain different perspectives and develop appropriate beliefs that members can synthesize in order to help solve the problem. Controversy, replacement of old beliefs with new ones, and the synthesis of new beliefs are all essential.

## BRAINSTORMING

Within the problem-solving process there are times when divergent thinking is necessary, when it is incumbent upon members to produce many diverse ideas. There are other times, of course, when convergent thinking is necessary, when the group needs to agree about its course of action. **Brainstorming** is a procedure that encourages divergent thinking and the production of many different ideas in a short period of time. It is a method of generating ideas in quantity and gaining the full participation of all group members in doing so. In essence, all evaluation is suspended and ideas are allowed to develop freely on a particular issue. Brainstorming is a time for free association of ideas and for the opening of new avenues of thought. Some of the reasons why brainstorming helps problem-solving groups become more creative are as follows:

1. It increases member participation and involvement.
2. It is a means of getting the most ideas in a relatively short period of time.
3. It reduces the need to look for the "right" idea in order to impress authority figures in the group.
4. It makes problem solving more fun and stimulating.
5. It reduces the possibility of negative subgrouping, competition, and one-upmanship during the problem-solving process.

To assure that the brainstorming session will be a success, group members should be familiar with a number of ground rules:

1. All criticism or evaluation of ideas is ruled out. Ideas are simply placed before the group.
2. Wild ideas are expected in the spontaneity that evolves when the group suspends judgment. Practical considerations are not important at this point. The session is to be freewheeling.
3. The quantity of ideas counts, not their quality. All ideas should be expressed, and none should be screened out by any individual. A great number of ideas will increase the likelihood of the group discovering good ones.
4. Build on the ideas of other group members when possible. Pool your creativity. Everyone should be free to build onto ideas and to make interesting combinations from the various suggestions.
5. Focus on a *single* problem or issue. Don't skip around to various problems or try to brainstorm a complex, multiple problem.

6. Promote a congenial, relaxed, cooperative atmosphere.
7. Make sure that all members, no matter how shy and reluctant to contribute, get their ideas heard.
8. Record *all* ideas.

After the period of brainstorming all the ideas should be categorized and the group should critically evaluate them for possible use or application. The best critical judgment of the group members should be applied to the ideas, though members should seek clues to something sound in even the wildest idea. Priorities should be selected and the best ideas applied.

For new groups unfamiliar with brainstorming a warm-up session in which the rationale and rules are explained might be helpful. If groups are being formed for brainstorming, it is important that some diversity of opinion and background be present in each group.

Brainstorming is useful because many of the reasons that ideas are never born—or, once born, are quickly stifled—have nothing to do with their value. Domineering members, stereotypes of each other's expertise and intelligence, interpersonal conflicts, habitual patterns of uninvolvement and silence, fear of ridicule or evaluation—all can smother the majority of members in a group. It is like a vice-president in charge of a group of managers saying, "Those opposed will signify by clearing out their desks, putting on their hats, and saying 'I resign.'"

It is a common saying among social psychologists that there is no such thing as a creative person, only creative groups. The thinking of all of us is highly influenced by the thinking of those with whom we talk and otherwise interact. It is almost always possible to be part of a group process that encourages, supports, and rewards our potential for creativity. The ideas of others spark our own. The theory of one group member may help build a much more creative theory by touching off all sorts of new ideas among the rest of the members. When controversy is encouraged and diversity sought and used, a group can engage in untold amounts of creative problem solving.

## EXERCISE 7.11: BRAINSTORMING

The objective of this exercise is to come up with a large number of ideas or solutions to a problem by temporarily suspending criticism and evaluation—in other words, to experience the process of brainstorming. The procedure is as follows:

1. The ground rules for brainstorming are reviewed by the group.
2. The group is presented with a problem: one of the authors of this book has been cast ashore nude on a desert island with nothing but a glass peace symbol on a leather thong.
3. The group has 15 minutes to generate ideas as to what can be done with this object.
4. The group has another 15 minutes to critically select their best ideas.
5. The group discusses how well it applied the rules of brainstorming and what its results were. Was creativity enhanced? Did it help the group to discover interesting ways of using the object?

After initial exposure to brainstorming a group should pick a specific problem it is working on and apply brainstorming to it to see if new, creative perspectives can be gained. If, however, a second practice session is desired, the following story can be used:

> A small wholesaler in the hinterland of New Mexico called his buyer in Santa Fe and asked him to obtain a large order of pipe cleaners from Mexico. The buyer agreed. He also agreed to advance the wholesaler the money to finance the deal. A month later, just as the shipment of pipe cleaners was arriving, the buyer received a disastrous phone call from the wholesaler: His warehouse and outlet store had burned down and there simply was no more business. The buyer was suddenly faced with the prospect of trying to sell 20,000 pipe cleaners.

In 1 minute group members should generate as many ideas as possible (with a recorder counting the number of different ideas) for selling pipe cleaners. (A relatively spontaneous group will create approximately 25 ideas in a little more than a minute. If the group creates 15 ideas or less, it should be given more training in brainstorming.)

In brainstorming a group problem, it is important that the problem be well defined and specific. It must also be a problem that the group has the power to do something about. If possible, the group members should be notified in advance about the issue to be explored so that they will have given some thought to it.

## EXERCISE 7.12:
## CREATIVITY WARM-UP

Have you ever felt in a rut? Have you ever felt embarrassed about sharing new or wild ideas? Have you ever ignored your thinking because you felt it was too far out? Do you ever enjoy letting your imagination and thoughts run wild? Have you ever been so critical of your own thoughts that you could not get started?

Here are six short, fun exercises to loosen up group thinking and warm up group creativity:

1. The group sits in a circle (group size should be limited to eight members or so). The person nearest the window says the first thing that comes to his mind. The statement should be short, not over a sentence or two. Without pause the person to his left says what comes to her mind. Her statement must be relevant to something the first person said. The relevance may be of any kind—an association, a contrast, an alternative, a continuation, and so on. The process continues at high speed until at least three rounds have been completed. Members critique the process by discussing the feelings they had during the exercise.
2. The group sits in a circle and identifies a problem or issue. The person nearest the door states his solution. Each subsequent group member (to his left) states his or hers, using as many ideas of previous speakers as one can. The process is continued until a plan generally acceptable to all the group members is arrived at. When a member cannot add anything new, he or she passes. Finally, members' reactions to and feelings about the experience are discussed.
3. The group sits in a circle and a group problem or issue is identified. The first person states her solution to the problem. The next person immediately states what her opposition to the first person's solution is. The third person immediately states his or her opposition to the second person's opposition. The process is continued until everyone in the group has spoken at least three times. The emphasis is upon generating creative ideas in arguments. Members' reactions to and feelings about the experience are discussed.

4. The group lies on the floor, members' heads toward the center of the room. The first person begins with a fantasy about what the group could be like. After no more than two or three minutes the fantasy is passed on to the next group member, who continues it, adding his own associations and fantasies. The process continues until everyone has spoken at least three times. Members' reactions to and feelings about the exercise are examined.

5. The group has before it a number of assorted materials, such as clay, water paints, Tinker Toys, magazines, newspapers, and so on. It then creates something out of the materials—a mural, a collage, a design. If more than one group participates, they end the exercise by discussing one another's creations.

6. The group acts out a walk through the woods. Each member takes the leadership role for a while and directs the walk, indicating what he or she is experiencing and seeing. What the members learn about one another, the group, and walking through the woods should be discussed.

## EXERCISE 7.13:
## YOUR BEHAVIOR IN CONTROVERSIES (II)

How do you behave in controversies? Has your behavior changed as a result of your experiences connected with this chapter? How would you now describe your behavior?

1. When I find myself disagreeing with other members of my group, I

    _____ stand by my ideas and continue to defend my position, actively trying to get it accepted by the group and incorporated into any decisions made for as long as it takes to do so.

    _____ try to explore the points of agreement and disagreement and the feelings that other group members have about these points and why; I press a search for alternatives that take everyone's views into account.

2. Controversies are

    _____ valuable to clear the air and enhance involvement and commitment and, when productively handled, result in increased creativity.

    _____ destructive because opposition leads to dislike, and disagreement over ideas means personal rejection of other group members.

3. When I am involved in a controversy, I

    _____ feel rather fearful and concerned about how other members like me and whether I really like them.

    _____ feel angry at their ignorance and rather annoyed that I have to be around such stupid people.

    _____ am stimulated and feel full of excitement and fun as I think about the issues being discussed.

4. Which of the following is more typical of your behavior?

    _____ When I find myself in disagreement with other group members, I always state my position and feelings so that everything is out in the open.

_____    When I find myself in disagreement with other group members I keep quiet and "sit the discussion out."

5. When I get involved in a good argument, I

_____    find my ideas becoming more and more creative as I incorporate other members' ideas and notions and begin to see the issue from different perspectives.

_____    become more and more certain that I am correct and argue more and more strongly for my own point of view.

Compare your answers with the answers you gave to the questionnaire at the beginning of the chapter. Have you changed? How would you now describe your behavior in controversy situations? Write a description of your controversy behavior, and share it with two persons who know you well and who have participated in some of the controversy exercises with you. Ask them to add to and modify your self-description.

## SUMMARY

The materials in this chapter concentrated on the productive management of controversies among group members in order to increase a group's effectiveness in making creative, high-quality decisions. You have practiced dealing with controversies and making creative decisions. The next chapter will continue along this same theme by showing you how to negotiate in dealing with conflicts of interest.

# 8

# Conflicts of Interest

## BASIC CONCEPTS TO BE COVERED IN THIS CHAPTER

In this chapter a number of concepts are defined and discussed. The major ones are listed below. The procedure for learning these concepts is as follows:

1. Divide into heterogeneous pairs.
2. The task for each pair is to
   a. Define each concept, noting the page on which it is defined and discussed.
   b. Ensure that both members of the pair understand the meaning of each concept.
3. Combine into groups of four. Compare the answers of the two pairs. If there is disagreement, the members look up the concept in the chapter and clarify it until they all agree on the definition and understand it.

### CONCEPTS

1. Interests
2. Conflict of interests
3. Withdrawal
4. Forcing
5. Smoothing
6. Compromise
7. Confrontation
8. Negotiation
9. Goal dilemma
10. Dilemma of trust
11. Dilemma of openness and honesty
12. Norm of reciprocity
13. Steps of negotiating
14. Attribution theory
15. Fundamental attribution error
16. Frustration-aggression process
17. Stereotype
18. Superordinate goal
19. Mediation
20. Self-fulfilling prophecy

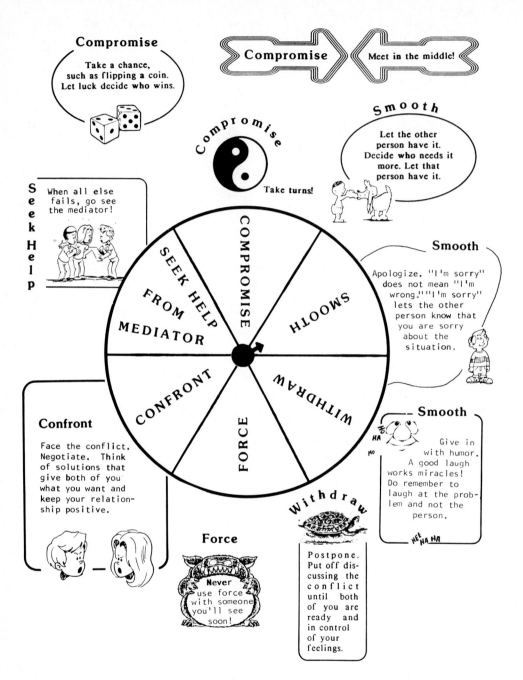

From D. W. Johnson and R. T. Johnson, *Creative Conflict*, (Edina, MN: Interaction Book Company, 1988). Used with permission of authors.

# WHAT ARE CONFLICTS OF INTEREST?

Imagine you are part of a group that has just been given $5,000 to spend in any way it wishes over the next two weeks. Your group has six members: Jane, Mary, Joe, John, Edythe, and yourself. Jane and Mary want to donate the money to the women's liberation movement. Edythe, John, and Joe want to give a series of parties for all their friends. You want the group to use the money for a college scholarship for your younger brother. Your group is in conflict, and it is more than just a matter of opposing opinions. There is a scarce resource (money) that the group must decide to allocate among the competing needs of the members. Since different members have vested interests in spending the money in different ways, your group has a conflict of interest.

The word conflict is derived from the Latin *conflictus*, meaning "striking together with force." There are times when group members' needs and preferences "strike together" and produce disruptive effects. We are all unique individuals with our separate needs and goals. Within the conflict literature, the term **interest** is used with the meaning of need, goal, benefit, profit, advantage, concern, right, or claim. Whenever we interact with another person, some of our needs and goals are congruent with theirs and some are incongruent. Within groups the various interests (i.e., needs and goals) of members at times are congruent and at times are in conflict. A **conflict of interest** exists when the actions of one person attempting to maximize his or her needs and benefits prevent, block, interfere with, injure, or in some way make less effective the actions of another person attempting to maximize his or her needs and benefits (Deutsch, 1973). When two members both want the same book, want to play the same position on an athletic team, want to achieve the same position, or want the greatest rewards, they have a conflict of interest. Conflicts among interests can be based on (1) differences in needs, values, and goals; (2) scarcities of certain resources, such as power, influence, money, time, space, popularity, and position; or (3) rivalry. When needs, values, and goals are incompatible, when certain resources (including power, time, space, popularity, money, and position) are scarce, and when competition for rewards and privileges is taking place, a conflict of interest exists. Within any group different persons will have different interests, and at times they will be in conflict with each other. In many groups, leaders structure a conflict of interest among members by having them compete for rewards. Ranking members from best to worse on their performance creates a conflict of interest among members by awarding a scarce commodity (i.e., rewards) to the few who do the "best." *Both because they occur naturally and because they are deliberately created, conflicts of interest are common.* The management of conflicts of interest is an important aspect of maintaining the cooperation among group members that is needed for group effectiveness.

All the potential values of conflict discussed at the beginning of Chapter 7 are applicable to conflicts of interest. Though not helpful in producing a creative, high-quality decision, a conflict of interest, if managed properly, can help to ensure that all group members are committed to implementing the group's decisions and that the group's problem-solving ability does not deteriorate during the decision-making process. In this chapter we shall focus on the use of negotiation to resolve conflicts of interest among group members and among groups. The use of interpersonal skills to resolve conflicts is covered in Johnson (1990). It focuses on increasing one's awareness of one's past and present styles of conflict management, confronting others constructively, defining a conflict constructively, getting an accurate perception of the other's position and feelings, making sure there is correct and effective communication in a conflict, developing a climate of trust, structuring cooperative interdependence in resolving the conflict, and managing stress and anger constructively.

## EXERCISE 8.1:
## YOUR CONFLICT STRATEGIES

Different persons learn different ways of managing conflicts. The strategies you use to manage conflicts may be quite different from those used by your friends and acquaintances. This exercise gives you an opportunity to increase your awareness of what conflict strategies you use and how they compare with the strategies used by others. The procedure is as follows:

1. With your classmates, form groups of six. Make sure you know the other members of the group. Do not join a group of strangers.
2. Working by yourself, complete the following questionnaire.
3. Working by yourself, read the accompanying discussion of conflict strategies. Then make five slips of paper. Write the names of the other five members of your group on the slips of paper, one name to a slip.
4. On each slip of paper write the conflict strategy that best fits the actions of the person named.
5. After all group members are finished, pass out your slips of paper to the persons whose names are on them. In turn you should end up with five slips of paper, each containing a description of your conflict style as seen by another group member. Likewise, each member of your group should end up with five slips of paper describing her conflict strategy.
6. Score your questionnaire, using the table that follows the discussion of conflict strategies. Rank the five conflict strategies from the one you use the most to the one you use the least. This will give you an indication of how you see your own conflict strategy. The second most frequently used strategy is your backup strategy, the one you use if your first one fails.
7. After drawing names to see who goes first, one member describes the results of his questionnaire. This is his view of his own conflict strategies. He then reads each of the five slips of paper on which are written the views of the group members about his conflict strategy. Next he asks the group to give specific examples of how they have seen him act in conflicts. The group members should use the rules for constructive feedback. The person to the left of the first member repeats this procedure, and so on around the group.
8. Each group discusses the strengths and weaknesses of each of the conflict strategies.

### How You Act in Conflicts

The proverbs listed below can be thought of as descriptions of some of the different strategies for resolving conflicts. Proverbs state traditional wisdom, and these proverbs reflect traditional wisdom for resolving conflicts. Read each of the proverbs carefully. Using the following scale, indicate how typical each proverb is of your actions in a conflict.

5 = very typical of the way I act in a conflict
4 = frequently typical of the way I act in a conflict
3 = sometimes typical of the way I act in a conflict
2 = seldom typical of the way I act in a conflict
1 = never typical of the way I act in a conflict

_____  1. It is easier to refrain than to retreat from a quarrel.

_____  2. If you cannot make a person think as you do, make him or her do as you think.

_____  3. Soft words win hard hearts.

_____  4. You scratch my back, I'll scratch yours.

_____  5. Come now and let us reason together.

_____  6. When two quarrel, the person who keeps silent first is the most praiseworthy.

_____  7. Might overcomes right.

_____  8. Smooth words make smooth ways.

_____  9. Better half a loaf than no bread at all.

_____ 10. Truth lies in knowledge, not in majority opinion.

_____ 11. He who fights and runs away lives to fight another day.

_____ 12. He hath conquered well that hath made his enemies flee.

_____ 13. Kill your enemies with kindness.

_____ 14. A fair exchange brings no quarrel.

_____ 15. No person has the final answer but every person has a piece to contribute.

_____ 16. Stay away from people who disagree with you.

_____ 17. Fields are won by those who believe in winning.

_____ 18. Kind words are worth much and cost little.

_____ 19. Tit for tat is fair play.

_____ 20. Only the person who is willing to give up his or her monopoly on truth can ever profit from the truths that others hold.

_____ 21. Avoid quarrelsome people as they will only make your life miserable.

_____ 22. A person who will not flee will make others flee.

_____ 23. Soft words ensure harmony.

_____ 24. One gift for another makes good friends.

## Scoring

| Withdrawing | Forcing | Smoothing | Compromising | Confronting |
|---|---|---|---|---|
| _____ 1. | _____ 2. | _____ 3. | _____ 4. | _____ 5. |
| _____ 6. | _____ 7. | _____ 8. | _____ 9. | _____ 10. |
| _____ 11. | _____ 12. | _____ 13. | _____ 14. | _____ 15. |
| _____ 16. | _____ 17. | _____ 18. | _____ 19. | _____ 20. |
| _____ 21. | _____ 22. | _____ 23. | _____ 24. | _____ 25. |
| _____ 26. | _____ 27. | _____ 28. | _____ 29. | _____ 30. |
| _____ 31. | _____ 32. | _____ 33. | _____ 34. | _____ 35. |
| _____ Total | _____ Total | _____ Total | _____ Total | _____ Total |

The higher the total score for each conflict strategy, the more frequently you tend to use that strategy. The lower the total score for each conflict strategy, the less frequently you tend to use that strategy.

_____ 25. Bring your conflicts into the open and face them directly; only then will the best solution be discovered.

_____ 26. The best way of handling conflicts is to avoid them.

_____ 27. Put your foot down where you mean to stand.

_____ 28. Gentleness will triumph over anger.

_____ 29. Getting part of what you want is better than not getting anything at all.

_____ 30. Frankness, honesty, and trust will move mountains.

_____ 31. There is nothing so important you have to fight for it.

_____ 32. There are two kinds of people in the world, the winners and the losers.

_____ 33. When one hits you with a stone, hit him or her with a piece of cotton.

_____ 34. When both give in halfway, a fair settlement is achieved.

_____ 35. By digging and digging, the truth is discovered.

## CONFLICT STRATEGIES: WHAT ARE YOU LIKE?

Different people use different strategies for managing conflicts. These strategies are learned, usually in childhood, and they seem to function automatically. Usually we are not aware of how we act in conflict situations. We just do whatever seems to come naturally. But we do have a personal strategy, and because it was learned, we can always change it by learning new and more effective ways of managing conflicts.

When you become engaged in a conflict, there are two major concerns you have to take into account:

1. *Reaching an agreement that satisfies one's needs and meets one's goals.* This is why one negotiates. Each person has personal goals that he or she wishes to achieve. You are in conflict because you have a goal or interests that conflict with another person's goal or interests. Your goal may be placed on a continuum between being of little importance to you to being highly important.

2. *Maintaining an appropriate relationship with the other person.* In a career setting such as a classroom and school, this means a caring and committed relationship. You have to live with the other person for at least a semester or year. You will thus need to interact effectively with the other person for some time. Your relationship with the other person, however, may be placed on a continuum between being of little importance to you or being highly important.

There are negotiation situations in which the persons in conflict have no future relationship. Buying a new car is a situation where negotiation over price is usually not affected by the need for future cooperation between the buyer and the salesman. Such one-time interactions are different from conflicts in a goal-oriented group (where members have a continuing relationship). How you manage the conflict of interest depends on whether or not you anticipate interacting with the other person again. If the conflict occurs with a career, family, community, or friendship setting, the ongoing relationship is more important than the outcome of any particular conflict. But when problems arise, the goals of each person and the quality of the ongoing relationship are in conflict. A major consequence of the "people problem" in negotiations is that the relationship between the individuals tends to become entangled with their discussions of their needs and goals.

## DECIDING HOW TO NEGOTIATE

Dealing with a conflict of interest is like going swimming in a cold lake. Some people like to test the water, stick their foot in, and enter slowly. Such people want to get used to the cold gradually. Other people like to take a running start and leap in. They want to get the cold shock over quickly. Different people use different strategies for managing conflicts. These strategies are learned, usually in childhood, and they seem to function automatically on a "preconscious" level. We just do whatever seems to come naturally. But we do have a personal strategy and, because it was learned, we can always change it by learning new and more effective ways of managing conflicts. How important your personal goals are to you and how important the relationship is perceived to be affect how you act in a conflict. Given these two concerns within a relationship, there are five basic strategies that may be used to manage conflicts (see Figure 8.1):

1. *The Turtle (Withdrawing).* Turtles withdraw into their shells to avoid conflicts. They give up their personal goals and relationships. They stay away from the issues over which the conflict is taking place and from the persons they are in conflict with. Turtles believe it is hopeless to try to resolve conflicts. They feel helpless. They believe it is easier to withdraw (physically and psychologically) from a conflict than to face it.

High
Importance

R
E
L
A
T
I
O
N
S
H
I
P
S

Low
Importance

GOALS

High
Importance

**FIGURE 8.1**  Strategies for managing conflicts.

2. *The Shark (Forcing).* Sharks try to overpower opponents by forcing them to accept their solution to the conflict. Their goals are highly important to them, and relationships are of minor importance. They seek to achieve their goals at all costs. They are not concerned with the needs of others. They do not care if others like or accept them. Sharks assume that conflicts are settled by one person winning and one person losing. They want to be the winner. Winning gives sharks a sense of pride and achievement. Losing gives them a sense of weakness, inadequacy, and failure. They try to win by attacking, overpowering, overwhelming, and intimidating others.

3. *The Teddy Bear (Smoothing).* To teddy bears the relationship is of great importance while their own goals are of little importance. Teddy bears want to be accepted and liked by others. They think that conflict should be avoided in favor of harmony and that people cannot discuss conflicts without damaging relationships. They are afraid that if the conflict continues, someone will get hurt, and that would ruin the relationship. They give up their goals to preserve the relationship. Teddy bears say, "I'll give up my goals and let you have what you want, in order for you to like me." Teddy bears try to smooth over the conflict out of fear of harming the relationship.

4. *The Fox (Compromising).* Foxes are moderately concerned with their own goals and their relationships with others. Foxes seek a compromise; they give up part of their goals and persuade the other person in a conflict to give up part of his goals. They seek a conflict solution in which both sides gain something—the middle ground between two extreme positions. They are willing to sacrifice part of their goals and relationships in order to find agreement for the common good.

5. *The Owl (Confronting).* Owls highly value their own goals and relationships. They view conflicts as problems to be solved and seek a solution that achieves both their own goals and the goals of the other person. Owls see conflicts as a means of improving relationships by reducing tension between two persons. They try to begin a discussion that identifies the conflict as a problem. By seeking solutions that satisfy both themselves and the other person, owls maintain the relationship. Owls are not satisfied until a solution is found that achieves their own goals and the other person's goals. And they are not satisfied until the tensions and negative feelings have been fully resolved.

A series of studies have compared confrontations with other strategies for dealing with conflicts of interest. Burke (1969) found that problem-solving confrontations were strongly associated with constructive resolution of conflicts, whereas forcing the other person to accept one's position was strongly associated with ineffective conflict management. Lawrence and Lorsch (1967) examined the use of confrontation, forcing the other person to accept one's position and smoothing over conflict in six organizations. They found that high organizational performance was associated with the use of confrontation in dealing with conflicts. Burke (1970) asked 74 managers to describe the way they and their immediate superiors dealt with conflicts. Although both effective and ineffective managers reported the use of confrontation, ineffective managers reported much higher use of forcing the other person to accept one's position.

Each conflict strategy, however, has its place. You do not want to be an overspecialized dinosaur who can deal with conflict in only one way. You need to be able to use any one of the five, depending on your goals and the relationship. In one conflict, you may wish to use one strategy, while in another conflict you may wish to use a different strategy. To be effective in resolving conflicts, you have to vary your actions according to what will work best in the situation. You need to be able to switch actions according to what will work best.

## EXERCISE 8.2:
## GROUP MEMBER EXCELLENCE

The objective of this exercise is to look at the dynamics of interpersonal negotiation in a group. The exercise can be conducted in less than one hour. The procedure for the coordinator is as follows:

1. Introduce the exercise as a chance to study the dynamics of negotiation among members of the same group. Divide the class into groups of 14: 12 participants and 2 observers. You need at least two groups. Distribute one copy of the accompanying instruction sheet to all members and observers and one copy of the observers' instructions to the observers. Without letting the groups know that they are getting different instructions, give half of them copies of the accompanying win-lose negotia-

tion instructions and the other half copies of the problem-solving negotiation instructions.

2. Meet with the observers to make sure they understand what they are expected to do.

3. Distribute a bag of marbles to each group member, using the accompanying table as a guide. Answer any questions members have about the exercise. Do *not*, however, tell them anything about the number of marbles or arrangement of colors in the bags or how to collect 15 marbles of the same color. Collect 25 cents from each participant, to be awarded to the members who finish the task. Announce that participants have 15 minutes to finish the task. Give the signal to begin.

4. At the end of 15 minutes announce that the time is up and the negotiations must end. Ask each participant to write two adjectives on her negotiation instruction sheet that describe her feelings during the negotiations. Gather the sheets and record how many participants completed the task and which type of negotiation instructions they had. Then divide the money among the members who completed the task.

5. Have each group meet separately with its observers to discuss the experience. The focus of the discussion should be upon the negotiation strategies used, how members reacted to one another's strategies, and how successful the different strategies were. Then, on a sheet of newsprint, summarize the strategies, their success, how members reacted to them, and any conclusions that can be drawn about their effectiveness.

6. Have the groups share their instructions for negotiation and the strategies members used, and ask them what conclusions they can make about the effectiveness of the different strategies. Announce how many persons with win-lose instructions completed the task and how many with problem-solving instructions completed it. The adjectives win-lose participants wrote down should be compared with the adjectives problem-solving participants used. An interesting subject to explore is how often coalitions formed in which two or more members pooled their marbles and negotiated with other members as a bloc. Sometimes a member will collect two colors of marbles in order to be flexible until the last few minutes. Summarize the major points of the discussion.

7. Have the participants read the subsequent sections on negotiation and compare their conclusions about the exercise with the material in those sections.

### General Instructions

Systems for evaluating the performance of group members have many shortcomings. Different members behave in different ways to accomplish their objectives. These variations make most comparisons difficult and unfair. To overcome this problem, we have developed a simulation that all members will participate in. From your behavior in this exercise we will be able to tell if you are a poor, average, good, or excellent group member. The exercise provides an impartial and equal measure of a participant's performance.

Here is how the exercise works: You are being issued a bag containing ten marbles of four different colors—red, green, blue, and rainbow. Different members have different proportions of the colors, but each person has 10 marbles. Your objective is to collect 15 marbles of the same color and turn them in to the coordinator of the exercise. You will have 15 minutes to do so. Extra points will be awarded for more than 15 marbles: you will receive a 10 percent bonus for each marble over the 15 that you collect. Thus, if you turn in 18 green marbles, you will receive the regular award for 15 marbles *plus* 30 percent more.

### Observers' Instructions

As an observer your task is to obtain as much information about what is taking place as possible. There are three areas on which you should concentrate: what strategies of negotiation are being used in the group, how members are reacting to each other's strategies, and how successful the strategies are. Observations of any other aspect of negotiating behavior will also be helpful. Write down your observations and make as many as possible.

### Distribution of Marbles to the Twelve Participants

| Member | Red | Blue | Green | Rainbow |
|:------:|:---:|:----:|:-----:|:-------:|
| 1 | 4 | 3 | 2 | 1 |
| 2 | 1 | 4 | 3 | 2 |
| 3 | 2 | 1 | 4 | 3 |
| 4 | 3 | 2 | 1 | 4 |
| 5 | 3 | 3 | 2 | 2 |
| 6 | 3 | 2 | 3 | 2 |
| 7 | 2 | 3 | 2 | 3 |
| 8 | 2 | 2 | 3 | 3 |
| 9 | 2 | 2 | 2 | 4 |
| 10 | 2 | 2 | 4 | 2 |
| 11 | 2 | 4 | 2 | 2 |
| 12 | 4 | 2 | 2 | 2 |

### Instructions for Problem-Solving Negotiation

In this exercise your group is to adopt a problem-solving negotiation strategy in which members try to define the task and find creative solutions to it that are satisfying to as many members as possible. In negotiating with other group members, try to make the problem solving as creative as possible. Communicate openly and honestly about your needs and try to find ways in which to help both your own and the other group members' success. Avoid all threats and deception, which might destroy trust among group members. The problem is to figure out how as many group members as possible can complete the task.

### Instructions for Win-Lose Negotiation

In this exercise your group is to adopt a win-lose negotiation strategy in which each member will try to obtain more marbles of the same color than anyone else. Obviously, some of the members of your group are going to win and some are going to lose. You want to be a winner. The use of deceit, threats, and force may be helpful in negotiating with the other members. During the negotiations try to achieve the best outcome for yourself, and use your power and skill in any way that helps you do so. Remember, if you keep the other group members from winning, you will increase your own chances of winning.

## EXERCISE 8.3:
## NEGOTIATION

This exercise consists of three situations in which members of the same organization or group have to negotiate a conflict of interest. In each situation the basic procedure for the coordinator is the same. The exercise takes less than one hour to complete.

1. Introduce the exercise as one in which the dynamics of negotiation among members of a group become apparent. Divide the class into groups of three (two participants and one observer) for case studies 1 and 2 and groups of four (three participants and one observer). You need at least two groups. Distribute the accompanying background sheets and role-playing sheets to the participants and observers. Give each observer one copy of the observers' instructions used in the previous exercise. Without letting the groups know that they are getting different instructions, give half of

them copies of the accompanying bargaining instructions and the other half copies of the role-reversal instructions.

2. Meet with the observers to make sure they understand what they are expected to do.

3. Give the signal to begin. Groups have up to 25 minutes to negotiate an agreement. If they finish before their time is up, note how long it took them to negotiate an agreement and what type of negotiation instructions they had.

4. At the end of 25 minutes announce that the time is up and the negotiations must end. Ask each participant to write on a sheet of paper two adjectives describing his feelings during the negotiations and hand it to you. Record how many groups negotiated an agreement and which type of instructions (bargaining or role reversal) they had.

5. Ask each group to discuss its experience with its observer. The main topics of the discussion should be the negotiation strategies used, how members reacted to one another's strategies, and how successful the different strategies were. Then, on a sheet of newsprint, have each group summarize its strategies, how successful they were, how members reacted to them, and any conclusions members can make about their effectiveness.

6. In a general session have each group share its instructions for negotiation, the strategies its members used, and its conclusions about their effectiveness. You can then reveal how participants with bargaining instructions reacted to the negotiations compared with participants with role-reversal instructions, how many groups with each type of instructions completed the negotiations successfully, and how long it took these groups to do so. Summarize the main points of the discussion.

7. Have the participants read the subsequent sections on negotiation and compare their conclusions with the material in those sections.

**Negotiation Exercise: Case Study 1**

**Background.**   Jim and Chris (a female) both work for a research firm but in different divisions. Chris has been assigned project leader of a study, and Jim has been assigned from the other division to work on it. This does not necessarily imply that Chris is Jim's boss. This arrangement has been in effect for about a year, and it is relatively unsatisfactory to Chris, who would like to have Jim taken off the project.

Meetings of the project team are often dominated by arguments between Chris and Jim. As a result Chris has often held meetings without notifying Jim.

Jim and Chris are meeting to see if the conflict between them can be resolved.

**Chris.**   Jim is a know-it all who is always trying to tell you how to run your project. You do not agree with his approach. What he wants to study is not the subject of the research.

You cannot stand Jim's voice. He has an extremely grating voice that he uses with imperious overtones. He is generally obnoxious.

He comes into meetings, slumps down in a chair, and demands that everyone pay attention to him, even if he is late and they have already started.

He doesn't give others a chance to talk, and always interrupts if they do get a chance.

He does not care about the project. If he finds something else to do that he likes better, he simply ignores his responsibilities for completing work on the project. The group had to miss one deadline because he chose to do something else, and in the report before, you had to rewrite one whole section because what he turned in was not adequate. He was busy working on something for the director of the organization just to make a name for himself. Meanwhile, he sacrificed your reputation by causing your project to be late and your group to produce inferior work.

**Jim.**   Chris thinks she is better than anyone else around here. She thinks she is some kind of prima donna and that only the research she is doing is any good. She thinks all the other work in the organization is "trash" except for hers.

You feel that what you were working on for the director was more important for the organization. But she is not willing to agree that anyone except herself can do anything well.

You do not agree with her approach to the project. Her main emphasis is on something that is not relevant to the problem. We need answers in order to make decisions today, not five years from now.

You do not really feel involved in the project. Chris accepts what everyone else on the project is doing, but she chooses your area to criticize.

### Negotiation Exercise: Case Study 2

**Background.**  Pat (a female) and Rich both work for a research organization. Originally the director of the organization was the leader of a project. Rich was interviewed for a position on that project and hired by the director. Pat also interviewed Rich, and strongly opposed his being hired for the project. Pat thought Rich wasn't competent to do the job.

Five or six months after work on the project began, the director decided she wanted to be relieved and proposed that Rich and Pat conduct it jointly. Pat agreed only reluctantly—with the stipulation that it be made clear she was not working for Rich. The director consented. They were to have a shared directorship.

Within a month Pat was angry because Rich was acting towards others as though he were the director of the entire project and she was working for him.

Pat and Rich are meeting to see if the conflict between them can be resolved.

**Pat.**  Right after the joint-leadership arrangement was reached with the director, Rich called a meeting of the project team without even consulting you about the time or content. He just told you when it was being held and said you should be there.

At the meeting Rich reviewed everyone's paper line by line—including yours, thus treating you as just another team member working for him.

He sends out letters and signs himself as project director, which obviously implies to others that you are working for him.

**Rich.**  You think Pat is all hung up with feelings of power and titles. Just because you are project director, or sign yourself that way, doesn't mean that she is working for you. You do not see anything to get excited about. What difference does it make?

She is too sensitive about everything. You call a meeting and right away she thinks you are trying to run everything.

Pat has other things to do—other projects to run—so she does not pay too much attention to this one. She mostly lets things slide. But when you take the initiative to set up a meeting, she starts jumping up and down about how you are trying to make her work for you.

### Negotiation Exercise: Bargaining Instructions

Bargaining is a process by which a person attempts to reach an agreement as favorable to herself as possible. It is aimed at producing an agreement with another person that settles what each is to give and receive in a transaction between them. Usually in a bargaining situation one person "wins" and the other person "loses." A variety of strategies can be used to influence the other bargainer in such a way as to reach an agreement as favorable to oneself as possible:

1. Presenting an opening offer very favorable to oneself and refusing to modify that position
2. Gathering information about what the other considers a "reasonable" agreement from the other's opening offer and proposals
3. Continually pointing out the validity of one's own position and the incorrectness of the other person's

4. Using a combination of threats and promises to convince the other person that he or she has to accept one's offer
5. Committing oneself to a position in such a way that if an agreement is to be reached, the other person has to agree to one's terms

In this exercise you are to bargain as toughly as you can to arrive at the best settlement possible for yourself.

**Negotiation Exercise: Role-Reversal Instructions**

Role reversal is defined as a negotiating action in which one person accurately and completely paraphrases, in a warm and involved way, the feelings and position of another. It is the expression of a sincere interest in understanding other person's position and feelings. The basic rule for role reversal is this: Each person speaks up for himself only after he has first restated the ideas and feelings of the other person accurately and to the other's satisfaction. In other words, before one person presents his point of view it is necessary for him to achieve the other person's perspective or frame of reference and to understand her position and feelings so well that he can paraphrase them accurately and completely. General guidelines for role reversal are as follows:

1. Restate the other person's expressed ideas and feelings in one's own words rather than parroting the words of the other person.
2. Preface your reflected remarks with "You think . . . ," "Your position is . . . ," "You feel . . . ," "It seems to you that . . . ," and so on.
3. Avoid any indication of approval or disapproval in paraphrasing the other person's statements. It is important to refrain from interpreting, blaming, persuading, or advising.
4. Make your nonverbal messages congruent with your verbal paraphrasing. Look attentive, be interested in and open to the other's ideas and feelings, and appear to be concentrating on what the other person is trying to communicate.

In this exercise you are to engage in role reversal during the entire negotiating session and use it to arrive at the solution to the problems you and the other person(s) are facing.

**EXERCISE 8.4:**
**CONFLICTS OF INTEREST**

The purpose of this exercise is to stimulate a discussion on how conflicts of interest should be managed. The procedure is as follows:

1. Brief descriptions of four conflicts of interest appear below. Read each one. Then, working by yourself, write a description of how you would handle each conflict if you were the teacher in the classroom. Assume the students are in high school.
2. With your classmates, form heterogeneous groups of four. Working as a group, discuss each conflict and come to a consensus how it should be managed. Write out the group's plan for handling each conflict.
3. Each group shares its solutions with the rest of the class.

**Conflict Descriptions**

1. My friend doesn't like to lose. But the teacher keeps giving tests and he comes out last. She posts the scores so everyone in the class knows my friend is dumb. So one day she was giving a test and he tossed a lighted firecracker under her seat. She

fainted. The principal came up to the class and said, "Who put that firecracker under Ms. Waterton's seat?" Several students started laughing, so the principal took them down to his office and called their parents. They got in trouble. But the look on the teacher's face when the firecracker went off was worth it. And you should have seen her face when she walked into the classroom the next day!

2. Two students begin to argue about who owns a pen. Both students claim it. The argument leads to a small fistfight. Both students end up feeling angry and rejected.

3. In your class you assigned each student a collage on a serious social problem, such as pollution, discrimination, drugs, or crime. The idea of the project was to get the students to express themselves and their ideas in a visual manner and to increase their awareness of how art can be an impressive and persuasive tool. A student raised his hand and said he didn't see the importance of this sort of thing. He said he wasn't going to do it because it sounded like a stupid waste of his time, and why couldn't you assign something more interesting and valuable.

4. Mary and George are members of a cooperative group. Yet they constantly put each other down, criticize each other, and even make fun of each other's contributions. They both want to be the group leader and spend most of their energy undermining each other's efforts to direct and control the group's activities.

## EXERCISE 8.5:
## MAKING A PROFIT

The purpose of this exercise is to give participants an opportunity to negotiate a profit-loss situation so that they may examine the dynamics of bargaining. The exercise can be conducted in less than half an hour. The procedure for the coordinator is as follows:

1. Introduce the exercise as an opportunity to study the dynamics of negotiation between two persons with different interests. The negotiation is between a buyer and a seller in a wholesale market.

2. Divide the class into heterogeneous groups of six. There needs to be an even number of members in each group (i.e., 2, 4, 6, 8, 10). Then divide each group into two subgroups of three members each. Assign one subgroup the role of buyers and the other subgroup the role of sellers. Instruct the subgroups that each member must prepare to negotiate with a member of the opposite subgroup. The purpose of the negotiation is to maximize the profits of the subgroup. The members of each subgroup will not be allowed to show their profit schedule to the negotiators from the other subgroup, and therefore must understand what possible agreements are advantageous for them. The profit schedules may be found on page 502 in the appendix.

3. Make three pairs from each group of six, each pair comprising one person from each subgroup. Have the negotiators meet face to face. Their task is to negotiate an agreement on the price for each commodity. They can say anything they want to each other, but they may *not* show each other their profit schedule.

4. After all pairs have finished negotiating, ask all participants to write down on a sheet of paper
   a. Which commodity was most important to the opponent.
   b. Which commodity was least important to the opponent.

5. Instruct participants to reform their groups of six and discuss the following questions:
   a. What were the agreements reached by the members of the group?
   b. What was the total joint outcome achieved by each buyer-and-seller pair? (The joint outcome is the sum of the profits of the buyer and the profits of the seller.) Which pair had the highest joint outcome?
   c. What negotiation strategies were used? Were they win-lose or problem-solving strategies?

    d. How did negotiators communicate information about their profit schedule, and how did they learn about the profit schedule of their opponent? Were their perceptions of what commodities were most and least important to their opponent correct? Was information exchange direct? (Did buyer and seller accurately tell each other their profit schedules?) Or was it indirect? (Did they deduce each other's profit schedule by comparing each other's responses to different package offers?)

    e. Did the negotiators make package deals or did they negotiate the commodities one at a time?

    f. What conclusions can the group make about negotiations on the basis of their experience and discussion?

6. Have each group share its conclusions with the rest of the class.

## CONFLICTS OF INTEREST: AVOID OR RESOLVE?

> Not everything that is faced can be changed but
> Nothing can be changed until it is faced.
> *James Baldwin*

When a conflict of interest arises, you will be faced with the decision of whether to avoid or resolve it. To make such a decision you will need to understand the circumstances that brought about the conflict and the entry state of the participants. The circumstances that surround the conflict include both the barriers to the beginning of negotiations and events that trigger expressions (Walton, 1987). **Internal barriers** include negative attitudes, values, fears, anxieties, and habitual patterns of avoiding conflict. **External barriers** may include task requirements, group norms for avoiding conflict, pressure to maintain a congenial public image, and faulty perceptions of one's vulnerability and others' strength. Physical separation is a frequently used barrier to the expression of conflicts of interest. Placing members in different locations, avoiding being in the same room with certain other members, and removing a member from the group, can all suppress a conflict of interest. A **triggering event** may be as simple as two group members being physically near each other or as complex as two members being in competition. Negative remarks, sarcasm, and criticism on sensitive points are common triggering events, as is the feeling of being deprived, neglected, or ignored. Some events may trigger a destructive cycle of conflict, and others may trigger problem solving; group members will want to maximize the latter type of triggering event.

    Since an important aspect of conflict management is choosing the right time and place for negotiations, an understanding of the barriers and triggering events allows you to suppress the expression of the conflict until the time and place is more appropriate, or to precipitate the expression when the time and place is appropriate. To avoid the conflict, you remove the triggering events and build up the barriers to negotiations. To resolve the conflict, you increase the frequency of the triggering events and decrease the barriers to negotiations. The diagnosis of a conflict involves discovering (1) the barriers to negotiation and (2) what triggers open expression of the conflict. From such knowledge group members can help choose the time and place for negotiations. If an appropriate time is not immediately available, the barriers to

**FIGURE 8.2**

expressing the conflict can be increased and the triggering events can be decreased in order to avoid the conflict temporarily. An analysis of events that surround or precede a conflict often provides clues to the basic issues of the conflict.

The entry state of the participants should be assessed by the group. The **entry state** of a group member is that person's ability to deal constructively with the conflict. Members' level of self-awareness, their ability to control their behavior, their skills in communicating and in other ways being interpersonally effective (see Johnson, 1990), their ability to withstand stress, and their ability to incorporate their strengths in constructive conflict behavior are all important aspects of their entry state. Your opponent may be too anxious, defensive, or psychologically unstable to negotiate effectively, or their motivation to change may be very low. Group support and consultation can raise the entry state of each participant.

Not every conflict of interest is negotiable. It is a mistake to assume that you can always openly negotiate the resolution of a conflict; there are times when conflicts are better avoided. But usually conflicts of interest can be settled constructively if participants attempt to do so.

## PROMOTING NEGOTIATIONS

Within any group, conflicts of interest will arise such that members will need to negotiate agreements with each other. Once you have decided to resolve a conflict of interest, you will find many procedures available—legal action, third-party roles (such as therapists, counselors, arbitrators, mediators, ombudsmen, and advocates), violence, and negotiation, among others. Negotiation is by far the most effective procedure for constructively resolving conflicts within a group. Each group member has needs and goals. Group members share many interests. But some of their interests are different. In order to resolve their different interests and continue to work together productively, negotiations must take place. To meet his or her needs and goals, each person makes proposals to others. The other persons evaluate the proposal on the basis of how well it meets their needs and goals and either agree or make a counterproposal. Given both shared and opposing interests, negotiation is a back-and-forth exchange of proposals aimed at reaching an agreement. In other words, **negotiation** is a process by which persons who (1) have both shared and opposing interests and (2) want to come to an agreement try to work out a settlement. Negotiations are aimed at achieving an agreement that specifies what each group member gives to and receives from each other. Negotiation may involve **distributive issues** where one member benefits only if the opponent agrees to make a concession or **integrative issues** where the two members are working together to seek a solution that will benefit everyone. Within groups, conflicts are usually of sufficient complexity that integrative resolutions are possible. A more complete discussion of the process of negotiation may be found in Johnson and Johnson (1987).

Not every group discussion involves negotiation. Negotiating is just one of many types of activity that take place within a group. So how do you recognize negotiations when you see them? You can tell whether or not you are negotiating by using the following checklist:

1. Is there another member involved?
2. Are both cooperative elements (we both wish to reach an agreement) and competitive elements (we both wish the agreement to be as favorable to ourselves as possible) present in the situation?
3. Does getting what you want depend upon the agreement of another member?
4. Are you in the dilemma of wanting to propose an agreement that is highly favorable to yourself but not wanting to risk making the other member so mad that she refuses to negotiate?
5. Are you dependent upon the other member to give you information about what is a reasonable agreement from her point of view?
6. Are there contractual norms on how negotiation should be conducted?
7. Do the negotiations have a beginning, a middle, and an end?

There are ten important points to be made about negotiations. The first is that it takes two to negotiate, whether it is two group members, two groups, two organizations, or two nations. You cannot negotiate by yourself. Second, within any negotiations, furthermore, there are both cooperative and competitive elements. Negotiations are typically mixed-motive situations (see Figure 8.2). A cooperative element exists when both members believe they will gain more by negotiating than by not negotiating; a competitive element exists when both members have conflicting preferences among or contending interests in the different possible agreements. In any negotiation a range of possible agreements can be made; it is the push for one particular agreement rather than another that signifies the competitive elements in the negotiation relationship.

Third, because both members must commit themselves to an agreement, each is dependent upon the other for the outcome. All negotiating is aimed at achieving certain outcomes for oneself, but those outcomes are possible only if the other negotiator agrees to them. This situation is called **outcome dependence.** The mutual outcome dependence highlights the fact that *the ultimate goal of negotiating is to gain benefits for all, not to create winners and losers*. Negotiators have to be concerned with both meeting their needs and goals and maintaining an appropriate relationship with the other person. In long-term relationships, maintaining an effective working relationship is usually more important than is meeting one's short-term needs and goals. One-sided settlements imposed by whomever has the most power at the moment are rarely stable or long lasting. What works are solutions that meet the needs of both persons. Otherwise you have to be careful when you go past dark alleys!

The fourth is that both primary and secondary gains must be attended to in negotiations. The *primary gain* is determined by the nature of the agreement: the more favorable the agreement is to a member's short-term goals, the greater the primary gain for her. The *secondary gain* is determined by the group: the more effective the group, the more the member's long-term goals will be met, and therefore the greater the long-term gain for her. Consequently, in negotiating a resolution to a conflict a group member has to be concerned not only with what is more desirable for him or her in the short term but also with what is most desirable for improving the effectiveness of the group.

A fifth characteristic of negotiations is the dilemma that participants face:

Each wants an agreement as favorable to himself as possible, but for one to attempt to maximize his outcome might result in such an unsatisfactory agreement for the other member that she would refuse to settle and would leave the negotiation relationship. For one negotiator not to attempt to maximize his outcome, however, would provide the other with too good an agreement; one would then be settling for less than necessary. In resolving the **goal dilemma,** participants must decide on a "reasonable" settlement, one that will not only get the most for one participant but also have a good chance of being acceptable to the other. Each participant seeks an agreement that is the best he or she can do in the face of the other's opposition. Inasmuch as there is rarely any obvious "correct" agreement that is accepted immediately by both members, each must decide during the negotiations what is a reasonable outcome for oneself and for the other negotiator. The problem is always that the more favorable the agreement to oneself the less favorable it is to the other person.

The sixth characteristic of negotiation relationship is **information dependence.** Negotiators are dependent upon each other not only for their outcomes but also for information about a possible agreement. Such information can be secured in one of two ways: negotiators can openly and honestly share their preferences, needs, and expectations, or they can attempt to hide their preferences, needs, and expectations in hopes of making an agreement as favorable to themselves as possible. This is a complicated issue because negotiators often do not know what their expectations should be until they learn what the other negotiator's expectations are. To the point that negotiators know both what the other wants and what is the least the other will accept, they will be able to develop an effective negotiating position. Information dependence sets up two more dilemmas, the dilemma of trust and the dilemma of honesty and openness. The *dilemma of trust* involves a choice between believing the other negotiator and risking potential exploitation or disbelieving the other negotiator and risking no agreement. To trust the other negotiator is to risk potential exploitation. By telling lies one participant can reduce the outcome for the other if her lies are believed. To distrust the other negotiator means that there is no possibility of any agreement being reached. The **dilemma of honesty and openness** involves the risk of either being exploited for disclosing too much too quickly or seriously damaging the negotiating relationship by refusing to disclose information and thereby seeming deceitful or distrusting.

The seventh characteristic of the negotiation relationship is the development of **contractual norms** that spell out the rules to be observed and the penalties for violating them. Thus, if violations occur the penalty can be assessed without destroying the possibility of further negotiations. Two norms quite common in negotiation situations are reciprocity and equity. The **norm of reciprocity** means that a negotiator should return the same benefit or harm given him or her by the other negotiator; "an eye for an eye and a kiss for a kiss" is an example of a norm of reciprocity. The **norm of equity** means that the benefits received or the costs assessed by the negotiators should be equal. Contractual norms provide clear ground rules for conducting the negotiations and managing the difficulties involved in reaching an agreement.

Eighth, the negotiation relationship has important time dimensions. It has a beginning, a middle, and an end. Negotiation begins when the parties acknowledge that a conflict of interest exists and either formally or informally make initial moves in the direction of its resolution. Negotiation ends when one or more of the parties chooses to leave the negotiating relationship. This may occur because an agreement has been reached and the parties conclude by mutual consent, or because one or more of the parties believes no satisfactory agreement is possible. Though ending a negotiating relationship, the parties may continue other relationships. For example, after they have negotiated an agreement, the two parties can work cooperatively toward a mutual goal. In conducting negotiations, therefore, the parties must always consider future relationships between them: It will do no good to negotiate an agreement highly favorable to one member if future cooperation is jeopardized or if the other member becomes so resentful that the agreement cannot be implemented.

The ninth is that negotiation is an ever-present function of human existence and groups and organizations are no exception. You cannot avoid negotiating. Negotiations are rarely formal. You are negotiating all the time on an informal basis. Negotiation is not something reserved for international or union-management disagreements. We all negotiate, and we spend a great deal of time negotiating. Every day group members face the choice of negotiating agreements or engaging in combat. Teachers negotiate with students over how much homework to give, parents negotiate with children about how frequently they clean up their rooms, managers negotiate with subordinates about how fast they will work to complete a project, and therapists negotiate with clients as to how fast they will implement changes in their lives. We negotiate at work and we negotiate in our personal lives with acquaintances, friends, parents and siblings, and spouse and children. We are even negotiating when we do not think of ourselves as doing so.

The tenth is that although negotiation takes place every day, it is not easy to do well. *Negotiating skills are one of your keys to success in life.* There is no overstating the importance of being able to negotiate well. A recent survey conducted for Accountemps (a large accounting, bookkeeping, and data processing temporary personnel service that is a division of Robert Half International, Inc.) of vice-presidents and personnel directors of 100 of the nation's 1,000 largest corporations found that the people who manage America's leading corporations spend over four working weeks a year dealing with the problems caused by employees who cannot resolve their conflicts with each other. In answer to the question, "What percent of management time is spent dealing with conflicts among employees?" respondents revealed that executives spend an average of 9.2 percent of their time or, based on a 40-hour week, 4.6 weeks a year attempting to deal with employee conflicts and the difficulties and disruptions they cause. In addition to taking up valuable management time, employee conflicts can seriously reduce any company's productivity and its ability to compete effectively in the marketplace. Knowing how to negotiate constructive resolutions to conflicts of interest is an essential skill for executives. Negotiation skills are required within any career and in building and maintaining meaningful and fulfilling personal relationships. Poor agreements are always breaking down. They bring nagging dissatisfaction and aggravation. But good agreements help you reach and exceed your own objectives while leaving others more satisfied at the same time.

# STEPS IN NEGOTIATING RESOLUTIONS
# OF CONFLICTS OF INTEREST

Storms are a natural and unavoidable aspect of the earth's weather system. Storms range in intensity from rainstorms to hurricanes. Some are accompanied by gentle rain, others by thunder and lightning. Similarly, interpersonal storms are a natural and unavoidable aspect of life within groups that vary in intensity from mild to severe. When faced with a storm among members, there are six basic steps in negotiating a resolution (Johnson & Johnson, 1987):

1. Jointly defining the conflict
2. Exchanging proposals and feelings
3. Reversing perspectives
4. Inventing options for mutual benefit
5. Reaching a wise agreement
6. Try, try again

## Step 1: Agreeing on a Definition of the Conflict

Sally Somnolent and Ms. Alert have a conflict. Sally sees it as very important that she get a good nap during geometry. Ms. Alert sees it as very important that Sally listens carefully in class to learn as much geometry as possible. "The problem is that no one understands or loves me," Sally says. "The problem is that students nowadays are rude and obnoxious," Ms. Alert says. Agreeing on the definition of a conflict is like putting gas in an airplane. Without it, conflict resolution will never get off the ground. To negotiate a resolution of the conflict you communicate to the other person:

1. There is a conflict.
2. You wish to resolve it (i.e., cooperative orientation).
3. Your perception of the conflict and how you feel about it (i.e., confrontation).
4. A request for a meeting in the near future (perhaps right now) so that the two could discuss it (i.e., setting a time).

After cooperative intentions are expressed, a confrontation takes place. A **confrontation** is the direct expression of one's view of the conflict and one's feelings about it and at the same time an invitation to the opposition to do the same. Confrontations involve clarifying and exploring the issues, the nature and strength of the underlying needs of the participants, and their current feelings. It is a deliberate attempt to begin a direct and problem-solving discussion about the conflict with the opposition. A time to discuss the conflict is set, and the people involved sit down to problem solve and negotiate. The first issue is to agree on a definition of the conflict. How the conflict is defined will influence how easy the conflict is to resolve.

*There are two steps in defining a conflict.* The first is to define the conflict by yourself. Your definition of the conflict will affect how you act and feel in trying to resolve it. With a poor definition, you will feel miserable and act in ways that will make the conflict worse. With a constructive definition, you will feel confident and

effective, and you will act in ways that resolve the conflict. It is important that you be able to define conflicts in a skillful way. The second is to agree with the other person on a joint definition. It takes two or more persons to create a conflict of interest, and two or more persons to resolve a conflict of interest. To reach an agreement how the conflict is to be resolved, one must define it in a way that both sides can accept. Here are five rules that will help you do so.

   **Rule 1: Describe the other person's actions.**   Do not label, accuse, or insult. Make sure the conflict is over issues and actions, not personalities. Focus on behavior, not on psychological states and personality characteristics. In trying to understand what causes the opponents to act the way they do, attributions are made. According to **attribution theory** (a theory of how people make inferences about the causes of behaviors and events), people continually formulate intuitive causal hypotheses so that they can understand and predict events that transpire in the group (Heider, 1958). Attributions become especially important in conflict, since attributions about causes influence group members' perceptions of their groupmates motives and intentions (Steiner, 1959) and partially mediate reactions to groupmates' behaviors (Horai, 1977; Messe, Stollak, Larson, & Michaels, 1979). If attributions are accurate, they help group members understand each other better. Attributions are, however, not always accurate. Perceptual biases regularly distort individuals' attributional inferences. The *fundamental attribution error* (Ross, 1977) is the attribution of the causes of other's behaviors to personal (disposition) factors while attributing the causes of your own behavior to situational (environmental) factors. When trying to understand the other's behavior, a person tends to overestimate the causal importance of personality, beliefs, attitudes, and values, and underestimates the causal importance of situational pressures. The opposite is done in trying to understand one's own behavior. Harold Kelley and his associates (Kelley, 1979, Orvis, Kelley, & Butler, 1976) demonstrated the impact of the fundamental attribution error on the resolution of conflict. Forty-one married couples were asked to recall and describe recent conflicts with each other. The typical conflict involved one person engaging in an action that the other reacted to negatively. The person who engaged in the negative action believed that the behavior was caused by extenuating circumstances, somebody else, or a desire to do the right thing. The other person explained the behavior as being caused by negative personal characteristics such as poor judgment, irresponsibility, selfishness, a lack of concern, a tendency to show off, and incompetence. Each person considered the other's attributions to be unfair and unreasonable and, therefore, the conflict invariably escalated.

Especially in conflicts, there is a tendency in defining conflicts to attribute the causes of the conflict to inner psychological states of the opponent (Blake & Mouton, 1962; Chesler & Franklin, 1968; Sherif & Sherif, 1969). Defining a conflict as the actions of a sick, perverted, and vicious troublemaker is less constructive than defining a conflict as a specific set of actions by an opponent. Like everyone else, opponents want to appear strong and capable to others, and if they believe you are trying to label them as sick, weak, incompetent, or ineffective they will refuse to compromise or negotiate flexibly (Brown, 1968; Pruitt & Johnson, 1970; Tjosvold, 1974, 1977).

Defining a conflict is like lacing your shoes. If you start out wrong, the whole thing gets messed up. Separate the person from the problem. Negotiate over issues, not personalities. Avoid personalized attacks. Keep the negotiations free of highly personal criticism, recriminations, abusive language, and especially those subtle jibes that inflict pain on the other. If you label the other person in negative ways, he or she will be defensive and hostile. Labeling creates mistrust, misunderstandings, and resentment. Do not label, accuse, or insult the other person! Describe the other's actions toward you! Conflicts must be defined as being over actions and issues, not personalities.

**Rule 2: Define the conflict as a mutual problem to be solved, not as a win-lose struggle.**   A conflict defined as a problem to be solved is much easier to resolve constructively than a conflict defined as a win-lose situation (Blake & Mouton, 1962; Deutsch & Lewicki, 1970). The total benefits for all sides in negotiations are higher than when problem-solving strategies are used (Lewis & Pruitt, 1971). Defining a conflict as a win-lose situation leads to adopting strategies such as making an opening proposal highly favorable to oneself, refusing to modify it, trying to persuade the opponent that one's position is reasonable, using threats and promises to coerce and entice the opponent to accept one's proposal, and ignoring all the opponent's arguments concerning the validity of his position (Chertkoff & Esser, 1976; Johnson, 1974; Rubin & Brown, 1975; Walton & McKersie, 1965). Although win-lose strategies often pay off in the short run, the damage they cause significantly reduces their secondary gain. Win-lose strategies commonly impose the position of the negotiator with the most power upon the other participants. They undermine trust, inhibit dialogue and communication, and generally diminish the likelihood that the conflict will be resolved constructively. In a win-lose negotiation every action of all participants is viewed as an attempt to dominate. Negotiators tend to deny the legitimacy of opponent's interests and consider only their own needs. They try to force the opponent to give in by augmenting their own power and undermining that of the opponent. Losers have little motivation to carry out the actions agreed upon, resent the winner, and often try to sabotage the agreement. The winner finds it hard to enforce the agreement. Severe damage to interpersonal relationships results. Winners and losers will generally be hostile toward each other in the future.

Despite their high probability of secondary losses, win-lose strategies are often used in schools. Both Gump (1964) and Flanders (1964) have observed that teachers try to dominate students by coercing them into doing what the teacher wants. Such negotiation strategies tend to provoke student resistance (Flanders, 1964). Rafalides and Hoy (1971), in a study of 45 high schools involving 3,000 teachers and administrators, concluded that when a school emphasizes authoritarian control and expects students to accept teacher decisions without question, students become alienated. DeCecco and Richards (1974) noted that 55 percent of the conflicts they studied were resolved by the imposing of decisions on students by school personnel. They concluded that coercion and threats of punishment by school personnel frequently escalated conflict and prevented negotiations.

Do not define a conflict as being a "win-lose" competition. Whenever you are trying to prove who is right and who is wrong and who is superior and who is inferior, you are in a win-lose competition. In the long run, neither good will result. The future relationship is always hurt by win-lose conflicts. You may feel great at first if you win. But the person who loses will feel resentful and will dislike the winner. A win-lose definition of a conflict promotes distrust, dislike, deception, rivalry, threats, and attempts to undermine each other's work. Trying to prove you are better than the other person will only make your marriage an unpleasant experience. Always try to define a conflict as a mutual problem to be solved. This will increase communication, trust, liking for each other, and cooperation. No one loses when you and the other person sit down to solve a mutual problem!

**Rule 3: Define the conflict in the smallest and most specific way possible.** The smaller and more precise the definition of a conflict, the easier it will be to resolve (Deutsch, Canavan, & Rubin, 1971). It is easier, for example, to resolve a conflict over a small rule infraction than one involving disrespect for adult authority. The more general and ambiguous the definition of the conflict, the harder it is to resolve constructively. Think small. The larger and vaguer the description of the other person's actions, the harder it is to resolve the conflict. When it comes to resolving conflicts, small is easy, large is hard! The more limited the definition of the conflict, the easier it is to resolve. The smaller and more specific the description of your spouse's actions, the easier it will be to find a way to resolve the conflict.

**Rule 4: Describe your feelings about, and reactions to, the other person's actions.** Do not expect the other person to be a mind reader. The only way he or she can know how you are feeling and reacting is if you tell him or her. What the other person does not know about, he or she cannot be blamed for. There is a tendency in conflicts to hide feelings and reactions. You often do not want the other person to know how upset you really are. But if the conflict is to be resolved, you need to share your feelings and reactions. This helps the other person understand how his or her actions are affecting you.

**Rule 5: Describe your actions (what you are doing and neglecting to do) that help create and continue the conflict.**   Who needs to change? You, the other person, or both? In a conflict, you may want the other person to change. But the easiest thing to change is your own actions. If you wish to resolve a conflict, you must begin with deciding how to change your actions. It would be nice if everyone else changed so we would never have to. But you do not have control over the actions of others. They do. What you do have control over is your own actions. You can change your actions much more easily than you can change the other person's actions! Knowing how your actions help create and continue the conflict is essential for planning how to resolve it! And neglecting to do something constructive helps create and continue the conflict just as much as doing something destructive!

These five rules provide a clear, useful way of defining a conflict. The more you follow these rules, the more skillful you will be in resolving them.

To define a conflict jointly, parties have to use a common language about conflicts. The group language may include such terms as win-lose, problem solve, confront, beltline, and gunnysack (i.e., to store up grievances for a long time and then unload them all on an offending group member). A common language about conflicts facilitates the identification of constructive and destructive strategies of negotiation. Groups may develop their own vocabulary for describing conflict behaviors and procedures.

## Step 2: Exchanging Proposals and Feelings

In exchanging proposals and feelings, both you and the other person have to

1. *Present your proposed agreements and feelings.* You have to be aware of your needs and goals, organize your thoughts and feelings into a coherent position, and persuasively present a proposal in hopes that the other person will agree. Typically your proposals are tentative based on current understanding of your interests and the interests of the other person. As you learn more about the other person's goals and needs, and about the situation in general, your goals and needs may shift and change.

How you present your proposed agreement, furthermore, has implications both for your commitment to your current position and the response to it by other group members. To persuade others you may overemphasize the factors that favor your position, and this overattention to positive arguments results in selective retention of position-consistent information. Arguing for your position, furthermore, tends to result in increased commitment to it (Hovland, Janis, & Kelley, 1953) and a belief that you are committed through self-perception (Bem, 1972). If you are too demanding in your presentation, however, your attempts to persuade may boomerang. Jack Brehm (1976; Brehm & Brehm, 1981) demonstrated that persuasive attempts that are viewed as coercive or biased often backfire by causing others to reject what you are saying and increase their commitment to their original positions. This intensification is called *psychological reactance*—the need to reestablish your freedom whenever it is threatened. In one of the Bem studies, for example, two teammates had to choose between two alternatives marked 1-A or 1-B. When the partner stated, "I prefer 1-A," 73 percent chose 1-A, but when the partner stated, "I think we should both do 1-A," only 40 percent chose 1-A (Brehm & Sensenig, 1966). Similarly, 83 percent of the members of a group refused to go along with a member who stated, "I think it's pretty obvious all of us are going to work on task A" (Worchel & Brehm, 1971).

2. *Listen to the other's proposals and feelings.* Your success as a negotiator depends largely on showing the other person how his or her needs and goals may be met through accepting your proposals. To make a persuasive case for your position, you have to understand clearly what the other person's interests and feelings are. This requires careful listening and being able to see the situation from the other person's perspective.

3. *Clarify, evaluate, refute each other's proposals.* To get other people to agree to your proposals, they have to see the inadequacies of their proposals. In clarifying the other's proposals a negotiator will often be trying to refute them. Thinking critically about the proposals of others often helps to eventually create an agreement that satisfies everyone's needs.

4. *Stay flexible, changing your position and feelings when persuaded to do so.* Negotiating is a rational process. You are seeking a way to satisfy your needs and reach your goals and the other person is doing the same. How successful you are in reaching an agreement good for you depends on how creatively you can think of alternatives that also are good for the other person. This requires flexibility and a willingness to change your mind when you are persuaded that it is rational to do so. It is very easy and quite common to become entrapped in your commitment to a position and close your mind to alternatives. Allan Teger (1980), for example, studied the entrapment process through conducting "dollar auctions." A dollar is auctioned off to the highest bidder with the rule that although the highest bidder gets to keep the dollar, the second highest bidder must pay the amount he or she bid. Thus, if a person bid 80 cents for the dollar and someone else bid 90 cents, the person is entrapped in bidding higher to avoid losing the 80 cents. Negotiators need to be vigilant against being entrapped by their commitment to old proposals and positions.

5. *Focus on Needs and Goals, Not Positions.* If you want to deal effectively with the other person, if you want to persuade him or her to meet your needs, if you want to negotiate an issue, you have to approach the other person with proposals based on his or her needs. *The heart of negotiations is meeting the needs of the other person while ensuring your needs are being met.* The success of negotiations depends on finding out what the other person really wants, and showing him or her a way to get it while you get what you want. For a wise decision, therefore, reconcile needs, not positions. For every need or goal, there usually exist several possible positions that could satisfy it. A common mistake is to assume that because the other person's position is opposed to yours, his or her needs and goals must also be opposed. Behind opposed positions lie shared and compatible goals, as well as conflicting ones. To identify the other person's needs and goals, ask "Why," ask, "Why not?" and think about his or her choices, and realize that the other person has many different needs and goals.

Focusing on needs and goals rather than positions eliminates many of the traps that cause conflicts to become destructive. One such trap is the aggression that arises from being frustrated by the opponent's refusal to agree with your position. The link between frustration and aggression is one of the oldest social-psychological explanations of hostility and physical violence. The **frustration-aggression process** may be summarized in the following way (Berkowitz, 1978). Individuals who are unable to attain the goals they desire because of personal limitations or external influences sometimes experience frustration. This frustration produces a readiness to respond in an aggressive manner which may boil over into hostility and violence if situational cues that serve as "releasers" are present. Negotiators can become frustrated and, at any sign of belligerence or hostility by others, release verbal and, in some cases, physical violence. What often prevents high levels of frustration is the continual clarification of needs and goals and the search from new positions that let all members reach their goals.

6. *Find out about the differences between your underlying needs and goals and those of the other person.* How and where are they incompatible? Conflicts cannot be resolved unless you understand what you are disagreeing about. *If you do not know how and where your needs and goals are incompatible with those of the other person, you cannot define the conflict and you cannot think of alternative agreements that might resolve it. If you do not know what you are disagreeing about, you cannot find a way to reach an agreement.* You must understand the differences between your needs and goals and the needs and goals of the other person. Only then will you be able to think of ways to combine ideas so that the conflict is resolved. Only if you understand the differences can you think of a way to resolve the conflict helpfully. Your ability to come up with satisfactory solutions depends on how the other person's thoughts, feelings, and needs are different from yours. Thus, in discussing a conflict you try to find the answers to these questions: (a) What are the differences between my needs and goals and those of the other person, (b) where are our needs and goals the same, (c) what actions of the other person do I find unacceptable, (d) what actions of mine does the other person find unacceptable, and (e) what are possible solutions that satisfy both my and the other person's needs and goals?

7. *Communicate cooperative intentions.* Numerous studies indicate that the unambiguous expression of cooperative intentions in negotiations and conflicts of interest results in agreements being reached in shorter periods of time. There is also a reduction of opponents' defensiveness and egocentrism; increased attitude change; reduction of the felt importance of having the "right" ideas about the issues being negotiated; greater comprehension and retention by an opponent of one's position and arguments; and increased perceptions by the opponent that one accurately understands the opponent's position, is an understanding and accepting person, and is a person the opponent would like to confide in (Johnson, 1971b, 1974; Johnson, McCarty, & Allen, 1976). It is a good idea, therefore, to communicate clearly one's motivations and intentions to cooperate.

The expression of competitive intentions, such as threats and punishments, tends to escalate the conflict. Morton Deutsch and Robert Krauss (1960, 1962) tested the hypothesis that the use of threats during a conflict will lead to increased hostility, counterthreats, and unwillingness to compromise. They studied pairs of female subjects playing the simple "Acme-Bolt Trucking Game." Each participant was to imagine herself as the owner of a trucking company—Acme or Bolt—that carried merchandise over the roads pictured in Figure 8.3. Each time a truck reached its destination, the subject would earn 60 cents minus the operating cost of 1 cent for each second taken up by the trip. To make money the subjects would have to use a stretch of one-lane road. If the trucks encountered each other on this one-lane road, one of the trucks had to back up to let the other through. Some pairs of subjects were provided with the power to threaten their opponents through a "gate" that they could close to block the road. Having a gate was of considerable advantage as it could be closed, forcing the other player to back up and take the alternate route, at which point the gate could be opened and the subject rapidly proceed to her destination. In the unilateral-threat condition, only one subject had a gate. In the bilateral-threat condition, both sides had the use of gates. In the control condition, no gates were present. When no gate was present, the subjects learned to alternate in their use of the one-lane road and both made a profit of about $1.00. When one subject had a gate, subjects lost an average of $2.03 per person, although the subject with the gate lost less than the subject without the gate. When both subjects had a gate, subjects lost an average of $4.38 per person. These results indicated that the use of threats was counterproductive, intensifying the destructive aspects of the conflict. In considering the use of threats, you may be advised to remember the advice of Niccolo Machiavelli, an advisor to sixteenth-century Florentine princes:

**FIGURE 8.3**  The road map in the Deutsch-Krauss trucking game.  From *The Resolution of Conflict: Constructive and Destructive Processes,* by M. Deutsch. Copyright 1973 by Yale University Press. Reprinted by permission.

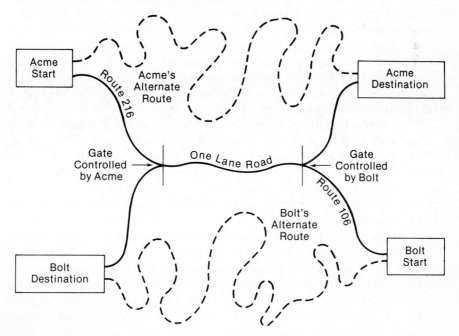

I hold it be a proof of great prudence for men to abstain from threats and insulting words toward anyone. For neither . . . diminishes the strength of the enemy; but the one makes him more cautious and the other increases his hatred of you and makes him more persevering in his efforts to injure you.

8. *Coordinate the motivation to negotiate in good faith.* There are often differences in motivation to resolve a conflict. You may want to resolve a conflict, but other group members couldn't care less. Your groupmate may be very concerned about resolving a conflict with you, but you may want to avoid the whole thing. Usually, a conflict cannot be resolved until both persons are motivated to resolve it at the same time. *The motivation to resolve a conflict is based on the costs and gains of continuing the conflict for each person.* The *costs* of continuing a conflict may be the loss of a friendship, loss of enjoyment from work, the loss of job productivity, the loss of a friend, or the loss of respect from the other person. The *gains* for continuing the conflict may be satisfaction in expressing your anger or resentment and the protection of the status quo. By protecting the status quo, you avoid the possibility that things will get worse when the conflict is resolved. Answering the following questions may help you clarify your motivation and the motivation of the other person to resolve the conflict:

    a.  What do I gain from continuing the conflict?
    b.  What does the other person gain from continuing the conflict?
    c.  What do I lose from continuing the conflict?
    d.  What does the other person lose from continuing the conflict?

A person's motivation to resolve a conflict can be changed. By increasing the costs of continuing the conflict or by increasing the gains for resolving it, the other person's motivation to resolve it can be increased. Through changing the costs and gains, you can change both your and the other person's motivation to resolve the conflict. By emphasizing costs and gains an optimal tension level can be maintained throughout the negotiations. A period of high tension generates motivation to negotiate in good faith, while a moderate level of tension ensures that participants have the ability to integrate and use information.

It is within the exchange of proposals and feelings that the dilemmas of trust and openness arise. The better negotiators understand each other's interests, the better the agreement that can ultimately be achieved. A negotiator faces the dilemmas of whether or not to (1) trust opponents to tell the truth about their interests and (2) tell the truth about his or her own interests to the opposing negotiators. Deutsch (1958, 1960, 1973) used the **Prisoner's Dilemma Game** (**PDG**) to study the issue of trust within conflict situations. The PDG derives its name from a hypothetical situation studied by mathematical game theorists (Luce & Raiffa, 1957). Once arrested, two villains (here named Butch and Sundance) are questioned in separate rooms (see Figure 8.4). Although the police are certain that Butch and Sundance are guilty of robbing a bank, they also realize that without a confession, the two criminals will have to be set free. The two prisoners are, therefore, presented with two alternatives: confess to the crime or remain silent. If Butch confesses and Sundance does not, then

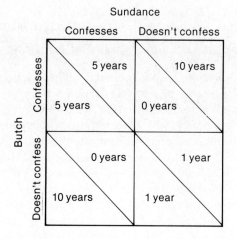
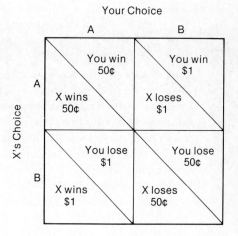

**FIGURE 8.4**  The Prisoner's Dilemma Game

Butch will go free but Sundance will get ten years in prison. Conversely, if Sundance confesses but Butch does not, then Sundance will go free and Butch will be locked away for ten years. If, however, both confess, then each will spend five years in prison, while if neither confesses, both will be tried on the minor charge that carries the light sentence of one year in prison. The dilemma for the each prisoner is that by confessing he will either end up with no sentence or an intermediate sentence, but by remaining silent he will get either one year or ten years. If both prisoners trust the other to keep his mouth shut, both will benefit.

To conduct research on trust, Deutsch used the prisoner's dilemma situation in a game format in which pairs of subjects were paid according to the combination of their choices (see Figure 8.3). If both choose A, both will receive 50 cents. If both choose B, both will lose 50 cents. If one chooses A and the other chooses B, the person choosing B wins one dollar and the person choosing A loses one dollar. Although the PDG was overused in research on conflict, it was a remarkable methodological breakthrough when Deutsch initiated its use. One of its most important uses was by Robert Axelrod (1984) in his studies of the evolution of cooperation (see Chapter 3). What the results of research using the PDG demonstrate is that the pursuit of self-interest by each group member leads to a poor outcome for all. In the long run, only cooperative behavior based on trust ensures the well-being of all group members.

## Step 3: Understanding the Other Person's Perspective

I have no special regard for Satan; but I can at least claim that I have no prejudice against him. It may even be that I lean a little his way, on account of his not having a fair show. All religions issue bibles against him, and say the most injurious things about him, but we never hear his side. We have none but the evidence for the prosecution, and yet we have rendered the verdict. To my mind, this is irregular. It is un-English; it is un-American; it is French . . . Of course Satan has some kind of a case, it goes without saying. It may be a poor one, but that is nothing; that can be said about any of us.

*Mark Twain, In Defense of Harriet Shelley and Other Essays*

In a relationship, to meet your needs you also have to meet the other person's needs. To meet the other person's needs you have to view the situation from the other person's shoes. Different people have different perspectives. No two people will see an issue in exactly the same way. Each person will interpret identical events differently. One person will see teasing as a sign of affection while another will see it as a sign of rejection. One person will believe that you only get angry at individuals you care about, while another person will believe that you only get angry at people you dislike. The other person will have one perspective, you will have another. You will conclude one thing from the other person's actions while the other person will see his or her behavior entirely differently. Conflicts will be most easily resolved when you are able to keep your own perspective and the other person's perspective in mind simultaneously.

Negotiation requires a realistic assessment of common and opposed interests. Often it requires the sacrifice of some of the opposed interests so that the common benefits, concerns, advantages, and needs may be built on. To be able to propose alternative agreements that will solve a problem, you must understand how the other person sees the problem and is thinking about it. To settle a conflict, it is necessary to have a clear understanding of all sides of the issue and an accurate assessment of their validity and relative merits. It is common to misunderstand the motivations behind the other person's actions. To understand the other person's actions and position, you will have to see the conflict from his or her perspective. To do so you must be sufficiently detached from your position that you can see the conflict from new perspectives. Understanding the other person's perspective, however, is not the same as agreeing with it.

One of the most important conflict resolution skills, therefore, is the ability to see the situation from the other person's perspective. People see what they want to see. Out of a mass of detailed information, they tend to pick out and focus on those facts that confirm their prior perceptions and to disregard or misinterpret those that call their perceptions into question. Each side in a negotiation tends to see only the merits of its case and only the faults of the other side. It is not enough to understand logically how the other person views the problem. *If you want to influence the other person, you also need to understand empathetically the power of his or her point of view and to feel the emotional force with which he or she believes in it.* You may see on the table a glass half full of water. The other person may see a dirty, half-empty glass about to cause a ring on the mahogany finish.

### RULES TO FOLLOW IN TRYING TO TAKE THE PERSPECTIVE OF THE OTHER PERSON:

1. Do not deduce the other person's intentions from your fears. People often tend to assume that whatever they fear, the other side intends to do.
2. Do not blame the other person for your problem. Blaming is an easy habit to fall into. Even if blaming is justified, it is counterproductive. It will make the other person defensive and closed-minded.

3. Discuss each other's perceptions.
4. Look for opportunities to act inconsistently with the other person's negative perceptions.
5. Give the other person a stake in the outcome by making sure they participate in the process. Agreement becomes much easier if both people feel ownership of the ideas.
6. Make your proposals consistent with the other person's goals and values and, thereby, help them "save face."

In their study of conflict within schools, DeCecco and Richards (1974) found that the inability to take the perspectives of others seriously impeded negotiations as a means of conflict resolution. The failure of teachers and administrators to perceive the interests of students correctly results in destructive procedures for managing conflicts. Without perspective taking, the common interests of school personnel and students were not recognized and sought after by either staff or students.

The most effective way to gain insight into the other person's perspective is to role play that you are the other person and present the other person's position and reasoning as if you were he or she. Then have the other person do the same. The more involved the two of you get in arguing for the other's position, the more you will understand how the conflict appears from the other person's viewpoint. Such role playing is invaluable in finding solutions that are mutually acceptable. A systematic series of studies on the impact of perspective reversal on the resolution of conflicts has been conducted (Johnson, 1971a). The results indicated that skillful role reversal increases cooperative behavior between negotiators, clarifies misunderstanding of the other's position, increases understanding of the other's position, and aids one's ability to perceive the issue from the other's frame of reference. He also found the role reversal skillfully used can result not only in a reevaluation of the issue and a change of attitude toward it, but also in the role reverser being perceived as a person who tries to understand the other's position, as an understanding person in general, a person as willing to compromise, and as a cooperative and trustworthy person. Temporarily arguing your opponent's position does result in insight into your opponent's perspective and changes your attitudes about the issues being negotiated.

There is nothing more important to resolving conflicts constructively than understanding how the conflict appears from the other person's perspective. Once you can view the conflict both from your own perspective and the other person's perspective, you can find mutually beneficial solutions. You can also communicate to the other person that you really understand his or her thoughts, feelings, and needs. It is usually much easier to resolve a conflict when the other person feels understood. The more skilled you are in seeing things from standing in other people's shoes, the more skilled you will be in resolving conflicts constructively.

## Step 4: Inventing Options for Mutual Gain

There are five steps in inventing options for mutual gain:

1. Focus on needs and goals, not positions.
2. Clarify differences before seeking similarities.

3. Empower the other person by
   a. Staying flexible in your choice of which option is best.
   b. Giving him or her choices.
4. Avoid the obstacles to creative thinking.
5. Invent a number of options to choose from.

**Focus on Needs and Goals, Not Positions**   Saxon is usually a compliant student in Mr. Norman's English class. Today, however, she comes up to Mr. Norman's desk and states, "I won't do this homework assignment. I don't care what you do to me, I'm not going to do it!" Mr. Norman, having read this book, immediately recognized that Saxon is presenting a position and Mr. Norman does not yet know what her goals and needs are. To negotiate successfully and reach an agreement that satisfies both people, you have to approach the other person on the basis of his or her needs and goals. For every need and goal, there exists several possible positions that could satisfy it. A common mistake is to assume that because the other person's position is opposed to yours, his or her needs and goals must also be opposed. Behind opposed positions lie shared and compatible goals, as well as conflicting ones. The heart of problem-solving negotiations is finding an option that meets the other person's needs and goals while ensuring that your goals and needs are met. *Success in problem-solving negotiations comes from finding out what the other person really wants, and showing him or her a way to get it while you get what you want.*

**Clarify Differences Before Exploring Similarities.**   Conflicts cannot be resolved unless you understand what you are disagreeing about. If you do not know what you are disagreeing about, you cannot find a way to reach an agreement. You must understand the differences between you and the other person. Only then will you be able to think of ways to combine ideas so that the conflict is resolved. Only if you understand the differences can you think of a way to resolve the conflict helpfully. Your ability to come up with satisfactory solutions depends on how the other person's thoughts, feelings, and needs are different from yours.

**Empower the Other Person.**   During negotiations it is important that you do not let the other person feel powerless. When a person is powerless, it is bad for everyone. Either he or she becomes hostile and tries to tear down the system or becomes apathetic and throws in the towel. You do not want the other person to do either one. The psychological costs of being helpless to resolve grievances include frustration, anxiety, and friction. We all need to believe that we have been granted a fair hearing and that we should have the power and the right to gain justice when we have been wronged. If it becomes evident that we cannot gain justice, frustration, anger, depression, and anxiety may result.

*There are two ways to empower the other person.* The first is by being open to negotiations and flexible about the option you like the best. If he or she can negotiate with you then he or she has power and options. Willingness to negotiate is based on being open to the possibility that there may be a better option available than you now realize. Staying tentative and flexible means that you do not become overcommitted to any one position until an agreement is reached. Some of the dangers in becoming convinced that your position is "right" and "just" are that it makes the other person feel powerless and helpless, that you do not listen to the whole range of options, and that you do not invent alternatives that present creative integrations of different positions. Keep your position tentative. Do not dig into a firm position and set up commitments that will result in a loss of face if changed later. Look for, and foster, flexibility. Suggest face-saving ways for the other person to be flexible. Second, you provide power through choice among options. Generate a variety of possible solutions before deciding what to do.

**Avoiding Obstacles.**    Inventing options does not come naturally. Not inventing options is the normal state of affairs, even within the easiest negotiations. In most negotiations there are four major obstacles that inhibit the inventing of a number of options:

1. *Judging prematurely.* Nothing is so harmful to inventing options as a critical attitude waiting to pounce on the drawbacks of any new idea. Premature criticism is the first impediment to creative thinking.
2. *Searching for the single answer.* Premature closure and fixation on the first proposal formulated as the single best answer is a sure short circuit of wise decision making.
3. *Assuming a fixed pie.* This inhibits creative thinking. Do not assume that the less for you, the more for me. Rarely, if ever, is this assumption true. Expanding the pie is a key to flexible problem solving.
4. *Being concerned only with your own immediate needs and goals.* In a relationship, to meet your needs you also have to meet the other person's needs. Shortsighted self-concern leads to partisan positions, partisan arguments, and one-sided solutions.

**Invent Creative Options.**    To invent creative options, you need to

1. *Separate the act of inventing options from the act of judging them.* Invent first, judge later.
2. *Broaden the options on the table rather than look for a single answer.* The more the options, the greater the room for negotiations. One of the keys to wise decision making is selecting from a great number and variety of options.
3. *Search for mutual gains.* There always exists the possibility of joint gain. Look for solutions that will leave the other person satisfied as well.
4. *Invent ways of making decisions easily.* Give them choices that are as painless as possible. If you want a horse to jump a fence, do not raise the fence! Propose "yesable" agreements.
5. *Propose package deals in which several issues being negotiated are all considered to be part of the agreement.* A package deal involving homework, in-class behavior, and helping another student may be easier to reach than trying to negotiate each separately.
6. *Propose tie-ins in which an issue considered extraneous by the other person is introduced and you offer to accept a certain settlement provided this extraneous issue will also be settled to one's satisfaction.* The opposite of a tie-in is to carve an issue out of a larger context, leaving the related issues unsettled.

After inventing a number of options, you and the other person will have to agree on which one to try out first. Some realistic assessment of the alternatives then takes place. In trying to decide which alternative to try first, it may help to remember Aesop's fable about the mice in trouble. The mice were saying, "It's terrible! Just terrible! We really must do something about it! But what?" The mice were talking about the cat. One by one they were falling into her claws. She would steal up softly, then spring suddenly, and there would be one mouse less. At last the mice held a meeting to decide what to do. After some discussion a young mouse jumped up. "I know what we should do! Tie a bell around the cat's neck! Then we would hear her coming and we could run away fast!" The mice clapped their little paws for joy. What a good idea! Why hadn't they thought of it before? And what a very clever little fellow this young mouse was! But now a very old mouse, who hadn't opened his mouth during the whole meeting, got up to speak. "Friends, I agree that the plan of the young mouse is very clever indeed. But I should like to ask one question. Which of us is going to tie the bell around the cat's neck?" The moral is: There is no use adopting an option that cannot be implemented by one or both persons.

## Step 5: Reaching a Wise Agreement

The conflict of interest is resolved when the participants reach an agreement. All participants need to be satisfied with the agreement and committed to abiding by it. The agreement should specify the joint position on the issues being adopted, the ways in which each participant will act differently in the future, and the ways cooperation will be restored if one of the participants slips and acts inappropriately. It should also include some provision for future meetings at which the participants can check how well the agreement is working and how cooperation can be improved.

Given that we are all separate individuals with our own unique needs and goals, whenever we interact with others, we will have some needs and goals that are congruent and other needs that are in conflict. It takes wisdom to manage the combination of shared and opposed needs and goals. Wise agreements are facilitated by using objective criteria, taking into account the needs and goals of both sides, and using a long-term perspective to ensure that the agreement is durable (Fisher & Ury, 1981). *Wise agreements are first of all based on some objective criteria.* Evaluate each of the proposed options on the basis of the standards of fairness, efficiency, community values, and scientific merit. Think through which standards are most appropriate to evaluate the options and make a decision based on principle. The more you do so, the more likely you are to produce a final agreement that is wise and fair. When all

else fails, and no objective criteria for evaluating options can be agreed on, try one of these methods:

1. One cuts, the other chooses.
2. Taking turns.
3. Flipping a coin.
4. Having a third party decide.

Trying one of these alternatives may result in clarifying what is "fair" and "just" from both sides of the issue. Remember King Solomon. One of the first problems the new King Solomon was presented with involved two women who both claimed the same baby. They wanted him to decide whose it was. Sitting on his throne, Solomon listened carefully. The two women lived together in the same house. Their babies had been born only three days apart. Then one of the babies died. The first woman said, "This woman's child died in the night. She then arose and took my son from beside me and placed the dead child next to me. When I woke to feed my baby, I found her dead child in my arms." "No!" the other woman cried frantically. "The living child is my son!" Solomon calmly said, "Bring me a sword and bring me the baby. Divide the living child in two and give half to the one and half to the other." Everyone was shocked. "No! Please don't!" screamed the real mother. "She can have the child. Don't kill it!" "No," the other woman said, "Let the child be neither mine nor yours, but divide it." "Aha!" said Solomon. "Now I know to whom the child belongs." Then pointing to the woman who had asked that the baby's life be spared, he said, "Give her the living child. She is its mother."

*The second requirement for a wise agreement is that it meet the legitimate needs of both sides and be viewed as fair by everyone involved.* In deciding which option to adopt keep in mind the importance of shared good feelings, preserving mutual interests, and preserving your shared history. Focus on a long-term perspective to ensure that the agreement is durable. *Durability is the third requirement of a wise agreement.* Point out that your long-term survival and happiness should not be jeopardized by any agreement reached. In reaching an agreement, the following points should be clearly understood (Deutsch, 1973; Johnson & Johnson, 1987):

1. The conflict is to end.
2. The ways in which you will act differently in the future are clear.
3. The ways in which the other person will act differently in the future are clear.
4. The ways in which cooperation will be restored if one person slips and acts inappropriately are clear.
5. The times the two of you will meet to discuss your relationship and to see if further steps can be taken to improve your cooperation with each other are spelled out.

You cannot be sure the agreement will work until you try it out. After you have tested it for a while, it is a good idea to set aside some time to talk over how things are going. You may find that you need to make some changes or even rethink the whole problem. The idea is to keep on top of the problem so that the two of you may creatively solve it.

It is important that both you and the other person understand which actions trigger anger and resentment in the other. Criticism, put downs, sarcasm, belittling, and other actions often trigger a conflict. If the two of you understand what not to do as well as what to do, the conflict will be resolved much more easily.

One way to understand how constructive agreements may be reached is to look at a few examples.

1. Roger was a coin collector; his wife, Ann, loved to raise and show championship rabbits. Their income did not leave enough money for both to practice their hobbies, and splitting the cash they did have would not have left enough for either. Solution: Put all the first year's money into the rabbits, and then after they were grown use the income from their litters and show prizes to pay for Roger's coins.
2. Edythe and Buddy shared an office but had different work habits. Edythe liked to do her work in silence while Buddy liked to socialize in the office and have the radio on. Solution: Mondays and Wednesdays Buddy would help keep silence in the office while on Tuesdays and Thursdays Edythe would work in a conference room that was free. On Fridays the two worked together on joint projects.
3. Keith loved to spend his evenings talking to people all over the world on his ham radio set. His wife, Simone, felt cheated out of the few hours of each day they could spend together. Keith did not want to give up his radio time, and Simone was not willing to forgo the time they had together. Solution: Four nights each week Keith stayed up late and talked to his ham radio friends after spending the evening with Simone. On the following mornings Simone drove Keith to work instead of having him go with a carpool, which allowed him to sleep later.

## Step 6: Try, Try Again

The final rule for negotiating in a problem solving way is: "Keep trying. Try, try again." No matter how far apart the two sides seem, no matter how opposed your interests seem to be with the interests of the other person, keep talking. With persistent discussion a viable and wise decision will eventually become clear.

## NEGOTIATING CONFLICTS OF INTEREST: A CHECKLIST FOR A PROBLEM-SOLVING STRATEGY

1. I understand what events "trigger" the conflict and what events prevent negotiations from happening. I can either trigger or avoid the conflict.
2. I am clear about my needs and goals and what I want from the other person.
3. I follow the rules:
   a. I do not withdraw or ignore the conflict.
   b. I do not engage in "win-lose" negotiations.
   c. I smooth if the other person's needs are greater than mine and the issue is not of great importance to me.
4. I confront the other person making sure I
   a. Do not "hit and run."
   b. Openly communicate my perceptions of and feelings about the issues, focusing on the issues and not on the other person as a person.
   c. Ask the other person to state their needs and goals and their perceptions of and feelings about the issues.
   d. Accurately and fully comprehend (paraphrase) the other person's views of and feelings about the conflict.

5.  I negotiate a joint definition of the conflict, making sure I
    a.  Describe the other person's actions without labeling, accusing, or insulting him or her. *I separate the other person from the issue.*
    b.  Define the conflict as a *mutual problem to be solved,* not as a win-lose struggle.
    c.  Define the conflict in the *smallest and most precise way* possible.
    d.  Describe the present conflict without bringing in the past. *The past is forgiven.*
6.  I ensure that we exchange our positions and feelings by
    a.  Fighting over issues, not personalities.
    b.  Finding out about our differences in needs and goals before exploring the similarities
    c.  Coordinating motivation to resolve the conflict, highlighting the costs of continuing the conflict and the gains for resolving it.
    d.  Making sure that the other person has the power to influence my thinking and conclusions.
    e.  Avoiding distractions such as anger and power issues.
    f.  Helping the other person "save face."
7.  I take the other person's perspective accurately and fully, making sure I understand it and that the other person knows I understand it. I paraphrase other person's position, needs, goals, and feelings, noting the changes that evolve as we problem solve the issue. In doing so,
    a.  I do not deduce the other person's intentions from my fears.
    b.  I do not blame the other person for the problem.
8.  I propose several optional agreements that clearly
    a.  Are consistent with person's needs and goals.
    b.  Can be demonstrated to be fair on the basis of objective criteria.
9.  We reach an agreement that is satisfactory to both of us and clearly specifies
    a.  The agreement.
    b.  The ways in which each person will act differently in the future.
    c.  The ways cooperation will be restored if one person slips and acts inappropriately.
    d.  When future meetings will be held so that we can check how well the agreement is working.

## FORCING: THE WIN-LOSE NEGOTIATING STRATEGY

When the negotiation is with a person whose continued goodwill and cooperation is not necessary, then forcing may be appropriate as a negotiating strategy. In the win-lose strategy, the goal of negotiations is to make an agreement more favorable to oneself than to the other negotiator. In all negotiations a sequence of behavior occurs in which one party presents a proposal, the other evaluates it and presents a counterproposal, the first party replies with a modified proposal, and so on until a settlement is reached. The negotiators use this sequence of behaviors to obtain information that helps resolve the dilemma of goals. On the basis of the other party's opening offer, the proposals one receives, and the counterproposals one offers, a negotiator can obtain an idea as to what sort of settlement the person will agree to. A common win-lose negotiating pattern is for both negotiators to set a relatively high but tentative goal at first; they can then change it on the basis of the other person's reactions and counterproposals. This sequence of behaviors, which allows one negotiator to assess the second negotiator's points of potential settlement, can also be used to influence the second negotiator's assessment of the first's point of potential settlement. Through their opening offers and their counterproposals, negotiators can influence the other's expectations of what they consider a "reasonable" agreement. The more one negotiator can convince the other that she will not make an agreement unless it is highly favorable to oneself, the more likely it is that the negotiator will obtain a profitable agreement. Thus, an opening offer by a negotiator that is extremely favorable to oneself, combined with a refusal to budge from that offer, may convince the other negotiators that if an agreement is to be reached they will have to modify considerably what they originally believed was a "reasonable" agreement. Ideally, a win-lose negotiator would like to obtain the maximal information about the other's preferences while disclosing the minimal, or misleading, information about her own preferences.

Other win-lose strategies include changing the other's evaluation of one's position, using threats and promises, and sticking doggedly to a committed position. When a win-lose negotiator makes an extreme opening offer and refuses to modify it very quickly, he must simultaneously try to convince the other negotiator of the correctness of his position. He does so by pointing out not only the validity of his own position but the wrongness or incorrectness of the other's. He must present, in other words, convincing rebuttals to the other's statements in order to try to change her evaluation of her position. In a *threat* a negotiator states that if the other negotiator performs an undesired act (such as refusing to agree to his proposed settlement), he will make sure the other is harmed. A negotiator may threaten that unless the other person agrees to accept a certain settlement he will not make an agreement at all. In a *promise* a negotiator states that if the other negotiator performs a desired act he will make sure the other receives benefits. A negotiator may promise that if the other person makes a certain compromise he will also compromise. Through the use of threats and promises win-lose negotiators attempt to persuade each other to make certain agreements. Another win-lose tactic for influencing the other negotiator to accept a certain agreement is for a negotiator to commit himself to a proposal that makes it clear that it is the other negotiator's last chance of avoiding "no agreement." Thus, he may make a proposal and plug up his ears until the other negotiator says yes.

For a goal-oriented group a win-lose strategy of negotiation has some fundamental shortcomings. Although it will often result in more favorable primary gains for some group members, the damage it can cause to future cooperation among group members significantly reduces its secondary gains. Because a win-lose strategy emphasizes power inequalities, it undermines trust, inhibits dialogue and communication, and diminishes the likelihood that the conflict will be resolved constructively. Attempts to create cooperative relations between negotiators are more effective if their power is equal. Walton (1987) notes that *when power is unequally distributed the low-power person will automatically distrust the high-power person because she knows that those with power have a tendency to use it for their own interests.* Usually, the greater the difference in power, the more negative the attitudes toward the high-power person. The high-power person, on the other hand, tends to underestimate the low-power person's positive intent. A negotiator's power advantage may make him more likely to interpret cooperative behavior by the other as compliant rather than volitional. The result is that the other's cooperative behavior has an effect on the high-power person that is less positive than it should be. Unequal power can also inhibit the weaker negotiator, and sometimes the stronger, from giving her views in a clear and forceful way. Finally, whenever one negotiator believes the other is trying to reduce his power, he is likely to react with competition and hostility.

## NEGOTIATING CONFLICTS OF INTEREST: A CHECKLIST
## FOR A WIN-LOSE STRATEGY

1. Identify triggering events and barriers to negotiations. Now, trigger the conflict at a moment when it is most advantageous to you and least advantageous to your opponent.
2. Clarify your goals, but publicly disguise or misrepresent them.
3. Begin a strategy to force the opponent into submission by presenting an extreme opening offer and indicating that you will rigidly adhere to it. Hit and run, mislead the opponent as to your position and feelings, and deliberately misunderstand the opponent's position and feelings when it helps you force the opponent into the agreement you want. Pursue your goals, ignoring goals held in common by you and the opponent.
4. Impose your definition of the conflict on the opponent. Label, accuse, and insult the opponent; define the conflict as a win-lose situation; and define the conflict in general and large ways when it is to your advantage to do so.
5. Concede and change slowly to force concessions from the opponent. Emphasize the superiority of your position, reasoning, and perspective. Use deceitful, inaccurate, and misleading communication of your goals, needs, position, and proposals. Use cooperative actions to grab a chance to exploit the opponent's cooperativeness.
6. Communicate competitive intentions. Use threats and hostility to obtain submission. Behave unpredictably to take advantage of the element of surprise. Increase ambiguity and uncertainty in an attempt to use deception and confusion to your advantage. Adopt a posture that allows you to exploit the opponent whenever possible.
7. Avoid all empathy and understanding of the opponent's position, needs, goals, feelings, and perspective.
8. Increase your opponent's willingness to concede by highlighting the costs of holding out and the gains for conceding. Try to arrange contact in which your power is greater. Try to increase your power over your opponent by emphasizing your independence from the opponent and the opponent's dependence on you. Isolate your opponent to reduce the possibility of his forming a coalition with third parties.
9. Make sure the agreement is as favorable to you and as unfavorable to your opponent as possible.

## EXERCISE 8.6:
## BREAKING BALLOONS

This exercise seeks to demonstrate a nonverbal conflict—which is a complete change from the previous highly verbal activities. The procedure is as follows:

Each participant is to blow up a balloon and tie it to his or her ankle with a string. Then, when the coordinator gives the signal, the participants are to try to break one another's balloons by stepping on them. The person whose balloon is broken is "out," and must sit and watch from the sidelines; the last person to have an unbroken balloon is the winner. The participants can then discuss their feelings of aggression, defense, defeat, and victory. Strategies for protecting one's balloon while attacking others should be noted. A variation on the exercise is to have teams with different colored balloons competing against each other.

## EXERCISE 8.7:
## INTERGROUP CONFLICT

This exercise studies the dynamics of intergroup conflict and negotiation among groups with conflicting positions. It takes two hours. The procedure for the coordinator is as follows:

1. Introduce the exercise as an experience in intergroup conflict and negotiation. Divide the participants into four groups of not less than six members each, and distribute a copy of one of the accompanying instruction sheets to each group. Emphasize that the exercise will determine which group is best.

2. Have each group meet separately to select a negotiator and to develop their proposals on the issue. They have half an hour to do this. At the end of this period give them the accompanying reaction form and ask them to answer only questions 1, 2, and 5 and to write the name of their group at the top.

3. Have the negotiators meet in the center of the room, each with her group sitting behind her. Give each group representative 5 minutes to present her group's proposals. After each representative has completed her presentation have all participants complete the reaction form, answering all questions.

4. Tell the groups to reconvene separately and brief their negotiator on the best way to proceed in a second presentation of their position. The groups have 15 minutes to confer. At the end of this period they again answer questions 1, 3, and 5 on the reaction form.

5. Have the negotiators again meet in the center of the room with their groups seated behind them. They have up to half an hour to reach an agreement. Group members can communicate with their negotiator through written notes. At the end of 15 minutes stop the negotiations and have everyone again complete the questionnaire. Negotiations then resume, and at the end of the 30-minute period everyone answers the reaction form for the last time.

6. Conduct a general session in which the results of the questionnaire are presented and discussed. Ask group members how they feel about the experience and then focus upon the experience of the negotiators.

7. Have the groups meet separately to discuss how well they worked together and what the experience was like for them. Develop a list of conclusions about intergroup conflict and place it on newsprint.

8. Again conduct a general session, this time to discuss the conclusions reached by each group.

### Instructions to Coordinator for Use of the Reaction Forms

1. Pick one person in each group—as many assistants as you need—to hand out and collect the reaction forms and to compute the group mean for each question each time the forms are used.

2. Copy the four accompanying charts on a blackboard or large sheets of newsprint. After each use of the reaction forms, calculate the group means and place them on the charts, using a different color for each group. The response to question 5 should be listed for use in the discussion sessions. Do not let the participants see the results until the general session in which the results are discussed.

3. In discussing the results of each question, look for certain trends. The response to question 1 should be somewhat high in the beginning, increase after comparison with other group's proposals, and drop off if agreement is reached. If no agreement is

reached it should not drop off. For question 2, look for the "hero-traitor" dynamic: satisfaction goes up if the negotiator convinces other groups that her proposals are best, and goes down if she compromises the group's position. It is often helpful to look at the notes passed to the negotiator to see how the group is reacting. The responses to question 3 should be the reverse of the responses to question 1 (if satisfaction with one's own group's proposal is high, satisfaction with the other groups' proposals is low and vice versa). This usually amounts to devaluating the other groups' proposals and a loss of objectivity in evaluation. Question 4 usually demonstrates overconfidence in one's own group's proposal, though this sense of superiority gradually slips from an initial high as negotiations progress.

### Intergroup Conflict Exercise: Teachers Group

You are residents of Engleston, a medium-sized but quickly growing suburban community that is within commuting distance of a large city. Engleston has recently been torn by a number of civil rights demonstrations centering on the issue of school integration. Two of the public schools in Engleston contain approximately 90 percent of the underprivileged, culturally different white and black children in the community. Moreover, the high school dropout rate (60 percent) has shown the inadequacy of the educational program for these youngsters. Acts of vandalism and other forms of juvenile delinquency have been pronounced, and costly to the town, and most of those responsible are among the dropouts.

Four opposing groups in the community, yours among them, have suggested various solutions to some of these problems. The school board has asked the four groups to get together and settle on a single set of four to six proposals, which it will then implement.

As a member of the teachers group, you are essentially opposed to breaking up the schools in any way. You are interested in creating better schools and are generally in favor of expanding the educational program.

Your group is to submit four to six recommendations for dealing with the problems at a meeting at which your representative and one from each of the other three groups will be present. You and your groupmates may prepare a simple chart of the *main* points you wish to emphasize.

Try to make your recommendations original and creative, because it will be to your advantage if the other groups accept your proposals. After the representatives have presented their group's proposals, they will negotiate a *composite proposal* of four to six points to be presented to the school board.

### Parents Group

You are residents of Engleston, a medium-sized but quickly growing suburban community that is within commuting distance of a large city. Engleston has recently been torn by a number of civil rights demonstrations centering on the issue of school integration. Two of the public schools in Engleston contain approximately 90 percent of the underprivileged, culturally different white and black children in the community. Moreover, the high school dropout rate (60 percent) has increasingly shown the inadequacy of the educational program for these youngsters. Acts of vandalism and other forms of juvenile delinquency have become pronounced, and costly to the town, and most of those responsible are among the dropouts.

Four opposing groups in the community, yours among them, have suggested various solutions to some of these problems. The school board has asked the four groups to get together and settle on a single set of four to six proposals, which it will then implement.

You are a member of the parents group. Because the tax rate is already one of the highest in the state, you favor solutions that will *not* increase your taxes. You feel that teachers and administrators have been lax, and that what is needed is more efficient and immediate use of the present resources. You are absolutely against any busing of students, and want all students to attend the school closest to their home.

Your group is to submit four to six recommendations for dealing with the problems at a meeting which your representative and one from each of the other three groups will be present. You and your groupmates may prepare a simple chart of the *main* points you wish to emphasize.

Try to make your recommendations original and creative, because it will be to your advantage if the other groups accept your proposals. After the representatives have presented their group's proposals, they will negotiate a *composite proposal* of four to six points to be presented to the school board.

## Civil Rights Group

You are residents of Engleston, a medium-sized but quickly growing suburban community that is within commuting distance of a large city. Engleston has recently been torn by a number of civil rights demonstrations centering on the issue of school integration. Two of the public schools in Engleston contain approximately 90 percent of the underprivileged, culturally different white and black children in the community. Moreover, the high school dropout rate (60 percent) has increasingly shown the inadequacy of the educational program for these youngsters. Acts of vandalism and other forms of juvenile delinquency have become pronounced, and costly to the town, and most of those responsible are among the dropouts.

Four opposing groups in the community, yours among them, have suggested various solutions to some of these problems. The school board has asked the four groups to get together and settle on a single set of four to six proposals, which it will then implement.

As a member of the civil rights group, you are totally committed to immediate integration. You believe the schools have to be integrated through immediate busing of students. You feel that reforms generally take place too slowly, and you are extremely dissatisfied with the present situation.

Your group is to submit four to six recommendations for dealing with the problems at a meeting at which your representative and one from each of the other three groups will be present. You and your groupmates may prepare a simple chart of the *main* points you wish to emphasize.

Try to make your recommendations original and creative, because it will be to your advantage if the other groups accept your proposals. After the representatives have presented their group's proposals, they will negotiate a *composite proposal* of four to six points to be presented to the school board.

## School Administrators Group

You are residents of Engleston, a medium-sized but quickly growing suburban community that is within commuting distance of a large city. Engleston has recently been torn by a number of civil rights demonstrations centering on the issue of school integration. Two of the public schools in Engleston contain approximately 90 percent of the underprivileged, culturally deprived white and black children in the community. Moreover, the high school dropout rate (60 percent) has increasingly shown the inadequacy of the educational program for these youngsters. Acts of vandalism and other forms of juvenile delinquency have become pronounced, and costly to the town, and most of those responsible are among the dropouts.

Four opposing groups in the community, yours among them, have suggested various solutions to some of these problems. The school board has asked the four groups to get together and settle on a single set of four to six proposals, which it will then implement.

As a member of the school administrators group, you are generally satisfied with the way things are and believe that anything but gradual and carefully planned change would lead to chaos. Moreover, you believe that the complaining has been done chiefly by extremist groups at work in the community. In your opinion all school policy decisions should be made by your group—and parents, teachers, and community groups should not butt in.

Your group is to submit four to six recommendations for dealing with the problems at a meeting at which your representative and one from each of the other three groups will be present. You and your groupmates may prepare a simple chart of the *main* points you wish to present.

Try to make your recommendations original and creative, because it will be to your advantage if the other groups accept your proposals. After the representatives have presented their group's proposals, they will negotiate a *composite proposal* of four to six points to be presented to the school board.

**Reaction Form**

Group _____

1. How satisfied are you with your own group's proposals?
   Very dissatisfied  1 : 2 : 3 : 4 : 5 : 6 : 7 : 8 : 9  Very satisfied
2. How satisfied are you with the negotiator your group has selected?
   Very dissatisfied  1 : 2 : 3 : 4 : 5 : 6 : 7 : 8 : 9  Very satisfied
3. How satisfied are you with the proposals of the other groups?
   Very dissatisfied  1 : 2 : 3 : 4 : 5 : 6 : 7 : 8 : 9  Very satisfied
4. How do you think the final composite proposal will compare with your group's proposals?
   Very inferior  1 : 2 : 3 : 4 : 5 : 6 : 7 : 8 : 9  Very superior
5. Write one adjective describing the way you now feel about what is taking place:

**Chart A: Satisfaction with Own Group's Proposals**

```
Very Satisfied    9
                  8
                  7
                  6
                  5
                  4
                  3
                  2
Very Dissatisfied 1 _____
                      1     2     3     4     5
```

**Chart B: Satisfaction with Negotiator**

```
Very Satisfied    9
                  8
                  7
                  6
                  5
                  4
                  3
                  2
Very Dissatisfied 1 _____
                      1     2     3     4     5
```

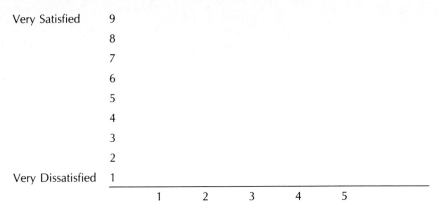

**Chart C: Satisfaction with Other Groups' Proposals**

Very Satisfied    9

8

7

6

5

4

3

2

Very Dissatisfied    1

       1      2      3      4      5

**Chart D: Satisfaction with Composite Proposal**

Very Satisfied    9

8

7

6

5

4

3

2

Very Dissatisfied    1

       1      2      3      4      5

## EXERCISE 8.8:
## BATTLESHIP

This exercise is designed to increase participants' understanding of a group's decision-making process during an intergroup conflict and to further their understanding of the dynamics of intergroup conflict. Here is the procedure for the coordinator:

1. Divide the class into groups of eight—six members and two observers. Introduce the exercise as an experience in group decision making during an intergroup conflict. State that each group will have the same task, the same instructions, and the same time limit. Performance on the task will be scored objectively. Each group member is to contribute fifty cents to a pool; the group with the highest score will collect 70 percent of the pool and the group with the next highest score will collect 30 percent. After the scores of the groups have been tabulated and the pool money distributed, the two winning groups must decide how to allocate their treasure by some rule other than dividing the money equally among group members. In other words, each

member of the winning groups must receive a different amount of money. Each group will have 20 minutes to plan its organization prior to performing the task; each will have 30 minutes to complete the task, including reading the instructions.

2.  While the groups begin organizing, brief the observers. They are to observe the task and maintenance behaviors of the group members (they will need copies of the task-behavior and maintenance-behavior forms in Chapter 5 for this), note the dynamics of the decision making within the groups, and record the effects of intergroup competition on intragroup functioning. These subjects are covered in this chapter and in Chapters 5 and 6. As soon as the briefing is over, the observers return to their groups.

3.  At the end of 20 minutes distribute copies of the accompanying instruction sheet and the grid sheet. Then take a grid sheet and draw the target mass anywhere on it, using the model on page 503 as an example. Record the salvos fired by each group and give the groups their total score for each salvo. Deal only with the official representatives of the groups. Do not accept more than four salvos from any one group.

4.  At the end of 30 minutes stop all action. Announce the winning groups and distribute the money between them. While the winning groups are parceling out the money among their members, ask the other groups to (a) describe the process by which they made decisions and (b) classify each person in the group in terms of the task and maintenance behaviors in which he engaged.

5.  Give each group 20 minutes to analyze its effectiveness. Groups should use the information gathered by their observers as a beginning point of the discussion. Conclusions about the impact of intergroup competition on intragroup functioning should be written on newsprint and shared with the other groups during the last few minutes of the exercise.

## Battleship Exercise Instructions

1.  The object of the exercise is to get the highest possible score from shooting 16 times at a target.

2.  The shots have to be fired in 4 salvos of 4 shots each. Any salvo may be fired at any time prior to the expiration of the 30 minutes. The coordinator will give a score of zero for any shots not fired before time expires.

3.  On the 10-by-10 square grid there is a target mass consisting of between 6 and 15 adjacent squares. *Adjacent* means horizontally or vertically, not diagonally.

4.  The squares in which the target is located differ in point value: Some are worth one point, some three points, and some five.

5.  A salvo is "fired" by being announced to the coordinator in terms of the coordinates of its targets (for example, A3, E5, C10, F2). The coordinator will then announce the *total* score obtained by the group for that salvo. He or she will *not* report the point value of an individual shot, only the *total salvo score.*

6.  Shots may continue to be fired at the same squares. For example, if a group fires a 4-shot salvo and gets a score of six points, it may continue to fire its remaining salvos at these same squares and obtain a score of six points for each salvo.

7.  Your group must select a representative who will announce the coordinates of all salvos to the coordinator. Only that person's "shots" will be accepted. If the representative announces a shot not on the grid—for example, P5—the coordinator will give a score of zero.

8.  Your group may mark its grid sheet in any way it chooses.

9.  Your group may not ask any questions of the coordinator. All the necessary instructions are contained on this sheet.

10. Remember, the 30-minute period began with the distribution of these instructions.

**Grid Sheet**

|    | A | B | C | D | E | F | G | H | I | J |
|----|---|---|---|---|---|---|---|---|---|---|
| 1  |   |   |   |   |   |   |   |   |   |   |
| 2  |   |   |   |   |   |   |   |   |   |   |
| 3  |   |   |   |   |   |   |   |   |   |   |
| 4  |   |   |   |   |   |   |   |   |   |   |
| 5  |   |   |   |   |   |   |   |   |   |   |
| 6  |   |   |   |   |   |   |   |   |   |   |
| 7  |   |   |   |   |   |   |   |   |   |   |
| 8  |   |   |   |   |   |   |   |   |   |   |
| 9  |   |   |   |   |   |   |   |   |   |   |
| 10 |   |   |   |   |   |   |   |   |   |   |

## OTHER EXERCISES IN INTERGROUP CONFLICT (8.9)

Other intergroup conflict exercises can easily be created around the general procedure given on pages 342–43. The task can be to state the five most important principles of leadership, the qualities of an effective supervisor, the five most important things for a teacher to know, and so on. The dynamics of intergroup conflict are so predictable that if people are divided into groups and told to compete, develop their position, and represent that position in negotiations, they are bound to be present.

## INTERGROUP CONFLICT

In 1863, in an isolated valley of the Appalachia mountains, a Hatfield stole some hogs from a McCoy (Rice, 1978). The McCoys countered by stealing hogs from another member of the Hatfield clan, but soon members of the two families began taking pot shots at one another. In 1865, Harmon McCoy was killed by an unknown assailant. Most of the residents assumed that Devil Anse, a Hatfield, was to blame. After this incident, the conflict cooled until 1878, when Randolph McCoy accused Floyd Hatfield of stealing more hogs, and filed a civil suit for damages. A jury composed of six Hatfields and six McCoys decided in favor of Floyd Hatfield. From that point on full-scale violence gripped the families. In the years between 1878 and 1890, more than ten men and women lost their lives as a direct result of the interfamily violence. Not all intergroup conflicts are as famous as that of the Hatfields and McCoys, but many deadly quarrels start over even more trivial reasons. Battles resulting in the death of street gang members have started from a perceived insult or the intrusion of a member of one gang into an area controlled by another gang.

How groups relate to one another within organizations has considerable bearing on the effectiveness of the organization. Groups are often in conflict. Production may be in conflict with sales, management may be in conflict with unionized employees, white and minority workers may be in conflict, male and female employees may be in conflict, and members of different project groups may compete with each other for resources. Just as cooperation is needed between different members of the same group, when two groups are part of the same organization or goal-directed effort, a high degree of cooperation between them is essential. The dynamics of intergroup conflict are about as destructive as they are predictable. Classifying people into categories is known as **social categorization.** Social categories function as cognitive "labor-saving devices" by helping you place other people into meaningful categories. While you may use a wide range of categories for classifying people (for example, male, friend, stranger, Christian, neighbor, political, athlete), two very basic social categorizations are (1) member of my group and (2) member of another group (Hamilton, 1979). Tajfel and Turner (1979, p. 38) demonstrated that a systematic in-group bias in groups where "the mere awareness of the presence of an out-group is sufficient to provoke intergroup competition or discriminatory responses on the part of the in-group." The more the intergroup conflict is defined as a win-lose situation, furthermore, the more predictable are the effects of the conflict on the relationships of members within the group, on relationships between the groups, on negotiations between the groups, on the group that wins, and on the group that loses (Sherif, 1966; Blake & Mouton, 1962; Watson & Johnson, 1972).

A group in the throes of an intergroup conflict experiences a strong upward shift in cohesion as the members join together to defend their group against defeat. The group becomes more closely knit and gleans greater loyalty from its members; members close ranks and "table," or put aside, some of their conflicts with one another. There is a sharpening and banding together of the ingroup power structure as militant leaders take control and group members become more willing to accept autocratic leadership. Maintenance needs become secondary to task needs, and the group becomes more tightly structured and organized. Satisfaction among the members runs high, along with their sense of identification with the group and with its position on the issues in the conflict. At the same time the opposing group and its positions are belittled and devalued. Conformity is demanded; "a solid front" must be presented.

Between the groups, an attitude of hostility develops. Each sees the other as the enemy. Inaccurate and uncomplimentary stereotypes form. Distortions in perception (see Johnson, 1990) increase. Each group sees only the best parts of itself and the worst parts of the other group. Interaction and communication decrease between members of the conflicting groups. Doubt is cast upon the validity of the position of the other group; its position is seen as distinctly inferior to that of one's own group. Group members tend to listen only to what supports their own position and stereotypes. They misperceive and fail to listen carefully to the other group's position. All these dynamics only intensify the conflict and deepen distrust.

In win-lose negotiations, there are distortions of judgment about the merits of the conflicting positions, with one's own position recognized as "good" and the other group's position assessed as "bad." Negotiators are relatively blind to points of agreement between their own and the other side's proposals, and they tend to emphasize the differences. The orientation of the negotiators for the two sides is to win for their group, not to reach an agreement that satisfies everyone. This stance inevitably results in the **hero-traitor dynamic**—the negotiator who "wins" is seen as a "hero" and the one who "loses" as a "traitor." When a neutral third party decides who is "right" and who is "wrong," the winner considers the third party to be impartial and objective; the loser views the third party as biased and thoughtless. Each side sees itself as objective and rational and the other side as unjust and irrational—thereby excluding from the negotiations any elements of genuine objectivity. With the only loyalty being to one's own group's position, the common result of win-lose negotiations is a deadlock. The win-lose strategy can result, of course, in the representative being caught in a conflict between his own beliefs and perceptions and the mandate given him by his group.

The group that "wins" becomes even more cohesive. It also tends to release tension, lose its fighting spirit, and become self-satisfied, casual, even playful. The leadership that was responsible for the victory is consolidated. Though there is a high concern for maintenance, there is little tendency to work. Members believe that winning has confirmed their positive stereotype of their group and the negative stereotype of the other group, and that as a result there is little need to reevaluate perceptions or reexamine group operations to learn how to improve them.

The group that "loses" frequently splinters, seeks the reasons for its defeat, and then reorganizes. Members bring to the surface unresolved conflicts among themselves in an effort to find the reasons for the defeat. Tension increases and the group begins to work even harder. Maintenance concerns abate as task concerns rise in a group effort to recover from defeat. The group often seeks someone to blame for the defeat—the leader, the judges, those who made the rules of the conflict situation, the least conforming members, and so on—and replaces the leadership responsible for the loss. If future victories seem impossible, members may become completely demoralized and assume a defeatist, apathetic attitude toward the group. The losing group tends to learn a great deal about itself because its positive stereotype of itself and its negative stereotype of the other group have been upset by the loss; it has therefore had to reevaluate its perceptions. Consequently, the losing group is likely to reorganize and become more cohesive and effective once it has accepted the loss realistically.

The most important point about intergroup conflict on a win-lose basis is that it should be prevented if at all possible. It is a lot easier to do this by making sure that the groups share a cooperative goal structure and that problem-solving methods are at work between them than it is to undo the conflict once the groups have gotten into a win-lose situation.

Though intergroup conflict has been discussed above from the point of view of the need to resolve it in a way that enhances cooperation among groups, it should be noted that intergroup competition can have many benefits. It often increases the involvement, fun, commitment, interest, and motivation of group members working on tasks. For a discussion of the use of such intergroup competition in school, see Johnson (1970) and Johnson and Johnson (1991).

## EXERCISE 8.10:
## INTERGROUP CONFRONTATION (I)

This procedure was developed by Blake and Mouton (1962), and has since been used quite successfully in conflicts in a variety of organizations. It has probably been applied to every type of intergroup conflict one can imagine. Its purpose is to change the win-lose orientation of intergroup conflict to the cooperative, problem-solving orientation. The exercise takes at least 2 or 3 hours to conduct (Blake and Mouton usually spend about 19 hours on it in actual union-management conflicts). The procedure for the coordinator is as follows:

1. Introduce the exercise as an experience in resolving conflicts between two or more groups. State that the objective is to change win-lose orientations to problem-solving orientations. You might discuss the previous success Blake and Mouton have had with the exercise in difficult union-management conflicts. Use the accompanying description of a union-management conflict to set up a role play that participants can use in the exercise.
2. Have each group meet separately and develop on newsprint how it sees itself as a group and how it sees the other group. Allow the groups at least 1 hour to complete this task.
3. Have the two groups come together and share their viewpoints. Have them compare, with your help, how each side sees itself with how the other side sees it. It is rather common for each group to see the other as unreasonable, unethical, and unwilling to cooperate while seeing itself as extraordinarily reasonable, ethical, and cooperative. The differences in the perception of how each group sees the other group are then clarified.
4. Ask the two groups to meet separately for at least 1 hour to diagnose their present relationship. They should answer such questions as, "What problems exist?" "Why aren't they being constructively handled?" "What does the other group contribute to the conflict?" "What does one's own group contribute to the conflict?" The groups should place this material on newsprint.
5. Have the groups meet together to share their diagnoses. Help them to summarize the key issues causing the conflicts between them and the main sources of friction. Keeping the material on constructive conflicts in mind, the two groups should plan the next stages of their cooperative solution of their conflict.
6. Ask the two groups to assess their reactions to the exercise and summarize what they have learned about resolving intergroup conflict. Conclusions about preventing intergroup conflict should also be presented and discussed.

### Union-Management Conflict

The teachers' union of a large city has asked the local board of education for certain across-the-board increases in pay and fringe benefits. The board has refused to meet these "excessive demands" and has made an offer that the union leadership considers unacceptable. Still without a contract agreement at midnight of the day school is to open, the union has voted to go on strike—and to remain on strike until a satisfactory agreement is reached. Divide into union and management groups and carry out the above procedures.

## THREE BASIC TRAPS

Blake and Mouton emphasize that those who use this procedure must avoid three basic traps that lead to increased, rather than decreased, conflict. The first to avoid is the *win-lose dynamic*—seeing every action of the other group as a move to dominate. The participants must learn to recognize win-lose attitudes and behaviors and be able to set norms that stress their avoidance. The second trap to avoid is the *psychodynamic fallacy*—seeing the motivation for the other group's behavior in terms of personality factors rather than the dynamics of intergroup conflict. It is much easier to blame the conflict on sick, vicious, power-hungry persons than to view the other group's behavior as a predictable result of intense intergroup conflict. The final trap to avoid is the use of a *self-fulfilling prophecy*. For example, one group assumes that the other is belligerent and proceeds to engage in hostile behavior in an attempt to defend itself by mounting a good offense, thereby provoking belligerence on the part of the other group, which confirms the original assumption.

## CROSS-ETHNIC CONFLICT

> You're going to find racism every place. In fact, I have never lived a day in my life that in some way—some small way, somewhere—someone didn't remind me that I'm Black.
>
> *Henry Aaron*

> To know one's self is wisdom, but to know one's neighbor is genius.
>
> *Minna Antrim*

Gordon W. Allport (1954, p. 226), in his classic treatise *The Nature of Prejudice*, stated, "realistic conflict is like a note on an organ. It sets all prejudices that are attuned to it into simultaneous vibration. The listener can scarcely distinguish the pure note from the surrounding jangle." He believed that even conflict rooted in objective characteristics of the situation will eventually create subjective biases that will divide the opposing groups. When the subjective biases exist before the realistic incident occurs, conflicts can light, flame, and burn quickly. The black residents of Liberty City in Miami, for example, attacked white residents and their businesses when several police officers accused of killing a black robbery suspect were not sent to prison. Rioting in Detroit in the late 1960s was precipitated by a police raid on a private drinking and gambling establishment (Goldberg, 1968). A crowd gathered during the arrests, and looting began after a window was broken by one spectator. Police withdrew for several hours in the hope that the residents would quiet down, but the looting continued. To quell the disorder, elite riot troops, complete with bayonets, swept through the streets. The black residents responded with a series of fire-bombings, and officials asked that the state police and national guard be brought in to control the mob. Rumors of sniping activity, the removal of restraints concerning the use of firearms, the lack of clear organization, and a desire for revenge prompted police violence, which in turn led to more widespread rioting.

The cross-ethnic prejudices that create and intensify such conflicts are typically reflected in stereotypes. A **stereotype** is a set of cognitive generalizations that summarize, organize, and guide the processing of information about members of a particular group. It is a set of expectations held by members of the ingroup regarding members of an outgroup. Woman have been stereotyped as being more emotional than men. Men have been stereotyped as being more competitive than women. Tall, dark, and handsome men have been stereotyped as being mysterious. Our impressions are initially based on surface characteristics, such as sex, ethnic membership, physical attractiveness, and appearance. We stereotype others on the basis of these surface characteristics. In many ways stereotypes function as social categories that lead to misunderstandings because they are inaccurate or biased. Stereotyping errors are particularly likely when emotions are running high and the tendency to overgeneralize about others is strong; their impact on intergroup conflict is considerable.

Stereotypes reflect an **illusionary correlation** between two unrelated factors, such as being poor and lazy. Usually stereotypes focus on negative traits that are easy to acquire and hard to lose. When you meet one poor person who is lazy you may tend to see all poor people as lazy. From then on, any poor person who is not hard at work the moment you notice him or her may be perceived to be lazy. Such prejudiced stereotypes such as poor people being lazy are protected in four ways.

First, stereotypes influence what we perceive and remember about the actions of outgroup members. The social categories we use to process information about the world controls what we tend to perceive and not perceive. Our prejudice makes us notice the negative traits we ascribe to the groups we are prejudiced against. When individuals expect members of an outgroup to behave in a certain way, furthermore, they tend to recall more accurately instances that confirm rather than disconfirm their expectations. Hence, if an outgroup is perceived to be of low intelligence, individuals would tend (1) to remember instances in which an outgroup member was confused in class or failed a test but would tend (2) to forget instances in which an outgroup member achieved a 4.0 grade point average or became class valedictorian (Rothbart, Evans, & Fulero, 1979).

Second, stereotypes create an oversimplified picture of outgroup members. The act of categorization itself leads people to assume similarity among the members of a category. Even when the distinctions between groups are arbitrary, people tend to minimize the differences they see among members of the same group and to accentuate the differences between members of two different groups (Wilder, 1986; Brewer & Kramer, 1985). When processing information about their ingroup and outgroups, people develop complex and extremely differentiated conceptions of their own groups but relatively simplistic and nonspecific pictures of outgroups (Linville, 1982; Linville & Jones, 1980; Quattrone & Jones, 1980). The larger the outgroup, the more likely oversimplifications will occur (Rothbart, Fulero, Jensen, Howard, & Birrell, 1978). Individuals, furthermore, do more than simply note the differences between their ingroup and the outgroups. They attempt to emphasize the differences, and take actions that will discriminate in favor of their own group.

Third, individuals tend to overestimate the similarity of behavior among outgroup members. Quattrone and Jones (1980) conducted a study to see whether or not individuals tended to overestimate the similarity of outgroups. He had subjects watch videotapes of a college student making a simple decision to either join a group, listen to music, or work on a problem. Half of the subjects were told the student was from their own college and half were led to believe that the student was from a rival university. The subjects were then asked to estimate the number of students at the person's college who would make the same decision. Subjects tended to think that other students would have made similar choices, especially if they were from the rival college. The researchers concluded that the people tend to assume that members of an outgroup will act in the same way. The tendency to overestimate the similarity of group members seems to be especially pronounced for outgroups in conflict. Since outgroups are perceived to be very homogeneous, the actions of one member can be generalized to all.

Fourth, people tend to have a **false consensus bias** by believing that most other people share their stereotypes (such as perceiving poor people as being lazy). Similarly, we egocentrically tend to see our own behavior and judgments as quite common and appropriate, and to view alternative responses as uncommon and often inappropriate.

Fifth, stereotypes tend to be self-fulfilling. Stereotypes subtly influence intergroup interactions in such a way that the stereotype is behaviorally confirmed. Expecting certain behaviors from an outgroup, individuals can behave in ways that elicit the expected actions, thus confirming their stereotype.

Sixth, stereotypes can lead to scapegoating. A **scapegoat** is a guiltless but defenseless group who is attacked to provide an outlet for pent-up anger and frustration caused by another group. The label is derived from the biblical guilt-transference ritual (Leviticus 16:21):

> And Aaron shall lay both his hands upon the head of the live goat, and confess over him all the iniquities of the children of Israel, and all their transgressions in all their sins, putting them upon the head of the goat, and shall send him away by the hand of a fit man into the wilderness.

In most instances, if Group 1 interfered with Group 2, 2 would respond by retaliating against 1. If, however, Group 1 is extremely powerful, too distant, or too difficult to locate, Group 2 may respond by turning its aggression onto Group 3. Group 3, although in no way responsible for the difficulties Group 2 experienced, would nonetheless be blamed and thereby become the target of 2's aggressive actions. Stereotypes of certain outgroups can create a continual scapegoat that is blamed for all problems and difficulties no matter what their origins.

Finally, we often develop a rationale and explanation to justify our stereotypes and prejudices.

In summary, intergroup conflict sets in motion a number of perceptual and behavioral reactions that tend to escalate the conflict in destructive ways. Clearer differentiations are drawn between the ingroup and the outgroup. Self-fulfilling stereotyped thinking results in the disputants selectively perceiving negative aspects of outgroup members' behaviors, developing oversimplified views of the outgroup, and overestimating the similarity among the outgroup members, believing that all others have the same stereotypes, and developing a readiness to scapegoat outgroup members. Given all these problems, the next question is: "How can conflict among groups be constructively resolved?"

## EXERCISE 8.11
## INTERGROUP CONFRONTATION (II)

A procedure has been established by Beckhard (1969) for determining the relevant cooperative goals toward which all groups can take committed action. Because he recommends that the exercise be used when groups are in conflict and the members are experiencing stress, the procedure is one of conflict management. The objective of the exercise is to get the groups moving toward a plan of action and a set of priorities for change and improvement that will resolve existing conflicts and establish cooperative goal accomplishment. Beckhard conducts the exercise as a one-day activity, but it can be shortened to a couple of hours when used strictly for learning. The procedure for the coordinator is as follows:

1. Introduce the exercise as an experience in setting cooperative goals among groups presently experiencing intergroup conflict. Stress that the exercise is an opportunity for the participants to influence the actions of their groups, and urge them to be open and honest with their feelings and ideas. The union-management situation used in the previous exercise can be applied here for role-playing purposes.
2. Divide the participants into groups of five or six and have them meet separately. The task of these conflicting groups is to think of ways in which life would be better for their members and for their relationship with other groups. Ask each group to make a list of its ideas and place them on newsprint. This phase takes between 30 and 45 minutes.
3. You or the participants should categorize the ideas listed.
4. Have the groups complete the following tasks:
   a. Go through the entire list and select three or four items that most affect you and your group. Determine what action your group will take on them, and establish a timetable for beginning work on those problems. Prepare to report your decisions in a general session.
   b. Go through the list again and select those items to which you think all groups should give highest priority. These items should be problems that your group cannot deal with alone.
5. In a general session have the groups share the results of their meetings. Combine the lists. The groups should then outline plans of action for implementing their decisions and determine the necessary follow-up procedures. In doing this they should emphasize intergroup cooperation.
6. Ask the groups to assess their reactions to the exercise and summarize what they have learned about resolving intergroup conflicts. Conclusions about preventing intergroup conflict should also be presented and discussed.

## INTERGROUP CONFLICT AND SUPERORDINATE GOALS

> We were wedded together on the basis of mutual work and goals.
>
> *Judy Chicago*

Perhaps the most interesting and best known studies of intergroup conflict were performed under the direction of Muzafer Sherif (1966). Sherif was born in 1906 in Izmir, Turkey. After attending Izmir International College, he studied at the University of Istanbul, receiving a master's degree in 1928. Awarded a fellowship in national competition for study abroad, he went to Harvard University in 1929, received another master's degree in 1932, and then traveled to Germany where he attended Kohler's lectures and the University of Berlin. He then taught in Turkey, returned to Harvard to conduct research, and then studied at Columbia University (1934–1936), where he received the Ph.D. degree in 1935. His dissertation was published as a book, *The Psychology of Group Norms* (discussed in Chapter 12). He studied in Paris, taught in Turkey until January 1945 when he returned to the United States. After a time at both Princeton and Yale, he became director of the Institute of Group Relations at the University of Oklahoma, a position he held from 1949 to 1966. In 1966 he moved to the Pennsylvania State University. It was during the years he spent at Oklahoma that he compiled his famous research on superordinate goals.

To study intergroup conflict and its resolution, Sherif, his students, and his colleagues ran a summer camp for 12-year-old boys in the early 1950s. All the boys were strangers to one another prior to attending the camp, so there were no established relationships among them. The camp setting, isolated from outside influences, afforded the experimenters a unique opportunity to manipulate the conditions and circumstances of interaction among the camp members. The investigators were interested in studying intergroup relations, and especially the effectiveness of various techniques for reducing hostility between groups. To create intergroup conflict, the experimenters divided up the campers into groups and instilled in each group an esprit de corps by such procedures as assigning names like Bull Dogs and Red Devils to the groups and structuring their daily activities so that interdependent, coordinated activity among the group members was necessary for achieving desired goals (the food, for example, needed to be cooked over a campfire and distributed among the group members).

Following the successful development in the camp of two ingroups characterized by mutual good feeling between their members, the experiments attempted to induce conflict between the two groups by requiring them to participate in competitive activities in which the winning group was rewarded and losing group was not. For a time the two groups displayed good sportsmanship, but in the course of the competitive activities they became increasingly hostile toward each other. Eventually the two groups were having garbage fights—throwing mashed potatoes, leftovers, bottle caps, and the like—in the dining hall.

Sherif (1966) and his associates next tested several different methods of reducing the conflict between the groups. To find out the effects of social contact between groups on intergroup conflict, Sherif devised several pleasant situations in which members of the rival groups could engage in such contact. These situations included eating together in the same dining room, watching a movie together, and shooting firecrackers in the same area. These contact situations had no effect in reducing intergroup conflict. If anything, they were utilized by members of both groups as opportunities for further name-calling and other forms of conflict. Sherif concluded that contact between groups in pleasant situations does not in itself decrease existing intergroup tension.

The next strategy researched by Sherif (1966) and his associates was the establishment of a common enemy. Sherif did demonstrate that it is possible to reduce the hostility between two groups by presenting them with a common enemy against whom they are banded together. He arranged a softball game in which the two groups in conflict were combined to play against a group of boys from a nearby town. The common enemy did bring the two groups of campers together and reduced some of the hostility between them. This approach, however, has little promise for conflict resolution, as it fails to resolve the conflict but only transfers it from two small groups to two larger groups. Bringing some groups together against another means larger and more devastating conflicts in the long run.

Sherif (1966) hypothesized that contact between the rival groups would resolve the conflict only when the groups came together to work cooperatively toward goals that were more important to the groups than the continuation of their conflict. Since cooperation toward common goals had been effective in forming the two in-groups, Sherif reasoned, it would be effective in reducing the conflict between the groups. Sherif therefore arranged a series of superordinate-goal situations for the two antagonistic groups of campers to engage in. He defined **superordinate goals** as goals that cannot be easily ignored by members of two antagonist groups, but whose attainment is beyond the resources and efforts of either group alone; the two groups, therefore, must join in a cooperative effort in order to attain the goals. One such goal was to repair the water-supply system, which the experimenters had earlier sabotaged. Another was to obtain money to rent a movie that both groups wanted to see. Still another was to push a truck to get it started after it had suddenly broken down on its way to a camp-out with food. After the campers had participated in a series of such activities their attitude toward members of the outgroup changed; several friendships among members of different groups were formed, members of the rival group were no longer disliked, and the friction between the groups disappeared.

The characteristics of the superordinate goals introduced by Sherif and his associates in their studies were as follows:

1. They were introduced by a more powerful third party (the experimenters).
2. They were perceived by campers to be natural events in no way identified with the third party.
3. They were not perceived by the two groups of campers as being aimed at resolving the conflict.
4. They transcended the conflict situation and restructured the competitive relationship between the groups into a cooperative one.

In most conflict situations such superordinate goals are not feasible alternatives. A third party, for example, rarely has the power to initiate goals with the above characteristics. Nor could a participant in a conflict easily initiate such a goal in an attempt to resolve the conflict.

Johnson and Lewicki (1969) compared the effectiveness of a superordinate goal having all of the characteristics of the superordinate goals used by Sherif with the effectiveness of a superordinate goal that was initiated by one of the groups in the conflict, was identified with the initiating group, and was perceived as being aimed at resolving the conflict. The subjects were a group of 36 college students who were participating in a four-day leadership-training program. An intergroup-competition exercise similar to ones used in the experiments of Blake and Mouton (1962) was used. Johnson and Lewicki found that although the Sherif-type superordinate goal was effective in reducing competition and hostility between groups, it tended to lead to a premature cooperation that left the basic conflict between the groups unresolved. They hypothesized that after the superordinate goals were accomplished the groups would still be faced with a basic conflict that might subsequently be reactivated. The second type of superordinate goal, on the other hand, became caught up in the competitiveness of the situation and increased, rather than decreased, the conflict. The group initiating the superordinate goal used it as a key argument in an attempt to reach an agreement with the opposing group. Believing that they had the best interests of both groups at heart and that initiating the superordinate goal was an initial concession on their part, they felt that the opposing group would be quite accommodating to their wishes. The opposing group, however, tended to view the superordinate goal as part of a competitive strategy aimed at furthering the initiating group's vested interests and refused to accept it. The result was an intensification of the conflict, increased misunderstanding, and a refusal by both groups to compromise. From the Johnson and Lewicki study it may be concluded that introducing superordinate goals to resolve a conflict between groups is a complex process that needs to include activities that resolve the differences between the groups and that needs to dissociate the superordinate goals from the negotiating ploys and strategies of the groups involved in the conflict.

Sherif's notion of resolving conflicts through the use of superordinate goals is an elaboration of the principle that groups that cooperate with one another toward the accomplishment of common goals will have harmonious and friendly relations. Deutsch's (1949, 1962) theory of cooperation and competition states such a principle, and a number of research studies support the principle's validity (Johnson & Johnson, 1987b). Deutsch's theory predicts that even when there is intense hostility between two groups, cooperative action to accomplish goals that are of vital importance to both will result in mutual liking and continued cooperation.

## THIRD-PARTY MEDIATION

**Mediation** exists when a neutral and impartial third party assists two or more parties in negotiating a constructive resolution of their conflict. Mediation is an extension of the negotiation process and is a collection of strategies to promote more efficient and effective negotiations. The main difference between negotiating and mediation is that a third party, the mediator, ensures that both parties engage in each step of the problem-solving negotiating process. Mediation is unlikely to be effective when the relationship between the two parties is poor and when resources are scarce. Under such conditions, the likelihood of finding a mutually acceptable compromise is not very high. Conversely, mediation is most likely to be successful when both parties are highly motivated to the mediation process. And in general, clients are likely to be satisfied with the mediation process, as most studies show satisfaction rates of 75 percent or higher (Kressel & Pruitt, 1985). Mediation facilitates conflict resolution in the following ways (Raven & Rubin, 1976, p. 462):

1. Reducing emotional upset by giving parties an opportunity to vent their feelings.
2. Presenting alternative solutions by recasting the issues in different or more acceptable terms.
3. Providing opportunities for "graceful retreat" or face-saving in the eyes of one's adversary, one's constituency, the public, or oneself.
4. Facilitating constructive communication among parties.
5. Controlling contact between the parties, including such aspects as the neutrality of the meeting site, the formality of the setting, the time constraints, and the number and kinds of people at the meeting.

To be successful, mediators need to possess certain characteristics and adopt particular strategies. Mediators need to be perceived as being trustworthy and able (Rubin & Brown, 1975). Mediators need to convey an impression of legitimacy, social position, and expertise in order to gain the confidence of both parties and to win acceptance for the proposed solution (Kolb, 1985). Mediators tailor tactics to particular situations. Mediators may lower hostility by being very directive and using humor but being nondirective with inexperienced parties who lack expertise in negotiating (Carnevale & Pegnetter, 1985). When mediation fails, an arbitrator may be brought in. **Arbitration** is a binding settlement of a conflict determined by a disinterested third party.

## EXERCISE 8.12:
## YOUR CONFLICT BEHAVIOR

Having completed this chapter on conflict, you may find it helpful to focus again on your behavior in conflict situations. To do so, form a group with two persons who know you well and who have participated with you in some of the exercises in this book. Then complete the following tasks, taking at least two hours to do so.

1. Give one another feedback about the animal, song, or book that each person reminds the other of on the basis of how he or she deals with conflict. Each person explains why he or she chose the animal, song, or book that he or she did.
2. Write down your individual strengths in handling conflicts constructively. Share your lists and see what you can add to the other members' lists.
3. Write down the individual skills you need to develop in order to handle conflict more constructively. Then share your lists and see what you can add to the other members' lists.
4. Discuss the feelings each of you have in conflict situations and why you react the way you do. Help each other think of alternative ways of feeling or reacting to conflict situations.
5. From magazine pictures and any other available materials build a collage about the way in which you behave in conflict situations. Share the collage with the others. Add ideas to their collages.

## SUMMARY

Now that you are acquainted with the dynamics involved in resolving conflicts of interest and have practiced resolving them, you are ready to encounter power. You will do so in the next chapter.

# 9

# The Use of Power

## BASIC CONCEPTS TO BE COVERED IN THIS CHAPTER

In this chapter a number of concepts are defined and discussed. The major ones are listed below. The procedure for learning these concepts is as follows:

1. The class forms heterogeneous groups of four.
2. Each group divides into two pairs.
3. The task for each pair is to
   a. Define each concept, noting the page on which it is defined and discussed.
   b. Make sure that both members of the pair understand the meaning of each concept.
4. In each group, members compare the answers of the two pairs. If there is disagreement, they look up the concept in the chapter and clarify it until they all agree on the definition and understand it.

### CONCEPTS

1. trait-factor view of power
2. dynamic-interdependence view of power
3. credibility
4. attractiveness
5. forewarning
6. inoculation
7. power
8. outcome dependence
9. information dependence
10. resistance
11. manipulation
12. rule of self-direction
13. strength
14. reward power
15. legitimate power

16. referent power

17. information power

18. expert power

19. coercion power

## EXERCISE 9.1:
## POWER ORIGIN: IS POWER A PERSONAL ATTRIBUTE OR AN ASPECT OF A RELATIONSHIP?

There has been some controversy over whether power is an attribute of a person or an aspect of a relationship between two or more persons. The purpose of this exercise is to structure a critical discussion of the issue. The procedure is as follows:

1. The class forms groups of four.
2. Each group is ultimately to write a report summarizing its position on whether power is a personal attribute or an aspect of a relationship. The report is to contain the group's overall conclusions and the facts and rationale supporting its position. The supporting facts and rationale may be obtained from this chapter, the entire book, and outside reading.
3. Each group divides into pairs. One pair is assigned the position that power is a personal attribute and the other pair the position that power is an aspect of a relationship between two or more persons. Each pair reviews the supporting sections of this chapter, the procedure for the exercise, and the guidelines for constructive controversy (p. 282).
4. The pairs meet separately to prepare as forceful a 3-minute presentation of their position as possible. They are to make sure that both members have contributed to building a persuasive case for their position and that it includes as many facts and research findings as possible. Both members need to master all the rationale supporting their position. Ten minutes are allowed for this phase.
5. The group of four meets. Each pair presents its position, being as forceful and persuasive as possible, while the other pair takes notes and asks for clarification of anything that is not fully understood. Each pair is allowed about 3 minutes to present its position.
6. The group of four has an open discussion of whether power is a personal attribute or an aspect of a relationship. Each side presents as many facts and research findings as it can to support its point of view. Members listen critically to the opposing position and ask for supporting facts for any conclusions made by the opposing pair. Participants should ensure that all the facts supporting both sides are brought out and discussed. The guidelines for constructive controversy should be followed. About 10 minutes are allowed for this phase.
7. The perspectives in each group are now reversed, each pair arguing the opposing pair's position. Members should be as forceful and persuasive as they can in arguing for the opposing pair's position. They should elaborate on the opposing position, seeing if they can think of any new arguments or facts that the opposing pair did not present. Each pair has about 3 minutes for its presentation.
8. Each group of four should derive a position that all members can agree on. The members should summarize the best arguments for each position, detailing as many facts as they can on whether power is a personal attribute or an aspect of a relationship. When they have consensus in their group, they should organize their arguments for presentation to the rest of the class. Since other groups will have other conclusions, each group may need to explain the validity of its position to the class. About 10 minutes are allowed for this phase.
9. The coordinator samples the decisions made by the groups of four by having several

of them present their position to the class. The class then discusses similarities and differences among the positions and the coordinator summarizes what the participants have learned about power and influence.

## INTRODUCTION

All human interaction involves power and influence. Yet many persons are unaware of the influence they exert on others, and many are unaware of how necessary and constructive mutual influence is in building effective groups and collaborative relationships among members. Being skillful in influencing other group members and taking responsibility for such influence are important parts of being a group member. In this chapter, power and influence (the two terms can be considered synonymous, and they are used interchangeably in this chapter) are defined from two points of view: the trait-factor perspective and the dynamic-interdependence perspective. The chapter begins with an explanation of these two views. The remainder of the chapter focuses on several topics concerning the use of power in a group in ways that increase the group's effectiveness and clarify conflicts that can then be resolved productively: personal power and personal-goal accomplishment, the bases of power, power and problem solving, interaction between high- and low-power members, and power and conflict.

## THE TRAIT-FACTOR APPROACH TO INFLUENCE

One night long, long ago a princess lay down to sleep on a bed that contained 13 mattresses. At the bottom of the pile of mattresses had been placed a tiny pea. The princess tossed and turned all night, unable to sleep. This fairy-tale princess was unable to sleep because it is part of the nature of princesses to be disturbed by provocations that those of us with mundane natures do not even notice. Winston Churchill could offer the people of England "blood, sweat, and tears" and inspire them to great effort and sacrifice during World War II because it is part of the nature of great leaders to influence others in ways that those of us with mundane natures cannot. The princess and Winston Churchill illustrate the trait-factor approach to power and influence. They are credited with having innately supernatural, religious, or instinctual dispositions. Who can deny their divine spark or conscience?

The **trait-factor approach to power** and influence may be traced to Aristotle, whose rhetoric dealt at some length with the characteristics of an effective influencer and gave detailed advice on the techniques of persuasion. From the trait-factor point of view, influence is a function of the characteristics of (1) the person exerting the influence, (2) the person receiving the influence, and (3) the influence attempt itself. The general approach of a trait-factor theory is to identify the factors that explain why an individual is as she is and how she became so, and to determine how these factors maintain her so, despite circumstances, fortune, and opportunities. The trait-factor approach is static, in that it focuses more on continuity than on change; atomistic, in that it assumes that complex phenomena can be analyzed into their component parts; historical, in that it assumes that causation of present behavior is a function of genetic and experiential factors acting cumulatively over relatively long periods of time; and inductive, in that it stresses accounting for empirically observed phenomena more than seeking empirical validation for general theoretical statements. According to the trait-factor approach, certain individuals are somehow born with a self-contained capacity to influence others.

The major post–World War II application of the trait-factor approach to power and influence was the Yale Attitude Change Program, which was headed by Carl Hovland immediately after World World II (Hovland, Lumsdaine, & Sheffield, 1949). Most of the research in this program focused on the area in which the trait-factor view is strongest—the effects of a single attempt to influence delivered through the mass media. In situations where a politician is giving a speech to an audience, an announcer is delivering a television commercial, or a health official is warning the public about a health danger, the findings from the Yale Program are quite useful. In each of these situations the contact between the communicator and the receiver of the communication is brief and not repeated. Moreover, the communication is one-way; there is no interaction between the two parties. Because single instances of one-way communication are essentially static, a trait-oriented theory is quite helpful in analyzing them.

Much of the post–World War II research on social influence stemmed from Hovland's wartime studies of propaganda and was organized around the theme question, "Who says what to whom with what effect?" Investigators have usually broken this question down into variables relating to the source (the characteristics of the communicator), the message (the characteristics of the communication), and the receiver (the characteristics of the person receiving the message). The exercise of power may thus be seen as a credible and attractive communicator's delivery of an effectively organized message to a vulnerable or influenceable audience. Trait-factor researchers assume that people are rational in the way they process information and are motivated to attend to a message, learn its contents, and incorporate it into their attitudes.

## The Effects of the Source

**Credibility.**   Aristotle noted that an effective communicator must be a person of good sense, goodwill, and good moral character. Following this notion, most of the research on the personal characteristics of the communicator has focused on the dimension of credibility. The **credibility** of a communicator is his perceived ability to know valid information and his perceived motivation to communicate this knowledge without bias. More specifically, credibility depends on the following factors (Giffin, 1967; Johnson, 1973a):

1. Objective indicators of *expertise* relevant to the topic under discussion (for example, a Ph.D. or an affiliation with a prestigious organization).
2. *Reliability* as an information source (for example, of communicator, or perceived character such as his dependability, predictability, and consistency).

3. The *motives* and *intentions* of the communicator. (Communicators who argue against their own self-interest or who appear not to be attempting to influence a receiver tend to be regarded as more trustworthy than communicators who overtly attempt to influence on the basis of self-interest).
4. The expression of *warmth* and *friendliness*.
5. The *dynamism* of the communicator. (A confident, forceful, and active communicator tends to be regarded as more credible than a self-conscious, listless communicator.)
6. The *majority opinion* of others concerning the expertness and trustworthiness of the communicator.

**Attractiveness.** The **attractiveness** of the communicator is also an important influence on her power to influence an audience. The following factors have been found to be determinants of how attractive one person appears to another:

1. *Cooperativeness and goal facilitation* (Johnson & Johnson, 1987b). A person likes others who are cooperating with him and facilitating his goal achievement.
2. *Physical appearance* (Berscheid & Walster, 1974). Other personal attributes being equal, physically attractive persons tend to be liked better than homely persons.
3. *Liking* (Byrne, 1969). If one person knows that she is liked by another, she is apt to reciprocate that liking.
4. *Similarity* (Byrne, 1969). Although the point is controversial, considerable evidence suggests that individuals who perceive themselves to be similar in basic values and other characteristics tend to like each other.
5. *Competence* (Blanchard, Weigel, & Cook, 1975). Persons who are perceived to be competent in important areas tend to be liked.
6. *Warmth* (Johnson, 1971a). Warm, friendly persons tend to be liked.
7. *Familiarity and propinquity* (Berscheid & Walster, 1969; Watson & Johnson, 1972). Although the point is equivocal, some findings suggest that a person likes others with whom he or she is familiar. "To know them is to love them."

## The Effects of the Message

Without a message there can be no influence exerted on another person. Like Aristotle, the Yale researchers were deeply concerned with the nature of arguments, their logical coherence and emotional appeal, and the language used by the communicator to convey these aspects of the message. Here are the basic findings from the research on message variables (Aronson, 1972; McGuire, 1969; Watson & Johnson, 1972):

1. In general, messages that inspire fear tend to be persuasive with receivers who have high self-esteem but not with those who have low self-esteem. High-fear appeals with specific instructions for action tend to be more persuasive than high-fear appeals without these instructions.
2. With intelligent receivers, messages that acknowledge opposing viewpoints (two-sided messages) are more persuasive than one-sided messages. With less intelligent receivers, one-sided messages tend to be more effective.
3. When a communicator is credible, the greater the discrepancy between the position she advocates and the receiver's initial position, the greater the change. If a communicator is not credible, she will be most effective with mildly discrepant positions.

## The Effects of the Receiver

Social psychologists have examined a multitude of personality characteristics and other differences among the receivers of persuasive communications for their effect on the acceptance of persuasion. Among the variety of findings, the most salient and consistent variables are these:

1. *Self-esteem* (McGuire, 1969; Watson & Johnson, 1972). When self-esteem is varied experimentally, the most frequent result is that receivers with low self-esteem are more persuasible than receivers with high self-esteem. When long-term self-esteem is measured and correlated with persuasion, this clearly negative relationship is less frequent and less pronounced.
2. *The receiver's present attitudes* (Watson & Johnson, 1972). Receivers may refuse to listen to messages that disagree with their present attitudes, or they may misinterpret what the communicator is stating. Attitudes that are integral to the individual's self-conception appear to be more difficult to change than less integral attitudes (Rokeach, 1968).
3. *Forewarning* (Watson & Johnson, 1972). Forewarning receivers of the communicator's intention of converting them to his or her point of view creates resistance to one's message.
4. *Role playing* (Watson & Johnson, 1972). Actively role playing a previously unacceptable position increases its acceptability to the receiver.
5. *Inoculation* (McGuire, 1964). Having receivers practice defending their position and then giving them additional arguments to support it decreases their susceptibility to attempt to influence them.
6. *Distraction* (Baron, Baron, & Miller, 1973). Receivers are generally more susceptible to influence when they are distracted during the communicator's statement of her message.
7. *Intelligence* (McGuire, 1969). Intelligence and influence are negatively related in the middle and upper portions of the IQ distribution and positively related in the lower portion.

## Summary

Attempts to exert power over other group members are enhanced if one is credible and attractive; if one phrases one's messages so that they are two sided, action oriented, and discrepant with members' current beliefs; and if the other group members have low self-esteem, see their attitudes under modification as peripheral to them, have no forewarning of the influence attempt, role play positions that agree with one's own, have not been inoculated, are distracted while one is presenting the message, and are not very intelligent. The trait-factor approach to influence, however, is weak both logically and empirically in situations where two or more individuals are constantly interacting. We thus turn next to the dynamic-interdependence approach to influence.

## THE DYNAMIC-INTERDEPENDENCE VIEW OF INFLUENCE

Group members adjust in many ways to one another. They take turns talking, they put aside individual interests to discuss mutual interests, they adjust their expression of their attitudes and beliefs to take into account the reactions of other members, they speed up or slow down their activity to stay coordinated with one another. Group members constantly modify their behavior to make it fit the group in which they are participating. When you are a member of a group you constantly influence and are influenced by the other group members. In fact, any two persons who interact constantly influence and are influenced by each other.

In the **dynamic-interdependence view of influence,** power is viewed as an aspect of a relationship between two or more persons. Relationships, and the exertion of influence within them, according to this view, are constantly changing as the group members modify and adjust their behavior to stay coordinated with one another. The relationships among group members are dynamic because the members are dependent on each other for the achievement of their joint goals. The basis of influence within a relationship is the mutual dependence of group members as they strive to achieve their mutual goals. Group members are interdependent and influence each other to the extent that they mediate or contribute to the attainment of important goals for each other. The degree of influence is dynamic: It is constantly changing as the group members make progress in obtaining their goals, as their costs (in energy, emotion, time, and so forth) of working collaboratively vary, and as other relationships and groups become available in which the goals of group members might be better achieved (Cartwright, 1959; Thibaut & Kelly, 1959). If the group members make progress toward achieving their goals and the costs of working together go down so that no other group would be as rewarding, the ability of members to influence each other increases. If, on the other hand, the group is not making progress toward goal accomplishment, if the costs to group members in terms of emotion and energy are high, and if other groups are available that are more effective and less demanding, the ability of group members to influence each other decreases. In the latter case, members may even terminate their membership and join other groups, thereby reducing to zero the capacity of the original group members to influence and be influenced by them.

From the dynamic-interdependence viewpoint, power is an attribute of a relationship, not of a person. It takes two persons for power to exist. A person cannot be an influencer if there is no influence. The exertion of power requires a relationship and some mutuality or goal interdependence. The dynamic-interdependence approach to power is *dynamic* in that it focuses more on the changing nature of influence within a relationship as the members strive to achieve their mutual goals than on who possesses power; *holistic*, in that it assumes that power is a complex phenomenon that has to be studied as a whole and that cannot be meaningfully broken into components; *phenomenological*, in that it stresses the immediate experience of group members and the ways they influence each other in the present rather than focusing on their history and genetic makeup; and *deductive*, in that it attempts to apply and validate theoretical principles concerning the nature and use of power.

Within a group, mutual power exists to the extent that one member can affect the goal accomplishment of other members. The more cooperative the group, the greater the goal interdependence of group members and the more influence members exert on each other. Through mutual influence the coordination of member behavior necessary for goal accomplishment is achieved. Leadership has been defined as the use of power to promote the goal accomplishment and maintenance of the

group. Decisions cannot be made without members influencing one another. Controversies and conflicts of interest cannot be managed or resolved without the use of influence. Even communication cannot take place without mutual influence. Thus, the use of power is essential to all aspects of group functioning. Power cannot be ignored, abdicated, or denied. Every group member should be aware of her power, accept it, and take responsibility for its use. The possession of power within a group is inevitable, and it is through the exercise of mutual influence that cooperation takes place and the group effectively achieves its goals.

## A DEFINITION OF POWER AND INFLUENCE

The terms power, influence, and control are sometimes defined differently and sometimes synonymously by social psychologists. **Power** has been defined variously as the actual control of another's behavior, the capacity to influence another's behavior, the capacity to affect another person's rewards and costs, the ability of one person to get others to behave in a particular way or to carry out certain actions, and the capacity to affect another's goal accomplishment. **Influence** has been defined as an attempt to use power to change another person in a desired direction. **Control** has been defined as having the influenced behaving as the influencer intended.

For the purposes of this chapter, however, power and influence will be defined as one person's control over resources valued by another. More specifically, individual A has power with respect to individual B when B perceives that A controls resources that B values. In turn, B's valuing of these resources depends on (1) the availability of alternative sources of these or similar resources at the same or a lower cost, and (2) the importance B attaches to the goals whose attainment is mediated by A's resources. Group member A influences group member B to the extent that A furnishes resources needed by B for the accomplishment of highly valued goals and to the extent that B cannot obtain these resources at a lower cost from other members or other groups. Social power and influence, then, depend on a need-resource correspondence among group members. When Helen and Frank, for example, are studying this chapter with Edythe and wish to understand the above definition of power, they are dependent on Edythe to the extent that she understands and can explain that definition; Edythe is thereby able to influence Helen and Frank's thinking about power. But if Helen and Frank are able to get a clearer explanation from Roger with less trouble, then Edythe's ability to influence their thinking is reduced.

In a group, members depend on one another for help in accomplishing their goals (outcome dependence) and for information about how to achieve their goals (information dependence). **Outcome dependence** is a function of the ability of others to affect one's costs of engaging in goal-directed behavior (that is, one's expenditure of energy, feelings of anxiety, and fear of displeasing important persons) and the benefits of that behavior. **Information dependence** is a function of the ability of others to supply one with the information one needs for determining which strategies to use in attempting to achieve one's goals, the costs of each strategy, and one's ability to implement the strategies. When other group members have the information one needs to make a decision about which strategy for achieving one's goals to adopt, a state of information dependence exists.

When group members are taking part in cooperative activities, and when their goals are compatible, they assert power in the same direction and there is little or no resistance to accepting the influence of another member. When group members have incompatible goals, however, or are in competition with one another, then their power assertions will conflict and there will be resistance to accepting another member's influence. **Resistance** is the psychological force aroused in a person that keeps him or her from accepting influence. Its magnitude is determined by the way in which power is exerted. Resistance can also be generated if the behavior desired of the members by the person exerting the power fails to help them achieve their goals.

A final point to be made about mutual dependence and power is that it is the *perception* of a group member's resources that affects the behavior of other members, not her actual resources. A member can have large resources that are unknown or ignored by other group members and therefore have little power over the others. On the other hand, a group member can have few vital resources but be seen as having many resources and thereby have a great deal of influence over the other group members.

## AVERSION TO THE USE OF DIRECT INFLUENCE

Although influence pervades all human relationships and although it has played a significant role in the lives of all members of succeeding civilizations, from antiquity to the present, some persons are averse to the planned use of direct influence. Our behavior is influenced by many forces—education, government, law, interpersonal expectations, religion, social norms, organizational-role requirements, and even advertising. But a group member consciously planning how best to influence other members may seem to some of us to be violating their freedom of choice and self-direction. London (1969) states that in our society there are at least three rules that oppose the influencing of others' behavior:

1. *The rule of noncoercion:* People should not be forced to do what others want but should be free to refuse them.
2. *The rule of explication:* People should not be seduced into compliance but should be told what is wanted of them.
3. *The rule of self-direction:* People should be free to decide for themselves how they want to guide their lives.

For some persons words like *power* and *influence* seem to violate these rules: Such persons frequently say they do not wish to have power over others.

Those who are averse to the exerting of power may actually be confusing the use of influence with manipulation. All human interaction involves mutual influence; manipulation is a certain type of influence. **Manipulation** is the managing or controlling of others by a shrewd use of influence, especially in an unfair or dishonest way, and for one's own purposes and profit. It is the influencing of others in ways they do not fully understand and with consequences that are undesirable for them but highly desirable for oneself. It is the use of power for one's own benefit at the expense of others. People characteristically react with anger, resentment, and retaliation if they find they have been manipulated. In proceeding through this chapter keep in mind that we are focusing on the constructive use of influence to increase cooperation among group members and group effectiveness: The use of manipulation is destructive in that it eventually decreases cooperation among members and causes severe maintenance problems for the group. The procedure for constructively influencing other group members without violating the three rules listed is presented in the following section.

## EXERCISE 9.2: PERSONAL POWER AND PERSONAL GOAL ACCOMPLISHMENT*

A basic need of every group member is some influence over what takes place in the group. A person joins a group to accomplish goals he cannot achieve, or cannot achieve as easily, without group membership. The power a person needs within a group is the power that will ensure that his goals are accomplished.

There is a definite process by which a person mobilizes her power in order to accomplish her goals. The process consists of (1) determining one's goals, (2) assessing one's resources and information level, (3) determining what coalitions will obtain the needed information and resources for accomplishing the goals, (4) contracting a coalition committed to accomplishing the goals, and (5) carrying out the activities necessary for the accomplishment of the goal. This exercise is an opportunity for you to acquire experience with this process, step by step.

### Step 1: Determining Your Goals

The first step in using your power within a group is to clarify your personal goals. Goals are based upon your needs, wants, and self-interests. The term goal is used here in the broadest possible sense to refer to the rewards consciously sought as well as the rewards obtained unconsciously through relationships with other group members. In order to plan to attain your

*This exercise was inspired by the work of George Peabody in this area.

goals you must be aware of them and accept them as valuable and worthwhile. Because many persons work for power they do not need and for goals they do not really want, it is essential that you first be clear about what you want. Group members have to deal realistically with what each of them wants; an effective group is one in which most members have their goals met. So, it is essential that a group member be clear about his or her goals, accept them as worthwhile, and be willing to enlist the aid of other group members to accomplish them. And in order to build and keep trust, a group member must be honest and accurate in his or her statements about personal goals and be willing to work openly for their accomplishment.

At this point, with your classmates divide into groups of four. Each person should first state all the desires, needs, wants, goals, and so on that he or she might work toward in this group. After everyone has had his or her say, each member should state which three goals he or she would like the group to accomplish first. Write these on newsprint, and include your name. Then go on to the next step.

### Step 2: Determining Your Resources

The second step in the process of mobilizing your power is to affirm the resources you bring to the group. You must be aware of and accept your resources in order to tell others about them. Moreover, awareness and acceptance of your resources are basic to an understanding by others of what you can contribute toward accomplishment of your goals and the goals of other group members. Using the resources of members is a key issue for effective groups. Not only should the group take an inventory of its resources before beginning work, but the individual members should also take a personal inventory to determine their ability to accomplish their own goals.

All of us have *many* different strengths upon which we base our interactions with others. All group members have solid strengths that are often unidentified and unused, both by the group and by themselves. The word *strength* refers to any skill, talent, ability, or personal trait that helps one function more productively. The object of this part of the exercise is to increase your awareness of your strengths. The procedure for each group is as follows:

1. Individually, think of all the things you do well, all the things you are proud of having done, all the things for which you feel a sense of accomplishment. List all your positive accomplishments and your successes.
2. Share your lists with one another. Then, with the help of the other three members, examine your past successes and identify the personal strengths you used to achieve them. Make a list of these strengths.
3. After you have all made your list of strengths, give one another feedback about additional strengths. Add to each persons's list the qualities, skills, and characteristics she has overlooked or undervalued.
4. Each member should then discuss the question "What might be keeping me from using all my strengths?" The group helps each person explore the ways in which she can free herself from constraints on the use of her strengths.
5. If possible, review the material on self-acceptance and the acceptance of others in Johnson (1981).

### Step 3: Determining Your Needed Coalitions

The third step in the process of mobilizing your power in a group is to assess what coalitions with other members are necessary for securing the information and resources you need in order to accomplish your goals. The question to ask yourself is, "Who has the information and resources I need, and how can I ally myself with them in order to help my goal accomplishment?" After identifying such persons ask yourself "What are their goals, and how might I contribute resources and information they need for their goal accomplishment?" Then ask yourself "What coalitions can I make with members who have compatible, similar, or complementary goals?"

To begin this step, take out the personal goal sheets you composed in step 1. Review your goals and change them in any way you believe appropriate. Then, as a group of four, look for similarities among your goals. Decide as a group upon the three goals that are most in accord with the personal goals of each member. List them on newsprint. Then review the strengths listed in step 2. Try to determine what resources are needed for the accomplishment of each of the three goals, and who has them. In determining these resources, you may find it helpful to read the following section on the bases of power and apply it to the strengths of your group's members. What are your bases of power? What are your resources? In what ways can you influence the goal achievement of the other group members? In what ways can they influence your goal achievement? How can you use your power to guarantee that your goals are met? In deciding which coalitions will help your goal accomplishment you should consider all of these questions.

In participating in this exercise you may experience either the frustration of finding little or no compatibility between your own goals and those of the other group members or the rejection of having your resources overlooked, undervalued, or underused. You may also experience the disappointment of finding that other members are more skillful in making coalitions. It is possible that two members will find themselves in basic disagreement with the other two group members. It is from such situations that conflicts are born. In the previous chapter we discussed at length the nature of such conflicts and how they can be managed productively. At this point the group should bring such conflicts out in the open, make them explicit, and be very clear about how they are to be dealt with.

Do not at this point make any formal coalitions with other group members. Limit yourself to determining what coalitions are needed. Then go on to the next step.

### Step 4: Contracting Help with Your Goals

The interdependence among group members should now be obvious. In contributing resources to the achievement of the group's three top goals, different members have different levels of motivation and different levels of energy in working toward goal accomplishment. The degree to which your personal goals are reflected in the group's goals and the degree to which your resources are recognized and used will usually determine the amount of energy you contribute to the accomplishment of the goals. In planning how resources will be utilized to help achieve a goal, group members often develop formal or informal contracts with one another. The forming of a contract is step 4 in the mobilization of one's power in a group. The contract usually includes at least three items: (1) what I want from the group members; (2) what the other group members want from me; (3) what we exchange so that everyone can accomplish his goals.

In the previous three steps you set group goals, surveyed resources, and made judgments about what coalitions needed to be formed in order for you to help your goal accomplishment. Now, in step 4, consciously work out formal contracts with other group members and form open coalitions. In doing so, focus specifically on the three items involved in a contract. Write your contracts on newsprint so that all members can see and read them. In essence, these contracts are a plan for group members to cooperatively apply their resources in certain ways toward the achievement of the group's goals.

Step 5, implementing the contracts, will not be discussed.

### Discussion

After completing the steps above, the groups should discuss their experiences. The following questions may be used to stimulate discussion:

1. How was power developed in the group?

2. How did members use power to form the group's goals and identify needed resources?
3. What was the outcome of the five steps? To what extent were everyone's goals integrated in the group's goals, and to what extent were everyone's resources committed to the accomplishment of the group's goals?
4. What are the present reactions and feelings of each group member to the five steps?
5. With the help of the other group members, each member should answer the following questions:
   a. What are my goals?
   b. What are my sources of power in the group?
   c. How did I apply my power in order to make sure my goals were accomplished?
   d. How successful was I?
   e. How can I do better for myself next time?
6. On the basis of the group's experiences, what conclusions can be made about the use of power in a group? Groups should write the answers to question 6 on newsprint. When all groups have finished their discussion, the conclusions should be shared.

# THE BASES OF POWER

In discussing how power is developed and used, many behavioral scientists have given particular attention to its sources (French & Raven, 1959; Raven & Kruglanski, 1970). According to them, there are six possible bases of a person's power: ability to reward and to coerce, his or her legal position, his or her capacity as a referent, his or her expertise, and his or her information.

A person has **reward power** over other group members if she has the ability to deliver positive consequences or remove negative consequences in response to their behavior. Her power will be greater the more the group members value the reward, the more they believe that she can dispense the reward, and the less their chances appear of getting the reward from someone else. The successful use of reward power will generally produce a "moving toward" the person. Group members will comply with the person's requests, seek her out, increase their liking for her, and communicate effectively with her. Under certain conditions, however, the reward power can backfire. Too many rewards or the development of suspicion on the part of the group members that they are being bribed or conned into going along can lead to a "moving away" or "moving against" the person.

A person has **coercive power** over other group members if he can mete out negative consequences or remove positive consequences in response to the behavior of group members. Punishment for a member who fails to get the group to go along with his wishes often increases the pressure on group members to engage in the desired behavior. Coercive power frequently causes the group to avoid the person and to like him less. Group members may do what he wants, but they tend to avoid interacting with him in the future. Only when the use of coercive power brings a conflict out into the open to be resolved can it have many positive effects.

When a person has **legitimate power** group members believe she ought to have influence over them because of her position in the group or organization (such as an employer) or because of her special role responsibilities (such as those of a policewoman). Group members invariably believe it their duty to follow the commands of a person with legitimate power, even when it means restricting themselves to a limited set of behaviors. Legitimate power is often used to reduce conflict—when the person with it plays the role of an arbitrator or mediator or when those with less power simply conform to her wishes.

When a person has **referent power** group members identify with or want to be like him and therefore do what he wants out of respect, liking, and wanting to be liked. Generally, the more the person is liked, the more the group members will identify with him.

When a person has **expert power** group members see her as having some special knowledge or skill and as being trustworthy. They believe she is not trying to deceive them for selfish purposes. The successful use of expert power results in movement toward the person, for the group members are convinced of the correctness of her request. Only if her expertise fosters feelings of inadequacy in the group members will it have negative effects.

When a person has **informational power** group members believe that he has resources of information that will be useful in accomplishing the goal and that are not available anywhere else. The power is based upon the logic of a person's arguments or the superiority of his demonstrated knowledge; it has effects similar to those that result from the use of expert power.

At this point, review the sources of power used in the previous exercise and classify them according to the bases of power discussed in this section. What power bases do you usually rely upon?

Match the following bases of power with their definitions (*answers at the end of the chapter*):

_____    1. Reward

_____    2. Coercive

_____    3. Legitimate

_____    4. Reference

_____    5. Expert

_____    6. Informational

a. Group members believe the person has useful knowledge not available elsewhere.
b. Group members believe the person ought to have power because of her position or responsibilities.
c. A person can deliver positive consequences or remove negative consequences.
d. Group members believe the person has a special knowledge or skill and is trustworthy.
e. Group members do what the person wants out of respect, liking, and wanting to be liked.
f. A person can deliver negative consequences or remove positive consequences.

## EXERCISE 9.3:
## UNEQUAL RESOURCES

This exercise gives participants a chance to observe how groups (1) use resources that have been unequally distributed and (2) negotiate to obtain the resources they need. It is conducted with four groups, each having two to four members. If there are more persons than needed for the exercise, they may participate without being group members. Should more than one cluster of four groups participate, the coordinator may wish to add the element of competition between as well as within the clusters. The exercise should take less than one hour. The procedure for the coordinator is as follows:

1. Introduce the exercise as an experience with the use of resources needed to accomplish a task that have been distributed unequally among groups. Form the groups. For each cluster have at least two observers. Groups should be placed far enough away from each other so that their negotiation positions are not compromised by casual observation.
2. Meet briefly with the observers and discuss what they might focus upon. Any aspect of negotiation and problem solving can be observed.
3. Distribute an envelope of materials and a copy of the accompanying task sheet to each group. Explain that each group has different materials, but that each must complete the same tasks. Explain that the groups may negotiate for the use of materials and tools in any way that is agreeable to everyone. Emphasize that the first group to finish all the tasks is the winner. (If clusters are competing, there will be both a group winner and a cluster winner.) Give the signal to begin.
4. When the groups have finished, declare the winner. Then conduct a discussion on using resources, sharing, negotiating, competing, and using power. Ask the observers to participate in the discussion. Then ask each cluster to summarize its conclusions about the use of power that manifested itself during the exercise.

### Group Materials

*Group 1:* scissors, ruler, paper clips, pencils, two 4-inch squares of red paper, and two 4-inch squares of white paper.

*Group 2:* scissors, glue, and two sheets each of gold paper, white paper, and blue paper, each $8\frac{1}{2}$ by 11 inches.

*Group 3:* felt-tipped markers and two sheets each of green paper, white paper, and gold paper, each $8\frac{1}{2}$ by 11 inches.

*Group 4:* five sheets of paper, $8\frac{1}{2}$ by 11 inches—one green, one gold, one blue, one red, and one purple.

### Unequal Resources Exercise Task Sheet

Each group is to complete the following tasks:

1. Make a 3- by 3-inch square of white paper.
2. Make a 4- by 2-inch rectangle of gold paper.
3. Make a 3- by 5-inch T-shaped piece of green and white paper.
4. Make a four-link paper chain, each link in a different color.
5. Make a 4- by 4-inch flag in any three colors.

The first group to complete all the tasks is the winner. Groups may negotiate with each other for the use of needed materials and tools on any mutually agreeable basis.

### EXERCISE 9.4:
### POWER POLITICS

The objective of this exercise is to examine the dynamics of negotiating for power. Group members with different amounts of power are to negotiate to form power coalitions with other group members. The exercise takes one and a half hours. Here is the procedure for the coordinator to follow:

1.  Introduce the exercise as a situation in which different group members have different amounts of power and are negotiating to form power coalitions in order to complete a task. Divide the participants into groups of 12. Each participant needs a pencil and a pad of paper for writing notes.
2.  Hand out a copy of the accompanying instruction sheet to each participant and have them read it. Then hand out a slip of paper with a number on it to each participant. The numbers on the slips are to range from 100 to 1,200. Announce that there will be two rounds of negotiations before the first vote is taken. The first round will be a 15-minute period in which members write notes to one another. No verbal communication is permitted. Members may write as many notes to as many other members as they wish. Notes should include the names of the sender and the receiver. These notes are not to be read until the end of the 15-minute period. Give the signal to begin round 1.
3.  At the end of fifteen minutes stop all note passing and allow members to read their notes. After they have done so, announce the beginning of round 2. The same rules apply. Round 2 lasts 15 minutes.
4.  At the end of round 2 ask the groups if they are ready to vote on their chairperson. If seven members want to vote, a vote is taken. All voting takes place by secret ballot. Members note the number of votes they control and how they commit them. If the group is not ready to vote, or if no one has enough votes to become chairperson, go to round 3.
5.  In round 3 members may negotiate verbally with one another. There are no restrictions on negotiations during this round, which also lasts for 15 minutes.
6.  At the end of round 3 call for a vote. The vote is again by secret ballot. If no one has enough votes to become chairperson, allow a 10-minute free-negotiation period. Then take a final vote.
7.  Have the groups discuss their experience, using the following questions as guides:
    a.  What deals were made for the 100 units of patronage? How was power used in making those deals?
    b.  What negotiation strategies were used?
    c.  How did members make their decision about whom to commit their votes to? What criteria did they use to make the decision?
    d.  What were the feelings and reactions of the members to the experience?
    e.  What feelings arose from the unequal distribution of votes? How did it feel to control a small number of votes? How did it feel to control a large number of votes?
    f.  How did members create allies and develop power blocs? What strategies did they use?
    g.  Who felt powerful? Who felt powerless?
    h.  What conclusions can you make about the use of power? (Write these on newsprint to share with other groups.)

### Power Politics Exercise Instruction Sheet

This is a game of power politics. Your group is to become the governing body of a political party, and you and the other group members must select a general chairperson. This is a crucial decision for the party. The person you elect will have extensive power and control over who gets how much patronage from the party. He or she will have 100 units of patronage to distribute among deserving members of the group. Members of your group may negotiate for votes and the distribution of the patronage. Each of you controls a different number of votes. One member controls 100 votes, a second controls 200, a third controls 300, and so on, with one member controlling 1,200 votes. The number of votes you have is on a slip of paper that will be given to you by the coordinator of the exercise. Keep this slip. *Do not show it to any other group member.* You may commit your votes to any member you wish; you may also split your votes among several members if you so desire. A member must receive 4,000 votes to become chairperson.

## POWER AND PROBLEM SOLVING

In the two previous exercises the resources of the group were distributed unequally among its members. This will be the case with most of the problems a group faces. Yet because resources are unequally distributed does not mean that there are members who are powerless. Every group member has some power; every group member is able to influence other group members in some way. Different group members will have different bases of power: Some, for example, may have a high degree of informational power, whereas others may have legitimate power. How a group manages the element of influence in member relationships has an important bearing on group effectiveness.

The effectiveness of any group is improved when (1) power is relatively balanced among its members, and (2) power is based upon competence, expertise, and information. Influence needs to be generally balanced or equal among all group members. A member's commitment to implementing a group decision depends upon her believing that she has influenced the decision. The ability of the group to solve problems increases as all group members come to feel that they share equally in influencing the direction of the group effort, and as the group climate becomes relatively free of domination by a few of the most powerful members. When members have equal power they are more cooperative in their interactions and more responsive to the cooperative initiatives of other members. Studies have found that even within organizations the satisfaction of subordinates increases when they believe they can influence particular aspects of the organization's decision making. Unequal power interferes with the trust and communication necessary for managing group conflicts constructively. Thus, the problem-solving ability of a group is improved when the group has flexible power patterns that in the long run equalize influence among group members.

A group's decisions are invariably of higher quality when power is based upon competence, expertise, and relevant information—not upon authority or popularity. The problem-solving capacity of many groups is seriously damaged when the member with the most authority is most influential at a time that calls for expertise and accurate information as the bases of power. The participation and involvement of all group members are dependent upon their being able to share the bases of power that will enable them to influence the decisions made by the group.

When power is not distributed equally among group members, or when the use of authority dominates and expertise and informational bases of power are ignored, group effectiveness is undermined. The next exercise deals with the unequal distribution of power and the consequences it can have for both high- and low-power group members.

## EXERCISE 9.5:
## POWER TO THE ANIMALS

The objective of this exercise is to examine the interaction among groups of different power as they negotiate with one another. The exercise takes 2 hours. The coordinator should read the accompanying instructions regarding the distribution of marbles and then follow this procedure:

1. Introduce the exercise as one that highlights interaction among groups having unequal power. Divide the class into groups of 12. Explain that within each group are three mammals, four birds, and five fish; the status of the members in each group is determined by how well they negotiate—for marbles. (Even if there are more than 12 participants in a group, keep the number of mammals under five.) Hand out a copy of the general instructions to every participant.
2. Distribute 12 bags of marbles randomly within each group. Make sure that the members understand their instructions. Give them time to examine what marbles they have, warning them not to let other group members see the marbles. Then begin negotiation session 1, which is to last 5 minutes.
3. During the negotiation session place on newsprint three headings: "Mammals," "Birds," and "Fish." After 5 minutes stop the negotiating and have the participants compute their scores. Take the three highest scores and place them, along with the persons' initials, under the heading "Mammals." (Even if there are more than 12 participants in a group, keep the number of mammals under five.) Place the next four scores, together with the persons' initials, under the heading "Birds." Place the remaining five scores, with the persons' initials, under the heading "Fish." Have each person make a name tag indicating what he is and put it on.
4. Begin negotiation session 2. After 5 minutes end it and ask for scores. Read just the individual scores, placing the three highest in the mammals column, the next four in the birds column, and the next five in the fish column. Members who change columns on the basis of their score will have to exchange their name tags.
5. Conduct negotiation session 3 in the same way.
6. Conduct negotiation session 4 in the same way.
7. Announce that the mammals now have the authority to make the rules for the exercise and that although anyone else can suggest rules, the mammals will decide which ones will be implemented. Inform the mammals that they may make any rules they wish, such as a rule that all marbles must be redistributed so that everyone has equal points, or a rule that all fish and birds must give mammals the marbles they ask for whether they want to or not. Have the mammals record their rules on newsprint.
8. After the new rules are established, conduct negotiation session 5. Then allow 5 minutes for the mammals to discuss and make any rule changes.
9. Repeat this cycle twice. Then give the birds and the fish copies of the list of strategies for influencing a high-power group. The birds and the fish have 10 minutes to discuss the strategies and decide which ones to adopt. Then continue with another negotiation session.
10. After a variety of strategies have been tried by the birds and the fish, or when they refuse to continue, conduct a discussion of the experience. The following questions may be used as guides:
    a. What were your feelings and your reactions to the experience?
    b. Are there any parallels between the system set up by the game and the system in which we live?
    c. Would it have made much difference if the members who were fish had been the mammals?
    d. Were the mammals acting with legitimate authority?

e. Are there any parallels between the exercise and the relations among racial groups, rich and poor, and adults and students?
f. What negotiation strategies were used?
g. What feelings arose from the unequal distribution of power? How did it feel to have high power? How did it feel to have low power?
h. How did the strategies for changing the high-power group work? What contributed to their effectiveness or ineffectiveness?
i. What conclusions about the use of power can be made from your experiences in the exercise?

## Distribution of Marbles

1. The total number of marbles needed is 72 (six times the number of group members).
2. The number of green marbles needed is 5 (the number of mammals plus two).
3. The number of yellow marbles needed is 10 (the number of birds plus the number of fish plus one).
4. The number of red, white, and blue marbles needed is 57, 19 of each.

Give each participant a bag of 6 marbles. Five bags are to contain 1 green marble, 1 yellow marble, and 4 marbles randomly selected from the colors red, white, and blue. Three bags are to contain 1 yellow marble and 5 marbles randomly selected from the colors red, white, and blue. The remaining 4 bags are to contain a random assortment of red, white, and blue marbles. These 12 bags are to be distributed at random within each group.

## General Instructions

In this exercise there are three levels of power, based on marbles in each group. Group members have the chance to progress from one level of power to another by obtaining marbles through negotiation. The three members who get the most power will be declared the winners when the exercise ends. You will be given 6 marbles each. The scoring system for the marbles is given below. Additional points are awarded if a member is able to get several marbles of the same color:

| Color | Points | Number of a Kind | Points |
|---|---|---|---|
| Green | 50 | 4 | 50 |
| Yellow | 25 | 3 | 30 |
| Red | 15 | 2 | 20 |
| White | 10 | 1 | 10 |
| Blue | 5 | | |

For example, a person's total score if she had six green marbles would be 300 (6 × 50) plus 50 (for 6 of a kind), or 350 points.

The rules for negotiation are as follows:

1. You have 5 minutes to improve your score.
2. You improve your score by negotiating with other group members.
3. Members must be holding hands to have an agreement.
4. Only one-for-one trades are legal. Two for one or any other combination is illegal.
5. Once a member touches the hand of another member, a marble of unequal value (or color) must be traded. If two members cannot make an agreement, they will have to hold hands for the entire negotiating round.
6. There is no talking unless hands are touching. This rule must be strictly followed.

7. Members with folded arms do not have to negotiate with other members.
8. All marbles must be hidden. This rule must be strictly followed.

### Strategies for Influencing a High-Power Group

1. Build your own organizations and resources in order to make the low-power group less vulnerable.
2. Form coalitions.
3. Change the attitudes of high-power group members through education or moral persuasion.
4. Use existing legal procedures to bring pressures for change.
5. Search for ways in which to make high-power group members dependent upon the low-power group.
6. Use harassment techniques to increase the high-power group's costs of sticking with the status quo.

## UNEQUAL POWER

When the distribution of power within a group is obviously unequal, both the high- and the low-power members have troubles. As we have seen, overall group effectiveness suffers, the gains members receive from being members decrease, and severe maintenance problems result. In discussions of theory and research pertaining to high and low power, the usual reference is to our society rather than to a small, problem-solving group. Yet the same dynamics between high-power and low-power persons can be found in a group of any size, even one as large as our society. In the previous exercise you yourself experienced, depending on your marbles, what it means to have a great deal of power or very little power. Compare your experience with the following discussions of high- and low-power group members.

### High-Power Members

Life generally seems good for high-power persons. Everything goes right, every problem is easily solved, everyone seems to like and appreciate them and everything they do. High-power persons are typically happy with their situation and tend not to see how much the use of power is involved in their relationships. They are convinced that low-power persons really do like them, that everyone communicates honestly with them, that no one hides information from them, and that they are really seen as "nice" persons. When this enjoyable world is threatened by dissatisfaction expressed by low-power persons, however, high-power persons tend not to react benevolently. They are hard to move toward cooperation, conciliation, and compromise, and they will largely ignore the efforts of their low-power groupmates to increase cooperative problem solving. To them, low-power persons somehow never learn to "know their place"; they insist on "rocking the boat" out of ignorance and spite.

There are at least two strategies that high-power group members use to make it more difficult for low-power members to reduce the differences in power between them (Jones & Gerard, 1967). The first is to institute norms or rules in the group that legitimize their power and make wrong any attempt by others to change the status quo. As you may have noticed in the previous exercise, the first action taken by most groups who attain power is to make their holding of it legitimate and to establish regulations and norms that make illegitimate any change in the existing power relationships. For example, in most communities the white power structure has established strong norms as to where minority-group members may live, what occupations they may have, and where they must go to school—as well as procedures for making both whites and nonwhites believe that the status quo is "legitimate" and "right." This strategy may be described as the "power-defines-justice" strategy, or the "might-is-right" strategy.

The second strategy high-power members employ to solidify their position is to make the risk of attempting to change the status quo so great that the low-power members are deterred from trying to do so. They can invoke this strategy by establishing severe penalties against those who might attempt to change the status quo, and by offering the low-power members a variety of benefits or rewards on the condition that they refrain from rebelliousness. Of the two, the second seems to be more effective. The threat of punishment has never worked effectively to deter behavior, but the paternalistic leadership that tries to keep everyone happy has been applied successfully in combating labor and racial unrest in many parts of the country. This strategy may be defined as the "this-hurts-me-more-than-it-will-hurt-you" strategy, or the "if-only-you-would-behave-neither-of-us-would-go-through-this-suffering" strategy.

In America, high power is believed to result in arrogance and corruption. "Power corrupts" is a common household saying, and most persons have seen the arrogance of those who have more power than they do (often secretaries in the office of their boss). There are many exceptions to these correlations, of course, but perhaps not nearly as many as high-power persons like to believe.

Halle (1967) makes the interesting suggestion that the greater a person's power, the more insufficient it is likely to seem, simply because the claims upon it increase faster than the power to fulfill them. The Ford Foundation, for example, though by far the richest of American foundations, is undoubtedly the most inadequately endowed in terms of the expectations it is called on to meet. High power may also have difficulty in handling small problems: It may become easier to drop an atom bomb on a mosquito than to use a can of bug spray.

A number of research studies have examined the effects of high power on group members. Kipnis (1972) found that powerful group members (1) made more attempts to influence the behavior of the low-power members, (2) devalued the performance of the low-power members, (3) attributed the efforts of the low-power members to their own use of power rather than to the low-power members' motivations to do well, (4) viewed the low-power members as objects of manipulation, and (5) expressed a preference for the maintenance of psychological distance from the low-power members. Participants who were randomly assigned to central positions in a communication network (the more powerful positions) not only viewed themselves as powerful but also rated themselves as more capable than the participants who were randomly assigned peripheral positions (Stotle, 1978). Tjosvold (1978) notes that high-power group members (1) feel more secure than low-power members, (2) underestimate the low-power members' positive intentions, (3) devalue the low-power person, (4) are inattentive to the communications of the low-power person, (5) are unresponsive to cooperative gestures by the low-power members, and (6) attempt to protect their superior power by rejecting demands for change. High-power group members also seem uninterested in learning about the intentions and plans of low-power members (Tjosvold & Sagaria, 1978).

## Low-Power Members

Group members subjected to the power of another generally find such a relationship threatening and debilitating. Tjosvold (1978) observes that members with low power are apt to feel frustrated and uncertain about their future goal facilitation because they depend heavily on the unpredictable behavior of the high-power members. These feelings of uncertainty and anxiety provoke (1) increased vigilance and attempts to understand and predict the high-power members' behavior, (2) distorted perceptions of the positive intent of the high-power members toward them, (3) attraction to, mixed with fear of, the high-power members, (4) stifling of criticism of the high-power members, (5) unwillingness to clarify one's position to the high-power members, (6) ingratiation, conformity, flattery, and effacing self-presentation so as to induce the high-power members to like and to reward them, and (7) the expectation of exploitation (low-power members tend to believe that, because they have no retaliatory capability, they are vulnerable and helpless and will be exploited). Low-power members have been found to direct much of their communication and attention to high-power members and to keep on good terms with them.

On the other hand, low-power group members have been found to resist

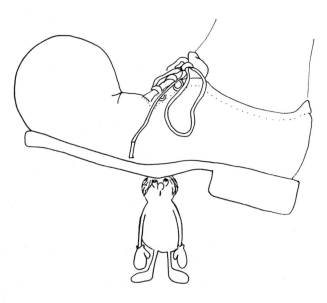

attempts by high-power members to control them. Tjosvold (1978) notes that low-power members have been found to defy threats, to counterthreaten, to refuse to comply with an influence attempt even when resistance is costly, to dislike the high-power members, and to perceive the relationship as competitive. Johnson and Allen (1972) found that low-power group members who believed they were equal to their high-power peers felt underrewarded and attempted to obtain increased rewards from the group while emphasizing the incompetence, uncooperativeness, lack of generosity, and unfairness of the high-power members. In addition, they disliked their high-power peers.

Deutsch (1969) assumes that the goal of low-power members is to establish authentic, cooperative, equal-power relationships with the high-power members. He states that the ability of low-power members to offer and engage in authentic cooperation means that they are aware that they are neither helpless nor powerless, even though they are at a disadvantage. Cooperative action requires a recognition that a person has the capacity to "go it alone" if necessary; unless a person has the freedom to choose not to cooperate, there can be no free choice to cooperate. Thus, the low-power members in a group need to build enough cohesiveness and strength to function independently of the high-power members if this is necessary. In addition, the high-power members must be motivated to cooperate with the low-power members. This means that the latter must find goals that are important to the high-power members, especially goals they cannot accomplish without the cooperation of the low-power members.

Deutsch (1969) notes that a variety of strategies for influencing high-power members are available to low-power members. By building their own organizations and developing their own resources, low-power members not only can make themselves less vulnerable to exploitation, but can also add to their power by providing themselves with alternatives that preclude their being dependent solely upon the high-power members. Low-power members can add to their power by allying themselves with third parties. Another strategy is to try to use existing legal procedures to bring pressures for change. Further, low-power members can search for attachments with the high-power members that, if made more obvious, could increase the latter's positive feelings toward or outcome dependence upon the low-power members. Low-power members can try to change the attitudes of those in high power through education or moral persuasion. Finally, the low-power members can use harassment techniques in order to increase the high-power members' costs of staying with the status quo. In planning how to increase their power in relation to the high-power members, low-power members of a group should first clarify their goals, take stock of their resources, and finally study how to make the high-power members more aware of their dependence on them and of their compatibility (if any) of goals.

## POWER AND CONFLICT

An intimate relationship exists between power and conflict. The use of power is always present in personal and group interaction. Group conflict does not exist, however, unless a group member wants something to happen that she does not have the power to make happen. If a person wants group members to do something and has the power to make them do it, there is no conflict. Also, if the person wants group members to do something and they want to do it, then even though she does not have the power to make sure they do it there is no conflict. But if a person wants other group members to do something they do not want to do and she does not have enough power to overcome their unwillingness, then a state of conflict exists. The successful attempt to use power can often end a conflict. The successful attempt to influence the group is one that helps resolve conflicts, whereas the unsuccessful attempt can increase the conflict. Conflicts are also increased when the desire to influence is not matched by the capacity to influence.

The destructive management of conflict is characterized by less and less mutual influence among group members. In a conflict situation that is being badly managed, informational power and expertise power are apt to be rejected because each participant sees the other as being untrustworthy and as trying to use his knowledge or expertise for personal goals. Hostility and distrust undermine legitimate power. The emphasis on differences among group members decreases mutual referent power. Reward power can arouse suspicions of bribery or suggest that one is attempting to increase another's dependence upon him. When the bases for these kinds of influence deteriorate, those with power begin to rely more and more on the use of coercive power.

The use of a coercive power base is a destructive way to manage a conflict for many reasons. It exacerbates the conflict, thereby increasing hostility, resentment, lies, threats, retaliation, revenge, and distrust. Threats often lead to aggression and counterthreats. Coercion and threats can sometimes cut short or control a conflict simply by getting behavioral compliance or by forcing a group member to leave the situation, but it will never lead to a productive resolution and cooperation. Communication decreases and becomes less reliable. Mutual influence also decreases, and the likelihood of a mutually satisfying settlement is diminished. Thus, whenever possible, attempts to exercise influence through the use of a coercive power base should be avoided in conflicts. One central strategy to resolve or control a conflict is to reestablish mutual influence among all those in the group.

## EXERCISE 9.6:
## FEMALES AT SUMMER CAMP

The purpose of this exercise is to provide an opportunity for a discussion as to how groups form, how leadership is developed, and how power is used within peer groups. It achieves this purpose by examining the interrelationships among ten female college students at summer camp. The procedure is as follows:

1. Form groups of six members. One member volunteers to be an observer. The task of the observer is to record the nature of leadership and power within the group as they complete the task.
2. Each participating group member (five in all) is given the description of two of the females (ten in all). The group as a whole is given a copy of the Characteristics Chart. The task of the group is to answer the following questions:
   a. Who are the members of each subgroup?

Characteristics of Females at the Summer Camp

| | | | | | | Girls | | | | |
|---|---|---|---|---|---|---|---|---|---|---|
| **Characteristics** | **Virginia** | **Renee** | **Pat** | **Debbie** | **Janice** | **Dianne** | **Gail** | **Cindy** | **Cathy** | **Heidi** |
| Religion | Catholic | Catholic | Nonsectarian | Methodist | Presbyterian | Baptist | Christian | Baptist | Catholic | Baptist |
| Attendance | Frequent | Occasional | Never | Frequent | Rare | Frequent | Occasional | Occasional | Occasional | Frequent |
| College major | Math | Education | Business Mgt. | Home Ec. | Accounting | History | Pre-Law | Languages | Home Ec. | Music |
| Grade average | B | C | A | B | A | B | A | B | C | C |
| Family income | Medium | Medium | Medium | Low | High | Medium | High | Medium | Low | Low |

     b. Who is the leader of each subgroup?

     c. What characterizes the interactions among members of different subgroups?

     Each group is to decide by consensus the answers to these questions with all members indicating that they know the answers to the questions and can explain how the group arrived at their conclusions.

3. When the group has finished step 2, write a description of leadership that includes answers to the following questions:

     a. What leadership qualities do the females identified as leaders have?

     b. How do the leaders of the subgroups exercise their leadership?

     Each group is to agree by consensus to all the points included in their written description of leadership.

4. When the group has finished step 3, write a description of power as it relates to social systems that includes the answers to the following questions:

     a. How do the females exert influence on each other?

     b. What bases of power do the females use?

     Each group is to agree by consensus to all the points included in their written description of power and influence.

5. The groups should share their descriptions of leadership and power with each other in a discussion involving the entire class.

## Females at Summer Camp Exercise Descriptions

Virginia is a social girl who often talks to others. She is quite attractive and dresses well. She dates often. When she has problems, she shares them with Renee or Pat. She sometimes borrows clothes from them. At night she is usually in her room or in Cathy's room. She sometimes sneaks out of camp at night and always gets back without being caught. She shares the food and liquor that she sneaks into the camp with Renee, Cathy, and sometimes Janice.

     Renee is a fairly attractive, rather insecure person. She smokes and drinks. She dates occasionally, often double-dating with Cathy. She borrows clothes from Virginia and Debbie. At night she is usually in Virginia or Cathy's room and confides in them. At times she sneaks out of camp at night and is helped by Virginia to get back in. She shares food and liquor with Cathy and Virginia.

     Pat is a clear-headed girl with a perceptive mind. She does not drink and is fairly traditional in her ideas. She is quiet and seldom dates; she never double-dates. She lends clothes to Janice, Virginia, Gail, and Heidi, but does not borrow them. She is a good listener and others confide in her, but she does not reciprocate. At night she can be found in her own room, but she is often accompanied by one of the other girls.

     Debbie is a rather wild girl who dates frequently, occasionally double-dating with Janice. She seems mostly interested in boys—her main topic of conversation. She shares clothes with Virginia and Janice, and at night can usually be found in one of their rooms. At times she sneaks out of camp at night and is helped to get back in by Virginia. She shares food with Janice, Virginia, and occasionally Cathy. She confides in Janice.

     Janice is a outgoing girl who is quite attractive and dresses well. She dates often and sometimes double-dates with Debbie. When she has problems she goes to see Pat. She borrows clothes from Pat or Debbie. At night she is usually in her own room. She is a good talker and is successful in debating most of the other girls. She is well versed in clothes, dating, and men and has lots of spending money. She shares food from home with Debbie, Virginia, and Gail.

     Dianne is a neat, well-groomed, modest girl with strong moral convictions. She seldom dates and does not smoke or drink. She is very active in church work and attends several times a week. When she has a personal problem, she goes to see Pat or her minister. She lends clothes to Cindy. At night she is usually in her own room. She likes to read and has been known to remind the girls about quiet hours, which has caused some resentment from Janice and Renee.

Gail is a wealthy, well-traveled, sophisticated girl who seems to relate well to everyone on a casual level. She dates occasionally but never double-dates. She sometimes borrows clothes from Pat, with whom she shares her problems. She is mature and understanding of others but does not seem to form very close friendships. At night she can be found in the rooms of Pat or Dianne. She shares food with Dianne, Pat, and sometimes Janice.

Cindy is a very shy girl who seldom dates. She doesn't smoke or drink. She occasionally goes to a movie with Dianne, sometimes Heidi. At night she can be found in Dianne's or Janice's room. She shares food with Dianne or Janice. She avoids Renee and Virginia.

Cathy is a rather loud, chunky girl. She often swears and is heard telling dirty jokes. She occasionally double-dates with Renee. She likes to smoke and drink. She shares her problems with Virginia and Renee. At night she is in her room or Virginia's room. She shares food with Virginia, Renee, and sometimes Debbie.

Heidi is an overweight girl who tries to be friendly with everyone. She goes out of her way to run errands and otherwise try to please the other girls. She does not smoke, drink, or date. She attends movies with Cindy or Dianne. She does not dress well, and Pat is the only one who will lend her clothes. At night she is either in her own room or Pat's or Dianne's room. She shares her problems with Pat or Dianne. She shares food with Dianne, Cindy, Gail, and Pat.

## EXERCISE 9.7:
## GROUP POWER

1. With your classmates, form groups of five. Place all the change the group members have in a hat. Decide who in the group gets all the money. Discuss the experience.
2. Stand by the walls of the room with your classmates. Each of you picks a spot in the center of the room in which you would like to sit. At a signal from a coordinator, go sit in that spot. Once all of you are settled, discuss your experience with the nearest person.
3. Stand in the circle with your classmates, touching fingertips with the person on either side. Pick a spot in the room to which you would like the group to go. Do not talk. When the signal is given, try to get the group to move to your chosen spot. Discuss what you have learned with a partner.
4. Stand in a circle with your classmates. Each member helps with one hand to hold a sheet of paper. No verbal communication is allowed. At the signal the paper suddenly becomes "power." See what happens and discuss.
5. Pair up with a classmate. Sit in chairs facing each other. You have 5 minutes to decide, nonverbally, who is going to sit on the floor. At the end of that time one person *must* be on the floor. See what happens and discuss.
6. Sit in a circle with your classmates. Each of you close your eyes and imagine you live in a small rural village. You have been handed an important message to deliver to someone in a much more powerful neighboring village. You begin to walk to the other village. You pass a girl on a bridge. You pass a man on a bicycle. You pass a family having a picnic. You hear the sound of birds singing, you see trees moving in the breeze, you smell the grass and the earth. Rounding a bend, you suddenly come upon a wall. It continues in both directions as far as you can see. The village you need to get to is beyond the wall. For a few minutes think of what happens. Then open your eyes and share stories of what happened at the wall. Discuss, from the standpoint of power.
7. Sit in a circle with your classmates. Each of you close your eyes and picture the group in which you are a member. In your fantasy, begin a game of follow-the-leader. At first see yourself as the leader and note what happens among the followers. Now shift leaders and see someone else at the head of the line. Keep going until all the members of your group have had a chance to be the leader. Then open your eyes and

discuss the following questions: What kinds of things did different persons lead the group to do? What feelings did you imagine among the followers? How did you picture the group behaving when you were the leader? Who seemed the most "natural" in the role? Who seemed the least "natural" in the role?

8. Divide into groups of four with your classmates. Make a picture or collage of power, using available resources—magazines, pencils, paints, crayons, newspapers, and so forth. At the end of 30 minutes discuss the picture of each group. If Polaroid cameras are available, instead of making a picture of power go out and take a picture of power. Then come back and discuss.

9. This exercise is for a group that has been working together on a task. Arrange yourselves in a line according to how powerful you see yourselves, from most powerful to least powerful. Before beginning mark one end of the line as the spot for the most powerful person so that all members will know how to arrange themselves. After the line has stabilized ask if anyone wants to move to a different location. Discuss self-perceptions and perceptions of others. How does your power as perceived by other members compare with how you see it? Were there disagreements among members about who is the most powerful? Does the group have certain biases about power, such as the richest person being seen as the most powerful?

## YOUR POWER BEHAVIOR

You have now participated in a series of exercises on power as well as having read a summary of much of the current theory and research on the use of power. Power has been discussed in several previous chapters. At this point, form a group with two of your classmates. Discuss what you have learned about yourself and your behavior in power situations. What are your feelings when you are being opposed and have to rely upon power to further your goals? How do you feel when others quickly conform to what you wish them to do? How do you react when others force you to comply to their wishes? What basis of power do you usually rely upon? Have you ever been manipulated or conned? If so, what did it feel like? Any question about power and its use should be discussed if it increases your understanding of yourself and the other members of your group. Write down your conclusions about yourself and your use of power.

## EXERCISE 9.8:
## DEVELOPING LAND AREAS

The purpose of this exercise is to examine the consequences of unequal power among nations of individuals. The exercise is actually a game, in which group members represent a large land area and strive to advance its standard of living. Materials needed are copies of the game board for each member (or one large one for each group, with 6 individual markers); 100 tokens for each group (coins, small strips of paper, etc.); resource cards—5 for each member, 30 for each group; 6 cards for each group with the land areas written on them; and copies of the rules for each group. Groups need six members each. The procedure for the coordinator is as follows:

1. Introduce the exercise as a game focusing upon the consequences of unequal power among nations or individuals. Each person will represent a land area and will attempt to improve the standard of living of his or her area.

2. Form groups of six. On 3- by 5-inch cards, write the names of the following land areas: Asia, Africa and Mideast, South America, Soviet Countries, Europe, and North America. Turn the cards face down and mix them. Each member chooses a card to find out which land area he or she will represent.

3. Tokens are distributed to the group members in the following way:
   a. Asia is given 1
   b. Africa and Mideast is given 2
   c. South America is given 2
   d. Soviet Countries is given 8
   e. Europe is given 13
   f. North America is given 26
   Tell the group members that these numbers represent the approximate gross national product of their areas divided by the population. Forty-eight additional tokens are put in the middle as a common bank from which members can draw according to game instructions.
4. Five resource cards marked with the land area are given to each member. These represent the natural resources of the area and can each either represent one token or can be used as collateral on loans from other land areas. In order to advance to level 7, however, members must possess all their resource cards.
5. Distribute a game board to each member. Members keep track of their progress by covering each square with a token. They must advance sequentially. (Alternative: Make one large game board per group and have members mark their places with representative markers.) Members begin on the square that represents the number of tokens they were initially given.
6. Go over the rules with the class. Give them a few minutes to study their positions, then have them begin.
7. After the game, discuss the following questions with the large group:
   a. How did it feel to begin the game with the number of tokens you did?
   b. How did the number of your tokens make a difference in the strategies you used?
   c. How difficult was it to develop an alliance or get a loan? Why?
   d. How many people called "Attack?" How successful was it as a strategy?
   e. What can you learn about the dynamics of unequal power from playing this game?

## Rules for Developing Land Areas Exercise

1. The purpose of this game is to advance your land area as many spaces as you can. You do this by gaining tokens; one token will advance you one space. You must keep all previous spaces filled, although you may go backward (by loaning tokens, for example) as well as forward. If you give as collateral a resource card you have used as a token, you must fill that empty space first.
2. You start out with the number of tokens which represent your land area's approximate wealth (according to the 1980 gross national product divided by population size). That number determines where you will start the game (put all your tokens on your game board to begin). In addition, you will each get five resource cards, which represent your area's natural resources. These can be used to add to your position by representing one token or can be used as collateral for loans from other countries. You can use a resource card you hold from another land area as collateral as one token.
3. There will be ten rounds. Appoint a timekeeper. Starting with Asia and rotating clockwise, you will each get 3 minutes to find a way to increase your tokens. Once you have added tokens, your turn is over. If you are unsuccessful at the end of three minutes, you lose your turn and the round continues. The game ends after ten rounds or if a stalemate develops.
4. You can gain tokens in four ways:
   a. Progress: When you fill a line with tokens, you get additional ones from the World Bank according to the number noted at the end of the line. If, in lending out or losing tokens, you fall below a line previously passed you do not have to repay

that token. You may collect (or recollect) tokens when you fill that line again. However, if you use resource cards as tokens, you may take them off a space only if you negotiate a loan and must thereby give the card to the lender.

b. Form an alliance: If you and another land area negotiate an alliance, you both get two tokens from the World Bank. You may negotiate an alliance only once with a particular land area.

c. Call an attack: If you call "Attack," each land area that does not hold any of your resource cards or is not in alliance with you must pay you one token. You may call an attack only twice during the game.

d. Negotiate a loan: Any land area can lend tokens to another land area in exchange for a resource card, which serves as collateral and can later be repurchased. The amount of the loan and the repurchase are negotiable.

| Level VII Nirvana | GAME BOARD FOR DEVELOPING LAND AREAS EXERCISE | | | | | | |
|---|---|---|---|---|---|---|---|
| | Self Sufficiency: *You can sit back and watch everyone else play, or . . .* | | | | | | |
| Level VI Secure | 31 Secure food | 32 Secure homes | 33 Secure work | 34 Secure health | 35 Secure education | 36 Secure energy | Buy back resource cards |
| Level V Specialized | 25 Extra food | 26 Luxury homes | 27 Confortable work | 28 Specialized medicine | 29 Specialized education | 30 Solar energy | Receive five tokens |
| Level IV Mass Production | 19 Abundant food | 20 Large houses | 21 Factories | 22 Hospitals | 23 Higher education | 24 Oil energy | Receive four tokens |
| Level III Mechanized | 13 Sufficient food | 14 Small houses | 15 Mechanized farms | 16 Health clinics | 17 Basic education | 18 Dam energy | Receive three tokens |
| Level II Basic | 7 Subsistance food | 8 Basic shelter | 9 Rudimentary farming | 10 Folk medicine | 11 Early education | 12 Forest energy | Receive two tokens |
| Level I Pre-development | 1 Malnutrition | 2 Lack of shelter | 3 Inefficient farming | 4 Disease | 5 Folklore | 6 Wood gathering | Receive one token |

# SUMMARY

You should now have a good understanding of power and how it can help or hinder a group. You have experienced high- and low-power situations and know the dangers of having either high or low power. In the next chapter you will learn more about how groups hold together and direct the behavior of their members.

## ANSWERS

*Page 374*: 1. c; 2. f; 3. b; 4. e; 5. d; 6. a.

# 10

## Leading Learning and Discussion Groups

### THE NATURE OF LEARNING GROUPS

Many groups have as their purpose the promotion of learning among group members. Group learning occurs in all sorts of educational settings, from preschool programs to postgraduate seminars, from athletic teams to special conferences, from consumer education meetings to wilderness survival programs. In one's school, career, leisure, and community life, participation in discussion groups is a pervasive experience. **Discussion groups** are one of the most important and versatile educational tools available, and as such are heavily used.

A **learning group** is a group whose purpose is to ensure that group members learn specific subject matter, information, knowledge, skills, and procedures. Learning is the primary purpose of the group. The whole point of having a discussion is to promote the learning of the members, and if such learning is not taking place, the group cannot be considered productive. The terms *learning group* and *discussion group* will be used interchangeably throughout this chapter.

There are three types of interaction within a discussion group: the interaction between the coordinator and the group members, the interaction between the group members and the curriculum materials, and the interaction among group members. Both the coordinator's role and the curriculum have received a great deal of attention in instructional theory (see Johnson, 1979), but the member-member interaction patterns have been largely ignored and often mismanaged by educators.

393

This chapter will focus on the structuring of constructive interaction among group members so as to ensure maximal learning by all members.

Despite the pervasiveness of learning in groups in our society, educators receive very little specific training on how to conduct discussion groups in ways that maximize members' learning. The all-too-common practice of simply asking group members to sit around a table and carry on a "meaningful" discussion is all too often unproductive. One major difficulty is that, although people spend much of their lives talking with one another, most persons have failed to develop the abilities and attitudes necessary for carrying on a worthwhile discussion for the purpose of learning new information, knowledge, skills, and procedures. People tend to be self-conscious, to be overly concerned with what others may think of their ideas, to listen carelessly to others, and to look for others to provide direction and leadership.

The development of a productive learning group must be preceded by the conscious development of an effective group. In order to be effective, a learning group must have the following elements:

1. A clear, cooperative goal structure
2. Accurate two-way communication among members
3. Widespread distribution participation and leadership among group members
4. The use of consensus to arrive at answers, solutions, and decisions
5. Power and influence based on expertise and access to information and social skills, not on authority
6. The frequent occurrence of controversy
7. The open confrontation and negotiation of conflicts of interest among members and between the group members and the coordinator
8. High cohesiveness
9. High trust among members
10. A climate of acceptance and support among members and between the group members and the coordinator
11. Group norms promoting individual responsibility and accountability, helping and sharing, and achievement
12. Generally high group and interpersonal skills among members

In other words, an effective learning group must possess all of the characteristics of an effective group listed in Chapter 1 and throughout this book. Discussion group members must be taught the fundamental skills and attitudes necessary for group effectiveness if they are to learn anything in a discussion group. They must know how to build an effective group.

In recent years there has been considerable development of effective procedures for structuring cooperative learning groups (Johnson & Johnson, 1978, 1987b). These procedures will be summarized in this chapter. Readers interested in further study are referred to Johnson and Johnson (1987b). Also available are two handbooks containing cooperatively structured lessons for classes from preschool through adult education (Chasnoff, 1979; Lyons, 1980), a movie demonstrating the use of cooperative learning groups (Johnson & Johnson, 1980), and a newsletter for educators wishing to exchange ideas with others interested in the use of cooperative learning procedures (*The Cooperative Link*).

In this chapter we shall first discuss the stages of development of cooperative learning groups. We then outline the basic procedures for structuring productive learning groups. Finally, we discuss the role of the coordinator in ensuring that learning groups operate successfully.

# THE STAGES OF DEVELOPMENT OF LEARNING GROUPS

Learning groups typically move through seven stages. These stages were derived from the application to cooperative learning groups of the stages of group development identified by Tuckman (1965). Tuckman reviewed approximately 50 studies on group development conducted in a wide variety of settings. Although the descriptions of the stages the groups went through varied widely on the surface (some studies identifying three stages and others identifying seven or eight), Tuckman found a surprising amount of agreement beneath the diversity. He identified four stages: forming, storming, norming, and performing. During the **forming stage,** there is a period of uncertainty in which members try to determine their place in the group and the procedures and rules of the group. During the **storming stage,** conflicts begin to arise as members resist the influence of the group and rebel against accomplishing the task. During the **norming stage,** the group establishes cohesiveness and commitment, discovering new ways to work together and setting norms for appropriate behavior. Finally, during the **performing stage** the group develops proficiency in achieving its goals and becomes more flexible in its patterns of working together. Virtually all the studies that Tuckman reviewed, however, involved group leaders who were passive and nondirective and who made no attempt to intervene in the group process. In most learning groups there is an instructor or coordinator who tries to ensure that the group functions productively.

In applying Tuckman's conclusions to cooperative learning groups, the authors (with the help of Roger Johnson and a number of other colleagues) identified seven stages of development: (1) defining and structuring procedures and becoming oriented, (2) conforming to procedures and getting acquainted, (3) recognizing mutuality and building trust, (4) rebelling and differentiating, (5) committing to and taking ownership for the goals, procedures, and other members, (6) functioning maturely and productively, and (7) terminating. Each of these stages is discussed in turn.

## Defining and Structuring Procedures and Becoming Oriented

When a discussion group begins, the members are usually concerned about what is expected of them and what the goals of the session are. Group members want to know what is going to happen; what is expected of them; whether or not they will be accepted, influential, and liked; how the group is going to function; and who the other group members are. Group members expect the coordinator to explain how the group is to function in a way that reassures them that their personal needs will be met. When a learning group first meets, therefore, the coordinator defines the procedures to be used, assigns participants to groups, communicates the task, establishes the cooperative interdependence among members, and generally organizes the group and announces the beginning of the group's work.

## Conforming to Procedures and Getting Acquainted

As group members follow the prescribed procedures and interact around the task, they become acquainted with one another and familiarize themselves with the procedures until they can follow them easily. They learn the strengths and weaknesses of the other group members. During this stage the group members are dependent on the coordinator for direction and clarification of the goals and procedures of the group. It is also during this stage that the coordinator stresses the following group norms: (1) taking responsibility for one's own learning and the learning of the other members of the group, (2) providing help and assistance to other members, (3) responding to other members in an accepting, supportive, and trustworthy way, (4) making decisions through consensus, and (5) confronting and solving problems in group functioning. During this stage the goals and procedures of the group are the coordinator's. The group members conform to the prescribed procedures and interact with each other, but they are not personally committed to the group's goals and each other.

## Recognizing Mutuality and Building Trust

The third stage of group development is marked by group members (1) recognizing their cooperative interdependence, and (2) building trust among themselves. A sense of mutuality is built as group members recognize that they are in fact interdependent and that they are in a sink-or-swim-together situation. Members begin to take responsibility for each other's learning and appropriate behavior. They accept and internalize the reality that, if *they* wish to do well, they have to ensure that all other group members learn the assigned material, complete the assigned work, and participate actively in discussions.

Trust is built through disclosing one's thoughts, ideas, conclusions, and feelings, and having the other group members respond with acceptance, support, and reciprocation of the disclosures. Trust is discussed at length in Chapter 12 and in Johnson (1986). While a group is in this stage, it is important that all members engage in trusting behavior and respond to other members with trustworthiness.

## Rebelling and Differentiating

The fourth stage of group development is marked by group members (1) rebelling against the coordinator and the procedures and (2) differentiating themselves from each other through disagreements and conflicts. On the road to maturity a group will go through a period (sometimes short, sometimes long) of challenging the authority of the coordinator. It is an ordinary occurrence and should be expected. This swing toward independence contrasts sharply with the dependence demonstrated by students during stage 2. Many group members may have the attitude that learning is a passive process in which they can slip by without doing much work. Participation in a cooperative learning group requires students to take responsibility for their own learning and the learning of the other members of their group and to participate actively in the group's work. Sometimes group members will resist these responsibilities and attempt to return to the more traditional passive, self-centered, minimal-effort student role. Students may say things like, "Do I have to help Roger?" "I don't like working in groups," "I won't work in groups unless I can work with my friends." "I'm not going to help her," "Why should I teach these dummies? That's your job," "I've learned the material, that's all I should be expected to do." Group members may wish to test and challenge the coordinator's sincerity and commitment to the procedures. Students may say things like, "It's not fair that I don't get an 'A' just because the other members didn't do their share," "I'm the only one doing my work," "Can't you get Roger out of our group?" and "You are being unjust and unfair by requiring me to take responsibility for the learning of the other group members." Students may become "counterdependent" and attempt to establish their independence by doing just the opposite of what the group-learning procedures call for.

On the road to group maturity members will almost inevitably go through a period of bickering with one another. In developing close and committed relationships there is first an effort to get to know each other and then often a pulling back in order to differentiate oneself from the other group members. Students may begin to say things to each other like, "I don't have to do what you say," "Just because you want to do it that way doesn't mean that I want to do it that way," "I can say no to you," "Can we disagree and still be friends?" "We don't have to like each other just because we work together," and "I'm tired of doing it your way, I want us to do it my way." Relationships among group members are often built through a cycle of becoming friendly, establishing independence through disagreement and conflict, and then committing oneself to a relationship. Differentiating is important for group members to establish boundaries where they stop and the other members begin and to establish their autonomy as individual and separate members of the group (Johnson, 1979, 1980a).

The coordinator can expect both rebelling against the discussion group procedures and conflict among group members as a natural and expected stage of group development. She will want to deal with both in an open and accepting way. Some advice for doing so includes the following:

1. Do not tighten control and try to force conformity to prescribed procedures; reason and negotiate.
2. Confront and problem solve when students become counterdependent and rebellious.
3. Mediate conflicts among members helping the group establish members' autonomy and individuality.
4. Work toward students taking ownership of the procedures and committing themselves to each other's success.

Coordinating a learning group at this stage is like teaching a child to ride a bicycle; one runs alongside to prevent the child from falling but one must let loose so the child can learn to balance on his or her own.

## Committing to and Taking Ownership for the Goals, Procedures, and Other Members

During this stage, dependence on the coordinator and conformity to the prescribed procedures are replaced by dependence on the other members of the group and personal commitment to the collaborative nature of the experience. The "changing hands" from the coordinator's group to our group that began in the previous stage is finalized in this stage. The group becomes "ours" rather than "hers." Group norms become internalized and group members enforce the norms on themselves; the coordinator no longer has to enforce the norms and encourage group members to cooperate with each other. The norms and procedures become internally imposed rather than externally imposed. Motivation to learn becomes intrinsic rather than extrinsic. Members become committed to the cooperative procedures and accept responsibility for maximizing the learning of all group members.

Group members also become personally committed to each other in this stage of group development. They become concerned about each other's welfare and learning, provide support and assistance (not because the coordinator wants them to but because they care about each other), believe that they can rely on the support and assistance of other group members, and truly become friends.

## Functioning Maturely and Productively

As members' commitment to one another and to the cooperative accomplishment of the group's goals increases, the group achieves maturity, autonomy, and productivity. A definite sense of group identity emerges as the group becomes a mature working unit possessing the skills and attitudes necessary for effective collaboration in maximizing all members' learning. Group members can work together to achieve a variety of learning tasks and can deal with controversy and conflicts of interest in constructive ways. The group's attention alternates between task and maintenance concerns. Group members clearly collaborate to achieve the group's goals while ensuring that their relationships with each other are maintained at a high quality level. The group can do without the assistance of the coordinator in managing problems that arise. The coordinator becomes a consultant to the group rather than a directive leader. The relationships among group members continue to improve, as does the relationship between the coordinator and the members.

In the maturely functioning group, all members participate and are influenced by each other according to the expertise and information each possesses. The actions of one group member truly substitute for the actions of other members as the group moves harmoniously, through a division of labor toward maximizing the learning of all members. Members freely ask for and give help and assistance. There is a sense of pride in the group's achievements and a sense of gratitude to other members for their contributions to the group's success. Members feel good about the group's efforts, each other, and themselves. Controversy is encouraged and looked forward to, and conflicts of interest are openly confronted and resolved. Leadership is shared and viewed as the responsibility of all members. All the group's decisions concerning the answers to problems being studied are made by consensus. All the criteria for effective groups are met.

Many discussion groups never reach this stage. Either the coordinator does not have the skills to establish the cooperative interdependence within the group or the group members do not have the group skills needed to function maturely. To establish an autonomous, productive, and mature discussion group, the coordinator manages each previous stage of development competently while at the same time ensures that members are mastering the group skills they need in order to interact effectively.

## Terminating

The life of every group is finite. The learning group eventually ends and the members go their separate ways. The more mature and cohesive the learning group, and the stronger the emotional bonds that have been formed among group members, the more potentially upsetting the termination period is. The ending of the group may be painful for members and the coordinator alike. Nevertheless, group members deal with the problems of separating so that they can leave the group experience behind them and move on to new experiences.

## Length of Each Stage

Not all stages last the same amount of time. Many groups move very quickly through the first five stages, spend considerable time functioning maturely, and then terminate quickly. The average amount of time discussion groups tend to spend in each stage is presented in Figure 10.1.

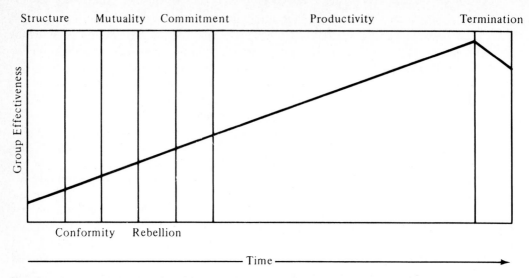

**FIGURE 10.1** Stages of Group Development

## Summary

The coordinator of a discussion group must, therefore, (1) introduce, define, and structure the learning group; (2) clarify procedures, reinforce members for conforming to the procedures, and help members become acquainted; (3) emphasize and highlight the cooperative interdependence among group members and encourage their engaging in both trusting and trustworthy behaviors; (4) accept the rebellion by and differentiation among group members as a normal process and use confrontation and constructive negotiation to help members establish their independence from each other and the prescribed procedures; (5) facilitate the members' committing themselves to and taking ownership for the group's goals, procedures, and other members; (6) be a consultant to the group providing needed material and informational resources for the group to function effectively; and (7) signal termination and help the members move on to future groups.

Another view of the coordinator's role is contained in the next section. There are a number of basic procedures the coordinator of a discussion group needs to carry out in building a productive group. These procedures further clarify the role of the coordinator.

## CHANGE OF OWNERSHIP FROM COORDINATOR TO GROUP MEMBERS

For a discussion group to be successful, the group members must commit themselves to the goals and procedures of the group. Group members need to come to believe that it is *their* goals the group is working toward and it is *their* procedures the group is using. The group members will then believe that it is *their* success when they are productive. The "changing of hands" of perceived ownership of goals and procedures from coordinator to group members is a gradual process that takes place as the group matures. Very briefly, during the first two stages the goals and procedures are basically the coordinator's, as the coordinator explains the goals and procedures of the discussion group and reinforces group members for engaging in appropriate task and maintenance action. When group members begin to recognize their mutuality and build trust the changing of hands begins. The rebellion is an essential aspect of the group members beginning to restate the goals and procedures in their terms and take ownership for them. Through the final three stages the group members perceive the group's goals and procedures as being essentially theirs, not the coordinator's.

## BASIC PROCEDURES FOR STRUCTURING DISCUSSION GROUPS

In conducting productive group discussions, the coordinator must follow certain basic procedures. These procedures ensure that the group is structured cooperatively and that the members have the needed group skills to function effectively. Many times learning groups are assumed to be cooperative when they are not. Cooperation is *not* having participants sit side by side and exchange comments as they learn. A learning group is *not* cooperative if members are instructed to learn on their own and help the slower members. Cooperation is *not* having group members share materials before a competitive examination. Cooperation is much more than being physically near other persons, discussing material with other members, helping other members, or sharing materials with other members, although each of these is an important aspect of cooperative learning.

The essence of cooperative learning is assigning a *group goal*, such as a single product (for example, answers to a single set of math problems, or a single report) or as high a group average on an examination as possible, and rewarding the entire group on the basis of the quality or quantity of their product according to a fixed standard of excellence. The coordinator, in other words, establishes a group goal and a criteria-referenced evaluation system and rewards group members on the basis of their group performance. The procedures for structuring an effective learning group are as follows.

### Specify Objectives

As far as possible, the coordinator must specify the objectives for the learning group.

### Select the Appropriate Group Size

The number of participants in a learning group has several important consequences for the success of the group. Optimum group size depends on the group's tasks, the composition of its members, the time available, the level of interpersonal and group skills of the members, and many other factors. Some of the more important effects of increasing group size are as follows (Johnson, 1980a):

1. As the size of the group increases, the total resources of the group increase, but not the usable resources. The range of abilities, expertise, and skills available to the group increases with an increase in group size, as well as the sheer number of "hands" available for acquiring and processing information. The usable resource per member, however, will often increase at a slower rate than the total resources and will often not increase at all beyond a certain point. Adding a new member to a group of three will have more impact, for example, than adding a new member to a group of 30.
2. As the size of the group increases, the heterogeneity of members increases. The probability that any given characteristic will appear increases as the size of the group increases, but the probability that all members have a given characteristic decreases as the size of the group increases.
3. As the size of the group increases, the opportunity for individual participation and reward decreases. The larger the group, the less opportunity each member has to participate in a discussion, the greater the feelings of threat and the greater the inhibition of impulses to participate, and the more a few members will dominate.
4. As the size of the group increases, the more members' energy must be directed toward coordinating and assembling the contributions of the individual members.
5. As the size of the group increases, the less liked, supported, and valued individual members will be, and the greater the absenteeism, formality, conflict, and dissatisfaction with the group. The larger the group, the less the interpersonal regard among members may become.
6. As the size of the group increases, the clarity of members' perceptions of each other's degree of mastery of the material being learned will decrease.

Taken in its entirety, the evidence concerning group size indicates that the optimal size of learning groups might be from four to six members. Such a group is large enough to ensure diversity and a variety of resources, and small enough that everyone's resources will be utilized and everyone will participate and receive rewards for his and her contributions. In a group of this size the energy needed to coordinate members' contributions is minimized, acceptance and support among members are highlighted, and the achievement level of each member is perceived by other group members. When group members are very young, however, or when there is a marked lack of the interpersonal and group skills necessary for working productively with others, pairs or triads may be more productive than larger groups.

## Assign Participants to Groups

Usually, the coordinator will wish to maximize the heterogeneity of learning groups. Although the research findings are not consistent, the overall weight of the evidence indicates that higher achievement by high-, medium-, and low-performing participants will result when they are placed in heterogeneous learning groups (Johnson, 1980a). Randomly assigning participants to groups usually ensures sufficient heterogeneity among members.

## Arrange the Room

The design and arrangement of space and furniture in a room affects the learning of group members in two ways (Johnson, 1979). First, they communicate a symbolic message of what is expected. The way in which chairs are arranged, for example, is a message to participants: Chairs in a row communicate a different message and expectation from chairs grouped in small circles. Second, room design can directly facilitate or interfere with learning. The way in which interior space is designed affects opportunities for social contact, patterns of participation in learning activities, patterns of communication among group members and between group members and the coordinator, the feelings (such as well-being, enjoyment, comfort, anger, and depression) of group members and the coordinator, the friendship patterns within the group, the ease of transition from one learning activity to another, the amount of time group members spend actually learning, the general morale of group members, the emergence of leadership, and the achievement of group members.

The design of the room is a tool that the coordinator can use to facilitate participant learning. In order to do so, the coordinator needs to know how to

1. Define patterns of work and social interaction through spatial arrangement, graphics, color, and physical boundaries.
2. Utilize physical arrangements to maximize learning.
3. Visually focus group members' attention on the coordinator, each other, or instructional materials, depending on the specific task.
4. Control levels of noise in the room.
5. Design patterns of circulation that will enable group members to have access to the social and material resources needed for learning.

Each of these factors is discussed in detail in Johnson (1979). In general, the coordinator will wish to cluster learning groups in such a way that they will not interfere with each other's functioning. Within the groups, members should be able to see the relevant materials, converse with each other, and exchange materials and ideas. Usually a circle is best; long or large tables should be avoided.

## Distribute Materials

Materials need to be distributed among group members in such a way that all members participate and master the assignment. When a group is mature and experienced, and when group members have a high level of group and interpersonal skills, the coordinator may not have to arrange materials in any special way. When a group is new or when group members are not very skilled, there are at least three ways in which a coordinator may arrange and distribute materials to group members:

1. The coordinator may arrange the material like a jigsaw puzzle and give each group member one piece (Aronson, Blaney, Stephan, Sikes, & Snapp, 1978). A learning group, for example, could be writing a report on Abe Lincoln, each group member having material on a different part of his life. For the report to be completed, all group members will have to contribute their material and make sure it is incorpo-

rated into the report. Many of the exercises in Chapter 4 are set up in a jigsaw manner.

2. The material may be structured as a controversy. Several of the controversy exercises in Chapter 7 are structured so that they may be used by learning groups. Because controversies were described in detail in that chapter, they will not be discussed here.

3. The materials may be structured in a game format and a tournament conducted among learning groups to see which group can learn the material the best and perform the best in the game. A procedure for developing instructional games is given by DeVries and Edwards (1973). They call their approach to structuring materials "Teams-Games-Tournament."

By arranging materials as a jigsaw puzzle or as a controversy, the coordinator creates a positive dependence of group members on each other for the information needed to complete the task. This resource interdependence of members ensures their collaboration.

## Assign Roles

Cooperative interdependence may also be arranged through the assignment of complementary and interconnected roles to group members. One group member, for example, could be assigned the role of reading the assigned material to the entire group, another member could be assigned the role of recording the group's answers, another member could be given the role of making sure that all members actively participate, and another member could be given the role of making sure all group members understand and can explain the group's answers. The assignment of such roles creates a role interdependence among group members that ensures their collaboration. Through the division of labor created by the assignment of interdependent roles, group members become cooperatively interdependent and must work on the achievement of the group's goals together.

## Explain the Cooperative Goal Structure and the Task

The task may be the successful completion of an assignment in any subject area. To explain the cooperative goal structure the coordinator will need to communicate that there is a group goal and a criteria-referenced evaluation system and that all the group members will be rewarded on the basis of the quality of the group's work. The group goal answers the question "Why do I have to work cooperatively with other group members?" The goal needs to be set carefully with statements such as "I want only one set of answers from each group" or "Help each other with the spelling words because your score is the number of words the four of you spell correctly." Because Chapter 3 contains considerable discussion of the cooperative goal structure, we will not examine that topic here.

If there is more than one learning group, the coordinator may wish to structure intergroup cooperation by stating that bonus points will be awarded if all the groups reach a certain criterion of learning. It is also important that group members be able to receive accurate feedback on the level of their individual achievement. In this way the members and the group as a whole know who to give added assistance and support to. Individual accountability is an important aspect of cooperative learning.

It is often helpful to describe five or six cooperative actions expected of group members while they work together. "Make sure everyone in the group knows the material and can explain the rationale," "Make sure all group members participate actively and have their say," and "Argue your point of view and don't change your mind unless you are logically persuaded" are examples of reminders that group members need from time to time. It is also a good idea to let group members know you are going to be watching for specific cooperative actions while they work together.

## Observe and Monitor the Behavior of Group Members

Just because the coordinator instructs group members to cooperate with each other does not mean that they will always do so. Much of the coordinator's time in cooperative learning situations is spent observing group members in order to see what problems they are having in working collaboratively. This book contains a variety of observation instruments and procedures that can be used for this purpose.

It is the monitoring and processing procedures that often motivate group members to engage in appropriate social skills while they are working together. The coordinator should keep in mind what member actions are to be observed, what observation and recording system he or she will use, and how the information gathered will be discussed and processed by group members.

## Intervene to Teach Needed Group Skills

At times the coordinator becomes a consultant to the group in order to help it function more effectively. When it is obvious that group members lack certain group and interpersonal skills that they need in order to cooperate with each other, the coordinator will want to intervene in order to help the members learn these social skills. These skills, along with activities that may be used in teaching them, are covered throughout this book and in Johnson (1986, 1987b). The specific process of teaching social skills is discussed in Chapter 2.

## Evaluate the Quality and Quantity of Group Productivity

The quality and quantity of the learning of group members needs to be evaluated, by a criteria-referenced system. The procedures for setting up and using such an evaluation system are given in Johnson and Johnson (1987b).

The product required from the group may be a report, the average of individual examination scores, or a single set of answers that all the group members agree to. One procedure that is effective in ensuring that all group members master the assigned material is the cooperative-test procedure to ensure that all group members understand the basic concepts in the chapter.

### Assess How Well the Group Functioned

After the learning of the group members is evaluated, it is necessary to discuss how effectively the members worked together. At this point the results of the coordinator's monitoring should be communicated to the group members and discussed by them. The more precise the feedback given to each group member and the more thorough the group processing of the coordinator's observations, the more effectively the group will function next time. Often it is also helpful to have one member of the group observe each group session so that both the coordinator's and the member's observations can be discussed and used to improve the effectiveness of the group.

One important aspect of group life to discuss in the processing sessions is group maintenance. Groups are often exclusively task oriented. Group sessions should be enjoyable, lively, and pleasant experiences. If no one is having fun, something is wrong. One of the major functions of controversy is to spark more involvement and enjoyment in a discussion. Group cohesion should be increasing with each session. Processing aspects of group functioning related to group maintenance usually improves the effectiveness of the group.

Another aspect of group life to assess is the attendance and preparation of group members. Members should attend a learning group regularly and come prepared. A productive group discussion is one in which members are present and prepared to discuss the material; only then can their resources be used fully. Absenteeism and lack of preparation, moreover, often demoralize other members. The greater the cooperativeness of group members, the more they will encourage and support each other's attendance and preparation.

Regular assessing of group's functioning should be accepted as an integral part of group functioning. A productive group is one that realizes that there will be process problems and is willing to evaluate its progress in managing these problems effectively. By assessing the group's functioning members learn what they must do to improve it and they gain a better understanding of how and when to contribute to its needs. Group skills, in other words, are improved through the processing of the coordinator's observations.

Finally, regular processing sessions facilitate the development of the group to higher levels of maturity.

## THE COORDINATOR'S ROLE: FINAL NOTES

For every discussion group there is usually a designated leader, or coordinator. Often this person is the teacher or the educator in charge of the instructional program. The responsibilities of such a person are hard to define specifically because he or she needs to promote a process in which a group or persons learn from their discussion and interaction with one another. Some of the coordinator's responsibilities are to introduce the discussion session, to be a task-oriented timekeeper who keeps the group moving so that it does not get sidetracked or bogged down, to restate and call attention to the main ideas of the discussion so that learning is focused, to promote a

climate of acceptance, openness, warmth, and support to facilitate learning, and to know when to provide a sense of closure.

Although all group members are responsible for behaving in ways that help one another learn, the coordinator may be more qualified than most other members to use four particular types of helpful behaviors. The first is the instructional behavior of resource expert. In most cases the coordinator will best know the materials, information, and readings that are most relevant and helpful for the group. Her second type of helpful behavior is that of a teacher—teaching the members of the group skills they need to function effectively in a discussion group. The coordinator may hold skill sessions in which members are given practice in fulfilling different functions in the group, or in which she makes periodic evaluations of the present functions and those needed to improve the quality of the group's performance. The third behavior is that of a process observer. As such, the coordinator must not only diagnose the present functioning of the group but also intervene in the group in ways that improve its effectiveness. The observation skills the coordinator needs in order to diagnose group effectiveness and questionnaires helpful in gathering members' perceptions of current group functioning are presented in previous chapters of this book. The intervention skills the coordinator needs in order to improve group functioning are also covered in previous chapters.

Finally, the coordinator may be the keeper of the group's physical structure. It is the discussion leader who will check to see that the group is sitting fairly close together in a circle without tables or desks between members, in a comfortable, pleasant room—perhaps with refreshments. This task is a vital part of promoting a productive session, for the physical setting can do much to help or obstruct learning in a discussion group.

In addition to these responsibilities, there are other ways in which a coordinator can assist the group. During the single discussion session the coordinator can be helpful, for example, in (1) beginning a discussion session, (2) keeping it going, and (3) ending it. As we have seen, in the early part of a session members are usually concerned about what is expected of them and what the goals of the session are. Group members also need to know clearly the coordinator's responsibilities and why he or she is there. Coordinators never want to be in the position of having all group maintenance and goal accomplishment left up to them. One of the easiest ways to make sure that all members will fulfill the responsibilities expected of them is to have the coordinator's role well defined.

Another part of beginning a discussion is setting a helpful climate. As we have noted, group members will not "open up" until they feel secure in expressing their attitudes and ideas and know they won't be ignored, ridiculed, criticized, or otherwise embarrassed by the other group members. Some of the ways in which a coordinator can promote a free and friendly climate are by helping members become better acquainted; dispensing with unnecessary formalities, such as raising hands for permission to speak; listening attentively to what each group member is saying; not evaluating the contributions of members or commenting on every contribution made; ruling out preaching, teaching, and moralizing; and avoiding forcing members into participation before they are ready.

A good discussion leader is prepared with several questions and stimulating comments for beginning a discussion, though she should not be in a hurry to use them. One of the critical points in a discussion group's development is freeing the members from dependence upon the coordinator's ideas and direction. Silence, therefore, should not disturb the coordinator. Many a discussion never got started because the coordinator didn't stop talking long enough for the group to "pick up the ball."

During the discussion the coordinator should help establish norms of participation by all members, model good communication skills, promote member-to-member interaction, and maintain the group's direction and agenda. He or she can encourage productive participation by watching the signs of a member's efforts to be heard and giving that person an opportunity to contribute; by being wary of those too eager to talk, as they can monopolize all the group's time; by encouraging and supporting all members who participate; by summarizing and clarifying the contributions; and by not dominating the discussion or commenting too frequently. Above all, a coordinator should show enthusiasm for the discussion and a sincere interest in the group members.

Often in a discussion group one member will obstruct the functioning of the group. And almost as often the other members will not be able to solve the problem constructively: they either support the obstructor or reject him—both of which are undesirable. The coordinator, then, may have to intervene if the situation is to be handled productively. The skills in handling interpersonal conflicts are discussed in Chapters 7 and 8 in this book and in Johnson (1986). The important point for the group to remember in such a situation is that the conflict must be processed, negotiated, and resolved to everyone's satisfaction.

A coordinator needs to be concerned with how the meeting ends. A few minutes before the group discussion is scheduled to close, or when it appears that the group has exhausted the subject, the session can be concluded with a summary of the significant points by a member or the coordinator. This summary should be brief, but it should not be a last-minute statement given to the tune of moving chairs and scuffling feet. The summary is vital because it leaves the group with a sense of achievement, it clarifies group thinking, and it tests the conclusions of the summarizer against those of other group members. After the summary the group should evaluate how it has functioned as a group. Finally, the coordinator may express his or her appreciation to the group. If the group is to meet again, the coordinator may wish to explain where and when. And if a final report is required, it should be presented before the fine points of the discussion are forgotten.

# 11

# Leading Growth and Counseling Groups

## INTRODUCTION

In the past 20 years there has been an explosion in people's participation in growth groups. It is estimated that over 5 million Americans have at one time or another participated in some type of group activity aimed at personal growth or change. Several million more are members of self-help groups, and tens of thousands have participated in counseling and psychotherapy groups. Special group experiences have been designed to help improve marriages, to bridge the gap between parents and children, to strengthen the communion and unity that have characterized religious organizations in the past, to help people handle conflict more constructively, and to increase people's ability to meditate, "center," and communicate through touch. Training in human relations has become mandatory for potential teachers, and intercultural experiences between minorities and whites are frequently offered as a means of improving teaching and cross-cultural relations. There are sensitivity groups, encounter groups, confrontation groups, personal growth groups, strength groups, consciousness-raising groups, and such a variety of other groups that no one can keep up with current labels. All such groups are generally referred to as **growth groups** in this book. With such a demand for small-group experiences, and with such an expansion in the types of group experiences available, it is difficult to conceive of a book on groups that does not cover growth groups.

To be an effective growth-group leader a person needs to (1) understand the unique powers of group experiences, (2) understand the events within groups that promote participant change and growth, (3) understand the goals of growth groups, and (4) perform competently a certain set of skills needed to lead a growth group. Each of these aspects of facilitating personal growth in a group context will be discussed in this chapter. We shall also discuss how one becomes a group facilitator and how the feelings, intuition, and conceptual frameworks of growth-group leaders are related.

## THE SOCIAL SKILLS BASIS OF PERSONAL GROWTH

Jane is a college sophomore who lives in a dorm. She is seeking to participate in a growth group because of her shyness. After a year and a half of college she has made only one friend and finds it hard to talk even to her roommate. Jane is very anxious about approaching others, and she lacks the small-group and interpersonal skills she needs in order to interact effectively with others. A social skills training approach would focus on teaching Jane how to initiate a conversation, how to show interest in another person, and how to build and maintain a relationship. The existence of Jane's anxiety is not ignored, but instead of focusing only on reducing the anxiety a growth group leader assumes that the anxiety will decrease as Jane acquires more effective skills in relating to others.

Most participants enter growth groups hoping to develop or refine certain skills in relating to others. It is their interpersonal interactions that have led them to depression, anger, anxiety, guilt, capriciousness, and other conflictive feelings. If they could resolve their conflicts with others, influence others in the ways they wish, or manage their feelings constructively, they would do so. Through either a lack of small-group and interpersonal skills or an inability to utilize the social skills they have, participants seek the help of a growth group.

It is our interpersonal relationships that provide the warmth, caring, support, and collaboration that give life its excitement and potential for joy and personal fulfillment. And it is in these relationships that both the origin of and the solution to participants' problems can usually be found. Psychological health can be defined as the ability of a person to build and maintain cooperative relationships with family, neighbors, friends, and fellow employees (Johnson, 1979, 1980b). The quality of one's relationships depends largely on one's interpersonal competence. Interpersonal and small-group skills form the basic nexus between the individual and others, and if participants are to cope with the stresses, strains, and conflicts involved in building and maintaining productive and fulfilling relationships, they must have a modicum of these skills. The underlying purpose of most growth groups, therefore, is to help participants achieve some kind of behavioral and cognitive change that increases their competence in managing their interpersonal relationships so that they can lead more productive, self-enhancing, and fulfilling lives. The advantages of and procedures for increasing one's interpersonal and small-group skills in a growth group form the body of this chapter.

## THE UNIQUE POWERS OF GROUP EXPERIENCES

Some persons seek isolation and privacy while they try to think through their problems and decide how they are going to improve their relationships. Others seek out a friend or a counselor and discuss their problems and plans in a dyad. Groups, however, have several unique advantages over solitary contemplation and dyadic discussion for those who want to grow, develop, and change. These unique capacities of groups are as follows.

1. Groups provide a more heterogeneous social setting in which interpersonal skills may be learned, mastered, and integrated into one's behavioral repertoire. Whereas in a dyad only one relationship has to be maintained, in a group several relationships have to be maintained and increased concern about rejection and exclusion for inappropriate behavior may result. In a dyad there is acceptance by only one person; in a group there may be acceptance by many persons. Different persons provoke different feelings and reactions, and in a group more feelings and reactions are generated. In a dyad there is one person to compare oneself with; in a group there are several. The greater number of relationships available in the group provide a richness and potential for learning not possible in a dyad or a solitary situation.

2. Groups generate a sense of community, belonging, support, acceptance, and assistance that eases the pain associated with therapeutic exploration and encourages risk taking in achieving growth goals (Lieberman, Lakin, & Whitaker, 1968). Groups offer a member acceptance by a number of persons, no matter what the member's history or behavior outside of the group. They provide the supportive climate that permits members to take risks and to reveal themselves. They provide the public esteem and acceptance that form the basis for increased self-esteem and self-acceptance. Members' confidence in their ability to grow and change may increase as they feel their groupmates become committed to assist and support them in doing so.

3. Groups influence the behavioral and attitudinal patterns of members. A

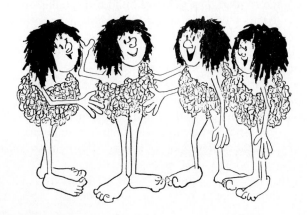

group is able to influence its members in a variety of ways beyond what one other person in a dyad can do. Social pressure to engage in more constructive behavior is greater in a group setting, the social approval of a number of persons is a more powerful reward than the social approval of one person, the authenticating affirmation of one's peers is more powerful than that of one person, and the threat of expulsion by a whole group is more powerful punishment than the threat of expulsion by one person. Within a group there are group norms that members will be influenced to conform to, and in a growth group the norms will encourage growth and the mastery of more constructive ways of behaving and thinking. Within a group there are a number of persons to identify with and imitate, whereas in a dyad there is only one.

4. Groups may induce and then reduce powerful feelings (Lieberman, Lakin, & Whitaker, 1968). Growth groups provide an environment in which participants may experience previously terrifying feelings with a new sense of acceptance. By finding that the previously feared feelings are not overwhelming or that the feared consequences do not occur, the participant has a corrective emotional experience. The wider variety of persons and the more diverse interpersonal events that take place within a group enable the group to induce more powerful emotions. Yet the support and acceptance within the group makes it likely that the emotions will not be completely overwhelming or terrorizing. The experiencing and discussing of the emotions in a supportive and caring environment usually reduce them and decrease their influence on the participant's future behavior and thinking.

5. Groups require the use of a wide variety of interpersonal skills and competencies. While contemplating problems by oneself, there are no interpersonal skills being used. Discussing problems with one person requires some interpersonal skills, but discussing problems and trying out new behaviors in a group requires a far broader range of interpersonal skills and competencies. Listening to others discuss their problems and helping them experiment with more constructive ways of behaving and thinking requires skills and competencies that may never be apparent in a dyadic relationship.

6. Groups provide opportunities for participants to understand and help their peers. In helping other group members to understand their destructive behavior and attitudinal patterns and facilitating their experimentation with more constructive ways of behaving and thinking, participants build self-esteem, self-insight, and increased interpersonal competence. Helping others is also an important opportunity for altruistic behavior that may be absent from their daily lives. By working to understand others in the group and by caring for the personal struggles that other members are going through, participants gain in a variety of ways.

7. Groups provide a variety of perspectives that stimulate insight into and understanding of one's problems and behavior. By providing labels for the participant's thoughts, feelings, and experiences and by helping the participant reflect on his interactions with them, the other group members help him understand his actions. A group adds to any insight achieved by a member through its consensual validation of the insight.

8. Groups provide sources of comparison for participants (Lieberman, Lakin, & Whitaker, 1968). Members of growth groups often compare their attitudes

toward their parents, spouses, children, and friends; their feelings about events within the group; the things that make them sad, happy, guilty, and angry; the ways each member typically deals with and expresses anger and affection; and so on. Such comparisons occur naturally within a group and facilitate possible new ways of feeling, perceiving, and behaving.

9. Groups provide a variety of sources of feedback (Lieberman, Lakin, & Whitaker, 1968). Within a group a person is provided the opportunity to engage in behavior or express observations and feelings, note the consequences of doing so, and hear from other members about his or her impact on them. In a group setting, participants can test their behavior and seek feedback from a variety of persons.

10. Groups provide a remedial environment for the solution of problems. It is within relationships that problems develop and people learn maladaptive patterns of thinking and behaving. A growth group enables participants to work on their problems immediately within a remedial environment. Besides understanding their problems, participants may take immediate corrective steps in their relationships with other members.

11. Groups provide the constructive peer relationships needed for healthy social and cognitive development (Johnson, 1980b). Peer relationships are an absolute necessity for healthy development, and group settings provide access to constructive relationships that may be absent in participants' lives.

## EVENTS THAT PROMOTE PARTICIPANT CHANGE

Within growth groups there are a series of events that promote participant change (Lieberman, 1980). Some of these events directly promote change; others reduce blocks to change. The events are as follows.

1. Change is promoted by the emotional expression of positive and negative feelings toward other group members and about important life events. Participants may express feelings toward other group members. They may also express feelings that they had previously blocked and thereby unburden themselves of an emotional restraint. If participants do not feel free to express positive and negative feelings such as caring and anger in the group, their ability to learn from each other and from their experiences in the group is markedly reduced. Unless participants are free to express both negative and positive feelings toward each other openly and directly, the road to change will be blocked.

2. Change is promoted by the experiencing of intense positive and negative emotions, whether or not they are expressed. Events within the group may unleash feelings certain participants have been previously unable or unwilling to experience. As we have seen, participants may find that such feelings are not overwhelming or that the feared consequences do not occur. Thus, a corrective emotional experience may result even when the feelings are not overtly expressed. Participants may learn a new acceptance of feelings they were previously afraid of.

3. Change is promoted by the observation of other group members having

significant emotional experiences. Participants often have beneficial experiences by observing other members having corrective emotional experiences. Other members' emotional experiences may clarify issues for a participant, who may then make use of the experiences in his or her own problematic areas.

4. Change is promoted by the inculcation of hope and a decrease in demoralization. To be demoralized is to be disheartened, bewildered, confused, disordered, and deprived of courage. The demoralized participant feels isolated, hopeless, and helpless. Group situations can generate events that inspire hope in participants, feelings that one can change, and beliefs that one can influence the causes of one's problems. Seeing other members in the group who have successfully grappled with problems or who have changed as a result of their participation in the group is one such event.

5. Change is promoted by the decrease in participants' egocentrism and the increase in their perspective-taking abilities. Through exchanges of ideas about problems and solutions within a context where participants feel understood and accepted, participants will be more aware of and open to other perspectives. Group leaders may also structure perspective-reversal situations in which participants switch positions and argue each other's point of view or take the perspective of a significant person outside of the group, such as a mother, boss, or spouse.

6. Change is promoted by self-disclosure, the realization that others have similar feelings, and insight into one's problems. In growth groups self-disclosure consists of the explicit communication of information (a) that a participant believes other group members would be unlikely to acquire unless she told it to them and (b) that she considers so highly private that she would exercise great caution regarding whom she told it to. Self-disclosure to a group of peers is quite different from self-disclosure to one other person. It feels less dramatic and is a less anxiety-laden action to reveal private information to a single person than to a group. The significance of self-disclosure is not what is disclosed, but rather the response of other members to what one has said. The therapeutic and growth value of self-disclosure lies in the sense of well-being, the trust and confidence in other human beings, and the acceptance by other members that one obtains after disclosing anxiety-producing information to the group and receiving a caring and supportive response from the other members. Self-disclosure can be cathartic when participants discover that no one is shocked by their deeply hidden secrets that have always made them feel ashamed, guilty, depressed, or angry. When several members of a group engage in self-disclosure on similar problems, they feel considerable relief when they discover that they are not the only ones who have reacted the way they have and who experience the feelings they do. There are times when discovering the similarities in their experiences, reactions, actions, and feelings reassures participants that they are normal. Finally, the disclosure of anxiety-producing information to a group facilitates the achievement of insight into one's problems and the dynamics of the situations being discussed.

In summary, self-disclosure helps provide participants with insight into their problems as they organize and think through their experiences in order to share them with others. It creates a sense of relief when participants discover that their problems are not unique and that they are not inherently evil for feeling and behaving as they do. It releases and frees one from anxiety-producing feelings when no one is shocked or horrified by them. Finally, self-disclosure that results in understanding and acceptance by others promotes a sense of personal well-being and trust in others.

7. Change is promoted by experimentation with new behavior and by feedback received from others. The availability of immediate information about how one is perceived by peers is unique to the group situation. There seems to be a basic human need to know how one stands with one's peers and how one is perceived by others. The feedback participants receive from other group members is an important ingredient in increasing their self-awareness and self-esteem. The nature and the value of constructive feedback is discussed at length in Johnson (1990) and Johnson (1978). Along with feedback, growth groups offer participants the opportunity to experiment with new patterns of behavior under low-risk conditions. Having experimented with new behavior patterns in the group, the participants will feel able to engage in the new behaviors in the outside world. Participants must feel that the group setting is safe enough for them to try out new ways of behaving, and they must identify problem areas and new ways of behaving in order to experiment with new behaviors. Feedback is a vital part of experimentation, for the participants need to find out how other members perceive the effectiveness of the new behavioral patterns they are trying out.

8. Change is promoted by other group members modeling constructive behavior and attitude patterns the participants wish to master. One of the best ways to learn new patterns of behaving and thinking is seeing them demonstrated by others. An important element of change, and of the maintaining of changes, is the internalization of how other participants and the group leader would have handled problem situations. Observing others use specific competencies to solve problems and relate more effectively to others can lead to considerable reflection and the discovery of alternative ways to achieve a goal.

9. Change is promoted by cognitive insight into one's problems, behavior patterns, and attitude patterns. Both increased understanding of oneself and the conscious implementation of interpersonal skills depend on cognitive learning. In their classic study of growth groups Lieberman, Yalom, and Miles (1973) found that it was self-disclosure involving some sort of cognitive mastery or understanding—not self-disclosure in and of itself—that was related to positive change. Many types of growth groups emphasize the learning of specific cognitive skills and frameworks as part of positive change.

## ESTABLISHING THE GOALS OF A GROWTH GROUP

When participants join a growth group both they and the group's leader have a set of goals for the group. The participants may wish to improve the state of their feelings or find a more meaningful career. The leader may wish to improve the participants' general interpersonal functioning, or even teach growth dynamics. Assuming that the goals of the participants and those of the group leader do not completely overlap, the two must negotiate a set of goals that they can mutually commit themselves to achieving. When participants and the leader have different goals, the goals may initially be cooperative (working to achieve the participants' goals facilitates the accomplishment of the leader's goals, and vice versa) or competitive (working to achieve the participants' goals interferes with the accomplishment of the leader's goals, and vice versa). For the growth group to be successful, the leader and the participants need to negotiate a set of cooperatively structured goals.

Some of the common goals that leaders of growth groups may have are (1) to facilitate participants' acquisition of self-enhancing patterns of attitudes and behaviors, (2) to facilitate participants' psychological health, (3) to increase participants' skills and competencies for creating humanizing relationships, (4) to increase participants' interpersonal effectiveness, and (5) to promote participants' self-actualization. Let's look briefly at each of these goals.

## Self-Enhancement

Many participants may have developed patterns of behaviors and attitudes that decrease their ability to build and maintain effective relationships with others. These patterns create and sustain negative and self-destructive consequences and ultimately lead to a more painful and troubled life. If a person has no opportunity to change, her self-defeating patterns of attitudes and behaviors will affect all aspects of her life. One of the goals of leaders of growth groups, then, is to help participants identify their self-defeating and self-destructive attitudinal and behavioral patterns and change them to **self-enhancing patterns.**

## Psychological Health

It is within interpersonal relationships that psychological illness or health is developed. **Psychological health** can be defined as the ability to be aware of and manage effectively one's cooperative interactions with others (Johnson, 1980b). To build and maintain the relationships so necessary for psychological health, individuals need to develop (Johnson, 1979)

1. A generalized interpersonal trust in the affection and support of others.
2. The perspective-taking abilities needed for an understanding of how a situation appears to another person and how that person is reacting cognitively and affectively.
3. A meaningful direction and purpose in life, a sense of "where I am going" that is valued by others and similar to the goals of the significant persons in one's life.
4. An awareness of meaningful cooperative interdependence with others.
5. An integrated and coherent sense of personal identity.

## Humanizing Relationships

**Humanizing relationships** reflect the qualities of kindness, mercy, consideration, tenderness, love, concern, compassion, responsiveness, and friendship. One goal of most group leaders is to create humanizing relationships within the group and to help participants build the competencies they need to form such relationships outside the group.

## Interpersonal Effectiveness

Interpersonal and group skills are based on a person's interpersonal effectiveness. **Interpersonal effectiveness** may be defined as the extent to which the consequences of a person's behavior match his intentions (Johnson, 1986). When two participants interact, for example, they have no choice but to make some impression on each other. When they make the impression they want, their interpersonal effectiveness is high; when they make an impression they do not want, their interpersonal effectiveness is low. All the group skills discussed in this book and the interpersonal skills discussed in Johnson (1990) are relevant to interpersonal effectiveness.

## Self-Actualization

**Self-actualization** may be defined as the psychological need for growth, development, and utilization of potential (Maslow, 1954). A self-actualizing participant will be moving toward the full use of her talents, capacities, and potentialities. Self-actualization involves both self-development and self-utilization: One develops potentialities and then uses them in order to actualize oneself.

# LEADING A GROWTH GROUP

Groups are uniquely suited to helping persons grow and change in constructive ways. As we have seen, a number of events may take place in a growth group that facilitate participant growth and help achieve the group's goals. But if these events are in fact to take place, the group leader needs several sets of complex skills:

1. Establishing the conditions for modifying participants' patterns of behavior and attitudes
2. Being a resource expert on how to learn and change within a group
3. Teaching needed interpersonal and small-group skills
4. Modeling the constructive use of small-group and interpersonal skills
5. Ensuring that members are provided with constructive confrontations and feedback
6. Helping define and diagnose the problems of participants
7. Making sure that members are provided with opportunities for self-disclosure and experimentation with new attitude and behavior patterns
8. Promoting corrective or reparative emotional experiences within the group
9. Engineering a problem-solving process with which participants can address their concerns
10. Negotiating changes in participants' patterns of attitude and behaviors
11. Engineering an effective group
12. Establishing and enforcing a contract with participants
13. Carrying out the executive functions of the group

Each of these sets of skills is discussed in turn.

## Establishing Conditions for Participant Change

This set of skills consists of establishing the conditions for change, helping partici-pants change, and then stabilizing the new and more appropriate patterns of behavior and attitudes. Establishing the conditions for change is discussed in detail in Johnson (1980b). These conditions are as follows:

1. A sufficient level of trust among group members to ensure that participants feel free to self-disclose, experiment with new patterns of thinking and behaving, and give and receive feedback. This includes a warm and supportive climate in which participants feel free to take risks.
2. A reduction of participants' egocentrism and the encouragement of their viewing problems and behavior patterns from a variety of perspectives.
3. A reduction of participants' demoralization and an increase in their sense of control and influence over themselves and their lives.
4. The promotion of positive identification by the participant with other members who have the skills and competencies she needs in order to solve the problems she is experiencing.

## Being a Resource Expert

An effective group leader must have the skills to act as a resource expert, an educator using inquiry and experiential methods, and a diagnoser of personal, interpersonal, and group dynamics. Any growth-group facilitator should be skilled in the use of inquiry and experiential methods of learning, a subject discussed in Chapters 1 and 2. Almost all types of growth groups emphasize inquiry into the experiences of the group members. This inquiry is usually based upon diagnoses of the personal, inter-personal, and group dynamics being experienced. To make such diagnoses, the facilitator applies a conceptual framework based upon theory and research to the behavior of the group members. And to apply such a framework, the facilitator must have expertise in one of the behavioral sciences, such as psychology or sociology. The presentation of conceptual frameworks enables members not only to gain insight into their behavior and their internal reactions to what occurs within the group, but to understand more fully the interpersonal and group dynamics they are involved in. Thus, a facilitator must have a solid knowledge of one of the behavioral sciences, an expertise in inquiry and experiential-learning methods, and the ability to use his knowledge and expertise to help the members understand what they are experienc-ing. Lieberman, Yalom, and Miles (1973) found that the most effective leaders had a great ability to present conceptualizations that gave meaning to the experiences the members were undergoing. This one ability was the most important variable in promoting member learning that they found in their study. Such conceptualizations are especially useful to members after the group experience has ended, when they are able to use them to understand more fully their day-to-day interpersonal and group situations. The conceptualizations presented in this book and in Johnson (1990) are examples of the types of conceptual frameworks a facilitator must be able to communicate to members.

## Teaching Group and Interpersonal Skills

One of the major keys to decreasing self-defeating behavior and increasing self-enhancing behavior is improving participants' group and interpersonal skills. It is often because participants lack social skills or are unable to utilize effectively the group and interpersonal skills they do have that they seek out a growth group to participate in. Improving participants' competency in and utilization of social skills can best be done in a group setting. In order to begin skill teaching growth-group leaders need to ask themselves questions such as these:

1. What are the group and interpersonal skills every person needs in order to function effectively in our society and lead a fulfilling and self-enhancing life? These skills are detailed in this book and in Johnson (1978, 1986, 1990).
2. What interpersonal and group skills are participants failing to utilize effectively?
3. What interpersonal and group skills do participants lack?
4. Will the learning and utilization of the apparently needed group and interpersonal skills reduce participants' self-defeating and self-destructive behavior and thinking and increase their ability to create for themselves a more productive, self-enhancing, and fulfilling life?

In some growth groups interpersonal and group skills are taught directly through exercises like the ones contained in this book. In other growth groups the skill building is conducted through reflection on members' interactions and relationships. Leading growth groups requires the capacity to facilitate the social-skill learning of the participants. Because such skill learning is discussed in depth in Chapters 1 and 2, it will not be discussed here.

## Modeling the Constructive Use of Social Skills

A fourth set of skills required of a facilitator consists of modeling the behaviors she hopes members will learn from their group experience. Social-learning theory (Bandura, 1969) emphasizes the importance of modeling desired behaviors and then reinforcing group members (for example, giving recognition and approval for imitating the facilitator); this procedure is probably the most effective way to teach new skills. The behaviors a facilitator may model are discussed in this book and in Johnson (1990). Such behaviors would include, for example, sending and receiving communications, self-disclosure, giving and receiving feedback, experimenting with alternative behaviors, and expressing acceptance and support for others. A willingness to model desired skills means that the facilitator will take an active part in interacting with other group members. Some research indicates that activeness on the part of the facilitator is to be preferred to passiveness (which, when it pertains to members, is associated with anxiety, dissatisfaction, silence, poor attendance, discontinuance, and lack of learning), except when the activeness turns into domination (Bierman, 1969). Peters (1966), in addition, found that members who imitate the facilitator learn more from growth groups than those who do not. Thus, the facilitator may want to be the "ideal member" in the group in order to promote members' skill development.

Finally, it should be noted that simply being an "authentic person" does not necessarily enable the facilitator systematically to present effective skills to be imitated by group members; a facilitator must be interpersonally effective in order to model desired skills.

## Providing Constructive Confrontations and Feedback

The facilitator must be able to make sure that members are provided with constructive feedback and confrontations. Helpful feedback is the sharing, upon request, of a description of how a person sees another person's behavior and its consequences, and a description of how the person is reacting to the other person's behavior. A confrontation is a deliberate attempt to help another person examine the consequences of some aspect of his or her behavior; it is an invitation to engage in self-examination. A confrontation originates from a desire to involve oneself more deeply with the person one is confronting, and it is intended to help the person behave in more fruitful or less destructive ways. The specific skills of feedback and confrontation are presented in Johnson (1990). The point to keep in mind when facilitating feedback and confrontations is the difference among the behavior being observed, the conceptual framework the observer is using, and the inferences and interpretations made about the person engaging in the behavior. A facilitator should never let group members confuse these three elements of giving feedback and confronting other members. The actual behavior being observed will be the same to all group members (assuming that the observations are valid), but the conceptual frameworks used to understand the behavior and to make interpretations and inferences about it can be widely disparate. Selling other group members on one interpretation of what is taking place is a much different activity from arriving at a consensus of what behavior is taking place.

## Defining and Diagnosing Participants' Problems

Creating meaning for participants by labeling feelings and events that they undergo and attributing meaning to experiences occurring within the group is a fundamental activity of leaders of growth groups. The increased understanding of participants resulting from such leader behavior reduces their fear and anxiety concerning emotional and interpersonal experiences and provides them with cognitive tools that they can use in becoming more effective persons. In helping participants understand their feelings and experiences, the leader must be careful about the way in which he or she attributes the causes of their problems and must pay attention to the resulting sense of personal control experienced by participants.

A participant's problems may be attributed to something within the participant (internal causation) or something outside of the participant (external causation). Causes may also be viewed as stable (incapable of change) or unstable (capable of change). Depending on the problem and the situation, a leader may wish to help the participant view a problem as having stable, external causes or unstable, internal causes. When a person is deeply depressed about a perceived failure, for example, the leader may wish to help that person focus on the external, unstable causes of the failure. But when he or she succeeds, the leader may wish to emphasize the internal, stable causes of the success in order to improve the person's self-esteem.

Participants' problems should usually be defined in ways that increase their sense of personal control in solving them. Most individuals seem to seek a sense of control over their lives. A belief that one is in control of one's life makes the world more predictable, and one tends to react more positively to the events that take place around oneself and the experiences one has. One of the reasons for severe depressions following major illnesses such as heart attacks is assumed to be the feeling that one has lost control over one's life (Glass, 1977). A belief in one's control over events affects performance on tasks (Glass & Singer, 1973), judgments of the pleasantness of one's surroundings and mood (Rodin, Solomon, & Metcalf, 1978), the positiveness of our reactions (Glass, 1977), how active, sociable, and vigorous we are (Langer & Rodin, 1976), and our general health and length of life (Rodin & Langer, 1977). The facilitator of a growth group will usually want to define and diagnose participants' problems in ways that maximize their sense of control over their lives.

Group leaders should also define participants' problems in ways that maximize their sense of freedom in solving them. Brehm (1966) has proposed the concept of psychological reactance to explain some of the reactions individuals have to a loss of control or freedom of choice. **Reactance** is a motivational state that is aroused whenever persons feel that their freedom has been abridged or threatened. Threats to personal freedom motivate persons to take actions that will help them regain their freedom and control. This motivation to regain freedom can be used to change self-defeating to self-enhancing patterns of attitudes and behavior. Being placed in a dependent position, on the other hand, can lead to a significant drop in later performance when one is asked to behave independently on one's own.

Confusion over their feelings and actions increases participants' anxiety and fear concerning their problems. A necessary skill of a growth-group leader, then, is to help participants apply to their actions and feelings, insights, and meaningful interpretations that will increase their sense of personal control and freedom.

## Ensuring Opportunities for Self-Disclosure and Experimentation

Many of the important experiences in growth groups come directly from participants' self-disclosures and experimentation with new patterns of thinking and behaving. An important function of the group leader, therefore, is to ensure that opportunities to do so are present in the group.

## Promoting Reparative Emotional Experiences

The facilitator needs to be able to promote corrective or reparative emotional experiences in the group. Highly personalized and relevant learning often arouses emotions—anxiety while the learning is taking place and happiness and satisfaction when it is achieved. To give and receive feedback, to confront and be confronted, to experiment with new behaviors, to bring out personal concerns to be problem solved—all promote considerable emotional reaction. High levels of warmth, anger, frustration, and anxiety are found in most growth-group experiences. A facilitator may stimulate emotional reaction by confronting group members, by supporting attempts to experiment with alternative behaviors, by promoting feedback and problem solving, by disclosing highly personal material about herself, and by expressing warmth and support for the members of the group. The most effective leaders in the Lieberman, Yalom, and Miles (1973) study engaged in a moderate amount of emotionally stimulating behavior. Though emotional experiences do not mean that learning will take place, genuine learning is often accompanied by emotionality. The facilitator needs to be certain that the members not only experience deep emotion but also are helped to look at the experience objectively, in such a way as to give it meaning for the future. She should emphasize reflection as well as experience and guide members in applying their present experiences. In managing the emotionality of the group, the facilitator must also moderately stimulate learning that arouses emotions and provide conceptualizations that will promote learning from emotional experiences.

## Engineering a Problem-Solving Process

Facilitators need to be able to engineer a problem-solving process with which participants can address their concerns. In such a problem-solving process it may be important to bring in information about the person's past behavior and feelings as well as his or her behavior and feelings in the group (Lieberman, Yalom, & Miles, 1973).

## Negotiating Changes in Participants' Patterns of Attitudes and Behaviors

Another set of skills for leaders of growth groups consists of helping participants clarify their current attitude and behavior patterns, determining how those patterns are affecting the participants' feelings and interactions with others, strengthening constructive patterns of attitudes and behaviors, and changing destructive patterns that lead to self-defeating cycles of behavior and cause such feelings as guilt, depression, anxiety, fear, anger, and resentment. Encouraging participants to actively take the perspectives of others with whom they are involved, communicating warmth and understanding, highlighting conflict between desired consequences and actual behavior and thinking, and initiating problem-solving discussions are all ways in which a group leader may facilitate participants' mastery of more self-enhancing patterns of attitudes and behaviors. For a more thorough discussion of these methods, see Johnson (1980b) and Johnson and Matross (1977).

## Engineering an Effective Group

The facilitator should be able to engineer an effective group. All the skills discussed in this book are useful here. Only in a growth group that is effective can the learning of members take place. The cohesion of the group; group norms that favor moderate emotional intensity, confrontation, and supportive peer control; the distribution of participation and leadership; the quality of communication; the management of conflict—these and all the other aspects of group effectiveness are extremely important for productive growth groups. A facilitator must be able to promote effective group behavior among the members.

### Establishing and Maintaining a Contract

It is sometimes useful for a facilitator to have a clear contract with participants concerning their responsibilities as group members. The contract might provide, for example, that members are (1) to be completely open to the group about both past and current behavior, (2) to take responsibility for themselves once they enter the group and not blame others or circumstances for their predicaments, and (3) to get involved with the other group members and cooperate in increasing their learning. When an explicit contract is made the facilitator becomes the "keeper of the contract" and should see to it that it is enforced.

### Carrying Out Executive Functions

Finally, a facilitator may have a variety of executive functions to carry out. Organizing the group, arranging for facilities in which it is to meet, providing it with needed materials, and conducting an evaluation of its success—all of which require a range of administrative and evaluative skills—may be the responsibilities of the facilitator.

## BECOMING A FACILITATOR

In the past two decades more and more persons have wanted to become qualified to conduct growth groups. One does not have to be a qualified growth-group facilitator to conduct inquiry- and experiential-learning activities. This book has organized material on group skills so that many different types of educational ventures can use it in the absence of a highly qualified staff. Yet being skilled in conducting inquiry- and experiential-learning activities does not mean that a person is qualified to conduct growth groups.

A person interested in being a facilitator should ask four basic questions. The first question is, "Do I have an adequate training in a behavioral science?" A facilitator should have a background in an applied behavioral science (such as social psychology) that places a heavy emphasis upon interpersonal relations and group dynamics. Ideally, one should have a basic knowledge of personality theory, psychopathology, group processes, and interpersonal dynamics. Ideally, the person should be connected with some organization, institution of higher education, or other agency that confirms his professional status. A serious commitment to growth groups should be part, but not all, of this person's professional activity. He or she should clearly know his or her intentions and goals as a facilitator, and he or she should understand all the ramifications of the client—facilitator relationship. A familiarity with the research on growth groups is also necessary.

The second question is, "How much experience have I had as a participant and a facilitator in growth groups?" Lakin (1972) recommends that before a person can legitimately function as a facilitator, he or she should have had a three-year training sequence something like this:

1. Participate as a member in at least two growth groups.
2. Observe group meetings of at least five growth groups and meet after the sessions with their facilitator to discuss the interactions of members and other relevant processes.
3. Co-lead five groups with experienced facilitators.
4. Lead five groups as sole facilitator, but be observed and discuss with the observer functioning in the facilitator role.
5. Undergo either psychotherapy or some equivalent sustained experiential self-study.
6. Be evaluated by well-qualified local facilitators who not only focus upon your general fitness of character and your preparation, but review with care evaluations others have made of you and their recommendations.
7. Keep up to date by periodically becoming involved in local seminars, supervision by more experienced professionals, and discussions of the ethics of the facilitator's role and function.

The third question is: "What is my personal level of sensitivity, self-awareness, self-understanding, and self-actualization?" No matter how much training a person has as a facilitator, if he or she is not self-aware and self-understanding, the person will not be able to resist indulging his or her own personal needs for such things as power and positive responses from participants. The personal qualities of sensitivity to and respect and liking for others are crucial for facilitators. Finally, Maslow (1962) states that a need-deficient person tends to see others in terms of the ways in which they can be of use; the self-actualized person, who is freer and more disinterested, is able to stand off and see others as they are—unique persons with their own problems who can be helped in various ways by various means.

The final question is: "Am I certified by a professional organization?" There are many professional organizations that to some extent certify members as being competent as growth-group facilitators. Also, many states license or certify practicing psychologists. A serious facilitator will take the time and trouble to become certified by a professional organization or licensed by his or her state.

## FEELINGS, INTUITION, AND CONCEPTUAL FRAMEWORKS

One major requisite of an effective facilitator is the ability to assess accurately his or her feelings, intuition, and conceptual frameworks. To a capable, well-trained, and experienced facilitator the three become integrated. Among poorly trained and inexperienced facilitators, feelings and intuition may be given a "mystical" sense of rightness and followed blindly as a form of emotional anarchy. Though this issue is closely related to the discussion of creativity in Chapter 7, it is important enough to be reviewed briefly at this point.

A person's feelings are great sources of information about what is happening within the group and what sorts of problems are occurring in the relationships among members. But feelings are not infallible. They are susceptible to bias, distortion, and misunderstanding, especially in situations where the person is threatened, defensive, anxious, or tense. Moreover, all people have their blind spots, and in certain situations, or under certain conditions, their feelings can be a reflection of their own fears and anxieties rather than of what is actually taking place in the group. It is important, therefore, for a facilitator to "calibrate" herself on the validity and reliability of her feelings in different situations, in response to different types of events, and under different conditions. When a person becomes highly emotional, she should be cautious about relying on the accuracy of her feelings, because it is then that they are most susceptible to distortion and bias. Understanding oneself and the potential causes of various feelings is important in learning to take action on the basis of one's intuitions and feelings.

Awareness of one's feelings and knowledge of the areas in which one can trust one's feelings lead to the issue of intuition as a base for judging what is taking place in the group and how and when to intervene in certain situations. Hunches often prompt a facilitator to intervene without his being able to explain the basis of its appropriateness. Intuition is a preconscious process: The person does not know quite how the conclusions or impulses were determined. Intuitive thinking characteristically does not advance in careful, well-defined steps: The person has an emotional and cognitive reaction to the total situation and arrives at an answer. He rarely can provide an adequate account of how the answer evolved, and he may be unaware of just what aspects of the problem situation he is responding to. Intuition results from an immersion in the group process and among the members, and from a strong identification with and empathy for what is occurring in the group. The greater the familiarity a person has with the issues that concern the group, the greater the likelihood of his intuitions being correct. A wide understanding of and acquaintance and empathy with both human nature and the nature of the group members will enhance one's intuition about the participants more than factual knowledge will. Experience in calibrating one's intuitive abilities is needed because one will find that one's intuition, like one's emotions, is sound on certain types of issues but misleading on others.

The overuse of intuition in leading growth groups has several short-comings. Facilitators who through lack of training or self-discipline do not have conceptual frameworks from the behavioral sciences or the skills to use such frameworks in gathering information about what is taking place in the group and among its members are ignoring these shortcomings. First, hunches often confuse observation with inference; a facilitator begins defending her intuitive inferences as if they were observations and facts. One cannot, for example, prove that a member is projecting his feelings into others. Second, facilitators may overrate the validity of their personal observations, believing them more accurate than the witnesses usually are. Research on rumors and testimony, for example, indicates that quite often eyewitnesses' perceptions, memory, and inferences are completely inaccurate even though the witnesses are convinced that they know exactly what happened. Third, the history of medicine and clinical psychology gives overwhelming evidence of the folly of treatments based upon intuition. For several centuries, for example, it was intuitively obvious not only that the insane were possessed by demons but that all diseases were in the blood and a sick person, therefore, could be cured by bleeding. What was intuitively obvious yesterday is often laughed at today. Fourth, the research on self-fulfilling prophecies indicates that people quite often engage in behavior that makes an originally false conclusion or perception become valid. Thus, a facilitator whose intuition is wrong may misunderstand a situation but set in action certain dynamics that create the very situation she is trying to correct but that confirm her original false intuition. A fifth shortcoming is that a person's intuitions give her no adequate basis for knowing whether they are accurate. The major fallacy in intuitive thought is not that it may be inaccurate (though we know that many hunches turn out to be mistaken); a person's intuitions may be quite accurate. It is rather that no basis exists for knowing if it is right or wrong. A facilitator who takes action on the basis of her intuition takes action before she can verify whether or not the action is appropriate. Finally, it must be recognized that intuition represents an internal logic based upon one's culture and frame of reference. Intuitive judgments about another culture or another frame of reference can be very misleading.

The need to use feelings and intuitions as a basis for action within the group, even though the dangers of doing so are recognized, reflects the necessity of conceptual frameworks and data-gathering skills that can be used to verify hunches. Facilitators must have the ability to clarify their intuitions to the degree that they are able to formulate hypotheses that can be verified or disproved. It is through conceptualizing what is happening within the group and among its members that the facilitator usually derives effective interventions. It is through the facilitator's communication of his conceptualizations, furthermore, that much of the learning of members takes place. Although facilitators vary in how much they rely on behavioral science conceptualizations and how much they rely on their feelings and intuitions, all have some conceptualization of what is taking place. One always has a set of assumptions from which to operate; the only question is how well formulated and explicit the conceptual framework is, and how systematically it is used to verify one's hunches.

A conceptual framework is nothing more than a way of looking at pieces of behavior in order to make some kind of sense out of them. Individual behaviors, when examined one by one, often have little or no value to the observer. When the pieces are conceptually connected, however, they become understandable and useful. The facilitator uses a conceptual framework to see the connections among and meaning of the individual behaviors of group members. All conceptualizations involve understanding relationships, grasping inherent meaning, or comprehending a structure. The value of conceptualization is that it provides an instrument for decision making. A facilitator is able to use her theoretical system to bring her interventions under rational control. She plans her actions in accordance with a system of related hypotheses rather than on the basis of an intuited procedure. The knowledge now available in the behavioral sciences provides facilitators with the means of organizing their perceptions, making observations systematically in order to promote member learning, checking out their hunches, and communicating their expertise to the members. There is no way to overemphasize the importance to facilitators of explicit conceptual schemes that they can use systematically in helping members learn from their experiences.

As with intuition, however, if facilitators use only their conceptualizations, their effectiveness may suffer. Their behavior in a group may become uncreative and overly structured. They may be pretending that the group is at a level of sophistication and knowledge that it is not, and they will be repressing their capacity for the kind of creativity that provides insights and alternative solutions to the problems the group faces. Though conceptual frameworks do help organize observations and do aid understanding and communication, they do not always help facilitators to draw upon the creativity they need in order to arrive at insights into members' behavior and put fire and zest into their own growth and actualization.

An effective facilitator should be aware of and accept his feelings. He should use them to spark his intuition about what is taking place in the group and among its members. He should also have expertise in using conceptual frameworks to verify hunches, to observe member behavior systematically, and to communicate with members in ways that facilitate their learning. Intuition and theory are both necessary and useful in generating effective interventions within a growth group. Neither should be slighted; neither should be overvalued when employed separately.

## GROWTH GROUPS AND PARTICIPANT ANXIETY

During the past 20 years there have been allegations that growth groups create levels of anxiety that are potentially damaging psychologically (Gottschalk, 1966). These allegations have not been supported by evidence. To determine how anxious college students are before and after participating in a growth group, Johnson, Kavanagh, and Lubin (1973), in two separate studies, compared the anxiety level of participants in a growth group with their anxiety level before and after taking a final examination in a course in group dynamics. They found that participant anxiety at the beginning of the growth group was less than that experienced before a final examination, and that participant anxiety after the growth group was over was considerably less than that experienced after a final examination. Participating in a growth group, then, seems less stressful than does taking course examinations.

# 12

# Team Development

## BASIC CONCEPTS TO BE COVERED IN THIS CHAPTER

In this chapter a number of concepts are defined and discussed. The major ones are listed below. The procedure for learning these concepts is as follows:

1. Divide into heterogeneous pairs.
2. The task for each pair is to
   a. Define each concept, noting the page on which it is defined and discussed.
   b. Ensure that both members of the pair understand the meaning of each concept.
3. Combine into groups of four. Compare the answers of the two pairs. If there is disagreement, the members look up the concept in the chapter and clarify it until they all agree on the definition and understand it.

### CONCEPTS

1. Organizational development
2. Organizational climate
3. Linking pin model of organizations
4. Team
5. Team building
6. Self-efficacy
7. Cohesion
8. Trust

# ORGANIZATIONAL DEVELOPMENT

> Our people's hard work is our most important resource.
>
> *Japanese management philosophy*

Team development typically takes place within organizations. It is one of several strategies used by organization development consultants to improve organizational functioning. For the past 20 years the area of organizational development has been steadily expanding in popularity. **Organizational development** is the use of diagnosis and intervention procedures to promote effective interpersonal, group, and intergroup behavior within the organization. Organization effectiveness is the extent to which the organization achieves its goals with the use of minimal resources. In doing so the organization has to achieve its goals, maintain effective cooperation among members, and adapt to the external environment. Organizational effectiveness depends on

1. Members having both the **interpersonal and small-group skills** (see all the chapters of this book and Johnson, 1990) and **personal attitudes** (i.e., commitment to the team and the organization, caring about colleagues, and caring about reliability and quality of one's work) and **technical competencies** needed to be effective contributors to the organization.
2. The **organizational structure** (i.e., roles and norms) supporting the use of the interpersonal and small-group skills and application of the personal attitudes.
3. The **organizational culture** supporting the new patterns of interaction and relating among members. The organizational culture is the patterns of interaction among members resulting from the organization's (a) norms and values, (b) history of internal and external conflicts, (c) types of people attracted to be members of the organization, (d) work processes and physical layout, (e) modes of communication, and (f) exercise of authority.
4. The **psychological energy** of members being activated for the organization's work. Members must be highly committed to contributing to the success of the organization.

Typically referred to as simply OD, organizational development utilizes the **action research** methodology pioneered by Kurt Lewin to improve the effectiveness of organizations. First, the vision and goals of the organization are clarified and their cooperative nature emphasized. Second, the action research methodology is implemented through the following steps:

1. *Diagnosis.* Diagnostic activities consist of a three-step process:
   a. Building a normative theory of how the group or organization should be functioning. Normative theories focus on such factors as cooperation, communication, leadership, decision making, and conflict resolution. Each chapter of this book presents such theories. Without knowledge of what effective leadership looks like, for example, a diagnosis of how effective the leadership of a group or organization is cannot take place.
   b. Measuring current group or organizational functioning by collecting data through interviews, observations, questionnaires, and diagnostic group sessions.
   c. Analyzing and organizing the data so that discrepancies between observed and ideal performance and the causes for the discrepancies can be identified.

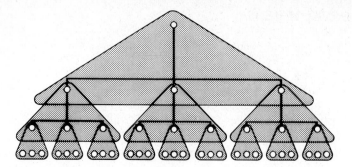

**FIGURE 12.1**    The Linking Pin Model of Organizational Structure

2. *Feedback.* The data are reported to those organizational members from whom the data were obtained to highlight the discrepancies between ideal and actual functioning (i.e., problems) of various work groups, departments, and the organization as a whole.
3. *Discussion and Planning.* The problems identified by the data are analyzed and the implications for improving the effectiveness of the relevant work groups and departments within the organization are discussed. A plan for improving organizational effectiveness is developed.
4. *Action.* The plan is implemented. Structural supports for the new behaviors and procedures are generated by changing role definitions and group norms. Interventions can be made on the person (skill training or attitude change), group (modifying group structure and procedures), or intergroup (intergroup problem-solving) levels.
5. *Rediagnosis.* New data are collected to determine if the plan (a) was implemented and (b) solved the problem. If not, the cycle is repeated.

This process should become continuous and ongoing within most work groups and organizations.

Organizations may be easily conceptualized as a hierarchy of work teams or "families" that are tied together by linking individuals who are leaders in one team but peer group members at the next highest organizational level (see Figure 12.1). These individuals are known as **linking pins** (Likert, 1961). Unlike many other organizational theories, Likert's model emphasizes group concepts such as group goals, leadership, group responsibility rather than individual concepts such as personal motivation and responsibility. Small groups of motivated individuals are the secret to organizational productivity.

## TYPES OF TEAMS

Productivity through people.

*Singapore management philosophy*

The Minnesota Timberwolves faced their first year as an NBA professional team with an emphasis on playing as a team. A game such as basketball requires elaborate teamwork if played with any degree of expertise. Each play must be practiced again and again until the athletes function as a single unit, and desire for personal success must be transformed into a desire for group success. Practices are designed to foster team spirit, formulate group goals, identify weaknesses in team play, build a desire for group success, and strive for better and better cooperation and integration.

Just as athletes must learn how to pool their individual abilities and energies to maximize the team's performance, employees must learn to coordinate their efforts with those of the other group members. A **team** is a set of interpersonal relationships structured to achieve established goals. The productivity of teams is not a simple function of team members' technical competencies and task abilities. Group goals must be set, work patterns structured and practiced, a desire for team success must be built, and a sense of group identity developed. While technical superstars are a great asset, unless all members pursue team success over their own personal stardom, the team suffers. There is no place for "lone rangers" on a team, whether the team is a family, in a business, or in any other organization. Individual members must learn how to coordinate their actions, identify any strains and stresses in working together, and continuously improve the integration of their efforts. The action research procedure that is the foundation of organizational development is also the foundation of team development. **Team building** emphasizes the analysis of work procedures and activities to improve productivity, relationships among members, the social competence of members, and the ability of the team to adapt to changing conditions and demands.

Teamwork is known by many different names in business and industry. It has been called employee involvement (EI), worker participation, and labor-management "jointness." Whatever it is called, teamwork is clearly troubling for many Americans. Not everyone is in favor of using teams within organizations. John Brodie, the president of United Paperworkers Local 448 in Chester, Pennsylvania, for example, stated

> What the company wants is for us to work like the Japanese. Everybody go out and do jumping jacks in the morning and kiss each other when they go home at night. You work as a team, rat on each other, and lose control of your destiny. That's not going to work in this country.

For most people in business and industry, however, teams are not only viewed as positive, they are also viewed as inevitable.

There are many different ways that work teams may be used within organizations. Three of the most common types are

1. *Problem-solving teams* consisting of 5 to 12 volunteers, hourly and salaried, drawn from different areas of a department. Problem-solving teams meet one to two hours a week to discuss ways of improving quality, efficiency, and work environment. They are "off-line" discussion groups that have no power to reorganize work or enlarge the role of workers in the production process. Problem-solving teams have been found to reduce costs and improve product quality, but to have little effect on how work is organized or how managers behave. Consequently, they have tended to fade away.

They were first implemented on a small scale in the 1920s and 1930s and, based on Japanese quality circles, adopted more widely in the late 1970s.

2. *Special-purpose teams* whose duties include such things as designing and introducing work reforms and new technology, meeting with suppliers and customers, and linking separate functions. In organizations that have unions, special-purpose teams have been used to facilitate collaboration between labor and management on operational decisions at all levels. Special-purpose teams involve works in decisions at ever-higher levels, creating an atmosphere for quality and productivity improvements. The teams create a foundation for self-managing work teams. Special-purpose teams have been implemented in the 1980s as the next step after problem-solving teams. They are still spreading, especially in companies with unions.

3. *Self-managing teams* of 5 to 15 employees who produce an entire product instead of subunits. Team members learn all tasks and rotate from job to job. The teams take over managerial duties, including work and vacation scheduling, the ordering of supplies and materials, and the hiring of new members. Self-managing teams can increase productivity 30 percent or more and substantially raise quality. They fundamentally change the way work is organized, giving employees control over their jobs, wiping out tiers of managers, and tearing down bureaucratic barriers between departments. A flatter organization results. Self-managing teams have been used by a few companies in the 1960s and 1970s and have rapidly spread in the mid to late 1980s. They appear to be the wave of the future.

Resistance to self-managing teams, however, has been widespread. Many managers resist self-managing teams because it means power sharing, less supervising, and fewer managers. Wall Street's focus on short-term results causes management to seek short-term strategies to increase productivity and ignore more long-term strategies. The takeovers of businesses also focus managers on short-term productivity rather than investing in long-term human capital programs such as the continual training that is needed to help workers improve their technical and social skills. Some employees resist self-managing teams because members have to accept considerable responsibility for production and quality control, members come under pressure from coworkers to produce more, and promotions are rare because there are few managerial positions. There is some doubt if many companies understand how deep the change in organizational functioning must be and really go after it. Using self-managing teams and providing continuous training of employees has to become their primary consideration.

## Self-Managing Teams in Manufacturing

The new manufacturing model emphasizes high-quality products produced in small lots in low-overhead facilities that are market driven with immediate response time capabilities and tailored to the specific consumer. If the United States is to become a world-class manufacturing nation, companies must be able to respond to niche markets by becoming specialist producers of products or services that emphasize (1) innovative design tailored for the specific market, (2) superior quality, and (3) exceptional service and responsiveness to customers. This contrasts with the traditional Model T Ford strategy—"any color as long as it's black." Quality, flexibility, and continuous improvements and innovations are the keys to success. Production will be handed over to small units of highly skilled workers who make incremental improvements in products and services. Products must continually change, as current products can become obsolete within one year. *Where before companies sold a "product," now they sell a "process."* The new basics of business are (1) world-class quality and service, (2) enhanced responsiveness to small markets through greatly increased flexibility, and (3) continuous, short-cycle innovation and improvement aimed at creating new markets for both new and apparently mature products and services. It no longer makes sense to develop large-volume mass production facilities that take weeks or even months to respond to a highly volatile marketplace.

In today's manufacturing world, any new technical breakthrough can be quickly copied all over the world. In the new global economy, nearly everyone has access to new breakthroughs and the machines and money to turn them into standardized products at about the same time and on roughly the same terms. Competitive advantage no longer lies in one-time technological breakthroughs. Workers in South Korea, Taiwan, or Mexico, furthermore, can churn out products just as well as American workers and for far lower wages. What cannot be copied or stolen is employees' ability to learn and adapt and respond to market needs. Competitive advantage lies in keeping a technology by elaborating on it continuously, developing variations and small improvements, so that particular needs of niche markets are better met. Companies compete on the basis of how quickly and well they can transform ideas into incrementally better products. This depends on the functioning of workers within teams.

The keys to today's and tomorrow's manufacturing are the team and the worker. To flourish, companies will need involved and committed workers, who are self-directed and creative thinkers, who continuously seek to upgrade their knowledge and skills, who rapidly and continuously improve products and services, and who are willing to move from job to job. Teamwork makes this possible because the employees usually are "cross-trained" to perform all tasks. They can fill in for absent coworkers and respond quickly to changes in models and production runs. They can make short production runs to create and service niche markets. They can teach knowledge and skills to each other. They can monitor members' actions and ensure high quality of work and products.

Self-managing teams mean radical change. The old system, based on principles developed by Frederick W. Taylor, involved the division of production work into simple, repetitive tasks performed by unskilled workers under close supervisory control. This system was based on the idea that efficient mass production inevitably breeds alienated workers who must be bought off with high pay. Taylorism had its critics from the beginning. Kurt Lewin, for example, in 1920 wrote an article discussing the "Taylor system" of eliminating superfluous effort through "scientific management." Lewin began the paper by observing that work has a central role in life as a person's capacity to work gives meaning and substance to his or her whole existence. Accordingly, Lewin believed that every job should sustain or enhance this "life value." Lewin argued that the emphasis on efficiency and increasing productivity and cutting down on the number of hours a person has to work ignores the value the worker places on what he or she is doing and the satisfaction derived from work.

Lewin believed that the inner value the person places on work is more important than such efficiency-enhancing procedures as time-and-motion studies of how the work should be done.

While few people listened to Lewin then, his viewpoint is being re-discovered today. The Taylor system has been disproved as a pattern for modern factory and office jobs. In self-management teams, workers have to be multiskilled and manage themselves. American companies are discovering that people, not technology or marketing ploys, are the keys to success in global competition.

## EXERCISE 12.1:
## TEAM STRUCTURE: APPLICATION EXERCISE

**Task:**   Given here are three ways of organizing the team. Describe the way team members would interact within each structure and predict the resulting productivity, morale, social support, and professional self-esteem.

**Cooperative:**   One answer from the three of you, everyone must agree, and everyone must be able to explain.

**Individual Accountability:**   One member of your group will be chosen randomly to explain the group's answers.

**Expected Behaviors:**   Everyone participates.

**Criterion for Success:**   Thoughtful answers that have a clear supporting rationale spelled out in detail.

### Situation 1: Merit Pay for the Best Team Member

Your organization has decided to implement a competitive merit pay system for employees. One hundred merit points are given to each team within the organization. You, the manager, are told that you are to rank the team members from best to worst in job performance and divide the bonus points among the team members accordingly. A team member could receive all 100 points or 0 points, depending on how his or her job performance is rated for that year. The more merit points given to one team member, the fewer available for the other team members.

To implement this system, criteria on which the team members are to be evaluated have to be determined. On the basis of the selected criteria, team members are ranked from most successful to least successful. The "most outstanding" member of the team receives 50 merit points, the first runner-up receives 30 points, and the second runner-up receives 20 merit points. The rest of the team members receive 0 merit points.

### Situation 2: Merit Pay for Outstanding Individual Efforts

Your organization has decided to implement an individualistic merit pay program for employees. You, the manager, are told to determine how many merit points each of your team members should receive. You decide to reward team members on the basis of how successful they have been this year. All team members who have demonstrated success will receive a merit bonus.

To implement this system, you set criteria for "excellent," "good," "average," "poor," and "terrible" performance. You evaluate the success of each team member. All "excellent" members are given 20 merit points, "good" members are given 10 merit points, "average" members are given 5 merit points, "poor" members are given 1 merit point, and "terrible" members are given 0 merit points.

### Situation 3: Merit Pay for Outstanding Group Efforts

Your organization decides to implement a cooperative merit pay program for employees. You, the manager, are told to determine how many merit points each of your team members should receive on the basis of how successful their team has been.

To implement the program, you organize all subordinates into teams. You then set criteria for "excellent," "good," "average," "poor," and "terrible" team performance. You evaluate the success of each team. Each member of the "excellent" teams is given 20 merit points, members of "good" teams are given 10 merit points, members of "average" teams are given 5 merit points, members of "poor" teams are given 1 merit point, and members of "terrible" teams are given 0 merit points.

### EXERCISE 12.2:
### THE COOPERATIVE TEAM SCENARIO

A responsibility of team leaders and members is to provide a vision of what the team will be like when the desired changes have been implemented. This vision must be clear and precise.

1. Working individualistically by yourself, write
   a. Your personal vision of what you hope the team will be.
   b. Your perception of the team's mission.
   c. The immediate goals your team is working to achieve.
   d. The unique talents, skills, competencies, and perspectives you bring to the team's work.
2. Form a triad. Working cooperatively, share your views of the team's mission and goals and come to a consensus as to what the mission and goals of the team should be.
3. In your triad,
   a. Write a detailed, behaviorally oriented, scenario that describes what you would expect to see, hear, and feel if most team members acted cooperatively most of the time. Include how interaction and relationships among team members would be affected. This description should be a personalized, realistic, and attainable description of what you are committed to achieving.
   b. It may be helpful to describe the team's mission, specify the environmental demands on your team, describe the current response to these demands, and then describe how cooperative efforts by team members will contribute to achieving the team's mission and responding to the current and future demands on your team.
   c. This is a cooperative effort. Form a group of three and write one description from the three of you. Everyone must contribute to the description, agree with it, and be able to explain it. Each will need their own copy of the scenario. Each will be individually accountable to present the group's scenario to another person. Plan how to do so effectively.

### EXERCISE 12.3:
### DEGREE OF INTERDEPENDENCE

**Task:** Decide which team analogy best describes your team and why.

**Cooperative:** One answer and rationale from the three of you, everyone must agree, and everyone must be able to explain.

**Individual Accountability:**   One member of your triad will be selected randomly to present the group's answer and rationale.

**Criterion for Success:**   A reasoned answer backed up by examples and information.

**Expected Behaviors:**   Everyone participates and contributes their ideas, analyses, and examples.

### TEAMS

1. **Golf Team:** Members all function independently of each other, working to promote as high an individual score as possible, so that when individual scores are combined into team scores, their team wins.
2. **Baseball Team:** Members are relatively independent of one another, and while all members are required to be on the field together, they virtually never interact together all at the same time.
3. **Football Team:** Members are divided into three subteams—offense, defense, and special teams. When the subteam is on the field, every player is involved in every play, but each has a set of specialized skills required by their individual position. But the teamwork required is centered in the subteam, not the total team.
4. **Basketball Team:** All members play on the team as a whole. Every player is involved in all aspects of the game, offense and defense, and all must pass, run, guard, and shoot. When a substitute comes in, all must play with the new person. True teamwork is like a basketball team where division of effort is meshed into a single coordinated result, where the whole is more than, and different from, the sum of its individual parts.

## EXERCISE 12.4:
## ROMAN ARMY

### The Reorganization of the Roman Army

As a popular and successful general, Caius Marius had been elected consul of the Roman republic five times. In 102 B.C., at the height of his popularity, he reorganized the Roman army—a reform that had been needed for about 50 years. The structural reorganization was relatively simple. The Roman legion consisted of about 6,000 men. Marius divided them into 60 centuries (100 men), each under a centurion. He grouped each century into ten cohorts, and he had the heads of the cohorts report directly to the general of the legion. This division made the army more efficient, but the real organization was based on changes in society.

Before the reorganization, the army was based on the draft, and under the Roman constitution, the draft applied only to citizens who owned a certain amount of property. But over time, the rich landowners, merchants, and others who were eligible no longer had either the aptitude or the taste for military service. The draft was kept, but Marius allowed the poor and unemployed to volunteer. Soon the reluctant farmers and merchants disappeared from the army. The volunteers were those who saw service under a successful general as a prospect for adventure or escape from poverty.

Then, the army began to supply equipment to the soldiers instead of having each individual furnish his own. This meant fewer distinctions based on wealth and ensured that both equipment and training were more standardized.

The bulk of the volunteers were farm laborers or small farmers so heavily in debt that they were in danger of losing their farms. In addition to the prospect of prizes from a successful campaign, a general in search of recruits could promise that, if the army were disbanded, the soldiers would be given an allotment of land. Thus the new Roman army gave more prominence to generals with established reputations whose names would bring in recruits.

The common soldier began to shift allegiance from the republic or the senate to the general. The senate might back down or delay on promises, but the soldiers could count on their generals to fight political battles for them. This made it almost impossible for one general to take an army from another or to remove another general from command.

Thus the army fell more and more under the control of the generals. In turn, the generals became servants of their own armies. They could not retire from public life if their own army were disbanded, since they had to fulfill the promises by which they had obtained volunteers.

Although the Roman soldier respected the constitution, the armies would not hesitate to support their generals against the government if the generals had good reason for attacking it. In 51 B.C., approximately 50 years later, Julius Caesar and Pompeius Magnus (Pompey) began a political struggle. In 50 B.C. Pompey violated the constitution, and Caesar's soldiers enthusiastically followed him. Caesar crossed the Rubicon and invaded Italy, and the civil war began. It ended in 44 B.C. with Caesar being voted a perpetual dictatorship. This was the beginning of the downfall of the Roman republic.*

**Questions**

1. Draw an organization chart based on the reorganized Roman army described in this case.
2. What social changes were particularly instrumental in changing the Roman army? How did socioeconomic conditions play a role in these changes?
3. Given hindsight, could the army have been reorganized differently and, perhaps, more effectively?
4. What does this case say about interactions between organizations and their environments?

## BUILDING PRODUCTIVE TEAMS

The Plains Indian People, known to whites as the Cheyenne, Crow, and Sioux, are truly the Painted Arrow, the Little Black Eagle, and the Brother People. They follow the **medicine wheel way.** The medicine wheel is pictured in Figure 12.2. Each of the stones within the medicine wheel represents one of the many things of the universe. All things are organized within the medicine wheel, and all things are equal within it. All things within the medicine wheel know of their harmony with every other thing, except for humans. Finding harmony involves recognizing the uniqueness of each person and their unity within the medicine wheel.

The medicine wheel way states that each person is unique in all ways but one. There is only one thing that all people possess equally, and that is loneliness. No two people on the face of this earth are alike in any one thing except for their loneliness. And the only way we can overcome our loneliness is through "touching" others. The medicine wheel way begins with touching others. Touching others means to be to each other a gift, as is the buffalo. Touching others means nourishing each other, that we all may grow. Through touching others we find our place within the universe and to be in harmony with all other things within the universe. We touch

*Source:* Edgar F. Huse, *The Modern Manager* (St. Paul, MN: West, 1979), pp. 58–59, as adapted from G. Ferrero, *The Greatness and Decline of Rome* (London: Heinemann, 1909) and F. Marsh, *A History of the Roman World* (New York: Barnes & Noble, 1963).

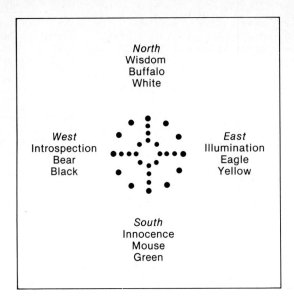

**FIGURE 12.2**
The Medicine Wheel

others by joining a team and seeing the unity of all members. We are all separate and unique individuals. We are all part of a larger harmony working with each other.

The Plains Indians are not the only ones who believe in unique individuals seeking harmony within a team. Personal productivity in most cases cannot take place without team productivity. A person cannot stand alone. He or she needs a team. Each person needs to be

1. A unique and valued individual successful in his or her own right.
2. Part of a successful (and great) team effort.

The combination of unique individuals who combine into a team fuels productivity. Team productivity depends on ensuring that a clear cooperative structure underlies team efforts and teaching team members the group skills (discussed in this book) they need to be contributing members. In other words, this whole book is about building productive teams. Clear cooperative goals, effective communication, good leadership, effective decision making, constructive conflict management, positive use of power, and so forth are all essential (see Figure 12.3). There are, however, a few issues that may be helpful in structuring teams:

1. Ensuring that the essential components of cooperative efforts are structured into the team.
2. Increasing team cohesion.
3. Establishing constructive norms.
4. Building trust.
5. Dealing with problem members.

*It takes a team to get extraordinary things done.* The productivity of teams is not a simple function of team members' technical competencies and task abilities.

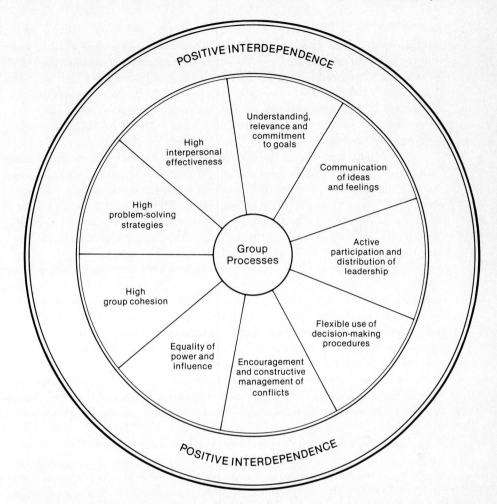

**FIGURE 12.3**   Components of an Effective Group   From D. W. Johnson and R. T. Johnson, *Cooperation and Competition: Theory and Research* (Edina, MN: Interaction Book Company, 1989). Used with permission of the authors.

Productivity is not guaranteed simply from team members being interested in attaining the team's goals. It takes more than just placing several people in the same room and telling them to work together to create a team effort. Successful team performance requires carefully structuring cooperation among team members.

Using a sales team as an example, there are three ways that relationships among team members may be structured. First, members of the sales team can *compete* with each other to see who is best. Members of the sales team could be ranked from highest to lowest in terms of sales for the month and be given bonuses accordingly. The person who sells the most, for example, would receive a bonus of $500, the second best salesperson $300, and the third best salesperson $100. The rest receive no bonus. When a sales staff competes, they will work against each other to be the "best." Since helping a competitor hurts one's own chances of winning, the salespersons will be tempted to hide potential customers from colleagues. If a salesperson has more promising leads that he or she can personally follow up in the near future, for example, the motivation will be toward hiding that information from colleagues in order to lower their sales and thereby increase one's own chances of being the top salesperson. The more one person sells, the less likely it is that others will receive a bonus.

Second, members of the sales team can work *individualistically* to achieve up to a preset criteria. When a sales staff works individualistically, each salesperson will be striving to meet a personal sales quota. A salesperson will receive $500 for selling over $5,000 of products, $300 for selling over $3,000 of products, and $100 for $1,000 of products. Everyone can succeed or everyone can fail, and the efforts of the salespeople are independent. How many sales one person makes has no positive or negative influence on the success of others.

Third, team members can work *cooperatively* to maximize the productivity of the team. Team members each receive a $500 bonus if the total sales of all members reach $30,000, $300 bonus if their total sales reach $30,000 and a $100 bonus if the team's total sales reach $10,000. When a sales team works cooperatively, they combine their efforts to maximize the sales of all members. Success depends not only on how many sales one member makes but also on the sales of all other team members. The more successful one's teammates, the more successful one is. If a salesperson has more promising leads that he or she can personally follow up in the near future, for example, he or she will be motivated to share that information with colleagues to increase their sales and thereby increase the overall performance of the team.

Teams structured cooperatively will be more productive than teams structured competitively or individualistically. As was discussed in Chapter 3, the more cooperative the team (as opposed to competitive or individualistic efforts), the greater the productivity, the more committed team members are to each other, and the greater members' social competencies. The positive results derived from cooperative efforts, however, do not happen automatically. Team efforts are made cooperative by carefully structuring five essential components: positive interdependence, face-to-face interaction, individual accountability, interpersonal and small-group skills, and group processing (Johnson & Johnson, 1989a).

## Positive Interdependence

> All for one and one for all.
>
> *Alexandre Dumas*

Within a football game, the quarterback who throws the pass and the receiver who catches the pass are positively interdependent. The success of one depends on the success of the other. It takes two to complete a pass. One player cannot succeed without the other. Both have to perform competently if their mutual success is to be assured. They sink or swim together.

The first requirement for any team is that members believe that they "sink or swim together." Team members are both responsible for their own productivity and for the productivity of teammates. The technical term for that dual responsibility is positive interdependence. **Positive interdependence** exists when members perceive that they are linked with groupmates in a way so that they cannot succeed unless their groupmates do (and vice versa) and/or that they must coordinate their efforts with the efforts of their groupmates to complete a task. Each member's work benefits all other members. As a result, team members (1) work together to get the job done, (2) share resources, (3) support and assist each other, and (4) celebrate joint success. When positive interdependence is clearly understood, it highlights

1. Each member's efforts are required and indispensable for group success (i.e., there can be no "free-riders") (Kerr & Bruun, 1983; Harkins & Petty, in press; Kerr, 1983; Sweeney, 1973).
2. Each member has a unique contribution to make to the joint effort because of his or her resources and/or role and task responsibilities (Harkins & Petty, 1982).

Poor teams have no overall goal—individual members work toward personal goals that have little or no relation to the goals of others. Good teams are characterized by mutual goals and positive interdependence. We, not me, has to dominate. Members of a cooperatively structured team perceive

1. They have **mutual goals.** Team members must believe that they "sink or swim together."
2. Group members are striving for **mutual benefit** so that all members of the group will gain. There is recognition that what helps other group members benefits oneself and what promotes one's own productivity benefits the other group members.
3. Group members share a **common fate** where they all gain or lose on the basis of the overall performance of group members. Either all succeed or all fail.
4. They are **mutually responsible** for each other's productivity as well as their own and, therefore, the productivity of group members is **mutually caused** by all members. All members are responsible for helping and assisting each other. No member works alone. Mutual effort and assistance result in mutual productivity. Each member's productivity is a combination of the individual's efforts and the assistance and encouragement of teammates. This mutual causation results in mutual responsibility for the performance of each member and **mutual obligation** to support the other group members. Group members have a **mutual investment** in each other.
5. Group members feel a **shared identity** based on group membership. Besides being a separate individual, one is a member of a team. The shared identity binds members together emotionally.
6. An expectation of **joint celebration** exists, based on mutual respect and appreciation for the success of group members. Being part of a team effort results in feelings of camaraderie, belonging, and pride. Feelings of success are shared, and pride is taken in others' accomplishments as well as one's own.

There are many paths to positive interdependence. Never take one when two are possible. The more types of interdependence structured within the team, the clearer the message will be to group members. The ways in which positive interdependence may be structured include (Johnson & Johnson, 1991; Johnson, Johnson, & Holubec, 1990)

1. *Positive goal interdependence,* where members perceive that they have a mutual set of goals that all are striving to accomplish and that success depends on all members reaching the goal. The goals for a self-managing team, for example, may be to build a product, develop a new product, adapt a product to the needs of a customer, or continuously refine and redesign the machines and processes the team is using to build its product.

2. *Positive reward interdependence,* where each member of the group is given the same reward for completing the task. A joint reward is given for successful group work. Everyone is rewarded or no one is rewarded. To structure positive reward interdependence among team members, (a) team members may all receive the equal rewards on the basis of total team performance or (b) team members may have a salary based on individual performance and receive·a regular bonus based on whether all team members meet a preset criteria for performance.
3. *Positive role interdependence,* where group members are assigned complementary and interconnected roles. Each member is assigned a responsibility that the group needs to function effectively.
4. *Positive task interdependence,* where a division of labor is created so that the actions of one group member have to be completed if the next group member is to complete his or her responsibilities.
5. *Positive resource interdependence,* where each member has only a portion of the information, resources, or materials necessary for the task to be completed.

## Face-to-Face Interaction

People who share the same goals are likely to come to care about one another on more than just a professional level. The more team members care about each other, the harder they will work to ensure team success. Extraordinary accomplishments result from team members getting personally involved with the task and with each other. The word "encouragement" has its root in the Latin word *cor*, which means "heart." When you encourage someone, you give them heart. Encouragement, help, assistance, and support mean more when they come from a person who cares about you and whom you care about.

Such promotive interaction has a number of effects. First, there are cognitive insights and understandings that can only come from explaining one's conclusions and views to others. Second, it is within face-to-face interaction that the opportunity for a wide variety of social influences and patterns emerge. Third, the verbal and nonverbal responses of other group members provide important feedback concerning each other's performance. Fourth, it provides an opportunity for peers to pressure unmotivated team members to do their share of the work. Fifth, it is the interaction involved in completing the work that allows team members to get to know each other as persons, which in turn forms the basis for caring and committed relationships among members. A poor team meets sporadically and members rarely interact. They are business associates only. A good team meets regularly so members can discuss their work with each other, identify and solve problems blocking success, and give and receive help and assistance. To obtain meaningful face-to-face interaction, the size of the team needs to be small (from two to six members). The smaller the team, the clearer it is to each member that his or her participation and efforts are needed.

## Individual Accountability

Among the early settlers of Massachusetts, there was a saying, "If you do not work, you do not eat." The third step in structuring a productive team is to ensure that all members are individually accountable for their share of the work. **Individual accountability** exists when the contributions each team member makes to the overall team effort are assessed and the results are given back to the group and the individual. It minimizes the likelihood of any member loafing and getting a free ride. A poor team has members who do not contribute and get a free ride. A poor team consists of members who do not do their share of the work and who do not learn or grow from their team experience. A good team consists of members who all do their share, who all contribute to the team's success, and who grow and learn from their experience. To ensure that each member is individually accountable to do their share of the work,

1. Assess how much effort each member is contributing to the group's work.
2. Provide feedback to the team and individual members.
3. Help the team avoid redundant efforts by members.
4. Ensure that every member is responsible for the final outcome.
5. Highlight and clarify the responsibilities of each member.

## Small-Group and Interpersonal Skills

The fourth essential component of cooperative efforts is the appropriate use of small-group and interpersonal skills. Teams cannot function effectively if members do not have and use the needed interpersonal and small-group skills. Placing socially un-skilled individuals on a team and telling them to collaborate does not guarantee that they are able to do so effectively. Many individuals have never been required to work as part of teams and, therefore, lack the needed cooperative skills for doing so. Other individuals may be socially skilled but not be motivated to provide the leadership, decision-making, trust-building, communication, and conflict-management skills needed to make the team productive. A poor team consists of interpersonally incom-petent individuals. A good team promotes the acquisition and use of interpersonal and small-group skills.

## Group Processing

No one learns from experience unless they stop and reflect on it. The fifth step in structuring a productive team is ensuring that the team has a specific time to discuss how well they are (1) achieving their goals and (2) maintaining effective working relationships among members. Teams need to describe what member actions were helpful and unhelpful and make decisions about what member actions to continue or change. Such processing enables teams to focus on group maintenance, facilitates the learning of social skills, ensures members receive feedback on their participation, and reminds members to practice social skills consistently. Some of the keys to successful processing are allowing sufficient time for processing to take place, making it specific rather than general, maintaining member involvement in processing and collabora-tive skills during processing, and communicating clear expectations for processing. A poor team never processes. A good team processes regularly.

Effective processing (1) promotes a sense of self-efficacy rather than helpless-ness and (2) focuses group members on positive rather than negative behaviors. One of the aims of group processing is to increase members' feelings of efficacy by em-powering group members to feel that they can increase their productivity. **Self-efficacy** is the expectation of successfully obtaining valued outcomes through person-al effort. Some of the consequences of an increased sense of self-efficacy are increased task orientation, increased persistence in completing learning tasks, greater confi-dence that one can successfully learn, and decreased self-doubt and self-preoccupa-tion, which may interfere with learning. **Group efficacy** is the expectation of suc-cessfully obtaining valued outcomes through the joint efforts of the group members. In team situations, the effort available includes one's own and the effort of one's collaborators. The knowledge that there is to be a team effort in achieving the group's goal provides added confidence that the group will be successful. The greater the sense of self- and joint efficacy promoted by group processing, the more productive and effective group members and the group as a whole become. Sarason and Potter (1983), for example, examined the impact of individual self-monitoring of thoughts on self-efficacy and successful performance and found that having individuals focus their attention on self-efficacious thoughts is related to greater task persistence and less cognitive interference. They concluded that the more that people are aware of what they are experiencing, the more aware they will be of their own role in determining their success.

Monitoring one's own and one's collaborators' actions begins with deciding which behaviors to direct one's attention toward. Knowing that certain behaviors are possible and reasonable can change a person's train of thought and cognitive focus. Individuals can focus either on positive and effective behaviors or on negative and ineffective behaviors. A focus on positive actions may result in feelings of satisfaction and efficacy. Positive monitoring is linked to the emission of thoughts and statements that reflect positively on oneself and one's collaborators. Someone whose attention is drawn to recent personal successes may come to attend to positive personal qualities. The more group members are aware of their competent, effective, successful actions, the more aware they will be of their own role in determining both their own and the group's success, and the more confident they will be in their ability to be productive and effective. Positive attributions (for example, "I'm an intelligent person who can do well on this task"; "We are a hard-working and committed group") are particularly effective in (1) countering the worrying and self-preoccupation that often cause poor performance and (2) fostering a sense of efficacy.

**Negative monitoring** (that is, monitoring unpleasant, unrewarding, frustrating, destructive, counterproductive behaviors) is linked to negative statements about oneself and others. A negative focus may result in feelings of dissatisfaction and incompetence and can exacerbate the group's difficulties. Negative monitoring may focus attention unduly on the stressful and unpleasant events in the group. Hypersensitivity to negative behaviors and attitudes and seeking to blame someone for any problems the group has in functioning may lead to destructive conflict, chronic complaining, and feelings of helplessness and dissatisfaction.

Sarason and Potter (1983) found that when individuals monitored their stressful experiences they were more likely to perceive a program as having been more stressful than did those who did not, but when individuals monitored their positive experiences they were more likely to perceive the group experience as involving less psychological demands, were more attracted to the group and had greater motivation to remain members, and felt less strained during the experience and more prepared for future group experiences. When individuals are anxious about being successful, and are then told they have failed, their performance tends to decrease significantly, but when individuals anxious about being successful are told they have succeeded, their performance tends to increase significantly (Turk & Sarason, 1983).

Processing is important both for the group as a whole and for individuals. Some of the most important reasons behind group processing include the following:

1. When groups first begin to work together, they tend to be very task oriented. Processing gives the groups the time they need to maintain effective working relationships.
2. Processing helps members become aware of and develop the collaborative skills they need to work effectively in teams.
3. Processing gives the members a chance to give each other positive feedback on their use of collaborative skills.
4. Processing reminds members to practice their new collaborative skills consistently, not just occasionally.

Processing will especially help individuals who have difficulty in appropriately relating to teammates. They will learn and practice acceptable behavior and start down the difficult path toward being more socially skilled.

Scheduling group processing involves two main elements. First, groups must set aside time to reflect on how well members are working together. Processing time (such as 10 minutes) may be scheduled at the end of each team meeting or, periodically, a longer duration of time (such as an hour) may be scheduled for an in-depth discussion. Second, groups must have a set of procedures for discussing how well the group is functioning and how well members are using collaborative skills. An example of such procedures is as follows (Johnson & Johnson, 1991):

1. *Decide* what group skills you are going to emphasize and observe for and *teach* (or *precue*) members the skills.
2. *Appoint* observers, *prepare* observation forms (one for each observer), *explain* observation form to observers.
3. *Observe* and *intervene* when necessary.
4. Group members *assess* how often and how well they performed the group skills.
5. Observer *reports* to the group the information gathered and group members report their impressions as to how they behaved.
6. Group members *reflect on* and *analyze* the effectiveness of their behavior by comparing their observed behavior with their own impressions of and expectations for their performance of the targeted group skills. Group members who used the skills frequently and appropriately are complimented (*reinforced*).
7. Group members publicly *set goals* for performing group skills in the next group session.

In addition to the five essential elements, effective teams need to implement norms that enhance the cooperative effort to maintain trust among members.

## NORM EXERCISE 1 (12.5)

With your classmates, divide into triads and list five "do's" and five "don'ts" for group members. Then meet as one group and have each triad present its list. As a group, decide which three "do's" and which three "don'ts" affect group cohesion the most.

## NORM EXERCISE 2 (12.6)

Several behaviors are listed below. For each one please indicate how appropriate or inappropriate you think it would be as a norm for your group. Write the number that shows your best estimate of how the group would feel: 5 if the behavior is definitely appropriate as a norm, 4 if the behavior is somewhat appropriate, 3 if it is questionable, 2 if it is somewhat inappropriate, and 1 if it is definitely inappropriate.

_____    1. Said little or nothing in most meetings.

_____    2. Talked about the details of her sex life.

_____    3. Brought up problems he had with others who weren't in the group.

_____   4. Kissed another group member.

_____   5. Asked for reactions or feedback ("How do you see me in this group?").

_____   6. Talked mostly about what was going on in the group.

_____   7. Frequently joked.

_____   8. Pleaded for help.

_____   9. Challenged other members' remarks.

_____   10. Said she was not getting anything out of being in the group.

_____   11. Described his reactions to what was taking place in the group.

_____   12. Highlighted opposition among ideas.

_____   13. Formed a contract with another member about the use of each other's resources in meeting both their needs and goals.

_____   14. Refused to be bound by a group decision.

_____   15. Asked for the goal to be clarified.

_____   16. Noted competition in the group and asked how it could be reduced.

_____   17. Gave advice to other group members about what to do.

_____   18. Interrupted a dialogue between two members.

_____   19. Told another member that she was unlikable.

_____   20. Was often absent.

_____   21. Shouted with anger at another member.

_____   22. With strong feelings, told another member how likable he was.

_____   23. Tried to manipulate the group to get her own way.

_____   24. Hit another group member.

_____   25. Acted indifferently to other members.

_____   26. Dominated the group's discussion for more than one session.

_____   27. Encouraged other group members to react to the topic being discussed.

_____   28. Tried to convince members of the rightness of a certain point of view.

_____   29. Talked a lot without showing his real feelings.

_____   30. Told the group off, saying that it was worthless.

_____ 31. Showed she had no intention of changing her behavior.

_____ 32. Resisted the suggestions of other members about procedures.

_____ 33. Commented that the decision-making procedure was not appropriate to the nature of the decision.

_____ 34. Asked that the causes of a group problem be analyzed.

_____ 35. Expressed affection for several group members.

After reacting to these items the members of your group may think of other behavioral norms to include. Once all members have rated the group norms, the group should discuss them and decide how each affects the cohesion of the group.

# GROUP NORMS

To be productive, team members must establish group norms that (1) promote conformity to norms structuring effective interaction among team members and (2) manage power in ways that preserve harmony among members.

## Conforming to Group Norms

> As for conforming outwardly, and living your own life inwardly, I do not think much of that.
>
> *Henry David Thoreau*

A man stands up and faces the group. "My name is Dale," he says. "I am an alcoholic. I have not had a drink for three years, two months, and six days." The group applauds. This is a meeting of Alcoholics Anonymous. One group norm is to take the "first step" and admit that you are an alcoholic. Another group norm is to stay sober, one day at a time. Dale has just publicly testified that he is conforming to these normative expectations. The group is giving him support and recognition for doing so. This scenario occurs countless times daily· in families, businesses, schools, churches, and all other groups. A group cannot exist, cannot survive, cannot function, and cannot be productive unless most members conform to its norms most of the time.

In our society conformity has acquired a generally negative connotation. Many people think of conformity as a blind, unreasoning, spineless, weak, slavish adherence to the demands of the majority of peers or of authority figures. Even among social psychologists there is a common conception of conformity as agreement with the majority or for the sake of agreement. Conformity to group norms is frequently viewed as a violation of one's principles in order to obtain group acceptance, or a selling out of one's individuality in order to get ahead. Much of the research on conformity is based on behaviors such as lying about one's perceptions or beliefs. These pejorative connotations of conformity, however, are inaccurate and are based on a misunderstanding of the complexity of the process of conforming to group norms. There are conditions under which conformity to group norms may violate important values and principles of an individual, and other conditions under which it will support these values and beliefs. **Conformity** is defined as changes in behavior that result from group influences. The changes include **compliance** (behavioral change without internal acceptance) and private acceptance (changes in both behavior and attitudes). Conforming to group norms frequently improves the functioning of a group at no expense to the individual's principles or beliefs. Conforming to a classroom norm that one should provide help and assistance to classmates, for example, is beneficial for the group and the students involved.

The classic studies on conformity under group pressures were conducted by Solomon Asch (1956). Asch was born in 1907 in Poland. He arrived in the United States at age 13. In 1928 he received a B.S. degree from City College of New York. In 1932 he received a Ph.D. degree from Columbia University. He was an unusually independent person, and of him it has often been said that it took the least conformant of social psychologists to defend conformity and to point out that an essential feature of social life is the willingness to trust the observations of others. In his experimental studies on conformity, he asked participants to choose which of several lines came closest in length to a line they had just seen (see Figure 12.4). There was an obvious right answer. Yet each participant found him or herself faced with most or all fellow group members (group size ranged from 3 to 15) agreeing on an obviously wrong answer. The participant was thus faced with a conflict: accepting the evidence of his or her own eyes or going along with the group's perception. Sixty-eight percent of the individual estimates remained independent; 32 percent were deflected part or all of the way to the unanimous judgment of the fellow group members. One-fourth of the participants made no concessions to the unanimous majority; one-third conformed in half or more the trials. Whether the majority consisted of 3 or 15 members made little difference, as long as it was unanimous. If one other member agreed with the participant, the tendency to err in the direction of the majority estimate dropped from 32 percent to 10 percent. If the participant reported his estimates secretly, furthermore, the promajority errors were fewer. The results of the Asch experiments were somewhat shocking, as they seemed to indicate that many persons would go along with an erroneous group judgment even when they knew it was false. Most social psychologists reacted to the results of Asch's studies as if they agreed with Thoreau.

In discussing conformity to group norms we must differentiate two dimensions: conformity versus anticonformity and independence versus dependence (Allen, 1965; Hollander & Willis, 1967). The conformers and anticonformers both react to the group norm and base their behavior on it: the conformers agree with the norm, the anticonformers disagree with the norm, and both behave accordingly. An independent person, on the other hand, does not give undue importance to the group norm in making her judgment.

Not all behavior is covered by group norms. Not many groups care what foods their members eat or whether they prefer one type of drink to another. Group norms deal primarily with the behavior affecting the accomplishment of the group's task and the ability of the group to maintain itself over time. In general, the more

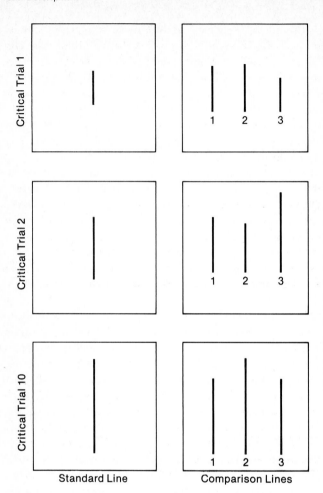

**FIGURE 12.4**   The Asch experiments. On 12 of the 18 trials, the majority of the group members purposely picked the incorrect comparison line. On the first of these critical trials, the standard line was 3 inches long, and Comparison Line 3 was the correct answer. However, the group chose Line 1, which was actually 3¾ inches long. On Critical Trial 2 the correct answer was 1, but the group unanimously answered with 2. Finally, the stimuli used in the tenth critical trial are also shown; the correct answer in this case was 2, but the group suggested 1.   From S. Asch, "An Experimental Investigation of Group Influence," in *Symposium on Preventive and Social Psychology,* Walter Reed Army Institute of Research (Washington, D.C.: U.S. Government Printing Office, 1957).

relevant the individual's behavior to the accomplishment of the group's task and the maintenance of the group, the more the pressures toward conformity. Many years ago observers in industrial organizations noted that members of male work groups typically established production standards (norms) that were adhered to by most members (Homans, 1950; Roethlisberger & Dickson, 1939). When a worker deviated too much from the standard, he was subjected to ridicule and other sanctions. If he produced too much he was referred to as a "speed king" or a "rate-buster"; if he produced too little, he was a "chiseler." Schachter (1951), Emerson (1954), and Schachter and his associates (1954) all found in their studies of deviation from group norms that the more relevant the deviation to the purposes of the group, the greater the rejection of the deviant by the group. Festinger (1950) and Allen (1965) concluded that there will be greater pressures to conform to task-related norms if goal attainment depends on the coordinated behavior of the group members. Raven and Rietsema (1957) found that the clearer the group goal and the path to the goal are to the group members, the stronger the pressures toward uniformity in task behavior will be. In general, nonconforming behaviors are accepted if they are perceived by the group's members as potentially improving the group's ability to accomplish its task and maintain itself; they are not accepted if they interfere with group maintenance and task accomplishment.

## Norms and Power

"What's it to be? Pizza or hamburgers?" Six friends who had just exited a movie theater were trying to decide what to eat. "Pizza!" immediately said five. "Hamburgers!" Keith answered. In rapid fire everyone talked to Keith. "We always get pizza." "Pizza is our group's official food." "You can have hamburger on your pizza." "We never eat hamburgers; hamburgers are for kids!" "Don't be a killjoy!" "OK," said Keith. "Let's get pizza." This scenario occurs many times a day. The majority of a group agree on a particular course of action that another member prefers not to do. The majority reminds the dissenter of group norms designed to pressure and persuade the member to adopt the group perspective. The incident concludes when the member capitulates and conforms to the group's norms.

Group norms often serve as substitutes for influence among group members (Thibaut & Kelley, 1959). Both the weaker and the stronger members tend to gain from having mutually acceptable norms that introduce regularity and control into their relationship without making direct interpersonal application of power necessary. The high-power members do not encounter the resistance and lack of wholehearted cooperation that often come from applying power in forceful ways. And the low-power members have more of a chance to influence the high-power members through the norms that specify their expected behavior and the limits of the use of power. Norms are a protection against the capricious or inconsistent use of influence by high-power members, but they also free the high-power members from constantly checking the behavior of low-power members to make sure they are conforming. Norms carry weight because they embody some of the personal power given up by group members. Individuals let themselves be influenced by norms in ways that they would never permit themselves to be influenced by others, for norms often take on the characteristics of moral obligations. At the very least, conformity to group norms is a requirement for continued membership in the group.

## Implementing Group Norms

There are several ways in which norms can be started in a group (Johnson, 1970). One frequent method is for a member to state it directly and tell other members to accept it. A member might say, for example, "I think we should express our feelings openly about this topic" and tell other members to do so. Norms can also be initiated through modeling, wherein members learn to conform to a group norm by watching others conform. Norms can also be imported from other groups. People usually learn cultural norms of social responsibility (you should help someone who is in need of help), fair play (don't kick someone when he's down), and reciprocity (if someone does you a favor, you should do her a favor in return) from others, and these norms can be incorporated into one's own group. All in all, however, perhaps the most effective way of starting group norms is through group discussion.

Johnson (1970) has presented a set of general guidelines for the establishment and support of group norms:

1. For members to accept group norms, they must recognize that they exist, see that the other members accept and follow them, and feel some internal commitment to them.
2. Members will accept and internalize norms to the extent that they see them as helping accomplish the goals and tasks to which they are committed. It is helpful, therefore, for a group to clarify how conformity to a norm will help goal accomplishment.
3. Members will accept and internalize norms for which they feel a sense of ownership. Generally, members will support and accept norms that they have helped set up.
4. Group members should enforce the norms on each other immediately after a violation. Enforcement should also be as consistent as possible.
5. Appropriate models and examples for conforming to the group norms should be present. Members should have the chance to practice the desired behaviors.
6. Cultural norms that promote goal accomplishment and group maintenance and growth should be imported into the group.
7. Because norms exist only to help group effectiveness, they should be flexible so that at any time more appropriate norms can be substituted.

## EXERCISE 12.7:
## YOUR COHESION BEHAVIOR (I)

How does your behavior affect group cohesion? When you want to increase group cohesion what do you do? How would you describe your behavior in influencing group cohesion?

The following questions should help you reflect upon how your behavior influences the cohesion of the groups to which you belong. Answer each question as honestly as possible.

1. I try to make sure that everyone enjoys being a member of the group.
   Never   1 : 2 : 3 : 4 : 5 : 6 : 7 : 8 : 9   Always
2. I discuss my ideas, feelings, and reactions to what is currently taking place within the group.
   Never   1 : 2 : 3 : 4 : 5 : 6 : 7 : 8 : 9   Always
3. I express acceptance and support when other members disclose their ideas, feelings, and reactions to what is currently taking place in the group.
   Never   1 : 2 : 3 : 4 : 5 : 6 : 7 : 8 : 9   Always
4. I try to make all members feel valued and appreciated.
   Never   1 : 2 : 3 : 4 : 5 : 6 : 7 : 8 : 9   Always
5. I try to include other members in group activities.
   Never   1 : 2 : 3 : 4 : 5 : 6 : 7 : 8 : 9   Always
6. I am influenced by other group members.
   Never   1 : 2 : 3 : 4 : 5 : 6 : 7 : 8 : 9   Always
7. I take risks in expressing new ideas and my current feelings.
   Never   1 : 2 : 3 : 4 : 5 : 6 : 7 : 8 : 9   Always
8. I express liking, affection, and concern for other members.
   Never   1 : 2 : 3 : 4 : 5 : 6 : 7 : 8 : 9   Always
9. I encourage group norms that support individuality and personal expression.
   Never   1 : 2 : 3 : 4 : 5 : 6 : 7 : 8 : 9   Always

These questions focus upon several ways of increasing group cohesion. The first question describes a general attempt to keep cohesion high. Questions 2 and 3 pertain to the expression of ideas and feelings and the support for others expressing ideas and feelings; such personal participation is essential for cohesiveness and for the development of trust. Questions 4 and 8 also focus upon support for, and liking of, other group members. Question 5 refers to the inclusion of other members, and question 6 takes up one's willingness to be influenced by other members. Questions 7 and 9 center on the acceptance of individuality within the group. All these factors are important for group cohesion. Discuss your answers with another group member. Then add all your answers together to get a total cohesion score. Keep your responses to these questions in mind as you proceed through this chapter.

## EXERCISE 12.8:
## THE LEVEL OF ACCEPTANCE IN YOUR GROUP

What is the level of acceptance in your group? The purpose of this exercise is to provide a way in which the level of acceptance in your group may be assessed and discussed. The procedure is as follows:

1. With the other members of your group, fill out the questionnaire below. Questionnaires should be unsigned so that no one's responses can be identified.
2. Tabulate the results in the summary table that follows the questionnaire.
3. Discuss the conclusions that can be drawn from the results. Consider these two questions:
   a. What is contributing to the present high or low level of acceptance in the group?
   b. How may the level of acceptance in the group be increased?

**Questionnaire: Level of Acceptance**

Think about the ways in which the members of your group normally behave toward you. In the parentheses in front of the statements below, place the number corresponding to your perceptions of the group as a whole, using the following scale:

5 = They *always* behave this way.
4 = They *typically* behave this way.
3 = They *usually* behave this way.
2 = They *seldom* behave this way.
1 = They *rarely* behave this way.
0 = They *never* behave this way.

My fellow group members:

1. (——) . . . . . . . . . . . . . . are completely honest with me.
2. . . . . (——) . . . . . . . . . understand what I am trying to communicate.
3. . . . . . . . . (——) . . . . interrupt and ignore my comments.
4. . . . . . . . . . . . . . . (——) accept me just the way I am.
5. (——) . . . . . . . . . . . . . . tell me when I bother them.
6. . . . . (——) . . . . . . . . . don't understand things I say or do.
7. . . . . . . . . (——) . . . . are interested in me.
8. . . . . . . . . . . . . . . (——) make it easy for me to be myself.
9. (——) . . . . . . . . . . . . . . don't tell me things that would hurt my feelings.
10. . . . . (——) . . . . . . . . understand who I really am.
11. . . . . . . . . (——) . . . . include me in what they are doing.
12. . . . . . . . . . . . . . . (——) evaluate whether I am acceptable or unacceptable.
13. (——) . . . . . . . . . . . . . . are completely open with me.

14.    .... (——) ........ immediately know when something is bothering me.
15.    ........ (——) .... value me as a person, apart from my skills or status.
16.    ............. (——) accept my differences or pecularities.

(——) Authenticity with me
(——) Understanding of me
(——) Valuing of me
(——) Accepting of me

Total the number of points in each column. Statements 3, 6, 9, and 12 are reversed in the scoring—subtract from 5 the rating given to each before placing the remainder in each column.

Summary Table: Level of Acceptance

| Score | Authenticity | Understanding | Valuing | Accepting |
|---|---|---|---|---|
| 0–4 | _____ | _____ | _____ | _____ |
| 5–8 | _____ | _____ | _____ | _____ |
| 9–12 | _____ | _____ | _____ | _____ |
| 13–16 | _____ | _____ | _____ | _____ |
| 17–20 | _____ | _____ | _____ | _____ |

## EXERCISE 12.9:
## HOW TRUSTING AND TRUSTWORTHY AM I?

When you are attempting to build a relationship with someone there is always the risk that the person will react in a rejecting and competitive way. In order for two group members to trust each other, each has to expect the other to be trustworthy and each has to engage in trusting behavior. This exercise allows you to compare the way you see your trust-building behavior in the group with the way other members see it. The procedure is as follows:

1. Complete the questionnaire below. Score your responses.
2. Then make a slip of paper for each member of your group. Fill out each slip as shown below, rating the members from 1 (low) to 7 (high) on how open and accepting you perceive him or her to be.

> **Member receiving feedback: Edythe**
> 1. Openness and sharing:          3
> 2. Acceptance, support, and
>    cooperativeness:          6

Base your rating on how you think the person has behaved during the entire time your group has met together.

3. Hand each member his or her slip. If there are six members in your group, you should receive five ratings of yourself, and each of the other members should likewise end up with five slips. Compute an average of how the other members see your behavior by adding all your ratings for openness and dividing up the number of slips and then doing the same with your ratings for acceptance.
4. In the diagram at the end of the exercise, you average openness and acceptance by (a) drawing a dotted line for the results of the feedback slips you received and (b) drawing a solid line for the results of your questionnaire.

5. Discuss with the other group members how similar your perception and their perceptions of your openness and acceptance are. If there is a difference between the two, ask the group to give you more specific feedback about your trust-building behavior in the group. Then discuss how to build trust with others in situations outside the group.

## Questionnaire

Here is a series of statements about your behavior in your group. Address each as honestly as you can. There are no right or wrong answers. It is important for you to describe your behavior as accurately as possible.

1. I offer facts, give my opinions and ideas, and provide suggestions and relevant information in order to promote the group discussion.
   Never   1 : 2 : 3 : 4 : 5 : 6 : 7 : 8 : 9   Always
2. I express my willingness to cooperate with other group members and my expectations that they will also be cooperative.
   Never   1 : 2 : 3 : 4 : 5 : 6 : 7 : 8 : 9   Always
3. I am open and candid in my dealings with the entire group.
   Never   1 : 2 : 3 : 4 : 5 : 6 : 7 : 8 : 9   Always
4. I give support to group members who are on the spot and struggling to express themselves intellectually or emotionally.
   Never   1 : 2 : 3 : 4 : 5 : 6 : 7 : 8 : 9   Always
5. I keep my thoughts, feelings, and reactions to myself during group discussions.
   Never   1 : 2 : 3 : 4 : 5 : 6 : 7 : 8 : 9   Always
6. I evaluate the contributions of other group members in terms of whether their contributions are useful to me and whether they are right or wrong.
   Never   1 : 2 : 3 : 4 : 5 : 6 : 7 : 8 : 9   Always
7. I take risks in expressing new ideas and my current feelings during a group discussion.
   Never   1 : 2 : 3 : 4 : 5 : 6 : 7 : 8 : 9   Always
8. I communicate to other group members that I am aware of, and appreciate, their abilities, talents, skills, and resources.
   Never   1 : 2 : 3 : 4 : 5 : 6 : 7 : 8 : 9   Always
9. I offer help to anyone in the group in order to bring up the performance of everyone.
   Never   1 : 2 : 3 : 4 : 5 : 6 : 7 : 8 : 9   Always
10. I accept and support the openness of other group members, support them for taking risks, and encourage individuality in them.
    Never   1 : 2 : 3 : 4 : 5 : 6 : 7 : 8 : 9   Always
11. I share any sources of information or other resources I have with the other group members in order to promote the success of individual members and the group as a whole.
    Never   1 : 2 : 3 : 4 : 5 : 6 : 7 : 8 : 9   Always
12. I often paraphrase or summarize what other members have said before I respond or comment.
    Never   1 : 2 : 3 : 4 : 5 : 6 : 7 : 8 : 9   Always
13. I level with other group members.
    Never   1 : 2 : 3 : 4 : 5 : 6 : 7 : 8 : 9   Always
14. I warmly encourage all members to participate, recognizing them for their contributions, demonstrating acceptance of and openness to their ideas, and generally being friendly and responsive to them.
    Never   1 : 2 : 3 : 4 : 5 : 6 : 7 : 8 : 9   Always

Reverse the scoring (subtract from 7 the rating given and place the remainder in the spaces provided) of questions 5 and 6. Then add the scores in the following way:

| OPENNESS AND SHARING | ACCEPTANCE AND SUPPORT |
|---|---|
| 1. _____ | 2. _____ |
| 3. _____ | 4. _____ |
| 5. _____ | 6. _____ |
| 7. _____ | 8. _____ |
| 9. _____ | 10. _____ |
| 11. _____ | 12. _____ |
| 13. _____ | 14. _____ |
| Total _____ | Total _____ |

If you have a score of 21 or over, you are trusting or trustworthy, whichever the case might be. If you have a score of less than 21, you are distrustful or untrustworthy, whichever the case may be.

### Johnson Trust Diagram, Part One

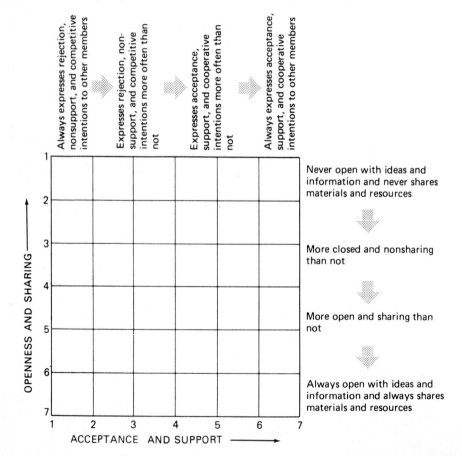

Johnson Trust Diagram, Part Two

|  | High Acceptance, Support, and Cooperative Intentions | Low Acceptance, Support, and Cooperative Intensions |
|---|---|---|
| **High Openness and Sharing** | Trusting and trustworthy | Trusting but untrustworthy |
| **Low Openness and Sharing** | Distrustful but trustworthy | Distrustful and untrustworthy |

## EXERCISE 12.10:
## PRACTICING TRUST-BUILDING SKILLS

This exercise is aimed at providing you with an opportunity to practice the trust-building skills that are needed in order for relationships to grow and develop. Here is the procedure:

1. With your classmates form groups of six members. Choose one member to observe.
2. Complete the task outlined below.
3. Discuss the following questions in your group:
    a. Who engaged in what types of trust-building behaviors?
    b. What feelings do members of the group have about their participation in the group?
    c. Was trust increased or decreased by participation in this exercise?

**Task**

Working as a group, estimate the number of persons in your city (or school) who possess each of the following genetic traits. Establish the frequency of occurrence of each genetic trait, first in your group and then in the entire room. On the basis of the percentage of occurrence in your group and the room, estimate the number of persons in your city (or school) who possess each trait.

Observation Sheet

| | | | | |
|---|---|---|---|---|
| 1. Contributes ideas | | | | |
| 2. Describes feelings | | | | |
| 3. Paraphrases | | | | |
| 4. Expresses acceptance and support | | | | |
| 5. Expresses warmth and liking | | | | |

Trusting behaviors = 1 and 2
Trustworthy behaviors = 3, 4, and 5

1. Dimples in the cheeks versus no dimples.
2. Brown (or hazel) eyes versus blue, gray, or green eyes.
3. Attached versus free earlobes (an earlobe is free if it dips below the point where it is attached).

4. Little-finger bend versus no bend. (Place your little fingers together with your palms toward you. If your little fingers bend away from each other at the tips, you have the famous little-finger bend.)
5. Tongue roll versus no tongue roll (if you can curl up both sides of your tongue to make a trough, you have it; it's not contagious).
6. Hairy versus nonhairy middle fingers (examine the back of the middle finger on each hand and look for hair between the first and second knuckles).
7. Widow's peak versus straight or curved hairline (examine the hairline across your forehead and look for a definite dip or point of hair extending down toward your nose).

**EXERCISE 12.11:**
**OPEN VERSUS CLOSED RELATIONSHIPS**

Are the relationships among group members open or closed? The purpose of this exercise is to provide participants with an opportunity to reflect on and to discuss this question. The procedure is as follows:

1. Read carefully the accompanying diagram of open and closed relationships.
2. Working by yourself, write down answers to the following questions:
   a. How open are your relationships with other group members?
   b. Are there relationships within the group you wish to make more open?
   c. Are there relationships within the group you wish to make more closed?
   d. What actions are needed to make a relationship more open?
   e. What actions are needed to make a relationship more closed?
3. Meet as a group and discuss each of these questions. Arrive at a group consensus on the answers to questions (d) and (e).
4. Each group shares its conclusions about open and closed relationships with the rest of the class.

For a more complete discussion of open and closed relationships, see Johnson (1990).

# GROUP COHESION

To function effectively a group has to cohere, "hang together," generate a "we feeling" among members, or have a positive emotional climate. The most frequently used term to describe a sense of member liking for and commitment to the group is cohesiveness. **Group cohesion** is all the forces (both positive and negative) that cause individuals to maintain their membership in specific groups. Group cohesion is the extent to which the influences on members to remain in the group are greater than the influences on members to leave the group. It is the sum of all the factors influencing members to stay in the group. When group members like one another and wish to remain in one another's presence, the group is cohesive.

Group cohesion is determined by the assessment of group members of the desirable and undesirable consequences of group membership. The more favorable the outcomes members can expect from membership, the more they will be attracted to the group. The outcomes expected from membership in a given group depend on such factors as the nature of the group and its goals, how clearly the goals are stated, how clear the procedures (or paths) are for achieving the goals, how likely it is that the goals will be successfully achieved, the past successes of the group in achieving its goals, how well the group members cooperate with each other, how constructively conflicts among members are managed, the attitude similarity of group members, and whether membership in other groups would provide greater benefits. Group cohesion is constantly changing because different members are attracted to the group to different degrees and the same member's attraction toward the group will vary at different times. Each event that occurs in the group alters the cohesion of the group to some extent.

The level of group cohesion is indicated in several ways. Attendance by group members, whether members arrive on time, the trust and support present among group members, the amount of individuality accepted in the group, the amount of fun members have—all may reflect the cohesion of the group. Cohesion can also be measured just by asking members whether they like one another, whether they want to continue their membership, and whether they are sure they can work effectively with the other group members in the future, and through sociometric devices.

A variety of research studies indicates that group cohesiveness has several definite consequences upon a group (Cartwright, 1968; Watson & Johnson, 1972). As cohesiveness increases, so too does the capacity of a group to keep its members—and the longer the group keeps its members, the greater the likelihood that it will achieve its goals. Highly cohesive groups are characterized by low turnover in membership and low absenteeism. They are less likely to be disrupted when one member does decide to leave. As cohesiveness increases, there is a corresponding rise in the participation of all group members—and the greater the participation of members, the more resources are available to the group to enhance goal accomplishment. Finally, the more cohesive the group, the more closely members will conform to the group's norms (see Figure 12.5). When the norms support productivity, members will work harder. When the norms support working slowly, group productivity will

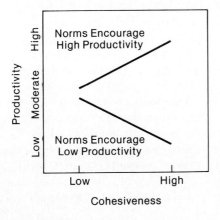

**FIGURE 12.5**  The hypothesized link between productivity and cohesiveness.

decrease. Typically, in a cooperatively structured team, group norms will require members to do their best to help the group be productive.

As cohesiveness increases, members also become more committed to the group's goals, accept assigned tasks and roles more readily, and conform to group norms more frequently. Members of cohesive groups put a greater value on the group's goals and stick more closely to the group's norms than do members of groups lacking cohesion. They are also more eager to protect the group's norms by putting pressure on or rejecting those who violate them. They are more loyal to the group and more willing to work toward a common goal. Unlike members of loosely assembled groups, members of cohesive groups take on group responsibilities more often, persist longer in working toward difficult goals, are more motivated to accomplish the group's tasks (if for no other reason than to live up to the expectations of their fellow group members), and are more satisfied with the work of the group. When the norms of a group favor productivity, those groups that are highly cohesive are more productive in accomplishing goals and in completing assigned tasks. Moreover, group members communicate more frequently and effectively in highly cohesive groups. Their interaction is more friendly, cooperative, and democratic. They are more likely to influence one another in making decisions, to be more willing to accept the opinions of the other members, and to be more willing to be influenced by other members. They are also more willing to endure pain or frustration on behalf of the group and more willing to defend the group against external criticism or attack. Finally, they are more satisfied with the group.

Highly cohesive groups are a source of security for members: They serve to reduce anxiety and to heighten self-esteem. Members of highly cohesive groups experience greater security and relief from tension in the group than do members of noncohesive groups. The awareness that one is liked, accepted, and valued and that others hold similar goals and values is an important aspect of psychological health. A person's acceptance by other group members is related in an important way to his or her participation in the group—the greater the group's acceptance, the more likely he or she is to participate, and the acceptance of the group becomes much more important psychologically after a person has disclosed oneself to the group through participation. Acceptance and approval are of utmost importance for any group member.

Although cohesive groups may show greater acceptance, intimacy, and understanding, there is also evidence that they allow greater development and expression of hostility and conflict than do noncohesive groups. Unless antagonism is openly expressed and conflicts are openly resolved, persistent and impenetrable hostile attitudes may develop that will increasingly hamper effective member cooperation and interaction. The result of a hostile attitude is often an avoidance of and an irrational dislike for the ideas of other members—and a refusal to communicate with them. At the most fundamental level, a person simply does not enjoy being with someone he or she dislikes, and the resulting lack of communication bars chances for the conflict to be resolved. These circumstances have been found to apply between groups as well as between members of a group. Cohesiveness affects such behavior because when the degree of cohesiveness is considerable, the members must mean enough to one another to be willing to bear the discomfort of working through the conflict. Regardless of how angry members of a cohesive group may become with one another, they are more apt to continue communication, which enables the group to resolve conflicts and capitalize upon controversies, both of which increase its productivity. Not only are members of cohesive groups better able to express hostility, but there is also evidence that they are better able to express hostility toward the leader (Pepitone & Reichling, 1955). All in all, cohesiveness in a group results in a better group, one in which members work more cooperatively on their tasks and resolve group difficulties.

How can a group increase its cohesion? There are several ways of doing so:

1. *Structuring cooperation among members.* One of the most predictable outcomes of cooperative interaction is that group members will like each other and value their membership in the group. Because cooperation is discussed in Chapter 3, it will not be discussed here.
2. *Successfully meeting the personal needs of members.* For a group to be cohesive, the members' needs for mutual inclusion, mutual influence, and mutual affection among themselves must be met.
3. *Maintaining a high level of trust among members.* Without a high level of trust, a group cannot be cohesive.
4. *Promoting group norms that encourage the expression of individuality, trusting and trustworthy behavior, and concern and affection among group members.* For a group to be cohesive, group members need to understand how to implement appropriate norms within the group.

Meeting the personal needs of group members, building and maintaining a high level of trust, and implementing appropriate group norms will all be discussed in this chapter.

## DEVELOPING AND MAINTAINING TRUST

An essential aspect of team effectiveness is developing and maintaining a high level of trust among group members. The more members trust each other, the more effectively they will work together (Deutsch, 1962, 1973; Johnson, 1974). Team effectiveness rests on every member's sharing resources, giving and receiving help, dividing the work, and contributing to the accomplishment of mutual goals. Such behaviors will occur when there is trust that everyone else is contributing to the group's progress and not using members' openness and sharing of resources for personal rather than group gain. Team members will more openly express their thoughts, feelings, reactions, opinions, information, and ideas when the trust level is high. When the trust level is low, group members will be evasive, dishonest, and inconsiderate in their communications. The development and maintenance of trust is discussed at length in Johnson (1990) and will therefore be reviewed only briefly at this point.

What is trust? Making a choice to trust another member involves the perception that the choice can lead to gains or losses, that whether you will gain or lose depends upon the behavior of the other member, that the loss will be greater than the gain, and that the other member will probably behave in such a way that you will gain rather than lose. Sounds complicated, doesn't it? In fact, there is nothing simple about trust: It is a complex concept and difficult to explain. An example may help. Imagine you are part of a small group that is supposed to decide which teachers to rehire for next year. You begin to contribute to the discussion, knowing you will gain if you contribute good ideas that other members accept but will lose if your ideas are laughed at and belittled. Whether you gain or lose depends upon the behavior of the other group members. You will feel more hurt if you are laughed at than you will feel satisfaction if your ideas are appreciated. Yet you expect the other group members to consider your ideas and accept them. The issue of trust is expressed in the question every member asks: "If I openly express myself, will what I say be used against me?"

In a team the crucial elements of trust are openness and sharing on the one hand and acceptance, support, and cooperative intentions on the other (see Table 12.1). Cooperative teamwork requires openness and sharing, which in turn are determined by the expression of acceptance, support, and cooperative intentions in the group. Openness is the sharing of information, ideas, thoughts, feelings, and reactions to the issue the group is pursuing. Sharing is the offering of your materials and resources to others in order to help them move the group toward total accomplishment. Acceptance is the communication of high regard for another person and his contributions to the group's work. Support is the communication to another person that you recognize her strengths and believe she has the capabilities she needs to manage productively the situation she is in. Cooperative intentions are the expectations that you are going to behave cooperatively and that every group member will also cooperate in achieving the group's goals. From these definitions, trusting behavior may be defined as openness and sharing and trustworthy behavior may be defined as the expression of acceptance, support, and cooperative intentions. In considering members' trustworthy behavior, you should remember that accepting and supporting the contributions of other group members does not mean that you agree with everything they say. You can express acceptance and support for the openness and sharing of other members and at the same time express different ideas and opposing points of view. This is an important point in building and maintaining trust.

## DEALING WITH PROBLEM BEHAVIORS

There are a number of obstacles to effective team functioning. *The first obstacle is maturity.* Groups ordinarily require some time to develop and stabilize their patterns of working. *The second obstacle is the group's history.* Norms rooted in past practice can sometimes adversely influence group members' current behavior. *The third obstacle is the mixed-motives of team members.* Individuals' motives are almost never purely cooperative. In varying degrees, members may desire team success, but at the same time each member may also desire to have his or her own interests satisfied. Each person may wish to be a star in order to secure individual rewards as well as contribute to the team's success. *Finally, obstructive individual behaviors may inter-*

**Table 12.1**  Open and Closed Relationships

Closed ← → Open

| | Closed | | | Open |
|---|---|---|---|---|
| Content being discussed | The content is of concern to no one (weather talk). | The content consists of technical aspects of work. | The content consists of the ideas and feelings of one person. | The content consists of the relationship between the two persons. |
| Time reference | No time reference (jokes and generalizations). | Distant past or future being discussed. | Recent past or future being discussed. | The immediate "here and now" being discussed. |
| Awareness of your sensing, interpreting, feeling, intending | You never listen to yourself and try to ignore, repress, and deny feelings and reactions. | | | You are constantly aware of what you are sensing, the interpretations you are making, your feelings, and your intentions about acting on your feelings. |
| Openness with own ideas, feelings, reactions | Your statements are generalizations, abstract ideas, intellectualizations; feelings are excluded as irrelevant and inappropriate and nonexistent. | | | Your personal reactions such as attitudes, values, preferences, feelings, experiences, and observations of the present are stated and focused upon; feelings are included as helpful information about the present. |
| Feedback from other people | Feedback from others is avoided, ignored, not listened to, and perceived as being hostile attacks on your personality. | | | Feedback from others is asked for, sought out, listened to, and used to increase your self-awareness; it is perceived as being a helpful attempt to add to your growth and effectiveness. |
| Acceptance of yourself | You believe that once you are known you will be disliked and rejected and, therefore, you hide your "real" self and try to make the impression you think will be most appreciated by other people. | | | You express confidence in your abilities and skills; can discuss your positive qualities without bragging and without false modesty; you understand how you have used your strengths in the past to achieve your goals and are confident you will do so again in the future. |
| Openness to others' ideas, feelings, reactions | You avoid and disregard others' reactions, ideas and feelings; you are embarrassed and put off by others' expressions of feelings; you reject other people and try to one-up and better them; you refuse to hear their feedback on their reactions to your behavior. | | | You listen to and solicit others' reactions, ideas, and feelings; you are interested and receptive to what others are saying and feeling; you express a desire to cooperate fully with them; you make it clear that you see their value and strengths even when you disagree with them; you ask others for feedback on their perceptions of your behavior. |
| Acceptance of other people | You evaluate the other person's actions, communicate that the other is unacceptable, show disregard for the other as a person. | | | You react without evaluation to the other's actions, communicate that the other is acceptable, value the other as a person. |

*fere with team effectiveness.* Despite good intentions, some people talk too much, argue too often, intimidate others, wander from the topic, become obsessed unnecessarily over detail, acquiesce too soon, stubbornly resist, and generally behave in a very human fashion, complete with neurotic and nonneurotic foibles that obstruct group functioning.

When individuals first start working in cooperative teams, they sometimes engage in unhelpful behaviors. Whenever inappropriate member behavior occurs, the team leader's first move should be toward strengthening the perceived interdependence within the work situation. Four of the most common behavioral problems are passive uninvolvement, active uninvolvement, independence, and taking charge.

## Passive Uninvolvement

When members are turning away from the group, not participating, not paying attention to the group's work, saying little or nothing, showing no enthusiasm, or not bringing their work or materials, other members may wish to

1. Jigsaw materials so that each group member has information the others need. If the passive and uninvolved member does not voluntarily contribute his or her information, the other group members will actively involve the student.
2. Divide up roles and assign to the passive, uninvolved member a role that is essential to the group's success.
3. Reward the group on the basis of its average performance, which will encourage other group members to derive strategies for increasing the problem member's involvement.

## Active Uninvolvement

When a member is talking about everything but work, leaving the group, attempting to sabotage the group's work by giving wrong answers or destroying the group's product, refusing to do work, or refusing to work with another group member, team leaders may wish to give a reward that this member or group finds especially attractive and structure the task so that all members must work steadily and contribute in order for the group to succeed and attain the reward. Assigning the member a specific role to fulfill, making the member a group observer with high accountability to collect data about group functioning, and sitting in on the group processing session and confronting the member are other possibilities.

## Independence

When you see a team member working alone and ignoring the group discussion, you may wish to

1. Limit the resources in the group. If there is only one set of materials or piece of equipment in the group, the member will be unable to work independently.
2. Jigsaw materials so that the member cannot do the work without the other members' information. To complete the task the independent member must interact and collaborate.

### Taking Charge

When one group member is doing all the work, refusing to let other members participate, ordering other members around, bullying other members, or making decisions for the group without checking to see if the other members agree, team leaders may wish to

1. Jigsaw resources so that the task cannot be completed without the staff member encouraging others to participate and the staff member listening carefully to the other members' contributions.
2. Assign roles so that other group members have the most powerful and dominant roles.
3. Reward the group on the basis of the lowest two performances by group members. This will place pressure on the person taking charge to encourage and help other members learn the material and complete the task.

## SUMMARY

A team is a set of interpersonal relationships structured to achieve established goals. Teams function as individual members interact. The productivity of teams is not a simple function of team members' technical competencies and task abilities. To be productive, team members must interact face-to-face, perceive strong positive interdependence, be individually accountable, employ their small-group skills, and process how effectively the group has been working. In addition, group members must ensure that the group is cohesive, that trust is built and maintained among group members, and that the group's norms enhance productivity. An effective group can be an extremely dynamic force and have strong psychological influence on its members, as you will find out in the next chapter.

# 13

# Psychological Benefits of Group Membership

## INTRODUCTION

There are many important psychological consequences of being a member of groups. This entire book has detailed many positive benefits of being a member of groups. Some of the psychological benefits include (Johnson & Johnson, 1987b):

1. It is within groups that competencies, attitudes, and values are learned. Personal autonomy results from the internalization of values derived from supportive and caring relationships and the acquisition of social competencies and sensitivity.
2. Interactions with other group members provide support, opportunities, and models for prosocial behavior. It is within interactions with other group members that you help, comfort, share with, take care of, assist, and give to others.
3. It is through interactions with others that all social and psychological development takes place, including the transitions to higher-level reasoning, taking the perspectives of others, and taking long-term time perspectives necessary for delaying gratification and controlling impulsive behavior.
4. It is within groups that the experimentation with a variety of behaviors, roles, and perspectives is conducted and thereby personal identity is developed. In addition, it is through group membership that a frame of reference for perceiving oneself is developed.
5. Positive relationships are formed within groups that can provide companionship, support, help, and assistance throughout one's life.

6. Acceptance by other group members is related to willingness to engage in social interaction, the ability of others to provide one with social rewards, and the utilization of abilities in achievement situations. Rejection by other group members is related to disruptive behavior, hostile and negative affect, and rejection of others. Isolation from others is related to high anxiety, low self-esteem, poor interpersonal skills, emotional handicaps, and psychological pathology.

Three of the most important direct consequences of the dynamics of group membership are social support, self-esteem, and psychological health. Each of these consequences is discussed in this chapter.

## SOCIAL SUPPORT

> A friend is one
> to whom one may pour
> out all the contents
> of one's heart,
> chaff and grain together
> knowing that the
> gentlest of hands
> will take and sift it,
> keep what is worth keeping
> and with a breath of kindness
> blow the rest away.
>                    *Arabian proverb*

Interpersonal relations are central to the quality of every person's life. As social beings, we require others to meet many of our needs. Evidence of the deleterious effects of isolation and the loss of important people in our lives reinforces the conclusion that relationships are critical to our well-being. Social support may provide an explanation as to why, for example, some people fare better than others when exposed to similar stressful circumstances. And social support provides a focus on interventions aimed at bolstering individuals' well-being by either helping people better adapt to adversity or by buffering the relationship between stressors and adverse outcomes. For example, support groups have formed for such diverse populations as cancer patients, first-time parents, the bereaved, rape victims, stepparents, and parents of acting-out teenagers.

One of the most important aspects of group membership is individuals' perceptions of social support. **Social support** is the exchange of resources intended to enhance mutual well-being and the existence and availability of people on whom one can rely for assistance, encouragement, acceptance, and caring. A social support system consists of significant others who collaboratively share people's tasks and goals, who provide individuals with resources (such as money, materials, tools, skills, information, and advice) that enhance their well-being and/or help them deal with the particular stressful situation to which they are exposed, and who help people mobilize their psychological resources in order to deal with their problems. Social support involves

1. Emotional concern such as attachment, reassurance, and a sense of being able to rely on and confide in a person, all of which contribute to the belief that one is loved and cared for.
2. Instrumental aid such as direct aid, goods, or services.
3. Informational aid such as facts or advice that may help to solve a problem.
4. Appraisal support such as feedback about the degree to which certain behavioral standards are met (information relevant to self-evaluation).

Social support has been conceptualized to include **quantity** of connections (number of friends), **quality** (having people one can trust), **utilization** (actually spending time with people), **meaning** (the importance of friends), **availability** (the likelihood of having someone there when needed), and **satisfaction** with one's support. Because not all interpersonal interactions are positive, it is assumed that social support is intended by the giver and perceived by the recipient as beneficial. **General cohesion** is another indication of social support, whereas **alienation,** whether from work, the organization, or other employees (school, schoolwork, and other students), indicates a lack of social support.

Through providing emotional concern, instrumental aid, information, and feedback, supportive people directly and indirectly promote your (Johnson & Johnson, 1987b)

1. Productivity by increasing motivation, morale, quality of cognitive reasoning, and job satisfaction while reducing job-related stress. Social support is related to achievement, successful problem solving, persistence on challenging tasks under frustrating conditions, lack of cognitive interference during problem solving, satisfaction, high morale, attendance or lack of absenteeism, retention, academic and career aspirations, more appropriate seeking of assistance, and greater compliance with regiments and behavioral patterns that increase health and productivity. Social support tends to increase group cohesion and thus affect, through group norms, the pressure towards productivity. Finally, social support reduces work-related stress and stress resulting from job loss and other distressful situations.
2. Psychological well-being and adjustment by providing belonging, clarity of self-identity, increased self-esteem; by preventing neuroticism and psychopathology; by reducing distress; and by providing resources such as confidants. Expressions of caring, love, understanding, concern, intimacy, and inclusion all lead to the secure feeling that you belong. Social support thus not only increases the quality of your life but also clarifies and maintains your positive sense of who you are and what you are like. Social support validates your sense of your own value and adequacy. Reassurance and affirmation of worth result from receiving expressions of approval, praise, and respect. If we are involved in ongoing, interdependent, supportive relationships that provide us with a sense of security, bolster our self-esteem, and strengthen our self-identity, we are less likely to be vulnerable to stressors. Social support, furthermore, is related to psychological health and adjustment, resilience in stressful situations, self-reliance and autonomy, a coherent and integrated self-identity, lack of neuroticism and psychopathology, increased interpersonal skills, greater psychological safety, higher self-

esteem, increased general happiness, reduction of psychological distress, and coping effectively with stressful situations. Probably the most underrated factor in the maintenance of psychological health is friends. The existence of an available confidant, for example, confers significant protection against the development of depression. Rates of mental hospitalization are roughly five to ten times greater for separated, divorced, and widowed persons as compared to married people.

3. Physical health; individuals involved in close relationships live longer, get sick less often, and recover from illness faster than do isolated individuals. Compared with people who maintain supportive relationships, socially isolated persons have two to three times the overall risk of dying prematurely. Social support is related to living longer lives and faster, more complete recovery from illness and injury. Investigators have consistently found that people who are connected with others live longer than single people in every age and ethnic group, and spanning all diseases. Social support is associated with recovery from illness or injury. Pregnant women under stress and without supportive, confiding personal relationships have two times the number of complications experienced by pregnant women undergoing similar levels of stress but with supportive personal relationships.

4. Constructive management of stress by providing the caring, resources, information, and feedback needed to cope with stress and by buffering the impact of stress on the individual. The relationship between social support and stress is discussed further in a subsequent section of this chapter.

There are two ways social support may be present in any situation:

1. Internalized supportive and caring relationships from the past.
2. The situation being structured cooperatively.

Social support may be felt through internalized past caring and committed relationships or through current collaborative relationships with others. Cooperative groups inherently provide a social support system for their members as they work together to maximize each other's productivity as well as their own. Each member gains from the efforts of their collaborators and it is in each member's interest to facilitate the productivity of other group members. As they work together emotional bonds form among group members that result in members relying on each other for assistance, support, and caring.

No matter how materially well off and interpersonally skilled we are, we need considerable social support to live productive and healthy lives. The question becomes, therefore, what are the sources of our social support. The sources of social support include superiors, peers, and subordinates. They may provide productivity and personal support. **Achievement/productivity support** is the providing of assistance and encouragement for productivity on assigned tasks. **Personal support** is the providing of personal liking and caring.

## SOCIAL SUPPORT AND STRESS

A direct relationship exists between the amount of stress within our lives and the amount of social support we need. Most stress has interpersonal origins, and reducing stress largely depends on the quality of the social support we can find. Our relationships with others provide the most powerful forces to either increase or decrease the stress we feel. Arguments with one's spouse, trouble with neighbors, problems getting along with coworkers, hassles from one's boss or supervisor, and difficulties with friends are all sources of stress. A significant source of stress among children is family pathology. Having an alcoholic or abusive parent can create stress that has deep and long-lasting effects. We may need more than our usual amount of support when confronted with certain events such as involving interpersonal losses (that is, the death of a loved one or divorce). Everyone, no matter how well adjusted and skilled the person is, at times experiences high levels of stress and a need for social support.

Perhaps the most powerful sources of stress are loneliness and interpersonal isolation. To feel unloved, alienated from others, isolated, lonely, and unknown is a powerful contributor to stress. In essence, this is the result of an individualistic orientation toward life, where each person works to achieve his or her own goals without any meaningful sense of interdependence or interconnnection with others. Within individualistic situations interpersonal relationships are nonexistent or minimal.

Stressful events can influence whether support is available. Serious distress can both elicit and discourage social support. Many job stresses, such as excessive amounts of work or working late shifts, can disrupt support from family and friends. Serving a jail term, being fired from one's work, moving, divorcing, being ill, retiring, or getting married alter the network of people with whom one comes into daily contact, and thus may undermine opportunities for receiving support.

Not all interpersonal encounters or their effects are positive. Other people can be sources of conflict; competitors can create obstacles in one's path; the efforts of well-intentioned cooperators can backfire if they do not fit one's situation. Moreover, if someone's support does not seem to help the recipient the support tends to be withdrawn.

When stress is being experienced, relationships that are primarily cooperative are essential. When stresses occur, social support is often sought out. And just because one needs the support and caring of others does not mean that it will be given. Stigmatizing events or conditions can reduce others' willingness to provide social support. For example, people suffering from cancer or mental illness make many other people uncomfortable when interacting with the victims.

Social support directly reduces stress by providing the caring, information, resources, and feedback individuals need to cope with stress and to flourish physically and psychologically. Indirect reduction of stress occurs when social support decreases the number or severity of stressful events in an individual's life. Rejection by one person, for example, may be easier to bear when one is loved and respected by many others. Social support and stress are related in that the greater the social support you have the less stress you experience and the better able you are to manage the stresses involved in your life. It is especially during transitions, furthermore, that stress is usually the highest and social support is usually most important.

Cooperative groups ensure that constructive relationships are available to reduce the frequency of stressful experiences, to lower the impact of stress when it occurs (build a defense against feeling stress), and to provide a reservoir of support after stress has occurred. Cooperative groups create relationships and norms that directly increase individuals' ability to deal with stress, indirectly serve as a buffering process, and are a resource to be tapped when stress occurs. An example of the seeking of group membership to manage stress is self-help groups.

## Self-Help Groups

Self-help groups provide emotional anchors and sources of identity and meaning for many individuals struggling with the ups and downs of daily life. It is estimated that in the United States there are over 500,000 self-help groups with about 15 million members. **Self-help groups** are voluntary gatherings of peers who share common problems and needs that are not being addressed by other groups and organizations. The general goals of self-help groups are to promote personal and/or social change for their members and/or society. Self-help groups include Alcoholics Anonymous, former mental patients, minority group members, parents of teenagers, divorced individuals, people on diets, single parents, families living in poverty, and persons with a debilitating illness. The groups are organized around a common need, handicap, or problem of their members. The groups provide the support, emotional nurturance, and sense of identity that members feel is lacking in their lives. People who join self-help groups must define themselves as in need of both help and support from others. They must affirm that they have a problem, need, or handicap, rather than deny its existence. They often must admit that it is a problem that they cannot manage by themselves. They must agree to conform to the norms and expectations of the group (such as not drinking or sticking with their diet). Belonging to a support group often empowers individuals by helping them cope with emotional stress, solve problems, and improve their lives. Membership in the group supports members' efforts to change, obtain a new identity, and enrich their lives. Support groups that provide people with a sense of identity, a way to assert themselves and their values, and a sense of empowerment have become increasingly essential in many people's lives.

In addition to providing social support and protecting one from stress, membership in groups affects individuals' self-esteem.

## SELF-ESTEEM

A person is not born with a sense of self. It is during the first two or three years of life that a kind of crude self-awareness develops, such as being able to make distinctions between what is part of his or her body and what is part of something else. It takes many years of maturation before full adult self-awareness comes into being. As people develop self-awareness, they formulate a self-conception and build processes through which they derive conclusions about their self-esteem. **Self-esteem** is a judgment about one's self-worth, one's competence or value, based on a process of conceptualizing and gathering information about oneself and one's experiences.

There are two major issues concerning self-esteem: the level of self-esteem and the processes through which individuals derive conclusions about their self-worth. It is important for individuals not only to learn to value themselves, but also to learn a constructive way of deciding on their worth from the information available about themselves. There are five basic processes:

1. **Reflected self-acceptance** is based on the way in which others perceive you and evaluate your worth. For example, a person who is perceived by family and friends to be intelligent will consider him- or herself as intelligent.
2. **Basic self-acceptance** is an intrinsic sense of unconditional self-worth.
3. **Conditional self-acceptance** is having one's self-acceptance contingent on meeting external standards and expectations.
4. **Comparative self-evaluation** is a person's estimate of how positively his or her attributes compare with those of peers.
5. **Real-ideal congruence** is the correspondence between what one thinks one is and what one thinks one should be.

Both the level of self-esteem and the process through which self-esteem is determined are derived through relationships and interaction with others. The groups to which one belongs, and the social support they provide, have important and powerful effects on one's self-esteem. Whether one is liked and respected and whether one's actions are effective and appreciated have marked impact on how one evaluates one's worth. There is considerable evidence that participation in cooperatively structured groups tends to promote higher self-esteem than does participation in competitive or individualistic situations (Johnson & Johnson, 1987b). In addition, cooperativeness tends to be related to basic unconditional self-acceptance and positive self-evaluation compared with peers, whereas competitiveness tends to be related to conditional self-acceptance. Avoidance of others tends to be related to basic self-rejection.

Similar to its effects on self-esteem, membership in groups has profound and important effects on psychological health and stability.

## PSYCHOLOGICAL HEALTH AND STABILITY

> A real friend is one who walks in
> When the rest of the world walks out.
>
> *Walter Winchell*

It is within groups that psychological health is developed or destroyed. **Psychological health** may be defined as the ability to be aware of and manage effectively one's collaborative relationships with others. A central component in developing and maintaining psychological health and stability is the social support present in the groups in which one belongs. It is through membership in groups such as the family, peer groups, educational settings, and career organizations that a person develops (Johnson & Johnson, 1987b)

1. The basic trust that he or she can rely on the affection and support of others.
2. The ability to view situations and problems from a variety of perspectives.
3. A meaningful sense of direction and purpose in life.
4. Awareness of mutual interdependence with others.
5. An integrated and coherent sense of personal identity.

A recent review of the literature found several studies indicating a relationship between (1) poor peer relations in childhood and (2) destructive social conduct in adolescence and psychological pathology in adulthood (Johnson & Johnson, 1987b). The more positive an individual's attitude toward cooperating with others, furthermore, the greater their psychological health. The more an individual is oriented toward avoiding interacting with others, the greater their psychological pathology.

One of the central tools in maintaining psychological health and stability is the enjoyment of humor.

## Humor

An important aspect of psychological health, and a unique aspect of group functioning, is **humor.** A healthy group is a humorous group. Humor can change everything, calm our anger, ease our embarrassment, relax our tensions, free us from boredom, dissolve our fears, establish rapport with strangers, and dramatically build more positive relationships. Like a sudden ray of sunshine that creates a rainbow in a thunderstorm, humor transforms our emotions from negative to positive, our perspective from egocentric to objective, and our relationships from cold to warm. Humor, when it is used appropriately, is a valuable tool. Within a group, humor may be used to redirect members away from potentially hostile, aggressive, or tense situations. It can be used to defuse a negative event or resolve a conflict among group members. Conversely, it can also be used to disorient other members, minimize their contributions, and emotionally hurt or injure them.

There are three major psychological theories of humor. **Incongruity-related theories** focus on the fact that, in many jokes, two seemingly incompatible phenomena are brought together. The audience is led along a certain path of comprehension and is then abruptly switched to another path by the punch line. An opposition between the two paths is highlighted. Psychologists who favor this theory talk about **incongruity-resolution mechanisms.** An example is a statement made by Woody Allen, "I don't know if I believe in an afterlife, but I'm taking a change of underwear."

**Disparagement-related theories** assume that humor is primarily an expression of human aggression, and that the purpose of jokes is to denigrate the audience or a third party. Thomas Hobbes, the English philosopher, is usually credited with this theory, although Plato, Aristotle, and Cicero mentioned it two millennia earlier. An opposition is created between "bad" and "good" individuals. For some adherents to this theory, humor is good because it replaces less civilized outlets for violence and aggression, such as physical combat or war. For other adherents, humor is bad because it still vents malice.

**Release-related theories** claim that laughter provides relief for mental, nervous, and psychic energy and thus restores balance and calm after struggle, tension, or strain. Freud, who developed the best known release theory, related humor to the sexual drive. Contemporary psychologists see this as part of **arousal-safety theory.** Laughter occurs when someone experiences heightened arousal but then evaluates the stimulus as safe or inconsequential. An opposition is created between obscene versus nonobscene, and is expressed in terms of sex, violence, bodily functions, and other taboos.

Humor is based on unpredictability. Catching us off guard is the essence of humor, which is created by presenting us with a paradox, a discrepancy between words and action, a startling event, a slight twist of perspective, or a sudden truth or personal insight.

Laughter is just plain good for you and your relationships. And it should be taken seriously as a means for building and maintaining both effective working relationships and friendships. Humor is a valuable asset to anyone who applies it. You may use humor to

1. Improve your personal health, well-being, and longevity. On a personal level, hearty laughter results in heart and blood circulation rates being elevated, muscles vibrating in a relaxing internal massage, and the brain emitting hormones that trigger the release of endorphins, the body's natural painkillers. Humor can release tensions, ease pain, and generally promote healing and health. Laughter provides relief for mental, nervous, and psychic energy, and thus restores balance and calm after struggle, tension, or strain. Laughing keeps you from cracking up or breaking down, vents your negative feelings, and promotes healthy self-acceptance. Learning to get more laughter from life enhances your motivation and morale. Laugher is a wonderful way of making today better and heading off stress and problems. Humor can help you keep life in perspective. Humor can expand awareness and broaden your perspective, thereby improving your ability to solve problems and relate effectively to others. The ability to find the humor in situations can go a long way toward helping you to avoid job burnout. The good health and relaxation achieved through laughing every day will tend to lengthen your life. Through humor you learn to accept yourself as a mortal, prone to failure and living with anxiety, yet always capable of coping anew.

2. Improve your relationships with other group members. Victor Borge once said, "Humor is the shortest distance between two people." Glasser (1984) states that humans have a basic need to have fun. Many long-term relationships grow empty because fun is neglected, taken for granted, or not felt as much needed by one of the partners as the other. Fun is a basic ingredient of group work. Successful group members are those who make group work fun for each other. Interpersonally, humor livens up your own and your associates' lives. Generally, the more humor you bring to relationships, the more positive and constructive they will be. People are perceived

to be more attractive, friendly, and desirable as friends when they offer others a chance for positive interactions. People tend to enjoy being around a person who creates an atmosphere that is optimistic, constructive, and happy.

3. Relieve stress and improve your problem-solving capabilities. In laughing or joking you separate yourself from annoying incidents. Humor is often an essential tool for reducing fear and anxiety. Trying to view one's problems with a sense of humor and laughing off setbacks and hurts are widely used means of reducing tension. The Roman philosopher Epictetus stated, "Men are disturbed not by things but by the view that they take of things." By choosing to react to anxiety-provoking events with humor, you can reduce your stress and preoccupation, thereby inducing creativity, alertness, and problem-solving ability. Learning to think funny when it's necessary to think straight—thereby relieving your mind of the grip of stress—can make the difference over the course of a career between retiring as a department manager or less and retiring as a corporate vice-president or more. Remember, "allow nonsense and sense is not far behind!"

4. Resolve interpersonal conflicts. Humor is an important tool for managing conflicts. First, humor can blunt the anger and calm the anxiety that you will often have when you are in conflict with other group members. It is hard to be angry, to be afraid, or to carry a grudge when you are laughing. When another member is angry at you, disagrees with you, or is rejecting of you, you can transform your negative reactions into laughter. Second, you may use humor to defuse the anger, hostility, and opposition of other group members. By the skillful use of humor you may redirect fellow members away from potentially hostile, aggressive, or tense reactions. When group members face each other in a competitive or hostile situation, humor may lessen the tension and allow them to make concessions without appearing weak or appeasing. Humor is often used as a tool of diplomacy to create a more relaxed and frank atmosphere in discussions. In direct negotiations, furthermore, humor has been found to produce more concessions and less resentment and anger on the part of opponents. One observer claims that Henry Kissinger made humor a tool of diplomacy. His banter inspired banter in others and usually led to a more relaxed atmosphere in the private, formal discussions or negotiations with world leaders. Humor opened the door to more frankness and less ritualized recitations as well. A laboratory study of bargaining supports this journalistic observation (O'Quin & Aronoff, 1981). Subjects acted as buyers and a confederate acted as seller of a landscape painting. The subjects were instructed to make a first bid of $10,000, and the seller began with a counteroffer of $70,000. When they were within $10,000 of one another, the seller made a final offer. In one condition, he simply said, "My offer is _____," and in the other condition he added, "and I'll throw in my pet frog." Subjects offered more for the painting when the seller had a sense of humor. Finally, Baron & Ball (1974) found that of two groups of individuals who were subjected separately to anger-inducing situations, the group that was shown a series of humorous cartoons later exhibited markedly less aggressive, less hostile behavior toward the object of anger.

5. Motivate yourself and your comembers. Humor energizes, freeing you from anger, resentment, hostility, disappointment, and other negative mood states so that you have more energy to work productively. Humor boosts enthusiasm and energy, which are stepping stones to greater motivation and productivity.

6. Gain attention. People may remember more of what you say when you are humorous. Your communications will have greater impact when they include humor. After-dinner speakers often begin their talks with a story or a joke. The idea is to relax the audience, gain its attention, and promote a positive impression. Yet evidence does not indicate that humor increases the effectiveness of persuasive communication

(Gruner, 1965). Lull (1940), for example, found that adding humor to speeches did not increase either the judged interest level of the speeches or their persuasiveness. Humor, however, was a very effective means of getting an audience's attention and goodwill.

7. Adjust to the insoluble problems in life. A sense of humor helps you survive until conditions change and problems are solved. Remember what William Makepeace Thackeray (a nineteenth-century English novelist) said, "A good laugh is sunshine in a house." Trying to view one's problems with a sense of humor and to laugh off setbacks and hurts are widely used means of dealing with problems that are currently beyond your power to solve.

Many people must relearn the humorous approach to life because it was squelched when they were children. "Wipe that smile off your face." "Don't laugh in church." "Don't be silly." "Settle down and get serious." These are statements all children tend to hear from their parents and other adults. Some good advice for you as an adult is to "put a smile on your face," "laugh often and deeply," "be silly whenever it is appropriate," and "be less serious." Relearn how to approach life with a sense of humor.

Humor is a skill that you can learn and use to your benefit. "There are three things that are real," wrote John F. Kennedy. "God, human folly, and laughter. The first two are beyond our comprehension. So we must do what we can with the third." To become skillful in being humorous, try the following:

1. Look for humor everywhere, in signs, newspapers, and daily events. Most of all, learn to guide your reaction to the events around you into a humorous outcome.
2. Set a goal of having 15 laughs a day. Joke books, a tape of your favorite comedian, or a phone call to a friend may help. Carry a small notebook with your favorite jokes and cartoons in it. At anytime during the day when a laugh may help, take out the notebook and look at it until you laugh.
3. Learn to be an "inverse paranoid." Believe that the world is out to do you good.
4. You can use humor to control your anger and to maintain at least a working relationship with people you must deal with regularly—even though you resent their attitude, disdain their ability, and dislike their looks. Do it this way. List their obnoxious traits in a notebook. Then match each trait with an expression of humor. Whenever you interact with them, think of the humor connected with them. You will find it much easier to relate to them in a relaxed and natural way.
5. Give each member of your family or workgroup a coupon book. Imprint the coupons with messages such as "Good for 10 minutes of silence—no matter how much I want to keep arguing," or "Hand me this and I won't say 'I told you so'."

For those interested in learning more about the productive use of humor, contact Joel Goodman, director of the Humor Project, 110 Spring Street, Saratoga Springs, NY 12866.

## CONSTRUCTIVE PEER RELATIONSHIPS AS PREVENTION

Many individuals feel isolated, disconnected from their family and peers, unattached to school and career, without purpose and direction, and lacking any distinct impression of who or what kind of person they are. At home, in school, at work, and in their community, they feel like an alien in their own native land, estranged from themselves, their families, their peers, and the activities that others are involved in. They are isolated not only by their own feelings of alienation but also by the stress and lack of support and caring present in their experiences.

The prevention of antisocial and psychologically disturbed behavior requires the building and maintaining of supportive and caring peer relationships in which the person is valued as a separate and unique individual. Having fellow group members and friends who value appropriate social goals (such as educational attainment, a productive career, and self-sufficiency), discouraging antisocial conduct, and behaving in competent and effective ways is essential for most individuals. Peer relationships are one of the most important influences on whether one engages in antisocial or prosocial actions; develops high ego-strength, psychological health, autonomy, and independence; acquires appropriate attitudes and values; and achieves academically and works productively. Being isolated from peers is one of the major signals of psychological distress and maladjustment. Deciding what groups to join, who one associates with, and who to be friends with are three of the most important actions one can take to ensure a productive and fulfilling life.

## SUMMARY

Besides the numerous benefits of belonging to groups detailed in this book, group membership provides many psychological benefits. Three of the most important are social support, self-esteem, and psychological health. Social support involves the exchange of resources intended to enhance mutual well-being and the existence of availability of people on whom one can rely for assistance, encouragement, acceptance, and caring. Through providing emotional concern, instrumental aid, information, and feedback, supportive people directly and indirectly promote your productivity, psychological well-being and adjustment, physical health, and ability to cope with stress. Social support and stress are related in that the greater your social support the less the stress you experience and the better able you are to manage the stresses involved in your life. Self-help groups are examples of how powerful the influences of social support can be. It is within groups, furthermore, that self-esteem is developed and enhanced. Self-esteem is derived through relationships and interaction with others. The level of self-esteem, and the reasoning process used to derive conclusions about self-worth, are both products of interpersonal interaction. The more cooperative your relationships with others, the higher your self-esteem will be and the more constructive will be your processes for deriving conclusions about your worth. Finally, psychological health depends on belonging to groups in which one is valued and respected. The basic attitudes and competencies necessary to maintain psychological health and stability are developed in groups. One often neglected aspect of health-producing relationships is humor. Psychological distress can be prevented or minimized through careful selection of the groups to which you belong and the people and friends with whom you spend time.

# Epilogue

I am cast upon a horrible, desolate island; void of all hope of recovery. I am singled out and separated, as it were, from all the world, to be miserable. I am divided from mankind, a solitary; one banished from human society. I have no soul to speak to or to relieve me.

*Daniel Defoe (1908, p. 51)*

When Robinson Crusoe was cast up on the shore of a tropical island, the lone survivor of a shipwreck, he had everything he needed for a comfortable life. He had more than adequate food, the climate was ideal, and the setting was beautiful. While he was thankful for being alive, he cursed his solitary life. He was emotionally miserable because he was no longer a member of any human group.

Humans are small group beings. We always have been and we always will be. The ubiquitousness of groups and the inevitability of being in them make groups one of the most important factors in our lives. As the effectiveness of our groups go, so goes the quality of our lives. Quite often groups are not very effective. To be effective, groups must have the following characteristics.

Groups must have clear goals that highlight the positive interdependence among members. Cooperation among group members is so fundamental that it is part of the definition of what a group is. The more cooperative group members are, as opposed to competitive or individualistic, the more productive the group is, the more members like each other, and the more psychologically healthy group members tend to be. Effective, two-way communication is the basis of all group functioning and interaction among group members. A group has to have shared leadership and the participation of all members. Groups need to balance their decision-making procedures with the time and resources available, the size and seriousness of the decision, and the commitment required to implement the decision. High-quality decisions require that all major alternatives are given a complete and fair hearing. That is ensured by the use of advocacy subgroups in the controversy process. The utilization of controversy enhances the quality and creativity of group decisions. There are, however, conflicts of interest among group members that must be resolved through negotiations. There are two types of negotiations: problem solving and win-lose. Through the use of problem-solving negotiations relationships among group members may be maintained while mutually acceptable agreements are worked out. Power needs to be used in positive ways to enhance mutual success. Group cohesion needs to be high.

To ensure that groups are effective, members must be highly skilled in small group skills. Humans are not born with these skills; they must be developed. You have now completed a variety of experiences aimed at increasing your group knowledge and skills. It is hoped that you are now a more effective group member. It is hoped that you are able to apply your increased skills and knowledge in a variety of groups and under a variety of conditions. You may wish to repeat many of the exercises in this book to reinforce your knowledge and to reread much of the material to gain a more complete understanding of how to utilize group skills. There are, however, two concluding exercises that may be helpful in applying the material covered in this book to the memberships you hold in groups.

## EXERCISE E.1:
## TERMINATING A GROUP

The goals of this exercise are to (1) complete any unfinished business in a group, (2) relive and remember the positive group experiences the group has had, (3) synthesize what group members have received from being part of the group, and (4) describe and express constructively group members' feelings about the termination of the group. The theme of the exercise is that although every group ends, the things you as a member have given and received, the ways in which you have grown, the skills you have learned, all continue with you. Terminating relationships may be sad, but the ways in which you have grown within your relationships with other group members can be applied to group situations in the future. Here is the procedure for the group to follow in the exercise:

1. Discuss the topic, "Is there anything that needs to be resolved, discussed, dealt with, or expressed before the group ends?"
2. Discuss these questions: "What have been the most significant experiences of the group? What have I gotten out of being a member of the group? How has being a part of this group facilitated my growth as a person? What skills have I learned from being in this group?" As alternatives to a discussion, group members might make a painting, a collage, or a poem describing their experiences.
3. Discuss how you feel about the group winding up its activities and what feelings you want to express about the termination. Personal styles of handling the dissolution of a group may be discussed. If you cannot discuss this issue, the following alternatives may generate a productive discussion:

a. Each of you in turn says good-bye to the group and leaves. Each of you then spends five minutes thinking about your feelings and returns to express anything you wanted to but did not express before.

b. Each of you nonverbally shows how you felt when you first joined the group and then shows nonverbally how you feel now.

4. As a closing exercise, stand up in a close circle. You are all to imagine that you have the magical power to give anything you wish to another group member. You are then to give the person on your right a parting gift, each taking your turn so that everyone in the group can hear what the gifts are. Examples of what individuals might give are moonbeams, a flower, a better self-concept, an ability to commit oneself to a relationship, comfort with conflict, more empathy with others, the perfect love affair, and so on. When giving the gift, extend your hands as if actually passing something to the other person.

5. Have a group hug.

**EXERCISE E.2:**
**SELF-CONTRACT**

Write a description of yourself as a group member. Mention all the strengths and skills you can think of and mention the areas in which you need to increase your skills. Then make a contract with yourself to make some changes in your life; the contract can involve starting something new, stopping something old, or changing some present aspect of your life. It should involve applying your group skills to the actual group situations you are now facing, or working to develop certain skills further. It may involve joining new groups and terminating old group memberships. In making the contract, pick several group memberships you now have and set a series of goals concerning how you will behave to increase your effectiveness and satisfaction as a group member. Write the contract down, place it in an envelope, address the envelope to yourself, and open it three months later.

# Appendix: Answers

## BROKEN SQUARES EXERCISE:
## DIRECTIONS FOR MAKING A SET OF SQUARES (3.6)

For each five-member group you will need a set of five envelopes containing pieces of cardboard that have been cut in different patterns and that, when properly arranged with pieces from some of the other four envelopes, will form five squares of equal size. To prepare a set, cut out five cardboard squares of equal size, approximately 6 by 6 inches. Place the squares in a row and make them as below, penciling the letters "a," "b," "c," and so on lightly so that they can later be erased.

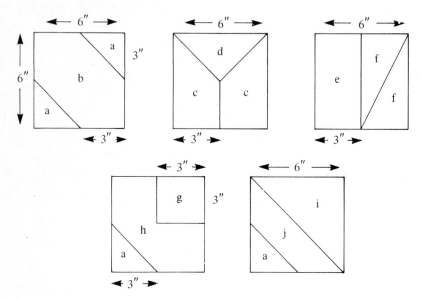

The lines should be so drawn that when the pieces are cut out, all pieces marked "a" will be exactly the same size, the pieces marked "c" will be the same size, and the pieces marked "f" will be the same size. By using multiples of 3 inches, several combinations will be possible that will enable participants to form one or two squares, but one combination is possible that will form five squares 6 by 6 inches.

After drawing the lines of the 6- by 6-inch squares and labeling them with the lowercase letters, cut each square as marked into smaller pieces to make the parts of the puzzle.

Mark the five envelopes "A," "B," "C," "D," and "E," and distribute the cardboard pieces among them as follows:

Envelope A has pieces i, h, e.
Envelope B has pieces a, a, a, c.
Envelope C has pieces a, j.
Envelope D has pieces d, f.
Envelope E has pieces g, b, f, c.

Erase the penciled letter from each piece and write on it instead its appropriate envelope letter. This relabeling will make it easy, when a group has completed the task, to return the pieces to the proper envelope for later use.

## GOAL STRUCTURES EXERCISE:
## ANSWERS (3.7)

Squares:  40
Biangles:  11
Triangles:  18

## BEWISE COLLEGE PROBLEM:
## SOLUTION (4.2)

| Name | Background | Education Degree | Teaching Experience | Public Relations Experience | Administrative Experience |
|------|-----------|------------------|---------------------|------------------------------|---------------------------|
| David Wolcott | Black American | Master's | 13 years | None | 8 years |
| Roger Thornton | Upper-class family | B.A., master's | 7 years | 9 years; politician | 16 years |
| Edythe Holubec | Community center director | None | 8 years | 2 years | 7 years |
| Frank Pierce | Neighborhood center worker; community relations | Master's | None | 14 years | 14 years |
| Helen Johnson | Childhood in slums | B.A., master's | 4 years | 5 years | 15 years |
| Keith Clement | Volunteer work; author of a book | B.A. | 5 years | 13 years | None |

Andrews College is the smallest college in the state, and therefore it had a completely black American student body in 1952.

As is evident from the table, all candidates but Helen Johnson are disqualified because they lack one of the qualifications outlined in the data sheets.

## SOLSTICE-SHENANIGANS MYSTERY:
## SOLUTION (4.3)

The Solstice Shenanigans Mystery Exercise appears on page 118. The painting by Artisimisso was stolen by Mr. Handsome, who took it with him when he left the party at 9:50. He took the painting because he was a kleptomaniac.

## LIEPZ AND BOUNZ EXERCISE:
## SOLUTION (4.4)

The Liepz and Bounz Exercise is on page 120. David jogged from Farmland to Muncie in 1 (5/5) jumpz.

**SQUARE ARRANGEMENT 1:**
**ONE-WAY COMMUNICATION (4.6)**

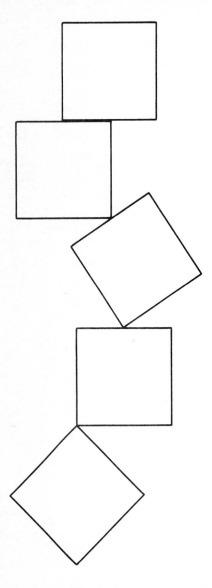

*Instructions:* Study the arrangement above. With your back to the group members, instruct them on how to draw the squares. Begin with the top square and describe each in succession, taking particular note of the placement of each in relation to the preceding one. No questions allowed.

**SQUARE ARRANGEMENT II:**
**TWO-WAY COMMUNICATION (4.6)**

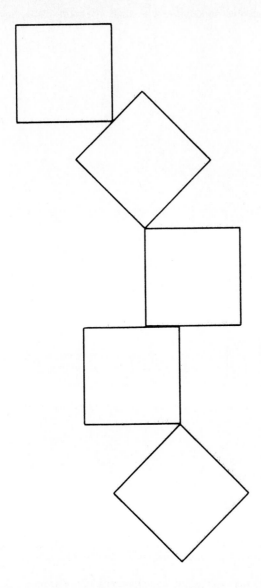

*Instructions:* Study the arrangement shown. Facing the group, instruct the members on how to draw the squares. Begin with the top square and describe each in succession, taking particular note of the placement of each in relation to the preceding one. Answer all questions from participants and repeat your description if necessary.

## FURNITURE FACTORY EXERCISE:
## SOLUTION (5.7)

The more directly Mr. Day involves the workers in the change, the more likely they are to support the change.

   a.  5
   b.  1
   c.  3
   d.  4
   e.  2

## HOLLOW SQUARE EXERCISE (5.11)

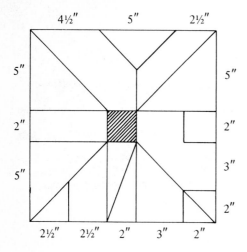

## WINTER SURVIVAL EXERCISE (6.3)

### Background Information for Coordinator

None of the information here should be given to participants until after they have completed the decision-making parts of the exercise. Mid-January is the coldest time of the year in Minnesota and Manitoba. The first problem the survivors face, therefore, is to preserve their body heat and protect themselves against its loss. This problem can be met by building a fire, minimizing movement and exertion, using as much insulation as possible, and constructing a shelter.

The participants have just crash-landed. Many individuals tend to overlook the enormous shock reaction this has upon the human body, and the death of the pilot and copilot increases the shock. Decision making under such conditions is extremely difficult. Such a situation requires a strong emphasis upon the use of reasoning, not only for making decisions, but also for reducing the fear and panic every survivor would naturally feel. Shock is manifested in feelings of helplessness, loneliness, and hopelessness as well as in fear. These feelings have brought about more fatalities than perhaps any other cause in survival situations. Through the use of reasoning, hope for survival and the will to live can be generated. Certainly the state of shock means that the movement of the survivors should be at a minimum and that an attempt to calm them should be made.

Before taking off, a pilot always has to file a flight plan. The flight plan contains the vital information regarding the flight, such as the course, speed, estimated time of arrival, type of aircraft, and number of persons on board. Search-and-rescue operations would begin shortly after the failure of the plane to appear at its destination at its estimated time of arrival.

The 20 miles to the nearest known town is a long walk even under ideal conditions, particularly if one is not used to walking such distances. Under the circumstances of being in shock, being dressed in city clothes, and having deep snow in the woods and a variety of water barriers to cross, to attempt to walk out would mean almost certain death from freezing and exhaustion. At temperatures of minus 25 to minus 40 degrees Fahrenheit the loss of body heat through exertion is a very serious matter.

Once the survivors have found ways in which to keep warm, their immediate problem is to attract the attention of search planes and search parties. Thus, all the items the group has salvaged must be assessed for their value in signaling the group's whereabouts.

## WINTER SURVIVAL EXERCISE: ANSWER KEY

| Item | Experts' Ranking | Your Ranking | Difference Score |
|---|---|---|---|
| Ball of steel wool | 2 | | |
| Newspapers (one per person) | 8 | | |
| Compass | 12 | | |
| Hand ax | 6 | | |
| Cigarette lighter (without fluid) | 1 | | |
| Loaded .45-caliber pistol | 9 | | |
| Sectional air map made of plastic | 11 | | |
| 20-ft by 20-ft piece of heavy-duty canvas | 5 | | |
| Extra shirt and pants for each survivor | 3 | | |
| Can of shortening | 4 | | |
| Quart of 100-proof whiskey | 10 | | |
| Family-size chocolate bar (one per person) | 7 | | |
| Total | | | _____ |

### Explanation of Answer Key

The following ranking of the survivors' items was made on the basis of information provided by Mark Wanvig and Roger Johnson and supplemented by Rutstrum (1973). Wanvig was an instructor in survival training for three years in the reconnaissance school in the 101st Division of the U.S. Army and later an instructor in wilderness survival for four years at the Twin City Institute for Talented Youth. He is now conducting wilderness-survival programs for Minneapolis teachers. Johnson is a national expert on environmental education.

1. *Cigarette lighter (without fluid).* The gravest danger facing the group is exposure to the cold. The greatest need is for a source of warmth and the second greatest need is for signaling devices. This makes building a fire the first order of business. Without matches something is needed to produce sparks to start a fire. Even without fluid the cigarette lighter can be used to produce sparks. The fire will provide not only warmth but also smoke for daytime signaling and firelight for nighttime signaling.

2. *Ball of steel wool.* To make a fire, the survivors need a means of catching the sparks made by the cigarette lighter. Steel wool is the best substance with which to catch a spark and support a flame, even if it is a little wet.

3. *Extra shirt and pants for each survivor.* Clothes are probably the most versatile items one can have in a situation like this. Besides adding warmth to the body they can be used for shelter, signaling, bedding, bandages, string when unraveled, and tinder to make fires. Even maps can be drawn on them. The versatility of clothes and the need for fires, signaling devices, and warmth make these items third in importance.

4. *Can of shortening.* This item has many uses—the most important being that a mirrorlike signaling device can be made from the lid. After shining the lid with the steel wool, the survivors can use it to produce an effective reflector of sunlight. A mirror is the most powerful tool they have for communicating their presence. In sunlight, a simple mirror can generate 5 to 7 million candlepower. The reflected sunbeam can be seen beyond the horizon. Its effectiveness is somewhat limited by the trees, but one member of the group could climb a tree and use the mirror to signal search planes. If the survivors had no other means of signaling than this, they would still have a better than 80 percent chance of being rescued within the first 24 hours.

   Other uses for this item are as follows: The shortening can be rubbed on exposed areas of the body, such as the face, lips, and hands, for protection from the cold. In desperation it could be eaten in small amounts. When melted into an oil the shortening is helpful in starting fires. When soaked into a piece of cloth, melted shortening will produce an effective candlewick. The can is useful in melting snow to produce drinking water. Even in winter water is important, as the body loses water in many ways, such as through perspiration, respiration, and shock. This water must be replenished, because dehydration affects one's ability to make clear decisions. The can is also useful as a cup.

5. *Twenty-by-twenty-foot piece of heavy-duty canvas.* The cold makes some form of shelter necessary. The canvas can be part of a shelter, protecting the survivors from the wind and possible snow. Spread on a frame and secured, it could make a good tent as well as a ground cover. Rigged as a wind screen, it could hold heat. Its squareness, contrasting with the surrounding terrain, might also be spotted in an air search, and this makes it an important signaling device.

6. *Hand ax.* The survivors need a continuous supply of wood in order to maintain the fire. The ax is useful in obtaining wood, and also for clearing a sheltered campsite, cutting boughs for ground insulation, and constructing a frame for the shelter.

7. *Family-size chocolate bars (one per person).* To gather wood for the fire and to set up signals, the survivors need energy. The chocolate will supply the energy to sustain them for some time. Because it contains mostly carbohydrates, it supplies energy without making digestive demands upon the body.

8. *Newspapers (one per person).* The newspaper can be used for starting a fire. It will also serve as an insulator: When rolled up and placed under the clothes around a person's legs and arms, it provides dead-air space for extra protection from the cold. The survivors can use the paper for recreation by reading it, memorizing it, folding it, or tearing it. They can roll it into a cone and yell through it as a signal device. They can also spread it around an area to help signal a rescue party.

9. *Loaded .45-caliber pistol.* The pistol provides a sound-signaling device. (The international distress signal is three shots fired in rapid succession.) There have been numerous cases of survivors going undetected because they were too weak to make a loud enough noise to attract attention. The butt of the pistol can be used as a hammer. The powder from the shells will assist in fire building. By placing a small bit of cloth in a cartridge emptied of its bullet, one can start a fire by firing the gun at dry wood on the ground. At night the muzzle blast of the gun is visible, and this provides another means of signaling.

The pistol's advantages are counterbalanced by its dangerous disadvantages. Anger, frustration, impatience, irritability, and lapses of rationality may increase as the group waits to be rescued. The availability of a lethal weapon is a substantial danger to the group under these conditions. Although the pistol could be used for hunting, it would take a highly skilled marksman to kill an animal with it. Even then the animal would have to be transported through the snow to the crash area, which would probably consume more energy than would be advisable.

10. *Quart of 100-proof whiskey.* The only uses of the whiskey are as an aid in fire building and as a fuel. A torch could be made from a piece of clothing soaked in the whiskey and attached to an upright pole. The danger of whiskey is that someone might try to drink it when it is cold. Alcohol takes on the temperature it is exposed to, and a drink of it at minus 30 degrees Fahrenheit would freeze a person's esophagus and stomach and do considerable damage to the mouth. Drinking it warm would cause dehydration. Alcohol, furthermore, mixes badly with cold because it dilates the blood vessels in the skin. This results in chilled blood being carried back to the heart, which in turn chills the heart and contributes to a rapid loss of body heat. An intoxicated person is much more likely to get hypothermia than a nonintoxicated person. The bottle may be used to store heated water.

11. *Compass.* Because the compass may also encourage some survivors to try to walk to the nearest town, it too is a dangerous item. The only redeeming feature of the compass is the possible use of its glass top as a reflector of sunlight to signal search planes, but this would be the least effective of the potential signaling devices available. That it might tempt survivors to walk away from the crash site makes it the least desirable of the 12 items.

12. *Sectional air map made of plastic.* This item is dangerous because it will encourage individuals to attempt to walk to the nearest town—thereby condemning them to almost certain death.

## THEY'LL NEVER TAKE US ALIVE EXERCISE: ANSWER KEY (6.4)

| Item | Experts' Ranking | Your Ranking | Difference Score |
|---|---|---|---|
| Swimming | 5 | | |
| Railroads | 7 | | |
| Police work | 11 | | |
| Home appliances | 9 | | |
| Alcohol | 2 | | |
| Nuclear power | 12 | | |
| Smoking | 1 | | |
| Motor vehicles | 3 | | |
| Pesticides | 15 | | |
| Handguns | 4 | | |
| Bicycles | 8 | | |
| Firefighting | 10 | | |
| Mountain climbing | 13 | | |
| Vaccinations | 14 | | |
| Surgery | 6 | | |
| Total | | _____ | |

## STRANDED IN THE DESERT EXERCISE:
## SCORING, KEY (7.3)

| Item | Experts' Ranking | Your Ranking | Difference Score |
|---|---|---|---|
| Magnetic compass | 12 | | |
| 20-ft by 20-ft piece of heavy-duty canvas | 7 | | |
| Book, *Plants of the Desert* | 10 | | |
| Rear-view mirror | 1 | | |
| Large knife | 5 | | |
| Flashlight (four battery size) | 8 | | |
| One jacket per person | 2 | | |
| One transparent plastic ground cloth (6 by 4 feet) per person | 4 | | |
| Loaded .38-caliber pistol | 9 | | |
| One 2-quart plastic canteen full of water per person | 3 | | |
| Acccurate map of the area | 11 | | |
| Large box of kitchen matches | 6 | | |
| Total | | | ——————— |

Score your group's ranking by finding the absolute difference between your ranking and the experts' ranking. An absolute difference is found by recording the difference between the two rankings while ignoring all plus or minus signs. After finding all the absolute differences, sum them. The lower your total score, the more accurate your ranking.

**Stranded in the Desert: Rationale for Experts' Ranking**

The group has just been through a traumatic situation that has had a shocking impact on all members. The fact that your advisor and the driver were killed would increase the shock reaction. Most, if not all, members of your group need to receive treatment for shock. Five of the more important problems for your group are as follows (Nesbitt, Pond, & Allen, 1959). One vital problem for the group members is dehydration from exposure to the sun, from bodily activity (causing perspiration and respiration), and from the hot dry air circulating next to the skin. To prevent dehydration the group members should (1) remain calm to reduce loss of moisture through respiration, (2) wear as many clothes as you can to reduce the loss of moisture through perspiration and having the dry desert air circulate next to your skin (by wearing sufficient clothes to keep the desert air away from your skin you can lengthen your survival time by at least a day), (3) stay in the shade, (4) minimize movement, especially during the day, and (5) drink as much water as you can. Any activity that increases heartbeat, respiration, and perspiration will speed up dehydration. Taking care to remain calm and in the shade, the group could probably survive three days without water. The need for clothes makes the jackets important. The need for shade makes the canvas important. To survive you must keep your body properly hydrated either with adequate water or by keeping body heat production down and keeping desert heat (from sun, air, and ground reflection) out. Once the jackets are on and the sunshade is up, everyone should be as calm and inactive as possible.

Another vital problem is signaling search parties of your whereabouts so that you may be rescued. The items that may be used to signal your presence are the mirror, the canvas, the flashlight, the revolver, and a fire (matches). The mirror is the most important signaling device the group has. As Nesbitt, Pond, and Allen (1959) state, "A signal mirror is the best, the simplest, the most important piece of survival equipment ever invented for the desert." In sunlight the mirror can generate 5 to 7 million candlepower of light, which may be seen beyond the horizon. It pays to flash the mirror at the horizon even when no plane is in view;

search planes have turned toward a mirror flash even when the survivors have neither seen or heard them. The canvas, when spread out to make a shelter, not only can reduce the temperature underneath it by as much as 20 degrees Fahrenheit but it can also be easily spotted from the air because it contrasts with the terrain. The flashlight provides a reliable and quick night signaling device. The pistol is an important sound signaling device, since speech becomes seriously impaired due to dehydration. In the desert setting there have been numerous occurrences of searchers not detecting the people they were looking for because the survivors could not make loud enough noises to attract the searchers' attention. There are important disadvantages to having the revolver in the hands of a group member who may become hysterical due to the trauma of the situation or delusional due to dehydration. Finally, building a fire at night and using smoke columns during the day will help attract the attention of searchers. "A column of smoke by day, a pillar of fire by night" is a biblical quotation worth remembering for desert signaling.

The third major problem is obtaining as much drinkable water as possible. The water you have in your canteens is enough to keep you rational for a while, but not enough to extend your survival time. That is, the water in the canteens is enough to hold off the effects of dehydration for a while; without water, within 24 hours you can expect to have impatience, nausea, and sleepiness interfere with rational decision making. The only way in which you may obtain purified water to drink from the shallow hole nearby is to build a solar still. The still is built by stretching the ground clothes a few inches above the waterhole and tilting them so that they drain into the canteens. The knife is helpful in cutting the stakes necessary to arrange the ground clothes. When the sun shines through the plastic onto the water, condensation forms on the underside of the plastic. The moisture is distilled and purified water.

The fourth problem is protecting yourself from the cold at night. Although the desert is hot during the day, it still gets cold at night. The jackets become important to protect the group members from the cold, as do the matches (to build a fire), and the canvas (to provide a shelter).

The fifth problem is gathering food if the group is not rescued in the first few days. It is important not to eat protein, as it takes considerable water to digest protein and flush out the waste products. The book on plants will be helpful in obtaining food. Hunting for animals, furthermore, would cause dehydration and would do far more harm than good.

If the group decides to walk out, traveling at night, all members will probably be dead by the second day. They will have walked less than 33 miles during the two nights. If group members decide to walk during the day, they will probably be dead by the next morning, after walking less than 12 miles. For the group to walk out, having just gone through a traumatic experience that has had a considerable impact on the body, having few if any members who have walked 45 miles before, and having to carry the canvas and wear the jackets to prevent dehydration, would be disastrous. One further fact of great importance: Once the members start walking, they will be much harder to spot by search parties. The compass and the map, therefore, are not helpful to the group's survival.

## FALLOUT SHELTER EXERCISE:
## ANSWERS (7.5)

<u>1</u> Containers of water. (The average person would need at least 1 quart of liquid per day. Each person should be allowed to drink according to need since studies have shown that nothing is gained by limiting the liquids below the amount demanded by the body. Two weeks is probably the maximum time needed to stay in the shelter. After that, other sources of water could be found.)

*This exercise is based on information in *Protection in the Nuclear Age* (Washington, D.C.: Department of Defense, Defense Civil Preparedness Agency, February 1977).

  2 Canned and dried foods. (Enough food should be on hand to feed everyone for two weeks, if possible. However, most people can get along on about half as much food as usual and can survive for several days without any. Therefore, this is not as important as the water.)

  3 1 large and 1 small garbage can with lids. (Next to water and food, the next most important concern is sanitation. Poor sanitation will attract diseases and vermin. The small garbage can can be used as a toilet and the large garbage can can be used to store garbage and human wastes until they can be taken outside and buried. Burial of the garbage is important to prevent spread of disease by rats or insects.)

  4 First-aid kit and iodine and medicines. (Useful if anyone gets hurt or falls ill; should include medicine for anyone with chronic illness. The iodine can be used to sterilize water.)

  5 Battery-powered radio. (Useful for obtaining information about what is happening outside the shelter and for information on when it is safe to come out. Useful for contact with outside world.)

  6 Soap and towels. (Useful and important for sanitation.)

  7 Liquid chlorine bleach. (Useful for sprinkling in the toilet to keep down odors and germs; it could also be used to sterilize any water which has become cloudy and thereby might contain bacteria.)

  8 Matches and candles. (They would help illuminate the shelter and thus make it more comfortable, particularly since there is not likely to be any natural source of light or electricity available.)

  9 Blankets. (They would be used for heat and comfort; would be of important but moderate use.)

 10 Flashlight and batteries. (Useful for illumination.)

 11 Cooking and eating utensils. (Useful in preparing and serving foods, but not essential.)

 12 Broom. (Useful for brushing radioactive fallout off anyone who had to leave the shelter for emergency reasons before they reentered.)

 13 Canned heat stove. (Useful if a heat supply is needed. However, it can only be used if there is adequate ventilation for the fumes; it could be dangerous.)

 14 Geiger counter. (Unnecessary. It could be used to check level of radiation outside the shelter to determine when it is safe to emerge, but the same information and more can be obtained from the radio. Also, fallout particles are visible and the radiation from them is given off quickly, so danger from radiation could be reduced by waiting 24 to 48 hours after the large particles have stopped falling.)

 15 Foam fire extinguisher. (Useful for fighting fires outside the shelter but could not be used within the shelter because of danger from the fumes.)

**THE JOHNSON SCHOOL EXERCISE:**
**SOLUTION (7.6)**

The following Johnsons coached the sports in the order listed.

1. Frank coached golf, basketball, wrestling, and track.
2. Roger coached basketball, golf, track, and wrestling.
3. David coached wrestling, track, basketball, and golf.
4. Helen coached track, wrestling, golf, and basketball.

**CREATIVITY PROBLEM:**
**SOLUTION (7.9)**

The solution of this problem is based upon the creative insight of going outside the obvious boundaries of the dots.

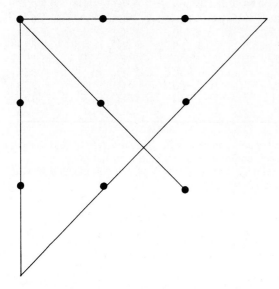

**JOE DOODLEBUG EXERCISE:**
**HINTS (7.10)**

1. Joe does not always have to face the food in order to eat it.
2. Joe can jump sideways and backward, as well as forward.
3. Read the problem again: Joe was moving east when the food was presented.

**JOE DOODLEBUG EXERCISE:**
**SOLUTION**

At the moment Joe's master set down the food, Joe had already jumped once to the east. He therefore has to jump sideways three times more to the east, and once sideways back to the west, landing on top of the food. He can now eat.

## MAKING A PROFIT EXERCISE:
## BUYER PROFIT SHEET (8.5)

| Oil | | Gas | | Coal | |
|---|---|---|---|---|---|
| Price | Profit | Price | Profit | Price | Profit |
| A | $4,000 | A | $2,000 | A | $1,000 |
| B | 3,500 | B | 1,750 | B | 875 |
| C | 3,000 | C | 1,500 | C | 750 |
| D | 2,500 | D | 1,250 | D | 625 |
| E | 2,000 | E | 1,000 | E | 500 |
| F | 1,500 | F | 750 | F | 375 |
| G | 1,000 | G | 500 | G | 250 |
| H | 500 | H | 250 | H | 125 |
| I | 0 | I | 0 | I | 0 |

The nine prices for each commodity are represented by the letters A to I. Next to each price is the profit you would make for each commodity if you sold it at that price.

You can say anything you wish during negotiations, but you may *not* show this profit sheet to the buyer you are negotiating with.

## MAKING A PROFIT EXERCISE:
## SELLER PROFIT SHEET

| Oil | | Gas | | Coal | |
|---|---|---|---|---|---|
| Price | Profit | Price | Profit | Price | Profit |
| A | $    0 | A | $    0 | A | $    0 |
| B | 125 | B | 250 | B | 500 |
| C | 250 | C | 500 | C | 1,000 |
| D | 375 | D | 750 | D | 1,500 |
| E | 500 | E | 1,000 | E | 2,000 |
| F | 625 | F | 1,250 | F | 2,500 |
| G | 750 | G | 1,500 | G | 3,000 |
| H | 875 | H | 1,750 | H | 3,500 |
| I | 1,000 | I | 2,000 | I | 4,000 |

**BATTLESHIP EXERCISE:**
**MODEL FOR COORDINATOR (8.8)**

|    | A | B | C | D | E | F | G | H | I | J |
|----|---|---|---|---|---|---|---|---|---|---|
| 1  |   |   |   |   |   |   |   |   |   |   |
| 2  |   |   |   |   |   |   |   |   |   |   |
| 3  |   |   |   |   |   |   |   |   |   |   |
| 4  |   |   |   | 1 |   |   |   |   |   |   |
| 5  |   |   | 1 | 3 | 1 |   |   |   |   |   |
| 6  |   |   | 1 | 5 | 1 |   |   |   |   |   |
| 7  |   |   | 1 | 5 | 1 |   |   |   |   |   |
| 8  |   |   | 1 | 3 | 1 |   |   |   |   |   |
| 9  |   |   |   | 1 |   |   |   |   |   |   |
| 10 |   |   |   |   |   |   |   |   |   |   |

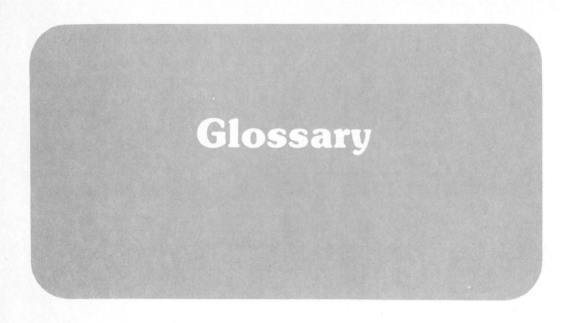

# Glossary

**Action research:**  The use of the scientific method in solving research questions that have significant social value.

**Action theory:**  Theory as to what actions are needed to achieve a desired consequence in a given situation.

**Additive tasks:**  Tasks for which group productivity represents the sum of individual member efforts.

**Aggregate:**  Collections of individuals who do not interact with one another.

**Arbitration:**  A form of third-party intervention in negotiations in which recommendations of the person intervening are binding on the parties involved.

**Assimilation:**  Changing a message to fit into your own cognitive frameworks and perspective.

**Attributional theory:**  A social psychological explanation of how individuals make inferences about the causes of behaviors and events.

**Authority:**  Legitimate power vested in a particular position to ensure that individuals in subordinate positions meet the requirements of their organizational role.

**Autocratic leader:**  A leader who dictates orders and determines all policy without involving group members in decision making.

**Bargaining:**  See *negotiations.*

**Cathexis:**  The investment of psychological energy in objects and events outside of oneself.

**Channel:**  The means of sending a message to another person, such as sound and sight.

**Charisma:**  An extraordinary power, as of working miracles.

**Charismatic leader:**  A person who has (1) an extraordinary power or vision and is able to communicate it to others or (2) unusual powers of practical leadership that will enable her to achieve the goals that will alleviate followers' distress.

**Cognitive dissonance:**  When a person possesses two cognitions that contradict each other. The theory developed by Leon Festinger predicts that dissonance is uncomfortable and a person will seek to reduce it.

**Cognitive structure:**  A set of principles and processes that organizes cognitive experience.

**Cohesiveness:**  All the forces (both positive and negative) that cause individuals to maintain their membership in specific groups. These include attraction to other group members and a close match between individuals' needs and the goals and activities of the group. The attractiveness that a group has for its members and that the members have for one another.

**Communication:**  A message sent by a person to a receiver(s) with the conscious intent of affecting the receiver's behavior.

**Communication networks:**  Representations of the acceptable paths of communication between persons in a group or organization.

**Competitive goal structure:** A negative correlation among group members' goal attainments; when group members perceive that they can obtain their goals if and only if the other members with whom they are competitively linked fail to obtain their goal.

**Compliance:** Behavior in accordance with a direct request. Behavioral change without internal acceptance.

**Consensus:** A collective opinion arrived at by a group of individuals working together under conditions that permit communications to be sufficiently open and the group climate to be sufficiently supportive for everyone in the group to feel that he or she has had a fair chance to influence the decision.

**Conformity:** Changes in behavior that result from group influences. Yielding to group pressures when no direct request to comply is made.

**Construct:** A concept, defined in terms of observable events, used by a theory to account for regularities or relationships in data.

**Conjunctive tasks:** Tasks for which group productivity is determined by the effort or ability of the weakest member.

**Concurrence seeking:** Situation where members of a decision-making group inhibit discussion to avoid any disagreement or arguments and emphasize agreement; there is a suppression of different conclusions, an emphasis on quick compromise, and a lack of disagreement within a decision-making group.

**Confrontation:** The direct expression of one's view of the conflict and one's feelings about it and at the same time an invitation to the opposition to do the same.

**Contingency theory of leadership:** A theory suggesting that leader effectiveness is determined both by characteristics of leaders and by several situational factors.

**Contractual norms:** Contracts that spell out the rules to be observed and the penalties for violating them.

**Controversy:** The situation that exists when one group member's ideas, information, conclusions, theories, and opinions are incompatible with those of another, and the two seek to reach an agreement.

**Cooperative goal structure:** A positive correlation among group members' goal attainments; when group members perceive that they can achieve their goal if and only if the other members with whom they are cooperatively linked obtain their goal.

**Critical path method:** Identifying the final goal and working backward to detail what must happen (tasks and subgoals) before it is achieved, what resources must be allocated, what the timetable for accomplishing each subgoal should be, and who should have what responsibilities.

**Debate:** Situation where group members present the best case for positions that are incompatible with one another and a winner is declared on the basis of who presented the best position.

**Decision making:** Obtaining some agreement among group members as to which of several courses of action is most desirable for achieving the group's goals.

The process through which groups identify problems in achieving the group's goals and attain solutions to them.

**Deindividuation:** A psychological state characterized by reduced self-awareness and major shifts in perception. It is encouraged by certain exernal conditions (e.g., anonymity) and enhances the performance of wild, impulsive forms of behavior.

**Democratic leader:** A leader who sets policies through group discussion and decision, encouraging and helping group members to interact, requesting the cooperation of others, and being considerate of members' feelings and needs.

**Deutsch, Morton:** Social psychologist who theorized about cooperative, competitive, and individualistic goal structures.

**Dilemma of honesty and openness:** The risk of either being exploited for disclosing too much too quickly or seriously damaging the negotiating relationship by refusing to disclose information and thereby seeming to be deceitful or distrusting.

**Dilemma of trust:** Choice between believing the other negotiator and risking potential exploitation or disbelieving the other negotiator and risking no agreement.

**Disjunctive tasks:** Tasks for which group performance is determined by the most competent or skilled member.

**Distributed-actions theory of leadership:** The performance of acts that help the group to complete its task and to maintain effective working relationships among its members.

**Effective communication:** When the receiver interprets the sender's message in the same way the sender intended it.

**Equity or merit view of distributing rewards:** Presented by Homans (1961) as a basic rule of distributive justice and equity theory: In a just distribution, rewards will be distributed among individuals in proportion to their contributions. In other words, those members who contribute the most to the group's success should receive the greatest benefits.

**Equality system of distributive justice:** All rewards are distributed equally among group members.

**Evaluation apprehension:** Concern over being evaluated by others. Such concern may increase arousal and may play an important role in social facilitation.

**Experiential learning:** Generating an action theory from your own experiences and then continually modifying it to improve your effectiveness.

**False consensus bias:** A belief (often false) that most other people think and feel very much as we do, such as sharing our stereotypes (such as believing that poor people are lazy).

**Force field analysis:** Portraying the problem as a balance between forces working in opposite directions—some helping the movement toward the desired state of affairs and others restraining such movement. The balance that results between the helping and restraining forces is the actual state of affairs—a **quasi-stationary equilibrium** that can be altered through changes in the forces.

**Frustration-aggression process:** Frustration due to the inability to achieve one's goals produces a readiness to respond in an aggressive manner which may boil over into hostility and violence if situational cues that serve as "releasers" are present.

**Fundamental attributional error:** The attribution of the causes of other's behaviors to personal (disposition) factors and the causes of one's own behavior to situational (environmental) factors. In explaining the causes of the other's behavior the attributor overestimates the causal importance of personality, beliefs, attitudes, and values, and underestimates the causal importance of situational pressures. The opposite is done in explaining the causes of one's own behavior.

**Gatekeeper:** Person who translates and interprets messages, information, and new developments to group-mates.

**Goal:** A desired place toward which people are working; a state of affairs that people value.

**Goal structure:** The type of social interdependence specified among individuals as they strive to achieve their goals.

**Great-person theory of leadership:** A theory suggesting that all great leaders share key traits that equip them for positions of power and authority.

**Group:** Two or more individuals in face-to-face interaction, each aware of his or her membership in the group, each aware of the others who belong to the group, and each aware of their positive interdependence as they strive to achieve mutual goals.

**Group dynamics:** The area of social science that focuses on advancing knowledge about the nature of group life. The scientific study of behavior in groups to advance our knowledge about the nature of groups, group development, and the interrelations between groups and individuals, other groups, and larger entities.

**Group effectiveness:** Success by the group in (1) achieving its goals, (2) maintaining good working relationships among members, and (3) developing and adapting to changing conditions to improve its ability to achieve 1 and 2.

**Group efficacy:** The expectation of successfully obtaining valued outcomes through the joint efforts of the group members.

**Group goal:** A future state of affairs desired by enough members of a group to motivate the group to work toward its achievement.

**Group influences:** The impact of groups on their members.

**Group polarization:** The tendency of group members to shift toward more extreme positions than those held initially, as a function of group discussion.

**Group processing:** Reflecting on a group session to (1) describe what member actions were helpful and unhelpful and (2) make decisions about what actions to continue or change.

**Group structure:** A stable pattern of interaction among group members created by a role structure and group norms.

**Groupthink:** The tendency of members of highly cohesive groups led by dynamic leaders to adhere to shared views so strongly that they totally ignore external information inconsistent with these views. A mode of thinking in which group members' strivings for unanimity override their motivation to appraise alternative courses of action realistically. A strong concurrence-seeking tendency that interferes with effective group decision making.

**Hawthorne effect:** A change in behavior that occurs when individuals know they are being observed by researchers.

**Hero-traitor dynamic:** The negotiator who "wins" is seen as a "hero" and the one who "loses" is perceived to be a "traitor."

**Hidden agendas:** Personal goals that are unknown to all the other group members and are at cross-purposes with the dominant group goals.

**Illusionary correlation:** Association perceived between two unrelated factors, such as being poor and being lazy, usually leading to stereotypes.

**Independent variable:** The variable manipulated by the researcher in an experiment; the causal factor in a cause-effect relationship.

**Individual accountability:** Assessing the quality and quantity of each member's contributions and giving the results to all group members.

**Individualization:** Maintaining a sense of unique individual identity.

**Individualistic goal structure:** No correlation among group members' goal attainments; when group members perceive that obtaining their goal is unrelated to the goal achievement of other members.

**Inducibility:** Openness to influence.

**Information dependence:** Dependence on others for information about their preferences, needs, and expectations so that an agreement can be reached.

**Influence leader:** A person who exerts more influence on other group members than they exert on him.

**Interest:** Need, goal, benefit, profit, advantage, concern, right, or claim.

**Integration:** Combining several positions into one new, creative position.

**Laissez-faire leader:** A leader who does not participate in group's decision making at all.

**Leader:** An individual in a group who exerts the greatest influence on other members.

**Leadership:** The process through which leaders exert their impact on other group members.

**Level of aspiration (LOA):** The compromise between ideal goals and more realistic expectations. A concept developed primarily by Kurt Lewin to explain how people set and revise goals themselves and for their groups. Generally, individuals enter situations with an ideal outcome in mind but revise their goals upward after success and downward after failure.

**Leveling:** Making a message shorter, more concise,

and more easily grasped and told. The reciprocal of sharpening.

**Lewin, Kurt:** Father of group dynamics; social psychologist who originated field theory, experimental group dynamics, and applied group dynamics.

**Machiavellian leadership:** Leadership based on the beliefs that (1) people are basically weak, fallible, and gullible, and not particularly trustworthy; (2) others are impersonal objects; and (3) one should manipulate others whenever it is necessary in order to achieve one's ends.

**Mediation:** A form of third-party intervention in negotiations in which a neutral person recommends a nonbinding agreement.

**Message:** Any verbal or nonverbal symbol that one person transmits to another; the subject matter being referred to in a symbolic way (all words are symbols).

**Need distribution of reward:** A situation in which the group members who are most in need of the rewards receive a disproportionate amount of them. A rule suggesting that individuals receive a share of available rewards reflecting their current needs.

**Negative monitoring:** Monitoring unpleasant, unrewarding, frustrating, destructive, counterproductive behaviors.

**Negotiating:** A process by which persons who want to come to an agreement try to work out a settlement by exchanging proposals and counterproposals.

**Noise:** Any element that interferes with the communication process.

**Norms:** The rules or expectations that specify appropriate behavior in the group; the standards by which group members regulate their actions.

**Norm of equity:** Norm specifying that the benefits received or the costs assessed by the negotiators should be equal.

**Norm of reciprocity:** Norm that a negotiator should return the same benefit or harm given him or her by the other negotiator; "an eye for an eye and a kiss for a kiss" is an example of a norm of reciprocity.

**Observational research:** The systematic description and recording of events that occur in groups by observers.

**Operational goals:** Goals for which specific steps to achievement are clear and identifiable.

**Organizational development:** The use of diagnosis and intervention procedures to promote effective interpersonal, group, and intergroup behavior within the organization.

**Outcome dependence:** Dependence on others to agree to one's proposals in negotiations. Because all parties must commit themselves to an agreement, each is dependent upon the others for the outcome.

**Package deal:** Several issues being negotiated are all included as part of the agreement.

**Participant observer:** A person who is skilled enough to both participate in group work and observe group process at the same time; analysis of the group process and functioning by a participating member of the group.

**Personal space:** The distance that people like to keep between themselves and others.

**Prisoner's dilemma game:** Nonzero-sum game used by Deutsch and others to investigate trust and conflict.

**Primary groups:** Small groups characterized by face-to-face interaction, interdependency, and strong group identification such as families and very close friends.

**Problem:** A discrepancy or difference between an actual state of affairs and a desired state of affairs.

**Process consultation:** An organizational development procedure of analyzing group functioning by an observing expert.

**Process loss:** Losses in members' performance due to their participation in the group.

**Promise:** The statement that if you do as I want, I will engage in an act that will benefit you. A negotiator stating that if the other performs a desired act the negotiator will make sure the other receives benefits.

**Psychodynamic fallacy:** Seeing the motivation for another's behavior in terms of personality factors rather than the dynamics of intergroup conflict.

**Reactance:** People's need to reestablish their freedom whenever it is threatened.

**Reference group:** A group people identify with, compare their attitudes to, and use as a means to evaluate those attitudes.

**Referent power:** Power based on the group members' identification with, attraction to, or respect for the powerholder.

**Resource attractor:** An attribute (such as ability or training) that tends to attract other resources because it gives the possessor an advantage in a competition for these other resources.

**Reward power:** Power based on the powerholder's control over the positive and negative reinforcements desired by other group members.

**Risky-shift:** The tendency for individuals to recommend riskier courses of action following group discussion than was true prior to such interaction. The tendency for groups to make riskier decisions than individuals.

**Role:** A set of expectations defining appropriate behaviors associated with a position within a group. The "part" played by a member of a group. Rules or understandings about the tasks persons occupying certain positions within a group are expected to perform.

**Scapegoat:** A guiltless but defenseless group who is attacked to provide an outlet for pent-up anger and frustration caused by another group.

**Self-efficacy:** The expectation of successfully obtaining valued outcomes through personal effort.

**Self-fulfilling prophecy:** A set of actions that provokes another into engaging in behavior that confirms one's original assumptions. An example is assuming that the other is belligerent and then proceeding to engage in hostile behavior thereby provoking the other into belligerent actions, which confirms the original assumption.

**Sharpening:** Selective perceiving and remembering of a few high points of a message while most of the rest is forgotten. The reciprocal of leveling.

**Situational approach to leadership:** The view that those members of a group most likely to become leaders are those who can best help it to reach its major goals.

**Social exchange:** A form of social interaction in which participants exchange something of value. What they exchange can range from specific goods or services through information, love, and approval.

**Social determinism:** The view that historic events are determined by social forces, social movements, and changing social values; see *zeitgeist*.

**Social facilitation:** The enhancement of well-learned responses in the presence of others. Effects on performance resulting from the presence of others.

**Social interaction:** Patterns of mutual influence linking two or more persons.

**Social loafing:** A reduction of individual effort when working with others on an additive group task.

**Social skills training:** A structured intervention designed to help participants to improve their interpersonal skills. It is generally conducted in group settings.

**Socioemotional activity:** Behavior that focuses on interpersonal relations in the group.

**Sociometry:** A measurement procedure developed by Moreno that is used to summarize graphically and mathematically patterns of interpersonal attraction in groups.

**Stereotypes:** A set of cognitive generalizations that summarize, organize, and guide the processing of information about members of a particular group. It is a set of expectations held by members of the ingroup regarding members of an outgroup.

**Superordinate goals:** Goals that cannot be easily ignored by members of two antagonistic groups, but whose attainment is beyond the resources and efforts of either group alone; the two groups, therefore, must join in a cooperative effort in order to attain the goals.

**Survey feedback:** An organizational development procedure that focuses on describing the current state of the organization through surveys or interviews and then sharing this descriptive information through feedback.

**Synthesizing:** Integrating a number of different positions containing diverse information and conclusions into a new, single, inclusive position that all group members can agree on and commit themselves to.

**Team:** A set of interpersonal relationships structured to achieve established goals.

**Team building:** The analysis of work procedures and activities to improve productivity, relationships among members, the social competence of members, and the ability of the team to adapt to changing conditions and demands.

**Threat:** The statement that unless you do as I want you to, I will engage in an act that will harm you. One individual informing another that negative actions will follow if the recipient of the threat does (or does not) behave in some manner. A negotiator stating that unless the other agrees to the proposed settlement, the negotiator will make sure the other is harmed.

**Tie-in:** In negotiations, an issue considered extraneous by the other person is introduced and you offer to accept a certain settlement provided this extraneous issue will also be settled to one's satisfaction.

**Transactional approach to leadership:** An approach suggesting that leadership involves a complex social relationship between leaders and followers in which each exerts influence on the other.

**Victim derogation:** The tendency for persons who take unfair advantage of others to view negatively the victims of their exploitation, believing that the victims somehow *deserve* such treatment.

**Triggering event:** An event (such as two group members being in competition or the expression of criticism on a sensitive point) that triggers the occurrence of a conflict.

**Win-lose dynamic:** Seeing every action of the other as a move to dominate.

**Zeitgeist:** Spirit or temper of the times.

# References

ACHENBACK, T., & EDELBROCK, C. (1981). Behavioral problems and competencies reported by parents of normal and disturbed children aged four through sixteen. *Monographs of the Society for Research in Child Development, 46* (1, Serial No. 188).

ALLEN, V. (1965). Situational factors in conformity. In L. Berkowitz (Ed.), *Advances in experimental social psychology* (Vol. 2). New York: Academic Press.

ALLPORT, F. (1924). *Social psychology.* Boston: Houghton Mifflin.

ALLPORT, G. (1954). *The nature of prejudice.* Reading, MA: Addison-Wesley.

————, & POSTMAN, L. (1945). The basic psychology of rumor. *Transactions of New York Academic Sciences,* Series II, *8,* 61–81.

ARONSON, E. (1972). *The social animal.* San Francisco: W. H. Freeman.

————, BLANEY, N., STEPHAN, C., SIKES, J., & SNAPP, M. (1978). *The jigsaw classroom.* Beverly Hills, CA: Sage Publications.

ASARNOW, J., & CALLAN, J. (1985). Boys with peer adjustment problems: Social cognitive processes. *Journal of Consulting and Clinical Psychology, 53,* 80–87.

ASCH, S. (1956). Studies of independence and conformity: A minority of one against a unanimous majority. *Psychological Monographs, 70,* 416.

————. (1957). An experimental investigation of group influence. In *Symposium on Preventive and Social Psychiatry,* Walter Reed Army Institute of Research. Washington, D.C.: U.S. Government Printing Office.

ATKINSON, J., & RAYNOR, J. (EDS.). (1974). *Motivation and achievement.* Washington, D.C.: Winston.

AXELROD, R. (1984). *The evolution of cooperation.* New York: Basic Books.

BABCHUK, N., & GOODE, W. (1951). Work incentives in a self-determined group. *American Journal of Sociology, 16,* 679–687.

BAHN, C. (1965). *The interaction of creativity and social facilitation in creative problem solving* (doctoral dissertation, Columbia University). Dissertation Abstracts International. (University Microfilms No. 65-7499.)

BALDERSTON, G. (1930). *Group incentives, some variations in the use of group bonus and gang piece work.* Philadelphia: University of Pennsylvania Press.

BALES, R. (1950). *Interaction process analysis.* Reading, MA: Addison-Wesley.

————. (1952). Some uniformities of behavior in small social systems. In G. Swanson, T. Newcomb, & E. Hartley (Eds.), *Readings in social psychology.* New York: Holt.

———. (1955). How people interact in conferences. *Scientific American, 192,* 31–35.

———. (1965). The equilibrium problem in small groups. In A. Hare, E. Borgatta, & R. Bales (Eds.), *Small groups: Studies in social interaction.* New York: Alfred A. Knopf.

———, & BORGATTA, E. (1955). Size of group as a factor in the interaction profile. In A. Hare, E. Borgatta, & R. Bales (Eds.), *Small groups.* New York: Knopf.

BANAS, P. (1988). Employee involvement: A sustained labor/management initiative at the Ford Motor Company. In J. Campbell & R. Campbell (Eds.), *Productivity in organizations: New perspectives from industrial and organizational psychology* (pp. 388–416). San Francisco: Jossey-Bass.

BANDURA, A. (1965). Vicarious processes: A case of no-trial learning. In L. Berkowitz (Ed.), *Advances in experimental social psychology* (Vol. 2). New York: Academic Press.

———. (1969). *Principles of behavior modification.* New York: Holt, Rinehart and Winston.

BARNLUND, D. (1959). A comparative study of individual, majority and group judgment. *Journal of Abnormal and Social Psychology, 58,* 55.

BARON, R., & BALL, R. (1974). The aggression-inhibiting influence of nonhostile humor. *Journal of Experimental Social Psychology, 10*(1), 23–33.

———, BARON, P., & MILLER, N. (1973). The relation between distraction and persuasion. *Psychological Bulletin, 80,* 310–323.

BARTLETT, F. (1932). *Remembering.* Cambridge: Cambridge University Press.

BASS, B. (1960). *Leadership, psychology, and organizational behavior.* New York: Harper & Row.

BAVELAS, A. (1942). Morale and training of leaders. In G. Watson (Ed.), *Civilian morale.* Boston: Houghton Mifflin.

———. (1948). A mathematical model for group structures. *Applied Anthropology, 7,* 16–30.

———, HOSTORF, A., GROSS, A., & KITE, W. (1965). Experiments on the alteration of group structure. *Journal of Experimental Social Psychology, 1,* 55–70.

BECKHARD, R. (1969). *Organizational development.* Reading, MA: Addison-Wesley.

BEKHTEREV, W. (1924). Die ergebnisse des experiments auf dem gebiet der kollektiven reflexologie. *Zeitschrift fur Angewandte Psychologie.*

BEM, D. (1972). Self-perception theory. In L. Berkowitz (Ed.), *Advances in experimental social psychology* (Vol. 6). New York: Academic Press.

BENNETT, E. (1955). Discussion, decision, commitment and consensus in "group decision." *Human Relations, 8,* 251.

BERKOWITZ, L. (1978). Whatever happened to the frustration-aggression hypothesis? *American Behavioral Scientist, 32,* 691–708.

BERLYNE, D. (1965). Curiosity and education. In J. Krumboltz (Ed.), *Learning and the educational process.* Chicago: Rand McNally.

———. (1966). Notes on intrinsic motivation and intrinsic reward in relation to instruction. In J. Bruner (Ed.), *Learning about learning* (Cooperative Research Monograph No. 15). Washington, D.C.: U.S. Department of Health, Education, and Welfare, Office of Education.

———. (1971). *Aesthetics and psychobiology.* New York: Appleton-Century-Crofts.

BERSCHEID, E., & WALSTER, E. (1969). *Interpersonal attraction.* Reading, MA: Addison-Wesley.

———, & WALSTER, E. (1974). Physical attractiveness. In L. Berkowitz (Ed.), *Advances in experimental social psychology* (Vol. 7). New York: Academic Press.

BIERMAN, R. (1969). Dimensions for interpersonal facilitation in psychotherapy in child development. *Psychological Bulletin, 72,* 338–352.

BION, W. (1961). *Experiences in groups.* New York: Basic Books.

BIRD, C. (1940). *Social psychology.* New York: Appleton-Century-Crofts.

BLAKE, R., & MOUTON, J. (1962a). Comprehension of points of commonality in competing solutions. *Sociometry, 25,* 56–63.

———. (1962b). The intergroup dynamics of win-lose conflict and problem-solving collaboration in union-management relations. In M. Sherif (Ed.), *Intergroup relations and leadership.* New York: John Wiley.

BLANCHARD, F., WEIGAL, R., & COOK, S. (1975). The effect of relative competence of group members upon interpersonal attraction in cooperating interracial groups. *Journal of Personality and Social Psychology, 32,* 519–530.

BLAU, P. (1954). Co-operation and competition in a bureaucracy. *American Journal of Sociology, 59,* 530–535.

BOLEN, L., & TORRANCE, E. (1976, April). *An experimental study of the influence of locus of control, dyadic interaction, and sex on creative thinking.* Paper presented at the Annual Meeting of the American Educational Research Association, San Francisco.

BONNER, H. (1959). *Group dynamics: Principles and applications.* New York: Ronald Press.

BOTKIN, B. (1957). *A treasury of American anecdotes.* New York: Random House.

BREHM, J. (1966). *A theory of psychological reactance.* New York: Academic Press.

———. (1976). Responses to loss of freedom: A theory of psychological reactance. In J. Thibaut, J. Spence, & R. Carson (Eds.), *Contemporary topics in social psychology.* Morristown, NJ: General Learning Press.

———, & SENSENIG, J. (1966). Social influence as a

function of attempted and implied usurpation of choice. *Journal of Personality and Social Psychology, 4,* 703–707.

BREHM, S., & BREHM, J. (1981). *Psychological reactance: A theory of freedom and control.* New York: Academic Press.

BREWER, M., & KRAMER, R. (1985). The psychology of intergroup attitudes and behavior. *Annual review of psychology, 36,* 219–243.

BRICKNER, M., HARKINS, S. & OSTROM, T. (1986). Effects of personal involvement: Thought-provoking implications for social loafing. *Journal of Personality and Social Psychology, 51,* 763–769.

BRONOWSKI, J. (1973). *The ascent of man.* Boston: Little Brown.

BROWN, B. (1968). The effects of the need to maintain face on interpersonal bargaining. *Journal of Experimental Social Psychology, 4,* 107–122.

BRUNER, J., & MINTURN, A. (1955). Perceptual identification and perceptual organization. *Journal of Genetic Psychology, 53,* 21–28.

BURKE, P. (1972). Leadership role differentiation. In C. McClintock (Ed.), *Experimental social psychology* (pp. 514–546). New York: Holt, Rinehart and Winston.

———. (1974). Participation and leadership in small groups. *American Sociological Review, 39,* 832–842.

BURKE, R. (1969, July). Methods of resolving interpersonal conflict. *Personnel Administration,* 48–55.

———. (1970). Methods of resolving superior-subordinate conflict: The constructive use of subordinate differences and disagreements. *Organizational Behavior and Human Performance, 5,* 393–411.

BYRNE, D. (1969). Attitudes and attraction. In L. Berkowitz (Ed.), *Advances in experimental social psychology* (Vol. 4, pp. 36–90). New York: Academic Press.

CANTRELL, V., & PRINZ, R. (1985). Multiple perspectives of rejected, neglected, and accepted children: Relation between sociometric status and behavioral characteristics. *Journal of Consulting and Clinical Psychology, 53,* 884–889.

CARNEVALE, P., & PEGNETTER, R. (1985). The selection of mediation tactics in public sector disputes: A contingency analysis. *Journal of Social Issues, 41*(2), 65–81.

CARTWRIGHT, D. (1959). A field theoretical conception of power. In D. Cartwright (Ed.), *Studies in social power.* Ann Arbor: University of Michigan, Institute for Social Research.

———. (1968). The nature of group cohesiveness. In D. Cartwright and A. Zander (Eds.), *Group dynamics: Research and theory* (3rd ed.). New York: Harper & Row.

———. & Zander, A. (Eds.). (1968). *Group dynamics: Research and theory* (3rd ed.). New York: Harper & Row.

CASSEL, R., & SHAFER, A. (1961). An experiment in leadership training. *Journal of Psychology, 51,* 299–305.

———. (1951). New concepts for measuring leadership, in terms of group syntality. *Human Relations, 4,* 161–184.

CHASNOFF, R. (ED.) (1979). *Structuring cooperative learning: The 1979 handbook.* New Brighton, MN: Interaction Book Company.

CHERTKOFF, J., & ESSER, J. (1976). A review of experiments in explicit bargaining. *Journal of Experimental Social Psychology, 12,* 464–487.

CHESLER, M., & FRANKLIN, J. (1968, August). *Interracial and intergenerational conflict in secondary schools.* Paper presented at the Annual Meeting of the American Sociological Association, Boston.

CHRISTIE, R., & GEIS, F. (1970). *Studies in Machiavelianism.* New York: Academic Press.

COCH, L., & FRENCH, J. (1948). Overcoming resistance to change. *Human Relations, 1,* 512–533.

COIE, J., & KUPERSMIDT, J. (1983). A behavioral analysis of emerging social status in boys' groups. *Child Development, 54,* 1400–1416.

COLLINS, B. (1970). *Social psychology.* Reading, MA: Addison-Wesley.

COTTRELL, N., WACK, D., SEKERAK, G., & RITTLE, R. (1968). Social facilitation of dominant responses by the presence of an audience and the mere presence of others. *Journal of Personality and Social Psychology, 9,* 245–250.

Cox, C. (1926). *The early mental traits of three hundred geniuses.* Stanford, CA: Stanford University Press.

DANCE, F. (1970). The "concept" of communication. *Journal of Communication, 20,* 201–210.

DAVID, G., & HOUTMAN, S. (1968). *Thinking creatively: A guide to training imagination.* Madison: Wisconsin Research and Development Center for Cognitive Learning.

DeCECCO, J., & RICHARDS, A. (1974). *Growing pains: Uses of school conflict.* New York: Aberdeen Press.

———, & RICHARDS, A. (1975). Civil war in the high schools. *Psychology Today, 9,* 51–81.

DEUTSCH, M. (1949a). A theory of cooperation and competition. *Human Relations, 2,* 129–152.

———. (1949b). An experimental study of the effects of cooperation and competition upon group process. *Human Relations, 2,* 199–231.

———. (1958). Trust and suspicion. *Journal of Conflict Resolution, 2,* 265–279.

———. (1960). The effects of motivational orientation upon trust and suspicion. *Human Relations, 13,* 123–139.

———. (1962). Cooperation and trust: Some theoretical notes. In M. R. Jones (Ed.), *Nebraska Symposium on Motivation.* Lincoln: University of Nebraska Press.

———. (1969). Conflicts: Productive and destructive. *Journal of Social Issues, 25,* 7–43.

———. (1973). *The resolution of conflict.* New Haven, CT: Yale University Press.

———. (1975). Equity, equality, and need: What determines which value will be used as the basis of distributive justice? *Journal of Social Issues, 31,* 137–149.

———. (1979). Education and distributive justice: Some reflections on grading systems. *American Psychologist, 34,* 391–401.

———. (1985). *Distributive justice: A social psychological perspective.* New Haven, CT: Yale University Press.

———, CANAVAN, D., & RUBIN, J. (1971). The effects of size of conflict and sex of experimenter upon interpersonal bargaining. *Journal of Experimental Social Psychology, 7,* 258–267.

———, & KRAUSS, R. (1960). The effect of threat upon interpersonal bargaining. *Journal of Abnormal and Social Psychology, 61,* 181–189.

———, & KRAUSS, R. (1962). Studies of interpersonal bargaining. *Journal of Conflict Resolutions, 6,* 52–76.

———, & LEWICKI, R. (1970). "Locking in" effects during a game of chicken. *Journal of Conflict Resolution, 14,* 367–378.

DEVRIES, D., & EDWARDS, K. (1973). Learning games and student teams: Their effects on classroom process. *American Educational Research Journal, 10,* 307–318.

———, & EDWARDS, K. (1974). Student teams and learning games: Their effects on cross-race and cross-sex interaction. *Journal of Educational Psychology, 66,* 741–749.

DIESING, P. (1962). *Reason in society.* Urbana: University of Illinois Press.

DODGE, K. (1983). Behavioral antecedents of peer social status. *Child Development, 54,* 1386–1389.

———, COIE, J., & BAKKE, N. (1982). Behavior patterns of socially rejected and neglected preadolescents: The roles of social approach and aggression. *Journal of Abnormal Child Psychology, 10,* 389–409.

DRUCKER, P. (1974). Multinationals and developing countries: Myths and realities. *Foreign Affairs, 53,* 121–134.

DUNNETTE, M., CAMPBELL, J., & JAASTAD, K. (1963). The effect of group participation on brainstorming effectiveness of two industrial samples. *Journal of Applied Psychology, 47,* 30–37.

DUNNING, D., & ROSS, L. (1988). Overconfidence in individual and group prediction: Is the collective any wiser? Unpublished manuscript, Cornell University.

DURKHEIM, E. (1897, 1966). *Suicide.* New York: Free Press.

———. (1898). Representations individuelles et representations collectives. *Revue de Metaphysique, 6,* 274–302. In D. F. Pocock (trans.), *Sociology and philosophy.* New York: Free Press, 1953.

EHRLICH, H., & LEE, D. (1969). Dogmatism, learning, and resistance to change: A review and a new paradigm. *Psychological Bulletin, 71*(4), 249–260.

EICHLER, G., & MERRILL, R. (1933). Can social leadership be improved by instruction in its technique? *Journal of Educational Sociology, 7,* 233–236.

EMERSON, R. (1954). Deviation and rejection: An experimental replication. *American Sociological Review, 19,* 688–693.

FALK, D., & JOHNSON, D. W. (1977). The effects of perspective-taking and egocentrism on problem solving in heterogeneous and homogeneous groups. *Journal of Social Psychology, 102,* 63–72.

FAY, B. (1929). *Benjamin Franklin: The apostle of modern times.* Boston: Little, Brown.

FESTINGER, L. (1950). Informal social communication. *Psychological Review, 57,* 271–292.

———. (1954). A theory of social comparison processes. *Human Relations, 7,* 117–140.

———. (1957). *A theory of cognitive dissonance.* Evanston, IL: Row, Peterson.

FIEDLER, F. (1964). A contingency model of leadership effectiveness. In L. Berkowitz (Ed.), *Advances in experimental social psychology* (Vol. 1). New York: Academic Press.

———. (1967). *A theory of leadership effectiveness.* New York: McGraw-Hill.

———. (1969). Style of circumstance: The leadership enigma. *Psychology Today, 2*(10), 38–46.

———. (1978). Recent developments in research on the contingency model. In L. Berkowitz (Ed.), *Group processes.* New York: Academic Press.

FISHER, R., & URY, W. (1981). *Getting to yes: Negotiating agreement without giving in.* Boston: Houghton Mifflin.

FLANDERS, N. (1964). Some relationships among teacher influence, pupil attitudes, and achievement. In B. Biddle & W. Ellena (Eds.), *Contemporary research on teacher effectiveness.* New York: Holt, Rinehart and Winston.

FOLEY, J., & MACMILLAN, F. (1943). Mediated generalization and the interpretation of verbal behavior: V. Free association as related to differences in professional training. *Journal of Experimental Psychology, 33,* 299–310.

FOOTLICK, J. (1989). What happened to the family? *Newsweek,* Special Issue, 14–20.

FOX, D., & LORGE, I. (1962). The relative quality of decisions written by individuals and by groups as the available time for problem solving is increased. *Journal of Social Psychology, 57,* 227–242.

FRANKFORT, H., FRANKFORT, H., WILSON, J., & JACOBSON, T. (1949). *Before philosophy.* Baltimore: Penguin.

FRASER, C. (1971). Group risk-taking and group polarization. *European Journal of Social Psychology, 1,* 493–510.

FREEMAN, E. (1936). *Social psychology.* New York: Holt.

FRENCH, J. (1941). The disruption and cohesion of groups. *Journal of Abnormal Social Psychology, 36,* 361–377.

———, & COCH, L. (1948). Overcoming resistance to change. *Human Relations, 1,* 512–532.

———, & RAVEN, B. (1959). The basis of social power. In D. Cartwright (Ed.), *Studies in social power.* Ann Arbor: University of Michigan Press.

GARDIN, J., KAPLAN, K., FIRESTONE, I., & COWAN, G. (1973). Proxemic effects on cooperation, attitude, and approach-avoidance in a prisoner's dilemma game. *Journal of Personality and Social Psychology, 27,* 13–18.

GEEN, R. (1980). The effects of being observed on performance. In P. Paulus (Ed.), *Psychology of group influence.* Hillsdale, NJ: Erlbaum.

GIBB, J. (1961). Defensive communication. *Journal of Communication, 11,* 141–148.

GIFFIN, K. (1967). The contribution of studies of source credibility to a theory of interpersonal trust in the communication process. *Psychological Bulletin, 68,* 104–121.

GLASS, D., & SINGER, J. (1973). Experimental studies of uncontrollable and unpredictable noise. *Representative Research in Social Psychology, 4*(1), 165–183.

GLASS, G. (1977). Integrating findings: The meta-analysis of research. In L. Schulman (Ed.), *Review of research in education.* Itasca, IL: F. E. Peacock.

GLIDEWELL, J. (1953). *Group emotionality and productivity.* Unpublished doctoral dissertation, University of Chicago.

GOLDBERG, L (1968). Ghetto riots and others: The faces of civil disorder in 1967. *Journal of Peace Research, 2,* 116–132.

GOLDMAN, M. (1965). A comparison of individual and group performance for varying combinations of initial ability. *Journal of Personality and Social Psychology, 1,* 210–216.

GORDON, K. (1924). Group judgments in the field of lifted weights. *Journal of Experimental Psychology, 7,* 398–400.

GORDON, W. (1961). *Synectics.* New York: Harper & Row.

GOTTSCHALK, L. (1966). Psychoanalytic notes on T-groups at the Human Relations Laboratory, Bethel, Maine. *Comprehensive Psychiatry, 7*(6), 472–487.

GREEN, D. (1977). The immediate processing of sentences. *Quarterly Journal of Experimental Psychology, 29,* 135–146.

GRUNER, C. (1965). An experimental study of satire as persuasion. *Speech Monographs, 32*(2), 149–153.

GUMP, P. (1964). Environmental guidance of the classroom behavioral system. In B. Biddle and W. Ellena (Eds.), *Contemporary research on teacher effectiveness.* New York: Holt, Rinehart and Winston.

HACKMAN, J., & WALTON, R. (1986). Leading groups in organizations. In P. Goodman (Ed.), *Designing effective work groups* (pp. 72–119). San Francisco: Jossey-Bass.

HALLE, L. J. (1967). Overestimating the power of power. *The New Republic,* June 10, 15–17.

HAMILTON, D. (1979). A cognitive-attributional analysis of stereotyping. In L. Berkowitz (Ed.), *Advances in experimental social psychology* (Vol. 12). New York: Academic Press.

HARE, A. (1976). *Handbook of small group research* (2nd ed.). New York: Free Press.

HARKINS, S., & PETTY, R. (1982). The effects of task difficulty and task uniqueness on social loafing. *Journal of Personality and Social Psychology, 43,* 1214–1229.

———, & PETTY, R. (in press). The role of intrinsic motivation in eliminating social loafing. *Journal of Personality and Social Psychology.*

HASTORF, A., & CANTRIL, H. (1954). They saw a game. *Journal of Abnormal and Social Psychology, 49,* 129–134.

HEIDER, F. (1958). *The psychology of interpersonal relations.* New York: John Wiley.

HERSEY, P., & BLANCHARD, K. (1977). *Management of organizational behavior: Utilizing human resources* (3rd ed.). Englewood Cliffs, NJ: Prentice-Hall.

HILL, G. (1982). Group versus individual performance: Are N + 1 heads better than one? *Psychological Bulletin, 91,* 517–539.

HILL, W., & GRUNER, L. (1973). A study of development in open and closed groups. *Small Group Behavior, 4,* 355–381.

HOFFMAN, L. (1961). Conditions for creative problem solving. *Journal of Psychology, 52,* 429–444.

———, HARBURG, E., & MAIER, N. (1962). Differences and disagreement as factors in creative problem solving. *Journal of Abnormal and Social Psychology, 64,* 206–214.

———, & WILLIS, R. (1967). Some current issues in the psychology of conformity and nonconformity. *Psychological Bulletin, 68,* 62–76.

HOMANS, G. (1950). *The human group.* New York: Harcourt, Brace.

———. (1961). *Social behaviors: Its elementary forms.* New York: Harcourt, Brace & World.

———. (1974). *Social behaviors: Its elementary forms* (rev. ed.). New York: Harcourt Brace Jovanovich.

HOOK, S. (1955). *The hero in history.* Boston: Beacon Press.

HORAI, J. (1977). Attributional conflict. *Journal of Social Issues, 33*(1), 88–100.

HORWITZ, M. (1954). The recall of interrupted group tasks: An experimental study of individual motivation in relation to group goals. *Human Relations, 7,* 3–38.

HOVLAND, C., JANIS, I., & KELLEY, H. (1953). *Communication and persuasion.* New Haven, CT: Yale University Press.

———, LUMSDAINE, A., & SHEFFIELD, F. (1949). *Ex-*

*periment on mass communication*. Princeton, NJ: Princeton University Press.

HOWELLS, L., & BECKER, S. (1962). Seating arrangement and leadership emergence. *Journal of Personality and Social Psychology, 64,* 148–150.

HUNT, P., & HILLERY, J. (1973). Social facilitation in a coaction setting: An examination of the effects over learning trials. *Journal of Experimental Social Psychology, 9,* 563–571.

ILLING, H. (1957). C. Jung on the present trends in group psychotherapy. *Human Relations, 10,* 77–84.

IVERSON, M., & SCHWAB, H. (1967). Ethnocentric dogmatism and binocular fusion of sexually and racially discrepant stimuli. *Journal of Personality and Social Psychology, 7,* 73–81.

JACKSON, J., & WILLIAMS, K. (1985). Social loafing on difficult tasks: Working collectively can improve performance. *Journal of Personality and Social Psychology, 49,* 937–942.

———, & WILLIAMS, K. (1988). A review and theoretical analysis of social loafing. Bronx, NY: Fordham University.

JANIS, I. (1971). Groupthink. *Psychology today,* 5(6), 43–46, 74–76.

———. (1972). *Victims of groupthink.* Boston: Houghton Mifflin.

———. (1982). *Groupthink* (revised and enlarged edition of *Victims of groupthink*). Boston: Houghton Mifflin.

———, & MANN, L. (1977). *Decision making.* New York: Free Press.

JANZ, T., & TJOSVOLD, D. (1985). Costing effective vs. ineffective work relationships: A method and first look. *Canadian Journal of Administrative Sciences, 2,* 53–51.

JOHNSON, D. W. (1970). *The social psychology of education.* New York: Holt, Rinehart and Winston.

———. (1971a). Role reversal: A summary and review of the research. *International Journal of Group Tensions, 1,* 318–334.

———. (1971b). The effectiveness of role reversal: The actor or the listener. *Psychological Reports, 28,* 275–282.

———. (1972). *The effects of role reversal on seeing a conflict from the opponent's frame of reference.* Unpublished manuscript. University of Minnesota, Minneapolis.

———. (1973). *Contemporary social psychology.* Philadelphia: J. B. Lippincott.

———. (1974). Communication and the inducment of cooperative behavior in conflicts. *Speech Monographs, 41,* 64–78.

———. (1977). Distribution and exchange of information in problem solving dyads. *Communication Research, 4,* 283–298.

———. (1978, 1987, 1991). *Human relations and your career* (1st, 2nd, 3rd eds.). Englewood Cliffs, NJ: Prentice-Hall.

———. (1979). *Educational psychology.* Englewood Cliffs, NJ: Prentice-Hall.

———. (1980a). Group processes: Influences on student-student interaction on school outcomes. In J. McMillan (Ed.), *Social psychology of school learning.* New York: Academic Press.

———. (1980b). Attitude modification methods. In F. Kanfer and A. Goldstein (Eds.), *Helping people change.* Elmsford, NY: Pergamon Press.

———. (1972, 1981, 1986, 1990). *Reaching out: Interpersonal effectiveness and self-actualization* (1st, 2nd, 3rd, 4th eds.). Englewood Cliffs, NJ: Prentice-Hall.

———, & ALLEN, S. (1972). Deviation from organizational norms concerning the relations between status and power. *Sociological Quarterly, 13,* 174–182.

———, & JOHNSON, F. (1987). *Joining together: Group theory and group skills* (3rd ed.). Englewood Cliffs, NJ: Prentice-Hall.

———, & JOHNSON, R. (1975, 1987, 1991). *Learning together and alone: Cooperation and competition, and individualization* (1st, 2nd, 3rd eds.). Englewood Cliffs, NJ: Prentice-Hall.

———, & JOHNSON, R. (1978). Cooperative, competitive, and individualistic learning. *Journal of Research and Development in Education, 12,* 3–15.

———, & JOHNSON, R. (1979). Conflict in the classroom: Controversy and learning. *Review of Educational Research, 49,* 51–70.

———, & JOHNSON, R. (1980). *Belonging* (16mm film). New Brighton, MN: Interaction Book Company.

———, & JOHNSON, R. (1983). The socialization and achievement crisis: Are cooperative learning experiences the solution? In L. Bickman (Ed.), *Applied Social Psychology Annual 4.* Beverly Hills, CA: Sage Publications.

———, & JOHNSON, R. (1987). *Creative conflict.* Edina, MN: Interaction Book Company.

———, & JOHNSON, R. (1989a). *Cooperation and competition: Theory and research.* Edina, MN: Interaction Book Company.

———, & JOHNSON, R. (1989b). *Leading the cooperative school.* Edina, MN: Interaction Book Company.

———, JOHNSON, R., BUCKMAN, L., & RICHARDS, P. (1986). The effect of prolonged implementation of cooperative learning on social support within the classroom. *Journal of Psychology, 119,* 405–411.

———, JOHNSON, R., & HOLUBEC, E. (1988). *Cooperation in the classroom.* Edina, MN: Interaction Books.

———, JOHNSON, R., & HOLUBEC, E. (1990). *Circles of learning: Cooperation in the classroom* (3rd ed.). Edina, MN: Interaction Book Company.

———, JOHNSON, R., & SMITH, K. (1987). Academic conflict among students: Controversy and learning. In R. Feldman (Ed.), *Social psychological applications to education.* Cambridge: Cambridge University Press.

————, JOHNSON, R. STANNE, M., & GARIBALDI, A. (in press). The impact of leader and member group processing on achievement in cooperative groups. *Journal of Social Psychology.*

————, KAVANAGH, J., & LUBIN, B. (1973). Tests, T-groups, and tension. *Comparative Group Studies, 4,* 81–88.

————, & LEWICKI, R. (1969). The initiation of superordinate goals. *Journal of Applied Behavioral Science, 5,* 9–24.

————, MARUYAMA, G., JOHNSON, R., NELSON, D., & SKON, L. (1981). Effects of cooperative, competitive, and individualistic goal structures on achievement: A meta-analysis. *Psychological Bulletin, 89,* 47–62.

————, & MATROSS, R. (1977). The interpersonal influence of the psychotherapist. In A. Gurman and A. Razin (Eds.), *The effective therapist: A handbook.* Elmsford, NY: Pergamon Press.

————, McCARTY, K., & ALLEN, T. (1976). Congruent and contradictory verbal and nonverbal communications of cooperativeness and competitiveness in negotiations. *Communication Research, 3,* 275–292.

————, SKON, L., & JOHNSON, R. (1980). The effects of cooperative, competitive and individualistic goal structures on student achievement on different types of tasks. *American Educational Research Journal, 17,* 83–93.

JONES, E., & GERARD, H. (1967). *Foundations of social psychology.* New York: John Wiley.

KELLEY, H. (1968). Interpersonal accommodation. *American Psychologist, 23,* 399–410.

————. (1979). *Personal relationships.* Hillsdale, NJ: Erlbaum.

————, & STRAHELSKI, A. (1970). Social interaction basis of cooperators' and competitors' beliefs about others. *Journal of Personality and Social Psychology, 16,* 66–91.

KERR, N. (1983). The dispensability of member effort and group motivation losses: Free-rider effects. *Journal of Personality and Social Psychology, 44,* 78–94.

————, ATKIN, R., STASSER, G., MEEK, D., HOLT, R., & DAVIS, J. (1976). Guilt beyond a reasonable doubt: Effects of concept definition and assigned decision rule on the judgments of mock jurors. *Journal of Personality and Social Psychology, 34,* 282–294.

————, & BRUUN, S. (1981). Ringelmann revisited: Alternative explanations for the social loafing effect. *Personality and Social Psychology Bulletin, 7,* 224–231.

————, & BRUUN, S. (1983). The dispensability of member effort and group motivation losses: Free-rider effects. *Journal of Personality and Social Psychology, 44,* 78–94.

KIPNIS, D. (1972). Does power corrupt? *Journal of Personality and Social Psychology, 24,* 33–41.

KOLB, D. (1985). To be a mediator: Expressive tactics in mediation. *Journal of Social Issues, 41*(2), 11–26.

KOSTICK, M. (1957). An experiment in group decision. *Journal of Teacher Education, 8,* 67–72.

KOUZES, J., & POSNER, B. (1987). *The leadership challenge.* San Francisco: Jossey-Bass.

KRAUSE, C. (1978). *Guyana massacre: The eyewitness account.* The Washington Post.

KRESSEL, K., & PRUITT, D. (1985). Themes in the mediation of social conflict. *Journal of Social Issues, 41*(2), 179–198.

LABARRE, W. (1972). *The ghost dance.* New York: Delta.

LAKIN, M. (1972). *Interpersonal encounter: Theory and practice in sensitivity training.* New York: McGraw-Hill.

LAMM, H., & TROMMSDORFF, G. (1973). Group versus individual performance on tasks requiring ideational proficiency (brainstorming): A review. *European Journal of Social Psychology, 3,* 361–388.

LANGER, E., & BENEVENTO, A. (1978). Self-induced dependence. *Journal of Personality and Social Psychology, 36,* 886–893.

————, BLANK, A., & CHANOWITZ, B. (1978). The mindlessness of ostensibly thoughtful action: The role of "placebic" information in interpersonal interaction. *Journal of Personality and Social Psychology, 36,* 635–642.

————, & RODIN, J. (1976). The effects of choice and enhanced personal responsibility for the aged: A field experiment in an institutional setting. *Journal of Personality and Social Psychology, 34*(2), 191–198.

LATANE, B., WILLIAMS, K., & HARKINS, S. (1979). Many hands make light the work: The causes and consequences of social loafing. *Journal of Personality and Social Psychology, 37,* 822–832.

LATHAM, G., & BALDES, J. (1975). The "practical significance" of Locke's theory of goal setting. *Journal of Applied Psychology, 60,* 122–124.

LAUGHLIN, P. (1980). Social combination processes of cooperative problem-solving groups on verbal intellective tasks. In M. Fishbein (Ed.), *Progress in social psychology* (Vol. 1). Hillsdale, NJ: Erlbaum.

————, & ADAMOPOULOS, J. (1980). Social combination processes and individual learning for six-person cooperative groups on an intellective task. *Journal of Personality and Social Psychology, 38,* 941–947.

————, BRANCH, L., & JOHNSON, H. (1969). Individual versus triadic performance on a unidimensional complementary task as a function of initial ability level. *Journal of Personality and Social Psychology, 12,* 144–150.

LAWRENCE, P., & LORSCH, J. (1967). *Organization and environment: Managing differentiation and integration.* Cambridge, MA: Harvard University, Division of Research, Graduate School of Business Administration.

LEAVITT, H. (1951). Some effects of certain communication patterns on group performance. *Journal of Abnormal and Social Psychology, 46,* 38–50.

LEVINE, J., & BUTLER, J. (1952). Lecture vs. group

decision in changing behavior. *Journal of Applied Psychology, 36,* 29–33.

LEVINE, R., CHEIN, I., & MURPHY, G. (1942). The relation of the intensity of a need to the amount of perceptual distortion: A preliminary report. *Journal of Psychology, 13,* 283–293.

LEW, M., MESCH, D., JOHNSON, D. W., & JOHNSON, R. (1986a). Positive interdependence, academic and collaborative-skills group contingencies and isolated students. *American Educational Research Journal, 23,* 476–488.

———, MESCH, D., JOHNSON, D. W., & JOHNSON, R. (1986b). Components of cooperative learning: Effects of collaborative skills and academic group contingencies on achievement and mainstreaming. *Contemporary Educational Psychology, 11,* 229–239.

LEWIN, K. (1935). *A dynamic theory of personality.* New York: McGraw-Hill.

———. (1943). Forces behind food habits and methods of change. *Bulletin of the National Research Council, 108,* 35–65.

———. (1944). Dynamics of group action. *Educational Leadership, 1,* 195–200.

———. (1948). *Resolving social conflicts: Selected papers on group dynamics.* New York: Harper.

———. (1951). *Field theory in social science.* New York: Harper.

———, DEMBO, T., FESTINGER, L., & SEARS, P. (1944). Level of aspiration. In J. Hunt (Ed.), *Personality and the behavior disorders.* New York: Ronald Press.

———, & GRABBE, P. (1945). Conduct, knowledge, and acceptance of new values. *Journal of Social Issues, 1,* 56–64.

———, LIPPETT, R., & WHITE, R. (1939). Patterns of aggressive behavior in experimentally created "social climates." *Journal of Social Psychology, 10,* 271–299.

LEWIS, H. (1944). An experimental study of the role of the ego in work. I. The role of the ego in cooperative work. *Journal of Experimental Psychology, 34,* 113–126.

———, & FRANKLIN, M. (1944). An experimental study of the role of the ego in work. II. The significance of task-orientation in work. *Journal of Experimental Psychology, 34,* 195–215.

LEWIS, S., & PRUITT, D. (1971). Organization, aspiration level, and communication freedom in integrative bargaining. *Proceedings of the 79th Annual Convention of the American Psychological Association, 6,* 221–222.

LIEBERMAN, M. (1980). Group methods. In F. Kanfer and A. Goldstein (Eds.), *Helping people change.* New York: Pergamon Press.

———, LAKIN, M., & WHITAKER, D. (1968). The group as a unique context for therapy. *Psychotherapy: Theory, Research and Practice, 5*(1), 29–36.

———, YALOM, I., & MILES, M. (1973). *Encounter groups: First facts.* New York: Basic Books.

———, YALOM, I., & MILES, M. (1980). Group methods. In F. Kanfer and A. Goldstein (Eds.), *Helping people change.* New York: Pergamon Press.

LICKERT, R. (1961). *New patterns of management.* New York: McGraw-Hill.

LINDBLOOM, D. (1959). The science of muddling through. *Public Administrative Review, 15,* 79–88.

LINVILLE, P. (1982). The complexity-extremity effect and age-based stereotyping. *Journal of Personality and Social Psychology, 42,* 193–211.

———, & JONES, E. (1980). Polarized appraisals of outgroup members. *Journal of Personality and Social Psychology, 38,* 689–703.

LISSNER, K. (1933). The resolution of needs by substitutive acts: Studies of action and affect psychology, edited by K. Lewin. *Psychologische Forschung, 18,* 27–87.

LONDON, P. (1969). *Behavior control.* New York: Harper & Row.

LORD, C., ROSS, L., & LEPPER, M. (1979). Biased assimilation and attitude polarization: The effects of prior theories on subsequently considered evidence. *Journal of Personality and Social Psychology, 37*(11), 2098–2109.

LUCE, R., & RAIFFA, H. (1957). *Games and decisions.* New York: John Wiley.

LUCHINS, A. (1942). Mechanization in problem solving: The effect of Einstellung. *Psychological Monographs, 54,* Whole No. 248.

LULL, P. E. (1940). The effectiveness of humor in persuasive speech. *Speech Monographs, 7,* 20–40.

LYONS, V. (1980). *Structuring cooperative learning: The 1980 handbook.* New Brighton, MN: Interaction Book Company.

MAGNUSON, E. (1986, March 10). A serious deficiency: The Rogers Commission faults NASA's flawed decision-making process. *Time,* pp. 40–42, international edition.

MAHLER, W. (1933). Substitution acts of a different degree of reality. Students of action and affect psychology, edited by K. Lewin. *Psychologische Forschung, 18,* 27–89.

MAIER, N. (1930). Reasoning in humans. *Journal of Comparative Psychology, 10,* 115–143.

———. (1950). The quality of group decisions as influenced by the discussion leader. *Human Relations, 3,* 155–174.

———. (1970). *Problem solving and creativity in individuals and group.* Belmont, CA: Brooks/Cole.

———, & HOFFMAN, L. (1964). Financial incentives and group decision in motivating change. *Journal of Social Psychology, 64,* 369–378.

———, & SOLEM, A. (1952). The contribution of a discussion leader to the quality of group thinking: The effective use of minority opinions. *Human Relations, 5,* 277–288.

———, & THURBER, J. (1969). Innovative problem-solving by outsiders: A study of individuals and groups. *Personal Psychology, 22*(3), 237–249.

MANN, L., & JANIS, I. (1983). Decisional conflict in organizations. In D. Tjosvold and D. Johnson (Eds.), *Productive conflict management*. New York: Irvington.

MANN, R. (1959). A review of the relationship between personality and performance in small groups. *Psychological Bulletin, 56*, 241–270.

MARKUS, H. (1978). The effect of mere presence on social facilitation: An unobtrusive test. *Journal of Experimental Social Psychology, 14*, 389–397.

MARROW, A. (1957). *Making management human*. New York: McGraw-Hill.

MASLOW, A. (1954). *Motivation and personality*. New York: Harper & Row.

———. (1962). *Toward a psychology of being*. Princeton, NJ: Van Nostrand.

McCLELLAND, D., & ATKINSON, J. (1948). The projective expression of needs: I. The effect of different intensities of the hunger drive on perception. *Journal of Psychology, 25*, 205–222.

McDAVID, J., & HARARI, H. (1968). *Social psychology: Individuals, groups, societies*. New York: Harper & Row.

McGREGOR, D. (1967). *The human side of enterprise*. New York: McGraw-Hill.

McGUIRE, W. (1964). Inducing resistance to persuasion. In L. Berkowitz (Ed.), *Advances in experimental social psychology* (Vol. 1, pp. 192–232). New York: Academic Press.

———. (1969). The nature of attitudes and attitude change. In B. Lindsey and E. Aronson (Eds.), *Handbook of social psychology* (Vol. 3). Reading, MA: Addison-Wesley.

MESCH, D., LEW, M., JOHNSON, D. W., & JOHNSON, R. (1986). Isolated teenagers, cooperative learning and the training of social skills. *Journal of Psychology, 120*, 323–334.

———, JOHNSON, D. W., & JOHNSON, R. (1988). Impact of positive interdependence and academic group contingencies on achievement. *Journal of Social Psychology, 128*, 345–352.

MESSE, L., STOLLAK, G., LARSON, R., & MICHAELS, G. (1979). Interpersonal consequences of person perception in two social contexts. *Journal of Personality and Social Psychology, 37*, 369–379.

MESSICK, D., & BREWER, M. (1983). Solving social dilemmas: A review. In L. Wheeler & P. Shaver (Eds.), *Review of personality and social psychology* (Vol. 4, pp. 11–44). Newbury Park, CA: Sage Publications.

MICHENER, H., & BURT, M. (1975). Components of "authority" as determinants of compliance. *Journal of Personality Psychology, 31*, 606–614.

MILLS, T. (1967). *The sociology of small groups*. Englewood Cliffs, NJ: Prentice-Hall.

MOEDE, W. (1920). *Experimentelle massenpsychologie*. Leipzig: S. Hirzel.

———. (1927). Die richtlinien der leistungspsychologie. *Industrielle Psychotechnik, 4*, 193–207.

MYERS, D. (1982). Polarizing effects of social interaction. In H. Brandstatter, J. Davis, & G. Stocker-Kreichgauer (Eds.), *Group decision making*. New York: Academic Press.

———, & BISHOP, G. (1970). Discussion effects on racial attitudes. *Science, 169*, 778–789.

———, & LAMM, H. (1976). The group polarization phenomenon. *Psychological Bulletin, 83*, 602–627.

MYERS, R. (1969). *Some effects of seating arrangements in counseling*. Unpublished doctoral dissertation, University of Florida-Gainesville.

MYRDAL, G. (1944). *An American dilemma: The Negro problem and modern democracy*. New York: Harper.

NATIONAL CENTER FOR MANUFACTURING SCIENCES. (1989). *Making the grade: Student perspectives on the state of manufacturing engineering education in American*. Ann Arbor, MI, p. 1.

NEISSER, U. (1954). On experimental distinction between perceptual process and verbal response. *Journal of Experimental Psychology, 47*, 399–402.

NEMETH, C. (1977). Interaction between jurors as a function of majority vs. unanimity decision rules. *Journal of Applied Social Psychology, 7*, 38–56.

NESBITT, P., POND, A., & ALLEN, W. (1959). *The survival book*. New York: Funk & Wagnalls.

NEWCOMB, T. (1943). *Personality and social change*. New York: Dryden.

ORVIS, B., KELLEY, H., & BUTLER, D. (1976). Attributional conflict in young couples. In J. Harvey, W. Ickles, & R. Kidd (Eds.), *New directions in attribution research* (Vol. 1). Hillsdale, NJ: Erlbaum.

O'QUIN, K., & ARONOFF, J. (1981). Humor as a technique of social influence. *Social Psychology Quarterly, 44*(4), 349–357.

OUISIANKINA, M. (1928). Investigations on the psychology of action and affection. VI. The resumption of interrupted acts, edited by K. Lewin. *Psychologische Forschung, 18*, 302–389.

PELZ, E. (1958). Some factors in "group decision." In E. Maccoby, T. Newcomb, and E. Hartley (Eds.), *Readings in social psychology*. New York: Holt.

PENNINGTON, D., HARAVEY, F., & BASS, B. (1958). Some effects of decision and discussion on coalescence, change, and effectiveness. *Journal of Applied Psychology, 42*, 404–408.

PEPINSKI, P., HEMPHILL, J., & SHEVITZ, R. (1958). Attempts to lead, group productivity, and morale under conditions of acceptance and rejection. *Journal of Abnormal and Social Psychology, 57*, 47–54.

PEPITONE, A. (1952). *Responsibility to the group and its effects on the performance of members*. Unpublished doctoral dissertation, University of Michigan, Ann Arbor.

———, & REICHLING, G. (1955). Group cohesiveness and the expression of hostility. *Human Relations, 8*, 327–337.

PEPITONE, E. (ED.) (1980). *Children in cooperation and competition*. Lexington, MA: Lexington Books.

PETERS, D. (1966). *Identification and personal change in laboratory training.* Unpublished doctoral dissertation, Massachusetts Institute of Technology, Cambridge.

PETERS, T. (1987). *Thriving on chaos.* New York: Alfred A. Knopf.

PETTY, M., HARKINS, S., WILLIAMS, K., & LATANE, B. (1977). Effects of group size on cognitive effort and evaluation. *Journal of Personality and Social Psychology, 3*(4), 579–582.

PRESTON, M., & HEINTZ, R. (1949). Effects of participatory vs. supervisory leadership on group judgment. *Journal of Abnormal and Social Psychology, 44,* 345–355.

PRUITT, D., & JOHNSON, D. W. (1970). Mediation as an aid to face saving in negotiation. *Journal of Personality and Social Psychology, 14,* 239–246.

PUTALLAZ, M. (1983). Predicting children's sociometric status from their behavior. *Child Development, 54,* 1417–1426.

PUTNAM, J., JOHNSON, D. W., RYNDERS, J., & JOHNSON, R. (1989). Collaborative skills instruction for promoting positive interactions between mentally handicapped and nonhandicapped children. *Exceptional Children, 55,* 550–557.

QUATTRONE, G., & JONES, E. (1980). The perception of variability within in-groups and out-groups: Implications for the law of small numbers. *Journal of Personality and Social Psychology, 38,* 141–152.

RADKE, M., & KLISURICH, D. (1947). Experiments in changing food habits. *Journal of the American Dietetics Association, 23,* 403–409.

RAFALIDES, M., & HOY, W. (1971). Student sense of alienation and pupil control orientation of high schools. *The High School Journal, 55*(3), 102.

RAVEN, B., & KRUGLANKSI, A. (1970). Conflict and power. In P. Swingle (Ed.), *The structure of conflict.* New York: Academic Press.

———, & RIETSEMA, J. (1957). The effects of varied clarity of group goal and group path upon the individual and his relation to his group. *Human Relations, 10,* 29–44.

———, & RUBIN, J. (1976). *Social psychology: People in groups.* New York: John Wiley.

RAWLS, J. (1971). *A theory of justice.* Cambridge, MA: Harvard University Press.

READ, P. (1974). *Alive.* New York: Avon.

RICE, O. (1978). *The Hatfields and the McCoys.* Lexington: University Press of Kentucky.

ROBINS, J., ET AL. (1984). Lifetime prevalence of specific psychiatric disorders in three sites. *Archives of General Psychiatry, 41,* 949–958.

RODIN, J., & LANGER, E. (1977). Long-term effects of a control-relevant intervention with the institutionalized aged. *Journal of Personality and Social Psychology, 35,* 897–902.

———, SOLOMON, J., & METCALF, J. (1978). Role of control in mediating perceptions of density. *Journal of Personality and Social Psychology, 36*(9), 988–999.

ROETHLISBERGER, F., & DICKSON, W. (1939). *Management and the worker.* Cambridge, MA: Harvard University Press.

ROFF, J., & WIRT, R. (1984). Childhood aggression and social adjustment antecedents of delinquency. *Journal of Abnormal Child Psychology, 12*(1), 111–126.

ROGERS, C. (1970). Towards a theory of creativity. In P. Vernon (Ed.), *Readings in creativity.* London: Penguin.

ROKEACH, M. (1954). The nature and meaning of dogmatism. *Psychological Review, 61,* 194–204.

———. (1960). *The open and closed mind.* New York: Basic Books.

———. (1968). *Beliefs, attitudes, and values.* San Francisco: Jossey-Bass.

ROSS, L. (1977). The intuitive psychologist and his shortcomings: Distortions in the attributional process. In L. Berkowitz (Ed.), *Advances in experimental social psychology,* (Vol. 10). New York: Academic Press.

ROTHBART, M., EVANS, M., & FULERO, S. (1979). Recall for confirming events: Memory processes and the maintenance of social stereotypes. *Journal of Experimental Social Psychology, 15,* 343–355.

———, FULERO, S., JENSEN, C., HOWARD, J., & BIRRELL, P. (1978). From individual to group impressions: Availability heuristics in stereotype formation. *Journal of Experimental Social Psychology, 14,* 237–255.

RUBIN, J., & BROWN, B. (1975). *The social psychology of bargaining and negotiation.* New York: Academic Press.

RUTSTROM, C. (1973). *The new ways of the wilderness.* New York: Collier.

SALOMON, G. (1981). *Communication and education: Social and psychological interactions.* Beverley Hills, CA: Sage Publications.

SANDERS, G., & BARON, R. (1975). The motivating effects of distraction on task performance. *Journal of Personality and Social Psychology, 32,* 956–963.

SARACHEK, G. (1968). Greek concepts of leadership. *Academy of Management Journal, 11,* 39–48.

SARASON, I., & POTTER, E. (1983). *Self-monitoring: Cognitive processes and performance.* Seattle: University of Washington, research report.

SCHACHTER, S. (1951). Deviation, rejection, and communication. *Journal of Abnormal and Social Psychology, 46,* 190–207.

———, ELLERTSON, N., McBRIDE, D., & GREGORY, D. (1951). An experimental study of cohesiveness and productivity. *Human Relations, 4,* 229–238.

———, NUTTIN, J., DEMONCHAUX, C., MAUCORPS, P., OSMER, DIEDRICH, DUIJKER, HUBERTUR, ROMMETVEIT, RAGNAR, ISRAEL, & JOACHIM. (1954). Cross-cultural experiments on threat and rejection. *Human Relations, 7,* 403–439.

SCHEIN, E. (1969). *Process consultation.* Reading, MA: Addison-Wesley.

SCHNEIDER, J. (1937). The cultural situation as a condition for the achievement of fame. *American Sociological Review, 2,* 480–491.

SEASHORE, S. (1954). *Group cohesiveness in the industrial work group.* Ann Arbor, MI: Institute for Social Research.

SELIGMAN, M. (1988). Boomer blues. *Psychology Today, 22,* 50–55.

SELMAN, R. (1981). The development of interpersonal competence: The role of understanding in conduct. *Departmental Review, 1,* 401–422.

SETA, J., PAULUS, P., & SCHKADE, J. (1976). Effects of group size and proximity under cooperative and competitive conditions. *Journal of Personality and Social Psychology, 34,* 47–53.

SHAMBAUGH, P. (1978). The development of the small group. *Human Relations, 31,* 283–295.

SHAW, M. (1932). A comparison of individuals and small groups in the rational solution of complex problems. *American Journal of Psychology, 44,* 491–504.

———. (1964). Communication networks. In L. Berkowitz (Ed.), *Advances in experimental social psychology* (Vol. 1). New York: Academic Press.

———. (1976). *Group dynamics.* New York: McGraw-Hill.

SHEINGOLD, K., HAWKINS, J., & CHAR, C. (1984). "I'm the thinkist, you're the typist": The interaction of technology and the social life of classrooms. *Journal of Social Issues, 40(3),* 49–61.

SHERIF, M. (1936a). *The psychology of group norms.* New York: Harper.

———. (1936b). *The psychology of social norms.* New York: Harper.

———. (1966). *In common predicament.* Boston: Houghton Mifflin.

———, & SHERIF, C. (1956). *An outline of social psychology.* New York: Harper & Row.

———, & SHERIF, C. (1969). *Social psychology.* New York: Harper & Row.

SIMON, H. (1976). *Administrative behavior: A study of decision-making processes in administrative organization* (3rd ed.). New York: Free Press.

SIMONTON, D. (1979). Multiple discovery and invention: Zeitgeist, genius or chance? *Journal of Personality and Social Psychology, 37,* 1603–1616.

SKON, L., JOHNSON, D. W., & JOHNSON, R. (1981). Cooperative peer interaction versus individual competition and individualistic efforts: Effects of the acquisition of cognitive reasoning strategies. *Journal of Educational Psychology, 73,* 83–92.

SLAVIN, R. (1986). *Using student team learning.* Baltimore, MD: Center for Research on Elementary & Middle Schools, Johns Hopkins University.

SMITH, K., JOHNSON, D. W., & JOHNSON, R. (1982). Effects of cooperative and individualistic instruction on the achievement of handicapped, regular, and gifted students. *Journal of Social Psychology, 116,* 277–283.

SMITH, M. (1945). Social situation, social behavior, and social group. *Psychological Review, 52,* 224–229.

SORRENTINO, R., & BOUTILLIER, R. (1975). The effect of quantity and quality of verbal interaction on ratings of leadership ability. *Journal of Experimental Social Psychology, 11,* 403–411.

SOUTH, E. (1972). Some psychological aspects of committee work. *Journal of Applied Psychology, 11,* 348–368; 437–464.

STEIN, M. (1968). *The creative individual.* New York: Harper & Row.

STEIN, R., & HELLER, T. (1979). An empirical analysis of the correlations between leadership status and participation rates reported in the literature. *Journal of Personality and Social Psychology, 37,* 1993–2002.

STEINER, I. (1959). Human interaction and interpersonal perception. *Sociometry, 22,* 230–235.

———. (1972). *Group process and productivity.* New York: Academic Press.

———. (1976). Task-performing groups. In J. Thibaut, J. Spence, & R. Carson (Eds.), *Contemporary topics in social psychology.* Morristown, NJ: General Learning Press.

STEINZOR, B. (1950). The spatial factor in face-to-face discussion groups. *Journal of Abnormal and Social Psychology, 45,* 552–555.

STEVENS, C. (1963). *Strategy and collective bargaining negotiation.* New York: McGraw-Hill.

STOGDILL, R. (1959). *Individual behavior and group achievement.* New York: Oxford University Press.

———. (1974). *Handbook of leadership.* New York: Free Press.

STONER, J. (1961). *A comparison of individual and group decisions involving risk.* Unpublished master's thesis, Massachusetts Institute of Technology, Cambridge.

STOTLE, J. (1978). Power structure and personal competence. *Journal of Social Psychology, 38,* 72–83.

STRODTBECK, F., & HOOK, L. (1961). The social dimensions of a twelve man jury table. *Sociometry, 24,* 397–415.

SWEENEY, J. (1973). An experimental investigation of the free-rider problem. *Social Science Research, 2,* 277–292.

TAJFEL, H., & TURNER, J. (1979). An integrative theory of intergroup conflict. In W. Austin & S. Worchel (Eds.), *The social psychology of intergroup conflict.* Monterey, CA.: Brooks/Cole.

TAYLOR, S. (1980). The interface of cognitive and social psychology. In J. H. Harvey (Ed.), *Cognition, social behavior, and the environment* (pp. 189–211). Hillsdale, NJ: Erlbaum.

TAGER, A. (1980). *Too much invested to quit.* Elmsford, NY: Pergamon Press.

TERMAN, L., & ODOR, M. (1947). *The gifted child grows up.* Stanford, CA: Stanford University Press.

THIBAUT, J., & KELLY, H. (1959). *The social psychology of groups.* New York: John Wiley.

THOMAS, K., & SCHMIDT, W. (1976). A survey of managerial interests with respect to conflict. *Academy of Management Journal, 19,* 315–318.

THORNDIKE, R. (1938). On what type of task will a group do well? *Journal of Abnormal Social Psychology, 30,* 409–413.

TJOSVOLD, D. (1974). Threat as a low-power person's strategy in bargaining: Social face and tangible outcomes. *International Journal of Group Tensions, 4,* 494–510.

———. (1977). Low-power person's strategies in bargaining: Negotiability of demand, maintaining face, and race. *International Journal of Group Tensions, 7,* 29–42.

———. (1978). Alternative organizations for schools and classrooms. In D. Bart-Tal and L. Saxe, (Eds.), *Social psychology of education.* Washington, D.C.: Hemisphere.

———. (1982). Effects of approach to controversy on superiors' incorporation of subordinates' information in decision making. *Journal of Applied Psychology, 67,* 189–193.

———. (1990). *The team organization: Applying group research to the workplace.* New York: John Wiley.

———, & JOHNSON, D. W. (1978). Controversy within a cooperative or competitive context and cognitive perspective-taking. *Contemporary Educational Psychology, 3,* 376–386.

———, & SAGARIA, D. (1978). Effects of relative power of cognitive perspective-taking. *Personality and Social Psychology Bulletin, 4,* 256–259.

TORRANCE, E. (1954). Some consequences of power differences in decision making in permanent and temporary three-man groups. *Research Studies, State College of Washington, 22,* 130–140.

———. (1957). Group decision-making and disagreement. *Social Forces, 35,* 314–318.

TREFFINGER, D., SPEEDIE, S., & BRUNNER, W. (1974). Improving children's creative problem solving ability: The Purdue creativity project. *The Journal of Creative Behavior, 8,* 20–29.

TRIANDIS, H., BASS, A., EWEN, R., & MIEKSELE, E. (1963). Teaching creativity as a function of the members. *Journal of Applied Psychology, 47,* 104–110.

TRIPLETT, N. (1898). The dynamogenic factors in peacemaking and competition. *American Journal of Psychology, 9,* 507–533.

TUCKMAN, B. (1965). Developmental sequence in small groups. *Psychological Bulletin, 63,* 384–399.

———, & JENSEN, M. (1977). Stages of small group development revisited. *Group and Organizational Studies, 2,* 419–427.

TURK, S., & SARASON, I. (1983). *Test anxiety and causal attributions.* Unpublished manuscript, University of Washington, Department of Psychology, Seattle, WA.

TVERSKY, A., & KAHNEMAN, D. (1981, January). The framing of decisions and the psychology of choice. *Science, 211,* 453–458.

VACCHIANO, R. B., STRAUSS, P. S., & HOCHMAN, L. (1968). The open and closed mind: A review of dogmatism. *Psychological Bulletin, 71*(4), 261–273.

VAN BLERKOM, M., & TJOSVOLD, D. (1981). The effects of social context on engaging in controversy. *Journal of Psychology, 107,* 141–145.

VILLASENOR, V. (1977). *Jury: The people vs. Juan Corona.* New York: Bantam.

VON MISES, L. (1949). *Human action: A treatise on economics.* New Haven, CT: Yale University Press.

VROOM, V., & YETTON, P. (1973). *Leadership and decision making.* Pittsburgh, PA: University of Pittsburgh Press.

WALLACH, M., KOGAN, N., & BEM, D. (1962). Group influence on individual risk taking. *Journal of Abnormal and Social Psychology, 65,* 75–86.

WALTON, R. (1969). *Interpersonal peacemaking.* Reading, MA: Addison-Wesley.

———. (1987). *Managing conflict.* Reading, MA: Addison-Wesley.

———, & MCKERSIE, R. (1965). *A behavioral theory of labor negotiations.* New York: McGraw-Hill.

WATSON, G. (1928). Do groups think more effectively than individuals? *Journal of Abnormal and Social psychology, 23,* 328–336.

———. (1931). Do groups think more effectively than individuals? In G. Murphy & L. Murphy (Eds.), *Experimental social psychology.* New York: Harper.

———, & JOHNSON, D. W. (1972). *Social psychology: Issues and insights* (2nd ed.). Philadelphia: J. B. Lippincott.

WEBB, N., ENDER, P., & LEWIS, S. (1986). Problem-solving strategies and group processes in small group learning computer programming. *American Educational Research Journal, 23*(2), 243–261.

WHEELER, R., & RYAN, F. (1973). Effects of cooperative and competitive classroom environments on the attitudes and achievement of elementary school students engaged in social studies inquiry activities. *Journal of Educational Psychology, 65,* 402–407.

WHYTE, W. (1943). *Street corner society.* Chicago: University of Chicago Press.

WIGGAM, A. (1931). The biology of leadership. In H. Metcalf (Ed.), *Business leadership.* New York: Pitman.

WILDER, D. (1986). Social categorization: Implications for creation and reduction of intergroup bias. *Advances in Experimental Social psychology, 19,* 291–355.

WILLIAMS, K. (1981). Developmental characteristics of a forward roll. *Research Quarterly for Exercise and Sport, 51*(4), 703–713.

———, HARKINS, S., & LATANE, B. (1981). Identifiability as a deterrent to social loafing: Two cheering experiments. *Journal of Personality and Social Psychology, 40,* 303–311.

WOODS, F. (1913). *The influence of monarchs.* New York: Macmillan.

WORCHEL, S., & BREHM, J. (1971). Direct and implied social restoration of freedom. *Journal of Personality and Social Psychology, 18,* 294–304.

WRIGHT, J. (1979). *On a clear day you can see General Motors.* New York: Avon.

YAGER, S., JOHNSON, D. W., & JOHNSON, R. (1985). Oral discussion, group-to-individual transfer, and achievement in cooperative learning groups. *Journal of Educational Psychology, 77,* 60–66.

ZACCARO, S. (1984). Social loafing: The role of task attractiveness. *Personality and Social Psychology Bulletin, 10,* 99–106.

ZAJONC, R. (1965). Social facilitation. *Science, 149,* 269–272.

ZANDER, A. (1971). *Motives and goals in groups.* New York: Academic Press.

——. (1974). Team spirit vs. the individual achiever. *Psychology Today, 8*(6), 64–68.

——. (1977). *Groups at work.* San Francisco: Jossey-Bass.

——. (1979). The psychology of group process. In A. Inkeles, J. Coleman, & R. Turner (Eds.), *Annual review of sociology* (Vol. 5). Palo Alto, CA: Annual Review.

——, & ARMSTRONG, W. (1972). Working for group pride in a slipper factory. *Journal of Applied Social Psychology, 2,* 293–307.

——, & MEDOW, H. (1963). Individual and group levels of aspiration. *Human Relation, 16,* 89–105.

ZDEP, S., & OAKES, W. (1967). Reinforcement of leadership behavior in group discussion. *Journal of Experimental Social Psychology, 3,* 310–320.

ZELENY, L. (1940). Experimental appraisal of a group learning plan. *Journal of Educational Research, 34,* 37–42.

ZILLER, R. (1957). Group size: A determinant of the quality and stability of group decision. *Sociometry, 20,* 165–173.

# Index